The Editor

RICHARD H. MILLINGTON is Professor of English at Smith College. He is the author of *Practicing Romance: Narrative Form and Cultural Engagement in Hawthorne's Fiction*, and of essays on Hawthorne and Willa Cather. He is the editor of *The Cambridge Companion to Nathaniel Hawthorne*, the co-editor of *Hitchcock's America*, which includes his essay on *North by Northwest*, and a past president of the Nathaniel Hawthorne Society.

A NORTON CRITICAL EDITION

Nathaniel Hawthorne

THE BLITHEDALE ROMANCE

AN AUTHORITATIVE TEXT
CONTEXTS
CRITICISM

Edited by

RICHARD H. MILLINGTON

SMITH COLLEGE

W. W. NORTON & COMPANY
New York • London

W. W. Norton & Company has been independent since its founding in 1923, when William Warder Norton and Mary D. Herter Norton first published lectures delivered at the People's Institute, the adult education division of New York City's Cooper Union. The firm soon expanded its program beyond the Institute, publishing books by celebrated academics from America and abroad. By mid-century, the two major pillars of Norton's publishing program—trade books and college texts—were firmly established. In the 1950s, the Norton family transferred control of the company to its employees, and today—with a staff of four hundred and a comparable number of trade, college, and professional titles published each year—W. W. Norton & Company stands as the largest and oldest publishing house owned wholly by its employees.

Composition by TexTech, Inc.
Manufacturing by the Courier Companies—Westford division
Production manager: Eric Pier-Hocking

Library of Congress Cataloging-in-Publication Data

Hawthorne, Nathaniel, 1804–1864.
    The Blithedale romance : an authoritative text, contexts, criticism /
Nathaniel Hawthorne ; edited by Richard H. Millington. — 1st ed.
        p. cm. — (A Norton critical edition)
    Includes bibliographical references.
    ISBN 978-0-393-92861-7 (pbk.)
    1. Communal living—Fiction. 2. Collective farms—Fiction.
3. Farm life—Fiction. 4. Massachusetts—Fiction. 5. Hawthorne,
Nathaniel, 1804–1864. Blithedale romance. I. Millington, Richard H.,
1953– II. Title.
    PS1855.A2M56 2010
    813'.3—dc22

W. W. Norton & Company, Inc., 500 Fifth Avenue
New York, N.Y. 10110-0017
wwnorton.com

W. W. Norton & Company Ltd., Castle House
75/76 Wells Street, London W1T 3QT

2 3 4 5 6 7 8 9 0

Contents

Criticism

Contents

Introduction

On July 17, 1852, three days after the publication of *The Blithedale Romance*, Herman Melville sent Hawthorne his first reaction to the just-received novel:

> I have not yet got far into the book but enough to see that you have most admirably employed materials which are richer than I had fancied them. Especially at this day, the volume is welcome, as an antidote to the mooniness of some dreamers—who are merely dreamers——Yet who the devel aint a dreamer?

Melville's reaction—admiration for his friend's skill in managing his artistic materials, followed by a moment of cryptic unease as he glimpses the sweep of the narrative's mordant critique of its era's optimism ("who the devel aint a dreamer?")—seems to forecast in miniature the novel's contemporary reception. A similar, though more moralistic note is struck by a remarkable essay in London's *Westminster Review*, which fully acknowledges Hawthorne's writerly brilliance but accuses him of a kind of analytic cruelty ("the poetry of the dissecting room") and laments his betrayal of the novelist's obligation to exemplify and promote moral beauty. *The Blithedale Romance*, of course, had its champions (as the Contemporary Responses section of this Norton Critical Edition will reveal), and the favorable British reviews in particular led Hawthorne to proclaim to a supporter that "your friend stands foremost there, as an American fiction-monger." Yet the pattern of sales of the book during Hawthorne's life also seems to trace a curve of waning enthusiasm, starting out strong but lagging well behind *The Scarlet Letter* and *The House of the Seven Gables* as the years unfolded; "I hope," wrote Hawthorne's publisher James T. Fields late in 1852, "that Hawthorne will give us no more Blithedales."[1]

Time has been good to this brilliantly innovative, absorbing, off-putting book, with its maddening narrator, its elusive plot, and its

1. *Correspondence: The Writings of Herman Melville*, vol. 14, ed. Lynn Horth (1993), 230–31 (herein, p. 255); "Contemporary Literature of America," *Westminster Review* 58, 592–98 (herein, p. 262); Hawthorne to Horatio Bridge, October 13, 1852, in *The Letters, 1843–53*, ed. Thomas Woodson et al. (1985), 604 (herein, p. 254); James T. Fields to Mary Russell Mitford, October 24, 1852, The Huntington Library (herein, p. 258).

powerful but self-thwarted characters. The very uneasiness that it
induced in some of its first readers has come to seem, as more recent
readers and scholars have turned their attention to the novel, not its
characteristic problem but its most significant legacy, its most inviting challenge to interpretation, its chief claim to our interest. The
previous Norton Critical Edition of *The Blithedale Romance*, edited
by Seymour Gross and Rosalie Murphy Baum and published in
1978, showed its readers, in its rich selection of critical essays from
the 1950s through the 1970s, the first "generation" of this resurgent
interest, and I have included brief excerpts from some of the essays
they reprinted in the "Selections from Classic Criticism" section of
this Norton Critical Edition. Not merely the passage of time but a
significant development within the history of literary study calls for a
new critical edition of the novel. While readers of *Blithedale* have all
along been interested in its account of its historical moment, particularly of the reform movements (Melville's "dreamers") of which
utopian communities were a part, and while a number of the essays
presented by Gross and Baum are concerned with the novel as a
"cultural document," in the 1980s literary scholarship began to turn
emphatically, then almost exclusively, to the exploration of a book's
meaning in intense and particular relation to the historical moment
of its composition, often subordinating formal and aesthetic questions to that "historicist" or "contextualizing" enterprise. In the case
of *The Blithedale Romance*, this was an especially productive critical
turn, and not only because the novel is itself so full of phenomena—
utopian socialism, feminism, mesmerism, emerging market capitalism, urban growth—that seem to call for the attention of a cultural
historian. Seen afresh through the lens of this new critical practice,
the novel itself appeared with new force to be engaged in a kind of
critical work very like that of the scholars who were turning their
attention to it: the tracking, through its characters, episodes, and
modes of attention, of the complex ways that changing forms of economic, social, and political arrangements came to speak in the emotions, in the consciousness, of the people who lived within them—the
writing, this is to say, of the inner history of its time.

In selecting the essays that appear in the "Recent Criticism" section, I have followed this critical turn. Rather than seeking to represent a menu of critical approaches, I chose what seemed to me to
be the most influential or powerful instances of this prevailing,
history-focused strain of scholarship; this, finally, was where the
richest, most challenging work seemed to be. Still, these essays produce anything but a critical consensus: their authors deliver a striking range of interpretations of the novel, of intellectual strategies
and commitments, of historical materials to put in productive relation to it, and, finally, very different versions of the Hawthorne that

we infer from within or glimpse behind the text. My selection of essays does, nevertheless, start well before this definitive change in scholarly direction. The first version of Nina Baym's essay was written in the late sixties (it is, in fact, included in Gross and Baum's edition), but in retrospect it is her work (along with Frederick Crews's groundbreaking psychoanalytic study, *The Sins of the Fathers*) that gave late-twentieth-century readers a new Hawthorne, one deeply critical of the orthodoxies and pieties of his era, and her interpretation of *Blithedale*, in its vigorous argument for the subversive relation between the novel and its culture, is one that all subsequent readers have had to reckon with. Several of the essays I have selected—those by Joel Pfister, Richard Brodhead, and Lauren Berlant—were published right around 1990, when the still-new burst of scholarly invention that gave us the turn toward historicism produced some of its most powerful and lasting insights. The most recent essays in this selection, by Russ Castronovo and Robert S. Levine, at once carry on this critical tradition and reflect upon it, as Castronovo follows the novel's interest in mesmerism into the deepest layers of antebellum political psychology, and Levine, returning to the question raised by Nina Baym, reclaims a new kind of subversiveness for the novel, showing us a Coverdale who is not a symptom of a deeply underlying cultural illness but an acute and ironic analyst of it. I have also departed slightly from chronology in the ordering of the essays so as to enable readers to track a difference in critical method: I begin with two essays—Nina Baym's and my own—that depend for their insights upon close attention to features of the text of the novel, and then move to those that work by bringing that text into generative relation with a particular set of historical materials.

Like other Norton Critical Editions, this edition of *The Blithedale Romance* offers a selection of historical materials that will enable readers to draw their own connections between the novel and the rapidly changing, revealingly conflicted culture it addresses, and a set of critical responses, from the contemporary to the current, that enable us to chart the trajectory of thought and feeling that the novel has provoked in its readers over the years since its original publication. The "Contexts" section arranges its materials under four rubrics; each of these includes some additional writings by Hawthorne, which, in a number of cases, found their way into the novel. The first of these rubrics, "The Brook Farm Community and the Ferment of Antebellum Social Reform," introduces its readers to the ideals, ambitions, and experimental fervor of antebellum reform movements by beginning with Brook Farm itself, the utopian community that Hawthorne joined in the spring of 1841, left in the fall of the same year, and later used as the model for the novel's Blithedale. This section starts by recording a failed attempt by

George Ripley, Brook Farm's founder, to recruit Ralph Waldo Emerson, the era's most influential intellectual seeker, to join the community, and then offers a glimpse, through additional selections, of other manifestations of and perspectives on the reform impulse, including Hawthorne's own bemused but respectful portrayal of it in one of his sketches, "The Hall of Fantasy." The following section, "Nathaniel Hawthorne at Brook Farm," focuses on Hawthorne's own experience at the community, rendered most vividly in letters to his fiancée, Sophia Peabody, and on the early life of the community as seen in those letters, Hawthorne's notebook entries, and a lively memoir by one of the students in the community's extraordinary school. While Hawthorne made significant use of these writings as he transformed Brook Farm into Blithedale, they are interesting also for capturing the exhilaration of this social experiment in its first days, and for providing an intimate sense of both the enthusiasm and the disappointment that attended his sojourn there.

The following sections of "Contexts" zoom back out, so to speak, to explore some of the other aspects of antebellum cultural life that figure significantly in the novel. In "The Woman Question," an excerpt from a powerful essay by Margaret Fuller, the era's leading feminist intellectual, enables us to recapture the debates about the nature and social role of women, crucial to both the culture and to the novel's characters—to hear, in a sense, one of the speeches Zenobia might have delivered off the book's own stage—while a stunning account from Hawthorne's notebooks of the suicide by drowning of a young Concord woman reveals his sympathetic understanding of how the restrictions of contemporary gender roles expressed themselves in daily misery. The section on "Mesmerism" permits us to witness a contemporary instance of this curious form of popular entertainment and to hear a practitioner's account of the theory and practice of his mysterious art—with its links to reform culture's perfectionism, to medical practice and scientific speculation, to understandings of gender and the nature of selfhood, to emerging forms of mass culture—which Hawthorne put at the center of the novel's action. We hear, too, in an impassioned letter to Sophia Peabody—written from Brook Farm—imploring her *not* to seek the curative services of a mesmerist, both Hawthorne's skepticism about this cultural phenomenon and his deeply felt anxiety about what it might reveal about the vulnerability of the individual psyche. The materials gathered in "Urban Observation," which evoke the Coverdale-like figure of the *flâneur*—the detached connoisseur of city life memorably described by Baudelaire—and feature some of Hawthorne's vivid accounts of his own Boston wanderings, will remind us how full this novel set at an agrarian commune is of the distinctive experiences and emotions of a new American urban life—and, beyond that, of how richly its interests and observations, its characters and forms of feeling, compose an exploration of an emerging American modernity. I have already explained the principles of selection that led me to the essays that appear under the "Recent Criticism" heading of the "Criticism" section of this book. The responses, reviews, and critical essays sampled in "Contemporary Responses" and "Selections from Classic Studies" enable us to see the different ways that *The Blithedale Romance* has been valued and criticized in the years since its publication—but this array of responses also begins to sketch a kind of history of the way generations of Hawthorne's readers have thought about novels and the kind of work they might do—or fail to do—for their readers and their times.

There is, in addition to the shift in the goals and strategies of literary study that I have described, a second change in the cultural landscape—how lasting or ephemeral we don't yet know—that makes this an interesting time to think again about *The Blithedale Romance*. Hawthorne's novel had its genesis in his brief experience at Brook Farm. Despite his skeptical turn of mind, he was one of the founding members of a utopian community, organized by George Ripley and richly connected to the radically experimental intellectual atmosphere of 1840s Boston, that set out—some eight miles from that city—to invent and to demonstrate a way of life that would be a beautiful, sustainable, and humane alternative to the competitive, exploitative world that, these experimenters felt, an emerging market capitalism was already producing all around them. *The Blithedale Romance*, this is to say, had its origin in a historical moment where a profound sense of the inhumanity of prevailing economic and social arrangements met an energetic optimism about the ability of right-thinking and right-feeling Americans to transform those arrangements—to remake, to reform, even to perfect the America that would take shape around them. It is hard not to hear echoes—as citizens throughout the world confront the implications of global warming, as college students spend their summers laboring on organic farms, as young people try to imagine a way to make a living compatible with their convictions, as a kind of optimism animates, who knows how briefly, our political life—of Hawthorne's 1840s in our current moment. For the current generation of scholars *The Blithedale Romance* has presented a single, absorbing question: what does this book teach us about mid-nineteenth-century America? That leaves a no-less-interesting question unclaimed: what is it that this book has to say to us today? I leave that question to this novel's newest readers, and to the classrooms in which this Norton Critical Edition hopes to do its work.

A Note on the Text
and Annotations

The text of *The Blithedale Romance* presented in this Norton Critical Edition is that of the *Centenary Edition of the Works of Nathaniel
Hawthorne*, a publication of the Ohio State University Center for
Textual Studies and the Ohio State University Press. The Centenary
edition is accepted by most scholars as the best available text of
Hawthorne's works and is accordingly cited in almost all scholarly
articles. This text of *The Blithedale Romance* was published in 1964,
under the general editorship of William Charvat, Roy Harvey
Pearce, and Claude M. Simpson; the chief textual editor was Fred-
son Bowers. The editors of the Centenary edition set out to establish
a text that is closest to the author's intention. In the case of *The
Blithedale Romance*, they worked from Hawthorne's manuscript of
the novel (held in the Pierpont Morgan Library), comparing it to the
first edition published by Ticknor, Reed, and Fields on July 14,
1852, and drawing informed conclusions about which changes from
the manuscript were likely to have been made by Hawthorne as he
corrected the proof sheets. (Those proof sheets have not survived, so
we cannot be absolutely certain of which changes were, in fact,
Hawthorne's, and which were introduced by an editor or printer). In
attempting to reconstruct Hawthorne's intentions, the editors made
a controversial decision: they chose to restore three passages—a
phrase referring to hard liquor, a sentence enhancing Coverdale's
description of Zenobia's erotic presence, and a longer passage
expressing skepticism about the temperance movement—which
appear in the manuscript but are absent from the first edition.
Though Hawthorne must have accepted these deletions, the editors
propose that these were not changes made for literary reasons but at
the censorious suggestion of some other person—their candidate is
Hawthorne's wife Sophia—and that they thus depart from his
deeper intentions. (These restored passages are identified in the
notes to this Norton Critical Edition). In any case, readers of this
text of the novel should note that no one read this exact text until
1964; Hawthorne's contemporaries read the text established for the

Ticknor, Reed, and Fields first edition, while his late-nineteenth and earlier-twentieth-century readers would have seen the text of the Riverside edition, first published by Houghton, Mifflin in 1883.

The footnotes in this Norton Critical Edition aim to offer concise information that will help the reader with Hawthorne's many historical and literary references, and with other possible sources of difficulty in the text; in some cases I have used the footnotes to direct the reader to appropriate material in the "Contexts" section. I have also annotated those materials, as well as those in the "Contemporary Responses" and "Selections from Classic Studies" sections. In the case of the essays reprinted in the "Recent Criticism" section, all the footnotes belong to the authors of the respective essays, unless otherwise indicated.

Acknowledgments

Thanks, first, to the scholars whose work is found in the "Recent Criticism" section of this Norton Critical Edition. I value the chance to present their essays to a new set of readers and to learn from their writing once again. The difficulty of selecting these essays from the rich array of recent scholarly writing on *The Blithedale Romance* has given me a vivid appreciation for the work of my fellow Hawthorne scholars—a community that is also remarkable for its congeniality, and I am grateful for the friendships that have emerged from our shared work. I have learned a great deal from editing this volume: excellent collections of materials relating to Brook Farm by Joel Myerson and Henry W. Sams, and William Cain's selection of broader cultural materials in his Bedford edition of the novel were very helpful as I chose the material for the "Contexts" section, and the historical introductions and annotations provided by the editors of *The Centenary Edition of the Works of Nathaniel Hawthorne* were indispensable as I wrote my own notes and headnotes. My thanks to the librarians at the American Antiquarian Society for their help in locating several of the documents reproduced in the "Mesmerism" and "Urban Observation" sections, and to Natalie Russel and David S. Zeidberg of the Huntington Library for help with and permission to reprint a letter from James T. Fields; I also received valuable advice and encouragement along the way from John Idol and Bob Levine. I am indebted to Carol Bemis, my editor at Norton, for her guidance, judgment, and—especially—patience; to her assistant, Rivka Genesen, for her good humor and her excellent work on permissions and guiding the book toward and through production; and to Katherine Ings for her alertness and skill as copyeditor. For astute advice and encouragement closer to home, I thank Callie Millington and Nalini Bhushan and, for his own inimitable contributions to the enterprise, Ajay Rosenfeld.

This edition hopes to do much of its work in the classroom. I therefore dedicate it to two of my teachers, Richard Brodhead and Alan Trachtenberg, who guided my study of Hawthorne; I continue to learn from their example.

The Text of
THE BLITHEDALE
ROMANCE

Preface

In the 'BLITHEDALE' of this volume, many readers will probably suspect a faint and not very faithful shadowing of BROOK FARM, in Roxbury, which (now a little more than ten years ago) was occupied and cultivated by a company of socialists.[1] The Author does not wish to deny, that he had this Community in his mind, and that (having had the good fortune, for a time, to be personally connected with it) he has occasionally availed himself of his actual reminiscences, in the hope of giving a more lifelike tint to the fancy-sketch in the following pages. He begs it to be understood, however, that he has considered the Institution itself as not less fairly the subject of fictitious handling, than the imaginary personages whom he has introduced there. His whole treatment of the affair is altogether incidental to the main purpose of the Romance;[2] nor does he put forward the slightest pretensions to illustrate a theory, or elicit a conclusion, favorable or otherwise, in respect to Socialism.[3]

In short, his present concern with the Socialist Community is merely to establish a theatre, a little removed from the highway of ordinary travel, where the creatures of his brain may play their phantasmagorical antics, without exposing them to too close a comparison with the actual events of real lives. In the old countries, with which Fiction has long been conversant, a certain conventional privilege seems to be awarded to the romancer; his work is not put exactly side by side with nature; and he is allowed a license with regard to every-day Probability, in view of the improved effects which he is bound to produce thereby. Among ourselves, on the

---

1. Brook Farm (1841–1847) was an experimental community, based on principles of shared labor and economic cooperation, located on 170 acres in West Roxbury, Massachusetts, eight miles from the center of Boston. Hoping to secure time to write and to establish a home with his fiancée, Sophia Peabody, Hawthorne invested $1,000 in the community, and lived there from April to late October 1841. For more on Brook Farm and Hawthorne's time there, see the "Contexts" section of this Norton Critical Edition, pp. 173–216.
2. Hawthorne's preferred term for his kind of fiction writing; in contrast to the realistic novel's faithful reproduction of everyday life, "romance" claims the latitude to incorporate mysterious, supernatural, or symbolic elements into its exploration of experience.
3. A plan of social and economic life emphasizing communal cooperation, in contrast to the individualism and competitiveness of marketplace capitalism—not yet, as in current usage, a political and economic system in which the primary means of producing and distributing goods are owned collectively by the state.

3

contrary, there is as yet no such Faery Land, so like the real world, that, in a suitable remoteness, one cannot well tell the difference, but with an atmosphere of strange enchantment, beheld through which the inhabitants have a propriety of their own. This atmosphere is what the American romancer needs. In its absence, the beings of imagination are compelled to show themselves in the same category as actually living mortals; a necessity that generally renders the paint and pasteboard of their composition but too painfully discernible. With the idea of partially obviating this difficulty, (the sense of which has always pressed very heavily upon him,) the Author has ventured to make free with his old, and affectionately remembered home, at BROOK FARM, as being, certainly, the most romantic episode of his own life—essentially a day-dream, and yet a fact—and thus offering an available foothold between fiction and reality. Furthermore, the scene was in good keeping with the personages whom he desired to introduce.

These characters, he feels it right to say, are entirely fictitious. It would, indeed, (considering how few amiable qualities he distributes among his imaginary progeny,) be a most grievous wrong to his former excellent associates, were the Auther to allow it to be supposed that he has been sketching any of their likenesses. Had he attempted it, they would at least have recognized the touches of a friendly pencil. But he has done nothing of the kind. The self-concentrated Philanthropist; the high-spirited Woman, bruising herself against the narrow limitations of her sex; the weakly Maiden, whose tremulous nerves endow her with Sibylline[4] attributes; the Minor Poet, beginning life with strenuous aspirations, which die out with his youthful fervor—all these might have been looked for, at BROOK FARM, but, by some accident, never made their appearance there.

The Author cannot close his reference to this subject, without expressing a most earnest wish that some one of the many cultivated and philosophic minds, which took an interest in that enterprise, might now give the world its history. Ripley, with whom rests the honorable paternity of the Institution, Dana, Dwight, Channing, Burton, Parker,[5] for instance—with others, whom he dares not name, because they veil themselves from the public eye—among

---

4. Prophetic, clairvoyant; Sibyls were women regarded as prophetesses by the ancient Greeks and Romans.
5. George Ripley (1802–1880) left the Unitarian ministry to found Brook Farm and headed the community throughout its life; Charles A. Dana (1819–1897), a founding member of the community and deeply involved in its management, later became owner and editor of the *New York Sun*. John Sullivan Dwight (1813–1893), a pioneering American music critic, lived there from 1841 to 1847; Warren Burton (1800–1866), educator and Unitarian minister, was an early member of the community. William Henry Channing (1810–1884) and Theodore Parker (1810–1860), both Unitarian ministers and influential reformers, were frequent visitors to Brook Farm but not members.

these is the ability to convey both the outward narrative and the inner truth and spirit of the whole affair, together with the lessons which those years of thought and toil must have elaborated, for the behoof of future experimentalists. Even the brilliant Howadji[6] might find as rich a theme in his youthful reminiscenses of BROOK FARM, and a more novel one—close at hand as it lies—than those which he has since made so distant a pilgrimage to seek, in Syria, and along the current of the Nile.

CONCORD (Mass.), May, 1852.

6. Pen name (Arabic for "traveler") of George William Curtis (1824–1892), who wrote two popular travel narratives, *Nile Notes of a Howadji* (1851) and *Howadji in Syria* (1852); later the reform-minded editor of *Harper's Weekly*; boarded at Brook Farm from 1842 to 1843.

The Blithedale Romance

I. Old Moodie

The evening before my departure for Blithedale,[1] I was returning to my bachelor-apartments, after attending the wonderful exhibition of the Veiled Lady, when an elderly-man of rather shabby appearance met me in an obscure part of the street.

"Mr. Coverdale,"[2] said he, softly, "can I speak with you a moment?"

As I have casually alluded to the Veiled Lady, it may not be amiss to mention, for the benefit of such of my readers as are unacquainted with her now forgotten celebrity, that she was a phenomenon in the mesmeric line;[3] one of the earliest that had indicated the birth of a new science, or the revival of an old humbug. Since those times, her sisterhood have grown too numerous to attract much individual notice; nor, in fact, has any one of them ever come before the public under such skilfully contrived circumstances of stage-effect, as those which at once mystified and illuminated the remarkable performances of the lady in question. Now-a-days, in the management of his 'subject,' 'clairvoyant,' or 'medium,' the exhibitor affects the simplicity and openness of scientific experiment; and even if he profess to tread a step or two across the boundaries of the spiritual world, yet carries with him the laws of our actual life, and extends them over his preternatural conquests. Twelve or fifteen years ago, on the contrary, all the arts of mysterious arrangement, of picturesque disposition, and artistically contrasted light and shade, were made available in order to set the apparent miracle in the strongest attitude of opposition to ordinary facts. In the case of the

---

1. Hawthorne's name for the community combines the words "blithe"—"happy," "joyous"—and "dale"—a term for a small valley.
2. The historical Miles Coverdale (1488–1569), priest and bishop in the Church of England, authored the first complete English translation of the Bible (1535).
3. A set of beliefs and practices that grew out of the theories of the Austrian physician Franz Mesmer (1734–1815), which held that an invisible substance, or "ether," made communication between souls or with the spirit world possible. Phenomena in the "mesmeric line" ranged from private therapeutic encounters between patient and healer to the kind of public demonstrations depicted in the novel. For more on Mesmerism in America, see the "Contexts" section of this Norton Critical Edition, pp. 226–39.

Veiled Lady, moreover, the interest of the spectator was further wrought up by the enigma of her identity, and an absurd rumor (probably set afloat by the exhibitor, and at one time very prevalent) that a beautiful young lady, of family and fortune, was enshrouded within the misty drapery of the veil. It was white, with somewhat of a subdued silver sheen, like the sunny side of a cloud; and falling over the wearer, from head to foot, was supposed to insulate her from the material world, from time and space, and to endow her with many of the privileges of a disembodied spirit.

Her pretensions, however, whether miraculous or otherwise, have little to do with the present narrative; except, indeed, that I had propounded, for the Veiled Lady's prophetic solution, a query as to the success of our Blithedale enterprise. The response, by-the-by, was of the true Sibylline stamp, nonsensical in its first aspect, yet, on closer study, unfolding a variety of interpretations, one of which has certainly accorded with the event. I was turning over this riddle in my mind, and trying to catch its slippery purport by the tail, when the old man, above-mentioned, interrupted me.

"Mr. Coverdale!—Mr. Coverdale!" said he, repeating my name twice, in order to make up for the hesitating and ineffectual way in which he uttered it—"I ask your pardon, sir—but I hear you are going to Blithedale tomorrow?"

I knew the pale, elderly face, with the red-tipt nose, and the patch over one eye, and likewise saw something characteristic in the old fellow's way of standing under the arch of a gate, only revealing enough of himself to make me recognize him as an acquaintance. He was a very shy personage, this Mr. Moodie; and the trait was the more singular, as his mode of getting his bread necessarily brought him into the stir and hubbub of the world, more than the generality of men.

"Yes, Mr. Moodie," I answered, wondering what interest he could take in the fact, "it is my intention to go to Blithedale tomorrow. Can I be of any service to you, before my departure?"

"If you pleased, Mr. Coverdale," said he, "you might do me a very great favor."

"A very great one!" repeated I, in a tone that must have expressed but little alacrity of beneficence, although I was ready to do the old man any amount of kindness involving no special trouble to myself. "A very great favor, do you say? My time is brief, Mr. Moodie, and I have a good many preparations to make. But be good enough to tell me what you wish."

"Ah, sir," replied old Moodie, "I don't quite like to do that; and, on further thoughts, Mr. Coverdale, perhaps I had better apply to some older gentleman, or to some lady, if you would have the kindness to make me known to one, who may happen to be going to Blithedale. You are a young man, sir!"

"Does that fact lessen my availability for your purpose?" asked I. "However, if an older man will suit you better, there is Mr. Hollingsworth, who has three or four years the advantage of me in age, and is a much more solid character, and a philanthropist to boot. I am only a poet, and, so the critics tell me, no great affair at that! But what can this business be, Mr. Moodie? It begins to interest me; especially since your hint that a lady's influence might be found desirable. Come; I am really anxious to be of service to you."

But the old fellow, in his civil and demure manner, was both freakish and obstinate; and he had now taken some notion or other into his head that made him hesitate in his former design.

"I wonder, sir," said he, "whether you know a lady whom they call Zenobia?"[4]

"Not personally," I answered, "although I expect that pleasure tomorrow, as she has got the start of the rest of us, and is already a resident at Blithedale. But have you a literary turn, Mr. Moodie?—or have you taken up the advocacy of women's rights?—or what else can have interested you in this lady? Zenobia, by-the-by, as I suppose you know, is merely her public name; a sort of mask in which she comes before the world, retaining all the privileges of privacy—a contrivance, in short, like the white drapery of the Veiled Lady, only a little more transparent. But it is late! Will you tell me what I can do for you?"

"Please to excuse me to-night, Mr. Coverdale," said Moodie. "You are very kind; but I am afraid I have troubled you, when, after all, there may be no need. Perhaps, with your good leave, I will come to your lodgings tomorrow-morning, before you set out for Blithedale. I wish you a good-night, sir, and beg pardon for stopping you."

And so he slipt away; and, as he did not show himself, the next morning, it was only through subsequent events that I ever arrived at a plausible conjecture as to what his business could have been. Arriving at my room, I threw a lump of cannel coal[5] upon the grate, lighted a cigar, and spent an hour in musings of every hue, from the brightest to the most sombre; being, in truth, not so very confident as at some former periods, that this final step, which would mix me up irrevocably with the Blithedale affair, was the wisest that could possibly be taken. It was nothing short of midnight when I went to bed, after drinking a glass of particularly fine Sherry, on which I used to pride myself, in those days. It was the very last bottle; and I finished it, with a friend, the next forenoon, before setting out for Blithedale.

---

4. Third-century Queen of Palmyra, a major city in the Roman Empire, located in what is now Syria, whose forces conquered Egypt and invaded Asia Minor; her rebellion against Roman authority was defeated by the Emperor Aurelian in C.E. 272. Depicted in Gibbon's *Decline and Fall of the Roman Empire* as a woman remarkable for her beauty, heroism, and learning, she was a figure of fascination in nineteenth-century England and America.
5. A form of bituminous coal that burns with a bright flame (from "candle coal").

II. Blithedale

There can hardly remain for me, (who am really getting to be a frosty bachelor, with another white hair, every week or so, in my moustache,) there can hardly flicker up again so cheery a blaze upon the hearth, as that which I remember, the next day, at Blithedale. It was a wood-fire, in the parlor of an old farm-house, on an April afternoon, but with the fitful gusts of a wintry snow-storm roaring in the chimney. Vividly does that fireside re-create itself, as I rake away the ashes from the embers in my memory, and blow them up with a sigh, for lack of more inspiring breath. Vividly, for an instant, but, anon, with the dimmest gleam, and with just as little fervency for my heart as for my finger-ends! The staunch oaken-logs were long ago burnt out. Their genial glow must be represented, if at all, by the merest phosphoric glimmer, like that which exudes, rather than shines, from damp fragments of decayed trees, deluding the benighted wanderer through a forest. Around such chill mockery of a fire, some few of us might sit on the withered leaves, spreading out each a palm towards the imaginary warmth, and talk over our exploded scheme for beginning the life of Paradise anew.

Paradise, indeed! Nobody else in the world, I am bold to affirm—nobody, at least, in our bleak little world of New England—had dreamed of Paradise, that day, except as the pole suggests the tropic. Nor, with such materials as were at hand, could the most skilful architect have constructed any better imitation of Eve's bower, than might be seen in the snow-hut of an Esquimaux. But we made a summer of it, in spite of the wild drifts.

It was an April day, as already hinted, and well towards the middle of the month. When morning dawned upon me, in town, its temperature was mild enough to be pronounced even balmy, by a lodger—like myself—in one of the midmost houses of a brick-block; each house partaking of the warmth of all the rest, besides the sultriness of its individual furnace-heat. But, towards noon, there had come snow, driven along the street by a north-easterly blast, and whitening the roofs and sidewalks with a business-like perseverance that would have done credit to our severest January tempest. It set about its task, apparently as much in earnest as if it had been guaranteed from a thaw, for months to come. The greater, surely, was my heroism, when, puffing out a final whiff of cigar-smoke, I quitted my cosey pair of bachelor-rooms—with a good fire burning in the grate, and a closet right at hand, where there was still a bottle or two in the champagne-basket, and a residuum of claret in a box, and somewhat of proof in the concavity of a big demijohn[1]—quitted, I say, these comfortable quarters, and plunged into the heart of the pitiless snow-storm, in quest of a better life.

The better life! Possibly, it would hardly look so, now; it is enough if it looked so, then. The greatest obstacle to being heroic, is the doubt whether one may not be going to prove one's self a fool; the truest heroism is, to resist the doubt—and the profoundest wisdom, to know when it ought to be resisted, and when to be obeyed.

Yet, after all, let us acknowledge it wiser, if not more sagacious, to follow out one's day-dream to its natural consummation, although, if the vision have been worth the having, it is certain never to be consummated otherwise than by a failure. And what of that! Its airiest fragments, impalpable as they may be, will possess a value that lurks not in the most ponderous realities of any practicable scheme. They are not the rubbish of the mind. Whatever else I may repent of, therefore, let it be reckoned neither among my sins nor follies, that I once had faith and force enough to form generous hopes of the world's destiny—yes!—and to do what in me lay for their accomplishment; even to the extent of quitting a warm fireside, flinging away a freshly lighted cigar, and travelling far beyond the strike of city-clocks, through a drifting snow-storm.

There were four of us who rode together through the storm; and Hollingsworth, who had agreed to be of the number, was accidentally delayed, and set forth at a later hour, alone. As we threaded the streets, I remember how the buildings, on either side, seemed to press too closely upon us, insomuch that our mighty hearts found barely room enough to throb between them. The snow-fall, too, looked inexpressibly dreary, (I had almost called it dingy,) coming down through an atmosphere of city-smoke, and alighting on the sidewalk, only to be moulded into the impress of somebody's patched boot or over-shoe. Thus, the track of an old conventionalism was visible on what was freshest from the sky. But—when we left the pavements, and our muffled hoof-tramps beat upon a desolate extent of country-road, and were effaced by the unfettered blast, as soon as stamped—then, there was better air to breathe. Air, that had not been breathed, once and again! Air, that had not been spoken into words of falsehood, formality, and error, like all the air of the dusky city!

1. A few bottles of red wine ("claret") and some whiskey in a large, narrow-necked, wicker-encased bottle. The phrase referring to the "demijohn" ("somewhat of proof . . .") was deleted from the manuscript, perhaps at Sophia Hawthorne's suggestion, when Hawthorne copied it for the printer. The editors of the Centenary edition have restored this phrasing and two others, a sentence emphasizing Zenobia's erotic presence and a passage criticizing the temperance movement. See p. 14, note 1 and p. 120, note 2.

"How pleasant it is!" remarked I, while the snow-flakes flew into my mouth, the moment it was opened. "How very mild and balmy is this country-air!"

"Ah, Coverdale, don't laugh at what little enthusiasm you have left," said one of my companions. "I maintain that this nitrous atmosphere[2] is really exhilarating; and, at any rate, we can never call ourselves regenerated men, till a February north-easter shall be as grateful to us as the softest breeze of June."

So we all of us took courage, riding fleetly and merrily along, by stone-fences that were half-buried in the wave-like drifts; and through patches of woodland, where the tree-trunks opposed a snow-encrusted side towards the north-east; and within ken of deserted villas, with no foot-prints in their avenues; and past scattered dwellings, whence puffed the smoke of country fires, strongly impregnated with the pungent aroma of burning peat. Sometimes, encountering a traveller, we shouted a friendly greeting; and he, unmuffling his ears to the bluster and the snow-spray, and listening eagerly, appeared to think our courtesy worth less than the trouble which it cost him. The churl![3] He understood the shrill whistle of the blast, but had no intelligence for our blithe tones of brotherhood. This lack of faith in our cordial sympathy, on the traveller's part, was one among the innumerable tokens how difficult a task we had in hand, for the reformation of the world. We rode on, however, with still unflagging spirits, and made such good companionship with the tempest, that, at our journey's end, we professed ourselves almost loth to bid the rude blusterer good bye. But, to own the truth, I was little better than an icicle, and began to be suspicious that I had caught a fearful cold.

And, now, we were seated by the brisk fireside of the old farm-house; the same fire that glimmers so faintly among my reminiscences, at the beginning of this chapter. There we sat, with the snow melting out of our hair and beards, and our faces all a-blaze, what with the past inclemency and present warmth. It was, indeed, a right good fire that we found awaiting us, built up of great, rough logs, and knotty limbs, and splintered fragments of an oak-tree, such as farmers are wont to keep for their own hearths; since these crooked and unmanageable boughs could never be measured into merchantable cords for the market. A family of the old Pilgrims might have swung their kettle over precisely such a fire as this, only, no

2. Charged with niter, or potassium nitrate, a compound used to make gunpowder; hence, a bracing or exhilarating atmosphere.
3. A rude, surly, ill-bred man. An antiquated term, even in the nineteenth century; typical of Coverdale's "poetical" language throughout this scene.

doubt, a bigger one; and, contrasting it with my coal-grate, I felt, so much the more, that we had transported ourselves a world-wide distance from the system of society that shackled us at breakfast-time.

Good, comfortable Mrs. Foster (the wife of stout Silas Foster, who was to manage the farm, at a fair stipend, and be our tutor in the art of husbandry) bade us a hearty welcome. At her back—a back of generous breadth—appeared two young women, smiling most hospitably, but looking rather awkward withal, as not well knowing what was to be their position in our new arrangement of the world. We shook hands affectionately, all round, and congratulated ourselves that the blessed state of brotherhood and sisterhood, at which we aimed, might fairly be dated from this moment. Our greetings were hardly concluded, when the door opened, and Zenobia—whom I had never before seen, important as was her place in our enterprise— Zenobia entered the parlor.

This (as the reader, if at all acquainted with our literary biography, need scarcely be told) was not her real name. She had assumed it, in the first instance, as her magazine-signature; and as it accorded well with something imperial which her friends attributed to this lady's figure and deportment, they, half-laughingly, adopted it in their familiar intercourse with her. She took the appellation in good part, and even encouraged its constant use, which, in fact, was thus far appropriate, that our Zenobia—however humble looked her new philosophy—had as much native pride as any queen would have known what to do with.

III. A Knot of Dreamers

Zenobia bade us welcome, in a fine, frank, mellow voice, and gave each of us her hand, which was very soft and warm. She had something appropriate, I recollect, to say to every individual; and what she said to myself was this:—

"I have long wished to know you, Mr. Coverdale, and to thank you for your beautiful poetry, some of which I have learned by heart;— or, rather, it has stolen into my memory, without my exercising any choice or volition about the matter. Of course—permit me to say— you do not think of relinquishing an occupation in which you have done yourself so much credit. I would almost rather give you up, as an associate, than that the world should lose one of its true poets!"

"Ah, no; there will not be the slightest danger of that, especially after this inestimable praise from Zenobia!" said I, smiling and blushing, no doubt, with excess of pleasure. "I hope, on the contrary, now, to produce something that shall really deserve to be called poetry—true, strong, natural, and sweet, as is the life which we are going to lead—something that shall have the notes of wild-birds twittering through it, or a strain like the wind-anthems in the woods, as the case may be!"

"Is it irksome to you to hear your own verses sung?" asked Zenobia, with a gracious smile. "If so, I am very sorry; for you will certainly hear me singing them, sometimes, in the summer evenings."

"Of all things," answered I, "that is what will delight me most."

While this passed, and while she spoke to my companions, I was taking note of Zenobia's aspect; and it impressed itself on me so distinctly, that I can now summon her up like a ghost, a little wanner than the life, but otherwise identical with it. She was dressed as simply as possible, in an American print, (I think the dry-goods people call it so,) but with a silken kerchief, between which and her gown there was one glimpse of a white shoulder. It struck me as a great piece of good-fortune that there should be just that glimpse. Her hair—which was dark, glossy, and of singular abundance—was put up rather soberly and primly, without curls, or other ornament, except a single flower. It was an exotic, of rare beauty, and as fresh as if the hot-house gardener had just clipt it from the stem. That flower has struck deep root into my memory. I can both see it and smell it, at this moment. So brilliant, so rare, so costly as it must have been, and yet enduring only for a day, it was more indicative of the pride and pomp, which had a luxuriant growth in Zenobia's character, than if a great diamond had sparkled among her hair.

Her hand, though very soft, was larger than most women would like to have—or than they could afford to have—though not a whit too large in proportion with the spacious plan of Zenobia's entire development. It did one good to see a fine intellect (as hers really was, although its natural tendency lay in another direction than towards literature) so fitly cased. She was, indeed, an admirable figure of a woman, just on the hither verge of her richest maturity, with a combination of features which it is safe to call remarkably beautiful, even if some fastidious persons might pronounce them a little deficient in softness and delicacy. But we find enough of those attributes, everywhere. Preferable—by way of variety, at least—was Zenobia's bloom, health, and vigor, which she possessed in such overflow that a man might well have fallen in love with her for their sake only. In her quiet moods, she seemed rather indolent; but when really in earnest, particularly if there were a spice of bitter feeling, she grew all alive, to her finger-tips.

"I am the first-comer," Zenobia went on to say, while her smile beamed warmth upon us all; "so I take the part of hostess, for to-day, and welcome you as if to my own fireside. You shall be my guests, too, at supper. Tomorrow, if you please, we will be brethren and sisters, and begin our new life from day-break."

"Have we our various parts assigned?" asked some one.

"Oh, we of the softer sex," responded Zenobia, with her mellow, almost broad laugh—most delectable to hear, but not in the least like an ordinary woman's laugh—"we women (there are four of us here, already) will take the domestic and indoor part of the business, as a matter of course. To bake, to boil, to roast, to fry, to stew—to wash, and iron, and scrub, and sweep, and, at our idler intervals, to repose ourselves on knitting and sewing—these, I suppose, must be feminine occupations for the present. By-and-by, perhaps, when our individual adaptations begin to develop themselves, it may be that some of us, who wear the petticoat, will go afield, and leave the weaker brethren to take our places in the kitchen!"

"What a pity," I remarked, "that the kitchen, and the house-work generally, cannot be left out of our system altogether! It is odd enough, that the kind of labor which falls to the lot of women is just that which chiefly distinguishes artificial life—the life of degener-ated mortals—from the life of Paradise. Eve had no dinner-pot, and no clothes to mend, and no washing-day."

"I am afraid," said Zenobia, with mirth gleaming out of her eyes, "we shall find some difficulty in adopting the Paradisiacal system, for at least a month to come. Look at that snow-drift sweeping past the window! Are there any figs ripe, do you think? Have the pine-apples been gathered, to-day? Would you like a bread-fruit, or a cocoa-nut? Shall I run out and pluck you some roses? No, no, Mr. Coverdale, the only flower hereabouts is the one in my hair, which I got out of a green-house, this morning. As for the garb of Eden," added she, shiv-ering playfully, "I shall not assume it till after May-day!"

Assuredly, Zenobia could not have intended it—the fault must have been entirely in my imagination—but these last words, together with something in her manner, irresistibly brought up a pic-ture of that fine, perfectly developed figure, in Eve's earliest gar-ment. I almost fancied myself actually beholding it.[1] Her free, careless, generous modes of expression often had this effect of cre-ating images which, though pure, are hardly felt to be quite deco-rous, when born of a thought that passes between man and woman. I imputed it, at that time, to Zenobia's noble courage, conscious of no harm, and scorning the petty restraints which take the life and color out of other women's conversation. There was another peculi-arity about her. We seldom meet with women, now-a-days, and in this country, who impress us as being women at all; their sex fades away and goes for nothing, in ordinary intercourse. Not so with Zenobia. One felt an influence breathing out of her, such as we

---

1. This sentence was deleted from the original manuscript but restored for the Centenary edition.

might suppose to come from Eve, when she was just made, and her Creator brought her to Adam, saying—'Behold, here is a woman!' Not that I would convey the idea of especial gentleness, grace, modesty, and shyness, but of a certain warm and rich characteristic, which seems, for the most part, to have been refined away out of the feminine system.

"And now," continued Zenobia, "I must go and help get supper. Do you think you can be content—instead of figs, pine-apples, and all the other delicacies of Adam's supper-table—with tea and toast, and a certain modest supply of ham and tongue, which, with the instinct of a housewife, I brought hither in a basket? And there shall be bread-and-milk, too, if the innocence of your taste demands it."

The whole sisterhood now went about their domestic avocations, utterly declining our offers to assist, farther than by bringing wood, for the kitchen-fire, from a huge pile in the back-yard. After heaping up more than a sufficient quantity, we returned to the sitting-room, drew our chairs closer to the hearth, and began to talk over our prospects. Soon, with a tremendous stamping in the entry, appeared Silas Foster, lank, stalwart, uncouth, and grisly-bearded. He came from foddering the cattle, in the barn, and from the field, where he had been ploughing, until the depth of the snow rendered it impossible to draw a furrow. He greeted us in pretty much the same tone as if he were speaking to his oxen, took a quid[2] from his iron tobacco-box, pulled off his wet cow-hide boots, and sat down before the fire in his stocking-feet. The steam arose from his soaked garments, so that the stout yeoman looked vaporous and spectre-like.

"Well, folks," remarked Silas, "you'll be wishing yourselves back to town again, if this weather holds!"

And, true enough, there was a look of gloom, as the twilight fell silently and sadly out of the sky, its gray or sable flakes intermingling themselves with the fast descending snow. The storm, in its evening aspect, was decidedly dreary. It seemed to have arisen for our especial behoof; a symbol of the cold, desolate, distrustful phantoms that invariably haunt the mind, on the eve of adventurous enterprises, to warn us back within the boundaries of ordinary life.

But our courage did not quail. We would not allow ourselves to be depressed by the snow-drift, trailing past the window, any more than if it had been the sigh of a summer wind among rustling boughs. There have been few brighter seasons for us, than that. If ever men might lawfully dream awake, and give utterance to their wildest visions, without dread of laughter or scorn on the part of the audience—yes, and speak of earthly happiness, for themselves and

2. A wad of chewing tobacco.

mankind, as an object to be hopefully striven for, and probably attained—we, who made that little semi-circle round the blazing fire, were those very men. We had left the rusty iron frame-work of society behind us. We had broken through many hindrances that are powerful enough to keep most people on the weary tread-mill of the established system, even while they feel its irksomeness almost as intolerable as we did. We had stept down from the pulpit; we had flung aside the pen; we had shut up the ledger; we had thrown off that sweet, bewitching, enervating indolence, which is better, after all, than most of the enjoyments within mortal grasp. It was our purpose—a generous one, certainly, and absurd, no doubt, in full proportion with its generosity—to give up whatever we had hereto-fore attained, for the sake of showing mankind the example of a life governed by other than the false and cruel principles, on which human society has all along been based.

And, first of all, we had divorced ourselves from Pride, and were striving to supply its place with familiar love. We meant to lessen the laboring man's great burthen of toil, by performing our due share of it at the cost of our own thews[3] and sinews. We sought our profit by mutual aid, instead of wresting it by the strong hand from an enemy, or filching it craftily from those less shrewd than ourselves, (if, indeed, there were any such, in New England,) or winning it by self-ish competition with a neighbor; in one or another of which fashions, every son of woman both perpetrates and suffers his share of the common evil, whether he chooses it or no. And, as the basis of our institution, we purposed to offer up the earnest toil of our bodies, as a prayer, no less than an effort, for the advancement of our race.

Therefore, if we built splendid castles (phalansteries,[4] perhaps, they might be more fitly called,) and pictured beautiful scenes, among the fervid coals of the hearth around which we were clustering—and if all went to rack with the crumbling embers, and have never since arisen out of the ashes—let us take to ourselves no shame. In my own behalf, I rejoice that I could once think better of the world's improvability than it deserved. It is a mistake into which men sel-dom fall twice, in a lifetime; or, if so, the rarer and higher is the nature that can thus magnanimously persist in error.

Stout Silas Foster mingled little in our conversation; but when he did speak, it was very much to some practical purpose. For instance:—

---

3. Muscles.
4. Large, elaborately planned buildings each designed to house the 1,620 members of a "phalanx," the basic social unit of Charles Fourier's utopian society. The Brook Farm community adopted a modified Fourierism and began to plan for the construction of a scaled-down phalanstery in early 1844 (see p. 38, n. 3).

"Which man among you," quoth he, "is the best judge of swine? Some of us must go to the next Brighton fair, and buy half-a-dozen pigs!"

Pigs! Good heavens, had we come out from among the swinish multitude, for this? And again, in reference to some discussion about raising early vegetables for the market:—

"We shall never make any hand at market-gardening," said Silas Foster, "unless the women-folks will undertake to do all the weeding. We haven't team enough for that and the regular farm-work, reckoning three of you city-folks as worth one common field-hand. No, no, I tell you, we should have to get up a little too early in the morning, to compete with the market-gardeners round Boston!"

It struck me as rather odd, that one of the first questions raised, after our separation from the greedy, struggling, self-seeking world, should relate to the possibility of getting the advantage over the outside barbarians, in their own field of labor. But, to own the truth, I very soon became sensible, that, as regarded society at large, we stood in a position of new hostility, rather than new brotherhood. Nor could this fail to be the case, in some degree, until the bigger and better half of society should range itself on our side. Constituting so pitiful a minority as now, we were inevitably estranged from the rest of mankind, in pretty fair proportion with the strictness of our mutual bond among ourselves.

This dawning idea, however, was driven back into my inner consciousness by the entrance of Zenobia. She came with the welcome intelligence that supper was on the table. Looking at herself in the glass, and perceiving that her one magnificent flower had grown rather languid, (probably by being exposed to the fervency of the kitchen-fire,) she flung it on the floor, as unconcernedly as a village-girl would throw away a faded violet. The action seemed proper to her character; although, methought, it would still more have befitted the bounteous nature of this beautiful woman to scatter fresh flowers from her hand, and to revive faded ones by her touch. Nevertheless— it was a singular, but irresistible effect—the presence of Zenobia caused our heroic enterprise to show like an illusion, a masquerade, a pastoral, a counterfeit Arcadia,[5] in which we grown-up men and women were making a play-day of the years that were given us to live in. I tried to analyze this impression, but not with much success.

"It really vexes me," observed Zenobia, as we left the room, "that Mr. Hollingsworth should be such a laggard. I should not have thought him at all the sort of person to be turned back by a puff of contrary wind, or a few snow-flakes drifting into his face."

5. In classical and Renaissance poetry, a place of pastoral simplicity and harmonious contentment.

"Do you know Hollingsworth personally?" I inquired.

"No; only as an auditor—auditress, I mean—of some of his lectures," said she. "What a voice he has! And what a man he is! Yet not so much an intellectual man, I should say, as a great heart; at least, he moved me more deeply than I think myself capable of being moved, except by the stroke of a true, strong heart against my own. It is a sad pity that he should have devoted his glorious powers to such a grimy, unbeautiful, and positively hopeless object as this reformation of criminals, about which he makes himself and his wretchedly small audiences so very miserable. To tell you a secret, I never could tolerate a philanthropist,[6] before. Could you?"

"By no means," I answered; "neither can I now!"

"They are, indeed, an odiously disagreeable set of mortals," continued Zenobia. "I should like Mr. Hollingsworth a great deal better, if the philanthropy had been left out. At all events, as a mere matter of taste, I wish he would let the bad people alone, and try to benefit those who are not already past his help. Do you suppose he will be content to spend his life—or even a few months of it—among tolerably virtuous and comfortable individuals, like ourselves?"

"Upon my word, I doubt it," said I. "If we wish to keep him with us, we must systematically commit at least one crime apiece! Mere peccadillos will not satisfy him."

Zenobia turned, sidelong, a strange kind of a glance upon me; but, before I could make out what it meant, we had entered the kitchen, where, in accordance with the rustic simplicity of our new life, the supper-table was spread.

IV. The Supper-Table

The pleasant firelight! I must still keep harping on it.

The kitchen-hearth had an old-fashioned breadth, depth, and spaciousness, far within which lay what seemed the butt of a good-sized oak-tree, with the moisture bubbling merrily out of both ends. It was now half-an-hour beyond dusk. The blaze from an armfull of substantial sticks, rendered more combustible by brush-wood and pine, flickered powerfully on the smoke-blackened walls, and so cheered our spirits that we cared not what inclemency might rage and roar, on the other side of our illuminated windows. A yet sultrier warmth was bestowed by a goodly quantity of peat, which was crumbling to white ashes among the burning brands, and incensed the kitchen

---

6. A person devoted to helping others through acts of charity or self-devotion—a new and controversial social type in nineteenth-century America.

with its not ungrateful fragrance. The exuberance of this household fire would alone have sufficed to bespeak us no true farmers; for the New England yeoman, if he have the misfortune to dwell within practicable distance of a wood-market, is as niggardly of each stick as if it were a bar of California gold.

But it was fortunate for us, on that wintry eve of our untried life, to enjoy the warm and radiant luxury of a somewhat too abundant fire. If it served no other purpose, it made the men look so full of youth, warm blood, and hope, and the women—such of them, at least, as were anywise convertible by its magic—so very beautiful, that I would cheerfully have spent my last dollar to prolong the blaze. As for Zenobia, there was a glow in her cheeks that made me think of Pandora,[1] fresh from Vulcan's workshop, and full of the celestial warmth by dint of which he had tempered and moulded her.

"Take your places, my dear friends all," cried she; "seat yourselves without ceremony—and you shall be made happy with such tea as not many of the world's working-people, except yourselves, will find in their cups to-night. After this one supper, you may drink butter-milk, if you please. To-night, we will quaff this nectar, which, I assure you, could not be bought with gold."

We all sat down—grisly Silas Foster, his rotund helpmate, and the two bouncing handmaidens, included—and looked at one another in a friendly, but rather awkward way. It was the first practical trial of our theories of equal brotherhood and sisterhood; and we people of superior cultivation and refinement (for as such, I presume, we unhesitatingly reckoned ourselves) felt as if something were already accomplished towards the millennium of love. The truth is, however, that the laboring oar was with our unpolished companions; it being far easier to condescend, than to accept of condescension. Neither did I refrain from questioning, in secret, whether some of us—and Zenobia among the rest—would so quietly have taken our places among these good people, save for the cherished conscious-ness that it was not by necessity, but choice. Though we saw fit to drink our tea out of earthen cups to-night, and in earthen company, it was at our own option to use pictured porcelain and handle silver forks again, tomorrow. This same salvo, as to the power of regaining our former position, contributed much, I fear, to the equanimity with which we subsequently bore many of the hardships and humili-ations of a life of toil. If ever I have deserved—(which has not often been the case, and, I think, never)—but if ever I did deserve to be

1. Eve-like figure in Greek mythology, created out of clay by Vulcan, the god of fire, and endowed with gifts of beauty and guile by the other gods. Sent by Zeus to punish mankind for Prometheus's theft of fire, she opened a forbidden "jar" or "box," unleashing evil, hard work, and trouble upon the earth.

soundly cuffed by a fellow-mortal, for secretly putting weight upon some imaginary social advantage, it must have been while I was striving to prove myself ostentatiously his equal, and no more. It was while I sat beside him on his cobbler's bench, or clinked my hoe against his own, in the cornfield, or broke the same crust of bread, my earth-grimed hand to his, at our noontide lunch. The poor, proud man should look at both sides of sympathy like this.

The silence, which followed upon our sitting down to table, grew rather oppressive; indeed, it was hardly broken by a word, during the first round of Zenobia's fragrant tea.

"I hope," said I, at last, "that our blazing windows will be visible a great way off. There is nothing so pleasant and encouraging to a solitary traveller, on a stormy night, as a flood of firelight, seen amid the gloom. These ruddy window-panes cannot fail to cheer the hearts of all that look at them. Are they not warm and bright with the beacon-fire which we have kindled for humanity?"

"The blaze of that brush-wood will only last a minute or two longer," observed Silas Foster; but whether he meant to insinuate that our moral illumination would have as brief a term, I cannot say.

"Meantime," said Zenobia, "it may serve to guide some wayfarer to a shelter."

And, just as she said this, there came a knock at the house-door.

"There is one of the world's wayfarers!" said I.

"Aye, aye, just so!" quoth Silas Foster. "Our firelight will draw stragglers, just as a candle draws dor-bugs,[2] on a summer night."

Whether to enjoy a dramatic suspense, or that we were selfishly contrasting our own comfort with the chill and dreary situation of the unknown person at the threshold—or that some of us city-folk felt a little startled at the knock which came so unseasonably, through night and storm, to the door of the lonely farm-house—so it happened, that nobody, for an instant or two, arose to answer the summons. Pretty soon, there came another knock. The first had been moderately loud; the second was smitten so forcibly that the knuckles of the applicant must have left their mark in the door-panel.

"He knocks as if he had a right to come in," said Zenobia, laughing. "And what are we thinking of? It must be Mr. Hollingsworth!"

Hereupon, I went to the door, unbolted, and flung it wide open. There, sure enough, stood Hollingsworth, his shaggy great-coat all covered with snow; so that he looked quite as much like a polar bear as a modern philanthropist.

"Sluggish hospitality, this!" said he, in those deep tones of his, which seemed to come out of a chest as capacious as a barrel. "It would have served you right if I had lain down and spent the night

2. Beetles that fly with a buzzing sound.

on the door-step, just for the sake of putting you to shame. But here is a guest, who will need a warmer and softer bed."

And stepping back to the wagon, in which he had journeyed hither, Hollingsworth received into his arms, and deposited on the door-step, a figure enveloped in a cloak. It was evidently a woman; or rather—judging from the ease with which he lifted her, and the little space which she seemed to fill in his arms—a slim and unsubstantial girl. As she showed some hesitation about entering the door, Hollingsworth, with his usual directness and lack of ceremony, urged her forward, not merely within the entry, but into the warm and strongly lighted kitchen.

"Who is this?" whispered I, remaining behind with him, while he was taking off his great-coat.

"Who? Really, I don't know," answered Hollingsworth, looking at me with some surprise. "It is a young person who belongs here, however; and, no doubt, she has been expected. Zenobia, or some of the women-folks, can tell you all about it."

"I think not," said I, glancing towards the new-comer and the other occupants of the kitchen. "Nobody seems to welcome her. I should hardly judge that she was an expected guest."

"Well, well," said Hollingsworth, quietly. "We'll make it right."

The stranger, or whatever she were, remained standing precisely on that spot of the kitchen-floor, to which Hollingsworth's kindly hand had impelled her. The cloak falling partly off, she was seen to be a very young woman, dressed in a poor, but decent gown, made high in the neck, and without any regard to fashion or smartness. Her brown hair fell down from beneath a hood, not in curls, but with only a slight wave; her face was of a wan, almost sickly hue, betokening habitual seclusion from the sun and free atmosphere, like a flower-shrub that had done its best to blossom in too scanty light. To complete the pitiableness of her aspect, she shivered either with cold, or fear, or nervous excitement, so that you might have beheld her shadow vibrating on the fire-lighted wall. In short, there has seldom been seen so depressed and sad a figure as this young girl's; and it was hardly possible to help being angry with her, from mere despair of doing anything for her comfort. The fantasy occurred to me, that she was some desolate kind of a creature, doomed to wander about in snow-storms, and that, though the ruddiness of our window-panes had tempted her into a human dwelling, she would not remain long enough to melt the icicles out of her hair.

Another conjecture likewise came into my mind. Recollecting Hollingsworth's sphere of philanthropic action, I deemed it possible that he might have brought one of his guilty patients, to be wrought upon, and restored to spiritual health, by the pure influences which our mode of life would create.

As yet, the girl had not stirred. She stood near the door, fixing a pair of large, brown, melancholy eyes upon Zenobia—only upon Zenobia!—she evidently saw nothing else in the room, save that bright, fair, rosy, beautiful woman. It was the strangest look I ever witnessed; long a mystery to me, and forever a memory. Once, she seemed about to move forward and greet her—I know not with what warmth, or with what words;—but, finally, instead of doing so, she drooped down upon her knees, clasped her hands, and gazed piteously into Zenobia's face. Meeting no kindly reception, her head fell on her bosom.

I never thoroughly forgave Zenobia for her conduct on this occasion. But women are always more cautious, in their casual hospitalities, than men.

"What does the girl mean?" cried she, in rather a sharp tone. "Is she crazy? Has she no tongue?"

And here Hollingsworth stept forward.

"No wonder if the poor child's tongue is frozen in her mouth," said he—and I think he positively frowned at Zenobia—"The very heart will be frozen in her bosom, unless you women can warm it, among you, with the warmth that ought to be in your own!"

Hollingsworth's appearance was very striking, at this moment. He was then about thirty years old, but looked several years older, with his great shaggy head, his heavy brow, his dark complexion, his abundant beard, and the rude strength with which his features seemed to have been hammered out of iron, rather than chiselled or moulded from any finer or softer material. His figure was not tall, but massive and brawny, and well befitting his original occupation, which—as the reader probably knows—was that of a blacksmith. As for external polish, or mere courtesy of manner, he never possessed more than a tolerably educated bear; although, in his gentler moods, there was a tenderness in his voice, eyes, mouth, in his gesture, and in every indescribable manifestation, which few men could resist, and no woman. But he now looked stern and reproachful; and it was with that inauspicious meaning in his glance, that Hollingsworth first met Zenobia's eyes, and began his influence upon her life.

To my surprise, Zenobia—of whose haughty spirit I had been told so many examples—absolutely changed color, and seemed mortified and confused.

"You do not quite do me justice, Mr. Hollingsworth," said she, almost humbly. "I am willing to be kind to the poor girl. Is she a protégée of yours? What can I do for her?"

"Have you anything to ask of this lady?" said Hollingsworth, kindly, to the girl. "I remember you mentioned her name, before we left town."

"Only that she will shelter me," replied the girl, tremulously. "Only that she will let me be always near her!"

"Well, indeed," exclaimed Zenobia, recovering herself, and laughing, "this is an adventure, and well worthy to be the first incident in our life of love and free-heartedness! But I accept it, for the present, without further question—only," added she, "it would be a convenience if we knew your name!"

"Priscilla," said the girl; and it appeared to me that she hesitated whether to add anything more, and decided in the negative. "Pray do not ask me my other name—at least, not yet—if you will be so kind to a forlorn creature."

Priscilla! Priscilla! I repeated the name to myself, three or four times; and, in that little space, this quaint and prim cognomen had so amalgamated itself with my idea of the girl, that it seemed as if no other name could have adhered to her for a moment. Heretofore, the poor thing had not shed any tears; but now that she found herself received, and at least temporarily established, the big drops began to ooze out from beneath her eyelids, as if she were full of them. Perhaps it showed the iron substance of my heart, that I could not help smiling at this odd scene of unknown and unaccountable calamity, into which our cheerful party had been entrapped, without the liberty of choosing whether to sympathize or no. Hollingsworth's behavior was certainly a great deal more creditable than mine.

"Let us not pry farther into her secrets," he said to Zenobia and the rest of us, apart—and his dark, shaggy face looked really beautiful with its expression of thoughtful benevolence—"Let us conclude that Providence has sent her to us, as the first fruits of the world, which we have undertaken to make happier than we find it. Let us warm her poor, shivering body with this good fire, and her poor, shivering heart with our best kindness. Let us feed her, and make her one of us. As we do by this friendless girl, so shall we prosper! And, in good time, whatever is desirable for us to know will be melted out of her, as inevitably as those tears which we see now."

"At least," remarked I, "you may tell us how and where you met with her."

"An old man brought her to my lodgings," answered Hollingsworth, "and begged me to convey her to Blithedale, where—so I understood him—she had friends. And this is positively all I know about the matter."

Grim Silas Foster, all this while, had been busy at the supper-table, pouring out his own tea, and gulping it down with no more sense of its exquisiteness than if it were a decoction of catnip; helping himself to pieces of dipt toast on the flat of his knife-blade, and dropping half of it on the table-cloth; using the same serviceable implement to cut slice after slice of ham; perpetrating terrible enormities with the butter-plate; and, in all other respects, behaving less like a civilized Christian than the worst kind of an ogre. Being, by this time, fully gorged, he crowned his amiable exploits with a draught from the water-pitcher, and then favored us with his opinion about the business in hand. And, certainly, though they proceeded out of an unwiped mouth, his expressions did him honor.

"Give the girl a hot cup of tea, and a thick slice of this first-rate bacon," said Silas, like a sensible man as he was. "That's what she wants. Let her stay with us as long as she likes, and help in the kitchen, and take the cow-breath at milking-time; and, in a week or two, she'll begin to look like a creature of this world!"

So we sat down again to supper, and Priscilla along with us.

V. Until Bedtime

Silas Foster, by the time we concluded our meal, had stript off his coat and planted himself on a low chair by the kitchen-fire, with a lap-stone, a hammer, a piece of sole-leather, and some waxed ends, in order to cobble an old pair of cow-hide boots; he being, in his own phrase, 'something of a dab'[1] (whatever degree of skill that may imply) at the shoemaking-business. We heard the tap of his hammer, at intervals, for the rest of the evening. The remainder of the party adjourned to the sitting-room. Good Mrs. Foster took her knitting-work, and soon fell fast asleep, still keeping her needles in brisk movement, and, to the best of my observation, absolutely footing a stocking out of the texture of a dream. And a very substantial stocking it seemed to be. One of the two handmaidens hemmed a towel, and the other appeared to be making a ruffle, for her Sunday's wear, out of a little bit of embroidered muslin, which Zenobia had probably given her.

It was curious to observe how trustingly, and yet how timidly, our poor Priscilla betook herself into the shadow of Zenobia's protection. She sat beside her on a stool, looking up, every now and then, with an expression of humble delight at her new friend's beauty. A brilliant woman is often an object of the devoted admiration—it might almost be termed worship, or idolatry—of some young girl, who perhaps beholds the cynosure only at an awful distance, and has as little hope of personal intercourse as of climbing among the stars of heaven. We men are too gross to comprehend it. Even a woman, of mature age, despises or laughs at such a passion. There occurred to me no mode of accounting for Priscilla's behavior, except by supposing that she had read some of Zenobia's stories, (as

1. Expert.

such literature goes everywhere,) or her tracts in defence of the sex, and had come hither with the one purpose of being her slave. There is nothing parallel to this, I believe—nothing so foolishly disinterested, and hardly anything so beautiful—in the masculine nature, at whatever epoch of life; or, if there be, a fine and rare development of character might reasonably be looked for, from the youth who should prove himself capable of such self-forgetful affection.

Zenobia happening to change her seat, I took the opportunity, in an under tone, to suggest some such notion as the above.

"Since you see the young woman in so poetical a light," replied she, in the same tone, "you had better turn the affair into a ballad. It is a grand subject, and worthy of supernatural machinery. The storm, the startling knock at the door, the entrance of the sable knight Hollingsworth and this shadowy snow-maiden, who, precisely at the stroke of midnight, shall melt away at my feet, in a pool of ice-cold water, and give me my death with a pair of wet slippers! And when the verses are written, and polished quite to your mind, I will favor you with my idea as to what the girl really is."

"Pray let me have it now," said I. "It shall be woven into the ballad."

"She is neither more nor less," answered Zenobia, "than a seamstress from the city, and she has probably no more transcendental purpose than to do my miscellaneous sewing; for I suppose she will hardly expect to make my dresses."

"How can you decide upon her so easily?" I inquired.

"Oh, we women judge one another by tokens that escape the obtuseness of masculine perceptions," said Zenobia. "There is no proof, which you would be likely to appreciate, except the needle marks on the tip of her forefinger. Then, my supposition perfectly accounts for her paleness, her nervousness, and her wretched fragility. Poor thing! She has been stifled with the heat of a salamander-stove,[2] in a small, close room, and has drunk coffee, and fed upon dough-nuts, raisins, candy, and all such trash, till she is scarcely half-alive; and so, as she has hardly any physique, a poet, like Mr. Miles Coverdale, may be allowed to think her spiritual!"

"Look at her now!" whispered I.

Priscilla was gazing towards us, with an inexpressible sorrow in her wan face, and great tears running down her cheeks. It was difficult to resist the impression, that, cautiously as we had lowered our voices, she must have overheard and been wounded by Zenobia's scornful estimate of her character and purposes.

"What ears the girl must have!" whispered Zenobia, with a look of vexation, partly comic and partly real. "I will confess to you that I cannot quite make her out. However, I am positively not

2. Small portable stove for heating rooms.

an ill-natured person, unless when very grievously provoked; and as you, and especially Mr. Hollingsworth, take so much interest in this odd creature—and as she knocks, with a very slight tap, against my own heart, likewise—why, I mean to let her in! From this moment, I will be reasonably kind to her. There is no pleasure in tormenting a person of one's own sex, even if she do favor one with a little more love than one can conveniently dispose of;—and that, let me say, Mr. Coverdale, is the most troublesome offence you can offer to a woman."

"Thank you!" said I, smiling. "I don't mean to be guilty of it."

She went towards Priscilla, took her hand, and passed her own rosy finger-tips, with a pretty, caressing movement, over the girl's hair. The touch had a magical effect. So vivid a look of joy flushed up beneath those fingers, that it seemed as if the sad and wan Priscilla had been snatched away, and another kind of creature substituted in her place. This one caress, bestowed voluntarily by Zenobia, was evidently received as a pledge of all that the stranger sought from her, whatever the unuttered boon might be. From that instant, too, she melted in quietly amongst us, and was no longer a foreign element. Though always an object of peculiar interest, a riddle, and a theme of frequent discussion, her tenure at Blithedale was thenceforth fixed; we no more thought of questioning it, than if Priscilla had been recognized as a domestic sprite, who had haunted the rustic fireside, of old, before we had ever been warmed by its blaze.

She now produced, out of a work-bag that she had with her, some little wooden instruments, (what they are called, I never knew,) and proceeded to knit, or net, an article which ultimately took the shape of a silk purse. As the work went on, I remembered to have seen just such purses, before. Indeed, I was the possessor of one. Their peculiar excellence, besides the great delicacy and beauty of the manufacture, lay in the almost impossibility that any uninitiated person should discover the aperture; although, to a practised touch, they would open as wide as charity or prodigality might wish. I wondered if it were not a symbol of Priscilla's own mystery.

Notwithstanding the new confidence with which Zenobia had inspired her, our guest showed herself disquieted by the storm. When the strong puffs of wind spattered the snow against the windows, and made the oaken frame of the farm-house creak, she looked at us apprehensively, as if to inquire whether these tempestuous outbreaks did not betoken some unusual mischief in the shrieking blast. She had been bred up, no doubt, in some close nook, some inauspiciously sheltered court of the city, where the uttermost rage of a tempest, though it might scatter down the slates of the roof into the bricked area, could not shake the casement of her little room. The sense of vast, undefined space, pressing from the outside against the black panes of our uncurtained windows, was fearful to the poor girl, heretofore accustomed to the narrowness of human limits, with the lamps of neighboring tenements glimmering across the street. The house probably seemed to her adrift on the great ocean of the night. A little parallelogram of sky was all that she had hitherto known of nature; so that she felt the awfulness that really exists in its limitless extent. Once, while the blast was bellowing, she caught hold of Zenobia's robe, with precisely the air of one who hears her own name spoken, at a distance, but is unutterably reluctant to obey the call.

We spent rather an incommunicative evening. Hollingsworth hardly said a word, unless when repeatedly and pertinaciously addressed. Then, indeed, he would glare upon us from the thick shrubbery of his meditations, like a tiger out of a jungle, make the briefest reply possible, and betake himself back into the solitude of his heart and mind. The poor fellow had contracted this ungracious habit from the intensity with which he contemplated his own ideas, and the infrequent sympathy which they met with from his auditors; a circumstance that seemed only to strengthen the implicit confidence that he awarded to them. His heart, I imagine, was never really interested in our socialist scheme, but was forever busy with his strange, and, as most people thought it, impracticable plan for the reformation of criminals, through an appeal to their higher instincts. Much as I liked Hollingsworth, it cost me many a groan to tolerate him on this point. He ought to have commenced his investigation of the subject by perpetrating some huge sin, in his proper person, and examining the condition of his higher instincts, afterwards.

The rest of us formed ourselves into a committee for providing our infant Community with an appropriate name; a matter of greatly more difficulty than the uninitiated reader would suppose. Blithedale was neither good nor bad. We should have resumed the old Indian name of the premises, had it possessed the oil-and-honey flow which the aborigines were so often happy in communicating to their local appellations; but it chanced to be a harsh, ill-connected, and interminable word, which seemed to fill the mouth with a mixture of very stiff clay and very crumbly pebbles. Zenobia suggested 'Sunny Glimpse,' as expressive of a vista into a better system of society. This we turned over and over, for awhile, acknowledging its prettiness, but concluded it to be rather too fine and sentimental a name (a fault inevitable by literary ladies, in such attempts) for sun-burnt men to work under. I ventured to whisper 'Utopia,' which, however, was unanimously scouted down,[3] and the proposer very harshly

---

3. Coverdale's proposal that the community be named after the ideal society of Thomas More's *Utopia* (1516) is ridiculed ("scouted down") by his companions.

maltreated, as if he had intended a latent satire. Some were for calling our institution 'The Oasis,' in view of its being the one green spot in the moral sand-waste of the world; but others insisted on a proviso for reconsidering the matter, at a twelvemonth's end; when a final decision might be had, whether to name it 'The Oasis,' or 'Saharah.' So, at last, finding it impracticable to hammer out anything better, we resolved that the spot should still be Blithedale, as being of good augury enough.

The evening wore on, and the outer solitude looked in upon us through the windows, gloomy, wild, and vague, like another state of existence, close beside the littler sphere of warmth and light in which we were the prattlers and bustlers of a moment. By-and-by, the door was opened by Silas Foster, with a cotton handkerchief about his head, and a tallow candle in his hand.

"Take my advice, brother-farmers," said he, with a great, broad, bottomless yawn, "and get to bed as soon as you can. I shall sound the horn at day-break; and we've got the cattle to fodder, and nine cows to milk, and a dozen other things to do, before breakfast."

Thus ended the first evening at Blithedale. I went shivering to my fireless chamber, with the miserable consciousness (which had been growing upon me for several hours past) that I had caught a tremendous cold, and should probably awaken, at the blast of the horn, a fit subject for a hospital. The night proved a feverish one. During the greater part of it, I was in that vilest of states when a fixed idea remains in the mind, like the nail in Sisera's brain,[4] while innumerable other ideas go and come, and flutter to-and-fro, combining constant transition with intolerable sameness. Had I made a record of that night's half-waking dreams, it is my belief that it would have anticipated several of the chief incidents of this narrative, including a dim shadow of its catastrophe. Starting up in bed, at length, I saw that the storm was past, and the moon was shining on the snowy landscape, which looked like a lifeless copy of the world in marble.

From the bank of the distant river, which was shimmering in the moonlight, came the black shadow of the only cloud in heaven, driven swiftly by the wind, and passing over meadow and hillock— vanishing amid tufts of leafless trees, but reappearing on the hither side—until it swept across our door-step.

How cold an Arcadia was this!

4. In the Bible, Sisera, commander of the army of the Canaanites (enemies of the Israelites), is killed when the heroic woman Jael drives a tent nail through his head as he sleeps (Judges 4).

VI. Coverdale's Sick-Chamber

The horn sounded at day-break, as Silas Foster had forewarned us, harsh, uproarious, inexorably drawn out, and as sleep-dispelling as if this hard-hearted old yeoman had got hold of the trump of doom.[1]

On all sides, I could hear the creaking of the bedsteads, as the brethren of Blithedale started from slumber, and thrust themselves into their habiliments, all awry, no doubt, in their haste to begin the reformation of the world. Zenobia put her head into the entry, and besought Silas Foster to cease his clamor, and to be kind enough to leave an armful of firewood and a pail of water at her chamber-door. Of the whole household—unless, indeed, it were Priscilla, for whose habits, in this particular, I cannot vouch—of all our apostolic society, whose mission was to bless mankind, Hollingsworth, I apprehend, was the only one who began the enterprise with prayer. My sleeping-room being but thinly partitioned from his, the solemn murmur of his voice made its way to my ears, compelling me to be an auditor of his awful privacy with the Creator. It affected me with a deep reverence for Hollingsworth, which no familiarity then existing, or that afterwards grew more intimate between us—no, nor my subsequent perception of his own great errors—ever quite effaced. It is so rare, in these times, to meet with a man of prayerful habits, (except, of course, in the pulpit,) that such an one is decidedly marked out by a light of transfiguration, shed upon him in the divine interview from which he passes into his daily life.

As for me, I lay abed, and, if I said my prayers, it was backward, cursing my day as bitterly as patient Job[2] himself. The truth was, the hot-house warmth of a town-residence, and the luxurious life in which I indulged myself, had taken much of the pith out of my physical system; and the wintry blast of the preceding day, together with the general chill of our airy old farm-house, had got fairly into my heart and the marrow of my bones. In this predicament, I seriously wished—selfish as it may appear—that the reformation of society had been postponed about half-a-century, or at all events, to such a date as should have put my intermeddling with it entirely out of the question.

What, in the name of common-sense, had I to do with any better society than I had always lived in! It had satisfied me well enough. My pleasant bachelor-parlor, sunny and shadowy, curtained and carpeted, with the bed-chamber adjoining; my centre-table, strewn

---

1. In the prophetic biblical book of Revelation, the end of the world is announced by an angel blowing a trumpet (Revelation 11:15).
2. Old Testament figure whom God allows Satan to torment as a test of his faith; Job triumphs—though not without considerable complaint.

with books and periodicals; my writing-desk, with a half-finished poem in a stanza of my own contrivance; my morning lounge at the reading-room or picture-gallery; my noontide walk along the cheery pavement, with the suggestive succession of human faces, and the brisk throb of human life, in which I shared; my dinner at the Albion, where I had a hundred dishes at command, and could banquet as delicately as the wizard Michael Scott,[3] when the devil fed him from the King of France's kitchen; my evening at the billiard-club, the concert, the theatre, or at somebody's party, if I pleased:— what could be better than all this? Was it better to hoe, to mow, to toil and moil amidst the accumulations of a barn-yard, to be the chambermaid of two yoke of oxen and a dozen cows, to eat salt-beef and earn it with the sweat of my brow, and thereby take the tough morsel out of some wretch's mouth, into whose vocation I had thrust myself? Above all, was it better to have a fever, and die blaspheming, as I was like to do?

In this wretched plight, with a furnace in my heart, and another in my head, by the heat of which I was kept constantly at the boiling point—yet shivering at the bare idea of extruding so much as a finger into the icy atmosphere of the room—I kept my bed until breakfast-time, when Hollingsworth knocked at the door, and entered.

"Well, Coverdale," cried he, "you bid fair to make an admirable farmer! Don't you mean to get up to-day?"

"Neither to-day nor tomorrow," said I, hopelessly. "I doubt if I ever rise again!"

"What is the matter now?" he asked.

I told him my piteous case, and besought him to send me back to town, in a close carriage.

"No, no!" said Hollingsworth, with kindly seriousness. "If you are really sick, we must take care of you."

Accordingly, he built a fire in my chamber, and having little else to do while the snow lay on the ground, established himself as my nurse. A doctor was sent for, who, being homeopathic,[4] gave me as much medicine, in the course of a fortnight's attendance, as would have lain on the point of a needle. They fed me on water-gruel[5] and I speedily became a skeleton above ground. But, after all, I have many precious recollections connected with that fit of sickness.

Hollingsworth's more than brotherly attendance gave me inexpressible comfort. Most men—and, certainly, I could not always

---

3. Medieval scholar, translator, philosopher, astrologer—and, according to legend, magician, capable of commanding spirits to provide his guests with food from royal courts or ring the bells of Notre Dame Cathedral. Birthdate unknown; died c. 1235.
4. Subscribing to the theory that illnesses could be cured by administering minute doses of medicines that would, in larger amounts, cause symptoms like those of the disease being treated.
5. A thin, easily digested broth made by cooking cereal in water.

claim to be one of the exceptions—have a natural indifference, if not an absolutely hostile feeling, towards those whom disease, or weakness, or calamity of any kind, causes to faulter and faint amid the rude jostle of our selfish existence. The education of Christianity, it is true, the sympathy of a like experience, and the example of women, may soften, and possibly subvert, this ugly characteristic of our sex. But it is originally there, and has likewise its analogy in the practice of our brute brethren, who hunt the sick or disabled member of the herd from among them, as an enemy. It is for this reason that the stricken deer goes apart, and the sick lion grimly withdraws himself into his den. Except in love, or the attachments of kindred, or other very long and habitual affection, we really have no tenderness. But there was something of the woman moulded into the great, stalwart frame of Hollingsworth; nor was he ashamed of it, as men often are of what is best in them, nor seemed ever to know that there was such a soft place in his heart. I knew it well, however, at that time; although, afterwards, it came nigh to be forgotten. Methought there could not be two such men alive, as Hollingsworth. There never was any blaze of a fireside that warmed and cheered me, in the down-sinkings and shiverings of my spirit, so effectually as did the light out of those eyes, which lay so deep and dark under his shaggy brows.

Happy the man that has such a friend beside him, when he comes to die! And unless a friend like Hollingsworth be at hand, as most probably there will not, he had better make up his mind to die alone. How many men, I wonder, does one meet with, in a lifetime, whom he would choose for his death-bed companions! At the crisis of my fever, I besought Hollingsworth to let nobody else enter the room, but continually to make me sensible of his own presence by a grasp of the hand, a word—a prayer, if he thought good to utter it—and that then he should be the witness how courageously I would encounter the worst. It still impresses me as almost a matter of regret, that I did not die, then, when I had tolerably made up my mind to it; for Hollingsworth would have gone with me to the hither verge of life, and have sent his friendly and hopeful accents far over on the other side, while I should be treading the unknown path. Now, were I to send for him, he would hardly come to my bedside; nor should I depart the easier, for his presence.

"You are not going to die, this time," said he, gravely smiling. "You know nothing about sickness, and think your case a great deal more desperate than it is."

"Death should take me while I am in the mood," replied I, with a little of my customary levity.

"Have you nothing to do in life," asked Hollingsworth, "that you fancy yourself so ready to leave it?"

"Nothing," answered I—"nothing, that I know of, unless to make pretty verses, and play a part, with Zenobia and the rest of the amateurs, in our pastoral. It seems but an unsubstantial sort of business, as viewed through a mist of fever. But, dear Hollingsworth, your own vocation is evidently to be a priest, and to spend your days and nights in helping your fellow-creatures to draw peaceful dying-breaths."

"And by which of my qualities," inquired he, "can you suppose me fitted for this awful ministry?"

"By your tenderness," I said. "It seems to me the reflection of God's own love."

"And you call me tender!" repeated Hollingsworth, thoughtfully. "I should rather say, that the most marked trait in my character is an inflexible severity of purpose. Mortal man has no right to be so inflexible, as it is my nature and necessity to be!"

"I do not believe it," I replied.

But, in due time, I remembered what he said.

Probably, as Hollingsworth suggested, my disorder was never so serious as, in my ignorance of such matters, I was inclined to consider it. After so much tragical preparation, it was positively rather mortifying to find myself on the mending hand.

All the other members of the Community showed me kindness, according to the full measure of their capacity. Zenobia brought me my gruel, every day, made by her own hands, (not very skilfully, if the truth must be told,) and, whenever I seemed inclined to converse, would sit by my bedside, and talk with so much vivacity as to add several gratuitous throbs to my pulse. Her poor little stories and tracts never half did justice to her intellect; it was only the lack of a fitter avenue that drove her to seek development in literature. She was made (among a thousand other things that she might have been) for a stump-oratress. I recognized no severe culture in Zenobia; her mind was full of weeds. It startled me, sometimes, in my state of moral, as well as bodily faint-heartedness, to observe the hardihood of her philosophy; she made no scruple of oversetting all human institutions, and scattering them as with a breeze from her fan. A female reformer, in her attacks upon society, has an instinctive sense of where the life lies, and is inclined to aim directly at that spot. Especially, the relation between the sexes is naturally among the earliest to attract her notice.

Zenobia was truly a magnificent woman. The homely simplicity of her dress could not conceal, nor scarcely diminish, the queenliness of her presence. The image of her form and face should have been multiplied all over the earth. It was wronging the rest of mankind, to retain her as the spectacle of only a few. The stage would have been her proper sphere. She should have made it a point of duty, moreover, to sit endlessly to painters and sculptors, and preferably to the latter; because the cold decorum of the marble would consist with the utmost scantiness of drapery, so that the eye might chastely be gladdened with her material perfection, in its entireness. I know not well how to express, that the native glow of coloring in her cheeks, and even the flesh-warmth over her round arms, and what was visible of her full bust—in a word, her womanliness incarnated—compelled me sometimes to close my eyes, as if it were not quite the privilege of modesty to gaze at her. Illness and exhaustion, no doubt, had made me morbidly sensitive.

I noticed—and wondered how Zenobia contrived it—that she had always a new flower in her hair. And still it was a hot-house flower—an outlandish flower—a flower of the tropics, such as appeared to have sprung passionately out of a soil, the very weeds of which would be fervid and spicy. Unlike as was the flower of each successive day to the preceding one, it yet so assimilated its richness to the rich beauty of the woman, that I thought it the only flower fit to be worn; so fit, indeed, that Nature had evidently created this floral gem, in a happy exuberance, for the one purpose of worthily adorning Zenobia's head. It might be, that my feverish fantasies clustered themselves about this peculiarity, and caused it to look more gorgeous and wonderful than if beheld with temperate eyes. In the height of my illness, as I well recollect, I went so far as to pronounce it preternatural.

"Zenobia is an enchantress!" whispered I once to Hollingsworth. "She is a sister of the Veiled Lady! That flower in her hair is a talisman. If you were to snatch it away, she would vanish, or be transformed into something else!"

"What does he say?" asked Zenobia.

"Nothing that has an atom of sense in it," answered Hollingsworth. "He is a little beside himself, I believe, and talks about your being a witch, and of some magical property in the flower that you wear in your hair."

"It is an idea worthy of a feverish poet," said she, laughing, rather compassionately, and taking out the flower. "I scorn to owe anything to magic. Here, Mr. Hollingsworth:—you may keep the spell, while it has any virtue in it; but I cannot promise you not to appear with a new one, tomorrow. It is the one relic of my more brilliant, my happier days!"

The most curious part of the matter was, that, long after my slight delirium had passed away—as long, indeed, as I continued to know this remarkable woman—her daily flower affected my imagination, though more slightly, yet in very much the same way. The reason must have been, that, whether intentionally on her part, or not, this favorite ornament was actually a subtle expression of Zenobia's character.

One subject, about which—very impertinently, moreover—I perplexed myself with a great many conjectures, was, whether Zenobia had ever been married. The idea, it must be understood, was unauthorized by any circumstance or suggestion that had made its way to my ears. So young as I beheld her, and the freshest and rosiest woman of a thousand, there was certainly no need of imputing to her a destiny already accomplished; the probability was far greater, that her coming years had all life's richest gifts to bring. If the great event of a woman's existence had been consummated, the world knew nothing of it, although the world seemed to know Zenobia well. It was a ridiculous piece of romance, undoubtedly, to imagine that this beautiful personage, wealthy as she was, and holding a position that might fairly enough be called distinguished, could have given herself away so privately, but that some whisper and suspicion, and, by degrees, a full understanding of the fact, would eventually be blown abroad. But, then, as I failed not to consider, her original home was at a distance of many hundred miles. Rumors might fill the social atmosphere, or might once have filled it, there, which would travel but slowly, against the wind, towards our northeastern metropolis, and perhaps melt into thin air before reaching it.

There was not, and I distinctly repeat it, the slightest foundation in my knowledge for any surmise of the kind. But there is a species of intuition—either a spiritual lie, or the subtle recognition of a fact—which comes to us in a reduced state of the corporeal system. The soul gets the better of the body, after wasting illness, or when a vegetable diet may have mingled too much ether in the blood.[6] Vapors then rise up to the brain, and take shapes that often image falsehood, but sometimes truth. The spheres of our companions have, at such periods, a vastly greater influence upon our own, than when robust health gives us a repellent and self-defensive energy. Zenobia's sphere, I imagine, impressed itself powerfully on mine, and transformed me, during this period of my weakness, into something like a mesmerical clairvoyant.[7]

Then, also, as anybody could observe, the freedom of her deportment (though, to some tastes, it might commend itself as the utmost perfection of manner, in a youthful widow, or a blooming matron) was not exactly maidenlike. What girl had ever laughed as Zenobia

---

6. According to some contemporary medical theories, a meatless diet generated "ether" in the body, increasing a person's receptiveness to the spiritual world.
7. Throughout this description of the effects of his illness, Coverdale borrows the vocabulary associated with "mesmerism," which imagines that the spiritual energy of one person might communicate with or exert power over the "sphere" of another (see p. 6, n. 3).

did! What girl had ever spoken in her mellow tones! Her uncon-
strained and inevitable manifestation, I said often to myself, was
that of a woman to whom wedlock had thrown wide the gates of
mystery. Yet, sometimes, I strove to be ashamed of these conjectures.
I acknowledged it as a masculine grossness—a sin of wicked interpretation, of which man is often guilty towards the other sex—thus
to mistake the sweet, liberal, but womanly frankness of a noble and
generous disposition. Still, it was of no avail to reason with myself,
nor to upbraid myself. Pertinaciously the thought—'Zenobia is a
wife! Zenobia has lived, and loved! There is no folded petal, no latent
dew-drop, in this perfectly developed rose!'—irresistibly that
thought drove out all other conclusions, as often as my mind
reverted to the subject.

Zenobia was conscious of my observation, though not, I presume,
of the point to which it led me.

"Mr. Coverdale," said she, one day, as she saw me watching her,
while she arranged my gruel on the table, "I have been exposed to a
great deal of eye-shot in the few years of my mixing in the world, but
never, I think, to precisely such glances as you are in the habit of
favoring me with. I seem to interest you very much; and yet—or else
a woman's instinct is for once deceived—I cannot reckon you as an
admirer. What are you seeking to discover in me?"

"The mystery of your life," answered I, surprised into the truth by
the unexpectedness of her attack. "And you will never tell me."

She bent her head towards me, and let me look into her eyes, as if
challenging me to drop a plummet-line down into the depths of her
consciousness.

"I see nothing now," said I, closing my own eyes, "unless it be the
face of a sprite, laughing at me from the bottom of a deep well."

A bachelor always feels himself defrauded, when he knows, or
suspects, that any woman of his acquaintance has given herself
away. Otherwise, the matter could have been no concern of mine. It
was purely speculative; for I should not, under any circumstances,
have fallen in love with Zenobia. The riddle made me so nervous,
however, in my sensitive condition of mind and body, that I most
ungratefully began to wish that she would let me alone. Then, too,
her gruel was very wretched stuff, with almost invariably the smell of
pine-smoke upon it, like the evil taste that is said to mix itself up
with a witch's best concocted dainties. Why could not she have
allowed one of the other women to take the gruel in charge? Whatever else might be her gifts, Nature certainly never intended Zenobia
for a cook. Or, if so, she should have meddled only with the richest
and spiciest dishes, and such as are to be tasted at banquets,
between draughts of intoxicating wine.

VII. The Convalescent

As soon as my incommodities allowed me to think of past occurrences, I failed not to inquire what had become of the odd little
guest, whom Hollingsworth had been the medium of introducing
among us. It now appeared, that poor Priscilla had not so literally
fallen out of the clouds, as we were at first inclined to suppose. A letter, which should have introduced her, had since been received from
one of the city-missionaries, containing a certificate of character, and
an allusion to circumstances which, in the writer's judgment, made it
especially desirable that she should find shelter in our Community.
There was a hint, not very intelligible, implying either that Priscilla
had recently escaped from some particular peril, or irksomeness of
position, or else that she was still liable to this danger or difficulty,
whatever it might be. We should ill have deserved the reputation of a
benevolent fraternity, had we hesitated to entertain a petitioner in
such need, and so strongly recommended to our kindness; not to
mention, moreover, that the strange maiden had set herself diligently
to work, and was doing good service with her needle. But a slight mist
of uncertainty still floated about Priscilla, and kept her, as yet, from
taking a very decided place among creatures of flesh and blood.

The mysterious attraction, which, from her first entrance on our
scene, she evinced for Zenobia, had lost nothing of its force. I often
heard her footsteps, soft and low, accompanying the light, but
decided tread of the latter, up the staircase, stealing along the passage-
way by her new friend's side, and pausing while Zenobia entered
my chamber. Occasionally, Zenobia would be a little annoyed by
Priscilla's too close attendance. In an authoritative and not very
kindly tone, she would advise her to breathe the pleasant air in a
walk, or to go with her work into the barn, holding out half a promise
to come and sit on the hay with her, when at leisure. Evidently,
Priscilla found but scanty requital for her love. Hollingsworth was
likewise a great favorite with her. For several minutes together, sometimes, while my auditory nerves retained the susceptibility of delicate
health, I used to hear a low, pleasant murmur, ascending from the
room below, and at last ascertained it to be Priscilla's voice, babbling
like a little brook to Hollingsworth. She talked more largely and freely
with him than with Zenobia, towards whom, indeed, her feelings
seemed not so much to be confidence, as involuntary affection. I
should have thought all the better of my own qualities, had Priscilla
marked me out for the third place in her regards. But, though she
appeared to like me tolerably well, I could never flatter myself with
being distinguished by her, as Hollingsworth and Zenobia were.

One forenoon, during my convalescence, there came a gentle tap at
my chamber-door. I immediately said—"Come in, Priscilla!"—with an

acute sense of the applicant's identity. Nor was I deceived. It was really Priscilla, a pale, large-eyed little woman, (for she had gone far enough into her teens to be, at least, on the outer limit of girlhood,) but much less wan than at my previous view of her, and far better conditioned both as to health and spirits. As I first saw her, she had reminded me of plants that one sometimes observes doing their best to vegetate among the bricks of an enclosed court, where there is scanty soil, and never any sunshine. At present, though with no approach to bloom, there were indications that the girl had human blood in her veins.

Priscilla came softly to my bedside, and held out an article of snow-white linen, very carefully and smoothly ironed. She did not seem bashful, nor anywise embarrassed. My weakly condition, I suppose, supplied a medium in which she could approach me.

"Do not you need this?" asked she. "I have made it for you."

It was a night-cap!

"My dear Priscilla," said I, smiling, "I never had on a night-cap in my life! But perhaps it will be better for me to wear one, now that I am a miserable invalid. How admirably you have done it! No, no; I never can think of wearing such an exquisitely wrought night-cap as this, unless it be in the day-time, when I sit up to receive company!"

"It is for use, not beauty," answered Priscilla. "I could have embroidered it and made it much prettier, if I pleased."

While holding up the night-cap, and admiring the fine needle-work, I perceived that Priscilla had a sealed letter, which she was waiting for me to take. It had arrived from the village post-office, that morning. As I did not immediately offer to receive the letter, she drew it back, and held it against her bosom, with both hands clasped over it, in a way that had probably grown habitual to her. Now, on turning my eyes from the night-cap to Priscilla, it forcibly struck me that her air, though not her figure, and the expression of her face, but not its features, had a resemblance to what I had often seen in a friend of mine, one of the most gifted women of the age. I cannot describe it. The points, easiest to convey to the reader, were, a certain curve of the shoulders, and a partial closing of the eyes, which seemed to look more penetratingly into my own eyes, through the narrowed apertures, than if they had been open at full width. It was a singular anomaly of likeness co-existing with perfect dissimilitude.

"Will you give me the letter, Priscilla?" said I.

She started, put the letter into my hand, and quite lost the look that had drawn my notice.

"Priscilla," I inquired, "did you ever see Miss Margaret Fuller?"[1]

---

1. Leading American intellectual and pioneering feminist; Fuller (1810–1850), a close friend of Emerson and a key figure in the Transcendentalist movement, was a frequent visitor to Brook Farm. For an example of her writing, see "Contexts," pp. 218–21.

"No," she answered.

"Because," said I, "you reminded me of her, just now, and it happens, strangely enough, that this very letter is from her!"

Priscilla, for whatever reason, looked very much discomposed.

"I wish people would not fancy such odd things in me!" she said, rather petulantly. "How could I possibly make myself resemble this lady, merely by holding her letter in my hand?"

"Certainly, Priscilla, it would puzzle me to explain it," I replied. "Nor do I suppose that the letter had anything to do with it. It was just a coincidence—nothing more."

She hastened out of the room; and this was the last that I saw of Priscilla, until I ceased to be an invalid.

Being much alone, during my recovery, I read interminably in Mr. Emerson's Essays, the Dial, Carlyle's works, George Sand's romances,[2] (lent me by Zenobia,) and other books which one or another of the brethren or sisterhood had brought with them. Agreeing in little else, most of these utterances were like the cry of some solitary sentinel, whose station was on the outposts of the advance-guard of human progression; or, sometimes, the voice came sadly from among the shattered ruins of the past, but yet had a hopeful echo in the future. They were well adapted (better, at least, than any other intellectual products, the volatile essence of which had heretofore tinctured a printed page) to pilgrims like ourselves, whose present bivouâc was considerably farther into the waste of chaos than any mortal army of crusaders had ever marched before. Fourier's works,[3] also, in a series of horribly tedious volumes, attracted a good deal of my attention, from the analogy which I could not but recognize between his system and our own. There was far less resemblance, it is true, than the world chose to imagine; inasmuch as the two theories differed, as widely as the zenith from the nadir, in their main principles.

I talked about Fourier to Hollingsworth, and translated, for his benefit, some of the passages that chiefly impressed me.

2. Coverdale, as befits the advanced views prevalent at Blithedale, is reading some of the most progressive, liberal-minded writers of the day. Ralph Waldo Emerson's *Essays* (1841, 1844) set out key elements of his transcendence-seeking individualism; *The Dial* (1840–44) was the journal sponsored by Boston's Transcendental Club (edited first by Margaret Fuller, then by Emerson); Thomas Carlyle (1795–1881) was an influential Scottish historian and critic of modern, materialistic society; George Sand (the pen-name of Amandine Aurore Lucile Dupin, Baronne Dudevant, 1804–1876) was a French novelist famous for her advocacy of feminism and socialism and for her unconventional private life.

3. In his many writings, Charles Fourier (1772–1837), French social theorist, offered a scathing critique of the inequities of modern life and devised a complex system of communal living and working designed to achieve complete social harmony. Fourier based his system on matching work assignments and living arrangements with the individual "passions" of the community's members (see also p. 16, n. 4 and "Contexts," pp. 183–84).

"When, as a consequence of human improvement," said I, "the globe shall arrive at its final perfection, the great ocean is to be converted into a particular kind of lemonade, such as was fashionable at Paris in Fourier's time. He calls it *limonade à cèdre*.[4] It is positively a fact! Just imagine the city-docks filled, every day, with a flood-tide of this delectable beverage!"

"Why did not the Frenchman make punch of it, at once?" asked Hollingsworth. "The jack-tars[5] would be delighted to go down in ships, and do business in such an element."

I further proceeded to explain, as well as I modestly could, several points of Fourier's system, illustrating them with here and there a page or two, and asking Hollingsworth's opinion as to the expediency of introducing these beautiful peculiarities into our own practice.

"Let me hear no more of it!" cried he, in utter disgust. "I never will forgive this fellow! He has committed the Unpardonable Sin! For what more monstrous iniquity could the Devil himself contrive, than to choose the selfish principle—the principle of all human wrong, the very blackness of man's heart, the portion of ourselves which we shudder at, and which it is the whole aim of spiritual discipline to eradicate—to choose it as the master-workman of his system? To seize upon and foster whatever vile, petty, sordid, filthy, bestial, and abominable corruptions have cankered into our nature, to be the efficient instruments of his infernal regeneration! And his consummated Paradise, as he pictures it, would be worthy of the agency which he counts upon for establishing it. The nauseous villain!"[6]

"Nevertheless," remarked I, "in consideration of the promised delights of his system—so very proper, as they certainly are, to be appreciated by Fourier's countrymen—I cannot but wonder that universal France did not adopt his theory, at a moment's warning. But is there not something very characteristic of his nation in Fourier's manner of putting forth his views? He makes no claim to inspiration. He has not persuaded himself—as Swedenborg[7] did, and as any other than a Frenchman would, with a mission of like

---

4. Coverdale's account of this passage is mildly inaccurate. In a long footnote in *Theory of the Four Movements*, Fourier theorizes that various climatic effects will accompany the achievement of full social harmony, among them the dissemination of "boreal citric acid" which will combine with salt to give sea water the taste of a kind of lemonade made from the fruit of the citron tree and known as *"aigre 'de cèdre'"* (not *"limonade à cèdre"*).

5. Sailors.

6. Hollingsworth objects to a key feature of Fourier's plan: in Fourier's ideal community, harmony was to be achieved by the organized expression, rather than the restraint, of individual desires ("the selfish principle," in Hollingsworth's phrasing).

7. Emanuel Swedenborg (1688–1772), Swedish scientist and mystical thinker; his "doctrine of correspondence" between the physical and spiritual worlds was based on direct, visionary experience.

importance to communicate—that he speaks with authority from above. He promulgates his system, so far as I can perceive, entirely on his own responsibility. He has searched out and discovered the whole counsel of the Almighty, in respect to mankind, past, present, and for exactly seventy thousand years to come, by the mere force and cunning of his individual intellect!"

"Take the book out of my sight!" said Hollingsworth, with great virulence of expression, "or, I tell you fairly, I shall fling it in the fire! And as for Fourier, let him make a Paradise, if he can, of Gehenna,[8] where, as I conscientiously believe, he is floundering at this moment!"

"And bellowing, I suppose," said I—not that I felt any ill-will towards Fourier, but merely wanted to give the finishing touch to Hollingsworth's image—"bellowing for the least drop of his beloved *limonade à cèdre!*"

There is but little profit to be expected in attempting to argue with a man who allows himself to declaim in this manner; so I dropt the subject, and never took it up again.

But had the system, at which he was so enraged, combined almost any amount of human wisdom, spiritual insight, and imaginative beauty, I question whether Hollingsworth's mind was in a fit condition to receive it. I began to discern that he had come among us, actuated by no real sympathy with our feelings and our hopes, but chiefly because we were estranging ourselves from the world, with which his lonely and exclusive object in life had already put him at odds. Hollingsworth must have been originally endowed with a great spirit of benevolence, deep enough, and warm enough, to be the source of as much disinterested good, as Providence often allows a human being the privilege of conferring upon his fellows. This native instinct yet lived within him. I myself had profited by it, in my necessity. It was seen, too, in his treatment of Priscilla. Such casual circumstances, as were here involved, would quicken his divine power of sympathy, and make him seem, while their influence lasted, the tenderest man and the truest friend on earth. But, by-and-by, you missed the tenderness of yesterday, and grew drearily conscious that Hollingsworth had a closer friend than ever you could be. And this friend was the cold, spectral monster which he had himself conjured up, and on which he was wasting all the warmth of his heart, and of which, at last—as these men of a mighty purpose so invariably do—he had grown to be the bond-slave. It was his philanthropic theory!

This was a result exceedingly sad to contemplate, considering that it had been mainly brought about by the very ardor and exuberance

8. Hell.

of his philanthropy. Sad, indeed, but by no means unusual. He had taught his benevolence to pour its warm tide exclusively through one channel; so that there was nothing to spare for other great manifestations of love to man, nor scarcely for the nutriment of individual attachments, unless they could minister, in some way, to the terrible egotism which he mistook for an angel of God. Had Hollingsworth's education been more enlarged, he might not so inevitably have stumbled into this pit-fall. But this identical pursuit had educated him. He knew absolutely nothing, except in a single direction, where he had thought so energetically, and felt to such a depth, that, no doubt, the entire reason and justice of the universe appeared to be concentrated thitherward.

It is my private opinion, that, at this period of his life, Hollingsworth was fast going mad; and, as with other crazy people, (among whom I include humorists of every degree,) it required all the constancy of friendship to restrain his associates from pronouncing him an intolerable bore. Such prolonged fiddling upon one string; such multiform presentation of one idea! His specific object (of which he made the public more than sufficiently aware, through the medium of lectures and pamphlets) was to obtain funds for the construction of an edifice, with a sort of collegiate endowment. On this foundation, he purposed to devote himself and a few disciples to the reform and mental culture of our criminal brethren. His visionary edifice was Hollingsworth's one castle in the air; it was the material type, in which his philanthropic dream strove to embody itself; and he made the scheme more definite, and caught hold of it the more strongly, and kept his clutch the more pertinaciously, by rendering it visible to the bodily eye. I have seen him, a hundred times, with a pencil and sheet of paper, sketching the façade, the side-view, or the rear of the structure, or planning the internal arrangements, as lovingly as another man might plan those of the projected home, where he meant to be happy with his wife and children. I have known him to begin a model of the building with little stones, gathered at the brookside, whither we had gone to cool ourselves in the sultry noon of haying-time. Unlike all other ghosts, his spirit haunted an edifice which, instead of being time-worn, and full of storied love, and joy, and sorrow, had never yet come into existence.

"Dear friend," said I, once, to Hollingsworth, before leaving my sick-chamber, "I heartily wish that I could make your schemes my schemes, because it would be so great a happiness to find myself treading the same path with you. But I am afraid there is not stuff in me stern enough for a philanthropist—or not in this peculiar direction—or, at all events, not solely in this. Can you bear with me, if such should prove to be the case?"

"I will, at least, wait awhile," answered Hollingsworth, gazing at me sternly and gloomily. "But how can you be my life-long friend, except you strive with me towards the great object of my life?"

Heaven forgive me! A horrible suspicion crept into my heart, and stung the very core of it as with the fangs of an adder. I wondered whether it were possible that Hollingsworth could have watched by my bedside, with all that devoted care, only for the ulterior purpose of making me a proselyte to his views!

VIII. A Modern Arcadia

May-day[1]—I forget whether by Zenobia's sole decree, or by the unanimous vote of our Community—had been declared a moveable festival. It was deferred until the sun should have had a reasonable time to clear away the snow-drifts, along the lee of the stone-walls, and bring out a few of the readiest wild-flowers. On the forenoon of the substituted day, after admitting some of the balmy air into my chamber, I decided that it was nonsense and effeminacy to keep myself a prisoner any longer. So I descended to the sitting-room, and finding nobody there, proceeded to the barn, whence I had already heard Zenobia's voice, and along with it a girlish laugh, which was not so certainly recognizable. Arriving at the spot, it a little surprised me to discover that these merry outbreaks came from Priscilla.

The two had been a-maying together. They had found anemones in abundance, houstonias by the handfull, some columbines, a few long-stalked violets, and a quantity of white everlasting-flowers, and had filled up their basket with the delicate spray of shrubs and trees.[2] None were prettier than the maple-twigs, the leaf of which looks like a scarlet-bud, in May, and like a plate of vegetable gold in October. Zenobia—who showed no conscience in such matters— had also rifled a cherry-tree of one of its blossomed boughs; and, with all this variety of sylvan ornament, had been decking out Priscilla. Being done with a good deal of taste, it made her look more charming than I should have thought possible, with my recollection of the wan, frost-nipt girl, as heretofore described. Nevertheless, among those fragrant blossoms, and conspicuously, too, had been stuck a weed of evil odor and ugly aspect, which, as soon as I detected it, destroyed the effect of all the rest. There was a gleam of latent mischief—not to call it deviltry—in Zenobia's eye, which seemed to indicate a slightly malicious purpose in the arrangement.

1. May 1; date of a spring festival, celebrated in English holiday tradition by picking wild flowers ("a-maying"), crowning a May queen, and dancing around a Maypole.
2. All varieties of flowering plants and herbs commonly found in New England in the spring.

As for herself, she scorned the rural buds and leaflets, and wore nothing but her invariable flower of the tropics.

"What do you think of Priscilla now, Mr. Coverdale?" asked she, surveying her as a child does its doll. "Is not she worth a verse or two?"

"There is only one thing amiss," answered I.

Zenobia laughed, and flung the malignant weed away.

"Yes; she deserves some verses now," said I, "and from a better poet than myself. She is the very picture of the New England spring, subdued in tint, and rather cool, but with a capacity of sunshine, and bringing us a few alpine blossoms, as earnest of something richer, though hardly more beautiful, hereafter. The best type of her is one of those anemones."

"What I find most singular in Priscilla, as her health improves," observed Zenobia, "is her wildness. Such a quiet little body as she seemed, one would not have expected that! Why, as we strolled the woods together, I could hardly keep her from scrambling up the trees like a squirrel! She has never before known what it is to live in the free air, and so it intoxicates her as if she were sipping wine. And she thinks it such a Paradise here, and all of us, particularly Mr. Hollingsworth and myself, such angels! It is quite ridiculous, and provokes one's malice, almost, to see a creature so happy—especially a feminine creature."

"They are always happier than male creatures," said I.

"You must correct that opinion, Mr. Coverdale," replied Zenobia, contemptuously, "or I shall think you lack the poetic insight. Did you ever see a happy woman in your life? Of course, I do not mean a girl—like Priscilla, and a thousand others, for they are all alike, while on the sunny side of experience—but a grown woman. How can she be happy, after discovering that fate has assigned her but one single event, which she must contrive to make the substance of her whole life? A man has his choice of innumerable events."

"A woman, I suppose," answered I, "by constant repetition of her one event, may compensate for the lack of variety."

"Indeed!" said Zenobia.

While we were talking, Priscilla caught sight of Hollingsworth, at a distance, in a blue frock[3] and with a hoe over his shoulder, returning from the field. She immediately set out to meet him, running and skipping, with spirits as light as the breeze of the May-morning, but with limbs too little exercised to be quite responsive; she clapt her hands, too, with great exuberance of gesture, as is the custom of young girls, when their electricity overcharges them. But, all at once, midway to Hollingsworth, she paused, looked round about her,

3. A loose overshirt, typically worn by workmen; the standard outfit for men at Brook Farm.

towards the river, the road, the woods, and back towards us, appearing to listen, as if she heard some one calling her name, and knew not precisely in what direction.

"Have you bewitched her?" I exclaimed.

"It is no sorcery of mine," said Zenobia. "But I have seen the girl do that identical thing, once or twice before. Can you imagine what is the matter with her?"

"No; unless," said I, "she has the gift of hearing those 'airy tongues that syllable men's names'—which Milton tells about."[4]

From whatever cause, Priscilla's animation seemed entirely to have deserted her. She seated herself on a rock, and remained there until Hollingsworth came up; and when he took her hand and led her back to us, she rather resembled my original image of the wan and spiritless Priscilla, than the flowery May Queen of a few moments ago. These sudden transformations, only to be accounted for by an extreme nervous susceptibility, always continued to characterize the girl, though with diminished frequency, as her health progressively grew more robust.

I was now on my legs again. My fit of illness had been an avenue between two existences; the low-arched and darksome doorway, through which I crept out of a life of old conventionalisms, on my hands and knees, as it were, and gained admittance into the freer region that lay beyond. In this respect, it was like death. And, as with death, too, it was good to have gone through it. No otherwise could I have rid myself of a thousand follies, fripperies, prejudices, habits, and other such worldly dust as inevitably settles upon the crowd along the broad highway, giving them all one sordid aspect, before noontime, however freshly they may have begun their pilgrimage, in the dewy morning. The very substance upon my bones had not been fit to live with, in any better, truer, or more energetic mode than that to which I was accustomed. So it was taken off me and flung aside, like any other worn out or unseasonable garment; and, after shivering a little while in my skeleton, I began to be clothed anew, and much more satisfactorily than in my previous suit. In literal and physical truth, I was quite another man. I had a lively sense of the exultation with which the spirit will enter on the next stage of its eternal progress, after leaving the heavy burthen of its mortality in an earthly grave, with as little concern for what may become of it, as now affected me for the flesh which I had lost.

Emerging into the genial sunshine, I half fancied that the labors of the brotherhood had already realized some of Fourier's predictions. Their enlightened culture of the soil, and the virtues with which

4. Coverdale quotes a line from John Milton's *Comus* (performed as a courtly masque in 1634), a poem in which the "virtuous mind" of the young heroine protects her from a sorcerer's enchantments.

they sanctified their life, had begun to produce an effect upon the material world and its climate. In my new enthusiasm, man looked strong and stately!—and woman, oh, how beautiful!—and the earth, a green garden, blossoming with many-colored delights! Thus Nature, whose laws I had broken in various artificial ways, comported herself towards me as a strict, but loving mother, who uses the rod upon her little boy for his naughtiness, and then gives him a smile, a kiss, and some pretty playthings, to console the urchin for her severity.

In the interval of my seclusion, there had been a number of recruits to our little army of saints and martyrs. They were mostly individuals who had gone through such an experience as to disgust them with ordinary pursuits, but who were not yet so old, nor had suffered so deeply, as to lose their faith in the better time to come. On comparing their minds, one with another, they often discovered that this idea of a Community had been growing up, in silent and unknown sympathy, for years. Thoughtful, strongly-lined faces were among them, sombre brows, but eyes that did not require spectacles, unless prematurely dimmed by the student's lamplight, and hair that seldom showed a thread of silver. Age, wedded to the past, incrusted over with a stony layer of habits, and retaining nothing fluid in its possibilities, would have been absurdly out of place in an enterprise like this. Youth, too, in its early dawn, was hardly more adapted to our purpose; for it would behold the morning radiance of its own spirit beaming over the very same spots of withered grass and barren sand, whence most of us had seen it vanish. We had very young people with us, it is true—downy lads, rosy girls in their first teens, and children of all heights above one's knee;—but these had chiefly been sent hither for education, which it was one of the objects and methods of our institution to supply. Then we had boarders, from town and elsewhere, who lived with us in a familiar way, sympathized more or less in our theories, and sometimes shared in our labors.

On the whole, it was a society such as has seldom met together; nor, perhaps, could it reasonably be expected to hold together long. Persons of marked individuality—crooked sticks, as some of us might be called—are not exactly the easiest to bind up into a faggot. But, so long as our union should subsist, a man of intellect and feeling, with a free nature in him, might have sought far and near, without finding so many points of attraction as would allure him hitherward. We were of all creeds and opinions, and generally tolerant of all, on every imaginable subject. Our bond, it seems to me, was not affirmative, but negative. We had individually found one thing or another to quarrel with, in our past life, and were pretty well agreed as to the inexpediency of lumbering along with the old system any farther. As to what should be substituted, there was much less unanimity. We did not greatly care—at least, I never did—for the written constitution under which our millennium had commenced. My hope was, that, between theory and practice, a true and available mode of life might be struck out, and that, even should we ultimately fail, the months or years spent in the trial would not have been wasted, either as regarded passing enjoyment, or the experience which makes men wise.

Arcadians though we were, our costume bore no resemblance to the be-ribboned doublets, silk breeches and stockings, and slippers fastened with artificial roses, that distinguish the pastoral people of poetry and the stage. In outward show, I humbly conceive, we looked rather like a gang of beggars or banditti, than either a company of honest laboring men or a conclave of philosophers. Whatever might be our points of difference, we all of us seemed to have come to Blithedale with the one thrifty and laudable idea of wearing out our old clothes. Such garments as had an airing, whenever we strode afield! Coats with high collars, and with no collars, broad-skirted or swallow-tailed, and with the waist at every point between the hip and armpit; pantaloons of a dozen successive epochs, and greatly defaced at the knees by the humiliations of the wearer before his lady-love;—in short, we were a living epitome of defunct fashions, and the very raggedest presentment of men who had seen better days. It was gentility in tatters. Often retaining a scholarlike or clerical air, you might have taken us for the denizens of Grub-street, intent on getting a comfortable livelihood by agricultural labor; or Coleridge's projected Pantisocracy, in full experiment; or Candide and his motley associates, at work in their cabbage-garden,[5] or anything else that was miserably out at elbows, and most clumsily patched in the rear. We might have been sworn comrades to Falstaff's ragged regiment.[6] Little skill as we boasted in other points of husbandry, every mother's son of us would have served admirably to stick up for a scarecrow. And the worst of the matter was, that the first energetic movement, essential to one downright stroke of real labor, was sure to put a finish to these poor habiliments. So we gradually flung them all aside, and took to honest homespun and linsey-woolsey, as preferable, on the whole, to the plan recommended,

---

5. In *Candide* (1759), a satirical novel by the French philosopher Voltaire (1694–1778), the main characters finally retire to their own garden after a series of disastrous misfortunes out in the world. *Grub-street*: a London street occupied by hack writers. *Pantisocracy*: a system of government in which all members share power equally; name chosen by the English poets Samuel Taylor Coleridge (1772–1834) and Robert Southey (1774–1843) for the utopian community they hoped to establish along the Susquehanna River in Pennsylvania.
6. The tattered, hopelessly unqualified recruits that Falstaff leads into battle in Shakespeare's *Henry IV, Part I* 4.2.

I think, by Virgil—'Ara nudus; sere nudus[7]—which, as Silas Foster remarked when I translated the maxim, would be apt to astonish the women-folks.

After a reasonable training, the yeoman-life throve well with us. Our faces took the sunburn kindly; our chests gained in compass, and our shoulders in breadth and squareness; our great brown fists looked as if they had never been capable of kid gloves. The plough, the hoe, the scythe, and the hay-fork, grew familiar to our grasp. The oxen responded to our voices. We could do almost as fair a day's work as Silas Foster himself, sleep dreamlessly after it, and awake at daybreak with only a little stiffness of the joints, which was usually quite gone by breakfast-time.

To be sure, our next neighbors pretended to be incredulous as to our real proficiency in the business which we had taken in hand. They told slanderous fables about our inability to yoke our own oxen, or to drive them afield, when yoked, or to release the poor brutes from their conjugal bond at nightfall. They had the face to say, too, that the cows laughed at our awkwardness at milking-time, and invariably kicked over the pails; partly in consequence of our putting the stool on the wrong side, and partly because, taking offence at the whisking of their tails, we were in the habit of holding these natural flyflappers with one hand, and milking with the other. They further averred, that we hoed up whole acres of Indian corn and other crops, and drew the earth carefully about the weeds; and that we raised five hundred tufts of burdock,[8] mistaking them for cabbages; and that, by dint of unskilful planting, few of our seeds ever came up at all, or if they did come up, it was stern foremost, and that we spent the better part of the month of June in reversing a field of beans, which had thrust themselves out of the ground in this unseemly way. They quoted it as nothing more than an ordinary occurrence for one or other of us to crop off two or three fingers, of a morning, by our clumsy use of the hay-cutter. Finally, and as an ultimate catastrophe, these mendacious rogues circulated a report that we Communitarians were exterminated, to the last man, by severing ourselves asunder with the sweep of our own scythes!—and that the world had lost nothing by this little accident.

But this was pure envy and malice on the part of the neighboring farmers. The peril of our new way of life was not lest we should fail in becoming practical agriculturalists, but that we should probably cease to be anything else. While our enterprise lay all in theory, we had pleased ourselves with delectable visions of the spiritualization

7. "Strip to plow and strip to sow"—advice to the farmer offered in the Roman poet Virgil's *Georgics* (1.299), a poem paying tribute to the value of rural life; *linsey-woolsey*: coarse, sturdy fabric made of a mix of linen or cotton and wool and used for work clothes.
8. A troublesome weed, producing purple flowers and burrs that stick to animals and clothing.

of labor. It was to be our form of prayer, and ceremonial of worship. Each stroke of the hoe was to uncover some aromatic root of wisdom, heretofore hidden from the sun. Pausing in the field, to let the wind exhale the moisture from our foreheads, we were to look upward, and catch glimpses into the far-off soul of truth. In this point of view, matters did not turn out quite so well as we anticipated. It is very true, that, sometimes, gazing casually around me, out of the midst of my toil, I used to discern a richer picturesqueness in the visible scene of earth and sky. There was, at such moments, a novelty, an unwonted aspect on the face of Nature, as if she had been taken by surprise and seen at unawares, with no opportunity to put off her real look, and assume the mask with which she mysteriously hides herself from mortals. But this was all. The clods of earth, which we so constantly belabored and turned over and over, were never etherealized into thought. Our thoughts, on the contrary, were fast becoming cloddish. Our labor symbolized nothing, and left us mentally sluggish in the dusk of the evening. Intellectual activity is incompatible with any large amount of bodily exercise. The yeoman and the scholar—the yeoman and the man of finest moral culture, though not the man of sturdiest sense and integrity—are two distinct individuals, and can never be melted or welded into one substance.

Zenobia soon saw this truth, and gibed me about it, one evening, as Hollingsworth and I lay on the grass, after a hard day's work.

"I am afraid you did not make a song, to-day, while loading the hay-cart," said she, "as Burns did, when he was reaping barley."[9]

"Burns never made a song in haying-time," I answered, very positively. "He was no poet while a farmer, and no farmer while a poet."

"And, on the whole, which of the two characters do you like best?" asked Zenobia. "For I have an idea that you cannot combine them, any better than Burns did. Ah, I see, in my mind's eye, what sort of an individual you are to be, two or three years hence! Grim Silas Foster is your prototype, with his palm of sole-leather, and his joints of rusty iron, (which, all through summer, keep the stiffness of what he calls his winter's rheumatize,) and his brain of—I don't know what his brain is made of, unless it be a Savoy cabbage;[1] but yours may be cauliflower, as a rather more delicate variety. Your physical man will be transmuted into salt-beef and fried pork, at the rate, I should imagine, of a pound and a half a day; that being about the average which we find necessary in the kitchen. You will make your toilet for the day (still like this delightful Silas Foster) by rinsing your fingers and the front part of your face in a little tin-pan

9. In addition to writing poems of rural Scottish life, Robert Burns (1759–1796) put in hard years of labor as a farmer.
1. A variety of common cabbage, with crinkled leaves and a compact head, grown for winter use.

of water, at the door-step, and teasing your hair with a wooden pocket-comb, before a seven-by-nine-inch looking-glass. Your only pastime will be, to smoke some very vile tobacco in the black stump of a pipe!"

"Pray spare me!" cried I. "But the pipe is not Silas's only mode of solacing himself with the weed."

"Your literature," continued Zenobia, apparently delighted with her description, "will be the Farmer's Almanac;[2] for, I observe, our friend Foster never gets so far as the newspaper. When you happen to sit down, at odd moments, you will fall asleep, and make nasal proclamation of the fact, as he does; and invariably you must be jogged out of a nap, after supper, by the future Mrs. Coverdale, and persuaded to go regularly to bed. And on Sundays; when you put on a blue coat with brass buttons, you will think of nothing else to do, but to go and lounge over the stone-walls and rail-fences, and stare at the corn growing. And you will look with a knowing eye at oxen, and will have a tendency to clamber over into pig-sties, and feel of the hogs, and give a guess how much they will weigh, after you shall have stuck and dressed them. Already, I have noticed, you begin to speak through your nose, and with a drawl. Pray, if you really did make any poetry to-day, let us hear it in that kind of utterance!"

"Coverdale has given up making verses, now," said Hollingsworth, who never had the slightest appreciation of my poetry. "Just think of him penning a sonnet, with a fist like that! There is at least this good in a life of toil, that it takes the nonsense and fancy-work out of a man, and leaves nothing but what truly belongs to him. If a farmer can make poetry at the plough-tail, it must be because his nature insists on it; and if that be the case, let him make it, in Heaven's name!"

"And how is it with you?" asked Zenobia, in a different voice; for she never laughed at Hollingsworth, as she often did at me.—"You, I think, cannot have ceased to live a life of thought and feeling."

"I have always been in earnest," answered Hollingsworth. "I have hammered thought out of iron, after heating the iron in my heart! It matters little what my outward toil may be. Were I a slave at the bottom of a mine, I should keep the same purpose—the same faith in its ultimate accomplishment—that I do now. Miles Coverdale is not in earnest, either as a poet or a laborer."

"You give me hard measure, Hollingsworth," said I, a little hurt. "I have kept pace with you in the field; and my bones feel as if I had been in earnest, whatever may be the case with my brain!"

2. A book, appearing yearly, containing a calendar of days, planting and tide tables, times of sunrise and sunset, weather forecasts, and other information useful to the farmer, along with whimsical humor, recipes, and comment on the issues of the day; first published in Massachusetts by Robert Bailey Thomas (1766–1846) in 1792 (with predictions for the year 1793) and still available today.

"I cannot conceive," observed Zenobia, with great emphasis— and, no doubt, she spoke fairly the feeling of the moment—"I cannot conceive of being, so continually as Mr. Coverdale is, within the sphere of a strong and noble nature, without being strengthened and ennobled by its influence!"

This amiable remark of the fair Zenobia confirmed me in what I had already begun to suspect—that Hollingsworth, like many other illustrious prophets, reformers, and philanthropists, was likely to make at least two proselytes, among the women, to one among the men. Zenobia and Priscilla! These, I believe, (unless my unworthy self might be reckoned for a third,) were the only disciples of his mission; and I spent a great deal of time, uselessly, in trying to conjecture what Hollingsworth meant to do with them—and they with him!

IX. Hollingsworth, Zenobia, Priscilla

It is not, I apprehend, a healthy kind of mental occupation, to devote ourselves too exclusively to the study of individual men and women. If the person under examination be one's self, the result is pretty certain to be diseased action of the heart, almost before we can snatch a second glance. Or, if we take the freedom to put a friend under our microscope, we thereby insulate him from many of his true relations, magnify his peculiarities, inevitably tear him into parts, and, of course, patch him very clumsily together again. What wonder, then, should we be frightened by the aspect of a monster, which, after all—though we can point to every feature of his deformity in the real personage—may be said to have been created mainly by ourselves!

Thus, as my conscience has often whispered me, I did Hollingsworth a great wrong by prying into his character, and am perhaps doing him as great a one, at this moment, by putting faith in the discoveries which I seemed to make. But I could not help it. Had I loved him less, I might have used him better. He—and Zenobia and Priscilla, both for their own sakes and as connected with him—were separated from the rest of the Community, to my imagination, and stood forth as the indices of a problem which it was my business to solve. Other associates had a portion of my time; other matters amused me; passing occurrences carried me along with them, while they lasted. But here was the vortex of my meditations around which they revolved, and whitherward they too continually tended. In the midst of cheerful society, I had often a feeling of loneliness. For it was impossible not to be sensible, that, while these three characters figured so largely on my private theatre, I—though probably reckoned as a friend by all—was at best but a secondary or tertiary personage with either of them.

I loved Hollingsworth, as has already been enough expressed. But it impressed me, more and more, that there was a stern and dreadful peculiarity in this man, such as could not prove otherwise than pernicious to the happiness of those who should be drawn into too intimate a connection with him. He was not altogether human. There was something else in Hollingsworth, besides flesh and blood, and sympathies and affections, and celestial spirit.

This is always true of those men who have surrendered themselves to an over-ruling purpose. It does not so much impel them from without, nor even operate as a motive power within, but grows incorporate with all that they think and feel, and finally converts them into little else save that one principle. When such begins to be the predicament, it is not cowardice, but wisdom, to avoid these victims. They have no heart, no sympathy, no reason, no conscience. They will keep no friend, unless he make himself the mirror of their purpose; they will smite and slay you, and trample your dead corpse under foot, all the more readily, if you take the first step with them, and cannot take the second, and the third, and every other step of their terribly straight path. They have an idol, to which they consecrate themselves high-priest, and deem it holy work to offer sacrifices of whatever is most precious, and never once seem to suspect—so cunning has the Devil been with them—that this false deity, in whose iron features, immitigable to all the rest of mankind, they see only benignity and love, is but a spectrum[1] of the very priest himself, projected upon the surrounding darkness. And the higher and purer the original object, and the more unselfishly it may have been taken up, the slighter is the probability that they can be led to recognize the process, by which godlike benevolence has been debased into all-devouring egotism.

Of course, I am perfectly aware that the above statement is exaggerated, in the attempt to make it adequate. Professed philanthropists have gone far; but no originally good man, I presume, ever went quite so far as this. Let the reader abate whatever he deems fit. The paragraph may remain, however, both for its truth and its exaggeration, as strongly expressive of the tendencies which were really operative in Hollingsworth, and as exemplifying the kind of error into which my mode of observation was calculated to lead me. The issue was, that, in solitude, I often shuddered at my friend. In my recollection of his dark and impressive countenance, the features grew more sternly prominent than the reality, duskier in their depth and shadow, and more lurid in their light; the frown, that had

1. Image.

merely flitted across his brow, seemed to have contorted it with an adamantine wrinkle. On meeting him again, I was often filled with remorse, when his deep eyes beamed kindly upon me, as with the glow of a household fire that was burning in a cave.—"He is a man, after all!" thought I—"his Maker's own truest image, a philanthropic man!—not that steel engine of the Devil's contrivance, a philanthropist!"—But, in my wood-walks, and in my silent chamber, the dark face frowned at me again.

When a young girl comes within the sphere of such a man, she is as perilously situated as the maiden whom, in the old classical myths, the people used to expose to a dragon. If I had any duty whatever, in reference to Hollingsworth, it was, to endeavor to save Priscilla from that kind of personal worship which her sex is generally prone to lavish upon saints and heroes. It often requires but one smile, out of the hero's eyes into the girl's or woman's heart, to transform this devotion, from a sentiment of the highest approval and confidence, into passionate love. Now, Hollingsworth smiled much upon Priscilla; more than upon any other person. If she thought him beautiful, it was no wonder. I often thought him so, with the expression of tender, human care, and gentlest sympathy, which she alone seemed to have power to call out upon his features. Zenobia, I suspect, would have given her eyes, bright as they were, for such a look; it was the least that our poor Priscilla could do, to give her heart for a great many of them. There was the more danger of this, inasmuch as the footing, on which we all associated at Blithedale, was widely different from that of conventional society. While inclining us to the soft affections of the Golden Age,[2] it seemed to authorize any individual, of either sex, to fall in love with any other, regardless of what would elsewhere be judged suitable and prudent. Accordingly, the tender passion was very rife among us, in various degrees of mildness or virulence, but mostly passing away with the state of things that had given it origin. This was all well enough; but, for a girl like Priscilla, and a woman like Zenobia, to jostle one another in their love of a man like Hollingsworth, was likely to be no child's play.

Had I been as cold-hearted as I sometimes thought myself, nothing would have interested me more than to witness the play of passions that must thus have been evolved. But, in honest truth, I would really have gone far to save Priscilla, at least, from the catastrophe in which such a drama would be apt to terminate.

Priscilla had now grown to be a very pretty girl, and still kept budding and blossoming, and daily putting on some new charm, which you no sooner became sensible of, than you thought it worth all that

2. In classical mythology, the first and best era of earthly life—a time of abundance, joy, harmony, and health.

she had previously possessed. So unformed, vague, and without substance, as she had come to us, it seemed as if we could see Nature
shaping out a woman before our very eyes, and yet had only a more
reverential sense of the mystery of a woman's soul and frame. Yesterday, her cheek was pale; to-day, it had a bloom. Priscilla's smile, like
a baby's first one, was a wondrous novelty. Her imperfections and
short-comings affected me with a kind of playful pathos, which was
as absolutely bewitching a sensation as ever I experienced. After she
had been a month or two at Blithedale, her animal spirits waxed
high, and kept her pretty constantly in a state of bubble and ferment, impelling her to far more bodily activity than she had yet
strength to endure. She was very fond of playing with the other girls,
out-of-doors. There is hardly another sight in the world so pretty, as
that of a company of young girls, almost women grown, at play, and
so giving themselves up to their airy impulse that their tiptoes barely
touch the ground.

Girls are incomparably wilder and more effervescent than boys,
more untameable, and regardless of rule and limit, with an ever-
shifting variety, breaking continually into new modes of fun, yet with
a harmonious propriety through all. Their steps, their voices, appear
free as the wind, but keep consonance with a strain of music, inaudible to us. Young men and boys, on the other hand, play according
to recognized law, old, traditionary games, permitting no caprioles[3]
of fancy, but with scope enough for the outbreak of savage instincts.
For, young or old, in play or in earnest, man is prone to be a brute.

Especially is it delightful to see a vigorous young girl run a race,
with her head thrown back, her limbs moving more friskily than they
need, and an air between that of a bird and a young colt. But
Priscilla's peculiar charm, in a foot-race, was the weakness and
irregularity with which she ran. Growing up without exercise, except
to her poor little fingers, she had never yet acquired the perfect use
of her legs. Setting buoyantly forth, therefore, as if no rival less swift
than Atalanta[4] could compete with her, she ran faulteringly, and
often tumbled on the grass. Such an incident—though it seems too
slight to think of—was a thing to laugh at, but which brought the
water into one's eyes, and lingered in the memory after far greater
joys and sorrows were swept out of it, as antiquated trash. Priscilla's
life, as I beheld it, was full of trifles that affected me in just this way.

When she had come to be quite at home among us, I used to fancy
that Priscilla played more pranks, and perpetrated more mischief,
than any other girl in the Community. For example, I once heard

3. Frolicsome leaps.
4. In classical mythology, a maiden capable of outrunning all her suitors—until one of them
   distracts her by dropping golden apples during their race.

Silas Foster, in a very gruff voice, threatening to rivet three horse-shoes round Priscilla's neck and chain her to a post, because she, with some other young people, had clambered upon a load of hay and caused it to slide off the cart. How she made her peace, I never knew; but very soon afterwards, I saw old Silas, with his brawny hands round Priscilla's waist, swinging her to-and-fro and finally depositing her on one of the oxen, to take her first lesson in riding. She met with terrible mishaps in her efforts to milk a cow; she let the poultry into the garden; she generally spoilt whatever part of the dinner she took in charge; she broke crockery; she dropt our biggest pitcher into the well; and—except with her needle, and those little wooden instru-ments for purse-making—was as unserviceable a member of society as any young lady in the land. There was no other sort of efficiency about her. Yet everybody was kind to Priscilla; everybody loved her, and laughed at her, to her face, and did not laugh, behind her back; everybody would have given her half of his last crust, or the bigger share of his plum-cake. These were pretty certain indications that we were all conscious of a pleasant weakness in the girl, and considered her not quite able to look after her own interests, or fight her battle with the world. And Hollingsworth—perhaps because he had been the means of introducing Priscilla to her new abode—appeared to recognize her as his own especial charge.

Her simple, careless, childish flow of spirits often made me sad. She seemed to me like a butterfly, at play in a flickering bit of sunshine, and mistaking it for a broad and eternal summer. We sometimes hold mirth to a stricter accountability than sorrow; it must show good cause, or the echo of its laughter comes back drearily. Priscilla's gaiety, moreover, was of a nature that showed me how delicate an instrument she was, and what fragile harp-strings were her nerves. As they made sweet music at the airiest touch, it would require but a stronger one to burst them all asunder. Absurd as it might be, I tried to reason with her, and persuade her not to be so joyous, thinking that, if she would draw less lavishly upon her fund of happiness, it would last the longer. I remember doing so, one summer evening, when we tired laborers sat looking on, like Goldsmith's old folks under the village thorn-tree, while the young people were at their sports.[5]

"What is the use or sense of being so very gay?" I said to Priscilla, while she was taking breath after a great frolic. "I love to see a suffi-cient cause for everything; and I can see none for this. Pray tell me, now, what kind of a world you imagine this to be, which you are so merry in?"

---

5. Coverdale alludes to the opening sequence of "The Deserted Village" (1770; ll. 1–34), a poem by Oliver Goldsmith (1730–1774) depicting an idyllic English rural life, now endangered by a mercantile economy and its resulting inequalities.

"I never think about it at all," answered Priscilla, laughing. "But this I am sure of—that it is a world where everybody is kind to me, and where I love everybody. My heart keeps dancing within me; and all the foolish things, which you see me do, are only the motions of my heart. How can I be dismal, if my heart will not let me?"

"Have you nothing dismal to remember?" I suggested. "If not, then, indeed, you are very fortunate!"

"Ah!" said Priscilla, slowly.

And then came that unintelligible gesture, when she seemed to be listening to a distant voice.

"For my part," I continued, beneficently seeking to over-shadow her with my own sombre humor, "my past life has been a tiresome one enough; yet I would rather look backward ten times, than forward once. For, little as we know of our life to come, we may be very sure, for one thing, that the good we aim at will not be attained. People never do get just the good they seek. If it come at all, it is something else, which they never dreamed of, and did not particularly want. Then, again, we may rest certain that our friends of to-day will not be our friends of a few years hence; but, if we keep one of them, it will be at the expense of the others—and, most probably, we shall keep none. To be sure, there are more to be had! But who cares about making a new set of friends, even should they be better than those around us?"

"Not I!" said Priscilla. "I will live and die with these!"

"Well; but let the future go!" resumed I. "As for the present moment, if we could look into the hearts where we wish to be most valued, what should you expect to see? One's own likeness, in the innermost, holiest niche? Ah, I don't know! It may not be there at all. It may be a dusty image, thrust aside into a corner, and by-and-by to be flung out-of-doors, where any foot may trample upon it. If not today, then tomorrow! And so, Priscilla, I do not see much wisdom in being so very merry in this kind of a world!"

It had taken me nearly seven years of worldly life, to hive up the bitter honey which I here offered to Priscilla. And she rejected it!

"I don't believe one word of what you say!" she replied, laughing anew. "You made me sad, for a minute, by talking about the past. But the past never comes back again. Do we dream the same dream twice? There is nothing else that I am afraid of."

So away she ran, and fell down on the green grass, as it was often her luck to do, but got up again without any harm.

"Priscilla, Priscilla!" cried Hollingsworth, who was sitting on the door-step. "You had better not run any more to-night. You will weary yourself too much. And do not sit down out of doors; for there is a heavy dew beginning to fall!"

At his first word, she went and sat down under the porch, at Hollingsworth's feet, entirely contented and happy. What charm was there, in his rude massiveness, that so attracted and soothed this shadowlike girl? It appeared to me—who have always been curious in such matters—that Priscilla's vague and seemingly causeless flow of felicitous feeling was that with which love blesses inexperienced hearts, before they begin to suspect what is going on within them. It transports them to the seventh heaven;[6] and if you ask what brought them thither, they neither can tell nor care to learn, but cherish an ecstatic faith that there they shall abide forever.

Zenobia was in the door-way, not far from Hollingsworth. She gazed at Priscilla, in a very singular way. Indeed, it was a sight worth gazing at, and a beautiful sight too, as the fair girl sat at the feet of that dark, powerful figure. Her air, while perfectly modest, delicate, and virginlike, denoted her as swayed by Hollingsworth, attracted to him, and unconsciously seeking to rest upon his strength. I could not turn away my own eyes, but hoped that nobody, save Zenobia and myself, were witnessing this picture. It is before me now, with the evening twilight a little deepened by the dusk of memory.

"Come hither, Priscilla!" said Zenobia. "I have something to say to you!"

She spoke in little more than a whisper. But it is strange how expressive of moods a whisper may often be. Priscilla felt at once that something had gone wrong.

"Are you angry with me?" she asked, rising slowly and standing before Zenobia in a drooping attitude. "What have I done? I hope you are not angry!"

"No, no, Priscilla!" said Hollingsworth, smiling. "I will answer for it, she is not. You are the one little person in the world, with whom nobody can be angry!"

"Angry with you, child? What a silly idea!" exclaimed Zenobia, laughing. "No, indeed! But, my dear Priscilla, you are getting to be so very pretty that you absolutely need a duenna;[7] and as I am older than you, and have had my own little experience of life, and think myself exceedingly sage, I intend to fill the place of a maiden-aunt. Every day, I shall give you a lecture, a quarter-of-an-hour in length, on the morals, manners, and proprieties of social life. When our pastoral shall be quite played out, Priscilla, my worldly wisdom may stand you in good stead!"

"I am afraid you are angry with me," repeated Priscilla, sadly; for, while she seemed as impressible as wax, the girl often showed a persistency in her own ideas, as stubborn as it was gentle.

---

6. In Jewish and Muslim theology, the highest level of heaven, the abode of God and the angels; hence, a place or condition of supreme happiness.
7. Chaperone; derived from the Spanish term for the older female companion of a marriageable young woman.

"Dear me, what can I say to the child!" cried Zenobia, in a tone of humorous vexation. "Well, well; since you insist on my being angry, come to my room, this moment, and let me beat you!"

Zenobia bade Hollingsworth good night very sweetly, and nodded to me with a smile. But, just as she turned aside with Priscilla into the dimness of the porch, I caught another glance at her countenance. It would have made the fortune of a tragic actress, could she have borrowed it for the moment when she fumbles in her bosom for the concealed dagger, or the exceedingly sharp bodkin, or mingles the ratsbane[8] in her lover's bowl of wine, or her rival's cup of tea. Not that I in the least anticipated any such catastrophe; it being a remarkable truth, that custom has in no one point a greater sway than over our modes of wreaking our wild passions. And, besides, had we been in Italy, instead of New England, it was hardly yet a crisis for the dagger or the bowl.

It often amazed me, however, that Hollingsworth should show himself so recklessly tender towards Priscilla, and never once seem to think of the effect which it might have upon her heart. But the man, as I have endeavored to explain, was thrown completely off his moral balance, and quite bewildered as to his personal relations, by his great excrescence of a philanthropic scheme. I used to see, or fancy, indications that he was not altogether obtuse to Zenobia's influence as a woman. No doubt, however, he had a still more exquisite enjoyment of Priscilla's silent sympathy with his purposes, so unalloyed with criticism, and therefore more grateful than any intellectual approbation, which always involves a possible reserve of latent censure. A man—poet, prophet, or whatever he may be—readily persuades himself of his right to all the worship that is voluntarily tendered. In requital of so rich benefits as he was to confer upon mankind, it would have been hard to deny Hollingsworth the simple solace of a young girl's heart, which he held in his hand, and smelled to,[9] like a rosebud. But what if, while pressing out its fragrance, he should crush the tender rosebud in his grasp!

As for Zenobia, I saw no occasion to give myself any trouble. With her native strength, and her experience of the world, she could not be supposed to need any help of mine. Nevertheless, I was really generous enough to feel some little interest likewise for Zenobia. With all her faults, (which might have been a great many, besides the abundance that I knew of,) she possessed noble traits, and a heart which must at least have been valuable while new. And she seemed ready to fling it away, as uncalculatingly as Priscilla herself.

---

8. Rat poison, usually a compound of arsenic; *bodkin*: a sharp, pointed instrument for making holes in cloth; or, a long, ornamental hairpin.
9. An antiquated use of "to smell" as an intransitive verb; Hollingsworth takes in the "fragrance" of Priscilla's heart, as if it were a flower held in his hand.

I could not but suspect, that, if merely at play with Hollingsworth, she was sporting with a power which she did not fully estimate. Or, if in earnest, it might chance, between Zenobia's passionate force and his dark, self-delusive egotism, to turn out such earnest as would develop itself in some sufficiently tragic catastrophe, though the dagger and the bowl should go for nothing in it.

Meantime, the gossip of the Community set them down as a pair of lovers. They took walks together, and were not seldom encountered in the wood-paths; Hollingsworth deeply discoursing, in tones solemn and sternly pathetic. Zenobia, with a rich glow on her cheeks, and her eyes softened from their ordinary brightness, looked so beautiful, that, had her companion been ten times a philanthropist, it seemed impossible but that one glance should melt him back into a man. Oftener than anywhere else, they went to a certain point on the slope of a pasture, commanding nearly the whole of our own domain, besides a view of the river and an airy prospect of many distant hills. The bond of our Community was such, that the members had the privilege of building cottages for their own residence, within our precincts, thus laying a hearth-stone and fencing in a home, private and peculiar, to all desirable extent; while yet the inhabitants should continue to share the advantages of an associated life. It was inferred, that Hollingsworth and Zenobia intended to rear their dwelling on this favorite spot.

I mentioned these rumors to Hollingsworth in a playful way.

"Had you consulted me," I went on to observe, "I should have recommended a site further to the left, just a little withdrawn into the wood, with two or three peeps at the prospect, among the trees. You will be in the shady vale of years, long before you can raise any better kind of shade around your cottage, if you build it on this bare slope."

"But I offer my edifice as a spectacle to the world," said Hollingsworth, "that it may take example and build many another like it. Therefore I mean to set it on the open hill-side."

Twist these words how I might, they offered no very satisfactory import. It seemed hardly probable that Hollingsworth should care about educating the public taste in the department of cottage-architecture, desirable as such improvement certainly was.

X. A Visitor from Town

Hollingsworth and I—we had been hoeing potatoes, that forenoon, while the rest of the fraternity were engaged in a distant quarter of the farm—sat under a clump of maples, eating our eleven o'clock lunch, when we saw a stranger approaching along the edge of the field. He had admitted himself from the road-side, through a turn-stile, and seemed to have a purpose of speaking with us.

And, by-the-by, we were favored with many visits at Blithedale; especially from people who sympathized with our theories, and perhaps held themselves ready to unite in our actual experiment, as soon as there should appear a reliable promise of its success. It was rather ludicrous, indeed, (to me, at least, whose enthusiasm had insensibly been exhaled, together with the perspiration of many a hard day's toil,) it was absolutely funny, therefore, to observe what a glory was shed about our life and labors, in the imagination of these longing proselytes. In their view, we were as poetical as Arcadians, besides being as practical as the hardest-fisted husbandmen in Massachusetts. We did not, it is true, spend much time in piping to our sheep, or warbling our innocent loves to the sisterhood. But they gave us credit for imbuing the ordinary rustic occupations with a kind of religious poetry, insomuch that our very cow-yards and pig-sties were as delightfully fragrant as a flower-garden. Nothing used to please me more than to see one of these lay enthusiasts snatch up a hoe, as they were very prone to do, and set to work with a vigor that perhaps carried him through about a dozen ill-directed strokes. Men are wonderfully soon satisfied, in this day of shameful bodily enervation, when, from one end of life to the other, such multitudes never taste the sweet weariness that follows accustomed toil. I seldom saw the new enthusiasm that did not grow as flimsy and flaccid as the proselyte's moistened shirt-collar, with a quarter-of-an-hour's active labor, under a July sun.

But the person, now at hand, had not at all the air of one of these amiable visionaries. He was an elderly man, dressed rather shabbily, yet decently enough, in a gray frock-coat, faded towards a brown hue, and wore a broad-brimmed white hat, of the fashion of several years gone by. His hair was perfect silver, without a dark thread in the whole of it; his nose, though it had a scarlet tip, by no means indicated the jollity of which a red nose is the generally admitted symbol. He was a subdued, undemonstrative old man, who would doubtless drink a glass of liquor, now and then, and probably more than was good for him; not, however, with a purpose of undue exhilaration, but in the hope of bringing his spirits up to the ordinary level of the world's cheerfulness. Drawing nearer, there was a shy look about him, as if he were ashamed of his poverty, or, at any rate, for some reason or other, would rather have us glance at him sidelong than take a full-front view. He had a queer appearance of hiding himself behind the patch on his left eye.

"I know this old gentleman," said I to Hollingsworth, as we sat observing him—"that is, I have met him a hundred times, in town, and have often amused my fancy with wondering what he was, before he came to be what he is. He haunts restaurants and such places, and has an odd way of lurking in corners or getting behind a door, whenever practicable, and holding out his hand, with some little article in it, which he wishes you to buy. The eye of the world seems to trouble him, although he necessarily lives so much in it. I never expected to see him in an open field."

"Have you learned anything of his history?" asked Hollingsworth.

"Not a circumstance," I answered. "But there must be something curious in it. I take him to be a harmless sort of a person, and a tolerably honest one; but his manners, being so furtive, remind me of those of a rat—a rat without the mischief, the fierce eye, the teeth to bite with, or the desire to bite. See, now! He means to skulk along that fringe of bushes, and approach us on the other side of our clump of maples."

We soon heard the old man's velvet tread on the grass, indicating that he had arrived within a few feet of where we sat.

"Good morning, Mr. Moodie," said Hollingsworth, addressing the stranger as an acquaintance. "You must have had a hot and tiresome walk from the city. Sit down, and take a morsel of our bread and cheese!"

The visitor made a grateful little murmur of acquiescence, and sat down in a spot somewhat removed; so that, glancing round, I could see his gray pantaloons and dusty shoes, while his upper part was mostly hidden behind the shrubbery. Nor did he come forth from this retirement during the whole of the interview that followed. We handed him such food as we had, together with a brown jug of molasses-and-water, (would that it had been brandy, or something better, for the sake of his chill old heart!) like priests offering dainty sacrifice to an enshrined and invisible idol. I have no idea that he really lacked sustenance; but it was quite touching, nevertheless, to hear him nibbling away at our crusts.

"Mr. Moodie," said I, "do you remember selling me one of those very pretty little silk purses, of which you seem to have a monopoly in the market? I keep it, to this day, I can assure you."

"Ah, thank you!" said our guest. "Yes, Mr. Coverdale, I used to sell a good many of those little purses."

He spoke languidly, and only those few words, like a watch with an inelastic spring, that just ticks, a moment or two, and stops again. He seemed a very forlorn old man. In the wantonness of youth, strength, and comfortable condition—making my prey of people's individualities, as my custom was—I tried to identify my mind with the old fellow's, and take his view of the world, as if looking through a smoke-blackened glass at the sun. It robbed the landscape of all its life. Those pleasantly swelling slopes of our farm, descending towards the wide meadows, through which sluggishly circled the brimfull tide of the Charles, bathing the long sedges on its hither and farther shores; the broad, sunny gleam over the winding water; that peculiar picturesqueness of the scene, where capes and headlands put themselves boldly forth upon the perfect level of the meadow, as into a green lake, with inlets between the promontories; the shadowy woodland, with twinkling showers of light falling into its depths; the sultry heat-vapor, which rose everywhere like incense, and in which my soul delighted, as indicating so rich a fervor in the passionate day, and in the earth that was burning with its love:—I beheld all these things as through old Moodie's eyes. When my eyes are dimmer than they have yet come to be, I will go thither again, and see if I did not catch the tone of his mind aright, and if the cold and lifeless tint of his perceptions be not then repeated in my own.

Yet it was unaccountable to myself, the interest that I felt in him.

"Have you any objection," said I, "to telling me who made those little purses?"

"Gentlemen have often asked me that," said Moodie, slowly; "but I shake my head, and say little or nothing, and creep out of the way, as well as I can. I am a man of few words; and if gentlemen were to be told one thing, they would be very apt, I suppose, to ask me another. But it happens, just now, Mr. Coverdale, that you can tell me more about the maker of those little purses, than I can tell you."

"Why do you trouble him with needless questions, Coverdale?" interrupted Hollingsworth. "You must have known, long ago, that it was Priscilla. And so, my good friend, you have come to see her? Well, I am glad of it. You will find her altered very much for the better, since that wintry evening when you put her into my charge. Why, Priscilla has a bloom in her cheeks, now!"

"Has my pale little girl a bloom?" repeated Moodie, with a kind of slow wonder. "Priscilla with a bloom in her cheeks! Ah, I am afraid I shall not know my little girl. And is she happy?"

"Just as happy as a bird," answered Hollingsworth.

"Then, gentlemen," said our guest, apprehensively, "I don't think it well for me to go any further. I crept hitherward only to ask about Priscilla; and now that you have told me such good news, perhaps I can do no better than to creep back again. If she were to see this old face of mine, the child would remember some very sad times which we have spent together. Some very sad times indeed! She has forgotten them, I know—them and me—else she could not be so happy, nor have a bloom in her cheeks. Yes—yes—yes," continued he, still with the same torpid utterance; "with many thanks to you, Mr. Hollingsworth, I will creep back to town again."

"You shall do no such thing, Mr. Moodie!" said Hollingsworth, bluffly. "Priscilla often speaks of you; and if there lacks anything to make her cheeks bloom like two damask roses,[1] I'll venture to say, it is just the sight of your face. Come; we will go and find her."

1. Roses known for their deep pink color.

"Mr. Hollingsworth!" said the old man, in his hesitating way.

"Well!" answered Hollingsworth.

"Has there been any call for Priscilla?" asked Moodie; and though his face was hidden from us, his tone gave a sure indication of the mysterious nod and wink with which he put the question. "You know, I think, sir, what I mean."

"I have not the remotest suspicion what you mean, Mr. Moodie," replied Hollingsworth. "Nobody, to my knowledge, has called for Priscilla, except yourself. But, come; we are losing time, and I have several things to say to you, by the way."

"And, Mr. Hollingsworth!" repeated Moodie.

"Well, again!" cried my friend, rather impatiently. "What now?"

"There is a lady here," said the old man; and his voice lost some of its wearisome hesitation. "You will account it a very strange matter for me to talk about; but I chanced to know this lady, when she was but a little child. If I am rightly informed, she has grown to be a very fine woman, and makes a brilliant figure in the world, with her beauty, and her talents, and her noble way of spending her riches. I should recognize this lady, so people tell me, by a magnificent flower in her hair!"

"What a rich tinge it gives to his colorless ideas, when he speaks of Zenobia!" I whispered to Hollingsworth. "But how can there possibly be any interest or connecting link between him and her?"

"The old man, for years past," whispered Hollingsworth, "has been a little out of his right mind, as you probably see."

"What I would inquire," resumed Moodie, "is, whether this beautiful lady is kind to my poor Priscilla."

"Very kind," said Hollingsworth.

"Does she love her?" asked Moodie.

"It should seem so," answered my friend. "They are always together."

"Like a gentlewoman and her maid servant, I fancy?" suggested the old man.

There was something so singular in his way of saying this, that I could not resist the impulse to turn quite round, so as to catch a glimpse of his face; almost imagining that I should see another person than old Moodie. But there he sat, with the patched side of his face towards me.

"Like an elder and younger sister, rather," replied Hollingsworth.

"Ah," said Moodie, more complaisantly—for his latter tones had harshness and acidity in them—"it would gladden my old heart to witness that. If one thing would make me happier than another, Mr. Hollingsworth, it would be, to see that beautiful lady holding my little girl by the hand."

"Come along," said Hollingsworth, "and perhaps you may."

After a little more delay on the part of our freakish visitor, they set forth together; old Moodie keeping a step or two behind Hollingsworth, so that the latter could not very conveniently look him in the face. I remained under the tuft of maples, doing my utmost to draw an inference from the scene that had just passed. In spite of Hollingsworth's off-hand explanation, it did not strike me that our strange guest was really beside himself, but only that his mind needed screwing up, like an instrument long out of tune, the strings of which have ceased to vibrate smartly and sharply. Me-thought it would be profitable for us, projectors of a happy life, to welcome this old gray shadow, and cherish him as one of us, and let him creep about our domain, in order that he might be a little merrier for our sakes, and we, sometimes, a little sadder for his. Human destinies look ominous, without some perceptible intermix-ture of the sable or the gray. And then, too, should any of our frater-nity grow feverish with an over-exulting sense of prosperity, it would be a sort of cooling regimen to slink off into the woods, and spend an hour, or a day, or as many days as might be requisite to the cure, in uninterrupted communion with this deplorable old Moodie!

Going homeward to dinner, I had a glimpse of him behind the trunk of a tree, gazing earnestly towards a particular window of the farm-house. And, by-and-by, Priscilla appeared at this window, play-fully drawing along Zenobia, who looked as bright as the very day that was blazing down upon us, only not, by many degrees, so well advanced towards her noon. I was convinced that this pretty sight must have been purposely arranged by Priscilla, for the old man to see. But either the girl held her too long, or her fondness was resented as too great a freedom; for Zenobia suddenly put Priscilla decidedly away, and gave her a haughty look, as from a mistress to a dependant. Old Moodie shook his head—and again, and again, I saw him shake it, as he withdrew along the road—and, at the last point whence the farm-house was visible, he turned, and shook his uplifted staff.

XI. The Wood-Path

Not long after the preceding incident, in order to get the ache of too constant labor out of my bones, and to relieve my spirit of the irksome-ness of a settled routine, I took a holiday. It was my purpose to spend it, all alone, from breakfast-time till twilight, in the deepest wood-seclusion that lay anywhere around us. Though fond of society, I was so constituted as to need these occasional retirements, even in a life like that of Blithedale, which was itself characterized by a remoteness from the world. Unless renewed by a yet farther withdrawal towards the inner circle of self-communion, I lost the better part of my individuality. My thoughts became of little worth, and my sensibilities grew as arid as a tuft of moss, (a thing whose life is in the shade, the rain, or the noontide dew,) crumbling in the sunshine, after long expectance of a shower. So, with my heart full of a drowsy pleasure, and cautious not to dissipate my mood by previous intercourse with any one, I hurried away, and was soon pacing a wood-path, arched overhead with boughs, and dusky brown beneath my feet.

At first, I walked very swiftly, as if the heavy floodtide of social life were roaring at my heels, and would outstrip and overwhelm me, without all the better diligence in my escape. But, threading the more distant windings of the track, I abated my pace and looked about me for some side-aisle, that should admit me into the innermost sanctuary of this green cathedral; just as, in human acquaintanceship, a casual opening sometimes lets us, all of a sudden, into the long-sought intimacy of a mysterious heart. So much was I absorbed in my reflections—or rather, in my mood, the substance of which was as yet too shapeless to be called thought—that footsteps rustled on the leaves, and a figure passed me by, almost without impressing either the sound or sight upon my consciousness.

A moment afterwards, I heard a voice at a little distance behind me, speaking so sharply and impertinently that it made a complete discord with my spiritual state, and caused the latter to vanish, as abruptly as when you thrust a finger into a soap-bubble.

"Halloo, friend!" cried this most unseasonable voice. "Stop a moment, I say! I must have a word with you!"

I turned about, in a humor ludicrously irate. In the first place, the interruption, at any rate, was a grievous injury; then, the tone displeased me. And, finally, unless there be real affection in his heart, a man cannot—such is the bad state to which the world has brought itself—cannot more effectually show his contempt for a brother-mortal, nor more gallingly assume a position of superiority, than by addressing him as 'friend.' Especially does the misapplication of this phrase bring out that latent hostility, which is sure to animate peculiar sects, and those who, with however generous a purpose, have sequestered themselves from the crowd; a feeling, it is true, which may be hidden in some dog-kennel of the heart, grumbling there in the darkness, but is never quite extinct, until the dissenting party have gained power and scope enough to treat the world generously. For my part, I should have taken it as far less an insult to be styled 'fellow,' 'clown,' or 'bumpkin.' To either of these appellations, my rustic garb (it was a linen blouse, with checked shirt and striped pantaloons, a chip-hat[1] on my head, and a rough hickory-stick in my

---

1. A brimmed hat, woven of thin strips of wood, palm leaf, or straw.

hand) very fairly entitled me. As the case stood, my temper darted at once to the opposite pole; not friend, but enemy!

"What do you want with me?" said I, facing about.

"Come a little nearer, friend!" said the stranger, beckoning.

"No," answered I. "If I can do anything for you, without too much trouble to myself, say so. But recollect, if you please, that you are not speaking to an acquaintance, much less a friend!"

"Upon my word, I believe not!" retorted he, looking at me with some curiosity; and lifting his hat, he made me a salute, which had enough of sarcasm to be offensive, and just enough of doubtful courtesy to render any resentment of it absurd.—"But I ask your pardon! I recognize a little mistake. If I may take the liberty to suppose it, you, sir, are probably one of the Æsthetic—or shall I rather say ecstatic?—laborers, who have planted themselves hereabouts. This is your forest of Arden; and you are either the banished Duke, in person, or one of the chief nobles in his train. The melancholy Jacques, perhaps?[2] Be it so! In that case, you can probably do me a favor."

I never, in my life, felt less inclined to confer a favor on any man.

"I am busy!" said I.

So unexpectedly had the stranger made me sensible of his presence, that he had almost the effect of an apparition, and certainly a less appropriate one (taking into view the dim woodland solitude about us) than if the salvage man of antiquity, hirsute and cinctured with a leafy girdle, had started out of a thicket.[3] He was still young, seemingly a little under thirty, of a tall and well-developed figure, and as handsome a man as ever I beheld. The style of his beauty, however, though a masculine style, did not at all commend itself to my taste. His countenance—I hardly know how to describe the peculiarity—had an indecorum in it, a kind of rudeness, a hard, coarse, forth-putting freedom of expression, which no degree of external polish could have abated, one single jot. Not that it was vulgar. But he had no fineness of nature; there was in his eyes (although they might have artifice enough of another sort) the naked exposure of something that ought not to be left prominent. With these vague allusions to what I have seen in other faces, as well as his, I leave the quality to be comprehended best—because with an intuitive repugnance—by those who possess least of it.

His hair, as well as his beard and moustache, was coal-black; his eyes, too, were black and sparkling, and his teeth remarkably

2. In Shakespeare's *As You Like It*, a deposed Duke leads a band of loyal courtiers—including the sharp-tongued Jacques—to a life of supposed pastoral simplicity in the Forest of Arden.
3. The "salvage man" was the conventional representation of the savage in traditional English pageantry and heraldry. Coverdale refers to two of this figure's typical visual features: a wild hairiness (hence, he is "hirsute"), and a belt ("cincture") of ivy leaves.

brilliant. He was rather carelessly, but well and fashionably dressed, in a summer-morning costume. There was a gold chain, exquisitely wrought, across his vest. I never saw a smoother or whiter gloss than that upon his shirt-bosom, which had a pin in it, set with a gem that glimmered, in the leafy shadow where he stood, like a living tip of fire. He carried a stick with a wooden head, carved in vivid imitation of that of a serpent. I hated him, partly, I do believe, from a comparison of my own homely garb with his well-ordered foppishness.

"Well, sir," said I, a little ashamed of my first irritation, but still with no waste of civility, "be pleased to speak at once, as I have my own business in hand."

"I regret that my mode of addressing you was a little unfortunate," said the stranger, smiling; for he seemed a very acute sort of person, and saw, in some degree, how I stood affected towards him. "I intended no offence, and shall certainly comport myself with due ceremony hereafter. I merely wish to make a few inquiries respecting a lady, formerly of my acquaintance, who is now resident in your Community, and, I believe, largely concerned in your social enterprise. You call her, I think, Zenobia."

"That is her name in literature," observed I—"a name, too, which possibly she may permit her private friends to know and address her by;—but not one which they feel at liberty to recognize, when used of her, personally, by a stranger or casual acquaintance."

"Indeed!" answered this disagreeable person; and he turned aside his face, for an instant, with a brief laugh, which struck me as a noteworthy expression of his character. "Perhaps I might put forward a claim, on your own grounds, to call the lady by a name so appropriate to her splendid qualities. But I am willing to know her by any cognomen that you may suggest."

Heartily wishing that he would be either a little more offensive, or a good deal less so, or break off our intercourse altogether, I mentioned Zenobia's real name.

"True," said he; "and, in general society, I have never heard her called otherwise. And, after all, our discussion of the point has been gratuitous. My object is only to inquire when, where, and how, this lady may most conveniently be seen?"

"At her present residence, of course," I replied. "You have but to go thither and ask for her. This very path will lead you within sight of the house:—so I wish you good morning."

"One moment, if you please," said the stranger. "The course you indicate would certainly be the proper one, in an ordinary morning-call. But my business is private, personal, and somewhat peculiar. Now, in a Community like this, I should judge that any little occurrence is likely to be discussed rather more minutely than would quite suit my views. I refer solely to myself, you understand, and without intimating that it would be other than a matter of entire indifference to the lady. In short, I especially desire to see her in private. If her habits are such as I have known them, she is probably often to be met with in the woods, or by the river-side; and I think you could do me the favor to point out some favorite walk, where, about this hour, I might be fortunate enough to gain an interview."

I reflected, that it would be quite a super-erogatory piece of quixotism,[4] in me, to undertake the guardianship of Zenobia, who, for my pains, would only make me the butt of endless ridicule, should the fact ever come to her knowledge. I therefore described a spot which, as often as any other, was Zenobia's resort, at this period of the day; nor was it so remote from the farm-house as to leave her in much peril, whatever might be the stranger's character.

"A single word more!" said he; and his black eyes sparkled at me, whether with fun or malice I knew not, but certainly as if the Devil were peeping out of them. "Among your fraternity, I understand, there is a certain holy and benevolent blacksmith; a man of iron, in more senses than one; a rough, cross-grained, well-meaning individual, rather boorish in his manners—as might be expected—and by no means of the highest intellectual cultivation. He is a philanthropical lecturer, with two or three disciples, and a scheme of his own, the preliminary step in which involves a large purchase of land, and the erection of a spacious edifice, at an expense considerably beyond his means; inasmuch as these are to be reckoned in copper or old iron, much more conveniently than in gold or silver. He hammers away upon his one topic, as lustily as ever he did upon a horse-shoe! Do you know such a person?"

I shook my head, and was turning away.

"Our friend," he continued, "is described to me as a brawny, shaggy, grim, and ill-favored personage, not particularly well-calculated, one would say, to insinuate himself with the softer sex. Yet, so far has this honest fellow succeeded with one lady, whom we wot[5] of, that he anticipates, from her abundant resources, the necessary funds for realizing his plan in brick and mortar!"

Here the stranger seemed to be so much amused with his sketch of Hollingsworth's character and purposes, that he burst into a fit of merriment, of the same nature as the brief, metallic laugh already alluded to, but immensely prolonged and enlarged. In the excess of his delight, he opened his mouth wide, and disclosed a gold band around the upper part of his teeth; thereby making it apparent that every one of his brilliant grinders and incisors was a sham. This discovery affected me very oddly. I felt as if the whole man were a moral and physical humbug; his wonderful beauty of face, for aught

---

4. An act of extravagant chivalry, romantic enthusiasm, or utter impracticality—in the manner of Don Quixote, the hero of Cervantes' novel; *super-erogatory*: superfluous; unnecessary.
5. Know.

I knew, might be removeable like a mask; and, tall and comely as his figure looked, he was perhaps but a wizened little elf, gray and decrepit, with nothing genuine about him, save the wicked expression of his grin. The fantasy of his spectral character so wrought upon me, together with the contagion of his strange mirth on my sympathies, that I soon began to laugh as loudly as himself.

By-and-by, he paused, all at once; so suddenly, indeed, that my own cachinnation[6] lasted a moment longer.

"Ah, excuse me!" said he. "Our interview seems to proceed more merrily than it began."

"It ends here," answered I. "And I take shame to myself, that my folly has lost me the right of resenting your ridicule of a friend."

"Pray allow me," said the stranger, approaching a step nearer, and laying his gloved hand on my sleeve. "One other favor I must ask of you. You have a young person, here at Blithedale, of whom I have heard—whom, perhaps, I have known—and in whom, at all events, I take a peculiar interest. She is one of those delicate, nervous young creatures, not uncommon in New England, and whom I suppose to have become what we find them by the gradual refining away of the physical system, among your women. Some philosophers choose to glorify this habit of body by terming it spiritual; but, in my opinion, it is rather the effect of unwholesome food, bad air, lack of out-door exercise, and neglect of bathing, on the part of these damsels and their female progenitors; all resulting in a kind of hereditary dyspepsia. Zenobia, even with her uncomfortable surplus of vitality, is far the better model of womanhood. But—to revert again to this young person—she goes among you by the name of Priscilla. Could you possibly afford me the means of speaking with her?"

"You have made so many inquiries of me," I observed, "that I may at least trouble you with one. What is your name?"

He offered me a card, with 'Professor Westervelt' engraved on it. At the same time, as if to vindicate his claim to the professorial dignity, so often assumed on very questionable grounds, he put on a pair of spectacles, which so altered the character of his face that I hardly knew him again. But I liked the present aspect no better than the former one.

"I must decline any further connection with your affairs," said I, drawing back. "I have told you where to find Zenobia. As for Priscilla, she has closer friends than myself, through whom, if they see fit, you can gain access to her."

"In that case," returned the Professor, ceremoniously raising his hat, "good morning to you."

He took his departure, and was soon out of sight among the windings of the wood-path. But, after a little reflection, I could not help

6. Convulsive laughter.

regretting that I had so peremptorily broken off the interview, while the stranger seemed inclined to continue it. His evident knowledge of matters, affecting my three friends, might have led to disclosures, or inferences, that would perhaps have been serviceable. I was particularly struck with the fact, that, ever since the appearance of Priscilla, it had been the tendency of events to suggest and establish a connection between Zenobia and her. She had come, in the first instance, as if with the sole purpose of claiming Zenobia's protection. Old Moodie's visit, it appeared, was chiefly to ascertain whether this object had been accomplished. And here, to-day, was the questionable Professor, linking one with the other in his inquiries, and seeking communication with both.

Meanwhile, my inclination for a ramble having been baulked, I lingered in the vicinity of the farm, with perhaps a vague idea that some new event would grow out of Westervelt's proposed interview with Zenobia. My own part, in these transactions, was singularly subordinate. It resembled that of the Chorus[7] in a classic play, which seems to be set aloof from the possibility of personal concernment, and bestows the whole measure of its hope or fear, its exultation or sorrow, on the fortunes of others, between whom and itself this sympathy is the only bond. Destiny, it may be—the most skilful of stage managers—seldom chooses to arrange its scenes, and carry forward its drama, without securing the presence of at least one calm observer. It is his office to give applause, when due, and sometimes an inevitable tear, to detect the final fitness of incident to character, and distil, in his long-brooding thought, the whole morality of the performance.

Not to be out of the way, in case there were need of me in my vocation, and, at the same time, to avoid thrusting myself where neither Destiny nor mortals might desire my presence, I remained pretty near the verge of the woodlands. My position was off the track of Zenobia's customary walk, yet not so remote but that a recognized occasion might speedily have brought me thither.

XII. Coverdale's Hermitage

Long since, in this part of our circumjacent wood, I had found out for myself a little hermitage. It was a kind of leafy cave, high upward into the air, among the midmost branches of a white-pine tree. A wild grape-vine, of unusual size and luxuriance, had twined and twisted itself up into the tree, and, after wreathing the entanglement

---

7. In Greek tragedy, a group that comments on the actions of the main characters of the play, often expressing sympathy, or traditional communal values and beliefs.

of its tendrils around almost every bough, had caught hold of three or four neighboring trees, and married the whole clump with a perfectly inextricable knot of polygamy. Once, while sheltering myself from a summer shower, the fancy had taken me to clamber up into this seemingly impervious mass of foliage. The branches yielded me a passage, and closed again, beneath, as if only a squirrel or a bird had passed. Far aloft, around the stem of the central pine, behold, a perfect nest for Robinson Crusoe or King Charles![1] A hollow chamber, of rare seclusion, had been formed by the decay of some of the pine-branches, which the vine had lovingly strangled with its embrace, burying them from the light of day in an aerial sepulchre of its own leaves. It cost me but little ingenuity to enlarge the interior, and open loop-holes through the verdant walls. Had it ever been my fortune to spend a honey-moon, I should have thought seriously of inviting my bride up thither, where our next neighbors would have been two orioles in another part of the clump.

It was an admirable place to make verses, tuning the rhythm to the breezy symphony that so often stirred among the vine-leaves; or to meditate an essay for the Dial, in which the many tongues of Nature whispered mysteries, and seemed to ask only a little stronger puff of wind, to speak out the solution of its riddle. Being so pervious to air-currents, it was just the nook, too, for the enjoyment of a cigar. This hermitage was my one exclusive possession, while I counted myself a brother of the socialists. It symbolized my individuality, and aided me in keeping it inviolate. None ever found me out in it, except, once, a squirrel. I brought thither no guest, because, after Hollingsworth failed me, there was no longer the man alive with whom I could think of sharing all. So there I used to sit, owl-like, yet not without liberal and hospitable thoughts. I counted the innumerable clusters of my vine, and fore-reckoned the abundance of my vintage. It gladdened me to anticipate the surprise of the Community, when, like an allegorical figure of rich October, I should make my appearance, with shoulders bent beneath the burthen of ripe grapes, and some of the crushed ones crimsoning my brow as with a blood-stain.[2]

Ascending into this natural turret, I peeped, in turn, out of several of its small windows. The pine-tree, being ancient, rose high above the rest of the wood, which was of comparatively recent growth. Even where I sat, about midway between the root and the topmost

---

1. After his forces lost the battle of Worcester (September, 1651), King Charles II of England evaded Oliver Cromwell's troops by hiding in an oak tree. *Robinson Crusoe*: in Daniel Defoe's *Robinson Crusoe* (1719), the title character, marooned on an island, looks for ships from a platform in a tree.
2. In "The Mutability Cantos," a fragment of Edmund Spenser's *The Faerie Queene* (1590, 1596)—one of Hawthorne's favorite poems—the allegorical figure of October appears, gleeful and tipsy from the new wine he has been making (*Mutabilitie* 7.39).

bough, my position was lofty enough to serve as an observatory, not for starry investigations, but for those sublunary matters in which lay a lore as infinite as that of the planets. Through one loop-hole, I saw the river lapsing calmly onward, while, in the meadow near its brink, a few of the brethren were digging peat for our winter's fuel. On the interior cart-road of our farm, I discerned Hollingsworth, with a yoke of oxen hitched to a drag of stones, that were to be piled into a fence, on which we employed ourselves at the odd intervals of other labor. The harsh tones of his voice, shouting to the sluggish steers, made me sensible, even at such a distance, that he was ill at ease, and that the baulked philanthropist had the battle-spirit in his heart.

"Haw Buck!" quoth he. "Come along there, ye lazy ones! What are ye about now? Gee!"

"Mankind, in Hollingsworth's opinion," thought I, "is but another yoke of oxen, as stubborn, stupid, and sluggish, as our old Brown and Bright. He vituperates us aloud, and curses us in his heart, and will begin to prick us with the goad stick, by-and-by. But, are we his oxen? And what right has he to be the driver? And why, when there is enough else to do, should we waste our strength in dragging home the ponderous load of his philanthropic absurdities? At my height above the earth, the whole matter looks ridiculous!"

Turning towards the farm-house, I saw Priscilla (for, though a great way off, the eye of faith assured me that it was she) sitting at Zenobia's window, and making little purses, I suppose, or perhaps mending the Community's old linen. A bird flew past my tree; and as it clove its way onward into the sunny atmosphere, I flung it a message for Priscilla.

"Tell her," said I, "that her fragile thread of life has inextricably knotted itself with other and tougher threads, and most likely it will be broken. Tell her that Zenobia will not be long her friend. Say that Hollingsworth's heart is on fire with his own purpose, but icy for all human affection, and that, if she has given him her love, it is like casting a flower into a sepulchre. And say, that, if any mortal really cares for her, it is myself, and not even I, for her realities—poor little seamstress, as Zenobia rightly called her!—but for the fancy-work with which I have idly decked her out!"

The pleasant scent of the wood, evolved by the hot sun, stole up to my nostrils, as if I had been an idol in its niche. Many trees mingled their fragrance into a thousand-fold odor. Possibly, there was a sensual influence in the broad light of noon that lay beneath me. It may have been the cause, in part, that I suddenly found myself possessed by a mood of disbelief in moral beauty or heroism, and a conviction of the folly of attempting to benefit the world, Our especial scheme of reform, which, from my observatory, I could take in with the bodily eye, looked so ridiculous that it was impossible not to laugh aloud.

"But the joke is a little too heavy," thought I. "If I were wise, I should get out of the scrape, with all diligence, and then laugh at my companions for remaining in it!"

While thus musing, I heard, with perfect distinctness, somewhere in the wood beneath, the peculiar laugh, which I have described as one of the disagreeable characteristics of Professor Westervelt. It brought my thoughts back to our recent interview. I recognized, as chiefly due to this man's influence, the sceptical and sneering view which, just now, had filled my mental vision in regard to all life's better purposes. And it was through his eyes, more than my own, that I was looking at Hollingsworth, with his glorious, if impracticable dream, and at the noble earthliness of Zenobia's character, and even at Priscilla, whose impalpable grace lay so singularly between disease and beauty. The essential charm of each had vanished. There are some spheres, the contact with which inevitably degrades the high, debases the pure, deforms the beautiful. It must be a mind of uncommon strength, and little impressibility, that can permit itself the habit of such intercourse, and not be permanently deteriorated; and yet the Professor's tone rep-resented that of worldly society at large, where a cold scepticism smothers what it can of our spiritual aspirations, and makes the rest ridiculous. I detested this kind of man, and all the more, because a part of my own nature showed itself responsive to him.

Voices were now approaching, through the region of the wood which lay in the vicinity of my tree. Soon, I caught glimpses of two figures—a woman and a man—Zenobia and the stranger—earnestly talking together as they advanced.

Zenobia had a rich, though varying color. It was, most of the while, a flame, and anon a sudden paleness. Her eyes glowed, so that their light sometimes flashed upward to me, as when the sun throws a dazzle from some bright object on the ground. Her gestures were free, and strikingly impressive. The whole woman was alive with a passionate intensity, which I now perceived to be the phase in which her beauty culminated. Any passion would have become her well, and passionate love, perhaps, the best of all. This was not love, but anger, largely intermixed with scorn. Yet the idea strangely forced itself upon me, that there was a sort of familiarity between these two companions, necessarily the result of an intimate love—on Zenobia's part, at least—in days gone by, but which had pro-longed itself into as intimate a hatred, for all futurity. As they passed among the trees, reckless as her movement was, she took good heed that even the hem of her garment should not brush against the stranger's person. I wondered whether there had always been a chasm, guarded so religiously, betwixt these two.

As for Westervelt, he was not a whit more warmed by Zenobia's passion, than a salamander by the heat of its native furnace.[3] He would have been absolutely statuesque, save for a look of slight perplexity tinctured strongly with derision. It was a crisis in which his intellectual perceptions could not altogether help him out. He failed to comprehend, and cared but little for comprehending, why Zenobia should put herself into such a fume; but satisfied his mind that it was all folly, and only another shape of a woman's manifold absurdity, which men can never understand. How many a woman's evil fate has yoked her with a man like this! Nature thrusts some of us into the world miserably incomplete, on the emotional side, with hardly any sensibilities except what pertain to us as animals. No passion, save of the senses; no holy tenderness, nor the delicacy that results from this. Externally, they bear a close resemblance to other men, and have perhaps all save the finest grace; but when a woman wrecks herself on such a being, she ultimately finds that the real womanhood, within her, has no corresponding part in him. Her deepest voice lacks a response; the deeper her cry, the more dead his silence. The fault may be none of his; he cannot give her what never lived within his soul. But the wretchedness, on her side, and the moral deterioration attendant on a false and shallow life, without strength enough to keep itself sweet, are among the most pitiable wrongs that mortals suffer.

Now, as I looked down from my upper region at this man and woman—outwardly so fair a sight, and wandering like two lovers in the wood—I imagined that Zenobia, at an earlier period of youth, might have fallen into the misfortune above indicated. And when her passionate womanhood, as was inevitable, had discovered its mistake, there had ensued the character of eccentricity and defiance, which distinguished the more public portion of her life.

Seeing how aptly matters had chanced, thus far, I began to think it the design of fate to let me into all Zenobia's secrets, and that therefore the couple would sit down beneath my tree, and carry on a conversation which would leave me nothing to inquire. No doubt, however, had it so happened, I should have deemed myself honorably bound to warn them of a listener's presence by flinging down a handful of unripe grapes; or by sending an unearthly groan out of my hiding-place, as if this were one of the trees of Dante's ghostly forest.[4] But real life never arranges itself exactly like a romance. In the first place, they did not sit down at all. Secondly, even while they passed beneath the tree,

---

3. Refers to the mythological salamander, a lizard-like animal supposedly able to endure or live in fire.
4. Dante writes of two woods in the *Inferno*, either of which might be Coverdale's "ghostly forest": one is the dark wood of Canto I, where the pilgrim loses his way and begins his journey; the other is the wood of the suicides, in Canto XIII, where the wailing voices of the punished souls, encased in trees and fed upon by Harpies, may be heard.

Zenobia's utterance was so hasty and broken, and Westervelt's so cool and low, that I hardly could make out an intelligible sentence, on either side. What I seem to remember, I yet suspect may have been patched together by my fancy, in brooding over the matter, afterwards.

"Why not fling the girl off," said Westervelt, "and let her go?"

"She clung to me from the first," replied Zenobia. "I neither know nor care what it is in me that so attaches her. But she loves me, and I will not fail her."

"She will plague you, then," said he, "in more ways than one."

"The poor child!" exclaimed Zenobia. "She can do me neither good nor harm. How should she?"

I know not what reply Westervelt whispered; nor did Zenobia's subsequent exclamation give me any clue, except that it evidently inspired her with horror and disgust.

"With what kind of a being am I linked!" cried she. "If my Creator cares aught for my soul, let him release me from this miserable bond!"

"I did not think it weighed so heavily," said her companion.

"Nevertheless," answered Zenobia, "it will strangle me at last!"

And then I heard her utter a helpless sort of moan; a sound which, struggling out of the heart of a person of her pride and strength, affected me more than if she had made the wood dolorously vocal with a thousand shrieks and wails.

Other mysterious words, besides what are above-written, they spoke together; but I understood no more, and even question whether I fairly understood so much as this. By long brooding over our recollections, we subtilize them into something akin to imaginary stuff, and hardly capable of being distinguished from it. In a few moments, they were completely beyond ear-shot. A breeze stirred after them, and awoke the leafy tongues of the surrounding trees, which forthwith began to babble, as if innumerable gossips had all at once got wind of Zenobia's secret. But, as the breeze grew stronger, its voice among the branches was as if it said—'Hush! Hush!'—and I resolved that to no mortal would I disclose what I had heard. And, though there might be room for casuistry,[5] such, I conceive, is the most equitable rule in all similar conjunctures.

XIII. Zenobia's Legend

The illustrious Society of Blithedale, though it toiled in downright earnest for the good of mankind, yet not unfrequently illuminated its laborious life with an afternoon or evening of pastime. Pic-nics under the trees were considerably in vogue; and, within doors, fragmentary

---

5. The working through of specific cases of right and wrong, through the application of ethical principles; often used pejoratively, to indicate specious or self-serving moral reasoning.

bits of theatrical performance, such as single acts of tragedy or comedy, or dramatic proverbs and charades. Zenobia, besides, was fond of giving us readings from Shakspeare, and often with a depth of tragic power, or breadth of comic effect, that made one feel it an intolerable wrong to the world, that she did not at once go upon the stage. *Tableaux vivants*[1] were another of our occasional modes of amusement, in which scarlet shawls, old silken robes, ruffs, velvets, furs, and all kinds of miscellaneous trumpery, converted our familiar companions into the people of a pictorial world. We had been thus engaged, on the evening after the incident narrated in the last chapter. Several splendid works of art—either arranged after engravings from the Old Masters,[2] or original illustrations of scenes in history or romance—had been presented, and we were earnestly entreating Zenobia for more.

She stood, with a meditative air, holding a large piece of gauze, or some such ethereal stuff, as if considering what picture should next occupy the frame; while at her feet lay a heap of many-colored garments, which her quick fancy and magic skill could so easily convert into gorgeous draperies for heroes and princesses.

"I am getting weary of this," said she, after a moment's thought. "Our own features, and our own figures and airs, show a little too intrusively through all the characters we assume. We have so much familiarity with one another's realities, that we cannot remove ourselves, at pleasure, into an imaginary sphere. Let us have no more pictures, to-night; but, to make you what poor amends I can, how would you like to have me trump up a wild, spectral legend, on the spur of the moment?"

Zenobia had the gift of telling a fanciful little story, off hand, in a way that made it greatly more effective, than it was usually found to be, when she afterwards elaborated the same production with her pen. Her proposal, therefore, was greeted with acclamation.

"Oh, a story, a story, by all means!" cried the young girls. "No matter how marvellous, we will believe it, every word! And let it be a ghost-story, if you please!"

"No; not exactly a ghost-story," answered Zenobia; "but something so nearly like it that you shall hardly tell the difference. And, Priscilla, stand you before me, where I may look at you, and get my inspiration out of your eyes. They are very deep and dreamy, to-night!"

I know not whether the following version of her story will retain any portion of its pristine character. But, as Zenobia told it, wildly and rapidly, hesitating at no extravagance, and dashing at absurdities which I am too timorous to repeat—giving it the varied emphasis of her inimitable voice, and the pictorial illustration of her mobile face, while, through it all, we caught the freshest aroma of the thoughts,

1. Elaborately presented scenes from literature, history, or works of art; the costumed participants remained silent and motionless as their scene was revealed to its audience.
2. Best-known western European painters of the thirteenth through the seventeenth centuries.

as they came bubbling out of her mind—thus narrated, and thus heard, the legend seemed quite a remarkable affair. I scarcely knew, at the time, whether she intended us to laugh, or be more seriously impressed. From beginning to end it was undeniable nonsense, but not necessarily the worse for that.

The Silvery Veil

You have heard, my dear friends, of the Veiled Lady, who grew suddenly so very famous, a few months ago. And have you never thought how remarkable it was, that this marvellous creature should vanish, all at once, while her renown was on the increase, before the public had grown weary of her, and when the enigma of her character, instead of being solved, presented itself more mystically at every exhibition? Her last appearance, as you know, was before a crowded audience. The next evening—although the bills had announced her, at the corner of every street, in red letters of a gigantic size—there was no Veiled Lady to be seen! Now, listen to my simple little tale; and you shall hear the very latest incident in the known life—(if life it may be called, which seemed to have no more reality than the candlelight image of one's self, which peeps at us outside of a dark window-pane)—the life of this shadowy phenomenon.

A party of young gentlemen, you are to understand, were enjoying themselves, one afternoon, as young gentlemen are sometimes fond of doing, over a bottle or two of champagne; and—among other ladies less mysterious—the subject of the Veiled Lady, as was very natural, happened to come up before them for discussion. She rose, as it were, with the sparkling effervescence of their wine, and appeared in a more airy and fantastic light, on account of the medium through which they saw her. They repeated to one another, between jest and earnest, all the wild stories that were in vogue; nor, I presume, did they hesitate to add any small circumstance that the inventive whim of the moment might suggest, to heighten the marvellousness of their theme.

"But what an audacious report was that," observed one, "which pretended to assert the identity of this strange creature with a young lady"—and here he mentioned her name—"the daughter of one of our most distinguished families!"

"Ah, there is more in that story than can well be accounted for!" remarked another. "I have it on good authority, that the young lady in question is invariably out of sight, and not to be traced, even by her own family, at the hours when the Veiled Lady is before the public; nor can any satisfactory explanation be given of her disappearance. And just look at the thing! Her brother is a young fellow of spirit. He cannot but be aware of these rumors in reference to his sister. Why, then, does he not come forward to defend her character, unless he is conscious that an investigation would only make the matter worse?"

It is essential to the purposes of my legend to distinguish one of these young gentlemen from his companions; so, for the sake of a soft and pretty name, (such as we, of the literary sisterhood, invariably bestow upon our heroes,) I deem it fit to call him 'Theodore.'

"Pshaw!" exclaimed Theodore. "Her brother is no such fool! Nobody, unless his brain be as full of bubbles as this wine, can seriously think of crediting that ridiculous rumor. Why, if my senses did not play me false, (which never was the case yet,) I affirm that I saw that very lady, last evening, at the exhibition, while this veiled phenomenon was playing off her juggling tricks! What can you say to that?"

"Oh, it was a spectral illusion that you saw!" replied his friends, with a general laugh. "The Veiled Lady is quite up to such a thing."

However, as the above-mentioned fable could not hold its ground against Theodore's downright refutation, they went on to speak of other stories, which the wild babble of the town had set afloat. Some upheld, that the veil covered the most beautiful countenance in the world; others—and certainly with more reason, considering the sex of the Veiled Lady—that the face was the most hideous and horrible, and that this was her sole motive for hiding it. It was the face of a corpse; it was the head of a skeleton; it was a monstrous visage, with snaky locks, like Medusa's,[3] and one great red eye in the centre of the forehead. Again, it was affirmed, that there was no single and unchangeable set of features, beneath the veil, but that whosoever should be bold enough to lift it, would behold the features of that person, in all the world, who was destined to be his fate; perhaps he would be greeted by the tender smile of the woman whom he loved; or, quite as probably, the deadly scowl of his bitterest enemy would throw a blight over his life. They quoted, moreover, this startling explanation of the whole affair:—that the Magician (who exhibited the Veiled Lady, and who, by-the-by, was the handsomest man in the whole world) had bartered his own soul for seven years' possession of a familiar fiend, and that the last year of the contract was wearing towards its close.

If it were worth our while, I could keep you till an hour beyond midnight, listening to a thousand such absurdities as these. But, finally, our friend Theodore, who prided himself upon his commonsense, found the matter getting quite beyond his patience.

"I offer any wager you like," cried he, setting down his glass so forcibly as to break the stem of it, "that, this very evening, I find out the mystery of the Veiled Lady!"

---

3. A female monster from Greek mythology, Medusa had snakes for hair and her gaze turned men to stone.

Young men, I am told, boggle at nothing, over their wine. So, after a little more talk, a wager of considerable amount was actually laid, the money staked, and Theodore left to choose his own method of settling the dispute.

How he managed it, I know not, nor is it of any great importance to this veracious legend; the most natural way, to be sure, was by bribing the door-keeper, or, possibly, he preferred clambering in at the window. But, at any rate, that very evening, while the exhibition was going forward in the hall, Theodore contrived to gain admittance into the private withdrawing-room, whither the Veiled Lady was accustomed to retire, at the close of her performances. There he waited, listening, I suppose, to the stifled hum of the great audience; and, no doubt, he could distinguish the deep tones of the Magician, causing the wonders that he wrought to appear more dark and intricate, by his mystic pretence of an explanation; perhaps, too, in the intervals of the wild, breezy music which accompanied the exhibition, he might hear the low voice of the Veiled Lady, conveying her Sibylline responses. Firm as Theodore's nerves might be, and much as he prided himself on his sturdy perception of realities, I should not be surprised if his heart throbbed at a little more than its ordinary rate!

Theodore concealed himself behind a screen. In due time, the performance was brought to a close; and whether the door was softly opened, or whether her bodiless presence came through the wall, is more than I can say; but, all at once, without the young man's knowing how it happened, a veiled figure stood in the centre of the room. It was one thing to be in presence of this mystery, in the hall of exhibition, where the warm, dense life of hundreds of other mortals kept up the beholder's courage, and distributed her influence among so many; it was another thing to be quite alone with her, and that, too, with a hostile, or, at least, an unauthorized and unjustifiable purpose. I rather imagine that Theodore now began to be sensible of something more serious in his enterprise than he had been quite aware of, while he sat with his boon-companions over their sparkling wine.

Very strange, it must be confessed, was the movement with which the figure floated to-and-fro over the carpet, with the silvery veil covering her from head to foot; so impalpable, so ethereal, so without substance, as the texture seemed, yet hiding her every outline in an impenetrability like that of midnight. Surely, she did not walk! She floated, and flitted, and hovered about the room;—no sound of a footstep, no perceptible motion of a limb;—it was as if a wandering breeze wafted her before it, at its own wild and gentle pleasure. But, by-and-by, a purpose began to be discernible, throughout the seeming vagueness of her unrest. She was in quest of something! Could it be, that a subtile presentiment had informed her of the young man's presence? And, if so, did the Veiled Lady seek, or did she shun him? The doubt in Theodore's mind was speedily resolved; for, after a moment or two of these erratic flutterings, she advanced, more decidedly, and stood motionless before the screen.

"Thou art here!" said a soft, low voice. "Come forth, Theodore!"

Thus summoned by his name, Theodore, as a man of courage, had no choice. He emerged from his concealment, and presented himself before the Veiled Lady, with the wine-flush, it may be, quite gone out of his cheeks.

"What wouldst thou with me?" she inquired, with the same gentle composure that was in her former utterance.

"Mysterious creature," replied Theodore, "I would know who and what you are!"

"My lips are forbidden to betray the secret!" said the Veiled Lady.

"At whatever risk, I must discover it!" rejoined Theodore.

"Then," said the Mystery, "there is no way, save to lift my veil!"

And Theodore, partly recovering his audacity, stept forward, on the instant, to do as the Veiled Lady had suggested. But she floated backward to the opposite side of the room, as if the young man's breath had possessed power enough to waft her away.

"Pause, one little instant," said the soft, low voice, "and learn the conditions of what thou art so bold to undertake! Thou canst go hence, and think of me no more; or, at thy option, thou canst lift this mysterious veil, beneath which I am a sad and lonely prisoner, in a bondage which is worse to me than death. But, before raising it, I entreat thee, in all maiden modesty, to bend forward, and impress a kiss, where my breath stirs the veil; and my virgin lips shall come forward to meet thy lips; and from that instant, Theodore, thou shalt be mine, and I thine, with never more a veil between us! And all the felicity of earth and of the future world shall be thine and mine together. So much may a maiden say behind the veil! If thou shrinkest from this, there is yet another way."

"And what is that?" asked Theodore.

"Dost thou hesitate," said the Veiled Lady, "to pledge thyself to me, by meeting these lips of mine, while the veil yet hides my face? Has not thy heart recognized me? Dost thou come hither, not in holy faith, nor with a pure and generous purpose, but in scornful scepticism and idle curiosity? Still, thou mayst lift the veil! But from that instant, Theodore, I am doomed to be thy evil fate; nor wilt thou ever taste another breath of happiness!"

There was a shade of inexpressible sadness in the utterance of these last words. But Theodore, whose natural tendency was towards scepticism, felt himself almost injured and insulted by the Veiled Lady's proposal that he should pledge himself, for life and eternity, to so questionable a creature as herself; or even that she should suggest an inconsequential kiss, taking into view the probability that her face was none of the most bewitching. A delightful idea, truly, that he should salute the lips of a dead girl, or the jaws of a skeleton, or the grinning cavity of a monster's mouth! Even should she prove a comely maiden enough, in other respects, the odds were ten to one that her teeth were defective; a terrible drawback on the delectableness of a kiss!

"Excuse me, fair lady," said Theodore—and I think he nearly burst into a laugh—"if I prefer to lift the veil first; and for this affair of the kiss, we may decide upon it, afterwards!"

"Thou hast made thy choice," said the sweet, sad voice, behind the veil; and there seemed a tender, but unresentful sense of wrong done to womanhood by the young man's contemptuous interpretation of her offer. "I must not counsel thee to pause; although thy fate is still in thine own hand!"

Grasping at the veil, he flung it upward, and caught a glimpse of a pale, lovely face, beneath; just one momentary glimpse; and then the apparition vanished, and the silvery veil fluttered slowly down, and lay upon the floor. Theodore was alone. Our legend leaves him there. His retribution was, to pine, forever and ever, for another sight of that dim, mournful face—which might have been his life-long, household, fireside joy—to desire, and waste life in a feverish quest, and never meet it more!

But what, in good sooth, had become of the Veiled Lady? Had all her existence been comprehended within that mysterious veil, and was she now annihilated? Or was she a spirit, with a heavenly essence, but which might have been tamed down to human bliss, had Theodore been brave and true enough to claim her? Hearken, my sweet friends—and hearken, dear Priscilla—and you shall learn the little more that Zenobia can tell you!

Just at the moment, so far as can be ascertained, when the Veiled Lady vanished, a maiden, pale and shadowy, rose up amid a knot of visionary people, who were seeking for the better life. She was so gentle and so sad—a nameless melancholy gave her such hold upon their sympathies—that they never thought of questioning whence she came. She might have heretofore existed; or her thin substance might have been moulded out of air, at the very instant when they first beheld her. It was all one to them; they took her to their hearts. Among them was a lady, to whom, more than to all the rest, this pale, mysterious girl attached herself.

But, one morning, the lady was wandering in the woods, and there met her a figure in an Oriental robe, with a dark beard, and holding in his hand a silvery veil. He motioned her to stay. Being a woman of some nerve, she did not shriek, nor run away, nor faint, as many ladies would have been apt to do, but stood quietly, and bade him speak. The truth was, she had seen his face before, but had never feared it, although she knew him to be a terrible magician.

"Lady," said he, with a warning gesture, "you are in peril!"

"Peril!" she exclaimed. "And of what nature?"

"There is a certain maiden," replied the Magician, "who has come out of the realm of Mystery, and made herself your most intimate companion. Now, the fates have so ordained it, that, whether by her own will, or no, this stranger is your deadliest enemy. In love, in worldly fortune, in all your pursuit of happiness, she is doomed to fling a blight over your prospects. There is but one possibility of thwarting her disastrous influence."

"Then, tell me that one method," said the lady.

"Take this veil!" he answered, holding forth the silvery texture. "It is a spell; it is a powerful enchantment, which I wrought for her sake, and beneath which she was once my prisoner. Throw it, at unawares, over the head of this secret foe, stamp your foot, and cry—'Arise, Magician, here is the Veiled Lady'—and immediately I will rise up through the earth, and seize her. And from that moment, you are safe!"

So the lady took the silvery veil, which was like woven air, or like some substance airier than nothing, and that would float upward and be lost among the clouds, were she once to let it go. Returning homeward, she found the shadowy girl, amid the knot of visionary transcendentalists,[4] who were still seeking for the better life. She was joyous, now, and had a rose-bloom in her cheeks, and was one of the prettiest creatures, and seemed one of the happiest, that the world could show. But the lady stole noiselessly behind her, and threw the veil over her head. As the slight, ethereal texture sank inevitably down over her figure, the poor girl strove to raise it, and met her dear friend's eyes with one glance of mortal terror, and deep, deep reproach. It could not change her purpose.

"Arise, Magician!" she exclaimed, stamping her foot upon the earth. "Here is the Veiled Lady!"

At the word, uprose the bearded man in the Oriental robes—the beautiful!—the dark Magician, who had bartered away his soul! He threw his arms around the Veiled Lady; and she was his bond-slave, forever more!

• • •

4. The phrase refers to the members of the Blithedale community. Strongly associated with Emerson, Margaret Fuller, and other Boston-area intellectuals, Transcendentalism was a loosely defined social and cultural movement, emerging in the 1830s and characterized by a distrust of established religious authority, a sense that nature was infused with spiritual meaning, an enthusiasm for various social reforms, and a commitment to individual self-realization. Several members of the Brook Farm Community, including founder George Ripley, were members of this group.

Zenobia, all this while, had been holding the piece of gauze, and so managed it as greatly to increase the dramatic effect of the legend, at those points where the magic veil was to be described. Arriving at the catastrophe, and uttering the fatal words, she flung the gauze over Priscilla's head; and, for an instant, her auditors held their breath, half expecting, I verily believe, that the Magician would start up through the floor, and carry off our poor little friend, before our eyes.

As for Priscilla, she stood, droopingly, in the midst of us, making no attempt to remove the veil.

"How do you find yourself, my love?" said Zenobia, lifting a corner of the gauze, and peeping beneath it, with a mischievous smile. "Ah, the dear little soul! Why, she is really going to faint! Mr. Coverdale, Mr. Coverdale, pray bring a glass of water!"

Her nerves being none of the strongest, Priscilla hardly recovered her equanimity during the rest of the evening. This, to be sure, was a great pity; but, nevertheless, we thought it a very bright idea of Zenobia's, to bring her legend to so effective a conclusion.

XIV. Eliot's Pulpit

Our Sundays, at Blithedale, were not ordinarily kept with such rigid observance as might have befitted the descendants of the Pilgrims, whose high enterprise, as we sometimes flattered ourselves, we had taken up, and were carrying it onward and aloft, to a point which they never dreamed of attaining.

On that hallowed day, it is true, we rested from our labors. Our oxen, relieved from their week-day yoke, roamed at large through the pasture; each yoke-fellow, however, keeping close beside his mate, and continuing to acknowledge, from the force of habit and sluggish sympathy, the union which the taskmaster had imposed for his own hard ends. As for us, human yoke-fellows, chosen companions of toil, whose hoes had clinked together throughout the week, we wandered off, in various directions, to enjoy our interval of repose. Some, I believe, went devoutly to the village-church. Others, it may be, ascended a city or a country-pulpit, wearing the clerical robe with so much dignity that you would scarcely have suspected the yeoman's frock to have been flung off, only since milking-time. Others took long rambles among the rustic lanes and by-paths, pausing to look at black, old farm-houses, with their sloping roofs; and at the modern cottage, so like a plaything that it seemed as if real joy or sorrow could have no scope within; and at the more pretending villa, with its range of wooden columns, supporting the needless insolence of a great portico. Some betook themselves into

the wide, dusky barn, and lay there, for hours together, on the odor-
ous hay; while the sunstreaks and the shadows strove together—
these to make the barn solemn, those to make it cheerful—and both
were conquerors; and the swallows twittered a cheery anthem, flash-
ing into sight, or vanishing, as they darted to-and-fro among the
golden rules of sunshine. And others went a little way into the
woods, and threw themselves on Mother Earth, pillowing their
heads on a heap of moss, the green decay of an old log; and dropping asleep, the humble-bees and musquitoes sung and buzzed
about their ears, causing the slumberers to twitch and start, without
awakening.

With Hollingsworth, Zenobia, Priscilla, and myself, it grew to be a
custom to spend the Sabbath-afternoon at a certain rock. It was
known to us under the name of Eliot's pulpit, from a tradition that
the venerable Apostle Eliot[1] had preached there, two centuries gone
by, to an Indian auditory. The old pine-forest, through which the
Apostle's voice was wont to sound, had fallen, an immemorial time
ago. But the soil, being of the rudest and most broken surface, had
apparently never been brought under tillage; other growths, maple,
and beech, and birch, had succeeded to the primeval trees; so that it
was still as wild a tract of woodland as the great-great-great-great
grandson of one of Eliot's Indians (had any such posterity been in
existence) could have desired, for the site and shelter of his wigwam.
These after-growths, indeed, lose the stately solemnity of the original
forest. If left in due neglect, however, they run into an entanglement
of softer wildness, among the rustling leaves of which the sun can
scatter cheerfulness, as it never could among the dark-browed pines.

The rock itself rose some twenty or thirty feet, a shattered granite
boulder, or heap of boulders, with an irregular outline and many fissures, out of which sprang shrubs, bushes, and even trees; as if the
scanty soil, within those crevices, were sweeter to their roots than
any other earth. At the base of the pulpit, the broken boulders
inclined towards each other, so as to form a shallow cave, within
which our little party had sometimes found protection from a summer shower. On the threshold, or just across it, grew a tuft of pale
columbines, in their season, and violets, sad and shadowy recluses,
such as Priscilla was, when we first knew her; children of the sun,
who had never seen their father, but dwelt among damp mosses,
though not akin to them. At the summit, the rock was overshadowed
by the canopy of a birch-tree, which served as a sounding-board for
the pulpit. Beneath this shade, (with my eyes of sense half shut, and

---

1. John Eliot (1604–1690), the Puritan minister of Roxbury, Massachusetts, was known as
the "Apostle to the Indians" for his missionary work among them; in order to preach
effectively, he learned the language of the Massachusetts Indians and translated the Bible
into their tongue. On the significance of this allusion, see the essay by Lauren Berlant in
the "Recent Criticism" section of this Norton Critical Edition.

those of the imagination widely opened,) I used to see the holy Apostle of the Indians, with the sunlight flickering down upon him through the leaves, and glorifying his figure as with the half-perceptible glow of a transfiguration.

I the more minutely describe the rock, and this little Sabbath solitude, because Hollingsworth, at our solicitation, often ascended Eliot's pulpit, and—not exactly preached—but talked to us, his few disciples, in a strain that rose and fell as naturally as the wind's breath among the leaves of the birch-tree. No other speech of man has ever moved me like some of those discourses. It seemed most pitiful—a positive calamity to the world—that a treasury of golden thoughts should thus be scattered, by the liberal handful, down among us three, when a thousand hearers might have been the richer for them; and Hollingsworth the richer, likewise, by the sympathy of multitudes. After speaking much or little, as might happen, he would descend from his gray pulpit, and generally fling himself at full length on the ground, face downward. Mean-while, we talked around him, on such topics as were suggested by the discourse.

Since her interview with Westervelt, Zenobia's continual inequalities of temper had been rather difficult for her friends to bear. On the first Sunday after that incident, when Hollingsworth had clambered down from Eliot's pulpit, she declaimed with great earnestness and passion, nothing short of anger, on the injustice which the world did to women, and equally to itself, by not allowing them, in freedom and honor, and with the fullest welcome, their natural utterance in public.

"It shall not always be so!" cried she. "If I live another year, I will lift up my own voice, in behalf of woman's wider liberty."

She, perhaps, saw me smile.

"What matter of ridicule do you find in this, Miles Coverdale?" exclaimed Zenobia, with a flash of anger in her eyes. "That smile, permit me to say, makes me suspicious of a low tone of feeling, and shallow thought. It is my belief—yes, and my prophecy, should I die before it happens—that, when my sex shall achieve its rights, there will be ten eloquent women, where there is now one eloquent man. Thus far, no woman in the world has ever once spoken out her whole heart and her whole mind. The mistrust and disapproval of the vast bulk of society throttles us, as with two gigantic hands at our throats! We mumble a few weak words, and leave a thousand better ones unsaid. You let us write a little, it is true, on a limited range of subjects. But the pen is not for woman. Her power is too natural and immediate. It is with the living voice, alone, that she can compel the world to recognize the light of her intellect and the depth of her heart!"

Now—though I could not well say so to Zenobia—I had not smiled from any unworthy estimate of woman, or in denial of the claims which she is beginning to put forth. What amused and puzzled me, was the fact, that women, however intellectually superior, so seldom disquiet themselves about the rights or wrongs of their sex, unless their own individual affections chance to lie in idleness, or to be ill at ease. They are not natural reformers, but become such by the pressure of exceptional misfortune. I could measure Zenobia's inward trouble, by the animosity with which she now took up the general quarrel of woman against man.

"I will give you leave, Zenobia," replied I, "to fling your utmost scorn upon me, if you ever hear me utter a sentiment unfavorable to the widest liberty which woman has yet dreamed of. I would give her all she asks, and add a great deal more, which she will not be the party to demand, but which men, if they were generous and wise, would grant of their own free motion. For instance, I should love dearly—for the next thousand years, at least—to have all government devolve into the hands of women. I hate to be ruled by my own sex; it excites my jealousy and wounds my pride. It is the iron sway of bodily force, which abases us, in our compelled submission. But, how sweet the free, generous courtesy, with which I would kneel before a woman-ruler!"

"Yes; if she were young and beautiful," said Zenobia, laughing. "But how if she were sixty, and a fright?"

"Ah; it is you that rate womanhood low," said I. "But let me go on. I have never found it possible to suffer a bearded priest so near my heart and conscience, as to do me any spiritual good. I blush at the very thought! Oh, in the better order of things, Heaven grant that the ministry of souls may be left in charge of women! The gates of the Blessed City will be thronged with the multitude that enter in, when that day comes! The task belongs to woman. God meant it for her. He has endowed her with the religious sentiment in its utmost depth and purity, refined from that gross, intellectual alloy, with which every masculine theologist—save only One, who merely veiled Himself in mortal and masculine shape, but was, in truth, divine—has been prone to mingle it. I have always envied the Catholics their faith in that sweet, sacred Virgin Mother, who stands between them and the Deity, intercepting somewhat of His awful splendor, but permitting His love to stream upon the worshipper, more intelligibly to human comprehension, through the medium of a woman's tenderness. Have I not said enough, Zenobia?"

"I cannot think that this is true," observed Priscilla, who had been gazing at me with great, disapproving eyes. "And I am sure I do not wish it to be true!"

"Poor child!" exclaimed Zenobia, rather contemptuously. "She is the type of womanhood, such as man has spent centuries in making it. He is never content, unless he can degrade himself by stooping towards what he loves. In denying us our rights, he betrays even more blindness to his own interests, than profligate disregard of ours!"

"Is this true?" asked Priscilla, with simplicity, turning to Hollingsworth. "Is it all true that Mr. Coverdale and Zenobia have been saying?"

"No, Priscilla," answered Hollingsworth, with his customary bluntness. "They have neither of them spoken one true word yet."

"Do you despise woman?" said Zenobia. "Ah, Hollingsworth, that would be most ungrateful!"

"Despise her?—No!" cried Hollingsworth, lifting his great shaggy head and shaking it at us, while his eyes glowed almost fiercely. "She is the most admirable handiwork of God, in her true place and character. Her place is at man's side. Her office, that of the Sympathizer; the unreserved, unquestioning Believer; the Recognition, withheld in every other manner, but given, in pity, through woman's heart, lest man should utterly lose faith in himself; the Echo of God's own voice, pronouncing—'It is well done!' All the separate action of woman is, and ever has been, and always shall be, false, foolish, vain, destructive of her own best and holiest qualities, void of every good effect, and productive of intolerable mischiefs! Man is a wretch without woman; but woman is a monster—and, thank Heaven, an almost impossible and hitherto imaginary monster— without man, as her acknowledged principal! As true as I had once a mother, whom I loved, were there any possible prospect of woman's taking the social stand which some of them—poor, miserable, abortive creatures, who only dream of such things because they have missed woman's peculiar happiness, or because Nature made them really neither man nor woman—if there were a chance of their attaining the end which these petticoated monstrosities have in view, I would call upon my own sex to use its physical force, that unmistakeable evidence of sovereignty, to scourge them back within their proper bounds! But it will not be needful. The heart of true womanhood knows where its own sphere is, and never seeks to stray beyond it!"

Never was mortal blessed—if blessing it were—with a glance of such entire acquiescence and unquestioning faith, happy in its completeness, as our little Priscilla unconsciously bestowed on Hollingsworth. She seemed to take the sentiment from his lips into her heart, and brood over it in perfect content. The very woman whom he pictured—the gentle parasite, the soft reflection of a more powerful existence—sat there at his feet.

I looked at Zenobia, however, fully expecting her to resent—as I felt, by the indignant ebullition of my own blood, that she ought— this outrageous affirmation of what struck me as the intensity of

masculine egotism. It centred everything in itself, and deprived
woman of her very soul, her inexpressible and unfathomable all, to
make it a mere incident in the great sum of man. Hollingsworth had
boldly uttered what he, and millions of despots like him, really felt.
Without intending it, he had disclosed the well-spring of all these
troubled waters. Now, if ever, it surely behoved Zenobia to be the
champion of her sex.

But, to my surprise, and indignation too, she only looked
humbled. Some tears sparkled in her eyes, but they were wholly of
grief, not anger.

"Well; be it so," was all she said. "I, at least, have deep cause to
think you right. Let man be but manly and godlike, and woman is
only too ready to become to him what you say!"

I smiled—somewhat bitterly, it is true—in contemplation of my
own ill-luck. How little did these two women care for me, who had
freely conceded all their claims, and a great deal more, out of the
fulness of my heart; while Hollingsworth, by some necromancy[2] of
his horrible injustice, seemed to have brought them both to his feet!

"Women almost invariably behave thus!" thought I. "What does
the fact mean? Is it their nature? Or is it, at last, the result of ages of
compelled degradation? And, in either case, will it be possible ever
to redeem them?"

An intuition now appeared to possess all the party, that, for this
time, at least, there was no more to be said. With one accord, we
arose from the ground, and made our way through the tangled
undergrowth towards one of those pleasant wood-paths, that wound
among the over-arching trees. Some of the branches hung so low as
partly to conceal the figures that went before, from those who followed. Priscilla had leaped up more lightly than the rest of us, and
ran along in advance, with as much airy activity of spirit as was typi-
fied in the motion of a bird, which chanced to be flitting from tree to
tree, in the same direction as herself. Never did she seem so happy
as that afternoon. She skipt, and could not help it, from very playful-
ness of heart.

Zenobia and Hollingsworth went next, in close contiguity, but not
with arm in arm. Now, just when they had passed the impending
bough of a birch-tree, I plainly saw Zenobia take the hand of
Hollingsworth in both her own, press it to her bosom, and let it fall
again!

The gesture was sudden and full of passion; the impulse had evidently taken her by surprise; it expressed all! Had Zenobia knelt
before him, or flung herself upon his breast, and gasped out—'I love
you, Hollingsworth!'—I could not have been more certain of what it

2. Sorcery.

meant. They then walked onward, as before. But, methought, as the declining sun threw Zenobia's magnified shadow along the path, I beheld it tremulous; and the delicate stem of the flower, which she wore in her hair, was likewise responsive to her agitation.

Priscilla—through the medium of her eyes, at least—could not possibly have been aware of the gesture above-described. Yet, at that instant, I saw her droop. The buoyancy, which just before had been so birdlike, was utterly departed; the life seemed to pass out of her, and even the substance of her figure to grow thin and gray. I almost imagined her a shadow, fading gradually into the dimness of the wood. Her pace became so slow, that Hollingsworth and Zenobia passed by, and I, without hastening my footsteps, overtook her.

"Come, Priscilla," said I, looking her intently in the face, which was very pale and sorrowful, "we must make haste after our friends. Do you feel suddenly ill? A moment ago, you flitted along so lightly that I was comparing you to a bird. Now, on the contrary, it is as if you had a heavy heart, and very little strength to bear it with. Pray take my arm!"

"No," said Priscilla, "I do not think it would help me. It is my heart, as you say, that makes me heavy; and I know not why. Just now, I felt very happy."

No doubt, it was a kind of sacrilege in me to attempt to come within her maidenly mystery. But as she appeared to be tossed aside by her other friends, or carelessly let fall, like a flower which they had done with, I could not resist the impulse to take just one peep beneath her folded petals.

"Zenobia and yourself are dear friends, of late," I remarked. "At first—that first evening when you came to us—she did not receive you quite so warmly as might have been wished."

"I remember it," said Priscilla. "No wonder she hesitated to love me, who was then a stranger to her, and a girl of no grace or beauty; she being herself so beautiful!"

"But she loves you now, of course," suggested I. "And, at this very instant, you feel her to be your dearest friend?"

"Why do you ask me that question?" exclaimed Priscilla, as if frightened at the scrutiny into her feelings which I compelled her to make. "It somehow puts strange thoughts into my mind. But I do love Zenobia dearly! If she only loves me half as well, I shall be happy!"

"How is it possible to doubt that, Priscilla?" I rejoined. "But, observe how pleasantly and happily Zenobia and Hollingsworth are walking together! I call it a delightful spectacle. It truly rejoices me that Hollingsworth has found so fit and affectionate a friend! So many people in the world mistrust him—so many disbelieve and ridicule, while hardly any do him justice, or acknowledge him for the wonderful man he is—that it is really a blessed thing for him to have won the sympathy of such a woman as Zenobia. Any man might be proud of that. Any man, even if he be as great as Hollingsworth, might love so magnificent a woman. How very beautiful Zenobia is! And Hollingsworth knows it, too!"

There may have been some petty malice in what I said. Generosity is a very fine thing, at a proper time, and within due limits. But it is an insufferable bore, to see one man engrossing every thought of all the women, and leaving his friend to shiver in outer seclusion, without even the alternative of solacing himself with what the more fortunate individual has rejected. Yes; it was out of a foolish bitterness of heart that I had spoken.

"Go on before!" said Priscilla, abruptly, and with true feminine imperiousness, which heretofore I had never seen her exercise. "It pleases me best to loiter along by myself. I do not walk so fast as you."

With her hand, she made a little gesture of dismissal. It provoked me, yet, on the whole, was the most bewitching thing that Priscilla had ever done. I obeyed her, and strolled moodily homeward, wondering—as I had wondered a thousand times, already—how Hollingsworth meant to dispose of these two hearts, which (plainly to my perception, and, as I could not but now suppose, to his) he had engrossed into his own huge egotism.

There was likewise another subject, hardly less fruitful of speculation. In what attitude did Zenobia present herself to Hollingsworth? Was it in that of a free woman, with no mortgage on her affections nor claimant to her hand, but fully at liberty to surrender both, in exchange for the heart and hand which she apparently expected to receive? But, was it a vision that I had witnessed in the wood? Was Westervelt a goblin? Were those words of passion and agony, which Zenobia had uttered in my hearing, a mere stage-declamation? Were they formed of a material lighter than common air? Or, supposing them to bear sterling weight, was it not a perilous and dreadful wrong, which she was meditating towards herself and Hollingsworth?

Arriving nearly at the farm-house, I looked back over the long slope of pasture-land, and beheld them standing together, in the light of sunset, just on the spot where, according to the gossip of the Community, they meant to build their cottage. Priscilla, alone and forgotten, was lingering in the shadow of the wood.

XV. A Crisis

Thus the summer was passing away; a summer of toil, of interest, of something that was not pleasure, but which went deep into my heart, and there became a rich experience. I found myself looking forward to years, if not to a lifetime, to be spent on the same system. The Community were now beginning to form their permanent plans. One of our purposes was to erect a Phalanstery (as I think we called it, after Fourier; but the phraseology of those days is not very fresh in my remembrance) where the great and general family should have its abiding-place. Individual members, too, who made it a point of religion to preserve the sanctity of an exclusive home, were selecting sites for their cottages, by the wood-side, or on the breezy swells, or in the sheltered nook of some little valley, according as their taste might lean towards snugness or the picturesque. Altogether, by projecting our minds outward, we had imparted a show of novelty to existence, and contemplated it as hopefully as if the soil, beneath our feet, had not been fathom-deep with the dust of deluded generations, on every one of which, as on ourselves, the world had imposed itself as a hitherto unwedded bride.

Hollingsworth and myself had often discussed these prospects. It was easy to perceive, however, that he spoke with little or no fervor, but either as questioning the fulfilment of our anticipations, or, at any rate, with a quiet consciousness that it was no personal concern of his. Shortly after the scene at Eliot's pulpit, while he and I were repairing an old stone-fence, I amused myself with sallying forward into the future time.

"When we come to be old men," I said, "they will call us Uncles, or Fathers—Father Hollingsworth and Uncle Coverdale—and we will look back cheerfully to these early days, and make a romantic story for the young people (and if a little more romantic than truth may warrant, it will be no harm) out of our severe trials and hardships. In a century or two, we shall every one of us be mythical personages, or exceedingly picturesque and poetical ones, at all events. They will have a great public hall, in which your portrait, and mine, and twenty other faces that are living now, shall be hung up; and as for me, I will be painted in my shirt-sleeves, and with the sleeves rolled up, to show my muscular development. What stories will be rife among them about our mighty strength," continued I, lifting a big stone and putting it into its place; "though our posterity will really be far stronger than ourselves, after several generations of a simple, natural, and active life! What legends of Zenobia's beauty, and Priscilla's slender and shadowy grace, and those mysterious qualities which make her seem diaphanous with spiritual light! In due course of ages, we must all figure heroically in an Epic Poem; and we will ourselves—at least, I will—bend unseen over the future poet, and lend him inspiration, while he writes it."

"You seem," said Hollingsworth, "to be trying how much nonsense you can pour out in a breath."

"I wish you would see fit to comprehend," retorted I, "that the profoundest wisdom must be mingled with nine-tenths of nonsense; else it is not worth the breath that utters it. But I do long for the cottages to be built, that the creeping plants may begin to run over them, and the moss to gather on the walls, and the trees—which we will set out—to cover them with a breadth of shadow. This spick-and-span novelty does not quite suit my taste. It is time, too, for children to be born among us. The first-born child is still to come! And I shall never feel as if this were a real, practical, as well as poetical, system of human life, until somebody has sanctified it by death."

"A pretty occasion for martyrdom, truly!" said Hollingsworth.

"As good as any other!" I replied. "I wonder, Hollingsworth, who, of all these strong men, and fair women and maidens, is doomed the first to die. Would it not be well, even before we have absolute need of it, to fix upon a spot for a cemetery? Let us choose the rudest, roughest, most uncultivable spot, for Death's garden-ground; and Death shall teach us to beautify it, grave by grave. By our sweet, calm way of dying, and the airy elegance out of which we will shape our funeral rites, and the cheerful allegories[1] which we will model into tombstones, the final scene shall lose its terrors; so that, hereafter, it may be happiness to live, and bliss to die. None of us must die young. Yet, should Providence ordain it so, the event shall not be sorrowful, but affect us with a tender, delicious, only half-melancholy, and almost smiling pathos!"

"That is to say," muttered Hollingsworth, "you will die like a Heathen, as you certainly live like one! But, listen to me, Coverdale. Your fantastic anticipations make me discern, all the more forcibly, what a wretched, unsubstantial scheme is this, on which we have wasted a precious summer of our lives. Do you seriously imagine that any such realities as you, and many others here, have dreamed of, will ever be brought to pass?"

"Certainly, I do," said I. "Of course, when the reality comes, it will wear the every-day, common-place, dusty, and rather homely garb, that reality always does put on. But, setting aside the ideal charm, I hold, that our highest anticipations have a solid footing on common-sense."

"You only half believe what you say," rejoined Hollingsworth; "and as for me, I neither have faith in your dream, nor would care the value of this pebble for its realization, were that possible. And what more do you want of it? It has given you a theme for poetry. Let that content you. But, now, I ask you to be, at last, a man of sobriety and earnestness, and aid me in an enterprise which is worth all our strength, and the strength of a thousand mightier than we!"

There can be no need of giving, in detail, the conversation that ensued. It is enough to say, that Hollingsworth once more brought forward his rigid and unconquerable idea; a scheme for the reformation of the wicked by methods moral, intellectual, and industrial, by the

---

1. Emblematic images to be carved upon or into tombstones.

sympathy of pure, humble, and yet exalted minds, and by opening to his pupils the possibility of a worthier life than that which had become their fate. It appeared, unless he over-estimated his own means, that Hollingsworth held it at his choice (and he did so choose) to obtain possession of the very ground on which we had planted our Community, and which had not yet been made irrevocably ours, by purchase. It was just the foundation that he desired. Our beginnings might readily be adapted to his great end. The arrangements, already completed, would work quietly into his system. So plausible looked his theory, and, more than that, so practical; such an air of reasonableness had he, by patient thought, thrown over it; each segment of it was contrived to dove-tail into all the rest, with such a complicated applicability; and so ready was he with a response for every objection—that, really, so far as logic and argument went, he had the matter all his own way.

"But," said I, "whence can you, having no means of your own, derive the enormous capital which is essential to this experiment? State-street,[2] I imagine, would not draw its purse-strings very liberally, in aid of such a speculation."

"I have the funds—as much, at least, as is needed for a commencement—at command," he answered. "They can be produced within a month, if necessary."

My thoughts reverted to Zenobia. It could only be her wealth which Hollingsworth was appropriating so lavishly. And on what conditions was it to be had? Did she fling it into the scheme, with the uncalculating generosity that characterizes a woman, when it is her impulse to be generous at all? And did she fling herself along with it? But Hollingsworth did not volunteer an explanation.

"And have you no regrets," I inquired, "in overthrowing this fair system of our new life, which has been planned so deeply, and is now beginning to flourish so hopefully around us? How beautiful it is, and, so far as we can yet see, how practicable! The Ages have waited for us, and here we are—the very first that have essayed to carry on our mortal existence, in love, and mutual help! Hollingsworth, I would be loth to take the ruin of this enterprise upon my conscience!"

"Then let it rest wholly upon mine!" he answered, knitting his black brows. "I see through the system. It is full of defects—irremediable and damning ones!—from first to last, there is nothing else! I grasp it in my hand, and find no substance whatever. There is not human nature in it!"

"Why are you so secret in your operations?" I asked. "God forbid that I should accuse you of intentional wrong; but the besetting sin of a philanthropist, it appears to me, is apt to be a moral obliquity.

---

2. Boston's banking and financial center during the nineteenth century.

His sense of honor ceases to be the sense of other honorable men. At some point of his course—I know not exactly when nor where—he is tempted to palter with the right, and can scarcely forbear persuading himself that the importance of his public ends renders it allowable to throw aside his private conscience. Oh, my dear friend, beware this error! If you meditate the overthrow of this establishment, call together our companions, state your design, support it with all your eloquence, but allow them an opportunity of defending themselves!"

"It does not suit me," said Hollingsworth. "Nor is it my duty to do so."

"I think it is!" replied I.

Hollingsworth frowned; not in passion, but like Fate, inexorably.

"I will not argue the point," said he. "What I desire to know of you is—and you can tell me in one word—whether I am to look for your co-operation in this great scheme of good. Take it up with me! Be my brother in it! It offers you (what you have told me, over and over again, that you most need) a purpose in life, worthy of the extremest self-devotion—worthy of martyrdom, should God so order it! In this view, I present it to you. You can greatly benefit mankind. Your peculiar faculties, as I shall direct them, are capable of being so wrought into this enterprise, that not one of them need lie idle. Strike hands with me; and, from this moment, you shall never again feel the languor and vague wretchedness of an indolent or half-occupied man! There may be no more aimless beauty in your life; but, in its stead, there shall be strength, courage, immitigable will—everything that a manly and generous nature should desire! We shall succeed! We shall have done our best for this miserable world; and happiness (which never comes but incidentally) will come to us unawares!"

It seemed his intention to say no more. But, after he had quite broken off, his deep eyes filled with tears, and he held out both his hands to me.

"Coverdale," he murmured, "there is not the man in this wide world, whom I can love as I could you. Do not forsake me!"

As I look back upon this scene, through the coldness and dimness of so many years, there is still a sensation as if Hollingsworth had caught hold of my heart, and were pulling it towards him with an almost irresistible force. It is a mystery to me, how I withstood it. But, in truth, I saw in his scheme of philanthropy nothing but what was odious. A loathsomeness that was to be forever in my daily work! A great, black ugliness of sin, which he proposed to collect out of a thousand human hearts, and that we should spend our lives in an experiment of transmuting it into virtue! Had I but touched his extended hand, Hollingsworth's magnetism would perhaps have penetrated me with his own conception of all these matters. But I stood aloof. I fortified myself with doubts whether his strength of purpose had not been too gigantic for his integrity, impelling him to trample on considerations that should have been paramount to every other.

"Is Zenobia to take a part in your enterprise?" I asked.

"She is," said Hollingsworth.

"She!—the beautiful!—the gorgeous!" I exclaimed. "And how have you prevailed with such a woman to work in this squalid element?"

"Through no base methods, as you seem to suspect," he answered, "but by addressing whatever is best and noblest in her."

Hollingsworth was looking on the ground. But, as he often did so—generally, indeed, in his habitual moods of thought—I could not judge whether it was from any special unwillingness now to meet my eyes. What it was that dictated my next question, I cannot precisely say. Nevertheless, it rose so inevitably into my mouth, and, as it were, asked itself, so involuntarily, that there must needs have been an aptness in it.

"What is to become of Priscilla?"

Hollingsworth looked at me fiercely, and with glowing eyes. He could not have shown any other kind of expression than that, had he meant to strike me with a sword.

"Why do you bring in the names of these women?" said he, after a moment of pregnant silence. "What have they to do with the proposal which I make you? I must have your answer! Will you devote yourself, and sacrifice all to this great end, and be my friend of friends, forever?"

"In Heaven's name, Hollingsworth," cried I, getting angry, and glad to be angry, because so only was it possible to oppose his tremendous concentrativeness and indomitable will, "cannot you conceive that a man may wish well to the world, and struggle for its good, on some other plan than precisely that which you have laid down? And will you cast off a friend, for no unworthiness, but merely because he stands upon his right, as an individual being, and looks at matters through his own optics, instead of yours?"

"Be with me," said Hollingsworth, "or be against me! There is no third choice for you."

"Take this, then, as my decision," I answered. "I doubt the wisdom of your scheme. Furthermore, I greatly fear that the methods, by which you allow yourself to pursue it, are such as cannot stand the scrutiny of an unbiassed conscience."

"And you will not join me?"

"No!"

I never said the word—and certainly can never have it to say, hereafter—that cost me a thousandth part so hard an effort as did that one syllable. The heart-pang was not merely figurative, but an absolute torture of the breast. I was gazing steadfastly at Hollingsworth. It seemed to me that it struck him, too, like a bullet. A ghastly paleness—always so terrific on a swarthy face—overspread his features. There was a convulsive movement of his throat, as if he were forcing down some words that struggled and fought for utterance. Whether words of anger, or words of grief, I cannot tell; although, many and many a time, I have vainly tormented myself with conjecturing which of the two they were. One other appeal to my friendship—such as once, already, Hollingsworth had made—taking me in the revulsion that followed a strenuous exercise of opposing will, would completely have subdued me. But he left the matter there.

"Well!" said he.

And that was all! I should have been thankful for one word more, even had it shot me through the heart, as mine did him. But he did not speak it; and, after a few moments, with one accord, we set to work again, repairing the stone-fence. Hollingsworth, I observed, wrought like a Titan; and, for my own part, I lifted stones which, at this day— or, in a calmer mood, at that one—I should no more have thought it possible to stir, than to carry off the gates of Gaza[3] on my back.

XVI. Leave-Takings

A few days after the tragic passage-at-arms between Hollingsworth and me, I appeared at the dinner-table, actually dressed in a coat, instead of my customary blouse; with a satin cravat, too, a white vest, and several other things that made me seem strange and outlandish to myself. As for my companions, this unwonted spectacle caused a great stir upon the wooden benches, that bordered either side of our homely board.

"What's in the wind now, Miles?" asked one of them. "Are you deserting us?"

"Yes, for a week or two," said I. "It strikes me that my health demands a little relaxation of labor, and a short visit to the seaside, during the dog-days."[1]

"You look like it!" grumbled Silas Foster, not greatly pleased with the idea of losing an efficient laborer, before the stress of the season was

---

3. Judges 16:1–3 records one of Samson's legendary feats of strength. While he visits a harlot in the enemy city of Gaza, its inhabitants lock the gates of the city, planning to kill him in the morning. Awaking at midnight, Samson simply picks up the gates and carries them on his shoulders to a nearby hill. *Titan*: in Greek mythology, one of the primordial gods deposed by Zeus and the Olympian deities; hence, a figure of gigantic strength.

1. The hottest, most sultry stretch of the summer, running from mid-July through August.

well over. "Now, here's a pretty fellow! His shoulders have broadened, a matter of six inches, since he came among us; he can do his day's work, if he likes, with any man or ox on the farm;—and yet he talks about going to the seashore for his health! Well, well, old woman," added he to his wife, "let me have a platefull of that pork and cabbage! I begin to feel in a very weakly way. When the others have had their turn, you and I will take a jaunt to Newport or Saratoga!"[2]

"Well, but, Mr. Foster," said I, "you must allow me to take a little breath."

"Breath!" retorted the old yeoman. "Your lungs have the play of a pair of blacksmith's bellows, already. What on earth do you want more? But go along! I understand the business. We shall never see your face here again. Here ends the reformation of the world, so far as Miles Coverdale has a hand in it!"

"By no means," I replied. "I am resolute to die in the last ditch, for the good of the cause."

"Die in a ditch!" muttered gruff Silas, with genuine Yankee intolerance of any intermission of toil, except on Sunday, the Fourth of July, the autumnal Cattle-show, Thanksgiving, or the annual Fast.[3] "Die in a ditch! I believe in my conscience you would, if there were no steadier means than your own labor to keep you out of it!"

The truth was, that an intolerable discontent and irksomeness had come over me. Blithedale was no longer what it had been. Everything was suddenly faded. The sun-burnt and arid aspect of our woods and pastures, beneath the August sky, did but imperfectly symbolize the lack of dew and moisture that, since yesterday, as it were, had blighted my fields of thought, and penetrated to the innermost and shadiest of my contemplative recesses. The change will be recognized by many, who, after a period of happiness, have endeavored to go on with the same kind of life, in the same scene, in spite of the alteration or withdrawal of some principal circumstance. They discover (what heretofore, perhaps, they had not known) that it was this which gave the bright color and vivid reality to the whole affair.

I stood on other terms than before, not only with Hollingsworth, but with Zenobia and Priscilla. As regarded the two latter, it was that dreamlike and miserable sort of change that denies you the privilege to complain, because you can assert no positive injury, nor lay your finger on anything tangible. It is a matter which you do not see, but feel, and which, when you try to analyze it, seems to lose its very existence, and resolve itself into a sickly humor of your own. Your

2. Newport, Rhode Island, a seaside resort, and Saratoga Springs, New York, a health spa offering mineral baths, were well-known sites of a new American custom: the vacation.
3. A holiday devoted each year, in some New England states, to fasting, prayer, and repentance—a practice inherited from the Puritan colonists. *Cattle-show*: days set aside for the exhibition and sale of livestock, the precursor to present-day state fairs.

understanding, possibly, may put faith in this denial. But your heart will not so easily rest satisfied. It incessantly remonstrates, though, most of the time, in a bass-note, which you do not separately distinguish; but, now-and-then, with a sharp cry, importunate to be heard, and resolute to claim belief. 'Things are not as they were!'—it keeps saying—'You shall not impose on me! I will never be quiet! I will throb painfully! I will be heavy, and desolate, and shiver with cold! For I, your deep heart, know when to be miserable, as once I knew when to be happy! All is changed for us! You are beloved no more!' And, were my life to be spent over again, I would invariably lend my ear to this Cassandra[4] of the inward depths, however clamorous the music and the merriment of a more superficial region.

My outbreak with Hollingsworth, though never definitely known to our associates, had really an effect upon the moral atmosphere of the Community. It was incidental to the closeness of relationship, into which we had brought ourselves, that an unfriendly state of feeling could not occur between any two members, without the whole society being more or less commoted[5] and made uncomfortable thereby. This species of nervous sympathy (though a pretty characteristic enough, sentimentally considered, and apparently betokening an actual bond of love among us) was yet found rather inconvenient in its practical operation; mortal tempers being so infirm and variable as they are. If one of us happened to give his neighbor a box on the ear, the tingle was immediately felt, on the same side of everybody's head. Thus, even on the supposition that we were far less quarrelsome than the rest of the world, a great deal of time was necessarily wasted in rubbing our ears.

Musing on all these matters, I felt an inexpressible longing for at least a temporary novelty. I thought of going across the Rocky Mountains, or to Europe, or up the Nile—of offering myself a volunteer on the Exploring Expedition[6]—of taking a ramble of years, no matter in what direction, and coming back on the other side of the world. Then, should the colonists of Blithedale have established their enterprise on a permanent basis, I might fling aside my pilgrim-staff and dusty shoon,[7] and rest as peacefully here as elsewhere. Or, in case Hollingsworth should occupy the ground with his School of Reform, as he now purposed, I might plead earthly guilt enough, by that time, to give me what I was inclined to think the only trustworthy

4. Daughter of King Priam of Troy, endowed with prophetic powers but condemned never to be believed.
5. Put into commotion; disturbed.
6. The U.S. government sponsored a number of expeditions involving world exploration in the early nineteenth century; in 1837, several of Hawthorne's influential friends sought unsuccessfully to get him a post as historian of an expedition to the South Seas and Antarctica.
7. Archaic plural of "shoe."

hold on his affections. Meanwhile, before deciding on any ultimate plan, I determined to remove myself to a little distance, and take an exterior view of what we had all been about.

In truth, it was dizzy work, amid such fermentation of opinions as was going on in the general brain of the Community. It was a kind of Bedlam,[8] for the time being; although, out of the very thoughts that were wildest and most destructive, might grow a wisdom, holy, calm, and pure, and that should incarnate itself with the substance of a noble and happy life. But, as matters now were, I felt myself (and having a decided tendency towards the actual, I never liked to feel it) getting quite out of my reckoning, with regard to the existing state of the world. I was beginning to lose the sense of what kind of a world it was, among innumerable schemes of what it might or ought to be. It was impossible, situated as we were, not to imbibe the idea that everything in nature and human existence was fluid, or fast becoming so; that the crust of the Earth, in many places, was broken, and its whole surface portentously upheaving; that it was a day of crisis, and that we ourselves were in the critical vortex. Our great globe floated in the atmosphere of infinite space like an unsubstantial bubble. No sagacious man will long retain his sagacity, if he live exclusively among reformers and progressive people, without periodically returning into the settled system of things, to correct himself by a new observation from that old stand-point.

It was now time for me, therefore, to go and hold a little talk with the conservatives, the writers of the North American Review, the merchants, the politicians, the Cambridge men,[9] and all those respectable old blockheads, who still, in this intangibility and mistiness of affairs, kept a death-grip on one or two ideas which had not come into vogue since yesterday-morning.

The brethren took leave of me with cordial kindness; and as for the sisterhood, I had serious thoughts of kissing them all round, but forbore to do so, because, in all such general salutations, the penance is fully equal to the pleasure. So I kissed none of them, and nobody, to say the truth, seemed to expect it.

"Do you wish me," I said to Zenobia, "to announce, in town, and at the watering-places,[1] your purpose to deliver a course of lectures on the rights of women?"

---

8. Popular name for the Hospital of St. Mary of Bethlehem, the famous London insane asylum; hence, a place of madness or confusion.
9. Men affiliated with Harvard University in Cambridge, Massachusetts, and thus part of the intellectual and cultural establishment of the era. *North American Review*: an ambitious literary, historical, and critical quarterly founded in 1815, predominantly conservative in its views and cultural affiliations.
1. Fashionable resorts.

"Women possess no rights," said Zenobia, with a half-melancholy smile; "or, at all events, only little girls and grandmothers would have the force to exercise them."

She gave me her hand, freely and kindly, and looked at me, I thought, with a pitying expression in her eyes; nor was there any settled light of joy in them, on her own behalf, but a troubled and passionate flame, flickering and fitful.

"I regret, on the whole, that you are leaving us," she said; "and all the more, since I feel that this phase of our life is finished, and can never be lived over again. Do you know, Mr. Coverdale, that I have been several times on the point of making you my confidant, for lack of a better and wiser one? But you are too young to be my Father Confessor; and you would not thank me for treating you like one of those good little handmaidens, who share the bosom-secrets of a tragedy-queen!"

"I would at least be loyal and faithful," answered I, "and would counsel you with an honest purpose, if not wisely."

"Yes," said Zenobia, "you would be only too wise—too honest. Honesty and wisdom are such a delightful pastime, at another person's expense!"

"Ah, Zenobia," I exclaimed, "if you would but let me speak!"

"By no means," she replied; "especially when you have just resumed the whole series of social conventionalisms, together with that straight-bodied coat. I would as lief open my heart to a lawyer or a clergyman! No, no, Mr. Coverdale; if I choose a counsellor, in the present aspect of my affairs, it must be either an angel or a madman; and I rather apprehend that the latter would be likeliest of the two to speak the fitting word. It needs a wild steersman when we voyage through Chaos![2] The anchor is up! Farewell!"

Priscilla, as soon as dinner was over, had betaken herself into a corner, and set to work on a little purse. As I approached her, she let her eyes rest on me, with a calm, serious look; for, with all her delicacy of nerves, there was a singular self-possession in Priscilla, and her sensibilities seemed to lie sheltered from ordinary commotion, like the water in a deep well.

"Will you give me that purse, Priscilla," said I, "as a parting keepsake?"

"Yes," she answered; "if you will wait till it is finished."

"I must not wait, even for that," I replied. "Shall I find you here, on my return?"

"I never wish to go away," said she.

2. A state of confusion and disorder; from the term, in Greek mythology, for the formless primordial condition that preceded the creation of the cosmos.

"I have sometimes thought," observed I, smiling, "that you, Priscilla, are a little prophetess; or, at least, that you have spiritual intimations respecting matters which are dark to us grosser people. If that be the case, I should like to ask you what is about to happen. For I am tormented with a strong foreboding, that, were I to return even so soon as tomorrow morning, I should find everything changed. Have you any impressions of this nature?"

"Ah, no!" said Priscilla, looking at me apprehensively. "If any such misfortune is coming, the shadow has not reached me yet. Heaven forbid! I should be glad if there might never be any change, but one summer follow another, and all just like this!"

"No summer ever came back, and no two summers ever were alike," said I, with a degree of Orphic[3] wisdom that astonished myself. "Times change, and people change; and if our hearts do not change as readily, so much the worse for us! Good bye, Priscilla!"

I gave her hand a pressure, which, I think, she neither resisted nor returned. Priscilla's heart was deep, but of small compass; it had room but for a very few dearest ones, among whom she never reckoned me.

On the door-step, I met Hollingsworth. I had a momentary impulse to hold out my hand, or, at least, to give a parting nod, but resisted both. When a real and strong affection has come to an end, it is not well to mock the sacred past with any show of those common-place civilities that belong to ordinary intercourse. Being dead henceforth to him, and he to me, there could be no propriety in our chilling one another with the touch of two corpse-like hands, or playing at looks of courtesy with eyes that were impenetrable beneath the glaze and the film. We passed, therefore, as if mutually invisible.

I can nowise explain what sort of whim, prank, or perversity it was, that, after all these leave-takings, induced me to go to the pig-stye and take leave of the swine! There they lay, buried as deeply among the straw as they could burrow, four huge black grunters, the very symbols of slothful ease and sensual comfort. They were asleep, drawing short and heavy breaths, which heaved their big sides up and down. Unclosing their eyes, however, at my approach, they looked dimly forth at the outer world, and simultaneously uttered a gentle grunt; not putting themselves to the trouble of an additional breath for that particular purpose, but grunting with their ordinary inhalation. They were involved, and almost stifled, and buried alive, in their own corporeal substance. The very unreadiness and oppression, wherewith these greasy citizens gained breath enough to

---

3. Prophetic, oracular; derived from Orphism, a mystical religion of ancient Greece, named for its founder Orpheus.

keep their life-machinery in sluggish movement, appeared to make them only the more sensible of the ponderous and fat satisfaction of their existence. Peeping at me, an instant, out of their small, red, hardly perceptible eyes, they dropt asleep again; yet not so far asleep but that their unctuous bliss was still present to them, betwixt dream and reality.

"You must come back in season to eat part of a spare-rib," said Silas Foster, giving my hand a mighty squeeze. "I shall have these fat fellows hanging up by the heels, heads downward, pretty soon, I tell you!"

"Oh, cruel Silas, what a horrible idea!" cried I. "All the rest of us, men, women, and live-stock, save only these four porkers, are bedev- illed with one grief or another; they alone are happy—and you mean to cut their throats, and eat them! It would be more for the general comfort to let them eat us; and bitter and sour morsels we should be!"

XVII. The Hotel

Arriving in town, (where my bachelor-rooms, long before this time, had received some other occupant,) I established myself, for a day or two, in a certain respectable hotel. It was situated somewhat aloof from my former track in life; my present mood inclining me to avoid most of my old companions, from whom I was now sundered by other interests, and who would have been likely enough to amuse themselves at the expense of the amateur working-man. The hotel- keeper put me into a back-room of the third story of his spacious establishment. The day was lowering, with occasional gusts of rain, and an ugly-tempered east-wind, which seemed to come right off the chill and melancholy sea, hardly mitigated by sweeping over the roofs, and amalgamating itself with the dusky element of city- smoke. All the effeminacy of past days had returned upon me at once. Summer as it still was, I ordered a coal-fire in the rusty grate, and was glad to find myself growing a little too warm with an artifi- cial temperature.

My sensations were those of a traveller, long sojourning in remote regions, and at length sitting down again amid customs once famil- iar. There was a newness and an oldness, oddly combining them- selves into one impression. It made me acutely sensible how strange a piece of mosaic-work had lately been wrought into my life. True; if you look at it in one way, it had been only a summer in the country. But, considered in a profounder relation, it was part of another age, a different state of society, a segment of an existence peculiar in its aims and methods, a leaf of some mysterious volume, interpolated into the current history which Time was writing off. At one moment, the very circumstances now surrounding me—my coal-fire, and the dingy room in the bustling hotel—appeared far off and intangible. The next instant, Blithedale looked vague, as if it were at a distance both in time and space, and so shadowy, that a question might be raised whether the whole affair had been anything more than the thoughts of a speculative man. I had never before experienced a mood that so robbed the actual world of its solidity. It nevertheless involved a charm, on which—a devoted epicure of my own emotions—I resolved to pause, and enjoy the moral sillabub[1] until quite dissolved away.

Whatever had been my taste for solitude and natural scenery, yet the thick, foggy, stifled element of cities, the entangled life of many men together, sordid as it was, and empty of the beautiful, took quite as strenuous a hold upon my mind. I felt as if there could never be enough of it. Each characteristic sound was too suggestive to be passed over, unnoticed. Beneath and around me, I heard the stir of the hotel; the loud voices of guests, landlord, or barkeeper; steps echoing on the staircase; the ringing of a bell, announcing arrivals or departures; the porter lumbering past my door with baggage, which he thumped down upon the floors of neighboring chambers; the lighter feet of chamber-maids scudding along the passages;—it is ridiculous to think what an interest they had for me. From the street, came the tumult of the pavements, pervading the whole house with a continual uproar, so broad and deep that only an unaccustomed ear would dwell upon it. A company of the city-soldiery, with a full military band, marched in front of the hotel, invisible to me, but stirringly audible both by its foot-tramp and the clangor of its instruments. Once or twice, all the city-bells jangled together, announcing a fire, which brought out the engine-men and their machines, like an army with its artillery rushing to battle. Hour by hour, the clocks in many steeples responded one to another. In some public hall, not a great way off, there seemed to be an exhibition of a mechanical diorama;[2] for, three times during the day, occurred a repetition of obstreperous music, winding up with the rattle of imitative cannon and musketry, and a huge final explosion. Then ensued the applause of the spectators, with clap of hands, and thump of sticks, and the energetic pounding of their heels. All this was just as valuable, in its way, as the sighing of the breeze among the birch-trees, that overshadowed Eliot's pulpit.

Yet I felt a hesitation about plunging into this muddy tide of human activity and pastime. It suited me better, for the present, to linger on

1. Sweet, frothy dessert made of cream and wine or cider.
2. A miniature, three-dimensional representation of a scene, viewed either through a small opening or (as above) in a specially designed space; "mechanical" dioramas had moving parts and changing lighting effects, and often featured urban vistas, battlefield scenes, or natural disasters.

the brink, or hover in the air above it. So I spent the first day, and the greater part of the second, in the laziest manner possible, in a rocking-chair, inhaling the fragrance of a series of cigars, with my legs and slippered feet horizontally disposed, and in my hand a novel, purchased of a railroad bibliopolist.[3] The gradual waste of my cigar accomplished itself with an easy and gentle expenditure of breath. My book was of the dullest, yet had a sort of sluggish flow, like that of a stream in which your boat is as often aground as afloat. Had there been a more impetuous rush, a more absorbing passion of the narrative, I should the sooner have struggled out of its uneasy current, and have given myself up to the swell and subsidence of my thoughts. But, as it was, the torpid life of the book served as an unobtrusive accompaniment to the life within me and about me. At intervals, however, when its effect grew a little too soporific—not for my patience, but for the possibility of keeping my eyes open—I bestirred myself, started from the rocking-chair, and looked out of the window.

A gray sky; the weathercock of a steeple, that rose beyond the opposite range of buildings, pointing from the eastward; a sprinkle of small, spiteful-looking raindrops on the window-pane! In that ebb-tide of my energies, had I thought of venturing abroad, these tokens would have checked the abortive purpose.

After several such visits to the window, I found myself getting pretty well acquainted with that little portion of the backside of the universe which it presented to my view. Over against the hotel and its adjacent houses, at the distance of forty or fifty yards, was the rear of a range of buildings, which appeared to be spacious, modern, and calculated for fashionable residences. The interval between was apportioned into grass-plots, and here and there an apology for a garden, pertaining severally to these dwellings. There were apple-trees, and pear and peach-trees, too, the fruit on which looked singularly large, luxuriant, and abundant; as well it might, in a situation so warm and sheltered, and where the soil had doubtless been enriched to a more than natural fertility. In two or three places, grape-vines clambered upon trellises, and bore clusters already purple, and promising the richness of Malta or Madeira[4] in their ripened juice. The blighting winds of our rigid climate could not molest these trees and vines; the sunshine, though descending late into this area, and too early intercepted by the height of the surrounding houses, yet lay tropically there, even when less than temperate in every other region. Dreary as was the day, the scene was illuminated by not a few sparrows and other birds, which spread their wings, and flitted and fluttered, and alighted now here, now there, and busily scratched their

3. Bookseller.
4. Islands, in the Mediterranean and Atlantic respectively, known for their fine wines.

food out of the wormy earth. Most of these winged people seemed to have their domicile in a robust and healthy buttonwood-tree.[5] It aspired upward, high above the roof of the houses, and spread a dense head of foliage half across the area.

There was a cat—as there invariably is, in such places—who evidently thought herself entitled to all the privileges of forest-life, in this close heart of city-conventionalisms. I watched her creeping along the low, flat roofs of the offices, descending a flight of wooden steps, gliding among the grass, and besieging the buttonwood-tree, with murderous purpose against its feathered citizens. But, after all, they were birds of city-breeding, and doubtless knew how to guard themselves against the peculiar perils of their position.

Bewitching to my fancy are all those nooks and crannies, where Nature, like a stray partridge, hides her head among the long-established haunts of men! It is likewise to be remarked, as a general rule, that there is far more of the picturesque, more truth to native and characteristic tendencies, and vastly greater suggestiveness, in the back view of a residence, whether in town or country, than in its front. The latter is always artificial; it is meant for the world's eye, and is therefore a veil and a concealment. Realities keep in the rear, and put forward an advance-guard of show and humbug. The posterior aspect of any old farm-house, behind which a rail-road has unexpectedly been opened, is so different from that looking upon the immemorial highway, that the spectator gets new ideas of rural life and individuality, in the puff or two of steam-breath which shoots him past the premises. In a city, the distinction between what is offered to the public, and what is kept for the family, is certainly not less striking.

But, to return to my window, at the back of the hotel. Together with a due contemplation of the fruit-trees, the grape-vines, the buttonwood-tree, the cat, the birds, and many other particulars, I failed not to study the row of fashionable dwellings to which all these appertained. Here, it must be confessed, there was a general sameness. From the upper-story to the first floor, they were so much alike that I could only conceive of the inhabitants as cut out on one identical pattern, like little wooden toy-people of German manufacture. One long, united roof, with its thousands of slates glittering in the rain, extended over the whole. After the distinctness of separate characters, to which I had recently been accustomed, it perplexed and annoyed me not to be able to resolve this combination of human interests into well-defined elements. It seemed hardly worth while for more than one of those families to be in existence; since they all

5. Sycamore.

had the same glimpse of the sky, all looked into the same area, all received just their equal share of sunshine through the front windows, and all listened to precisely the same noises of the street on which they bordered. Men are so much alike, in their nature, that they grow intolerable unless varied by their circumstances.

Just about this time, a waiter entered my room. The truth was, I had rung the bell and ordered a sherry-cobbler.[6]

"Can you tell me," I inquired, "what families reside in any of those houses opposite?"

"The one right opposite is a rather stylish boarding-house," said the waiter. "Two of the gentlemen-boarders keep horses at the stable of our establishment. They do things in very good style, sir, the people that live there."

I might have found out nearly as much for myself, on examining the house a little more closely. In one of the upper chambers, I saw a young man in a dressing-gown, standing before the glass and brushing his hair, for a quarter-of-an-hour together. He then spent an equal space of time in the elaborate arrangement of his cravat, and finally made his appearance in a dress-coat, which I suspected to be newly come from the tailor's, and now first put on for a dinner-party. At a window of the next story below, two children, prettily dressed, were looking out. By-and-by, a middle-aged gentleman came softly behind them, kissed the little girl, and playfully pulled the little boy's ear. It was a papa, no doubt, just come in from his counting-room or office; and anon appeared mamma, stealing as softly behind papa, as he had stolen behind the children, and laying her hand on his shoulder to surprise him. Then followed a kiss between papa and mamma, but a noiseless one; for the children did not turn their heads.

"I bless God for these good folks!" thought I to myself. "I have not seen a prettier bit of nature, in all my summer in the country, than they have shown me here in a rather stylish boarding-house. I will pay them a little more attention, by-and-by."

On the first floor, an iron balustrade ran along in front of the tall, and spacious windows, evidently belonging to a back drawing-room; and, far into the interior, through the arch of the sliding-doors, I could discern a gleam from the windows of the front apartment. There were no signs of present occupancy in this suite of rooms; the curtains being enveloped in a protective covering, which allowed but a small portion of their crimson material to be seen. But two house-maids were industriously at work; so that there was good prospect that the boarding-house might not long suffer from the absence of its most expensive and profitable guests. Meanwhile, until they

6. A drink made with sherry, lemon juice, sugar, and water, and served over ice.

should appear, I cast my eyes downward to the lower regions. There, in the dusk that so early settles into such places, I saw the red glow of the kitchen-range; the hot cook, or one of her subordinates, with a ladle in her hand, came to draw a cool breath at the back-door; as soon as she disappeared, an Irish man-servant, in a white jacket, crept slily forth and threw away the fragments of a china-dish, which unquestionably he had just broken. Soon afterwards, a lady, showily dressed, with a curling front of what must have been false hair, and reddish brown, I suppose, in hue—though my remoteness allowed me only to guess at such particulars—this respectable mistress of the boarding-house made a momentary transit across the kitchen-window, and appeared no more. It was her final, comprehensive glance, in order to make sure that soup, fish, and flesh, were in a proper state of readiness, before the serving up of dinner.

There was nothing else worth noticing about the house; unless it be, that, on the peak of one of the dormer-windows, which opened out of the roof, sat a dove, looking very dreary and forlorn; insomuch that I wondered why she chose to sit there, in the chilly rain, while her kindred were doubtless nestling in a warm and comfortable dove-cote. All at once, this dove spread her wings, and launching herself in the air, came flying so straight across the intervening space, that I fully expected her to alight directly on my window-sill. In the latter part of her course, however, she swerved aside, flew upward, and vanished, as did likewise the slight, fantastic pathos with which I had invested her.

XVIII. The Boarding-House

The next day, as soon as I thought of looking again towards the opposite house, there sat the dove again, on the peak of the same dormer-window!

It was by no means an early hour; for, the preceding evening, I had ultimately mustered enterprise enough to visit the theatre, had gone late to bed, and slept beyond all limit, in my remoteness from Silas Foster's awakening horn. Dreams had tormented me, throughout the night. The train of thoughts which, for months past, had worn a track through my mind, and to escape which was one of my chief objects in leaving Blithedale, kept treading remorselessly to-and-fro, in their old footsteps, while slumber left me impotent to regulate them. It was not till I had quitted my three friends that they first began to encroach upon my dreams. In those of the last night, Hollingsworth and Zenobia, standing on either side of my bed, had bent across it to exchange a kiss of passion. Priscilla, beholding this—for she seemed to be peeping in at the chamber-window—had melted gradually away, and left only the sadness of her expression in my heart. There it still lingered, after I awoke; one of those unreasonable sadnesses that you know not how to deal with, because it involves nothing for common-sense to clutch.

It was a gray and dripping forenoon; gloomy enough in town, and still gloomier in the haunts to which my recollections persisted in transporting me. For, in spite of my efforts to think of something else, I thought how the gusty rain was drifting over the slopes and valleys of our farm; how wet must be the foliage that overshadowed the pulpit-rock; how cheerless, in such a day, my hermitage—the tree-solitude of my owl-like humors—in the vine-encircled heart of the tall pine! It was a phase of home-sickness. I had wrenched myself too suddenly out of an accustomed sphere. There was no choice now, but to bear the pang of whatever heart-strings were snapt asunder, and that illusive torment (like the ache of a limb long ago cut off) by which a past mode of life prolongs itself into the succeeding one. I was full of idle and shapeless regrets. The thought impressed itself upon me, that I had left duties unperformed. With the power, perhaps, to act in the place of destiny, and avert misfortune from my friends, I had resigned them to their fate. That cold tendency, between instinct and intellect, which made me pry with a speculative interest into people's passions and impulses, appeared to have gone far towards unhumanizing my heart.

But a man cannot always decide for himself whether his own heart is cold or warm. It now impresses me, that, if I erred at all, in regard to Hollingsworth, Zenobia, and Priscilla, it was through too much sympathy, rather than too little.

To escape the irksomeness of these meditations, I resumed my post at the window. At first sight, there was nothing new to be noticed. The general aspect of affairs was the same as yesterday, except that the more decided inclemency of to-day had driven the sparrows to shelter, and kept the cat within doors, whence, however, she soon emerged, pursued by the cook, and with what looked like the better half of a roast chicken in her mouth. The young man in the dress-coat was invisible; the two children, in the story below, seemed to be romping about the room, under the superintendence of a nursery-maid. The damask curtains of the drawing-room, on the first floor, were now fully displayed, festooned gracefully from top to bottom of the windows, which extended from the ceiling to the carpet. A narrower window, at the left of the drawing-room, gave light to what was probably a small boudoir, within which I caught the faintest imaginable glimpse of a girl's figure, in airy drapery. Her arm was in regular movement, as if she were busy with her German worsted,[1] or some other such pretty and unprofitable handiwork.

---

1. Woolen yarn used in ornamental needlework.

While intent upon making out this girlish shape, I became sensible that a figure had appeared at one of the windows of the drawing-room. There was a presentiment in my mind; or perhaps my first glance, imperfect and sidelong as it was, had sufficed to convey subtle information of the truth. At any rate, it was with no positive surprise, but as if I had all along expected the incident, that, directing my eyes thitherward, I beheld—like a full-length picture, in the space between the heavy festoons of the window-curtains—no other than Zenobia! At the same instant, my thoughts made sure of the identity of the figure in the boudoir. It could only be Priscilla.

Zenobia was attired, not in the almost rustic costume which she had heretofore worn, but in a fashionable morning-dress. There was, nevertheless, one familiar point. She had, as usual, a flower in her hair, brilliant, and of a rare variety, else it had not been Zenobia. After a brief pause at the window, she turned away, exemplifying, in the few steps that removed her out of sight, that noble and beautiful motion which characterized her as much as any other personal charm. Not one woman in a thousand could move so admirably as Zenobia. Many women can sit gracefully; some can stand gracefully; and a few, perhaps, can assume a series of graceful positions. But natural movement is the result and expression of the whole being, and cannot be well and nobly performed, unless responsive to something in the character. I often used to think that music—light and airy, wild and passionate, or the full harmony of stately marches, in accordance with her varying mood—should have attended Zenobia's footsteps.

I waited for her re-appearance. It was one peculiarity, distinguishing Zenobia from most of her sex, that she needed for her moral well-being, and never would forego, a large amount of physical exercise. At Blithedale, no inclemency of sky or muddiness of earth had ever impeded her daily walks. Here, in town, she probably preferred to tread the extent of the two drawing-rooms, and measure out the miles by spaces of forty feet, rather than bedraggle her skirts over the sloppy pavements. Accordingly, in about the time requisite to pass through the arch of the sliding-doors to the front window, and to return upon her steps, there she stood again, between the festoons of the crimson curtains. But another personage was now added to the scene. Behind Zenobia appeared that face which I had first encountered in the wood-path; the man who had passed, side by side with her, in such mysterious familiarity and estrangement, beneath my vine-curtained hermitage in the tall pine-tree. It was Westervelt. And though he was looking closely over her shoulder, it still seemed to me, as on the former occasion, that Zenobia repelled him—that, perchance, they mutually repelled each other—by some incompatibility of their spheres.

This impression, however, might have been altogether the result of fancy and prejudice, in me. The distance was so great as to obliterate any play of feature, by which I might otherwise have been made a partaker of their counsels.

There now needed only Hollingsworth and old Moodie to complete the knot of characters, whom a real intricacy of events, greatly assisted by my method of insulating them from other relations, had kept so long upon my mental stage, as actors in a drama. In itself, perhaps, it was no very remarkable event, that they should thus come across me, at the moment when I imagined myself free. Zenobia, as I well knew, had retained an establishment in town, and had not unfrequently withdrawn herself from Blithedale, during brief intervals, on one of which occasions she had taken Priscilla along with her. Nevertheless, there seemed something fatal in the coincidence that had borne me to this one spot, of all others in a great city, and transfixed me there, and compelled me again to waste my already wearied sympathies on affairs which were none of mine, and persons who cared little for me. It irritated my nerves; it affected me with a kind of heart-sickness. After the effort which it cost me to fling them off—after consummating my escape, as I thought, from these goblins of flesh and blood, and pausing to revive myself with a breath or two of an atmosphere in which they should have no share—it was a positive despair, to find the same figures arraying themselves before me, and presenting their old problem in a shape that made it more insoluble than ever.

I began to long for a catastrophe. If the noble temper of Hollingsworth's soul were doomed to be utterly corrupted by the too powerful purpose, which had grown out of what was noblest in him; if the rich and generous qualities of Zenobia's womanhood might not save her; if Priscilla must perish by her tenderness and faith, so simple and so devout;—then be it so! Let it all come! As for me, I would look on, as it seemed my part to do, understandingly, if my intellect could fathom the meaning and the moral, and, at all events, reverently and sadly. The curtain fallen, I would pass onward with my poor individual life, which was now attenuated of much of its proper substance, and diffused among many alien interests.

Meanwhile, Zenobia and her companion had retreated from the window. Then followed an interval, during which I directed my eyes towards the figure in the boudoir. Most certainly it was Priscilla, although dressed with a novel and fanciful elegance. The vague perception of it, as viewed so far off, impressed me as if she had suddenly passed out of a chrysalis state and put forth wings. Her hands were not now in motion. She had dropt her work, and sat with her head thrown back, in the same attitude that I had seen several times before, when she seemed to be listening to an imperfectly distinguished sound.

Again the two figures in the drawing-room became visible. They were now a little withdrawn from the window, face to face, and, as I could see by Zenobia's emphatic gestures, were discussing some subject in which she, at least, felt a passionate concern. By-and-by, she broke away, and vanished beyond my ken. Westervelt approached the window, and leaned his forehead against a pane of glass, displaying the sort of smile on his handsome features which, when I before met him, had let me into the secret of his gold-bordered teeth. Every human being, when given over to the Devil, is sure to have the wizard mark upon him, in one form or another. I fancied that this smile, with its peculiar revelation, was the Devil's signet on the Professor.

This man, as I had soon reason to know, was endowed with a cat-like circumspection; and though precisely the most unspiritual quality in the world, it was almost as effective as spiritual insight, in making him acquainted with whatever it suited him to discover. He now proved it, considerably to my discomfiture, by detecting and recognizing me, at my post of observation. Perhaps I ought to have blushed at being caught in such an evident scrutiny of Professor Westervelt and his affairs. Perhaps I did blush. Be that as it might, I retained presence of mind enough not to make my position yet more irksome, by the poltroonery[2] of drawing back.

Westervelt looked into the depths of the drawing-room, and beckoned. Immediately afterwards, Zenobia appeared at the window, with color much heightened, and eyes which, as my conscience whispered me, were shooting bright arrows, barbed with scorn, across the intervening space, directed full at my sensibilities as a gentleman. If the truth must be told, far as her flight-shot was, those arrows hit the mark. She signified her recognition of me by a gesture with her head and hand, comprising at once a salutation and dismissal. The next moment, she administered one of those pitiless rebukes which a woman always has at hand, ready for an offence, (and which she so seldom spares, on due occasion,) by letting down a white linen curtain between the festoons of the damask ones. It fell like the drop-curtain of a theatre, in the interval between the acts.

Priscilla had disappeared from the boudoir. But the dove still kept her desolate perch, on the peak of the attic-window.

2. Cowardice.

XIX. Zenobia's Drawing-Room

The remainder of the day, so far as I was concerned, was spent in meditating on these recent incidents. I contrived, and alternately rejected, innumerable methods of accounting for the presence of Zenobia and Priscilla, and the connection of Westervelt with both. It must be owned, too, that I had a keen, revengeful sense of the insult inflicted by Zenobia's scornful recognition, and more particularly by her letting down the curtain; as if such were the proper barrier to be interposed between a character like hers, and a perceptive faculty like mine. For, was mine a mere vulgar curiosity? Zenobia should have known me better than to suppose it. She should have been able to appreciate that quality of the intellect and the heart, which impelled me (often against my own will, and to the detriment of my own comfort) to live in other lives, and to endeavor—by generous sympathies, by delicate intuitions, by taking note of things too slight for record, and by bringing my human spirit into manifold accordance with the companions whom God assigned me—to learn the secret which was hidden even from themselves.

Of all possible observers, methought, a woman, like Zenobia, and a man, like Hollingsworth, should have selected me. And, now, when the event has long been past, I retain the same opinion of my fitness for the office. True; I might have condemned them. Had I been judge, as well as witness, my sentence might have been stern as that of Destiny itself. But, still, no trait of original nobility of character; no struggle against temptation; no iron necessity of will, on the one hand, nor extenuating circumstance to be derived from passion and despair, on the other; no remorse that might co-exist with error, even if powerless to prevent it; no proud repentance, that should claim retribution as a meed—would go unappreciated. True, again, I might give my full assent to the punishment which was sure to follow. But it would be given mournfully, and with undiminished love. And, after all was finished, I would come, as if to gather up the white ashes of those who had perished at the stake, and to tell the world— the wrong being now atoned for—how much had perished there, which it had never yet known how to praise.

I sat in my rocking-chair, too far withdrawn from the window to expose myself to another rebuke, like that already inflicted. My eyes still wandered towards the opposite house, but without effecting any new discoveries. Late in the after-noon, the weathercock on the church-spire indicated a change of wind; the sun shone dimly out, as if the golden wine of its beams were mingled half-and-half with water. Nevertheless, they kindled up the whole range of edifices, threw a glow over the windows, glistened on the wet roofs, and, slowly withdrawing upward, perched upon the chimney-tops; thence they took a higher flight, and lingered an instant on the tip of the spire, making it the final point of more cheerful light in the whole sombre scene. The next moment, it was all gone. The twilight fell into the area like a shower of dusky snow; and before it was quite dark, the gong of the hotel summoned me to tea.

When I returned to my chamber, the glow of an astral lamp[1] was penetrating mistily through the white curtain of Zenobia's drawing-room. The shadow of a passing figure was now-and-then cast upon this medium, but with too vague an outline for even my adventurous conjectures to read the hieroglyphic that it presented.

All at once, it occurred to me how very absurd was my behavior, in thus tormenting myself with crazy hypotheses as to what was going on within that drawing-room, when it was at my option to be person-ally present there. My relations with Zenobia, as yet unchanged—as a familiar friend, and associated in the same life-long enterprise—gave me the right, and made it no more than kindly courtesy demanded, to call on her. Nothing, except our habitual independence of con-ventional rules, at Blithedale, could have kept me from sooner rec-ognizing this duty. At all events, it should now be performed.

In compliance with this sudden impulse, I soon found myself actually within the house, the rear of which, for two days past, I had been so sedulously watching. A servant took my card, and immedi-ately returning, ushered me up-stairs. On the way, I heard a rich, and, as it were, triumphant burst of music from a piano, in which I felt Zenobia's character, although heretofore I had known nothing of her skill upon the instrument. Two or three canary-birds, excited by this gush of sound, sang piercingly, and did their utmost to produce a kindred melody. A bright illumination streamed through the door of the front drawing-room; and I had barely stept across the thresh-old before Zenobia came forward to meet me, laughing, and with an extended hand.

"Ah, Mr. Coverdale," said she, still smiling, but, as I thought, with a good deal of scornful anger underneath, "it has gratified me to see the interest which you continue to take in my affairs! I have long recognized you as a sort of transcendental Yankee, with all the native propensity of your countrymen to investigate matters that come within their range, but rendered almost poetical, in your case, by the refined methods which you adopt for its gratification. After all, it was an unjustifiable stroke, on my part—was it not?—to let down the window-curtain!"

"I cannot call it a very wise one," returned I, with a secret bitter-ness which, no doubt, Zenobia appreciated. "It is really impossible to hide anything, in this world, to say nothing of the next. All that we

---

1. Oil lamp designed to cast a shadowless light on objects below it.

ought to ask, therefore, is, that the witnesses of our conduct, and the speculators on our motives, should be capable of taking the highest view which the circumstances of the case may admit. So much being secured, I, for one, would be most happy in feeling myself followed, everywhere, by an indefatigable human sympathy."

"We must trust for intelligent sympathy to our guardian angels, if any there be," said Zenobia. "As long as the only spectator of my poor tragedy is a young man, at the window of his hotel, I must still claim the liberty to drop the curtain."

While this passed, as Zenobia's hand was extended, I had applied the very slightest touch of my fingers to her own. In spite of an external freedom, her manner made me sensible that we stood upon no real terms of confidence. The thought came sadly across me, how great was the contrast betwixt this interview and our first meeting. Then, in the warm light of the country fireside, Zenobia had greeted me cheerily and hopefully, with a full sisterly grasp of the hand, conveying as much kindness in it as other women could have evinced by the pressure of both arms around my neck, or by yielding a cheek to the brotherly salute. The difference was as complete as between her appearance, at that time—so simply attired, and with only the one superb flower in her hair—and now, when her beauty was set off by all that dress and ornament could do for it. And they did much. Not, indeed, that they created, or added anything to what Nature had lavishly done for Zenobia. But, those costly robes which she had on, those flaming jewels on her neck, served as lamps to display the personal advantages which required nothing less than such an illumination, to be fully seen. Even her characteristic flower, though it seemed to be still there, had undergone a cold and bright transfiguration; it was a flower exquisitely imitated in jeweller's work, and imparting the last touch that transformed Zenobia into a work of art.

"I scarcely feel," I could not forbear saying, "as if we had ever met before. How many years ago it seems, since we last sat beneath Eliot's pulpit, with Hollingsworth extended on the fallen leaves, and Priscilla at his feet! Can it be, Zenobia, that you ever really numbered yourself with our little band of earnest, thoughtful, philanthropic laborers?"

"Those ideas have their time and place," she answered, coldly. "But, I fancy, it must be a very circumscribed mind that can find room for no others."

Her manner bewildered me. Literally, moreover, I was dazzled by the brilliancy of the room. A chandelier hung down in the centre, glowing with I know not how many lights; there were separate lamps, also, on two or three tables, and on marble brackets, adding their white radiance to that of the chandelier. The furniture was exceedingly rich. Fresh from our old farm-house, with its homely

board and benches in the dining-room, and a few wicker-chairs in
the best parlor, it struck me that here was the fulfilment of every fantasy of an imagination, revelling in various methods of costly self-
indulgence and splendid ease. Pictures, marbles, vases; in brief,
more shapes of luxury than there could be any object in enumerating, except for an auctioneer's advertisement—and the whole
repeated and doubled by the reflection of a great mirror, which
showed me Zenobia's proud figure, likewise, and my own. It cost me,
I acknowledge, a bitter sense of shame, to perceive in myself a positive effort to bear up against the effect which Zenobia sought to
impose on me. I reasoned against her, in my secret mind, and strove
so to keep my footing. In the gorgeousness with which she had surrounded herself—in the redundance of personal ornament, which
the largeness of her physical nature and the rich type of her beauty
caused to seem so suitable—I malevolently beheld the true character of the woman, passionate, luxurious, lacking simplicity, not
deeply refined, incapable of pure and perfect taste.

But, the next instant, she was too powerful for all my opposing
struggles. I saw how fit it was that she should make herself as
gorgeous as she pleased, and should do a thousand things that would
have been ridiculous in the poor, thin, weakly characters of other
women. To this day, however, I hardly know whether I then beheld
Zenobia in her truest attitude, or whether that were the truer one in
which she had presented herself at Blithedale. In both, there was
something like the illusion which a great actress flings around her.

"Have you given up Blithedale forever?" I inquired.

"Why should you think so?" asked she.

"I cannot tell," answered I; "except that it appears all like a dream
that we were ever there together."

"It is not so to me," said Zenobia. "I should think it a poor and
meagre nature, that is capable of but one set of forms, and must
convert all the past into a dream, merely because the present happens to be unlike it. Why should we be content with our homely life
of a few months past, to the exclusion of all other modes? It was
good; but there are other lives as good or better. Not, you will understand, that I condemn those who give themselves up to it more
entirely than I, for myself, should deem it wise to do."

It irritated me, this self-complacent, condescending, qualified
approval and criticism of a system to which many individuals—perhaps as highly endowed as our gorgeous Zenobia—had contributed
their all of earthly endeavor, and their loftiest aspirations. I determined to make proof if there were any spell that would exorcise her
out of the part which she seemed to be acting. She should be compelled to give me a glimpse of something true; some nature, some
passion, no matter whether right or wrong, provided it were real.

"Your allusion to that class of circumscribed characters, who can live only in one mode of life," remarked I, coolly, "reminds me of our poor friend Hollingsworth. Possibly, he was in your thoughts, when you spoke thus. Poor fellow! It is a pity that, by the fault of a narrow education, he should have so completely immolated himself to that one idea of his; especially as the slightest modicum of common-sense would teach him its utter impracticability. Now that I have returned into the world, and can look at his project from a distance, it requires quite all my real regard for this respectable and well-intentioned man to prevent me laughing at him—as, I find, society at large does!"

Zenobia's eyes darted lightning; her cheeks flushed; the vividness of her expression was like the effect of a powerful light, flaming up suddenly within her. My experiment had fully succeeded. She had shown me the true flesh and blood of her heart, by thus involuntarily resenting my slight, pitying, half-kind, half-scornful mention of the man who was all in all with her. She herself, probably, felt this; for it was hardly a moment before she tranquillized her uneven breath, and seemed as proud and self-possessed as ever.

"I rather imagine," said she, quietly, "that your appreciation falls short of Mr. Hollingsworth's just claims. Blind enthusiasm, absorption in one idea, I grant, is generally ridiculous, and must be fatal to the respectability of an ordinary man; it requires a very high and powerful character, to make it otherwise. But a great man—as, perhaps, you do not know—attains his normal condition only through the inspiration of one great idea. As a friend of Mr. Hollingsworth, and, at the same time, a calm observer, I must tell you that he seems to me such a man. But you are very pardonable for fancying him ridiculous. Doubtless, he is so—to you! There can be no truer test of the noble and heroic, in any individual, than the degree in which he possesses the faculty of distinguishing heroism from absurdity."

I dared make no retort to Zenobia's concluding apothegm. In truth, I admired her fidelity. It gave me a new sense of Hollingsworth's native power, to discover that his influence was no less potent with this beautiful woman, here, in the midst of artificial life, than it had been, at the foot of the gray rock, and among the wild birch-trees of the wood-path, when she so passionately pressed his hand against her heart. The great, rude, shaggy, swarthy man! And Zenobia loved him!

"Did you bring Priscilla with you?" I resumed. "Do you know, I have sometimes fancied it not quite safe, considering the susceptibility of her temperament, that she should be so constantly within the sphere of a man like Hollingsworth? Such tender and delicate natures, among your sex, have often, I believe, a very adequate appreciation of the heroic element in men. But, then, again, I should suppose them as likely as any other women to make a recip-rocal impression. Hollingsworth could hardly give his affections to a person capable of taking an independent stand, but only to one whom he might absorb into himself. He has certainly shown great tenderness for Priscilla."

Zenobia had turned aside. But I caught the reflection of her face in the mirror, and saw that it was very pale;—as pale, in her rich attire, as if a shroud were round her.

"Priscilla is here," said she, her voice a little lower than usual. "Have not you learnt as much, from your chamber-window? Would you like to see her?"

She made a step or two into the back drawing-room, and called:— "Priscilla! Dear Priscilla!"

XX. They Vanish

Priscilla immediately answered the summons, and made her appear-ance through the door of the boudoir. I had conceived the idea—which I now recognized as a very foolish one—that Zenobia would have taken measures to debar me from an interview with this girl, between whom and herself there was so utter an opposition of their dearest interests, that, on one part or the other, a great grief, if not likewise a great wrong, seemed a matter of necessity. But, as Priscilla was only a leaf, floating on the dark current of events, with-out influencing them by her own choice or plan—as she probably guessed not whither the stream was bearing her, nor perhaps even felt its inevitable movement—there could be no peril of her commu-nicating to me any intelligence with regard to Zenobia's purposes.

On perceiving me, she came forward with great quietude of man-ner; and when I held out my hand, her own moved slightly towards it, as if attracted by a feeble degree of magnetism.

"I am glad to see you, my dear Priscilla," said I, still holding her hand. "But everything that I meet with, now-a-days, makes me won-der whether I am awake. You, especially, have always seemed like a figure in a dream—and now more than ever."

"Oh, there is substance in these fingers of mine!" she answered, giving my hand the faintest possible pressure, and then taking away her own. "Why do you call me a dream? Zenobia is much more like one than I; she is so very, very beautiful! And, I suppose," added Priscilla, as if thinking aloud, "everybody sees it, as I do."

But, for my part, it was Priscilla's beauty, not Zenobia's, of which I was thinking, at that moment. She was a person who could be quite obliterated, so far as beauty went, by anything unsuitable in her attire; her charm was not positive and material enough to bear up against a mistaken choice of color, for instance, or fashion. It was safest, in her case, to attempt no art of dress; for it demanded the most perfect taste, or else the happiest accident in the world, to give her precisely the adornment which she needed. She was now dressed in pure white, set off with some kind of a gauzy fabric, which—as I bring up her figure in my memory, with a faint gleam on her shadowy hair, and her dark eyes bent shyly on mine, through all the vanished years—seems to be floating about her like a mist. I wondered what Zenobia meant by evolving so much loveliness out of this poor girl. It was what few women could afford to do; for, as I looked from one to the other, the sheen and splendor of Zenobia's presence took nothing from Priscilla's softer spell, if it might not rather be thought to add to it.

"What do you think of her?" asked Zenobia.

I could not understand the look of melancholy kindness with which Zenobia regarded her. She advanced a step, and beckoning Priscilla near her, kissed her cheek; then, with a slight gesture of repulse, she moved to the other side of the room. I followed.

"She is a wonderful creature," I said. "Ever since she came among us, I have been dimly sensible of just this charm which you have brought out. But it was never absolutely visible till now. She is as lovely as a flower!"

"Well; say so, if you like," answered Zenobia. "You are a poet—at least, as poets go, now-a-days—and must be allowed to make an opera-glass of your imagination, when you look at women. I wonder, in such Arcadian freedom of falling in love as we have lately enjoyed, it never occurred to you to fall in love with Priscilla! In society, indeed, a genuine American never dreams of stepping across the inappreciable air-line which separates one class from another. But what was rank to the colonists of Blithedale?"

"There were other reasons," I replied, "why I should have demonstrated myself an ass, had I fallen in love with Priscilla. By-the-by, has Hollingsworth ever seen her in this dress?"

"Why do you bring up his name, at every turn?" asked Zenobia, in an undertone, and with a malign look which wandered from my face to Priscilla's. "You know not what you do! It is dangerous, sir, believe me, to tamper thus with earnest human passions, out of your own mere idleness, and for your sport. I will endure it no longer! Take care that it does not happen again! I warn you!"

"You partly wrong me, if not wholly," I responded. "It is an uncertain sense of some duty to perform, that brings my thoughts, and therefore my words, continually to that one point."

"Oh, this stale excuse of duty!" said Zenobia, in a whisper so full of scorn that it penetrated me like the hiss of a serpent. "I have often heard it before, from those who sought to interfere with me, and I know precisely what it signifies. Bigotry; self-conceit; an insolent curiosity; a meddlesome temper; a cold-blooded criticism, founded on a shallow interpretation of half-perceptions; a monstrous scepticism in regard to any conscience or any wisdom, except one's own; a most irreverent propensity to thrust Providence aside, and substitute one's self in its awful place—out of these, and other motives as miserable as these, comes your idea of duty! But beware, sir! With all your fancied acuteness, you step blindfold into these affairs. For any mischief that may follow your interference, I hold you responsible!"

It was evident, that, with but a little further provocation, the lioness would turn to bay; if, indeed, such were not her attitude, already. I bowed, and, not very well knowing what else to do, was about to withdraw. But, glancing again towards Priscilla, who had retreated into a corner, there fell upon my heart an intolerable burthen of despondency, the purport of which I could not tell, but only felt it to bear reference to her. I approached her, and held out my hand; a gesture, however, to which she made no response. It was always one of her peculiarities that she seemed to shrink from even the most friendly touch, unless it were Zenobia's or Hollingsworth's. Zenobia, all this while, stood watching us, but with a careless expression, as if it mattered very little what might pass.

"Priscilla," I inquired, lowering my voice, "when do you go back to Blithedale?"

"Whenever they please to take me," said she.

"Did you come away of your own free-will?" I asked.

"I am blown about like a leaf," she replied. "I never have any free-will."

"Does Hollingsworth know that you are here?" said I.

"He bade me come," answered Priscilla.

She looked at me, I thought, with an air of surprise, as if the idea were incomprehensible, that she should have taken this step without his agency.

"What a gripe[1] this man has laid upon her whole being!" muttered I, between my teeth. "Well; as Zenobia so kindly intimates, I have no more business here. I wash my hands of it all. On Hollingsworth's head be the consequences! Priscilla," I added, aloud, "I know not that ever we may meet again. Farewell!"

As I spoke the word, a carriage had rumbled along the street, and stopt before the house. The door-bell rang, and steps were immediately afterwards heard on the staircase. Zenobia had thrown a shawl over her dress.

"Mr. Coverdale," said she, with cool courtesy, "you will perhaps excuse us. We have an engagement, and are going out."

1. Grip.

"Whither?" I demanded.

"Is not that a little more than you are entitled to inquire?" said she, with a smile. "At all events, it does not suit me to tell you."

The door of the drawing-room opened, and Westervelt appeared. I observed that he was elaborately dressed, as if for some grand entertainment. My dislike for this man was infinite. At that moment, it amounted to nothing less than a creeping of the flesh, as when, feeling about in a dark place, one touches something cold and slimy, and questions what the secret hatefulness may be. And, still, I could not but acknowledge, that, for personal beauty, for polish of manner, for all that externally befits a gentleman, there was hardly another like him. After bowing to Zenobia, and graciously saluting Priscilla in her corner, he recognized me by a slight, but courteous inclination.

"Come, Priscilla," said Zenobia, "it is time. Mr. Coverdale, good evening!"

As Priscilla moved slowly forward, I met her in the middle of the drawing-room.

"Priscilla," said I, in the hearing of them all, "do you know whither you are going?"

"I do not know," she answered.

"Is it wise to go?—and is it your choice to go?" I asked. "If not—I am your friend, and Hollingsworth's friend—tell me so, at once!"

"Possibly," observed Westervelt, smiling, "Priscilla sees in me an older friend than either Mr. Coverdale or Mr. Hollingsworth. I shall willingly leave the matter at her option."

While thus speaking, he made a gesture of kindly invitation; and Priscilla passed me, with the gliding movement of a sprite, and took his offered arm. He offered the other to Zenobia. But she turned her proud and beautiful face upon him, with a look which—judging from what I caught of it in profile—would undoubtedly have smitten the man dead, had he possessed any heart, or had this glance attained to it. It seemed to rebound, however, from his courteous visage, like an arrow from polished steel. They all three descended the stairs; and when I likewise reached the street-door, the carriage was already rolling away.

XXI. An Old Acquaintance

Thus excluded from everybody's confidence, and attaining no further, by my most earnest study, than to an uncertain sense of something hidden from me, it would appear reasonable that I should have flung off all these alien perplexities. Obviously, my best course was, to betake myself to new scenes. Here, I was only an intruder. Elsewhere, there might be circumstances in which I could establish a personal interest, and people who would respond, with a portion of their sympathies, for so much as I should bestow of mine.

Nevertheless, there occurred to me one other thing to be done. Remembering old Moodie, and his relationship with Priscilla, I determined to seek an interview, for the purpose of ascertaining whether the knot of affairs was as inextricable, on that side, as I found it on all others. Being tolerably well acquainted with the old man's haunts, I went, the next day, to the saloon of a certain establishment about which he often lurked. It was a reputable place enough, affording good entertainment in the way of meat, drink, and fumigation; and there, in my young and idle days and nights, when I was neither nice[1] nor wise, I had often amused myself with watching the staid humors and sober jollities of the thirsty souls around me.

At my first entrance, old Moodie was not there. The more patiently to await him, I lighted a cigar, and establishing myself in a corner, took a quiet, and, by sympathy, a boozy kind of pleasure in the customary life that was going forward. Human nature, in my opinion, has a naughty instinct that approves of wine, at least, if not of stronger liquor. The temperance-men may preach till doom's day; and still this cold and barren world will look warmer, kindlier, mellower, through the medium of a toper's[2] glass; nor can they, with all their efforts, really spill his draught upon the floor, until some hitherto unthought-of discovery shall supply him with a truer element of joy. The general atmosphere of life must first be rendered so inspiriting that he will not need his delirious solace. The custom of tippling has its defensible side, as well as any other question. But these good people snatch at the old, time-honored demijohn, and offer nothing—either sensual or moral—nothing whatever to supply its place; and human life, as it goes with a multitude of men, will not endure so great a vacuum as would be left by the withdrawal of that big-bellied convexity. The space, which it now occupies, must somehow or other be filled up. As for the rich, it would be little matter if a blight fell upon their vineyards; but the poor man—whose only glimpse of a better state is through the muddy medium of his liquor—what is to be done for him? The reformers should make their efforts positive, instead of negative; they must do away with evil by substituting good.

The saloon was fitted up with a good deal of taste. There were pictures on the walls, and among them an oil-painting of a beef-steak, with such an admirable show of juicy tenderness, that the beholder sighed to think it merely visionary, and incapable of ever being put

1. Refined, discriminating; *fumigation*: tobacco-smoking.
2. A toper is a hard drinker. This passage (beginning with "Human nature" and running to the end of the paragraph), skeptical of the efforts of temperance reformers, is the third of the manuscript passages restored by the editors of the Centenary edition (see p. 10, n. 1).

upon a gridiron. Another work of high art was the lifelike representation of a noble sirloin; another, the hind-quarters of a deer, retaining
the hoofs and tawny fur; another, the head and shoulders of a
salmon; and, still more exquisitely finished, a brace of canvassback
ducks, in which the mottled feathers were depicted with the accuracy of a daguerreotype.[3] Some very hungry painter, I suppose, had
wrought these subjects of still life, heightening his imagination with
his appetite, and earning, it is to be hoped, the privilege of a daily
dinner off whichever of his pictorial viands he liked best. Then there
was a fine old cheese, in which you could almost discern the mites;
and some sardines, on a small plate, very richly done, and looking as
if oozy with the oil in which they had been smothered. All these
things were so perfectly imitated, that you seemed to have the genuine article before you, and yet with an indescribable, ideal charm;
it took away the grossness from what was fleshiest and fattest, and
thus helped the life of man, even in its earthliest relations, to appear
rich and noble, as well as warm, cheerful, and substantial. There
were pictures, too, of gallant revellers, those of the old time, Flem-
ish, apparently, with doublets and slashed sleeves, drinking their
wine out of fantastic, long-stemmed glasses; quaffing joyously,
quaffing forever, with inaudible laughter and song; while the champagne bubbled immortally against their moustaches, or the purple
tide of Burgundy ran inexhaustibly down their throats.

But, in an obscure corner of the saloon, there was a little picture—
excellently done, moreover—of a ragged, bloated, New England
toper, stretched out on a bench, in the heavy, apoplectic sleep of
drunkenness. The death-in-life was too well portrayed. You smelt the
fumy liquor that had brought on this syncope.[4] Your only comfort lay
in the forced reflection, that, real as he looked, the poor caitiff[5] was
but imaginary, a bit of painted canvass, whom no delirium tremens,
nor so much as a retributive headache, awaited, on the morrow.

By this time, it being past eleven o'clock, the two bar-keepers of
the saloon were in pretty constant activity. One of these young men
had a rare faculty in the concoction of gin-cocktails. It was a spectacle to behold, how, with a tumbler in each hand, he tossed the
contents from one to the other. Never conveying it awry, nor spilling
the least drop, he compelled the frothy liquor, as it seemed to me, to
spout forth from one glass and descend into the other, in a great par-
abolic curve, as well-defined and calculable as a planet's orbit. He
had a good forehead, with a particularly large development just

3. The image produced by an early form of photography, named for its inventor, Louis-
Jacques-Mande Daguerre (1789–1851), who displayed the first such image in 1839.
4. Loss of consciousness.
5. Miserable or unfortunate person.

above the eyebrows; fine intellectual gifts, no doubt, which he had educated to this profitable end; being famous for nothing but gin-cocktails, and commanding a fair salary by his one accomplishment. These cocktails, and other artificial combinations of liquor, (of which there were at least a score, though mostly, I suspect, fantastic in their differences,) were much in favor with the younger class of customers, who, at farthest, had only reached the second stage of potatory life. The staunch, old soakers, on the other hand—men who, if put on tap, would have yielded a red alcoholic liquor, by way of blood—usually confined themselves to plain brandy-and-water, gin, or West India rum; and, oftentimes, they prefaced their dram with some medicinal remark as to the wholesomeness and stom-achic qualities of that particular drink. Two or three appeared to have bottles of their own, behind the counter; and winking one red eye to the bar-keeper, he forthwith produced these choicest and peculiar cordials, which it was a matter of great interest and favor, among their acquaintances, to obtain a sip of.

Agreeably to the Yankee habit, under whatever circumstances, the deportment of all these good fellows, old or young, was decorous and thoroughly correct. They grew only the more sober in their cups; there was no confused babble, nor boisterous laughter. They sucked in the joyous fire of the decanters, and kept it smouldering in their inmost recesses, with a bliss known only to the heart which it warmed and comforted. Their eyes twinkled a little, to be sure; they hemmed vigorously, after each glass, and laid a hand upon the pit of the stomach, as if the pleasant titillation, there, was what consti-tuted the tangible part of their enjoyment. In that spot, unquestion-ably, and not in the brain, was the acme of the whole affair. But the true purpose of their drinking—and one that will induce men to drink, or do something equivalent, as long as this weary world shall endure—was the renewed youth and vigor, the brisk, cheerful sense of things present and to come, with which, for about a quarter-of-an-hour, the dram permeated their systems. And when such quarters-of-an-hour can be obtained in some mode less baneful to the great sum of a man's life—but, nevertheless, with a little spice of impro-priety, to give it a wild flavor—we temperance-people may ring out our bells for victory!

The prettiest object in the saloon was a tiny fountain, which threw up its feathery jet, through the counter, and sparkled down again into an oval basin, or lakelet, containing several gold-fishes. There was a bed of bright sand, at the bottom, strewn with coral and rock-work; and the fishes went gleaming about, now turning up the sheen of a golden side, and now vanishing into the shadows of the water, like the fanciful thoughts that coquet with a poet in his dream. Never before, I imagine, did a company of water-drinkers remain so entirely uncontaminated by the bad example around them; nor could I help wondering that it had not occurred to any freakish ine-briate, to empty a glass of liquor into their lakelet. What a delightful idea! Who would not be a fish, if he could inhale jollity with the essential element of his existence!

I had begun to despair of meeting old Moodie, when, all at once, I recognized his hand and arm, protruding from behind a screen that was set up for the accommodation of bashful topers. As a matter of course, he had one of Priscilla's little purses, and was quietly insinu-ating it under the notice of a person who stood near. This was always old Moodie's way. You hardly ever saw him advancing towards you, but became aware of his proximity without being able to guess how he had come thither. He glided about like a spirit, assuming visibility close to your elbow, offering his petty trifles of merchandise, remain-ing long enough for you to purchase, if so disposed, and then taking himself off, between two breaths, while you happened to be thinking of something else.

By a sort of sympathetic impulse that often controlled me, in those more impressible days of my life, I was induced to approach this old man in a mode as undemonstrative as his own. Thus, when, according to his custom, he was probably just about to vanish, he found me at his elbow.

"Ah!" said he, with more emphasis than was usual with him. "It is Mr. Coverdale!"

"Yes, Mr. Moodie, your old acquaintance," answered I. "It is some time now since we ate our luncheon together, at Blithedale, and a good deal longer since our little talk together, at the street-corner."

"That was a good while ago," said the old man.

And he seemed inclined to say not a word more. His existence looked so colorless and torpid—so very faintly shadowed on the can-vass of reality—that I was half afraid lest he should altogether disap-pear, even while my eyes were fixed full upon his figure. He was certainly the wretchedest old ghost in the world, with his crazy hat, the dingy handkerchief about his throat, his suit of threadbare gray, and especially that patch over his right eye,[6] behind which he always seemed to be hiding himself. There was one method, however, of bringing him out into somewhat stronger relief. A glass of brandy would effect it. Perhaps the gentler influence of a bottle of claret might do the same. Nor could I think it a matter for the recording angel to write down against me, if—with my painful consciousness of the frost in this old man's blood, and the positive ice that had

6. In his prior appearance in the text (p. 59), Moodie is said to wear the patch over his left eye.

congealed about his heart—I should thaw him out, were it only for an hour, with the summer warmth of a little wine. What else could possibly be done for him? How else could he be imbued with energy enough to hope for a happier state, hereafter? How else be inspirited to say his prayers? For there are states of our spiritual system, when the throb of the soul's life is too faint and weak to render us capable of religious aspiration.

"Mr. Moodie," said I, "shall we lunch together? And would you like to drink a glass of wine?"

His one eye gleamed. He bowed; and it impressed me that he grew to be more of a man at once, either in anticipation of the wine, or as a grateful response to my good-fellowship in offering it.

"With pleasure," he replied.

The barkeeper, at my request, showed us into a private room, and, soon afterwards, set some fried oysters and a bottle of claret on the table; and I saw the old man glance curiously at the label of the bottle, as if to learn the brand.

"It should be good wine," I remarked, "if it have any right to its label."

"You cannot suppose, sir," said Moodie, with a sigh, "that a poor old fellow, like me, knows any difference in wines."

And yet, in his way of handling the glass, in his preliminary snuff at the aroma, in his first cautious sip of the wine, and the gustatory skill with which he gave his palate the full advantage of it, it was impossible not to recognize the connoisseur.

"I fancy, Mr. Moodie," said I, "you are a much better judge of wines than I have yet learned to be. Tell me fairly—did you never drink it where the grape grows?"

"How should that have been, Mr. Coverdale?" answered old Moodie, shyly; but then he took courage, as it were, and uttered a feeble little laugh. "The flavor of this wine," added he, "and its perfume, still more than its taste, makes me remember that I was once a young man!"

"I wish, Mr. Moodie," suggested I—not that I greatly cared about it, however, but was only anxious to draw him into some talk about Priscilla and Zenobia—"I wish, while we sit over our wine, you would favor me with a few of those youthful reminiscences."

"Ah," said he, shaking his head, "they might interest you more than you suppose. But I had better be silent, Mr. Coverdale. If this good wine—though claret, I suppose, is not apt to play such a trick—but if it should make my tongue run too freely, I could never look you in the face again."

"You never did look me in the face, Mr. Moodie," I replied, "until this very moment."

"Ah!" sighed old Moodie.

It was wonderful, however, what an effect the mild grape-juice wrought upon him. It was not in the wine, but in the associations which it seemed to bring up. Instead of the mean, slouching, furtive, painfully depressed air of an old city-vagabond, more like a gray kennel-rat[7] than any other living thing, he began to take the aspect of a decayed gentle-man. Even his garments—especially after I had myself quaffed a glass or two—looked less shabby than when we first sat down. There was, by-and-by, a certain exuberance and elaborate-ness of gesture, and manner, oddly in contrast with all that I had hitherto seen of him. Anon, with hardly any impulse from me, old Moodie began to talk. His communications referred exclusively to a long past and more fortunate period of his life, with only a few unavoidable allusions to the circumstances that had reduced him to his present state. But, having once got the clue, my subsequent researches acquainted me with the main facts of the following narrative; although, in writing it out, my pen has perhaps allowed itself a trifle of romantic and legendary license, worthier of a small poet than of a grave biographer.

XXII. Fauntleroy

Five-and-twenty years ago, at the epoch of this story, there dwelt, in one of the middle states, a man whom we shall call Fauntleroy;[1] a man of wealth, and magnificent tastes, and prodigal expenditure. His home might almost be styled a palace; his habits, in the ordinary sense, princely. His whole being seemed to have crystallized itself into an external splendor, wherewith he glittered in the eyes of the world, and had no other life than upon this gaudy surface. He had married a lovely woman, whose nature was deeper than his own. But his affection for her, though it showed largely, was superficial, like all his other manifestations and developments; he did not so truly keep this noble creature in his heart, as wear her beauty for the most brilliant ornament of his outward state. And there was born to him a child, a beautiful daughter, whom he took from the beneficent hand of God with no just sense of her immortal value, but as a man, already rich in gems, would receive another jewel. If he loved her, it was because she shone.

---

7. Gutter-rat (from "kennel" or "cannel," terms for a street or drainage gutter).
1. Hawthorne's choice of this name may have been suggested by the historical Henry Fauntleroy (1785–1824), a London banker hanged for forgery; the case was well publicized on both sides of the Atlantic, and 100,000 people are said to have attended his execution.

After Fauntleroy had thus spent a few empty years, corruscating[2] continually an unnatural light, the source of it—which was merely his gold—began to grow more shallow, and finally became exhausted. He saw himself in imminent peril of losing all that had heretofore distinguished him; and, conscious of no innate worth to fall back upon, he recoiled from this calamity, with the instinct of a soul shrinking from annihilation. To avoid it—wretched man!—or, rather, to defer it, if but for a month, a day, or only to procure himself the life of a few breaths more, amid the false glitter which was now less his own than ever—he made himself guilty of a crime. It was just the sort of crime, growing out of its artificial state, which society (unless it should change its entire constitution for this man's unworthy sake) neither could nor ought to pardon. More safely might it pardon murder. Fauntleroy's guilt was discovered. He fled; his wife perished by the necessity of her innate nobleness, in its alliance with a being so ignoble; and betwixt her mother's death and her father's ignominy, his daughter was left worse than orphaned.

There was no pursuit after Fauntleroy. His family-connections, who had great wealth, made such arrangements with those whom he had attempted to wrong, as secured him from the retribution that would have overtaken an unfriended criminal. The wreck of his estate was divided among his creditors. His name, in a very brief space, was forgotten by the multitude who had passed it so diligently from mouth to mouth. Seldom, indeed, was it recalled, even by his closest former intimates. Nor could it have been other-wise. The man had laid no real touch on any mortal's heart. Being a mere image, an optical delusion, created by the sunshine of prosperity, it was his law to vanish into the shadow of the first intervening cloud. He seemed to leave no vacancy; a phenomenon which, like many others that attended his brief career, went far to prove the illusive-ness of his existence.

Not, however, that the physical substance of Fauntleroy had liter-ally melted into vapor. He had fled northward, to the New England metropolis;[3] and had taken up his abode, under another name, in a squalid street, or court, of the older portion of the city. There he dwelt among poverty-stricken wretches, sinners, and forlorn, good people, Irish, and whomsoever else were neediest. Many families were clustered in each house together, above stairs and below, in the little peaked garrets, and even in the dusky cellars. The house, where Fauntleroy paid weekly rent for a chamber and a closet, had been a

2. Glittering.
3. Boston.

stately habitation, in its day. An old colonial Governor had built it, and lived there, long ago, and held his levees[4] in a great room where now slept twenty Irish bedfellows, and died in Fauntleroy's chamber, which his embroidered and white-wigged ghost still haunted. Tattered hangings, a marble hearth, traversed with many cracks and fissures, a richly-carved oaken mantel-piece, partly hacked-away for kindling-stuff, a stuccoed ceiling, defaced with great, unsightly patches of the naked laths;—such was the chamber's aspect, as if, with its splinters and rags of dirty splendor, it were a kind of practical gibe at this poor, ruined man of show.

At first, and at irregular intervals, his relatives allowed Fauntleroy a little pittance to sustain life; not from any love, perhaps, but lest poverty should compel him, by new offences, to add more shame to that with which he had already stained them. But he showed no tendency to further guilt. His character appeared to have been radically changed (as, indeed, from its shallowness, it well might) by his miserable fate; or, it may be, the traits now seen in him were portions of the same character, presenting itself in another phase. Instead of any longer seeking to live in the sight of the world, his impulse was to shrink into the nearest obscurity, and to be unseen of men, were it possible, even while standing before their eyes. He had no pride; it was all trodden in the dust. No ostentation; for how could it survive, when there was nothing left of Fauntleroy, save penury and shame! His very gait demonstrated that he would gladly have faded out of view, and have crept about invisibly, for the sake of sheltering himself from the irksomeness of a human glance. Hardly, it was averred, within the memory of those who knew him now, had he the hardihood to show his full front to the world. He skulked in corners, and crept about in a sort of noonday twilight, making himself gray and misty, at all hours, with his morbid intolerance of sunshine.

In his torpid despair, however, he had done an act which that condition of the spirit seems to prompt, almost as often as prosperity and hope. Fauntleroy was again married. He had taken to wife a forlorn, meek-spirited, feeble young woman, a seamstress, whom he found dwelling with her mother in a contiguous chamber of the old gubernatorial residence. This poor phantom—as the beautiful and noble companion of his former life had done—brought him a daughter. And sometimes, as from one dream into another, Fauntleroy looked forth out of his present grimy environment, into that past magnificence, and wondered whether the grandee of yesterday or the pauper of to-day were real. But, in my mind, the one and the

4. Morning assemblies held by a prince or person of distinction.

other were alike impalpable. In truth, it was Fauntleroy's fatality to behold whatever he touched dissolve. After a few years, his second wife (dim shadow that she had always been) faded finally out of the world, and left Fauntleroy to deal as he might with their pale and nervous child. And, by this time, among his distant relatives—with whom he had grown a weary thought, linked with contagious infamy, and which they were only too willing to get rid of—he was himself supposed to be no more.

The younger child, like his elder one, might be considered as the true offspring of both parents, and as the reflection of their state. She was a tremulous little creature, shrinking involuntarily from all mankind, but in timidity, and no sour repugnance. There was a lack of human substance in her; it seemed as if, were she to stand up in a sunbeam, it would pass right through her figure, and trace out the cracked and dusty window-panes upon the naked floor. But, nevertheless, the poor child had a heart; and from her mother's gentle character, she had inherited a profound and still capacity of affection. And so her life was one of love. She bestowed it partly on her father, but, in greater part, on an idea.

For Fauntleroy, as they sat by their cheerless fireside—which was no fireside, in truth, but only a rusty stove—had often talked to the little girl about his former wealth, the noble loveliness of his first wife, and the beautiful child whom she had given him. Instead of the fairy tales, which other parents tell, he told Priscilla this. And, out of the loneliness of her sad little existence, Priscilla's love grew, and tended upward, and twined itself perseveringly around this unseen sister; as a grape-vine might strive to clamber out of a gloomy hollow among the rocks, and embrace a young tree, standing in the sunny warmth above. It was almost like worship, both in its earnestness and its humility; nor was it the less humble, though the more earnest, because Priscilla could claim human kindred with the being whom she so devoutly loved. As with worship, too, it gave her soul the refreshment of a purer atmosphere. Save for this singular, this melancholy, and yet beautiful affection, the child could hardly have lived; or, had she lived, with a heart shrunken for lack of any sentiment to fill it, she must have yielded to the barren miseries of her position, and have grown to womanhood, characterless and worthless. But, now, amid all the sombre coarseness of her father's outward life, and of her own, Priscilla had a higher and imaginative life within. Some faint gleam thereof was often visible upon her face. It was as if, in her spiritual visits to her brilliant sister, a portion of the latter's brightness had permeated our dim Priscilla, and still lingered, shedding a faint illumination through the cheerless chamber, after she came back.

As the child grew up, so pallid and so slender, and with much unaccountable nervousness, and all the weaknesses of neglected infancy still haunting her, the gross and simple neighbors whispered strange things about Priscilla. The big, red, Irish matrons, whose innumerable progeny swarmed out of the adjacent doors, used to mock at the pale Western child. They fancied—or, at least, affirmed it, between jest and earnest—that she was not so solid flesh and blood as other children, but mixed largely with a thinner element. They called her ghost-child, and said that she could indeed vanish, when she pleased, but could never, in her densest moments, make herself quite visible. The sun, at mid-day, would shine through her; in the first gray of the twilight, she lost all the distinctness of her outline; and, if you followed the dim thing into a dark corner, behold! she was not there. And it was true, that Priscilla had strange ways; strange ways, and stranger words, when she uttered any words at all. Never stirring out of the old Governor's dusky house, she sometimes talked of distant places and splendid rooms, as if she had just left them. Hidden things were visible to her, (at least, so the people inferred from obscure hints, escaping unawares out of her mouth,) and silence was audible. And, in all the world, there was nothing so difficult to be endured, by those who had any dark secret to conceal, as the glance of Priscilla's timid and melancholy eyes.

Her peculiarities were the theme of continual gossip among the other inhabitants of the gubernatorial mansion. The rumor spread thence into a wider circle. Those who knew old Moodie—as he was now called—used often to jeer him, at the very street-corners, about his daughter's gift of second-sight and prophecy. It was a period when science (though mostly through its empirical professors) was bringing forward, anew, a hoard of facts and imperfect theories, that had partially won credence, in elder times, but which modern scepticism had swept away as rubbish. These things were now tossed up again, out of the surging ocean of human thought and experience. The story of Priscilla's preternatural manifestations, therefore, attracted a kind of notice of which it would have been deemed wholly unworthy, a few years earlier. One day, a gentleman ascended the creaking staircase, and inquired which was old Moodie's chamber-door. And, several times, he came again. He was a marvellously handsome man, still youthful, too, and fashionably dressed. Except that Priscilla, in those days, had no beauty, and, in the languor of her existence, had not yet blossomed into womanhood, there would have been rich food for scandal in these visits; for the girl was unquestionably their sole object, although her father was supposed always to be present. But, it must likewise be added, there was something about Priscilla that calumny could not meddle with; and thus far was she privileged, either by the preponderance of what was spiritual, or the thin and watery blood that left her cheek so pallid.

Yet, if the busy tongues of the neighborhood spared Priscilla, in one way, they made themselves amends by renewed and wilder babble, on another score. They averred that the strange gentleman was a wizard, and that he had taken advantage of Priscilla's lack of earthly substance to subject her to himself, as his familiar spirit, through whose medium he gained cognizance of whatever happened, in regions near or remote. The boundaries of his power were defined by the verge of the pit of Tartarus, on the one hand, and the third sphere of the celestial world, on the other.[5] Again, they declared their suspicion that the wizard, with all his show of manly beauty, was really an aged and wizened figure, or else that his semblance of a human body was only a necromantic, or perhaps a mechanical contrivance, in which a demon walked about. In proof of it, however, they could merely instance a gold band around his upper teeth, which had once been visible to several old women, when he smiled at them from the top of the Governor's staircase. Of course, this was all absurdity, or mostly so. But, after every possible deduction, there remained certain very mysterious points about the stranger's character, as well as the connection that he established with Priscilla. Its nature, at that period, was even less understood than now, when miracles of this kind have grown so absolutely stale, that I would gladly, if the truth allowed, dismiss the whole matter from my narrative.

We must now glance backward, in quest of the beautiful daughter of Fauntleroy's prosperity. What had become of her? Fauntleroy's only brother, a bachelor, and with no other relative so near, had adopted the forsaken child. She grew up in affluence, with native graces clustering luxuriantly about her. In her triumphant progress towards womanhood, she was adorned with every variety of feminine accomplishment. But she lacked a mother's care. With no adequate control, on any hand, (for a man, however stern, however wise, can never sway and guide a female child,) her character was left to shape itself. There was good in it, and evil. Passionate, self-willed, and imperious, she had a warm and generous nature; showing the richness of the soil, however, chiefly by the weeds that flourished in it, and choked up the herbs of grace. In her girlhood, her uncle died. As Fauntleroy was supposed to be likewise dead, and no other heir was known to exist, his wealth devolved on her, although, dying suddenly, the uncle left no will. After his death,

---

5. That is, from Tartarus, the infernal abyss below Hades, all the way up to the sphere of Venus, far above the earth. (In the Ptolemaic system, the earth is at the center of the universe, with the sun, moon, the planets, and the stars located in concentric spheres radiating out from it.)

there were obscure passages in Zenobia's history. There were whispers of an attachment, and even a secret marriage, with a fascinating and accomplished, but unprincipled young man. The incidents and appearances, however, which led to this surmise, soon passed away and were forgotten.

Nor was her reputation seriously affected by the report. In fact, so great was her native power and influence, and such seemed the careless purity of her nature, that whatever Zenobia did was generally acknowledged as right for her to do. The world never criticised her so harshly as it does most women who transcend its rules. It almost yielded its assent, when it beheld her stepping out of the common path, and asserting the more extensive privileges of her sex, both theoretically and by her practice. The sphere of ordinary womanhood was felt to be narrower than her development required.

A portion of Zenobia's more recent life is told in the foregoing pages. Partly in earnest—and, I imagine, as was her disposition, half in a proud jest, or in a kind of recklessness that had grown upon her, out of some hidden grief—she had given her countenance, and promised liberal pecuniary aid, to our experiment of a better social state. And Priscilla followed her to Blithedale. The sole bliss of her life had been a dream of this beautiful sister, who had never so much as known of her existence. By this time, too, the poor girl was enthralled in an intolerable bondage, from which she must either free herself or perish. She deemed herself safest near Zenobia, into whose large heart she hoped to nestle.

One evening, months after Priscilla's departure, when Moodie (or shall we call him Fauntleroy?) was sitting alone in the state-chamber of the old Governor, there came footsteps up the staircase. There was a pause on the landing-place. A lady's musical, yet haughty accents were heard making an inquiry from some denizen of the house, who had thrust a head out of a contiguous chamber. There was then a knock at Moodie's door.

"Come in!" said he.

And Zenobia entered. The details of the interview that followed, being unknown to me—while, notwithstanding, it would be a pity quite to lose the picturesqueness of the situation—I shall attempt to sketch it, mainly from fancy, although with some general grounds of surmise in regard to the old man's feelings.

She gazed, wonderingly, at the dismal chamber. Dismal to her, who beheld it only for an instant, and how much more so to him, into whose brain each bare spot on the ceiling, every tatter of the paper-hangings, and all the splintered carvings of the mantel-piece, seen wearily through long years, had worn their several prints! Inexpressibly miserable is this familiarity with objects that have been, from the first, disgustful.

"I have received a strange message," said Zenobia, after a moment's silence, "requesting, or rather enjoining it upon me, to come hither. Rather from curiosity than any other motive—and because, though a woman, I have not all the timidity of one—I have complied. Can it be you, sir, who thus summoned me?"

"It was," answered Moodie.

"And what was your purpose?" she continued. "You require charity, perhaps? In that case, the message might have been more fitly worded. But you are old and poor; and age and poverty should be allowed their privileges. Tell me, therefore, to what extent you need my aid."

"Put up your purse," said the supposed mendicant, with an inexplicable smile. "Keep it—keep all your wealth—until I demand it all, or none! My message had no such end in view. You are beautiful, they tell me; and I desired to look at you!"

He took the one lamp that showed the discomfort and sordidness of his abode, and approaching Zenobia, held it up, so as to gain the more perfect view of her, from top to toe. So obscure was the chamber, that you could see the reflection of her diamonds thrown upon the dingy wall, and flickering with the rise and fall of Zenobia's breath. It was the splendor of those jewels on her neck, like lamps that burn before some fair temple, and the jewelled flower in her hair, more than the murky yellow light, that helped him to see her beauty. But he beheld it, and grew proud at heart; his own figure, in spite of his mean habiliments, assumed an air of state and grandeur.

"It is well!" cried old Moodie. "Keep your wealth. You are right worthy of it. Keep it, therefore, but with one condition, only!"

Zenobia thought the old man beside himself, and was moved with pity.

"Have you none to care for you?" asked she. "No daughter?—no kind-hearted neighbor?—no means of procuring the attendance which you need? Tell me, once again, can I do nothing for you?"

"Nothing," he replied. "I have beheld what I wished. Now, leave me! Linger not a moment longer; or I may be tempted to say what would bring a cloud over that queenly brow. Keep all your wealth, but with only this one condition. Be kind—be no less kind than sisters are—to my poor Priscilla!"

And, it may be, after Zenobia withdrew, Fauntleroy paced his gloomy chamber, and communed with himself, as follows:—or, at all events, it is the only solution, which I can offer, of the enigma presented in his character.

"I am unchanged—the same man as of yore!" said he. "True; my brother's wealth, he dying intestate, is legally my own. I know it; yet, of my own choice, I live a beggar, and go meanly clad, and hide myself behind a forgotten ignominy. Looks this like ostentation? Ah, but, in Zenobia, I live again! Beholding her so beautiful—so fit to be adorned with all imaginable splendor of outward state—the cursed vanity, which, half-a-lifetime since, dropt off like tatters of once gaudy apparel from my debased and ruined person, is all renewed for her sake! Were I to re-appear, my shame would go with me from darkness into daylight. Zenobia has the splendor, and not the shame. Let the world admire her, and be dazzled by her, the brilliant child of my prosperity! It is Fauntleroy that still shines through her!"

But, then, perhaps, another thought occurred to him.

"My poor Priscilla! And am I just, to her, in surrendering all to this beautiful Zenobia? Priscilla! I love her best—I love her only!—but with shame, not pride. So dim, so pallid, so shrinking—the daughter of my long calamity! Wealth were but a mockery in Priscilla's hands. What is its use, except to fling a golden radiance around those who grasp it? Yet, let Zenobia take heed! Priscilla shall have no wrong!"

But, while the man of show thus meditated—that very evening, so far as I can adjust the dates of these strange incidents—Priscilla— poor, pallid flower!—was either snatched from Zenobia's hand, or flung wilfully away!

XXIII. A Village-Hall

Well! I betook myself away, and wandered up and down, like an exorcised spirit that had been driven from its old haunts, after a mighty struggle. It takes down the solitary pride of man, beyond most other things, to find the impracticability of flinging aside affections that have grown irksome. The bands, that were silken once, are apt to become iron fetters, when we desire to shake them off. Our souls, after all, are not our own. We convey a property in them to those with whom we associate, but to what extent can never be known, until we feel the tug, the agony, of our abortive effort to resume an exclusive sway over ourselves. Thus, in all the weeks of my absence, my thoughts continually reverted back, brooding over the by-gone months, and bringing up incidents that seemed hardly to have left a trace of themselves, in their passage. I spent painful hours in recall-ing these trifles, and rendering them more misty and unsubstantial than at first, by the quantity of speculative musing, thus kneaded in with them. Hollingsworth, Zenobia, Priscilla! These three had absorbed my life into themselves. Together with an inexpressible longing to know their fortunes, there was likewise a morbid resent-ment of my own pain, and a stubborn reluctance to come again within their sphere.

All that I learned of them, therefore, was comprised in a few brief and pungent squibs,[1] such as the newspapers were then in the habit of bestowing on our socialist enterprise. There was one paragraph which, if I rightly guessed its purport, bore reference to Zenobia, but was too darkly hinted to convey even thus much of certainty. Hollingsworth, too, with his philanthropic project, afforded the penny-a-liners[2] a theme for some savage and bloody-minded jokes; and, considerably to my surprise, they affected me with as much indignation as if we had still been friends.

Thus passed several weeks; time long enough for my brown and toil-hardened hands to re-accustom themselves to gloves. Old habits, such as were merely external, returned upon me with wonderful promptitude. My superficial talk, too, assumed altogether a worldly tone. Meeting former acquaintances, who showed themselves inclined to ridicule my heroic devotion to the cause of human welfare, I spoke of the recent phase of my life as indeed fair matter for a jest. But I also gave them to understand that it was, at most, only an experiment, on which I had staked no valuable amount of hope or fear; it had enabled me to pass the summer in a novel and agreeable way, had afforded me some grotesque specimens of artificial simplicity, and could not, therefore, so far as I was concerned, be reckoned a failure. In no one instance, however, did I voluntarily speak of my three friends. They dwelt in a profounder region. The more I consider myself, as I then was, the more do I recognize how deeply my connection with those three had affected all my being.

As it was already the epoch of annihilated space,[3] I might, in the time I was away from Blithedale, have snatched a glimpse at England, and been back again. But my wanderings were confined within a very limited sphere. I hopped and fluttered, like a bird with a string about its leg, gyrating round a small circumference, and keeping up a restless activity to no purpose. Thus, it was still in our familiar Massachusetts—in one of its white country-villages—that I must next particularize an incident.

The scene was one of those Lyceum-halls,[4] of which almost every village has now its own, dedicated to that sober and pallid, or, rather, drab-colored, mode of winter-evening entertainment, the Lecture. Of late years, this has come strangely into vogue, when the natural tendency of things would seem to be, to substitute lettered for oral

1. Short compositions of a witty or satirical cast.
2. Hack writers, paid by the line.
3. Steam power had significantly shortened the time required to cross the Atlantic; the Hawthornes' 1853 voyage from Boston to Liverpool, for example, took eleven days.
4. Buildings set aside for the delivery of popular lectures on literary, cultural, or scientific topics; Emerson had great success as a lyceum lecturer.

methods of addressing the public. But, in halls like this, besides the winter course of lectures, there is a rich and varied series of other exhibitions. Hither comes the ventriloquist, with all his mysterious tongues; the thaumaturgist, too, with his miraculous transformations of plates, doves, and rings, his pancakes smoking in your hat, and his cellar of choice liquors, represented in one small bottle. Here, also, the itinerant professor instructs separate classes of ladies and gentlemen in physiology, and demonstrates his lessons by the aid of real skeletons, and mannikins in wax, from Paris. Here is to be heard the choir of Ethiopian melodists, and to be seen, the diorama of Moscow or Bunker Hill, or the moving panorama of the Chinese wall. Here is displayed the museum of wax figures, illustrating the wide catholicism of earthly renown by mixing up heroes and statesmen, the Pope and the Mormon Prophet, kings, queens, murderers, and beautiful ladies; every sort of person, in short, except authors, of whom I never beheld even the most famous, done in wax. And here, in this many-purposed hall, (unless the selectmen of the village chance to have more than their share of the puritanism, which, however diversified with later patchwork, still gives its prevailing tint to New England character,) here the company of strolling players sets up its little stage, and claims patronage for the legitimate drama.[5]

But, on the autumnal evening which I speak of, a number of printed handbills—stuck up in the bar-room and on the sign-post of the hotel, and on the meeting-house porch, and distributed largely through the village—had promised the inhabitants an interview with that celebrated and hitherto inexplicable phenomenon, the Veiled Lady!

The hall was fitted up with an amphitheatrical descent of seats towards a platform, on which stood a desk, two lights, a stool, and a capacious, antique chair. The audience was of a generally decent and respectable character; old farmers, in their Sunday black coats, with shrewd, hard, sun-dried faces, and a cynical humor, oftener than any other expression, in their eyes; pretty girls, in many-colored attire; pretty young men—the schoolmaster, the lawyer, or student-at-law, the shopkeeper—all looking rather suburban than rural. In these days, there is absolutely no rusticity, except when the actual labor of the soil leaves its earth-mould on the person. There was likewise a considerable proportion of young and middle-aged women, many of

---

5. This paragraph describes an array of the new forms of entertainment that were emerging in nineteenth-century America. A "thaumaturgist" is a magician; "Ethiopian melodists" were minstrels, white performers in black-face make-up who performed songs, skits, and dances imitating or imagining African American cultural forms; panoramas and dioramas offered elaborate depictions of scenes from history or faraway places. Joseph Smith (1805–1844), the visionary founder of the Church of Jesus Christ of the Latter-Day Saints, is the wax museum's "Mormon Prophet."

them stern in feature, with marked foreheads, and a very definite line of eyebrow; a type of womanhood in which a bold intellectual development seems to be keeping pace with the progressive delicacy of the physical constitution. Of all these people I took note, at first, according to my custom. But I ceased to do so, the moment that my eyes fell on an individual who sat two or three seats below me, immoveable, apparently deep in thought, with his back, of course, towards me, and his face turned steadfastly upon the platform.

After sitting awhile, in contemplation of this person's familiar contour, I was irresistibly moved to step over the intervening benches, lay my hand on his shoulder, put my mouth close to his ear, and address him in a sepulchral, melodramatic whisper:—

"Hollingsworth! Where have you left Zenobia!"

His nerves, however, were proof against my attack. He turned half around, and looked me in the face, with great, sad eyes, in which there was neither kindness nor resentment, nor any perceptible surprise.

"Zenobia, when I last saw her," he answered, "was at Blithedale."

He said no more. But there was a great deal of talk going on, near me, among a knot of people who might be considered as representing the mysticism, or, rather, the mystic sensuality, of this singular age. The nature of the exhibition, that was about to take place, had probably given the turn to their conversation.

I heard, from a pale man in blue spectacles, some stranger stories than ever were written in a romance; told, too, with a simple, unimaginative steadfastness, which was terribly efficacious in compelling the auditor to receive them into the category of established facts. He cited instances of the miraculous power of one human being over the will and passions of another; insomuch that settled grief was but a shadow, beneath the influence of a man possessing this potency, and the strong love of years melted away like a vapor. At the bidding of one of these wizards, the maiden, with her lover's kiss still burning on her lips, would turn from him with icy indifference; the newly made widow would dig up her buried heart out of her young husband's grave, before the sods had taken root upon it; a mother, with her babe's milk in her bosom, would thrust away her child. Human character was but soft wax in his hands; and guilt, or virtue, only the forms into which he should see fit to mould it. The religious sentiment was a flame which he could blow up with his breath, or a spark that he could utterly extinguish. It is unutterable, the horror and disgust with which I listened, and saw, that, if these things were to be believed, the individual soul was virtually annihilated, and all that is sweet and pure, in our present life, debased, and that the idea of man's eternal responsibility was made ridiculous, and immortality rendered, at once, impossible, and not worth acceptance. But I would have perished on the spot, sooner than believe it.

The epoch of rapping spirits,[6] and all the wonders that have followed in their train—such as tables, upset by invisible agencies, bells, self-tolled at funerals, and ghostly music, performed on jew-sharps—had not yet arrived. Alas, my countrymen, methinks we have fallen on an evil age! If these phenomena have not humbug at the bottom, so much the worse for us. What can they indicate, in a spiritual way, except that the soul of man is descending to a lower point than it has ever before reached, while incarnate? We are pursuing a downward course, in the eternal march, and thus bring ourselves into the same range with beings whom death, in requital of their gross and evil lives, has degraded below humanity. To hold intercourse with spirits of this order, we must stoop, and grovel in some element more vile than earthly dust. These goblins, if they exist at all, are but the shadows of past mortality, outcasts, mere refuse-stuff, adjudged unworthy of the eternal world, and, on the most favorable supposition, dwindling gradually into nothingness. The less we have to say to them, the better; lest we share their fate!

The audience now began to be impatient; they signified their desire for the entertainment to commence, by thump of sticks and stamp of boot-heels. Nor was it a great while longer, before, in response to their call, there appeared a bearded personage in Oriental robes, looking like one of the enchanters of the Arabian Nights.[7] He came upon the platform from a side-door—saluted the spectators, not with a salaam, but a bow—took his station at the desk—and first blowing his nose with a white handkerchief, prepared to speak. The environment of the homely village-hall, and the absence of many ingenious contrivances of stage-effect, with which the exhibition had heretofore been set off, seemed to bring the artifice of this character more openly upon the surface. No sooner did I behold the bearded enchanter, than laying my hand again on Hollingsworth's shoulder, I whispered in his ear:—

"Do you know him?"

"I never saw the man before," he muttered, without turning his head.

But I had seen him, three times, already. Once, on occasion of my first visit to the Veiled Lady; a second time, in the wood-path at

6. In "spirit rapping," the participants, in the presence of a medium, put questions to spirits, often their dead relatives; the spirits answer by knocking or rapping in coded patterns. The first spirit rapping took place in 1848, and such spiritual "investigations" became widely popular in the 1850s.
7. Collection of tales, translated from Arabic and derived from Persian, Indian, and Arabian folk traditions; framed by the story of Scheherazade, who tells the stories to keep her sultan-husband from putting her to death, the collection includes the tales of Ali Baba and Aladdin.

Blithedale; and, lastly, in Zenobia's drawing-room. It was Westervelt. A quick association of ideas made me shudder, from head to foot; and, again, like an evil spirit, bringing up reminiscences of a man's sins, I whispered a question in Hollingsworth's ear.

"What have you done with Priscilla?"

He gave a convulsive start, as if I had thrust a knife into him, writhed himself round on his seat, glared fiercely into my eyes, but answered not a word.

The Professor began his discourse, explanatory of the psychological phenomena, as he termed them, which it was his purpose to exhibit to the spectators. There remains no very distinct impression of it on my memory. It was eloquent, ingenious, plausible, with a delusive show of spirituality, yet really imbued throughout with a cold and dead materialism. I shivered, as at a current of chill air, issuing out of a sepulchral vault and bringing the smell of corruption along with it. He spoke of a new era that was dawning upon the world; an era that would link soul to soul, and the present life to what we call futurity, with a closeness that should finally convert both worlds into one great, mutually conscious brotherhood. He described (in a strange, philosophical guise, with terms of art, as if it were a matter of chemical discovery) the agency by which this mighty result was to be effected; nor would it have surprised me, had he pretended to hold up a portion of his universally pervasive fluid, as he affirmed it to be, in a glass phial.

At the close of his exordium, the Professor beckoned with his hand—one, twice, thrice—and a figure came gliding upon the platform, enveloped in a long veil of silvery whiteness. It fell about her, like the texture of a summer cloud, with a kind of vagueness, so that the outline of the form, beneath it, could not be accurately discerned. But the movement of the Veiled Lady was graceful, free, and unembarrassed, like that of a person accustomed to be the spectacle of thousands. Or, possibly, a blindfold prisoner within the sphere with which this dark, earthly magician had surrounded her, she was wholly unconscious of being the central object to all those straining eyes.

Pliant to his gesture, (which had even an obsequious courtesy, but, at the same time, a remarkable decisiveness,) the figure placed itself in the great chair. Sitting there, in such visible obscurity, it was perhaps as much like the actual presence of a disembodied spirit as anything that stage-trickery could devise. The hushed breathing of the spectators proved how high-wrought were their anticipations of the wonders to be performed, through the medium of this incomprehensible creature. I, too, was in breathless suspense, but with a far different presentiment of some strange event at hand.

"You see before you the Veiled Lady," said the bearded Professor, advancing to the verge of the platform. "By the agency of which I have just spoken, she is, at this moment, in communion with the spiritual world. That silvery veil is, in one sense, an enchantment, having been dipt, as it were, and essentially imbued, through the potency of my art, with the fluid medium of spirits. Slight and ethereal as it seems, the limitations of time and space have no existence within its folds. This hall—these hundreds of faces, encompassing her within so narrow an amphitheatre—are of thinner substance, in her view, than the airiest vapor that the clouds are made of. She beholds the Absolute!"

As preliminary to other, and far more wonderful psychological experiments, the exhibitor suggested that some of his auditors should endeavor to make the Veiled Lady sensible of their presence by such methods—provided, only, no touch were laid upon her person—as they might deem best adapted to that end. Accordingly, several deep-lunged country-fellows, who looked as if they might have blown the apparition away with a breath, ascended the platform. Mutually encouraging one another, they shouted so close to her ear, that the veil stirred like a wreath of vanishing mist; they smote upon the floor with bludgeons; they perpetrated so hideous a clamor, that methought it might have reached, at least a little way, into the eternal sphere. Finally, with the assent of the Professor, they laid hold of the great chair, and were startled, apparently, to find it soar upward, as if lighter than the air through which it rose. But the Veiled Lady remained seated and motionless, with a composure that was hardly less than awful, because implying so immeasurable a distance betwixt her and these rude persecutors.

"These efforts are wholly without avail," observed the Professor, who had been looking on with an aspect of serene indifference. "The roar of a battery of cannon would be inaudible to the Veiled Lady. And yet, were I to will it, sitting in this very hall, she could hear the desert-wind sweeping over the sands, as far off as Arabia; the ice-bergs grinding one against the other, in the polar seas; the rustle of a leaf in an East Indian forest; the lowest whispered breath of the bashfullest maiden in the world, uttering the first confession of her love! Nor does there exist the moral inducement, apart from my own behest, that could persuade her to lift the silvery veil, or arise out of that chair!"

Greatly to the Professor's discomposure, however, just as he spoke these words, the Veiled Lady arose. There was a mysterious tremor that shook the magic veil. The spectators, it may be, imagined that she was about to take flight into that invisible sphere, and to the society of those purely spiritual beings, with whom they reckoned her so near akin. Hollingsworth, a moment ago, had mounted the platform, and now stood gazing at the figure, with a sad intentness that brought the whole power of his great, stern, yet tender soul, into his glance.

"Come!" said he, waving his hand towards her. "You are safe!"

She threw off the veil, and stood before that multitude of people, pale, tremulous, shrinking, as if only then had she discovered that a thousand eyes were gazing at her. Poor maiden! How strangely had she been betrayed! Blazoned abroad as a wonder of the world, and performing what were adjudged as miracles—in the faith of many, a seeress and a prophetess–in the harsher judgment of others, a mountebank—she had kept, as I religiously believe, her virgin reserve and sanctity of soul, throughout it all. Within that encircling veil, though an evil hand had flung it over her, there was as deep a seclusion as if this forsaken girl had, all the while, been sitting under the shadow of Eliot's pulpit, in the Blithedale woods, at the feet of him who now summoned her to the shelter of his arms. And the true heart-throb of a woman's affection was too powerful for the jugglery that had hitherto environed her. She uttered a shriek and fled to Hollingsworth, like one escaping from her deadliest enemy, and was safe forever!

XXIV. The Masqueraders

Two nights had passed since the foregoing occurrences, when, in a breezy September forenoon, I set forth from town, on foot, towards Blithedale.

It was the most delightful of all days for a walk, with a dash of invigorating ice-temper in the air, but a coolness that soon gave place to the brisk glow of exercise, while the vigor remained as elastic as before. The atmosphere had a spirit and sparkle in it. Each breath was like a sip of ethereal wine, tempered, as I said, with a crystal lump of ice. I had started on this expedition in an exceedingly sombre mood, as well befitted one who found himself tending towards home, but was conscious that nobody would be quite overjoyed to greet him there. My feet were hardly off the pavement, however, when this morbid sensation began to yield to the lively influences of air and motion. Nor had I gone far, with fields yet green on either side, before my step became as swift and light as if Hollingsworth were waiting to exchange a friendly hand-grip, and Zenobia's and Priscilla's open arms would welcome the wanderer's re-appearance. It has happened to me, on other occasions, as well as this, to prove how a state of physical well-being can create a kind of joy, in spite of the profoundest anxiety of mind.

The pathway of that walk still runs along, with sunny freshness, through my memory. I know not why it should be so. But my mental eye can even now discern the September grass, bordering the pleasant roadside with a brighter verdure than while the summer-heats were scorching it; the trees, too, mostly green, although, here and there, a branch or shrub has donned its vesture of crimson and gold, a week or two before its fellows. I see the tufted barberry bushes, with their small clusters of scarlet fruit; the toadstools, likewise, some spotlessly white, others yellow or red—mysterious growths, springing suddenly from no root or seed, and growing nobody can tell how or wherefore. In this respect, they resembled many of the emotions in my breast. And I still see the little rivulets, chill, clear, and bright, that murmured beneath the road, through subterranean rocks, and deepened into mossy pools where tiny fish were darting to-and-fro, and within which lurked the hermit-frog. But, no—I never can account for it—that, with a yearning interest to learn the upshot of all my story, and returning to Blithedale for that sole purpose, I should examine these things so like a peaceful-bosomed naturalist. Nor why, amid all my sympathies and fears, there shot, at times, a wild exhilaration through my frame!

Thus I pursued my way, along the line of the ancient stone-wall that Paul Dudley[1] built, and through white villages, and past orchards of ruddy apples, and fields of ripening maize, and patches of woodland, and all such sweet rural scenery as looks the fairest, a little beyond the suburbs of a town. Hollingsworth, Zenobia, Priscilla! They glided mistily before me, as I walked. Sometimes, in my solitude, I laughed with the bitterness of self-scorn, remembering how unreservedly I had given up my heart and soul to interests that were not mine. What had I ever had to do with them? And why, being now free, should I take this thraldom on me, once again? It was both sad and dangerous, I whispered to myself, to be in too close affinity with the passions, the errors, and the misfortunes, of individuals who stood within a circle of their own, into which, if I stept at all, it must be as an intruder, and at a peril that I could not estimate.

Drawing nearer to Blithedale, a sickness of the spirits kept alternating with my flights of causeless buoyancy. I indulged in a hundred odd and extravagant conjectures. Either there was no such place as Blithedale, nor ever had been, nor any brotherhood of thoughtful laborers, like what I seemed to recollect there; or else it was all changed, during my absence. It had been nothing but dream-work and enchantment. I should seek in vain for the old farm-house, and for the greensward, the potatoe-fields, the root-crops, and acres of Indian corn, and for all that configuration of the land which I had imagined. It would be another spot, and an utter strangeness.

---

1. Paul Dudley (1675–1751), an important figure in the legal and political life of the Massachusetts Bay Colony, retired to a large country estate in Roxbury (on the road to "Blithedale" from Boston).

These vagaries were of the spectral throng, so apt to steal out of an unquiet heart. They partly ceased to haunt me, on my arriving at a point whence, through the trees, I began to catch glimpses of the Blithedale farm. That, surely, was something real. There was hardly a square foot of all those acres, on which I had not trodden heavily in one or another kind of toil. The curse of Adam's posterity—and, curse or blessing be it, it gives substance to the life around us—had first come upon me there. In the sweat of my brow, I had there earned bread and eaten it, and so established my claim to be on earth, and my fellowship with all the sons of labor. I could have knelt down, and have laid my breast against that soil. The red clay, of which my frame was moulded, seemed nearer akin to those crumbling furrows than to any other portion of the world's dust. There was my home; and there might be my grave.

I felt an invincible reluctance, nevertheless, at the idea of presenting myself before my old associates, without first ascertaining the state in which they were. A nameless foreboding weighed upon me. Perhaps, should I know all the circumstances that had occurred, I might find it my wisest course to turn back, unrecognized, unseen, and never look at Blithedale more. Had it been evening, I would have stolen softly to some lighted window of the old farm-house, and peeped darkling in, to see all their well-known faces round the supper-board. Then, were there a vacant seat, I might noiselessly unclose the door, glide in, and take my place among them, without a word. My entrance might be so quiet, my aspect so familiar, that they would forget how long I had been away, and suffer me to melt into the scene, as a wreath of vapor melts into a larger cloud. I dreaded a boisterous greeting. Beholding me at table, Zenobia, as a matter of course, would send me a cup of tea, and Hollingsworth fill my plate from the great dish of pan-dowdy,[2] and Priscilla, in her quiet way, would hand the cream, and others help me to the bread and butter. Being one of them again, the knowledge of what had happened would come to me, without a shock. For, still, at every turn of my shifting fantasies, the thought stared me in the face, that some evil thing had befallen us, or was ready to befall.

Yielding to this ominous impression, I now turned aside into the woods, resolving to spy out the posture of the Community, as craftily as the wild Indian before he makes his onset. I would go wandering about the outskirts of the farm, and, perhaps catching sight of a solitary acquaintance, would approach him amid the brown shadows of the trees, (a kind of medium fit for spirits departed and revisitant, like myself,) and entreat him to tell me how all things were.

2. Deep-dish apple pie or pudding.

The first living creature that I met, was a partridge, which sprung up beneath my feet, and whirred away; the next was a squirrel, who chattered angrily at me, from an overhanging bough. I trod along by the dark, sluggish river, and remember pausing on the bank, above one of its blackest and most placid pools—(the very spot, with the barkless stump of a tree aslantwise over the water, is depicting itself to my fancy, at this instant)—and wondering how deep it was, and if any over-laden soul had ever flung its weight of mortality in thither, and if it thus escaped the burthen, or only made it heavier. And per-haps the skeleton of the drowned wretch still lay beneath the inscrutable depth, clinging to some sunken log at the bottom with the gripe of its old despair. So slight, however, was the track of these gloomy ideas, that I soon forgot them in the contemplation of a brood of wild ducks, which were floating on the river, and anon took flight, leaving each a bright streak over the black surface. By-and-by, I came to my hermitage, in the heart of the white-pine tree, and clambering up into it, sat down to rest. The grapes, which I had watched throughout the summer, now dangled around me in abun-dant clusters of the deepest purple, deliciously sweet to the taste, and though wild, yet free from that un-gentle flavor which distin-guishes nearly all our native and uncultivated grapes. Methought a wine might be pressed out of them, possessing a passionate zest, and endowed with a new kind of intoxicating quality, attended with such bacchanalian ecstasies as the tamer grapes of Madeira, France, and the Rhine, are inadequate to produce. And I longed to quaff a great goblet of it, at that moment!

While devouring the grapes, I looked on all sides out of the peep-holes of my hermitage, and saw the farm-house, the fields, and almost every part of our domain, but not a single human figure in the landscape. Some of the windows of the house were open, but with no more signs of life than in a dead man's unshut eyes. The barn-door was ajar, and swinging in the breeze. The big, old dog—he was a relic of the former dynasty of the farm—that hardly ever stirred out of the yard, was nowhere to be seen. What, then, had become of all the fraternity and sisterhood? Curious to ascertain this point, I let myself down out of the tree, and going to the edge of the wood, was glad to perceive our herd of cows, chewing the cud, or grazing, not far off. I fancied, by their manner, that two or three of them recognized me, (as, indeed, they ought, for I had milked them, and been their chamberlain, times without number;) but, after star-ing me in the face, a little while, they phlegmatically began grazing and chewing their cuds again. Then I grew foolishly angry at so cold a reception, and flung some rotten fragments of an old stump at these unsentimental cows.

Skirting farther round the pasture, I heard voices and much laughter proceeding from the interior of the wood. Voices, male and feminine; laughter, not only of fresh young throats, but the bass of grown people, as if solemn organ-pipes should pour out airs of merriment. Not a voice spoke, but I knew it better than my own; not a laugh, but its cadences were familiar. The wood, in this portion of it, seemed as full of jollity as if Comus and his crew[3] were holding their revels, in one of its usually lonesome glades. Stealing onward as far as I durst, without hazard of discovery, I saw a concourse of strange figures beneath the overshadowing branches; they appeared, and vanished, and came again, confusedly, with the streaks of sunlight glimmering down upon them.

Among them was an Indian chief, with blanket, feathers and war-paint, and uplifted tomahawk; and near him, looking fit to be his woodland-bride, the goddess Diana,[4] with the crescent on her head, and attended by our big, lazy dog, in lack of any fleeter hound. Drawing an arrow from her quiver, she let it fly, at a venture, and hit the very tree behind which I happened to be lurking. Another group consisted of a Bavarian broom-girl, a negro of the Jim Crow order, one or two foresters of the middle-ages, a Kentucky woodsman in his trimmed hunting-shirt and deerskin leggings, and a Shaker elder,[5] quaint, demure, broad-brimmed, and square-skirted. Shepherds of Arcadia, and allegoric figures from the Faerie Queen,[6] were oddly mixed up with these. Arm in arm, or otherwise huddled together, in strange discrepancy, stood grim Puritans, gay Cavaliers, and Revolutionary officers, with three-cornered cocked-hats, and queues longer than their swords.[7] A bright-complexioned, dark-haired, vivacious little gipsy, with a red shawl over her head, went from one group to another, telling fortunes by palmistry; and Moll Pitcher, the renowned old witch of Lynn,[8] broomstick in hand, showed herself prominently in the midst, as if announcing all these apparitions to be the offspring of her necromantic art. But Silas Foster, who leaned against a tree near by, in his customary blue

---

3. The enchanter and his riotous attendants (men and women he has given the heads of beasts) from John Milton's *Comus* (1634).
4. Roman goddess of woodland and wild nature; a protector of women, she was also associated with hunting and the moon.
5. Prominent member of an American religious sect; Shakers were known for the sobriety and skill of their daily life, their commitment to total celibacy, and the "shaking" involved in their dance-like worship. *negro of the Jim Crow order*: that is, a white person in blackface make-up, imitating one of the stock characters of the nineteenth-century minstrel show.
6. Edmund Spenser's allegorical epic poem, *The Faerie Queene* (1590, 1596).
7. During the English Revolution (1642–49), the Puritans supported Parliament while the "Cavaliers" fought for King Charles I; the "Revolutionary officers," though, are figures from the American Revolution.
8. Clairvoyant (d. 1813) who practiced in Lynn, Massachusetts; though famous throughout New England for the uncanny accuracy of her predictions, she was not in actuality the stereotypical "witch" that legend made her.

frock, and smoking a short pipe, did more to disenchant the scene, with his look of shrewd, acrid, Yankee observation, than twenty witches and necromancers could have done, in the way of rendering it weird and fantastic.

A little further off, some old-fashioned skinkers and drawers, all with portentously red noses, were spreading a banquet on the leaf-strewn earth; while a horned and long-tailed gentleman (in whom I recognized the fiendish musician, erst seen by Tam O'Shanter)[9] tuned his fiddle, and summoned the whole motley rout to a dance, before partaking of the festal cheer. So they joined hands in a circle, whirling round so swiftly, so madly, and so merrily, in time and tune with the Satanic music, that their separate incongruities were blended all together; and they became a kind of entanglement that went nigh to turn one's brain, with merely looking at it. Anon, they stopt, all of a sudden, and staring at one another's figures, set up a roar of laughter; whereat, a shower of the September leaves (which, all day long, had been hesitating whether to fall or no) were shaken off by the movement of the air, and came eddying down upon the revellers.

Then, for lack of breath, ensued a silence; at the deepest point of which, tickled by the oddity of surprising my grave associates in this masquerading trim, I could not possibly refrain from a burst of laughter, on my own separate account.

"Hush!" I heard the pretty gipsy fortuneteller say. "Who is that laughing?"

"Some profane intruder!" said the goddess Diana. "I shall send an arrow through his heart, or change him into a stag, as I did Actaeon,[1] if he peeps from behind the trees!"

"Me take his scalp!" cried the Indian chief, brandishing his toma-hawk, and cutting a great caper in the air.

"I'll root him in the earth, with a spell that I have at my tongue's end!" squeaked Moll Pitcher. "And the green moss shall grow all over him, before he gets free again!"

"The voice was Miles Coverdale's," said the fiendish fiddler, with a whisk of his tail and a toss of his horns. "My music has brought him hither. He is always ready to dance to the devil's tune!"

Thus put on the right track, they all recognized the voice at once, and set up a simultaneous shout.

"Miles! Miles! Miles Coverdale, where are you?" they cried. "Zenobia! Queen Zenobia! Here is one of your vassals lurking in the wood. Command him to approach, and pay his duty!"

---

9. In Robert Burns's poem "Tam O'Shanter" (1791), the drunken title character encounters the Devil providing the music for a dance of witches and warlocks. *skinkers and drawers*: servers of drink.
1. In classical mythology, the young hunter turned into a stag and torn apart by his own dogs after he happens upon the goddess Diana bathing.

The whole fantastic rabble forthwith streamed off in pursuit of me, so that I was like a mad poet hunted by chimaeras.[2] Having fairly the start of them, however, I succeeded in making my escape, and soon left their merriment and riot at a good distance in the rear. Its fainter tones assumed a kind of mournfulness, and were finally lost in the hush and solemnity of the wood. In my haste, I stumbled over a heap of logs and sticks that had been cut for firewood, a great while ago, by some former possessor of the soil, and piled up square, in order to be carted or sledded away to the farm-house. But, being forgotten, they had lain there, perhaps fifty years, and possibly much longer; until, by the accumulation of moss, and the leaves falling over them and decaying there, from autumn to autumn, a green mound was formed, in which the softened outline of the wood-pile was still perceptible. In the fitful mood that then swayed my mind, I found something strangely affecting in this simple circumstance. I imagined the long-dead woodman, and his long-dead wife and children, coming out of their chill graves, and essaying to make a fire with this heap of mossy fuel!

From this spot I strayed onward, quite lost in reverie, and neither knew nor cared whither I was going, until a low, soft, well-remembered voice spoke, at a little distance.

"There is Mr. Coverdale!"

"Miles Coverdale!" said another voice—and its tones were very stern—"Let him come forward, then!"

"Yes, Mr. Coverdale," cried a woman's voice—clear and melodious, but, just then, with something unnatural in its chord—"You are welcome! But you come half-an-hour too late, and have missed a scene which you would have enjoyed!"

I looked up, and found myself nigh Eliot's pulpit, at the base of which sat Hollingsworth, with Priscilla at his feet, and Zenobia standing before them.

XXV. The Three Together

Hollingsworth was in his ordinary working-dress. Priscilla wore a pretty and simple gown, with a kerchief about her neck, and a calash,[1] which she had flung back from her head, leaving it suspended by the strings. But Zenobia (whose part among the masquers, as may be supposed, was no inferior one) appeared in a costume of fanciful magnificence, with her jewelled flower as the central ornament of what resembled a leafy crown, or coronet. She

2. Unreal creatures of the imagination.
1. A hood or bonnet designed to fold forward to cover the head or backward to rest on the shoulders.

represented the Oriental princess, by whose name we were accustomed to know her. Her attitude was free and noble, yet, if a queen's, it was not that of a queen triumphant, but dethroned, on trial for her life, or perchance condemned, already. The spirit of the conflict seemed, nevertheless, to be alive in her. Her eyes were on fire; her cheeks had each a crimson spot, so exceedingly vivid, and marked with so definite an outline, that I at first doubted whether it were not artificial. In a very brief space, however, this idea was shamed by the paleness that ensued, as the blood sank suddenly away. Zenobia now looked like marble.

One always feels the fact, in an instant, when he has intruded on those who love, or those who hate, at some acme of their passion that puts them into a sphere of their own, where no other spirit can pretend to stand on equal ground with them. I was confused—affected even with a species of terror—and wished myself away. The intentness of their feelings gave them the exclusive property of the soil and atmosphere, and left me no right to be or breathe there.

"'Hollingsworth—Zenobia—I have just returned to Blithedale," said I, "and had no thought of finding you here. We shall meet again at the house. I will retire."

"This place is free to you," answered Hollingsworth.

"As free as to ourselves," added Zenobia. "This long while past, you have been following up your game, groping for human emotions in the dark corners of the heart. Had you been here a little sooner, you might have seen them dragged into the daylight. I could even wish to have my trial over again, with you standing by, to see fair-play! Do you know, Mr. Coverdale, I have been on trial for my life?"

She laughed, while speaking thus. But, in truth, as my eyes wandered from one of the group to another, I saw in Hollingsworth all that an artist could desire for the grim portrait of a Puritan magistrate, holding inquest of life and death in a case of witchcraft;[2]—in Zenobia, the sorceress herself, not aged, wrinkled, and decrepit, but fair enough to tempt Satan with a force reciprocal to his own;—and, in Priscilla, the pale victim, whose soul and body had been wasted by her spells. Had a pile of faggots[3] been heaped against the rock, this hint of impending doom would have completed the suggestive picture.

"It was too hard upon me," continued Zenobia, addressing Hollingsworth, "that judge, jury, and accuser, should all be comprehended in one man! I demur, as I think the lawyers say, to the jurisdiction. But let the learned Judge Coverdale seat himself on the top of the rock, and you and me stand at its base, side by side, pleading our cause before him! There might, at least, be two criminals, instead of one."

2. As in the Salem witch trials of 1692.
3. Bundles of twigs, sticks, or branches used for fire.

"You forced this on me," replied Hollingsworth, looking her sternly in the face. "Did I call you hither from among the masqueraders yonder? Do I assume to be your judge? No; except so far as I have an unquestionable right of judgment, in order to settle my own line of behavior towards those, with whom the events of life bring me in contact. True; I have already judged you, but not on the world's part—neither do I pretend to pass a sentence!"

"Ah, this is very good!" said Zenobia, with a smile. "What strange beings you men are, Mr. Coverdale!—is it not so? It is the simplest thing in the world, with you, to bring a woman before your secret tribunals, and judge and condemn her, unheard, and then tell her to go free without a sentence. The misfortune is, that this same secret tribunal chances to be the only judgment-seat that a true woman stands in awe of, and that any verdict short of acquittal is equivalent to a death-sentence!"

The more I looked at them, and the more I heard, the stronger grew my impression that a crisis had just come and gone. On Hollingsworth's brow, it had left a stamp like that of irrevocable doom, of which his own will was the instrument. In Zenobia's whole person, beholding her more closely, I saw a riotous agitation; the almost delirious disquietude of a great struggle, at the close of which, the vanquished one felt her strength and courage still mighty within her, and longed to renew the contest. My sensations were as if I had come upon a battle-field, before the smoke was as yet cleared away.

And what subjects had been discussed here? All, no doubt, that, for so many months past, had kept my heart and my imagination idly feverish. Zenobia's whole character and history; the true nature of her mysterious connection with Westervelt; her later purposes towards Hollingsworth, and, reciprocally, his in reference to her; and, finally, the degree in which Zenobia had been cognizant of the plot against Priscilla, and what, at last, had been the real object of that scheme. On these points, as before, I was left to my own conjectures. One thing, only, was certain. Zenobia and Hollingsworth were friends no longer. If their heart-strings were ever intertwined, the knot had been adjudged an entanglement, and was now violently broken.

But Zenobia seemed unable to rest content with the matter, in the posture which it had assumed.

"Ah! Do we part so?" exclaimed she, seeing Hollingsworth about to retire.

"And why not?" said he, with almost rude abruptness. "What is there further to be said between us?"

"Well; perhaps nothing!" answered Zenobia, looking him in the face, and smiling. "But we have come, many times before, to this gray rock, and we have talked very softly, among the whisperings of the birch-trees. They were pleasant hours! I love to make the latest of them, though not altogether so delightful, loiter away as slowly as may be. And, besides, you have put many queries to me, at this, which you design to be our last interview; and being driven, as I must acknowledge, into a corner, I have responded with reasonable frankness. But, now, with your free consent, I desire the privilege of asking a few questions in my turn."

"I have no concealments," said Hollingsworth.

"We shall see!" answered Zenobia. "I would first inquire, whether you have supposed me to be wealthy?"

"On that point," observed Hollingsworth, "I have had the opinion which the world holds."

"And I held it, likewise," said Zenobia. "Had I not, Heaven is my witness, the knowledge should have been as free to you as me. It is only three days since I knew the strange fact that threatens to make me poor; and your own acquaintance with it, I suspect, is of at least as old a date. I fancied myself affluent. You are aware, too, of the disposition which I purposed making of the larger portion of my imaginary opulence;—nay, were it all, I had not hesitated. Let me ask you further, did I ever propose or intimate any terms of compact, on which depended this—as the world would consider it—so important sacrifice?"

"You certainly spoke of none," said Hollingsworth.

"Nor meant any," she responded. "I was willing to realize your dream, freely—generously, as some might think—but, at all events, fully—and heedless though it should prove the ruin of my fortune. If, in your own thoughts, you have imposed any conditions of this expenditure, it is you that must be held responsible for whatever is sordid and unworthy in them. And, now, one other question! Do you love this girl?"

"Oh, Zenobia!" exclaimed Priscilla, shrinking back, as if longing for the rock to topple over, and hide her.

"Do you love her?" repeated Zenobia.

"Had you asked me that question, a short time since," replied Hollingsworth, after a pause, during which, it seemed to me, even the birch-trees held their whispering breath, "I should have told you—'No!' My feelings for Priscilla differed little from those of an elder brother, watching tenderly over the gentle sister whom God has given him to protect."

"And what is your answer, now?" persisted Zenobia.

"I do love her!" said Hollingsworth, uttering the words with a deep, inward breath, instead of speaking them outright. "As well declare it thus, as in any other way. I do love her!"

"Now, God be judge between us," cried Zenobia, breaking into sudden passion, "which of us two has most mortally offended Him!

At least, I am a woman—with every fault, it may be, that a woman ever had, weak, vain, unprincipled, (like most of my sex; for our virtues, when we have any, are merely impulsive and intuitive,) passionate, too, and pursuing my foolish and unattainable ends, by indirect and cunning, though absurdly chosen means, as an hereditary bond-slave must—false, moreover, to the whole circle of good, in my reckless truth to the little good I saw before me—but still a woman! A creature, whom only a little change of earthly fortune, a little kinder smile of Him who sent me hither, and one true heart to encourage and direct me, might have made all that a woman can be! But how is it with you? Are you a man? No; but a monster! A cold, heartless, self-beginning and self-ending piece of mechanism!"

"With what, then, do you charge me?" asked Hollingsworth, aghast, and greatly disturbed at this attack. "Show me one selfish end in all I ever aimed at, and you may cut it out of my bosom with a knife!"

"It is all self!" answered Zenobia, with still intenser bitterness. "Nothing else; nothing but self, self, self! The fiend, I doubt not, has made his choicest mirth of you, these seven years past, and especially in the mad summer which we have spent together. I see it now! I am awake, disenchanted, disenthralled! Self, self, self! You have embodied yourself in a project. You are a better masquerader than the witches and gipsies yonder; for your disguise is a self-deception. See whither it has brought you! First, you aimed a death-blow, and a treacherous one, at this scheme of a purer and higher life, which so many noble spirits had wrought out. Then, because Coverdale could not be quite your slave, you threw him ruthlessly away. And you took me, too, into your plan, as long as there was hope of my being available, and now fling me aside again, a broken tool! But, foremost, and blackest of your sins, you stifled down your inmost consciousness!— you did a deadly wrong to your own heart!—you were ready to sacrifice this girl, whom, if God ever visibly showed a purpose, He put into your charge, and through whom He was striving to redeem you!"

"This is a woman's view," said Hollingsworth, growing deadly pale—"a woman's, whose whole sphere of action is in the heart, and who can conceive of no higher nor wider one!"

"Be silent!" cried Zenobia, imperiously. "You know neither man nor woman! The utmost that can be said in your behalf—and because I would not be wholly despicable in my own eyes, but would fain excuse my wasted feelings, nor own it wholly a delusion, therefore I say it—is, that a great and rich heart has been ruined in your breast. Leave me, now! You have done with me, and I with you. Farewell!"

"Priscilla," said Hollingsworth, "come!"

Zenobia smiled; possibly, I did so too. Not often, in human life, has a gnawing sense of injury found a sweeter morsel of revenge, than was conveyed in the tone with which Hollingsworth spoke those two words. It was the abased and tremulous tone of a man, whose faith in himself was shaken, and who sought, at last, to lean on an affection. Yes; the strong man bowed himself, and rested on this poor Priscilla. Oh, could she have failed him, what a triumph for the lookers-on!

And, at first, I half imagined that she was about to fail him. She rose up, stood shivering, like the birch-leaves that trembled over her head, and then slowly tottered, rather than walked, towards Zenobia. Arriving at her feet, she sank down there, in the very same attitude which she had assumed on their first meeting, in the kitchen of the old farm-house. Zenobia remembered it.

"Ah, Priscilla," said she, shaking her head, "how much is changed since then! You kneel to a dethroned princess. You, the victorious one! But he is waiting for you. Say what you wish, and leave me."

"We are sisters!" gasped Priscilla.

I fancied that I understood the word and action; it meant the offering of herself, and all she had, to be at Zenobia's disposal. But the latter would not take it thus.

"True; we are sisters!" she replied; and, moved by the sweet word, she stooped down and kissed Priscilla—but not lovingly; for a sense of fatal harm, received through her, seemed to be lurking in Zenobia's heart—"We had one father! You knew it from the first; I, but a little while—else some things, that have chanced, might have been spared you. But I never wished you harm. You stood between me and an end which I desired. I wanted a clear path. No matter what I meant. It is over now. Do you forgive me?"

"Oh, Zenobia," sobbed Priscilla, "it is I that feel like the guilty one!"

"No, no, poor little thing!" said Zenobia, with a sort of contempt. "You have been my evil fate; but there never was a babe with less strength or will to do an injury. Poor child! Methinks you have but a melancholy lot before you, sitting all alone in that wide, cheerless heart, where, for aught you know—and as I, alas! believe—the fire which you have kindled may soon go out. Ah, the thought makes me shiver for you! What will you do, Priscilla, when you find no spark among the ashes?"

"Die!" she answered.

"That was well said!" responded Zenobia, with an approving smile. "There is all a woman in your little compass, my poor sister. Meanwhile, go with him, and live!"

She waved her away, with a queenly gesture, and turned her own face to the rock. I watched Priscilla, wondering what judgment she would pass, between Zenobia and Hollingsworth; how interpret his behavior, so as to reconcile it with true faith both towards her sister and herself; how compel her love for him to keep any terms whatever with her sisterly affection! But, in truth, there was no such difficulty as I imagined. Her engrossing love made it all clear. Hollingsworth could have no fault. That was the one principle at the centre of the universe. And the doubtful guilt or possible integrity of other people, appearances, self-evident facts, the testimony of her own senses— even Hollingsworth's self-accusation, had he volunteered it—would have weighed not the value of a mote of thistle-down, on the other side. So secure was she of his right, that she never thought of comparing it with another's wrong, but left the latter to itself.

Hollingsworth drew her arm within his, and soon disappeared with her among the trees. I cannot imagine how Zenobia knew when they were out of sight; she never glanced again towards them. But, retaining a proud attitude, so long as they might have thrown back a retiring look, they were no sooner departed—utterly departed—than she began slowly to sink down. It was as if a great, invisible, irresistible weight were pressing her to the earth. Settling upon her knees, she leaned her forehead against the rock, and sobbed convulsively; dry sobs, they seemed to be, such as have nothing to do with tears.

XXVI. Zenobia and Coverdale

Zenobia had entirely forgotten me. She fancied herself alone with her great grief. And had it been only a common pity that I felt for her—the pity that her proud nature would have repelled, as the one worst wrong which the world yet held in reserve—the sacredness and awfulness of the crisis might have impelled me to steal away, silently, so that not a dry leaf should rustle under my feet. I would have left her to struggle, in that solitude, with only the eye of God upon her. But, so it happened, I never once dreamed of questioning my right to be there, now, as I had questioned it, just before, when I came so suddenly upon Hollingsworth and herself, in the passion of their recent debate. It suits me not to explain what was the analogy that I saw, or imagined, between Zenobia's situation and mine; nor, I believe, will the reader detect this one secret, hidden beneath many a revelation which perhaps concerned me less. In simple truth, however, as Zenobia leaned her forehead against the rock, shaken with that tearless agony, it seemed to me that the self-same pang, with hardly mitigated torment, leaped thrilling from her heart-strings to my own. Was it wrong, therefore, if I felt myself consecrated to the priesthood, by sympathy like this, and called upon to minister to this woman's affliction, so far as mortal could?

But, indeed, what could mortal do for her? Nothing! The attempt would be a mockery and an anguish. Time, it is true, would steal away her grief, and bury it, and the best of her heart in the same grave. But Destiny itself, methought, in its kindliest mood, could do no better for Zenobia, in the way of quick relief, than to cause the impending rock to impend a little further, and fall upon her head. So I leaned against a tree, and listened to her sobs, in unbroken silence. She was half prostrate, half kneeling, with her forehead still pressed against the rock. Her sobs were the only sound; she did not groan, nor give any other utterance to her distress. It was all involuntary.

At length, she sat up, put back her hair, and stared about her with a bewildered aspect, as if not distinctly recollecting the scene through which she had passed, nor cognizant of the situation in which it left her. Her face and brow were almost purple with the rush of blood. They whitened, however, by-and-by, and, for some time, retained this deathlike hue. She put her hand to her forehead, with a gesture that made me forcibly conscious of an intense and living pain there.

Her glance, wandering wildly to-and-fro, passed over me, several times, without appearing to inform her of my presence. But, finally, a look of recognition gleamed from her eyes into mine.

"Is it you, Miles Coverdale?" said she, smiling. "Ah, I perceive what you are about! You are turning this whole affair into a ballad. Pray let me hear as many stanzas as you happen to have ready!"

"Oh, hush, Zenobia!" I answered. "Heaven knows what an ache is in my soul!"

"It is genuine tragedy, is it not?" rejoined Zenobia, with a sharp, light laugh. "And you are willing to allow, perhaps, that I have had hard measure. But it is a woman's doom, and I have deserved it like a woman; so let there be no pity, as, on my part, there shall be no complaint. It is all right now, or will shortly be so. But, Mr. Coverdale, by all means, write this ballad, and put your soul's ache into it, and turn your sympathy to good account, as other poets do, and as poets must, unless they choose to give us glittering icicles instead of lines of fire. As for the moral, it shall be distilled into the final stanza, in a drop of bitter honey."

"What shall it be, Zenobia?" I inquired, endeavoring to fall in with her mood.

"Oh, a very old one will serve the purpose," she replied. "There are no new truths, much as we have prided ourselves on finding some. A moral? Why, this:—that, in the battle-field of life, the downright stroke, that would fall only on a man's steel head-piece, is sure to light on a woman's heart, over which she wears no breastplate, and whose wisdom it is, therefore, to keep out of the conflict. Or this:— that the whole universe, her own sex and yours, and Providence, or Destiny, to boot, make common cause against the woman who swerves one hair's breadth out of the beaten track. Yes; and add, (for I may as well own it, now,) that, with that one hair's breadth, she goes all astray, and never sees the world in its true aspect, afterwards!"

"This last is too stern a moral," I observed. "Cannot we soften it a little?"

"Do it, if you like, at your own peril, not on my responsibility," she answered; then, with a sudden change of subject, she went on:—"After all, he has flung away what would have served him better than the poor, pale flower he kept. What can Priscilla do for him? Put passionate warmth into his heart, when it shall be chilled with frozen hopes? Strengthen his hands, when they are weary with much doing and no performance? No; but only tend towards him with a blind, instinctive love, and hang her little, puny weakness for a clog upon his arm! She cannot even give him such sympathy as is worth the name. For will he never, in many an hour of darkness, need that proud, intellectual sympathy which he might have had from me?—the sympathy that would flash light along his course, and guide as well as cheer him? Poor Hollingsworth! Where will he find it now?"

"Hollingsworth has a heart of ice!" said I, bitterly. "He is a wretch!"

"Do him no wrong!" interrupted Zenobia, turning haughtily upon me. "Presume not to estimate a man like Hollingsworth! It was my fault, all along, and none of his. I see it now! He never sought me. Why should he seek me? What had I to offer him? A miserable, bruised, and battered heart, spoilt long before he met me! A life, too, hopelessly entangled with a villain's! He did well to cast me off. God be praised, he did it! And yet, had he trusted me, and borne with me a little longer, I would have saved him all this trouble."

She was silent, for a time, and stood with her eyes fixed on the ground. Again raising them, her look was more mild and calm.

"Miles Coverdale!" said she.

"Well, Zenobia!" I responded. "Can I do you any service?"

"Very little," she replied. "But it is my purpose, as you may well imagine, to remove from Blithedale; and, most likely, I may not see Hollingsworth again. A woman in my position, you understand, feels scarcely at her ease among former friends. New faces—unaccustomed looks—those only can she tolerate. She would pine, among familiar scenes; she would be apt to blush, too, under the eyes that knew her secret; her heart might throb uncomfortably; she would mortify herself, I suppose, with foolish notions of having sacrificed the honor of her sex, at the foot of proud, contumacious[1] man. Poor womanhood, with its rights and wrongs! Here will be new matter for my course of lectures, at the idea of which you smiled, Mr. Coverdale, a month or two ago. But, as you have really a heart and sympathies, as far as they

1. Unyielding, headstrong.

go, and as I shall depart without seeing Hollingsworth, I must entreat you to be a messenger between him and me."

"Willingly," said I, wondering at the strange way in which her mind seemed to vibrate from the deepest earnest to mere levity. "What is the message?"

"True;—what is it?" exclaimed Zenobia. "After all, I hardly know. On better consideration, I have no message. Tell him—tell him something pretty and pathetic, that will come nicely and sweetly into your ballad—anything you please, so it be tender and submissive enough. Tell him he has murdered me! Tell him that I'll haunt him!"—she spoke these words with the wildest energy—"And give him—no, give Priscilla—this!"

Thus saying, she took the jewelled flower out of her hair; and it struck me as the act of a queen, when worsted in a combat, discrowning herself, as if she found a sort of relief in abasing all her pride.

"Bid her wear this for Zenobia's sake," she continued. "She is a pretty little creature, and will make as soft and gentle a wife as the veriest Bluebeard[2] could desire. Pity that she must fade so soon! These delicate and puny maidens always do. Ten years hence, let Hollingsworth look at my face and Priscilla's, and then choose betwixt them. Or, if he pleases, let him do it now!"

How magnificently Zenobia looked, as she said this! The effect of her beauty was even heightened by the over-consciousness and self-recognition of it, into which, I suppose, Hollingsworth's scorn had driven her. She understood the look of admiration in my face; and—Zenobia to the last—it gave her pleasure.

"It is an endless pity," said she, "that I had not bethought myself of winning your heart, Mr. Coverdale, instead of Hollingsworth's. I think I should have succeeded; and many women would have deemed you the worthier conquest of the two. You are certainly much the handsomest man. But there is a fate in these things. And beauty, in a man, has been of little account with me, since my earliest girlhood, when, for once, it turned my head. Now, farewell!"

"Zenobia, whither are you going?" I asked.

"No matter where," said she. "But I am weary of this place, and sick to death of playing at philanthropy and progress. Of all varieties of mock-life, we have surely blundered into the very emptiest mockery, in our effort to establish the one true system. I have done with it; and Blithedale must find another woman to superintend the laundry, and you, Mr. Coverdale, another nurse to make your gruel, the next time you fall ill. It was, indeed, a foolish dream! Yet it gave us

---

2. Character in a well-known fairy tale by Charles Perrault (1628–1703), who has murdered a series of wives and keeps their bodies in a secret room—where they are discovered by his current wife, whose curiosity almost costs her her life as well.

some pleasant summer days, and bright hopes, while they lasted. It can do no more; nor will it avail us to shed tears over a broken bubble. Here is my hand! Adieu!"

She gave me her hand, with the same free, whole-souled gesture as on the first afternoon of our acquaintance; and being greatly moved, I bethought me of no better method of expressing my deep sympathy than to carry it to my lips. In so doing, I perceived that this white hand—so hospitably warm when I first touched it, five months since—was now cold as a veritable piece of snow.

"How very cold!" I exclaimed, holding it between both my own, with the vain idea of warming it. "What can be the reason? It is really deathlike!"

"The extremities die first, they say," answered Zenobia, laughing. "And so you kiss this poor, despised, rejected hand! Well, my dear friend, I thank you! You have reserved your homage for the fallen. Lip of man will never touch my hand again. I intend to become a Catholic, for the sake of going into a nunnery. When you next hear of Zenobia, her face will be behind the black-veil; so look your last at it now—for all is over! Once more, farewell!"

She withdrew her hand, yet left a lingering pressure, which I felt long afterwards. So intimately connected, as I had been, with perhaps the only man in whom she was ever truly interested, Zenobia looked on me as the representative of all the past, and was conscious that, in bidding me adieu, she likewise took final leave of Hollingsworth, and of this whole epoch of her life. Never did her beauty shine out more lustrously, than in the last glimpse that I had of her. She departed, and was soon hidden among the trees.

But, whether it was the strong impression of the foregoing scene, or whatever else the cause, I was affected with a fantasy that Zenobia had not actually gone, but was still hovering about the spot, and haunting it. I seemed to feel her eyes upon me. It was as if the vivid coloring of her character had left a brilliant stain upon the air. By degrees, however, the impression grew less distinct. I flung myself upon the fallen leaves, at the base of Eliot's pulpit. The sunshine withdrew up the tree-trunks, and flickered on the topmost boughs; gray twilight made the wood obscure; the stars brightened out; the pendent boughs became wet with chill autumnal dews. But I was listless, worn-out with emotion on my own behalf, and sympathy for others, and had no heart to leave my comfortless lair, beneath the rock.

I must have fallen asleep, and had a dream, all the circumstances of which utterly vanished at the moment when they converged to some tragical catastrophe, and thus grew too powerful for the thin sphere of slumber that enveloped them. Starting from the ground, I found the risen moon shining upon the rugged face of the rock, and myself all in a tremble.

XXVII. Midnight

It could not have been far from midnight, when I came beneath Hollingsworth's window, and finding it open, flung in a tuft of grass, with earth at the roots, and heard it fall upon the floor. He was either awake, or sleeping very lightly; for scarcely a moment had gone by, before he looked out and discerned me standing in the moonlight.

"Is it you, Coverdale?" he asked. "What is the matter?"

"Come down to me, Hollingsworth!" I answered. "I am anxious to speak with you."

The strange tone of my own voice startled me, and him, probably, no less. He lost no time, and soon issued from the house-door, with his dress half-arranged.

"Again, what is the matter?" he asked, impatiently.

"Have you seen Zenobia," said I, "since you parted from her, at Eliot's pulpit?"

"No," answered Hollingsworth; "nor did I expect it."

His voice was deep, but had a tremor in it. Hardly had he spoken, when Silas Foster thrust his head, done up in a cotton handkerchief, out of another window, and took what he called—as it literally was— a squint at us.

"Well, folks, what are ye about here?" he demanded. "Aha, are you there, Miles Coverdale? You have been turning night into day, since you left us, I reckon; and so you find it quite natural to come prowl- ing about the house, at this time o' night, frightening my old woman out of her wits, and making her disturb a tired man out of his best nap. In with you, you vagabond, and to bed!"

"Dress yourself quietly, Foster," said I. "We want your assistance."

I could not, for the life of me, keep that strange tone out of my voice. Silas Foster, obtuse as were his sensibilities, seemed to feel the ghastly earnestness that was conveyed in it, as well as Hollingsworth did. He immediately withdrew his head, and I heard him yawning, muttering to his wife, and again yawning heavily, while he hurried on his clothes. Meanwhile, I showed Hollingsworth a delicate handker- chief, marked with a well-known cypher, and told where I had found it, and other circumstances which had filled me with a suspicion so terrible, that I left him, if he dared, to shape it out for himself. By the time my brief explanation was finished, we were joined by Silas Fos- ter, in his blue woollen frock.

"Well, boys," cried he, peevishly, "what is to pay now?"

"Tell him, Hollingsworth!" said I.

Hollingsworth shivered, perceptibly, and drew in a hard breath betwixt his teeth. He steadied himself, however, and looking the matter more firmly in the face than I had done, explained to Foster my suspicions and the grounds of them, with a distinctness from which, in spite of my utmost efforts, my words had swerved aside. The tough-nerved yeoman, in his comment, put a finish on the business, and brought out the hideous idea in its full terror, as if he were removing the napkin from the face of a corpse.

"And so you think she's drowned herself!" he cried.

I turned away my face.

"What on earth should the young woman do that for?" exclaimed Silas, his eyes half out of his head with mere surprise. "Why, she has more means than she can use or waste, and lacks nothing to make her comfortable, but a husband—and that's an article she could have, any day! There's some mistake about this, I tell you!"

"Come," said I, shuddering. "Let us go and ascertain the truth."

"Well, well," answered Silas Foster, "just as you say. We'll take the long pole, with the hook at the end, that serves to get the bucket out of the draw-well, when the rope is broken. With that, and a couple of long-handled hay-rakes, I'll answer for finding her, if she's anywhere to be found. Strange enough! Zenobia drown herself! No, no, I don't believe it. She had too much sense, and too much means, and enjoyed life a great deal too well."

When our few preparations were completed, we hastened, by a shorter than the customary route, through fields and pastures, and across a portion of the meadow, to the particular spot, on the river-bank, which I had paused to contemplate, in the course of my afternoon's ramble. A nameless presentiment had again drawn me thither, after leaving Eliot's pulpit. I showed my companions where I had found the handkerchief, and pointed to two or three footsteps, impressed into the clayey margin, and tending towards the water. Beneath its shallow verge, among the water-weeds, there were further traces, as yet unobliterated by the sluggish current, which was there almost at a stand-still. Silas Foster thrust his face down close to these footsteps, and picked up a shoe, that had escaped my observation, being half imbedded in the mud.

"There's a kid-shoe that never was made on a Yankee last,"[1] observed he. "I know enough of shoemaker's craft to tell that. French manufacture; and see what a high instep!—and how evenly she trod in it! There never was a woman that stept handsomer in her shoes than Zenobia did. Here," he added, addressing Hollingsworth, "would you like to keep the shoe?"

Hollingsworth started back.

"Give it to me, Foster," said I.

I dabbled it in the water, to rinse off the mud, and have kept it ever since. Not far from this spot, lay an old, leaky punt, drawn up on the oozy river-side, and generally half-full of water. It served the

---

1. A shoe made of the finest leather ("kid"), too fancy to have been manufactured in America (on a Yankee "last," a foot-shaped mold or form used for building or repairing shoes).

angler to go in quest of pickerel, or the sportsman to pick up his wild-ducks. Setting this crazy barque afloat, I seated myself in the stern, with the paddle, while Hollingsworth sat in the bows, with the hooked pole, and Silas Foster amidships, with a hay-rake.

"It puts me in mind of my young days," remarked Silas, "when I used to steal out of bed to go bobbing for horn-pouts[2] and eels. Heigh-ho!—well!—life and death together make sad work for us all. Then, I was a boy, bobbing for fish; and now I am getting to be an old fellow, and here I be, groping for a dead body! I tell you what, lads, if I thought anything had really happened to Zenobia, I should feel kind o' sorrowful."

"I wish, at least, you would hold your tongue!" muttered I.

The moon, that night, though past the full, was still large and oval, and having risen between eight and nine o'clock, now shone aslant-wise over the river, throwing the high, opposite bank, with its woods, into deep shadow, but lighting up the hither shore pretty effectually. Not a ray appeared to fall on the river itself. It lapsed imperceptibly away, a broad, black, inscrutable depth, keeping its own secrets from the eye of man, as impenetrably as mid-ocean could.

"Well, Miles Coverdale," said Foster, "you are the helmsman. How do you mean to manage this business?"

"I shall let the boat drift, broadside foremost, past that stump," I replied. "I know the bottom, having sounded it in fishing. The shore, on this side, after the first step or two, goes off very abruptly; and there is a pool, just by the stump, twelve or fifteen feet deep. The current could not have force enough to sweep any sunken object—even if partially buoyant—out of that hollow."

"Come, then," said Silas. "But I doubt whether I can touch bottom with this hay-rake, if it's as deep as you say. Mr. Hollingsworth, I think you'll be the lucky man, to-night, such luck as it is!"

We floated past the stump. Silas Foster plied his rake manfully, poking it as far as he could into the water, and immersing the whole length of his arm besides. Hollingsworth at first sat motionless, with the hooked-pole elevated in the air. But, by-and-by, with a nervous and jerky movement, he began to plunge it into the blackness that upbore us, setting his teeth, and making precisely such thrusts, methought, as if he were stabbing at a deadly enemy. I bent over the side of the boat. So obscure, however, so awfully mysterious, was that dark stream, that—and the thought made me shiver like a leaf—I might as well have tried to look into the enigma of the eternal world, to discover what had become of Zenobia's soul, as into the river's depths, to find her body. And there, perhaps, she lay, with her face upward, while the shadow of the boat, and my own pale face peering downward, passed slowly betwixt her and the sky.

2. Catfish.

Once, twice, thrice, I paddled the boat up stream, and again suffered it to glide, with the river's slow, funeral motion, downward. Silas Foster had raked up a large mass of stuff, which, as it came towards the surface, looked somewhat like a flowing garment, but proved to be a monstrous tuft of water-weeds. Hollingsworth, with a gigantic effort, upheaved a sunken log. When once free of the bottom, it rose partly out of water—all weedy and slimy, a devilish-looking object, which the moon had not shone upon for half a hundred years—then plunged again, and sullenly returned to its old resting-place, for the remnant of the century.

"That looked ugly!" quoth Silas. "I half thought it was the Evil One on the same errand as ourselves—searching for Zenobia!"

"He shall never get her!" said I, giving the boat a strong impulse.

"That's not for you to say, my boy!" retorted the yeoman. "Pray God he never has, and never may! Slow work this, however! I should really be glad to find something. Pshaw! What a notion that is, when the only good-luck would be, to paddle, and drift and poke, and grope, hereabouts, till morning, and have our labor for our pains! For my part, I shouldn't wonder if the creature had only lost her shoe in the mud, and saved her soul alive, after all. My stars, how she will laugh at us, tomorrow morning!"

It is indescribable what an image of Zenobia—at the breakfast-table, full of warm and mirthful life—this surmise of Silas Foster's brought before my mind. The terrible phantasm of her death was thrown by it into the remotest and dimmest back-ground, where it seemed to grow as improbable as a myth.

"Yes, Silas; it may be as you say!" cried I.

The drift of the stream had again borne us a little below the stump, when I felt—yes, felt, for it was as if the iron hook had smote my breast—felt Hollingsworth's pole strike some object at the bottom of the river. He started up, and almost overset the boat.

"Hold on!" cried Foster. "You have her!"

Putting a fury of strength into the effort, Hollingsworth heaved amain, and up came a white swash to the surface of the river. It was the flow of a woman's garments. A little higher, and we saw her dark hair, streaming down the current. Black River of Death, thou hadst yielded up thy victim! Zenobia was found!

Silas Foster laid hold of the body—Hollingsworth, likewise, grappled with it—and I steered towards the bank, gazing, all the while, at Zenobia, whose limbs were swaying in the current, close at the boat's side. Arriving near the shore, we all three stept into the water, bore her out, and laid her on the ground, beneath a tree.

"Poor child!" said Foster—and his dry old heart, I verily believe, vouchsafed a tear—"I'm sorry for her!"

Were I to describe the perfect horror of the spectacle, the reader might justly reckon it to me for a sin and shame. For more than twelve long years I have borne it in my memory, and could now reproduce it as freshly as if it were still before my eyes. Of all modes of death, methinks it is the ugliest. Her wet garments swathed limbs of terrible inflexibility. She was the marble image of a death-agony. Her arms had grown rigid in the act of struggling, and were bent before her, with clenched hands; her knees, too, were bent, and— thank God for it!—in the attitude of prayer. Ah, that rigidity! It is impossible to bear the terror of it. It seemed—I must needs impart so much of my own miserable idea—it seemed as if her body must keep the same position in the coffin, and that her skeleton would keep it in the grave, and that when Zenobia rose, at the Day of Judg- ment, it would be in just the same attitude as now!

One hope I had; and that, too, was mingled half with fear. She knelt, as if in prayer. With the last, choking consciousness, her soul, bubbling out through her lips, it may be, had given itself up to the Father, reconciled and penitent. But her arms! They were bent before her, as if she struggled against Providence in never-ending hostility. Her hands! They were clenched in immitigable defiance. Away with the hideous thought! The flitting moment, after Zenobia sank into the dark pool—when her breath was gone, and her soul at her lips—was as long, in its capacity of God's infinite forgiveness, as the lifetime of the world.

Foster bent over the body, and carefully examined it.

"You have wounded the poor thing's breast," said he to Hollingsworth. "Close by her heart, too!"

"Ha!" cried Hollingsworth, with a start.

And so he had, indeed, both before and after death.

"See!" said Foster. "That's the place where the iron struck her. It looks cruelly, but she never felt it!"

He endeavored to arrange the arms of the corpse decently by its side. His utmost strength, however, scarcely sufficed to bring them down; and rising again, the next instant, they bade him defiance, exactly as before. He made another effort, with the same result.

"In God's name, Silas Foster," cried I, with bitter indignation, "let that dead woman alone!"

"Why, man, it's not decent!" answered he, staring at me in amaze- ment. "I can't bear to see her looking so! Well, well," added he, after a third effort, "'tis of no use, sure enough; and we must leave the women to do their best with her, after we get to the house. The sooner that's done, the better."

We took two rails from a neighboring fence, and formed a bier by laying across some boards from the bottom of the boat. And thus we bore Zenobia homeward. Six hours before, how beautiful! At midnight, what a horror! A reflection occurs to me, that will show ludicrously, I doubt not, on my page, but must come in, for its sterling truth. Being the woman that she was, could Zenobia have foreseen all these ugly circumstances of death, how ill it would become her, the altogether unseemly aspect which she must put on, and, especially, old Silas Foster's efforts to improve the matter, she would no more have committed the dreadful act, than have exhibited herself to a public assembly in a badly-fitting garment! Zenobia, I have often thought, was not quite simple in her death. She had seen pictures, I suppose, of drowned persons, in lithe and graceful attitudes. And she deemed it well and decorous to die as so many village-maidens have, wronged in their first-love, and seeking peace in the bosom of the old, familiar stream—so familiar that they could not dread it— where, in childhood, they used to bathe their little feet, wading midleg deep, unmindful of wet skirts. But, in Zenobia's case, there was some tint of the Arcadian affectation that had been visible enough in all our lives, for a few months past.

This, however, to my conception, takes nothing from the tragedy. For, has not the world come to an awfully sophisticated pass, when, after a certain degree of acquaintance with it, we cannot even put ourselves to death in whole-hearted simplicity?

Slowly, slowly, with many a dreary pause—resting the bier often on some rock, or balancing it across a mossy log, to take fresh hold—we bore our burthen onward, through the moonlight, and, at last, laid Zenobia on the floor of the old farm-house. By-and-by, came three or four withered women, and stood whispering around the corpse, peering at it through their spectacles, holding up their skinny hands, shaking their night-capt heads, and taking counsel of one another's experience what was to be done.

With those tire-women,[3] we left Zenobia!

XXVIII. Blithedale-Pasture

Blithedale, thus far in its progress, had never found the necessity of a burial-ground. There was some consultation among us, in what spot Zenobia might most fitly be laid. It was my own wish, that she should sleep at the base of Eliot's pulpit, and that, on the rugged front of the rock, the name by which we familiarly knew her—ZENOBIA—and not another word, should be deeply cut, and left for the moss and lichens to fill up, at their long leisure. But Hollingsworth (to whose ideas, on

---

3. Literally, a lady's dressing assistants (from "attire"); in this context, women preparing and dressing the body for burial.

this point, great deference was due) made it his request that her grave might be dug on the gently sloping hill-side, in the wide pasture, where, as we once supposed, Zenobia and he had planned to build their cottage. And thus it was done, accordingly.

She was buried very much as other people have been, for hundreds of years gone by. In anticipation of a death, we Blithedale colonists had sometimes set our fancies at work to arrange a funereal ceremony, which should be the proper symbolic expression of our spiritual faith and eternal hopes; and this we meant to substitute for those customary rites, which were moulded originally out of the Gothic gloom, and, by long use, like an old velvet-pall, have so much more than their first death-smell in them. But, when the occasion came, we found it the simplest and truest thing, after all, to content ourselves with the old fashion, taking away what we could, but interpolating no novelties, and particularly avoiding all frippery of flowers and cheerful emblems. The procession moved from the farm-house. Nearest the dead walked an old man in deep mourning, his face mostly concealed in a white handkerchief, and with Priscilla leaning on his arm. Hollingsworth and myself came next. We all stood around the narrow niche in the cold earth; all saw the coffin lowered in; all heard the rattle of the crumbly soil upon its lid—that final sound, which mortality awakens on the utmost verge of sense, as if in the vain hope of bringing an echo from the spiritual world.

I noticed a stranger—a stranger to most of those present, though known to me—who, after the coffin had descended, took up a handful of earth, and flung it first into the grave. I had given up Hollingsworth's arm, and now found myself near this man.

"It was an idle thing—a foolish thing—for Zenobia to do!" said he. "She was the last woman in the world to whom death could have been necessary. It was too absurd! I have no patience with her."

"Why so?" I inquired, smothering my horror at his cold comment in my eager curiosity to discover some tangible truth, as to his relation with Zenobia. "If any crisis could justify the sad wrong she offered to herself, it was surely that in which she stood. Everything had failed her—prosperity, in the world's sense, for her opulence was gone—the heart's prosperity, in love. And there was a secret burthen on her, the nature of which is best known to you. Young as she was, she had tried life fully, had no more to hope, and something, perhaps, to fear. Had Providence taken her away in its own holy hand, I should have thought it the kindest dispensation that could be awarded to one so wrecked."

"You mistake the matter completely," rejoined Westervelt.

"What, then, is your own view of it?" I asked.

"Her mind was active, and various in its powers," said he; "her heart had a manifold adaptation; her constitution an infinite buoyancy, which (had she possessed only a little patience to await the reflux of her troubles) would have borne her upward, triumphantly, for twenty years to come. Her beauty would not have waned—or scarcely so, and surely not beyond the reach of art to restore it—in all that time. She had life's summer all before her, and a hundred varieties of brilliant success. What an actress Zenobia might have been! It was one of her least valuable capabilities. How forcibly she might have wrought upon the world, either directly in her own person, or by her influence upon some man, or a series of men, of controlling genius! Every prize that could be worth a woman's having—and many prizes which other women are too timid to desire—lay within Zenobia's reach."

"In all this," I observed, "there would have been nothing to satisfy her heart."

"Her heart!" answered Westervelt, contemptuously. "That troublesome organ (as she had hitherto found it) would have been kept in its due place and degree, and have had all the gratification it could fairly claim. She would soon have established a control over it. Love had failed her, you say! Had it never failed her before? Yet she survived it, and loved again—possibly, not once alone, nor twice either. And now to drown herself for yonder dreamy philanthropist!"

"Who are you," I exclaimed, indignantly, "that dare to speak thus of the dead? You seem to intend a eulogy, yet leave out whatever was noblest in her, and blacken, while you mean to praise. I have long considered you as Zenobia's evil fate. Your sentiments confirm me in the idea, but leave me still ignorant as to the mode in which you have influenced her life. The connection may have been indissoluble, except by death. Then, indeed—always in the hope of God's infinite mercy—I cannot deem it a misfortune that she sleeps in yonder grave!"

"No matter what I was to her," he answered, gloomily, yet without actual emotion. "She is now beyond my reach. Had she lived, and hearkened to my counsels, we might have served each other well. But there Zenobia lies, in yonder pit, with the dull earth over her. Twenty years of a brilliant lifetime thrown away for a mere woman's whim!"

Heaven deal with Westervelt according to his nature and deserts!—that is to say, annihilate him. He was altogether earthy, worldly, made for time and its gross objects, and incapable—except by a sort of dim reflection, caught from other minds—of so much as one spiritual idea. Whatever stain Zenobia had, was caught from him; nor does it seldom happen that a character of admirable qualities loses its better life, because the atmosphere, that should sustain it, is rendered poisonous by such breath as this man mingled with Zenobia's. Yet his reflections possessed their share of truth. It was a woful thought, that a woman of Zenobia's diversified capacity should have fancied herself irretrievably defeated on the broad battle-field of life, and with no refuge, save to fall on her own sword, merely because Love had gone against her. It is nonsense, and a miserable wrong—the result, like so many others, of masculine egotism—that the success or failure of woman's existence should be made to depend wholly on the affections, and on one species of affection; while man has such a multitude of other chances, that this seems but an incident. For its own sake, if it will do no more, the world should throw open all its avenues to the passport of a woman's bleeding heart.

As we stood around the grave, I looked often towards Priscilla, dreading to see her wholly overcome with grief. And deeply grieved, in truth, she was. But a character, so simply constituted as hers, has room only for a single predominant affection. No other feeling can touch the heart's inmost core, nor do it any deadly mischief. Thus, while we see that such a being responds to every breeze, with tremulous vibration, and imagine that she must be shattered by the first rude blast, we find her retaining her equilibrium amid shocks that might have overthrown many a sturdier frame. So with Priscilla! Her one possible misfortune was Hollingsworth's unkindness; and that was destined never to befall her—never yet, at least—for Priscilla has not died.

But, Hollingsworth! After all the evil that he did, are we to leave him thus, blest with the entire devotion of this one true heart, and with wealth at his disposal, to execute the long contemplated project that had led him so far astray? What retribution is there here? My mind being vexed with precisely this query, I made a journey, some years since, for the sole purpose of catching a last glimpse at Hollingsworth, and judging for myself whether he were a happy man or no. I learned that he inhabited a small cottage, that his way of life was exceedingly retired, and that my only chance of encountering him or Priscilla was, to meet them in a secluded lane, where, in the latter part of the afternoon, they were accustomed to walk. I did meet them, accordingly. As they approached me, I observed in Hollingsworth's face a depressed and melancholy look, that seemed habitual; the powerfully built man showed a self-distrustful weakness, and a childlike, or childish, tendency to press close, and closer still, to the side of the slender woman whose arm was within his. In Priscilla's manner, there was a protective and watchful quality, as if she felt herself the guardian of her companion, but, likewise, a deep, submissive, unquestioning reverence, and also a veiled happiness in her fair and quiet countenance.

Drawing nearer, Priscilla recognized me, and gave me a kind and friendly smile, but with a slight gesture which I could not help interpreting as an entreaty not to make myself known to Hollingsworth.

Nevertheless, an impulse took possession of me, and compelled me to address him.

"I have come, Hollingsworth," said I, "to view your grand edifice for the reformation of criminals. Is it finished yet?"

"No—nor begun!" answered he, without raising his eyes. "A very small one answers all my purposes."

Priscilla threw me an upbraiding glance. But I spoke again, with a bitter and revengeful emotion, as if flinging a poisoned arrow at Hollingsworth's heart.

"Up to this moment," I inquired, "how many criminals have you reformed?"

"Not one!" said Hollingsworth, with his eyes still fixed on the ground. "Ever since we parted, I have been busy with a single murderer!"

Then the tears gushed into my eyes, and I forgave him. For I remembered the wild energy, the passionate shriek, with which Zenobia had spoken those words—Tell him he has murdered me! Tell him that I'll haunt him!'—and I knew what murderer he meant, and whose vindictive shadow dogged the side where Priscilla was not.

The moral which presents itself to my reflections, as drawn from Hollingsworth's character and errors, is simply this:—that, admitting what is called Philanthropy, when adopted as a profession, to be often useful by its energetic impulse to society at large, it is perilous to the individual, whose ruling passion, in one exclusive channel, it thus becomes. It ruins, or is fearfully apt to ruin, the heart; the rich juices of which God never meant should be pressed violently out, and distilled into alcoholic liquor, by an unnatural process; but should render life sweet, bland, and gently beneficent, and insensibly influence other hearts and other lives to the same blessed end. I see in Hollingsworth an exemplification of the most awful truth in Bunyan's book[1] of such;—from the very gate of Heaven, there is a by-way to the pit!

But, all this while, we have been standing by Zenobia's grave. I have never since beheld it, but make no question that the grass grew all the better, on that little parallelogram of pasture-land, for the decay of the beautiful woman who slept beneath. How much Nature seems to love us! And how readily, nevertheless, without a sigh or a complaint, she converts us to a meaner purpose, when her highest one—that of conscious, intellectual life, and sensibility—has been untimely baulked! While Zenobia lived, Nature was proud of her, and directed all eyes upon that radiant presence, as her fairest handiwork. Zenobia perished. Will not Nature shed a tear? Ah, no! She

---

1. *The Pilgrim's Progress* (1678, 1684), a widely read allegory of the soul's progress toward Christian salvation by the English Puritan writer John Bunyan (1628–1688).

adopts the calamity at once into her system, and is just as well pleased, for aught we can see, with the tuft of ranker vegetation that grew out of Zenobia's heart, as with all the beauty which has bequeathed us no earthly representative, except in this crop of weeds. It is because the spirit is inestimable, that the lifeless body is so little valued.

XXIX. Miles Coverdale's Confession[1]

It remains only to say a few words about myself. Not improbably, the reader might be willing to spare me the trouble; for I have made but a poor and dim figure in my own narrative, establishing no separate interest, and suffering my colorless life to take its hue from other lives. But one still retains some little consideration for one's self; so I keep these last two or three pages for my individual and sole behoof.

But what, after all, have I to tell? Nothing, nothing, nothing! I left Blithedale within the week after Zenobia's death, and went back thither no more. The whole soil of our farm, for a long time afterwards, seemed but the sodded earth over her grave. I could not toil there, nor live upon its products. Often, however, in these years that are darkening around me, I remember our beautiful scheme of a noble and unselfish life, and how fair, in that first summer, appeared the prospect that it might endure for generations, and be perfected, as the ages rolled away, into the system of a people, and a world. Were my former associates now there—were there only three or four of those true-hearted men, still laboring in the sun—I sometimes fancy that I should direct my world-weary footsteps thitherward, and entreat them to receive me, for old friendship's sake. More and more, I feel that we had struck upon what ought to be a truth. Posterity may dig it up, and profit by it. The experiment, so far as its original projectors were concerned, proved long ago a failure, first lapsing into Fourierism, and dying, as it well deserved, for this infidelity to its own higher spirit. Where once we toiled with our whole hopeful hearts, the town-paupers, aged, nerveless, and disconsolate, creep sluggishly a-field. Alas, what faith is requisite to bear up against such results of generous effort!

My subsequent life has passed—I was going to say, happily—but, at all events, tolerably enough. I am now at middle-age—well, well, a

1. Hawthorne added this concluding chapter to the novel after April 30, 1852, when he had described the manuscript, which had then ended with the description of Zenobia's gravesite at the close of Chapter XXVIII, as finished. He sent the manuscript to Edwin P. Whipple, a trusted critic of his work, for comment, and may have added the chapter at Whipple's suggestion; whether inspired by Whipple's suggestion or by his own rethinking, this concluding chapter was added to the final, "fair-copy" manuscript before it was sent to the printer.

step or two beyond the midmost point, and I care not a fig who knows it!—a bachelor, with no very decided purpose of ever being otherwise. I have been twice to Europe, and spent a year or two, rather agreeably, at each visit. Being well to do in the world, and having nobody but myself to care for, I live very much at my ease, and fare sumptuously every day. As for poetry, I have given it up, notwithstanding that Doctor Griswold[2]—as the reader, of course, knows—has placed me at a fair elevation among our minor minstrelsy, on the strength of my pretty little volume, published ten years ago. As regards human progress, (in spite of my irrepressible yearnings over the Blithedale reminiscences,) let them believe in it who can, and aid in it who choose! If I could earnestly do either, it might be all the better for my comfort. As Hollingsworth once told me, I lack a purpose. How strange! He was ruined, morally, by an overplus of the very same ingredient, the want of which, I occasionally suspect, has rendered my own life all an emptiness. I by no means wish to die. Yet, were there any cause, in this whole chaos of human struggle, worth a sane man's dying for, and which my death would benefit, then—provided, however, the effort did not involve an unreasonable amount of trouble—methinks I might be bold to offer up my life. If Kossuth,[3] for example, would pitch the battle-field of Hungarian rights within an easy ride of my abode, and choose a mild, sunny morning, after breakfast, for the conflict, Miles Coverdale would gladly be his man, for one brave rush upon the levelled bayonets. Farther than that, I should be loth to pledge myself.

I exaggerate my own defects. The reader must not take my own word for it, nor believe me altogether changed from the young man, who once hoped strenuously, and struggled, not so much amiss. Frostier heads than mine have gained honor in the world; frostier hearts have imbibed new warmth, and been newly happy. Life, however, it must be owned, has come to rather an idle pass with me. Would my friends like to know what brought it thither? There is one secret—I have concealed it all along, and never meant to let the least whisper of it escape—one foolish little secret, which possibly may have had something to do with these inactive years of meridian manhood, with my bachelorship, with the unsatisfied retrospect that I fling back on life, and my listless glance towards the future. Shall I reveal it? It is an absurd thing for a man in his afternoon—a man of the world, moreover, with these three white hairs in his brown

---

2. Rufus Wilmot Griswold (1815–1857), a prominent journalist, editor, and anthologist, who published *The Poets and Poetry of America* in 1842.
3. Louis [Lajos] Kossuth (1802–1894), leading figure in the Hungarian revolution against Austrian rule (March, 1848); after the defeat of the Hungarian republic in 1849 and a period of imprisonment, Kossuth toured the United States in 1851–52 in an attempt to gain support for the restoration of Hungarian independence.

moustache, and that deepening track of a crow's foot on each temple—an absurd thing ever to have happened, and quite the absurdest for an old bachelor, like me, to talk about. But it rises in my throat; so let it come.

I perceive, moreover, that the confession, brief as it shall be, will throw a gleam of light over my behavior throughout the foregoing incidents, and is, indeed, essential to the full understanding of my story. The reader, therefore, since I have disclosed so much, is entitled to this one word more. As I write it, he will charitably suppose me to blush, and turn away my face:—[4]

I—I myself—was in love—with—Priscilla!

The End.

---

4. This paragraph appears in the first edition of the novel, but not in the manuscript Hawthorne had prepared for the printer; apparently he added it as he corrected the proof sheets.

CONTEXTS

The Brook Farm Community
and the Ferment of
Antebellum Social Reform

Though Hawthorne would insist that Blithedale was a fictional place, populated by invented characters, the novel grew out of his own experience at Brook Farm, a utopian community where he lived from early April to late October 1841. His time as a member of the Brook Farm community was Hawthorne's most direct encounter with the energies and ambitions of antebellum social reform—with the conviction, shared by advocates of, for instance, temperance, abolition, and prison reform, that the joint and voluntary effort of committed individuals might bring about a more humane, even perhaps a perfect social order. The founding members of the Brook Farm community sought to transform a social world distorted by the competition and inequity of an emergent market capitalism by creating an alternative economic model: all members of the community would share equally the burden of the labor necessary to sustain it and become the joint beneficiaries of the rich social, intellectual, and cultural life that such a fair distribution of work would bring about. This section permits us to listen to some of the voices of antebellum reform and to witness several responses to its claims. The convictions and ambitions that animated the Brook Farm community at its inception are expressed in a "recruitment" letter its founder George Ripley wrote to Ralph Waldo Emerson; we hear in Emerson's struggle to work out his answer both the powerful appeal of Ripley's idea and the tension between it and the intense commitment to individual freedom that was another engine of radical thought in this era. An excerpt from Hawthorne's "Hall of Fantasy" gives us his bemused but respectful take on the culture of reform, while passages from the writings of the French social theorist Charles Fourier, whose plans for a utopian community were adopted, in modified form, by the Brook Farm community late in its life, articulate a bold reconception of the nature and logistics of work. In the final selection, excerpts from a sermon given by Theodore Parker, an eminent minister and close friend of Ripley, provide a sense of what might have been Hollingsworth's arguments for the humane treatment of criminals. Apart from the skeptical Hawthorne and the Frenchman Fourier, the contributors to this section were all important figures in what their contemporaries called "the Newness"—the Boston-centered intellectual ferment (also referred to as "Transcendentalism") that encouraged exhilarating hopes for new forms of social organization and new possibilities of self-realization. Sterling Delano's *Brook Farm: The Dark Side of Utopia*, listed in this Norton Critical Edition's "Selected Bibliography," offers an excellent history of the Brook Farm community.

GEORGE RIPLEY

George Ripley (1802–1880) began his career as a Unitarian minister. He was active in Boston's intellectual life, joining Emerson and others in the Transcendental Club, writing for its associated journal, *The Dial*, and becoming well known as a spokesman for the radical strain of Unitarianism. In 1840, looking for a way to give practical expression to his criticisms of social injustice, he left the ministry and began working to establish a self-supporting agricultural and educational community that would permit its members to combine work and thought in a new way. His letter of invitation to Emerson is the fullest articulation of his hopes and ambitions for the community in its earliest phase, when Hawthorne became a member. After the financial failure of the Brook Farm community in 1847, Ripley went on to a successful career as a man of letters, reviewing books for the New York *Tribune* and collaborating on a popular encyclopedia.

Letter to Ralph Waldo Emerson, November 9, 1840[†]

MY DEAR SIR,—Our conversation in Concord was of such a general nature, that I do not feel as if you were in complete possession of the idea of the Association which I wish to see established.[1] As we have now a prospect of carrying it into effect, at an early period, I wish to submit the plan more distinctly to your judgment, that you may decide whether it is one that can have the benefit of your aid and coöperation.

Our objects, as you know, are to insure a more natural union between intellectual and manual labor than now exists; to combine the thinker and the worker, as far as possible, in the same individual; to guarantee the highest mental freedom, by providing all with labor, adapted to their tastes and talents, and securing to them the fruits of

---

† From Octavius Brooks Frothingham, *George Ripley* (Boston: Houghton, Mifflin, 1882), pp. 307–12.

1. Ripley and his wife Sophia had met with Emerson, Margaret Fuller, and Bronson Alcott—all influential figures in Transcendentalist circles—on October 18, 1840, at Emerson's Concord home to discuss their plans for the community.

their industry; to do away the necessity of menial services, by opening the benefits of education and the profits of labor to all; and thus
to prepare a society of liberal, intelligent, and cultivated persons,
whose relations with each other would permit a more simple and
wholesome life, than can be led amidst the pressure of our competitive institutions.

To accomplish these objects, we propose to take a small tract of land,
which, under skillful husbandry, uniting the garden and the farm, will
be adequate to the subsistence of the families; and to connect with this
a school or college, in which the most complete instruction shall be
given, from the first rudiments to the highest culture. Our farm would
be a place for improving the race of men that lived on it; thought would
preside over the operations of labor, and labor would contribute to the
expansion of thought; we should have industry without drudgery, and
true equality without its vulgarity.

An offer has been made to us of a beautiful estate, on very reasonable terms, on the borders of Newton, West Roxbury, and Dedham.[2]
I am very familiar with the premises, having resided on them a part of
last summer, and we might search the country in vain for anything
more eligible. Our proposal now is for three or four families to take
possession on the first of April next, to attend to the cultivation of the
farm and the erection of buildings, to prepare for the coming of as
many more in the autumn, and thus to commence the institution in
the simplest manner, and with the smallest number, with which it
can go into operation at all. It would thus be not less than two or
three years, before we should be joined by all who mean to be with
us; we should not fall to pieces by our own weight; we should grow up
slowly and strong; and the attractiveness of our experiment would
win to us all whose society we should want.

The step now to be taken at once is the procuring of funds for the
necessary capital. According to the present modification of our plan,
a much less sum will be required than that spoken of in our discussions at Concord. We thought then $50,000 would be needed; I find
now, after a careful estimate, that $30,000 will purchase the estate
and buildings for ten families, and give the required surplus for carrying on the operations for one year.

We propose to raise this sum by a subscription to a joint stock
company, among the friends of the institution, the payment of a
fixed interest being guaranteed to the subscribers, and the subscription itself secured by the real estate.[3] No man then will be in danger

---

2. The property occupied 170 acres in West Roxbury, eight miles west of the center of
   Boston; formerly a dairy farm, its sandy soil made it an unpromising site for the kind of
   cultivation Ripley had in mind.
3. Those who contributed funds to founding the community would become its joint
   owners, receiving shares of stock in return for their investment.

of losing; he will receive as fair an interest as he would from any investment, while at the same time he is contributing towards an institution, in which while the true use of money is retained, its abuses are done away. The sum required cannot come from rich capitalists; their instinct would protest against such an application of their coins; it must be obtained from those who sympathize with our ideas, and who are willing to aid their realization with their money, if not by their personal cooperation. There are some of this description on whom I think we can rely; among ourselves we can produce perhaps $10,000; the remainder must be subscribed for by those who wish us well, whether they mean to unite with us or not.

I can imagine no plan which is suited to carry into effect so many divine ideas as this. If wisely executed, it will be a light over this country and this age. If not the sunrise, it will be the morning star. As a practical man, I see clearly that we must have some such arrangement, or all changes less radical will be nugatory. I believe in the divinity of labor; I wish to "harvest my flesh and blood from the land;" but to do this, I must either be insulated and work to disadvantage, or avail myself of the services of hirelings, who are not of my order, and whom I can scarce make friends; for I must have another to drive the plough, which I hold. I cannot empty a cask of lime upon my grass alone. I wish to see a society of educated friends, working, thinking, and living together, with no strife, except that of each to contribute the most to the benefit of all.

Personally, my tastes and habits would lead me in another direction. I have a passion for being independent of the world, and of every man in it. This I could do easily on the estate which is now offered, and which I could rent at a rate, that with my other resources, would place me in a very agreeable condition, as far as my personal interests were involved. I should have a city of God, on a small scale of my own; and please God, I should hope one day to drive my own cart to market and sell greens. But I feel bound to sacrifice this private feeling, in the hope of a great social good. I shall be anxious to hear from you. Your decision will do much towards settling the question with me, whether the time has come for the fulfillment of a high hope, or whether the work belongs to a future generation. All omens now are favorable; a singular union of diverse talents is ready for the enterprise; everything indicates that we ought to arise and build; and if we let slip this occasion, the unsleeping Nemesis will deprive us of the boon we seek. For myself, I am sure that I can never give so much thought to it again; my mind must act on other objects, and I shall acquiesce in the course of fate, with grief that so fair a light is put out. A small pittance of the wealth which has been thrown away on ignoble objects, during this wild contest for political supremacy, would lay the cornerstone of a house, which would ere long become the desire of nations. * * * Pray write me with as much frankness as I have used towards you, and believe me ever your friend and faithful servant,

GEORGE RIPLEY.

P. S. I ought to add, that in the present stage of the enterprise no proposal is considered as binding. We wish only to know what can probably be relied on, provided always, that no pledge will be accepted until the articles of association are agreed on by all parties.

I recollect you said that if you were sure of compeers of the right stamp you might embark yourself in the adventure: as to this, let me suggest the inquiry, whether our Association should not be composed of various classes of men? If we have friends whom we love and who love us, I think we should be content to join with others, with whom our personal sympathy is not strong, but whose general ideas coincide with ours, and whose gifts and abilities would make their services important. For instance, I should like to have a good washerwoman in my parish admitted into the plot. She is certainly not a Minerva or a Venus; but we might educate her two children to wisdom and varied accomplishments, who otherwise will be doomed to drudge through life. The same is true of some farmers and mechanics, whom we should like with us.

RALPH WALDO EMERSON

Ralph Waldo Emerson (1803–1882) was one of America's most influential writers and thinkers. Like Ripley, he started out as a Unitarian minister in Boston; no longer able to conform even to the relatively liberal practices of his church, he left the ministry in 1832. After a trip to Europe that confirmed his affiliation to Romantic thought, with its belief in the power of the imagination and the capacity of the human soul to access truths beyond the limitations of sensory experience, Emerson began a remarkable, increasingly celebrated career as a lecturer, essayist, and explorer, on behalf of his readers and listeners, of pressing questions of meaning, morality, and freedom. He was important, too, as an intellectual mentor: his work and friendship influenced many contemporaries, among them Margaret Fuller, Henry David Thoreau, and Walt Whitman. In the journal entry and letter that follow, we witness Emerson working to articulate, as against Ripley's model of the transformative community, his conviction that the most crucial reforms are to be achieved within the heart and mind of the individual seeker.

Journal Entry, October 17, 1840[†]

Yesterday George and Sophia Ripley, Margaret Fuller and Alcott discussed here the Social Plans.[1] I wished to be convinced, to be thawed,
to be made nobly mad by the kindlings before my eye of a new dawn of
human piety. But this scheme was arithmetic and comfort: this was a
hint borrowed from the Tremont House and United States Hotel;[2] a
rage in our poverty and politics to live rich and gentlemanlike, an
anchor to leeward against a change of weather; a prudent forecast on
the probable issue of the great questions of Pauperism and Poverty.
And not once could I be inflamed, but sat aloof and thoughtless; my
voice faltered and fell. It was not the cave of persecution which is the
palace of spiritual power, but only a room in the Astor House hired for
the Transcendentalists. I do not wish to remove from my present
prison to a prison a little larger. I wish to break all prisons. I have not
yet conquered my own house. It irks and repents me. Shall I raise the
siege of this hencoop, and march baffled away to a pretended siege of
Babylon? It seems to me that so to do were to dodge the problem I am
set to solve, and to hide my impotency in the thick of a crowd. I can
see too, afar,—that I should not find myself more than now,—no, not
so much, in that select, but not by me selected, fraternity. Moreover,
to join this body would be to traverse all my long trumpeted theory,
and the instinct which spoke from it, that one man is a counterpoise
to a city,—that a man is stronger than a city, that his solitude is more
prevalent and beneficent than the concert of crowds.

Letter to George Ripley,
December 15, 1840[‡]

Concord

My dear Sir,

It is quite time I made an answer to your proposition that I should
join you in your new enterprise. The design appears to me so noble &
humane, proceeding, as I plainly see, from a manly & expanding

---

† From *The Journals of Ralph Waldo Emerson*, vol. 5, ed. E. W. Emerson (Boston:
Houghton Mifflin, 1911), pp. 473–74.
1. The plans for the Brook Farm community.
2. Boston hotels; like New York's Astor House, mentioned later in the passage, the Tremont
House was known for its luxury.
‡ From *The Letters of Ralph Waldo Emerson*, 2nd ed. Ralph L. Rusk (New York: Columbia
University Press, 1939), pp. 368–71. Reprinted, without indications of Emerson's revi-
sions, by permission of Columbia University Press.

heart & mind that it makes me & all men its friends & debtors It becomes a matter of conscience to entertain it friendly & to examine what it has for us.

I have decided not to join it & yet very slowly & I may almost say penitentially. I am greatly relieved by learning that your coadjutors are now so many that you will no longer ascribe that importance to the defection of individuals which you hinted in your letter to me. it might attach to mine.

The ground of my decision is almost purely personal to myself. I have some remains of skepticism in regard to the general practicability of the plan, but these have not much weighed with me. That which determines me is the conviction that the Community is not good for me. Whilst I see it may hold out many inducements for others it has little to offer me which with resolution I cannot procure for myself. It seems to me that it would not be worth my while to make the difficult exchange of my property in Concord for a share in the new Household. I am in many respects suitably placed. in an agreeable neighborhood, in a town which I have many reasons to love & which has respected my freedom so far that I may presume it will indulge me farther if I need it. Here I have friends & kindred. Here I have builded & planted: & here I have greater facilities to prosecute such practical enterprizes as I may cherish, than I could probably find by any removal. I cannot accuse my townsmen or my social position of my domestic grievances:—only my own sloth & conformity. It seems to me a circuitous & operose way of relieving myself of any irksome circumstances, to put on your community the task of my emancipation which I ought to take on myself.

The principal particulars in which I wish to mend my domestic life are in acquiring habits of regular manual labor, and in ameliorating or abolishing in my house the condition of hired menial service. I should like to come one step nearer to nature than this usage permits. I desire that my manner of living may be honest and agreeable to my imagination. But surely I need not sell my house & remove my family to Newton in order to make the experiment of labor & self help. I am already in the act of trying some domestic & social experiments which my present position favors. And I think that my present position has even greater advantages than yours would offer me for testing my improvements in those small private parties into which men are all set off already throughout the world.

—But I own I almost shrink from making any statement of my objections to our ways of living because I see how slowly I shall mend them. My own health & habits & those of my wife & my mother are not of that robustness which should give any pledge of enterprize & ability in reform. And whenever I am engaged in literary composition I find myself not inclined to insist with heat on new methods. Yet I think that all I shall solidly do, I must do alone. I do not think I should gain anything—I who have little skill to converse with people—by a plan of so many parts and which I comprehend so slowly & imperfectly as the proposed Association.

If the community is not good for me neither am I good for it. I do not look on myself as a valuable member to any community which is not either very large or very small & select I fear that yours would not find me as profitable & pleasant an associate as I should wish to be and as so important a project seems imperatively to require in all its constituents Moreover I am so ignorant & uncertain in my improvements that I would fain hide my attempts & failures in solitude where they shall perplex none or very few beside myself The result of our secretest improvements will certainly have as much renown as shall be due to them.

In regard to the plan as far as it respects the formation of a School or College, I have more hesitation, inasmuch as a concentration of scholars in one place seems to me to have certain great advantages. Perhaps as the school emerges to more distinct consideration out of the Farm, I shall yet find it attractive And yet I am very apt to relapse into the same skepticism as to modes & arrangements the same magnifying of the men—the men alone. According to your ability & mine, you & I do now keep school for all comers, & the energy of our thought & will measures our influence. In the community we shall utter not a word more—not a word less.

Whilst I refuse to be an active member of your company I must yet declare that of all the philanthropic projects of which I have heard yours is the most pleasing to me and if it is prosecuted in the same spirit in which it is begun, I shall regard it with lively sympathy & with a sort of gratitude.

Yours affectionately
R W Emerson.

NATHANIEL HAWTHORNE

In "The Hall of Fantasy," Hawthorne's narrator imagines himself transported, in mid-reverie, to a dreamy edifice inhabited by imaginers of all sorts and from all eras—poets, fiction writers, religious visionaries, inventors, and, as in the following passage, an array of reformers. The sketch unfolds as a tour conducted by one of the narrator's friends, also a resident, at least temporarily, of the Hall. The selection printed here includes a passage on Brook Farm and the Transcendentalists that was cut from the original magazine version of the sketch when it was reprinted in *Mosses from an Old Manse*, a collection of Hawthorne's stories and sketches published in 1846.

From The Hall of Fantasy[†]

* * *

Among the characters [present], were most of the noted reformers of the day, whether in physics, politics, morals, or religion. There is no surer method of arriving at the Hall of Fantasy, than to throw oneself into the current of a theory; for, whatever landmarks of fact may be set up along the stream, there is a law of nature that impels it thither. And let it be so; for here the wise head and capacious heart may do their work; and what is good and true becomes gradually hardened into fact, while error melts away and vanishes among the shadows of the hall. Therefore may none, who believe and rejoice in the progress of mankind, be angry with me because I recognized their apostles and leaders, amid the fantastic radiance of those pictured windows. I love and honor such men, as well as they.

There was a dear friend of mine among them, who has striven with all his might to wash away the blood-stain from the statute-book; and whether he finally succeed or fail, no philanthropist need blush to stand on the same footing with O'Sullivan.[1]

In the midst of these lights of the age, it gladdened me to greet my old friends of Brook Farm, with whom, though a recreant now, I had borne the heat of many a summer's day, while we labored together towards the perfect life. They seem so far advanced, however, in the realization of their idea, that their sun-burnt faces and toil-hardened frames may soon be denied admittance into the Hall of Fantasy. Mr. Emerson was like-wise there, leaning against one of the pillars, and surrounded by an admiring crowd of writers and readers of the Dial,[2] and all manner of Transcendentalists and disciples of the New-ness, most of whom betrayed the power of his intellect by its modifying influence upon their own. He had come into the hall, in search, I suppose, either of a fact or a real man; both of which he was as likely to find there as elsewhere. No more earnest seeker after truth than he, and few more successful finders of it; although, sometimes, the truth assumes a mystic unreality and shadowyness in his grasp. * * *

It would be endless to describe the herd of real or self-styled reformers, that peopled this place of refuge. They were the representatives of

[†] From *Mosses from an Old Manse*, ed. J. Donald Crowley et al. (Columbus: Ohio State University Press, 1974), pp. 180–81, 637–38. Reprinted with permission of the Ohio State University Press. "The Hall of Fantasy" first appeared in the February 1843 issue of *Pioneer* and was reprinted in the 1846 and 1854 editions of *Mosses from an Old Manse*.
1. John Louis O'Sullivan (1813–1895), close friend of Hawthorne and publisher, as editor of the *United States Magazine and Democratic Review*, of many of his early tales and sketches, was also an important advocate for the abolition of the death penalty.
2. Emerson followed Margaret Fuller as the editor of this journal, which, from its founding in 1840 to its demise in 1844, was the chief forum for the writers and thinkers associated with Transcendentalism.

an unquiet period, when mankind is seeking to cast off the whole tissue of ancient custom, like a tattered garment. Many of them had got possession of some crystal fragment of truth, the brightness of which so dazzled them, that they could see nothing else in the wide universe. Here were men, whose faith had embodied itself in the form of a potatoe; and others whose long beards had a deep spiritual significance. Here was the abolitionist, brandishing his one idea like an iron flail. In a word, there were a thousand shapes of good and evil, faith and infidelity, wisdom and nonsense,—a most incongruous throng.

Yet, withal, the heart of the stanchest conservative, unless he abjured his fellowship with man, could hardly have helped throbbing in sympathy with the spirit that pervaded these innumerable theorists. It was good for the man of unquickened heart to listen even to their folly. Far down, beyond the fathom of the intellect, the soul acknowledged that all these varying and conflicting developments of humanity were united in one sentiment. Be the individual theory as wild as fancy could make it, still the wiser spirit would recognize the struggle of the race after a better and purer life, than had yet been realized on earth. My faith revived, even while I rejected all their schemes. It could not be, that the world should continue forever what it has been; a soil where Happiness is so rare a flower, and Virtue so often a blighted fruit; a battle-field where the good principle, with its shield flung above its head, can hardly save itself amid the rush of adverse influences. In the enthusiasm of such thoughts, I gazed through one of the pictured windows; and, behold! the whole external world was tinged with the dimly glorious aspect that is peculiar to the Hall of Fantasy; insomuch that it seemed practicable, at that very instant, to realize some plan for the perfection of mankind. But, alas! if reformers would understand the sphere in which their lot is cast, they must cease to look through pictured windows. Yet they not only use this medium, but mistake it for the whitest sunshine.

"Come," said I to my friend, starting from a deep reverie,—"let us hasten hence, or I shall be tempted to make a theory—after which, there is little hope of any man."

* * *

CHARLES FOURIER

In his many writings, Charles Fourier (1772–1837), a French social theorist whose ideas attracted great interest and sparked debate among reform-minded American intellectuals, offered a scathing critique of the inequities of modern life and devised a complex system of communal living and working designed to achieve complete social harmony. His ideas attracted great interest among some reform-minded American intellectuals, though they typically left his cosmological speculations and bold ideas about sexuality out of the versions of his proposals that they adapted for American audiences. Fourier based his system on matching work assignments and living arrangements with the individual "passions" of community members. Hawthorne borrowed three volumes of Fourier's works as he began work on *The Blithedale Romance*, and he has Coverdale describe Fourier's theories to a disapproving Hollingsworth in Chapter 7. The Brook Farm community adopted a modified Fourierism and began to plan for the construction of a scaled-down phalanstery—the elaborately planned building designed to carry out Fourier's ideas—in early 1844, long after Hawthorne had left the community. The Blithedale community does not follow Fourier's model. This selection describes the reconception of labor at the heart of Fourier's system. For an account of the American reception of Fourier's ideas, see Carl J. Guaneri's *The Utopian Alternative: Fourierism in Nineteenth-Century America*, listed in the "Selected Bibliography."

From Attractive Labour[†]

In the civilised mechanism we find everywhere composite unhappiness instead of composite charm. Let us judge of it by the case of labour. It is, says the Scripture very justly, a punishment of man: Adam and his issue are condemned to earn their bread by the sweat of their brow. That, already, is an affliction; but this labour, this ungrateful labour upon which depends the earning of our miserable bread, we cannot even get it! a labourer lacks the labour upon which his maintenance depends,—he asks in vain for a tribulation! He suffers a second, that of obtaining work at times whose fruit is his master's and not his, or of being employed in duties to which he is entirely unaccustomed. . . . The civilised labourer suffers a third affliction through the maladies with which he is generally stricken by the excess of labour demanded by his master. . . . He suffers a fifth affliction, that of being despised and treated as a beggar because he lacks those necessaries which he consents to purchase by the anguish of repugnant labour. He

---

[†] From *Selections from the Works of Fourier*, ed. Charles Gide, trans. Julia Franklin (London: Swan Sonnenschein & Co., 1901), pp. 163–64. This early-twentieth-century British edition composes its chapters from selections of various works by Fourier. The chapter reprinted here begins with a paragraph from Fourier's manuscripts; the rest of the excerpt is taken from *Theorie de l'Unité Universelle* ("Theory of Universal Unity"), an 1838 edition of a text first published in 1822.

suffers, finally, a sixth affliction, in that he will obtain neither advancement nor sufficient wages, and that to the vexation of present suffering is added the perspective of future suffering, and of being sent to the gallows should he demand that labour which he may lack tomorrow.

Labour, nevertheless, forms the delight of various creatures, such as beavers, bees, wasps, ants, which are entirely at liberty to prefer inertia: but God has provided them with a social mechanism which attracts to industry, and causes happiness to be found in industry. Why should he not have accorded us the same favour as these animals? What a difference between their industrial condition and ours! A Russian, an Algerian, work from fear of the lash or the bastinado; an Englishman, a Frenchman, from fear of the famine which stalks close to his poor household; the Greeks and the Romans, whose freedom has been vaunted to us, worked as slaves, and from fear of punishment, like the negroes in the colonies to-day.

Associative labour,[1] in order to exert a strong attraction upon people, will have to differ in every particular from the repulsive conditions which render it so odious in the existing state of things. It is necessary, in order that it become attractive, that associative labour fulfil the following seven conditions:

1. That every labourer be a partner, remunerated by dividends and not by wages.

2. That every one, man, woman, or child, be remunerated in proportion to the three faculties, *capital, labour,* and *talent.*

3. That the industrial sessions be varied about eight times a day, it being impossible to sustain enthusiasm longer than an hour and a half or two hours in the exercise of agricultural or manufacturing labour.

4. That they be carried on by bands of friends, united spontaneously, interested and stimulated by very active rivalries.

5. That the workshops and husbandry offer the labourer the allurements of elegance and cleanliness.

6. That the division of labour be carried to the last degree, so that each sex and age may devote itself to duties that are suited to it.

7. That in this distribution, each one, man, woman, or child, be in full enjoyment of the right to labour or the right to engage in such branch of labour as they may please to select, provided they give proof of integrity and ability.

⋈[2] Finally, that, in this new order, people possess a guarantee of well-being, of a minimum sufficient for the present and the future, and that this guarantee free them from all uneasiness concerning themselves and their families.

* * *

1. Labor as conducted in Fourier's proposed harmonious community.
2. The sign ⋈, in the language of Fourier, serves to designate that which is "pivotal," that is to say, fundamental, in enumeration [note in original].

THEODORE PARKER

Theodore Parker (1810–1860) was a prominent Unitarian minister, a theological and political radical, and an impassioned spokesman for a range of social reforms. A close friend of George Ripley, Parker was a frequent visitor to Brook Farm, often walking over from his nearby farm for an afternoon of intense conversation. Parker was best known as an abolitionist and a resister of the Fugitive Slave Law, but his sermons and highly popular lectures also addressed an array of social and political questions, from the oppression of the poor to the justness of the Mexican War. In the sermon excerpted here—delivered not in his church but at Boston's leading concert and exhibition hall—Parker calls for the reform of the treatment of criminals.

[What Shall Be Done for Criminals?]†

What shall be done for Criminals, the backward children of society, who refuse to keep up with the moral or legal advance of mankind?

* * *

It seems to me that our whole method of punishing crimes is a false one; that but little good comes of it, or can come. We beat the stool which we have stumbled over. We punish a man in proportion to the loss or the fear of society; not in proportion to the offender's state of mind; not with a careful desire to improve that state of mind. This is wise if vengeance be the aim; if reformation, it seems sheer folly. I know our present method is the result of six thousand years' experience of mankind; I know how easy it is to find fault—how difficult to devise a better mode. Still the facts are so plain that one with half an eye cannot fail to see the falseness of the present methods. To remove the evil, we must remove its cause,—so let us look a little into this matter, and see from what quarter our criminals proceed.

Here are two classes.

I. There are the foes of society; men that are criminals in soul, born criminals, who have a bad nature. The cause of their crime therefore is to be found in their nature itself, in their organization if you will. All experience shows that some men are born with a depraved organization, an excess of animal passions, or a deficiency of other powers to balance them.

II. There are the victims of society; men that become criminals by circumstances, made criminals, not born; men who become criminals,

† From "A Sermon of the Dangerous Classes in Society. Preached at the Melodeon, on Sunday, January 31, 1847," collected in Theodore Parker, *Speeches, Addresses, and Occasional Sermons*, vol. 1 (Boston: Crosby and Nichols, 1852), pp. 201–38.

not so much from strength of evil in their soul, or excess of evil propensities in their organization, as from strength of evil in their circumstances. I do not say that a man's character is wholly determined by the circumstances in which he is placed, but all experience shows that circumstances, such as exposure in youth to good men or bad men, education, intellectual, moral, and religious, or neglect thereof entire or partial, have a vast influence in forming the character of men, especially of men not well endowed by nature.

Now the criminals in soul are the most dangerous of men, the born foes of society. I will not at this moment undertake to go behind their organization and ask, "How comes it that they are so ill-born?" I stop now at that fact. The cause of their crime is in their bodily constitution itself. This is always a small class. There are in New England perhaps five hundred men born blind or deaf. Apart from the idiots, I think there are not half so many who by nature and bodily constitution are incapable of attaining the average morality of the race at this day; not so many born foes of society as are born blind or deaf.

The criminals from circumstances become what they are by the action of causes which may be ascertained, guarded against, mitigated, and at last overcome and removed. These men are born of poor parents, and find it difficult to satisfy the natural wants of food, clothing, and shelter. They get little culture, intellectual or moral. The school-house is open, but the parent does not send the children, he wants their services, to beg for him, perhaps to steal, it may be to do little services which lie within their power. Besides, the child must be ill-clad, and so a mark is set on him. The boy of the perishing classes, with but common endowments, cannot learn at school as one of the thrifty or abounding class. Then he receives no stimulus at home; there everything discourages his attempts. He cannot share the pleasure and sport of his youthful fellows. His dress, his uncleanly habits, the result of misery, forbid all that. So the children of the perishing herd together, ignorant, ill-fed, and miserably clad. You do not find the sons of this class in your colleges, in your high schools where all is free for the people; few even in the grammar schools; few in the churches. Though born into the nineteenth century after Christ, they grow up almost in the barbarism of the nineteenth century before him. Children that are blind and deaf, though born with a superior organization, if left to themselves become only savages, little more than animals. What are we to expect of children, born indeed with eyes and ears, but yet shut out from the culture of the age they live in? In the corruption of a city, in the midst of its intenser life, what wonder that they associate with crime, that the moral instinct, baffled and cheated of its due, becomes so powerless in the boy or girl; what wonder that reason never gets developed there, nor conscience nor that blessed religious sense learns ever to assert its power? Think of the temptations that beset the boy; those yet more revolting which address the other sex. Opportunities for crime continually offer. Want impels, desire leagues with opportunity, and the result we know. Add to all this the curse that creates so much disease, poverty, wretchedness and so perpetually begets crime; I mean intemperance! That is almost the only pleasure of the perishing class. What recognized amusement have they but this, of drinking themselves drunk? Do you wonder at this? with no air, nor light, nor water, with scanty food and a miserable dress, with no culture, living in a cellar or a garret, crowded, stifling, and offensive even to the rudest sense, do you wonder that man or woman seeks a brief vacation of misery in the dram-shop and in its drunkenness? I wonder not. Under such circumstances how many of you would have done better?

* * *

Now, our present method is wholly inadequate to reform men exposed to such circumstances. You may punish the man, but it does no good. You can seldom frighten men out of a fever. Can you frighten them from crime, when they know little of the internal distinction between right and wrong; when all the circumstances about them impel to crime? Can you frighten a starving girl into chastity? You cannot keep men from lewdness, theft and violence, when they have no self-respect, no culture, no development of mind, heart, and soul. The jail will not take the place of the church, of the schoolhouse, of home. It will not remove the causes which are making new criminals. It does not reform the old ones. Shall we shut men in a jail, and when there treat them with all manner of violence, crush out the little self-respect yet left, give them a degrading dress, and send them into the world cursed with an infamous name, and all that because they were born in the low places of society and caught the stain thereof? The jail does not alter the circumstances which occasioned the crime, and till these causes are removed a fresh crop will spring out of the festering soil.

* * *

When the victims of society violated its laws, I would not torture a man for his misfortune, because his father was poor, his mother a brute; because his education was neglected. I would shut him out from society for a time. I would make him work for his own good and the good of others. The evil he had caught from the world I would overcome by the good that I would present to him. I would not clothe him with an infamous dress, crowd him with other men whom society had made infamous, leaving them to ferment and rot together. I would not set him up as a show to the public, for his enemy, or his rival, or some miserable fop to come and stare at with merciless and tormenting eye. I would not load him with chains, nor tear his flesh with a whip. I would not set soldiers with loaded gun to keep watch over him, insulting their brother by mocking and threats. I would treat the man with firmness, but with justice, with pity, with love. I would teach the man; what his family could not do for him, what society and the church had failed of, the jail should do, for the jail should be a manual labor school, not a dungeon of torture. I would take the most gifted, the most cultivated, the wisest and most benevolent, yes, the most Christian man in the State, and set him to train up these poor savages of civilization. The best man is the natural physician of the wicked. * * * I would set such a man, if I could find such another, to look after the dangerous classes of society. I would pay him for it; honor him for it. I would have a Board of Public Morals to look after this matter of crime, a Secretary of Public Morals, a Christian Censor, whose business it should be to attend to this class, to look after the jails and make them houses of refuge, of instruction, which should do for the perishing class what the school-house and the church do for others. I would send missionaries amongst the most exposed portions of mankind as well as amongst the savages of New Holland.[1]

* * *

I cannot think the method here suggested would be so costly as the present. It seems to me that institutions of this character might be made not only to support themselves, but be so managed as to leave a balance of income considerably beyond the expense. This might be made use of for the advantage of the criminal when he returned to society; or with it he might help make restitution of what he had once stolen. Besides being less costly, it would cure the offender and send back valuable men into society.

It seems to me that our whole criminal legislation is based on a false principle—force and not love; that it is eminently well adapted to revenge, not at all to correct, to teach, to cure. The whole apparatus for the punishment of offenders, from the gallows down to the House of Correction, seems to me wrong; wholly wrong, unchristian, and even inhuman. We teach crime while we punish it. Is it consistent for the State to take vengeance when I may not? Is it better for the State to kill a man in cold blood, than for me to kill my brother when in a rage? I cannot help thinking that the gallows and even the

1. Australia.

jail, as now administered, are practical teachers of violence and wrong! I cannot think it will always be so. Hitherto we have looked on criminals as voluntary enemies of mankind. We have treated them as wild beasts, not as dull or loitering boys. We have sought to destroy by death, to disable by mutilation or imprisonment, to terrify and subdue, not to convince, to reform, encourage, and bless.

* * *

To change the treatment of criminals, we must change every thing else. The dangerous class is the unavoidable result of our present civilization; of our present ideas of man and social life. To reform and elevate the class of criminals, we must reform and elevate all other classes. To do that, we must educate and refine men. We must learn to treat all men as brothers. This is a great work and one of slow achievement. It cannot be brought about by legislation, nor any mechanical contrivance and re-organization alone. There is no remedy for this evil and its kindred but keeping the laws of God; in one word, none but Christianity, goodness, and piety felt in the heart, applied in all the works of life, individually, socially, and politically. While educated and abounding men acknowledge no rule of conduct but self-interest, what can you expect of the ignorant and the perishing? * * * We must improve all classes to improve one; perhaps the highest first. Different men acting in the most various directions, without concert, often jealous one of another, and all partial in their aims, are helping forward this universal result. While we are contending against slavery, war, intemperance, or party rage, while we are building up hospitals, colleges, schools, while we are contending for freedom of conscience, or teaching abstractly the love of man and love of God, we are all working for the welfare of this neglected class. The gallows of the barbarian and the Gospel of Christianity cannot exist together. The times are full of promise. Mankind slowly fulfils what a man of genius prophesies; God grants what a good man asks, and when it comes, it is better than what he prayed for.

Nathaniel Hawthorne
at Brook Farm

Hawthorne arrived at Brook Farm on April 12, 1841; he left the community for good some six months later, having invested $1,000 of his scant funds (much of which he never recovered) in Association stock and having served, for a time, as the chairman of the Association's Finance Committee. With his fiancée, Sophia Peabody, Hawthorne had hoped to find, in the success of the community, an arrangement that would allow them to marry and find a home while he pursued what had so far been a distinctly unprofitable writing career. Yet, as his letters to Sophia and others reveal, his investment in the community was much more than strategic. Though he was quickly disillusioned, both about the possibility of combining writing and farm work and about the financial sustainability of the enterprise, his hope and enthusiasm were real (as the financial risk testifies), and he never lost his admiration and affection for Ripley and his other Brook Farm companions. These documents tell the story of Hawthorne's time at Brook Farm in four sections: Hawthorne's early letters, aspects of which turn up in Miles Coverdale's account of his first days at Blithedale, vividly capture the comedy and excitement of the early days of the community; selections from his Notebooks (several of which will also find their way into the novel) together with observations by other members of the community, give us a sense of daily life; selections from his later letters track his emerging skepticism about the community's capacity to meet his hopes for it, and recount his decision to leave.

FIRST DAYS AT BROOK FARM

NATHANIEL HAWTHORNE

Letters from Brook Farm

To Sophia Peabody, Boston, April 13, 1841[†]

Ownest love,

Here is thy poor husband in a polar Paradise![1] I know not how to interpret this aspect of Nature—whether it be of good or evil omen to our enterprise. But I reflect that the Plymouth pilgrims arrived in the midst of storm and stept ashore upon mountain snow-drifts; and nevertheless they prospered, and became a great people—and doubtless it will be the same with us. I laud my stars, however, that thou wilt not have thy first impressions of our future home from such a day as this. Thou wouldst shiver all thy life afterwards, and never realize that there could be bright skies, and green hills and meadows, and trees heavy with foliage, where now the whole scene is a great snow-bank, and the sky full of snow likewise. Through faith, I persist in believing that spring and summer will come in their due season; but the unregenerated man shivers within me, and suggests a doubt whether I may not have wandered within the precincts of the Arctic circle, and chosen my heritage among everlasting snows.[2] Dearest, provide thyself with a good stock of furs; and if thou canst obtain the skin of a polar bear, thou wilt find it a very suitable summer dress for this region. Thou must not hope ever to walk abroad, except upon snow-shoes, nor to find any warmth, save in thy husband's heart.

Belovedest, I have not yet taken my first lesson in agriculture, as thou mayst well suppose—except that I went to see our cows foddered, yesterday afternoon. We have eight of our own; and the number is now increased by a transcendental heifer, belonging to Miss Margaret Fuller.[3] She is very fractious, I believe, and apt to kick over the milk pail. Thou knowest best, whether, in these traits of character, she resembles her mistress. Thy husband intends to convert himself

---

[†] From *The Letters, 1813–1843*, ed. Thomas Woodson, L. Neal Smith, Norman Holmes Pearson (Columbus: Ohio State University Press, 1984), pp. 526–29. Reprinted by permission of The Ohio State University Press.

1. Though he and Sophia would not marry until July 1842, Hawthorne often refers, throughout these letters, to her as "wife" and himself as "husband."

2. Compare Coverdale's arrival at Blithedale, pp. 9–12.

3. Margaret Fuller (1810–1850), feminist writer and intellectual force, was a frequent visitor to Brook Farm.

into a milk-maid, this evening; but I pray heaven that Mr. Ripley may be moved to assign him the kindliest cow in the herd—otherwise he will perform his duty with fear and trembling.

Ownest wife, I like my brethren in affliction very well; and couldst thou see us sitting round our table, at meal-times, before the great kitchen-fire, thou wouldst call it a cheerful sight. Mrs. Barker[4] is a most comfortable woman to behold; she looks as if her ample person were stuffed full of tenderness—indeed, as if she were all one great, kind heart. Wert thou but here, I should ask for nothing more—not even for sunshine and summer weather; for thou wouldst be both, to thy husband. And how is that cough of thine, my belovedest? Hast thou thought of me, in my perils and wanderings? Thou must not think how I longed for thee, when I crept into my cold bed last night,—my bosom remembered thee,—and refused to be comforted without thy caresses. I trust that thou dost muse upon me with hope and joy, not with repining. Think that I am gone before, to prepare a home for my Dove, and will return for her, all in good time.

Thy husband has the best chamber in the house, I believe; and though not quite so good as the apartment I have left, it will do very well. I have hung up thy two pictures; and they give me a glimpse of summer and of thee. The vase I intended to have brought in my arms, but could not very conveniently do it yesterday; so that it still remains at Mrs. Hillards, together with my carpet. I shall bring them the next opportunity.

Now farewell, for the present, most beloved. * * *

April 14th. 10 A.M. Sweetest, I did not milk the cows last night, because Mr. Ripley was afraid to trust them to my hands, or me to their horns—I know not which. But this morning, I have done wonders. Before breakfast, I went out to the barn, and began to chop hay for the cattle; and with such "righteous vehemence" (as Mr. Ripley says) did I labor, that, in the space of ten minutes, I broke the machine. Then I brought wood and replenished the fires; and finally sat down to breakfast and ate up a huge mound of buckwheat cakes. After breakfast, Mr. Ripley put a four-pronged instrument into my hands, which he gave me to understand was called a pitch-fork; and he and Mr. Farley[5] being armed with similar weapons, we all three commenced a gallant attack upon a heap of manure. This affair being concluded, and thy husband having purified himself, he sits down to finish this letter to his most beloved wife. Dearest, I will never consent that thou come within half a mile of me, after such an

4. Elise Barker, a domestic worker from Boston, joined the community with the hope of bringing her family to live there.
5. Francis D. (Frank) Farley, a former mechanic and one of the most likable and versatile members of the community, would leave four months later, suffering from severe depression.

encounter as that of this morning. Pray Heaven that this letter retain none of the fragrance with which the writer was imbued. As for thy husband himself, he is peculiarly partial to the odor; but that whimsical little nose of thine might chance to quarrel with it.

Belovedest, Miss Fuller's cow hooks the other cows, and has made herself ruler of the herd, and behaves in a very tyrannical manner. Sweetest, I know not when I shall see thee; but I trust it will not be longer than till the end of next week. I love thee! I love thee! I would thou wert with me; for then would my labor be joyful—and even now, it is not sorrowful. Dearest, I shall make an excellent husband-man. I feel the original Adam reviving within me.

To Sophia Peabody, Boston, April 16, 1841[†]

* * *

Dearest, since I last wrote thee, there has been an addition to our community of four gentlemen in sables, who promise to be among our most useful and respectable members.[1] They arrived yesterday, about noon. Mr. Ripley had proposed to them to join us, no longer ago than that very morning. I had some conversation with them in the afternoon, and was glad to hear them express much satisfaction with their new abode, and all the arrangements. They do not appear to be very communicative, however—or perhaps it may be merely an external reserve, like that of thy husband, to shield their delicacy. Several of their prominent characteristics, as well as their black attire, lead me to believe that they are members of the clerical profession; but I have not yet ascertained, from their own lips, what has been the nature of their past lives. I trust to have much pleasure in their society, and, sooner or later, that we shall all of us derive great strength from our intercourse with them. I cannot too highly applaud the readiness with which these four gentlemen in black have thrown aside all the fopperies and flummeries, which have their origin in a false state of society. When I last saw them, they looked as heroically regardless of the stains and soils incident to our profession, as thy husband did when he emerged from the gold mine.[2]

Ownest wife, thy husband has milked a cow!!!

Belovedest, the herd have rebelled against the usurpation of Miss Fuller's cow; and whenever they are turned out of the barn, she is compelled to take refuge under our protection. So much did she

---

† From *The Letters, 1813–1843*, ed. Thomas Woodson, L. Neal Smith, Norman Holmes Pearson (Columbus: Ohio State University Press, 1984), pp. 530–32. Reprinted by permission of The Ohio State University Press.
1. Hawthorne refers here to four black pigs, just purchased by George Ripley.
2. Ripley's nickname for the manure pile.

impede thy husband's labors, by keeping close to him, that he found it necessary to give her two or three gentle pats with a shovel; but still she preferred to trust herself to my tender mercies, rather than venture among the horns of the herd. She is not an amiable cow; but she has a very intelligent face, and seems to be of a reflective cast of character. I doubt not that she will soon perceive the expediency of being on good terms with the rest of the sisterhood.

I have not yet been twenty yards from our house and barn; but I begin to perceive that this is a beautiful place. The scenery is of a mild and placid character, with nothing bold in its character; but I think its beauties will grow upon us, and make us love it the more, the longer we live here. There is a brook, so near the house that we shall be able to hear its ripple, in the summer evenings; and whenever we lie awake in the summer nights; but, for agricultural purposes, it has been made to flow in a straight and rectangular fashion, which does it infinite damage, as a picturesque object.

Naughtiest, it was a moment or two before I could think whom thou didst mean by Mr. Dismal View.[3] Why, he is one of the best of the brotherhood, so far as cheerfulness goes; for, if he do not laugh himself, he makes the rest of us laugh continually. He is the quaintest and queerest personage thou didst ever see—full of dry jokes, the humor of which is so incorporated with the strange twistifications of his physiognomy, that his sayings ought to be written down, accompanied with illustrations by Cruikshank.[4] Then he keeps quoting innumerable scraps of Latin, and makes classical allusions, while we are turning over the gold mine; and the contrast between the nature of his employment and the character of his thoughts is irresistibly ludicrous.

To Sophia Peabody, Boston, April 28, 1841[†]

* * *

Belovedest, thy husband was caught by a cold, during his visit to Boston.[1] It has not affected his whole frame, but took entire possession of his head, as being the weakest and most vulnerable part. Never didst thou hear anybody sneeze with such vehemence and frequency; and his poor brain has been in a thick fog—or rather, it seemed as if his head were stuffed with coarse wool. I know not when I have been so pestered before; and sometimes I wanted to

---

3. Warren Burton, a Unitarian minister and reformer, one of the first to leave the community.
4. English illustrator and caricaturist, known for his illustrations of Charles Dickens's writing.
† From *The Letters, 1813–1843*, ed. Thomas Woodson, L. Neal Smith, Norman Holmes Pearson (Columbus: Ohio State University Press, 1984), pp. 534–36. Reprinted by permission of The Ohio State University Press.
1. Compare Coverdale's first night at Blithedale, p. 28.

wrench off my head, and give it a great kick, like a foot-ball. This annoyance has made me endure the bad weather with even less than ordinary patience; and my faith was so far exhausted, that when they told me yesterday that the sun was setting clear, I would not even turn my eyes towards the west. But, this morning, I am made all over anew, and have no greater remnant of my cold, than will serve as an excuse for doing no work to-day. * * *

The family has been dismal and dolorous, throughout the storm. The night before last, William Allen[2] was stung by a wasp, on the eye-lid; whereupon, the whole side of his face swelled to an enormous magnitude; so that, at the breakfast table, one half of him looked like a blind giant (the eye being closed) and the other half had such a sor-rowful and ludicrous aspect, that thy husband was constrained to laugh out of sheer pity. The same day, a colony of wasps was discov-ered in thy husband's chamber, where they had remained throughout the winter, and were now just bestirring themselves, doubtless with the intention of stinging me from head to foot. Thou wilt readily believe, that not one of the accursed crew escaped my righteous vengeance. A similar discovery was made in Mr. Farley's room. In short, we seem to have taken up our abode in a wasp's nest. Thus thou seest, belovedest, that a rural life is not one of unbroken quiet and serenity.

If the middle of the day prove warm and pleasant, thy husband promises himself to take a walk, in every step of which thou shalt be his companion. Oh, how I long for thee to stray with me, in reality, among the hills, and dales, and woods, of our home. I have taken one walk, with Mr. Farley; and I could not have believed that there was such seclusion, at so short a distance from a great city. Many spots seem hardly to have been visited for ages—not since John Eliot[3] preached to the Indians here. If we were to travel a thousand miles, we could not escape the world more completely than we can here.

Sweetest, I long unspeakably to see thee—it is only the thought of thee that draws my spirit out of this solitude. Otherwise, I care noth-ing for the world nor its affairs. I read no newspapers, and hardly remember who is President, and feel as if I had no more concern with what other people trouble themselves about, than if I dwelt in another planet. But, still, thou drawest me to thee continually; and so I can realize how a departed spirit feels, while looking back from another world to the beloved ones of this. All other interests appear like shadows and trifles; but love is a reality, which makes the spirit still an inhabitant of the world which it has quitted.

2. The community's head farmer and a Brook Farm shareholder.
3. John Eliot (1604–1690), the Puritan minister of the town of Roxbury, was famous for his missionary work among the Indians; he learned the language of the Massachusetts Indi-ans and translated the Bible into their tongue.

To Louisa Hawthorne, Salem, May 3, 1841[†]

As the weather precludes all possibility of ploughing, hoeing, sowing, and other such operations, I bethink me that you may have no objection to hear something of my whereabout and whatabout. You are to know then, that I took up my abode here on the 12th ultimo, in the midst of a snow-storm, which kept us all idle for a day or two. At the first glimpse of fair weather, Mr. Ripley summoned us into the cow-yard, and introduced me to an instrument with four prongs, commonly called a dung-fork. With this tool, I have already assisted to load twenty or thirty carts of manure, and shall take part in loading nearly three hundred more. Besides, I have planted potatoes and pease, cut straw and hay for the cattle, and done various other mighty works. This very morning, I milked three cows; and I milk two or three every night and morning. The weather has been so unfavorable, that we have worked comparatively little in the fields; but, nevertheless, I have gained strength wonderfully—grown quite a giant, in fact—and can do a day's work without the slightest inconvenience. In short, I am transformed into a complete farmer.

This is one of the most beautiful places I ever saw in my life, and as secluded as if it were a hundred miles from any city or village. There are woods, in which we can ramble all day, without meeting anybody, or scarcely seeing a house. Our house stands apart from the main road; so that we are not troubled even with passengers looking at us. Once in a while, we have a transcendental visitor, such as Mr. Alcott[1] but, generally, we pass whole days without seeing a single face, save those of the brethren. At this present time, our effective force consists of Mr. Ripley, Mr. Farley, (a farmer from the far west,) Rev. Warren Burton (author of various celebrated works) three young men and boys, who are under Mr. Ripley's care, and William Allen, his hired man, who has the chief direction of our agricultural labors. In the female part of the establishment there is Mrs Ripley, and two women folks. The whole fraternity eat together; and such a delectable way of life has never been seen on earth, since the days of the early Christians. We get up at half-past four, breakfast at half past six, dine at half past twelve, and go to bed at nine.

The thin frock, which you made for me, is considered a most splendid article; and I should not wonder if it were to become the summer uniform of the community. I have a thick frock, likewise; but it is rather deficient in grace, though extremely warm and

† From *The Letters, 1813–1843*, ed. Thomas Woodson, L. Neal Smith, Norman Holmes Pearson (Columbus: Ohio State University Press, 1984), pp. 539–40. The recipient of this letter is Hawthorne's sister, Marie Louisa (1808–1852). Reprinted by permission of The Ohio State University Press.
1. A. Bronson Alcott (1799–1888), Transcendentalist visionary and reformer, father of novelist Louisa May Alcott.

comfortable. I wear a tremendous pair of cow-hide boots, with soles two inches thick. Of course, when I come to see you, I shall wear my farmer's dress.

* * *

Nath. Hawthorne,
Ploughman.

To Sophia Peabody, Boston, May 4, 1841[†]

Belovedest, as Mrs. Ripley is going to the city this afternoon, I cannot but write to thee, though I have but little time; for the cornfield will need me very soon. My cold no longer troubles me; and all the morning, I have been at work under the clear blue sky, on a hill side. Sometimes it almost seemed as if I were at work in the sky itself; though the material in which I wrought was the ore from our gold mine. Nevertheless, there is nothing so unseemly and disagreeable in this sort of toil, as thou wouldst think. It defiles the hands, indeed, but not the soul. This gold ore is a pure and wholesome substance; else our Mother Nature would not devour it so readily, and derive so much nourishment from it, and return such a rich abundance of good grain and roots in requital of it.

The farm is growing very beautiful now—not that we yet see anything of the pease or potatoes, which we have planted; but the grass blushes green on the slopes and hollows. I wrote that word blush almost unconsciously; so we will let it go as an inspired utterance. When I go forth afield, I think of my Dove, and look beneath the stone walls, where the verdure is richest, in hopes that a little company of violets, or some solitary bud, prophetic of the summer, may be there; to which I should award the blissful fate of being treasured for a time in thy bosom; for I doubt not, dearest, that thou wouldst admit any flower of thy husband's gathering into that sweetest place. But not a wild flower have I yet found. One of the boys gathered some yellow cowslips, last Sunday; but I am well content not to have found them; for they are not precisely what I should like to send my Dove, though they deserve honor and praise, because they come to us when no others will. We have our parlor here dressed in evergreen, as at Christmas. That beautifullest little flower vase of thine stands on Mr. Ripley's study table, at which I am now writing. It contains some daffodils and some willow blossoms. I brought it here, rather than kept it in my chamber; because I never sit there; and it gives me many pleasant emotions to look round and be surprised

[†] From The Letters, 1813–1843, ed. Thomas Woodson, L. Neal Smith, Norman Holmes Pearson (Columbus: Ohio State University Press, 1984), pp. 542–43. Reprinted by permission of The Ohio State University Press.

(for it is often a surprise, though I well know that it is there) by something which is connected with the idea of thee.

* * *

We had some tableaux last evening, the principal characters being sustained by Mr. Farley and Miss Ellen Slade.[1] They went off very well. I would like to see a tableaux, arranged by my Dove.

Dearest, I fear it is time for thy clod-compelling husband to take the field again. Good bye. * * *

Daily Life at Brook Farm

ORA GANNETT SEDGWICK

Ora Gannett came to Brook Farm as one of the first pupils at its extraordinary school and was a vivacious and well-liked member of the community. She left Brook Farm early in 1844, as it moved closer to the Fourierist model of organization, which emphasized industrial rather than agricultural work.

From A Girl of Sixteen at Brook Farm[†]

The Hive was the Ellis farmhouse, one of the lovely old New England houses with a broad hall running through the whole length, and having a door at each end. From the left side of this hall, as you entered, a staircase went straight up to the second floor. The walls of the hall were lined with open book-shelves filled with rare English, French, and German books, belonging to Mr. Ripley, who had, I imagine, one of the finest libraries in Boston at that time, especially in foreign works. After the Eyrie was built the Hive became merely the working headquarters, and this library was removed to the new building; but the books were always free to all, a fact which showed the real generosity of Mr. Ripley.

There was a comfortable sofa in the hall, under the stairs, on which Nathaniel Hawthorne, who then occupied the front room at the right, used to sit for hours at a time, with a book in his hand, not turning a leaf, but listening with sharp ears to the young people's talk,

---

1. In "tableaux," or "tableaux vivants" ("living paintings"), participants—in costume, but silent and motionless—presented scenes from literature, history, or works of art. The Blithedalers present tableaux in chapter 13 of the novel. Ellen Slade, a young woman of about 16, lived at Brook Farm with her sister.
† From *The Atlantic Monthly* 85(1900): 394–404.

which he seemed to enjoy immensely, perhaps with the satisfaction of Burns's "Chiel among ye takin' notes."[1] It is, however, but just to Mr. Hawthorne to say that, whatever use he made in Blithedale Romance of the scenery and "romantic atmosphere" of Brook Farm, he cannot be accused of violating the sanctities of the home and holding up to public observation exaggerated likenesses of his associates there. I spent some delightful hours with him the winter he died, when he assured me that Zenobia represented no one person there.

* * *

As I remember our meals, they were most delightful times for talk, humor, wit, and the interchange of pleasant nonsense. When our one table had grown into three, Charles A. Dana[2], who must have been a very orderly young man, organized a corps of waiters from among our nicest young people, whose meals were kept hot for them, and they in their turn were waited on by those whom they had served. I have seen Mr. Dana reading a small Greek book between the courses, though he was a faithful waiter. The table talk was most delightful and profitable to me. Looking back over a long and varied life, I think that I have rarely sat down with so many men and women of culture, so thoroughly unselfish, polite, and kind to one another, as I found at those plain but attractive tables. All seemed at rest and at their best. There was no man, tired with the stock market and his efforts to make or to increase a big fortune, coming home harassed or depressed, too cross or disappointed to talk. There was no woman vying with others in French gowns, laces, and diamonds. The fact that all felt that they were honored for themselves alone brought out more individuality in each, so that I have often said that I have never elsewhere seen a set of people of whom each seemed to possess some peculiar charm.

I do not recollect Hawthorne's talking much at the table. Indeed, he was a very taciturn man. One day, tired of seeing him sitting immovable on the sofa in the hall, as I was learning some verses to recite at the evening class for recitation formed by Charles A. Dana, I daringly took my book, pushed it into his hands, and said, "Will you hear my poetry, Mr. Hawthorne?" He gave me a sidelong glance from his very shy eyes, took the book, and most kindly heard me. After that he was on the sofa every week to hear me recite.

---

1. A line, referring to a note-taking antiquarian, from a poem by Robert Burns (1759–1796), "On Captain Grose's Peregrinations through Scotland."
2. Dana came to Brook Farm in the late summer of 1841, having completed his second year at Harvard College; he would quickly become deeply involved in the management of the community.

One evening he was alone in the hall, sitting on a chair at the farther end, when my roommate, Ellen Slade, and myself were going upstairs. She whispered to me, "Let's throw the sofa pillows at Mr. Hawthorne." Reaching over the banisters, we each took a cushion and threw it. Quick as a flash he put out his hand, seized a broom that was hanging near him, warded off our cushions, and threw them back with sure aim. As fast as we could throw them at him he returned them with effect, hitting us every time, while we could hit only the broom. He must have been very quick in his movements. Through it all not a word was spoken. We laughed and laughed, and his eyes shone and twinkled like stars. Wonderful eyes they were, and when anything witty was said I always looked quickly at Mr. Hawthorne; for his dark eyes lighted up as if flames were suddenly kindled behind them, and then the smile came down to his lips and over his grave face.

My memories of Mr. Hawthorne are among the pleasantest of my Brook Farm recollections. His manners to children were charming and kind. I saw him one day walking, as was his custom, with his hands behind his back, head bent forward, the two little Bancrofts and other children following him with pleased faces, and stooping every now and then with broad smiles, after which they would rise and run on again behind him. Puzzled at these manœuvres, I watched closely, and found that although he hardly moved a muscle except to walk, yet from time to time he dropped a penny, for which the children scrambled.

Among our regular visitors in that first year were: Emerson, who came occasionally to spend a day; Margaret Fuller, who passed weeks at a time with us; and Theodore Parker, who was a frequent caller. The last, a warm personal friend of Mr. Ripley, lived within walking distance, and we were often amused at the ceremonies of his leave-taking. When he took his departure, after spending two or three hours in close conversation with Mr. Ripley, the latter always started to accompany him part of the way; at the end of a mile or so, when Mr. Ripley turned back, Mr. Parker, in his turn, became escort, Mr. Ripley resuming the rôle when Brook Farm was reached. In this way, the two men, always absorbed in conversation, walked back and forth, until sometimes another couple of hours were added to the solid talk.

* * *

Perhaps my recollections of Brook Farm are tinted by the rose-colored optimism of sixteen, but as I have grown old, and, looking back to the general standard of half a century ago, have compared the lives led at Brook Farm with the most useful ones of these days, I am more and more convinced that my estimates are true, that there was very much "sweetness and light" there,—a light too bright for most people at that time to bear.

With the progress of time, as higher moral and scientific developments have improved the internal as well as the external vision, the
world is coming to see that living for others is true living. Certainly,
most of the persons whom I knew at Brook Farm lived on a higher
plane than their contemporaries, recognizing, as they did, others'
needs as of equal moment with their own. * * *

One may easily imagine the influence such a man as George P.
Bradford[3] had on the people assembled at Brook Farm. He knew the
woods and fields well,—indeed, all outdoor things; the flora, especially, which, as my memory recalls it, was very rich; astronomy, too.
Many, many nights he showed us the constellations, quietly talking
of all this beauty in a way that inspired love and reverence in us.

He loved the beautiful pine wood which we called the Cathedral,
using it as a magnificent hall, for our amusement. Hawthorne tells
in one of his Note-Books of the masquerade we had there, where
more beautiful people met, I think, than usually falls to one's lot to
see in a lifetime.

* * *

I have often wondered if such a place, so pure, refined, and entirely
democratic, could have been started nearly "sixty years since" in any
other place than the United States, and in Boston or its vicinity.

One thing I early learned there was to discern the small importance of outward worldly distinctions as compared with true worth
of character. This has helped me much in life in choosing friends,
finding them sometimes even among servants. It has enabled me to
treat them as if they were really equals, and to recognize sometimes
their superiority to myself. This lesson has done much to make the
practical part of my life run smoothly, I am sure. That such men as
George P. Bradford and George William Curtis should muffle themselves up in the stormy and freezing weather, and work hard in the
unaccustomed business of hanging out clothes, to save women,
some of whom had toiled all their lives, seems to me more chivalrous
than Raleigh's throwing his cloak in front of Elizabeth. I have never
seen such true politeness as prevailed there.

* * *

The teaching at Brook Farm was fine, and, to one who really wished
to learn, of the very best kind. It was not confined to daytime study
hours, for some, not only of the teachers, but of the scholars, used to
work a portion of each day on the farm. In order to get our work done
early enough for the evening pleasures, among which we reckoned
Mr. Ripley's classes, Georgiana Bruce, Sarah Stearns, and myself,

---

3. One of the first residents of Brook Farm, the Harvard-educated Bradford labored with
   Hawthorne in the fields and taught at the community's school.

whose duty it was to wash the tea dishes, used to hurry through the task with great rapidity, the young men helping by wiping them. I recollect particularly one evening in the moral philosophy class,—which must have been very interesting to rouse and keep the enthusiasm of a girl of sixteen,—when the question of free will came up. Mr. Ripley read aloud Jonathan Edwards's famous chapter on Golden, Silver, Wooden, and Pottery Vessels, and this was followed by a most exciting discussion between Mr. Ripley and Miss Bruce.[4]

* * *

Among the unwarranted calumnies formerly circulated about Brook Farm was the assertion that a good deal of flirting was carried on there. I have been much with young people in my life,—a teacher for some years, a mother with several children, and now a grandmother with hosts of grandchildren,—and I have never seen more truly gentlemanly and gentlewomanly relations between youths and maidens than at Brook Farm. I am sure not only that no harm was done, either to young men or maidens, by the healthful and simple intercourse that was invariable between them, but that very much good came, especially to the young men. There seemed a desire in each person to make Brook Farm a happy home. There were few of us who had not enough work each day, either manual or intellectual, generally both, to give a keen zest to the pleasures of the evening. It seems to me, as I look back upon the happy hours of recreation, that we were more amiable and content with ourselves and one another than any circle of people I have ever known since.

Among our daytime amusements were some charming picnics in the pine-tree grove, one of which is almost exactly described in The Blithedale Romance. Hawthorne's one variation from the facts was in making me, both there and in the American Note-Books, the gypsy fortune teller, whereas that part was really taken by Mrs. Ripley, and I was merely the messenger to bring persons to her; but it would seem that I must have done some talking on my own account.

In the happy Brook Farm evenings there were games for the young people at the Hive, while once or twice a week, at the same place, the older classes listened to Mr. Bradford's readings of Racine's and Molière's[5] plays,—delightful readings they were,—or to discussions in Mr. Ripley's moral philosophy class. At the Eyrie we had charming

4. Apparently, a chapter from *Freedom of the Will* (1754) by the American philosopher and theologian Jonathan Edwards (1703–1758), though no reference to "Golden, Silver, Wooden, and Pottery Vessels" (which figure in a parable found in 2 Timothy 2:20–21) appears in that text.
5. Molière: pen name of Jean Baptiste Poquelin (1622–1673), French comic dramatist; Jean Baptiste Racine (1639–1699): French playwright, famous for his classical tragedies.

singing by the two Curtis brothers,[6] occasional concerts given by people from "the world," talks by Margaret Fuller, William H. Channing, and others, sometimes dancing in moderation, and once in a while a fancy-dress party.

NATHANIEL HAWTHORNE

From The American Notebooks[†]

[*Sunday, September 26, 1841*]

* * *

A walk in the forenoon, along the edge of the meadow towards Cow Island. Large trees, almost a wood, principally of pine, with the green pasture glades intermixed, and cattle feeding. * * *

Within the verge of the meadow, mostly near the firm shore of pasture ground, I found several grape vines, hung with abundance of large purple grapes. The vines had caught hold of maples and alders, and climbed to the top, curling round about and interwreathing their twisted folds in so intimate a manner, that it was not easy to tell the parasite from the supporting tree or shrub.[1] Sometimes the same vine had enveloped several shrubs, and caused a strange tangled confusion, converting all these poor plants to the purposes of its own support, and hindering them growing to their own benefit and convenience. The broad vine-leaves, some of them yellow or yellowish-tinged, were seen apparently growing on the same stems with the silver maple leaves, and those of the other shrubs, thus married against their will by this conjugal twine; and the purple clusters of grapes hung down from above and in the midst, so that a man might gather grapes, if not of thorns, yet of as alien bushes. One vine had ascended almost to the tip-top of a large white pine tree, spreading its leaves and hanging its purple clusters among all its boughs—still climbing and clambering, as if it would not be content till it crowned the very summit of the tree with a wreath of

---

6. James Burrill Curtis and George William Curtis—Brook Farm's "young Greek gods"—arrived at Brook Farm at the ages of twenty and eighteen, respectively. George would become the influential editor of *Harper's Weekly*, Burrill an Anglican clergyman in England.
† From *The American Notebooks*, ed. Claude M. Simpson (Columbus: Ohio State University Press, 1972), pp. 196–204, 209–10. Reprinted by permission of The Ohio State University Press.
1. Compare this passage to the description of "Coverdale's Hermitage," pp. 69–71.

its own foliage and a cluster of grapes. I mounted high into the tree, and ate grapes there, while the vine wreathed still higher into the depths of the tree, above my head. The grapes were sour, being not yet fully ripe; some of them, however, were sweet and pleasant. The vine embraces the trees like a serpent.

[*Tuesday, September 28, 1841*]

A picnic party in the woods, yesterday, in honor of Frank Dana's birth-day, he being six years old.[2] I strolled into the woods, after dinner, with Mr. Bradford; and in a lonesome glade, we met the apparition of an Indian chief, dressed in appropriate costume of blanket, feathers, and paint, and armed with a musket. Almost at the same time a young gipsey fortune teller came from among the trees, and proposed to tell my fortune; which while she was doing, the goddess Diana (known on earth as Miss Ellen Slade) let fly an arrow and hit me smartly in the hand. This fortune teller and goddess were a fine contrast, Diana being a blonde, fair, quiet, with a moderate composure; and the gipsey (Ora Gannet) a bright, vivacious, dark-haired, rich-complexioned damsel—both of them very pretty; at least, pretty enough to make fifteen years enchanting. Accompanied by these denizens of the wild wood, we went onward, and came to a company of fantastic figures, arranged in a ring for a dance or game. There was a Swiss girl, an Indian squaw, a negro of the Jim Crow order,[3] one or two foresters; and several people in Christian attire; besides children of all ages. Then followed childish games, in which the grown people took part with mirth enough—while I, whose nature it is to be a mere spectator both of sport and serious business, lay under the trees and looked on. Meanwhile, Mr. Emerson and Miss Fuller, who had arrived an hour or two before, came forth into the little glade where we were assembled. Here followed much talk.

The ceremonies of the day concluded with a cold collation of cakes and fruit. * * * It has left a fantastic impression on my memory, this intermingling of wild and fabulous characters with real and homely ones, in the secluded nook of the woods. I remember them with the sunlight breaking through overshadowing branches, and they appearing and disappearing confusedly—perhaps starting out of the earth; as if the every day laws of Nature were suspended for this particular occasion. There are the children, too, laughing and sporting about, as if they were at home among such strange shapes—and

---

2. Compare the following passage to the novel's description of an open air masquerade party, pp. 144–45.
3. A white person in blackface make-up, imitating one of the stock characters of the nineteenth-century minstrel show.

anon bursting into loud uproar of lamentation, when the rude gambols of the merry-makers chance to overturn them. And, apart, with a shrewd Yankee observation of the scene, stands our friend Orange,[4] a thickset, sturdy figure, in his blue frock, enjoying the fun well enough, yet rather laughing with a perception of its nonsensicallness, than at all entering into the spirit of the thing.

* * *

I ought to have mentioned, among the diverse and incongruous guests of the picnic party, our two Spanish boys from Manilla—Lucas with his heavy features and almost mulatto complexion; and Jose, slighter, with rather a feminine face—not a gay-girlish one, but grave, reserved, eyeing you sometimes with an earnest, but secret expression, and causing you to question what sort of person he is. Make up the group with good, homely, sensible Mrs. Pratt, and her husband, every way fitted to her—pattern specimens of New England matrimony.

[Friday, October 1, 1841]

I have been looking at our four swine, not of the last lot, but those in process of fatting.[5] They lie among the clean rye straw in their stye, nestling close together; for they seem to be a sensitive beast to the cold; and this is a clear, bright, chrystal, north-west windy, cool morning. So there lie these four black swine, as deep among the straw as they can burrow, the very symbols of slothful ease and sensual comfort. They seem to be actually oppressed and over-burthened with comfort. They are quick to notice any one's approach to the stye, and utter a low grunt—not drawing a breath for that particular purpose, but grunting with their ordinary breath—at the same time turning an observant, though dull and sluggish eye upon the visitor. They seem to be involved and buried in their own corporeal substance, and to look dimly forth at the outer world. They breathe not easily, and yet not with difficulty or discomfort; for the very unreadiness and oppression with which their breath comes, appears to make them sensible of the deep sensual satisfaction which they feel. Swill, the remnant of their last meal, remains in their trough, denoting that their food is more abundant than even a hog can demand. Anon, they fall asleep, drawing short and heavy breaths, which heave their huge sides up and down; but at

---

4. The farmer T. J. Orange, a Brook Farm neighbor; compare the novel's depiction of Silas Foster at the masquerade, pp. 144–45.
5. Hawthorne makes use of this paragraph in Chapter XVI of the novel; see pp. 100–01.

the slightest noise, they sluggishly unclose their eyes, and give another gentle grunt. They also grunt among themselves, apparently without any external cause, but merely to express their swinish sympathy. I suppose it is the knowledge that these four grunters are doomed to die within two or three weeks, that gives them a sort of awfulness in my conception; it makes me contrast their present gross substance of fleshly life with the nothingness speedily to come.

Meantime, the four newly bought pigs are running about the cow-yard, lean, active, shrewd, investigating everything, as their nature is. When I throw apples among them, they scramble with one another for the prize; and the successful one scampers away to eat it at leisure. They thrust their snouts into the mud, and pick a grain of corn out of the filth. Nothing within their sphere do they leave unexamined—grunting all the time, with infinite variety of expression. Their language seems to be the most copious of that of any quadruped; and, indeed, there is something deeply and indefinably interesting in the swinish race. They appear the more a mystery, the longer you gaze at them; it seems as if there was an important meaning to them, if you could but find out. One interesting trait in swine, is their perfect independence of character. They care not for man, and will not adapt themselves to his notions, as other beasts do; but are true to themselves, and act out their hoggish nature.

[*Saturday, October 9, 1841*]

Still dismal weather. Our household, being composed in great measure of children and young people, is generally a cheerful one enough, even in gloomy weather. For a week past, we have been especially gladdened with a little sempstress from Boston,[6] about seventeen years old, but of such a petite figure that, at first view, one would take her to be hardly in her teens. She is very vivacious and smart, laughing, singing, and talking, all the time—talking sensibly, but still taking the view of matters that a city girl naturally would. If she were larger than she is, and of less pleasing aspect, I think she might be intolerable; but being so small, and with a white skin, healthy as a wild flower, she is really very agreeable; and to look at her face is like being shone upon by a ray of the sun. She never walks, but bounds and dances along; and this motion, in her small person, does not give the idea of violence. It is like a bird, hopping from twig to twig, and chirping merrily all the time. Sometimes she is a little vulgar; but even that works well enough into her character, and accords with it. On continued observation and acquaintance,

---

6. This passage finds its way into two of the novel's descriptions of Priscilla; see pp. 24–25, 52–54.

you discover that she is not a little girl, but really a little woman, with all the prerogatives and liabilities of a woman. This gives a new aspect to her character; while her girlish impression still continues, and is strangely combined with the sense that this frolicksome little maiden has the material for that sober character, a wife. She romps with the boys, runs races with them in the yard, and up and down the stairs, and is heard scolding laughingly at their rough play. She asks William Allen to put her "on top of that horse;" whereupon he puts his large brown hands about her waist, and, swinging her to-and-fro, places her on horseback. By the bye, William threatened to rivet two horse shoes round her neck, for having clambered, with the other girls and boys, upon a load of hay; whereby the said load lost its balance, and slided off the cart. She strings the seed-berries of roses together, making a scarlet necklace of them, which she wears about her neck. She gathers everlasting flowers, to wear in her hair or bonnet, arranging them with the skill of a dress-maker. In the evening, she sits singing by the hour together, with the musical part of the establishment—often breaking into laughter, whereto she is incited by the tricks of the boys. The last thing you hear of her, she is tripping up stairs, to bed, talking lightsomely or singing; and you meet her in the morning, the very image of lightsome morn itself, smiling briskly at you, so that one takes her for a promise of cheerfulness through the day. Be it said, among all the rest, there is a perfect maiden modesty in her deportment; though I doubt whether the boys, in their rompings with her, do not feel that she has past out of her childhood.

This lightsome little maid has left us this morning; and the last thing I saw of her was her vivacious face, peeping through the curtain of the carryall, and nodding a brisk farewell to the family, who were shouting their adieus at the door. With her other merits, she is an excellent daughter, and, I believe, supports her mother by the labor of her hands. It would be difficult to conceive, beforehand, how much can be added to the enjoyment of a household by mere sunniness of temper and smartness of disposition; for her intellect is very ordinary, and she never says anything worth hearing, or even laughing at, in itself. But she herself is an expression, well worth studying.

NATHANIEL HAWTHORNE

Letters from Brook Farm

To Sophia Peabody, Boston, June 1, 1841[†]

Very dearest,

I have been too busy to write thee a long letter by this opportunity; for I think this present life of mine gives me an antipathy to pen and ink, even more than my Custom House[1] experience did. I could not live without the idea of thee, nor without spiritual communion with thee; but, in the midst of toil, or after a hard day's work in the gold mine, my soul obstinately refuses to be poured out on paper. That abominable gold mine! Thank God, we anticipate getting rid of its treasurers, in the course of two or three days. Of all hateful places, that is the worst; and I shall never comfort myself for having spent so many days of blessed sunshine there. It is my opinion, dearest, that a man's soul may be buried and perish under a dung-heap or in a furrow of the field, just as well as under a pile of money. Well; that giant, Mr. George Bradford, will probably be here to-day; so that there will be no danger of thy husband being under the necessity of laboring more than he likes, hereafter. Meantime, my health is perfect, and my spirits buoyant, even in the gold mine.

* * *

Thy lovingest husband.

To G. S. Hillard, Boston, July 16, 1841[‡]

Dear Hillard,[1]

I have not written that infernal story. The thought of it has tormented me ever since I came here, and has deprived me of all the

---

[†] From *The Letters, 1813–1843*, ed. Thomas Woodson, L. Neal Smith, Norman Holmes Pearson (Columbus: Ohio State University Press, 1984), p. 545. Reprinted by permission of The Ohio State University Press.

1. Hawthorne refers to his stint in the position of measurer at the Boston Custom House, which he held from January 1839 through December 1840.

[‡] From *The Letters, 1813–1843*, ed. Thomas Woodson, L. Neal Smith, Norman Holmes Pearson (Columbus: Ohio State University Press, 1984), p. 550. Reprinted by permission of The Ohio State University Press.

1. George Stillman Hillard, a Boston lawyer, literary critic, and editor, was Hawthorne's friend and personal attorney; Hawthorne had promised him a story for the 1842 edition of *The Token*.

comfort I might otherwise have had, in my few moments of leisure. Thank God, it is now too late—so I disburthen my mind of it, now and forever.

You cannot think how exceedingly I regret the necessity of disappointing you; but what could be done? An engagement to write a story must in its nature be conditional; because stories grow like vegetables, and are not manufactured, like a pine table. My former stories all sprung up of their own accord, out of a quiet life. Now, I have no quiet at all; for when my outward man is at rest—which is seldom, and for short intervals—my mind is bothered with a sort of dull excitement, which makes it impossible to think continuously of any subject. You cannot make a silk purse out of a sow's ear; nor must you expect pretty stories from a man who feeds pigs.

My hands are covered with a new crop of blisters—the effect of raking hay; so excuse this scrawl.

Yours truly,
Nath. Hawthorne.

To David Mack, Cambridge, July 18, 1841[†]

My dear Sir,[1]

Your letter has this moment been put into my hands. I truly thank you for it, and wish to lose no time in correcting some misapprehensions which have been caused by your judging of my feelings through the medium of third persons—and partly from my brief and imperfect communications to you, last Sunday.

I have never felt that I was called upon by *Mr. Ripley* to devote so much of my time to manual labor, as has been done since my residence at Brook Farm; nor do I believe that others have felt constraint of that kind, from him personally. We have never looked upon him as a master, or an employer, but as a fellow laborer on the same terms as ourselves, with no more right to bid us perform any one act of labor, than we have to bid him. Our constraint has been merely that of circumstances, which were as much beyond his control as our own; and there was no way of escaping this constraint, except by leaving the farm at once; and this step none of us were prepared to take, because (though attributing less importance to the success of this immediate enterprise than

† From *The Letters, 1813–1843*, ed. Thomas Woodson, L. Neal Smith, Norman Holmes Pearson (Columbus: Ohio State University Press, 1984), pp. 552–54. Reprinted by permission of The Ohio State University Press.
1. David Mack, a teacher from Cambridge, had signed the articles of agreement that first established the Brook Farm community, but never carried out his intention to join; in 1842 he became one of the founders of the Northampton Association, a utopian community in western Massachusetts.

Mr. Ripley does) we still felt that its failure would be very inauspicious to the prospects of the community. For my own part, there are private and personal motives[2] which, without the influence of those shared by us all, would still make me wish to bear all the drudgery of this one summer's labor, were it much more onerous than I have found it. It is true that I not infrequently regret that the summer is passing with so little enjoyment of nature and my own thoughts, and with the sacrifice of some objects that I had hoped to accomplish. Such were the regrets to which I alluded, last Sunday; but Mr. Ripley cannot be held responsible for the disagreeable circumstances which cause them.

I recollect speaking very despondingly, or perhaps despairingly, of the prospects of the institution. My views in this respect vary somewhat with the state of my spirits; but I confess that, of late, my hopes are never very sanguine. I form my judgment, however, not from anything that has passed within the precincts of Brook Farm, but from external circumstances—from the improbability that adequate funds will be raised, or that any feasible plan can be suggested, for proceeding without a very considerable capital. I likewise perceive that there would be some very knotty points to be discussed, even had we capital enough to buy an estate. These considerations have somewhat lessened the heartiness and cheerfulness with which I formerly went forth to the fields, and perhaps have interposed a medium of misunderstanding between Mr. Ripley and us all. His zeal will not permit him to doubt of eventual success; and he perceives, or imagines, a more intimate connection between our present farming operations and our ultimate enterprise, than is visible to my perceptions. But, as I said before, the two things are sufficiently connected, to make me desirous of giving my best efforts to the promotion of the former.

You will see, I think, from what I have now stated, that there was no pressing necessity for me, or my fellow laborers, to dishearten Mr. Ripley, by expressing dissatisfaction with our present mode of life. It is our wish to give his experiment a full and fair trial; and if his many hopes are to be frustrated, we should be loth to give him reason to attribute the failure to lack of energy and perseverance in his associates. Nevertheless, we did, several days since (he and myself, I mean) have a conversation on the subject; and he is now fully possessed of my feelings, in respect to personal labor.

* * *

2. His wish to find a living situation that would enable him and Sophia to marry.

To Sophia Peabody, Lynn, Massachusetts, August 12, 1841[†]

Belovedest, I am very well, and not at all weary; for yesterday's rain gave us a holyday; and moreover the labors of the farm are not so pressing as they have been. And—joyful thought!—in a little more than a fortnight, thy husband will be free from his bondage[1]—free to think of his Dove— free to enjoy Nature—free to think and feel! I do think that a greater weight will then be removed from me, than when Christian's burthen fell off at the foot of the cross.[2] Even my Custom House experience was not such a thraldom and weariness; my mind and heart were freer. Oh; belovedest, labor is the curse of this world, and nobody can meddle with it, without becoming proportionably brutified. Dost thou think it a praiseworthy matter, that I have spent five golden months in providing food for cows and horses? Dearest, it is not so. Thank God, my soul is not utterly buried under a dung-heap. I shall yet rescue it, somewhat defiled, to be sure, but not utterly unsusceptible of purification.

* * *

Thine ownest.

To Sophia Peabody, Boston, August 22, 1841[‡]

* * *

Dearest wife, it is extremely doubtful whether Mr. Ripley will succeed in locating his community on this farm. He can bring Mr. Ellis to no terms; and the more they talk about the matter, the farther they appear to be from a settlement. Thou and I must form other plans for ourselves; for I can see few or no signs that Providence purposes to give us a home here. I am weary, weary, thrice weary of waiting so many ages. Yet what can be done? Whatever may be thy husband's gifts, he has not hitherto shown a single one that may avail to gather gold. I confess that I have strong hopes of good from this arrangement with Munroe;[1] but when I look at the scanty avails of my past literary efforts, I do not feel authorized to expect much from the future. Well; we shall see. Other persons have bought large estates and built splendid mansions

---

† From *The Letters, 1813–1843*, ed. Thomas Woodson, L. Neal Smith, Norman Holmes Pearson (Columbus: Ohio State University Press, 1984), pp. 557–58. Reprinted by permission of The Ohio State University Press.

1. Hawthorne had arranged with Ripley to begin paying for his board, freeing him from his labor obligations.

2. A scene from John Bunyan's *The Pilgrim's Progress* (1678).

‡ From *The Letters, 1813–1843*, ed. Thomas Woodson, L. Neal Smith, Norman Holmes Pearson (Columbus: Ohio State University Press, 1984), pp. 563–64. Reprinted by permission of The Ohio State University Press.

1. James Munroe, a Boston publisher with whom Hawthorne was negotiating.

with such little books as I mean to write; so perhaps it is not unreasonable to hope that mine may enable me to build a little cottage—or, at
least, to buy or hire one. But I am becoming more and more convinced, that we must not lean upon the community. What ever is to be
done, must be done by thy husband's own individual strength. Most
beloved, I shall not remain here through the winter, unless with an
absolute certainty that there will be a home ready for us in the spring.
Otherwise I shall return to Boston,—still, however, considering myself
an associate of the community; so that we may take advantage of any
more favorable aspect of affairs. Dearest, how much depends on those
little books! Methinks, if anything could draw out my whole strength,
it should be the motives that now press upon me. Yet, after all, I must
keep these considerations out of my mind, because an external pressure always disturbs, instead of assisting me.

Dearest, I have written the above in not so good spirits as sometimes; but now that I have so ungenerously thrown my despondency
on thee, my heart begins to throb more lightly. I doubt not that God
has great good in store for us; for He would not have given us so
much, unless He were preparing to give a great deal more. I love thee!
Thou lovest me! What present bliss! What sure and certain hope!

Thine ownest husband.

To Sophia Peabody, Boston, September 3, 1841[†]

* * *

Sweetest, it seems very long already since I saw thee; but thou hast
been all the time in my thoughts; so that my being has been contin-
uous. Therefore, in one sense, it does not seem as if we had parted at
all. But really, I should judge it to be twenty years since I left Brook
Farm,[1] and I take this to be one proof that my life there was an
unnatural and unsuitable, and therefore an unreal one. It already
looks like a dream behind me. The real Me was never an associate of
the community; there has been a spectral Appearance there, sounding the horn at day-break, and milking the cows, and hoeing potatoes, and raking hay, toiling and sweating in the sun, and doing me
the honor to assume my name. But be not thou deceived, Dove of
my heart. This Spectre was not thy husband. Nevertheless, it is
somewhat remarkable that thy husband's hands have, during this
past summer, grown very brown and rough; insomuch that many

[†] From *The Letters, 1813–1843*, ed. Thomas Woodson, L. Neal Smith, Norman Holmes
Pearson (Columbus: Ohio State University Press, 1984), p. 566. Reprinted by permission
of The Ohio State University Press.
1. Hawthorne writes from Salem, where he was visiting his mother and sisters.

people persist in believing that he, after all, was the aforesaid spectral horn-sounder, cow-milker, potatoe-hoer, and hay-raker.

To Sophia Peabody, Boston, September 22, 1841[†]

Dearest love, here is thy husband again, slowly adapting himself to the life of this queer community, whence he seems to have been absent half a life time—so utterly has he grown apart from the spirit and manners of the place. Thou knowest not how much I wanted thee, to give me a home-feeling in the spot—to keep a feeling of coldness and strangeness from creeping into my heart and making me shiver. Nevertheless, I was most kindly received; and the fields and woods looked very pleasant, in the bright sunshine of the day before yesterday. I had a friendlier disposition towards the farm, now that I am no longer obliged to toil in its stubborn furrows. Yesterday and to-day, however, the weather has been intolerable—cold, chill, sullen, so that it is impossible to be on kindly terms with mother Nature. Would I were with thee, mine own warmest and truest-hearted wife! I never shiver, while encircled in thine arms.

Belovedest, I doubt whether I shall succeed in writing another volume of Grandfather's Library,[1] while I remain at the farm. I have not the sense of perfect seclusion, which has always been essential to my power of producing anything. It is true, nobody intrudes into my room; but still I cannot be quiet. Nothing here is settled—everything is but beginning to arrange itself—and though thy husband would seem to have little to do with aught beside his own thoughts, still he cannot but partake of the ferment around him. My mind will not be abstracted. I must observe, and think, and feel, and content myself with catching glimpses of things which may be wrought out hereafter. Perhaps it will be quite as well that I find myself unable to set seriously about literary occupation for the present. It will be good to have a longer interval between my labor of the body and that of the mind. I shall work to the better purpose, after the beginning of November.[2] Meantime, I shall see these people and their enterprise under a new point of view, and perhaps be able to determine whether thou and I have any call to cast in our lot among them.

* * *

[†] From *The Letters, 1813–1843*, ed. Thomas Woodson, L. Neal Smith, Norman Holmes Pearson (Columbus: Ohio State University Press, 1984), pp. 575–77. Reprinted by permission of The Ohio State University Press.
1. *Biographical Stories for Children*, which would be published in April 1842.
2. Hawthorne intended to leave Brook Farm for the winter months.

We had some tableaux last night. They were very stupid, (as, indeed, was the case with all I have ever seen) but do not thou tell Mrs. Ripley so. She is a good woman, and I like her better than I did—her husband keeps his old place in my judgment. Farewell, thou gentlest Dove—thou perfectest woman—thou desirablest wife.

Thine ownest Husband.

To Sophia Peabody, Boston, September [30], 1841[†]

* * *

Dearest love, thy husband was elected to two high offices, last night—viz., to be a Trustee of the Brook Farm estate, and Chairman of the Committee of Finance!!!![1] Now dost thou not blush to have formed so much lower an opinion of my business talents, than is entertained by other discerning people? From the nature of my hoffice, I shall have the chief direction of all the money affairs of the community—the making of bargains—the supervision of receipts and expenditures &c. &c &c. Thou didst not think of this, when thou didst pronounce me unfit to make a bargain with that petty knave of a publisher. A prophet has no honor among them of his own kindred,[2] nor a financier in the judgment of his wife.

Belovedest, my accession to these august offices does not at all decide the question of my remaining here permanently. I told Mr. Ripley, that I could not spend the winter at the farm, and that it was quite uncertain whether I returned in the spring.

* * *

Thy truest husband.

[†] From *The Letters, 1813–1843*, ed. Thomas Woodson, L. Neal Smith, Norman Holmes Pearson (Columbus: Ohio State University Press, 1984), p. 582. Reprinted by permission of The Ohio State University Press.
1. At this same meeting, Hawthorne agreed to purchase two shares of stock in Brook Farm for $1,000.
2. In Matthew 13:57, Jesus observes that "a prophet is not without honor, save in his own country, and in his own house."

Decision

NATHANIEL HAWTHORNE

Letters, after Brook Farm

To David Mack, Northampton, Massachusetts, May 25, 1842[†]

My dear Sir,

When I last met you, I expressed my purpose of coming to Northampton, in the course of the present month, in order to gain information as to the situation and prospects of your community.[1] Since our interview, however, circumstances of various kinds have induced me to give up the design of offering myself as a member. As a matter of conscience, with my present impressions, I should hardly feel myself justified in taking such a step; for, though I have much faith in the general good tendency of institutions on this principle, yet I am troubled with many doubts (after my experience of last year) whether I, as an individual, am a proper subject for those beneficial influences. In an economical point of view, undoubtedly, I could not do so well anywhere else; but I feel that this ought not to be the primary consideration. A more important question is, how my intellectual and moral condition, and my ability to be useful, would be affected by merging myself in a community. I confess to you, my dear Sir, it is my present belief that I can best attain the higher ends of life, by retaining the ordinary relation to society.

With my best wishes for your prosperity and happiness,

I remain Yours sincerely,
Nath. Hawthorne.

† From *The Letters, 1813–1843*, ed. Thomas Woodson, L. Neal Smith, Norman Holmes Pearson (Columbus: Ohio State University Press, 1984), p. 624. Reprinted by permission of The Ohio State University Press.
1. By the time he wrote this letter, Hawthorne had decided not to return to Brook Farm; he had left the community for the winter in late October 1841. Mack had invited him to consider joining another utopian community, the Northampton Association of Education and Industry, which had begun its operation in April 1842.

216   NATHANIEL HAWTHORNE

To Charles A. Dana, Brook Farm, October 17, 1842[†]

I ought, some time ago, to have tendered my resignation as an associate of the Brook Farm Institute, but I have been unwilling to feel myself entirely disconnected with you. As I can see but little prospect, however, of returning to you, it becomes proper for me now to take the final step. But no longer a brother of your band, I shall always take the warmest interest in your progress, and shall heartily rejoice at your success—of which I can see no reasonable doubt.

[†] From *The Letters, 1813–1843*, ed. Thomas Woodson, L. Neal Smith, Norman Holmes Pearson (Columbus: Ohio State University Press, 1984), p. 655. Reprinted by permission of The Ohio State University Press.

The Woman Question

Through the characters of Zenobia and Priscilla, Hawthorne brings into *The Blithedale Romance* some of the questions about the social roles and moral and political rights of women that deeply concerned him and his contemporaries. These questions gather with particular force around Zenobia, who is presented as a well-known lecturer on women's rights and who delivers several impassioned speeches about the condition of women. The first of the selections in this section is an excerpt from Margaret Fuller's essay "The Great Lawsuit: Man *versus* Men. Women *versus* Women," which was published in the *Dial* in July 1843. Fuller, one of the leading intellectuals of her day and a pioneering feminist thinker, was a frequent visitor to Brook Farm, and readers of the novel have long speculated about her relation to Hawthorne's Zenobia (for an exploration of Fuller's presence in the novel, see *Hawthorne's Fuller Mystery*, by Thomas C. Mitchell, listed in the "Selected Bibliography"). We might think of this passage as giving us a chance to hear one of Zenobia's "off-stage" addresses on women's rights. The second passage, from a July 1845 entry in Hawthorne's notebooks, recounts his participation in the recovery of the body of Martha Hunt, who had drowned herself in the Concord River; he drew from this remarkable entry, which reveals a strong sense of the burdens borne by a young woman who failed to fit the social expectations of her time, in writing chapter 27 of the novel.

MARGARET FULLER

[What Woman Needs]†

Many women are considering within themselves what they need that they have not, and what they can have, if they find they need it. Many men are considering whether women are capable of being and having more than they are and have, and whether, if they are, it will be best to consent to improvement in their condition.

The numerous party, whose opinions are already labelled and adjusted too much to their mind to admit of any new light, strive, by lectures on some model-women of bridal-like beauty and gentleness, by writing or lending little treatises, to mark out with due precision the limits of woman's sphere, and woman's mission, and to prevent other than the rightful shepherd from climbing the wall, or the flock from using any chance gap to run astray.

Without enrolling ourselves at once on either side, let us look upon the subject from that point of view which to-day offers. No better, it is to be feared, than a high house-top. A high hill-top, or at least a cathedral spire, would be desirable.

It is not surprising that it should be the Anti-Slavery party that pleads for woman, when we consider merely that she does not hold property on equal terms with men; so that, if a husband dies without a will, the wife, instead of stepping at once into his place as head of the family, inherits only a part of his fortune, as if she were a child, or ward only, not an equal partner.

We will not speak of the innumerable instances, in which profligate or idle men live upon the earnings of industrious wives; or if the wives leave them and take with them the children, to perform the double duty of mother and father, follow from place to place, and threaten to rob them of the children, if deprived of the rights of a husband, as they call them, planting themselves in their poor lodgings, frightening them into paying tribute by taking from them the children, running into debt at the expense of these otherwise so overtasked helots.[1] Though such instances abound, the public opinion of his own sex is against the man, and when cases of extreme tyranny are made known, there is private action in the wife's favor. But if woman be, indeed, the weaker party, she ought to have legal protection, which would make such oppression impossible.

---

† From "The Great Lawsuit: Man *versus* Men. Woman *versus* Women," *Dial* (Boston: July 1843).
1. Slaves. This is an accurate description of the legal situation of women at this time.

And knowing that there exists, in the world of men, a tone of feeling towards women as towards slaves, such as is expressed in the common phrase, "Tell that to women and children;" that the infinite soul can only work through them in already ascertained limits; that the prerogative of reason, man's highest portion, is allotted to them in a much lower degree; that it is better for them to be engaged in active labor, which is to be furnished and directed by those better able to think, &c. &c.; we need not go further, for who can review the experience of last week, without recalling words which imply, whether in jest or earnest, these views, and views like these? Knowing this, can we wonder that many reformers think that measures are not likely to be taken in behalf of women, unless their wishes could be publicly represented by women?

That can never be necessary, cry the other side. All men are privately influenced by women; each has his wife, sister, or female friends, and is too much biased by these relations to fail of representing their interests. And if this is not enough, let them propose and enforce their wishes with the pen. The beauty of home would be destroyed, the delicacy of the sex be violated, the dignity of halls of legislation destroyed, by an attempt to introduce them there. Such duties are inconsistent with those of a mother; and then we have ludicrous pictures of ladies in hysterics at the polls, and senate chambers filled with cradles.

But if, in reply, we admit as truth that woman seems destined by nature rather to the inner circle, we must add that the arrangements of civilized life have not been as yet such as to secure it to her. Her circle, if the duller, is not the quieter. If kept from excitement, she is not from drudgery. Not only the Indian carries the burdens of the camp, but the favorites of Louis the Fourteenth accompany him in his journeys, and the washerwoman stands at her tub and carries home her work at all seasons, and in all states of health.

As to the use of the pen, there was quite as much opposition to woman's possessing herself of that help to free-agency as there is now to her seizing on the rostrum or the desk; and she is likely to draw, from a permission to plead her cause that way, opposite inferences to what might be wished by those who now grant it.

As to the possibility of her filling, with grace and dignity, any such position, we should think those who had seen the great actresses, and heard the Quaker preachers of modern times, would not doubt, that woman can express publicly the fulness of thought and emotion, without losing any of the peculiar beauty of her sex.

As to her home, she is not likely to leave it more than she now does for balls, theatres, meetings for promoting missions, revival meetings, and others to which she flies, in hope of an animation for her existence, commensurate with what she sees enjoyed by men.

Governors of Ladies' Fairs are no less engrossed by such a charge, than the Governor of the State by his; presidents of Washingtonian societies,[2] no less away from home than presidents of conventions. If men look straitly to it, they will find that, unless their own lives are domestic, those of the women will not be. The female Greek, of our day, is as much in the street as the male, to cry, What news? We doubt not it was the same in Athens of old. The women, shut out from the market-place, made up for it at the religious festivals. For human beings are not so constituted, that they can live without expansion; and if they do not get it one way, must another, or perish.

And, as to men's representing women fairly, at present, while we hear from men who owe to their wives not only all that is comfortable and graceful, but all that is wise in the arrangement of their lives, the frequent remark, "You cannot reason with a woman," when from those of delicacy, nobleness, and poetic culture, the contemptuous phrase, "Women and children," and that in no light sally of the hour, but in works intended to give a permanent statement of the best experiences, when not one man in the million, shall I say, no, not in the hundred million, can rise above the view that woman was made *for man*, when such traits as these are daily forced upon the attention, can we feel that man will always do justice to the interests of woman? Can we think that he takes a sufficiently discerning and religious view of her office and destiny, ever to do her justice, except when prompted by sentiment; accidentally or transiently, that is, for his sentiment will vary according to the relations in which he is placed. The lover, the poet, the artist, are likely to view her nobly. The father and the philosopher have some chance of liberality; the man of the world, the legislator for expediency, none.

Under these circumstances, without attaching importance in themselves to the changes demanded by the champions of woman, we hail them as signs of the times. We would have every arbitrary barrier thrown down. We would have every path laid open to woman as freely as to man. Were this done, and a slight temporary fermentation allowed to subside, we believe that the Divine would ascend into nature to a height unknown in the history of past ages, and nature, thus instructed, would regulate the spheres not only so as to avoid collision, but to bring forth ravishing harmony.

Yet then, and only then, will human beings be ripe for this, when inward and outward freedom for woman, as much as for man, shall be acknowledged as a right, not yielded as a concession. As the friend of the negro assumes that one man cannot, by right, hold another in bondage, should the friend of woman assume that man cannot, by right, lay even well-meant restrictions on woman. If the

2. Temperance organizations, which might well be headed by women.

negro be a soul, if the woman be a soul, apparelled in flesh, to one
master only are they accountable. There is but one law for all souls,
and, if there is to be an interpreter of it, he comes not as man, or son
of man, but as Son of God.

Were thought and feeling once so far elevated than man should
esteem himself the brother and friend, but nowise the lord and tutor
of woman, were he really bound with her in equal worship, arrangements as to function and employment would be of no consequence.
What woman needs is not as a woman to act or rule, but as a nature
to grow, as an intellect to discern, as a soul to live freely, and unim-
peded to unfold such powers as were given her when we left our
common home.

NATHANIEL HAWTHORNE

[For Want of Sympathy][†]

* * *

On the night of July 9th, a search for the dead body of a drowned girl.
She was a Miss Hunt, about nineteen years old; a girl of education
and refinement, but depressed and miserable for want of sympathy—
her family being an affectionate one, but uncultivated, and incapable
of responding to her demands. She was of a melancholic temperament, accustomed to solitary walks in the woods. At this time, she had
the superintendence of one of the district-schools, comprising sixty
scholars, particularly difficult of management. Well; Ellery Channing[1]
knocked at the door, between 9 and 10 in the evening, in order to get
my boat, to go in search of this girl's drowned body. He took the oars,
and I the paddle, and we went rapidly down the river, until, a good
distance below the bridge, we saw lights on the bank, and the dim
figures of a number of people waiting for us. Her bonnet and shoes
had already been found on this spot, and her handkerchief,
I believe, on the edge of the water; so that the body was probably at
no great distance, unless the current (which is gentle, and almost
imperceptible) had swept her down.

We took in General Buttrick,[2] and a young man in a blue frock,
and commenced the search; the general and the other man having

---

† From *The American Notebooks*, ed. Claude M. Simpson (Columbus: Ohio State University Press, 1972), pp. 261–67. Reprinted by permission of The Ohio State University Press.
1. William Ellery Channing (1817–1901), poet and friend of Hawthorne, living in Concord.
2. Probably General Joshua Buttrick, an officer in the local militia who owned a farm near the Concord River.

long poles, with hooks at the end, and Ellery a hay-rake, while I steered the boat. It was a very eligible place to drown one's self. On the verge of the river, there were water-weeds; but after a few steps, the bank goes off very abruptly, and the water speedily becomes fifteen or twenty feet deep. It must be one of the deepest spots in the whole river; and, holding a lantern over it, it was black as midnight, smooth, impenetrable, and keeping its secrets from the eye as perfectly as mid-ocean could. We caused the boat to float once or twice past the spot where the bonnet &c had been found; carefully searching the bottom at different distances from the shore—but, for a considerable time without success. Once or twice the poles or the rake caught in bunches of water-weed, which, in the star-light, looked like garments; and once Ellery and the General struck some substance at the bottom, which they at first mistook for the body; but it was probably a sod that had rolled in from the bank. All this time, the persons on the bank were anxiously waiting, and sometimes giving us their advice to search higher or lower, or at such and such a point. I now paddled the boat again past the point where she was supposed to have entered the river, and then turned it, so as to let it float broadside downwards, about midway from bank to bank. The young fellow in the blue frock sat on the next seat to me, plying his long pole.

We had drifted a little distance below the group of men on the bank, when this fellow gave a sudden start—"What's this?" cried he. I felt in a moment what it was; and I suppose the same electric shock went through everybody in the boat. "Yes; I've got her!" said he; and heaving up his pole with difficulty, there was an appearance of light garments on the surface of the water; he made a strong effort, and brought so much of the body above the surface, that there could be no doubt about it. He drew her towards the boat, grasped her arm or hand; and I steered the boat to the bank, all the while looking at this dead girl, whose limbs were swaying in the water, close at the boat's side. The fellow evidently had the same sort of feeling in his success as if he had caught a particularly fine fish; though mingled, no doubt, with horror. For my own part, I felt my voice tremble a little, when I spoke, at the first shock of the discovery; and at seeing the body come to the surface, dimly in the starlight. When close to the bank, some of the men stepped into the water and drew out the body; and then, by their lanterns, I could see how rigid it was. There was nothing flexible about it; she did not droop over the arms of those who supported her, with her hair hanging down, as a painter would have represented her; but was all as stiff as marble. And it was evident that her wet garments covered limbs perfectly inflexible. They took her out of the water, and deposited her under an oak-tree; and by the time we had got ashore, they were examining her by the light of two or three lanterns.

I never saw nor imagined a spectacle of such perfect horror. The rigidity, above spoken of, was dreadful to behold. Her arms had stiffened in the act of struggling; and were bent before her, with the hands clenched. She was the very image of a death-agony; and when the men tried to compose her figure, her arms would still return to that same position; indeed it was almost impossible to force them out of it for an instant. One of the men put his foot upon her arm, for the purpose of reducing it by her side; but, in a moment, it rose again. The lower part of the body had stiffened into a more quiet attitude; the legs were slightly bent, and the feet close together. But that rigidity!—it is impossible to express the effect of it; it seemed as if she would keep the same posture in the grave, and that her skeleton would keep it too, and that when she rose at the day of Judgment, it would be in the same attitude.

As soon as she was taken out of the water, the blood began to stream from her nose. Something seemed to have injured her eye, too; perhaps it was the pole, when it first struck the body. The complexion was a dark red, almost purple; the hands were white, with the same rigidity in their clench as in all the rest of the body. Two of the men got water, and began to wash away the blood from her face; but it flowed and flowed, and continued to flow; and an old carpenter, who seemed to be skilful in such matters, said that this was always the case, and that she would continue to "purge," as he called it, in this manner, until her burial, I believe. He said, too, that the body would swell, by morning, so that nobody would know her. Let it take what change it might, it could scarcely look more horrible than it did now, in its rigidity; certainly, she did not look as if she had gotten grace in the world whither she had precipitated herself; but rather, her stiffened death-agony was an emblem of inflexible judgment pronounced upon her. If she could have foreseen, while she stood, at 5 o'clock that morning, on the bank of the river, how her maiden corpse would have looked, eighteen hours afterwards, and how coarse men would strive with hand and foot to reduce it to a decent aspect, and all in vain—it would surely have saved her from this deed. So horribly did she look, that a middle-aged man, David Buttrick,[3] absolutely fainted away, and was found lying on the grass, at a little distance, perfectly insensible. It required much rubbing of hands and limbs to restore him.

Meantime, General Buttrick had gone to give notice to the family that the body was found; and others had gone in search of rails, to make a bier. Another boat now arrived, and added two or three more horror-struck spectators. There was a dog with them, who looked at the body, as it seemed to me, with pretty much the same feelings as

3. Another Concord farmer.

the rest of us—horror and curiosity. A young brother of the deceased, apparently about twelve or fourteen years old, had been on the spot from the beginning. He seemed not much moved, externally, but answered questions about his sister, and the number of the brothers and sisters, (ten in all,) with composure. No doubt, however, he was stunned and bewildered with the scene—to see his sister lying there, in such terrific guise, at midnight, under an oak, on the verge of the black river, with strangers clustering about her, holding their lanterns over her face; and that old carpenter washing the blood away, which still flowed forth, though from a frozen fountain. Never was there a wilder scene. All the while, we were talking about the circumstances, and about an inquest, and whether or no it was necessary, and of how many it should consist; and the old carpenter was talking of dead people, and how he would as lief handle them as living ones.

By this time, two rails had been procured, across which were laid some boards or broken oars from the bottom of a boat; and the body, being wrapt in an old quilt, was laid upon this rude bier. All of us took part in bearing the corpse, or in steadying it. From the bank of the river to her father's house, there was nearly half a mile of pasture-ground, on the ascent of the hill; and our burthen grew very heavy, before we reached the door. What a midnight procession it was! How strange and fearful it would have seemed, if it could have been foretold, a day beforehand, that I should help carry a dead body along that track! At last, we reached the door, where appeared an old gray-haired man, holding a light; he said nothing, seemed calm, and after the body was laid upon a large table, in what seemed to be the kitchen, the old man disappeared. This was the grandfather. Good Mrs. Pratt[4] was in the room, having been sent for to assist in laying out the body; but she seemed wholly at a loss how to proceed; and no wonder—for it was an absurd idea to think of composing that rigidly distorted figure into the decent quiet of the coffin. A Mrs. Lee had likewise been summoned, and shortly appeared, a withered, skin-and-bone looking woman; but she, too, though a woman of skill, was in despair at the job, and confessed her ignorance how to set about it. Whether the poor girl did finally get laid out, I know not, but can scarcely think it possible. I have since been told that, on stripping the body, they found a strong cord wound round the waist, and drawn tight—for what purpose is impossible to guess.

"Ah, poor child!"—that was the exclamation of an elderly man, as he helped draw her out of the water. I suppose one friend would have saved her; but she died for want of sympathy—a severe penalty

---

4. Maria T. Pratt; with her husband Minot, she had been at Brook Farm during Hawthorne's time there; they now had a farm in Concord.

for having cultivated and refined herself out of the sphere of her natural connections.

She is said to have gone down to the river at 5 in the morning, and to have been seen walking to and fro on the bank, so late as 7—there being all that space of final struggle with her misery. She left a diary, which is said to exhibit (as her whole life did) many high and remarkable traits. The idea of suicide was not a new one with her; she had before attempted, walking up to her chin into the water, but coming out again, in compassion to the agony of a sister, who stood on the bank. She appears to have been religious, and of a high morality.

The reason, probably, that the body remained so near the spot where she drowned herself, was, that it had sunk to the bottom of perhaps the deepest spot in the river, and so was out of the action of the current.

Mesmerism

"Mesmerism" refers to a set of beliefs and practices that grew out of the theories of the Austrian physician Franz Mesmer (1734–1815), which held that an invisible substance, or "ether," made potentially healing communication between souls or with the spirit world possible. Often referred to as "animal magnetism," a phrase that captures the ostensible power of the mesmerist to influence, or "magnetize," the interior spiritual substance ("anima") of his subject, mesmeric practices ranged from private therapeutic encounters between patient and healer to the kind of public demonstrations of "magnetic" phenomena depicted in the novel. Mesmerism was brought to the United States by Charles Poyen, a Frenchman who conducted a series of well-attended public demonstrations of mesmerism's trance-inducing power in various New England cities in 1836–37. While in Europe interest in mesmerism was confined to aristocratic circles, in America it found a broad middle-class audience, and its promise of access to a deeper reality attracted people attached to the concept of human perfectibility central to reform culture, while its implications about the permeability of the psyche and the nature of consciousness attracted the kind of psychological speculations and anxieties that we witness in the novel (see especially chapter 23). In the selection from Poyen's 1837 account of his New England tour provided here, he makes a case for the scientific validity of animal magnetism, and reprints a newspaper report of a successful—and notably theatrical—demonstration of the power of the magnetic trance. Poyen's account is followed by excerpts from a "Practical Magnetizer's" 1843 description of the theory and practice of his profession. In the final selection, Hawthorne, writing from Brook Farm, makes an impassioned plea that his fiancée Sophia Peabody, seeking treatment for her severe headaches, refrain from using the services of a mesmerical healer. Robert C. Fuller's *Mesmerism and the American Cure of Souls*, listed in the "Selected Bibliography," offers a valuable history of this phenomenon.

CHARLES POYEN

[The Proofs of Animal Magnetism]†

Animal Magnetism being * * * a science of observation, has not ceased to gain ground more and more rapidly, although violently and generally opposed, because the results of positive experiments proved stronger than all the arguments used against it. It is not advocated from "*a priori views*"[1] or on the ground that it agrees with the religious or philosophical prejudices of man, &c. On the contrary, it apparently attacks and overturns all the received notions of the present generation, all that has been inculcated upon us by philosophy and education! It changes materially, in several points, the mental constitution of mankind. Far from being enthusiastically led into a belief in the reality of it, those who begin the investigation of its claims, are at first decided skeptics; they proceed with diffidence and care in their examination, and, in order to satisfy their mind fully, they do not resort to reasoning, but to repeated, sifted, and positive experiments.

Some will reply, that "*witchcraft*," which is now generally acknowledge to have been a gross and lamentable superstition, was likewise pretended to be founded on facts; that it was, for centuries, believed in by all classes of society, and countenanced even by a crowd of distinguished men, some of whom were the greatest geniuses of their time, &c. We answer, that witchcraft originated from an "*a priori notion*," from a mere article of faith, viz. the belief in the existence of the devil, and in his influence on human affairs. This belief had been handed down from the very beginning of society; it was deeply impressed on the public mind through education, religious doctrines, and social institutions; it had thus become a profound and powerful element of the mental constitution of mankind. The infernal agency being admitted as an indisputable truth, people were forcibly led into the most serious and absurd errors; every thing that appeared strange, was immediately attributed to the diabolical interference; even on some occasions, the public mind was so much engrossed and perverted by that superstition, that they mistook very plain, yea, common natural effects, for evident proofs of an intercourse existing between certain individuals and the evil spirit. Such was, to quote an instance, the witchcraft delusion in Salem, Massachusetts. * * *

---

† From *Progress of Animal Magnetism in New England* (Boston: Weeks, Jordan & Co., 1837), pp. 27–29, 78–85. Poyen's footnotes have been deleted.
1. Views held prior to or independent of experience or observation.

Now Animal Magnetism did not originate, like witchcraft, from any preconceived idea or popular notion; its claims are not founded on a mere article of faith; and those who have assented to a belief in its reality, had not within themselves, like the partisans of witchcraft, a cause of error. Animal Magnetism, I repeat, sprung from observation; Mesmer and all his disciples have claimed for it the title of natural science; they have constantly endeavored to combat superstition, and remove all remaining prejudices concerning the influence of spiritual agents, by contending and showing that the phenomena once attributed to the action of the devil, are the results of a peculiar modification of which the nervous organization of man is susceptible, when placed in certain circumstances.

* * *

I offer the following statement, merely as a specimen of some of the experiments which I usually perform, and that have already been seen by upwards of one hundred individuals of this city [Boston].[2]

These experiments took place on Saturday evening, February 4th inst. I put Miss Gleason to the magnetic sleep towards a quarter past seven o'clock. The operation did not last more than a minute and a half. At half past seven, some company which I expected, arrived, and found the lady on her rocking-chair, motionless, with her eyes closed, and exactly as a person delivered up to the natural sleep. Among the gentlemen present, were Dr. C. T. Jackson, Dr. H. Dewar, Messrs, Clark, H. K. Horton, Andrew Morse, Jr., well known by his ingenious and useful inventions in mechanics, Wilson Dana, a lawyer in Charlestown.[3]

Various attempts were made to awake Miss Gleason, but without success. Dr. Jackson examined the state of her eyes, and it was found that the lids were firmly closed, and resisted very much against the efforts which were made to open them. Being thus partially opened, the eye-balls were seen turned upward, and convulsed; the white of the eye, only, could be seen.

Two gentlemen, in succession, shook her, spoke to her in a loud voice, and took her hand, but could not obtain a word from her. Then I approached and spoke to her, in a tone much lower, and she answered immediately the question I proposed to her.

2. Poyen reprints this account of his "experiment" from the *Boston Courier* of February 10, 1837.
3. Poyen's medium, or "somnambulist"—the receptive person through whom magnetism's insights were evoked by the mesmerist—was Cynthia Gleason, a young woman from Pawtucket, Rhode Island, who worked as a weaver in a cotton cloth factory. (In another newspaper article, Poyen had provided testimonials to her upright character.) The men mentioned are clearly prominent citizens, chosen to lend authority to the proceedings.

Some time having elapsed in general conversation, a gentleman came to me, and asked me whether I could make the somnambulist talk with another person, and cause her to cease speaking by my will. I answered, that I thought I could.

Two handkerchiefs, folded up several times, were tied over Miss Gleason's eyes and face, down to the opening of the nostrils. It was agreed that a gentleman should stand behind the somnambulist's chair, in order to give the signal when to act. One of the gentlemen took the position, holding a pencil-case in his hand. The signals agreed upon were, that when the pencil was held horizontally, I would cause Miss Gleason to speak; when it was held vertically, I would cause her to stop speaking.

Dr. Jackson sat by Miss Gleason's right side, and I stood about one foot and a half distant from her left side, stooping, with both my hands leaning on my knees; my mouth was about on the level with the top of Miss Gleason's head.

Dr. Jackson began to talk, but obtained no answer. The pencil was placed on the horizontal line. Dr. Jackson put some other question—then Miss Gleason turned her head towards him, and answered his questions readily. The pencil was placed vertically, immediately the somnambulist ceased speaking. The pencil was held again horizontally, and she resumed the conversation. These experiments were made four or five times in succession, and always successfully. They were pronounced satisfactory by all the gentlemen. The bandages were removed; then I said aloud to the somnambulist, "Why have you spoken with Dr. Jackson, at times?" She answered—"Because you *told me to.*" "Why did you cease to talk with him?" "Because you *told me to.*" Now, it is a fact, that I did not move my lips once. None of those who were around, watching my motions, could discover any thing of the kind; neither did I touch the somnambulist; consequently, she was influenced by my will only.

* * *

Some moments after this, Miss Gleason called me, and begged for some water. A tumbler was brought in; Dr. Jackson took it, and presented it to the somnambulist, even pressed it against her lips, but she took no notice of it. The tumbler was handed to me; I presented it to Miss Gleason, at some distance from her face, without speaking a word; then she stretched out her hand, grasped it, and drank part of the water. Dr. Dewar presented his hand to receive the tumbler; the somnambulist took no notice of him; he then took hold of the glass, and made considerable efforts to pull it, by force, from Miss Gleason's hand, but she resisted so strongly, that the gentleman was obliged to leave it off, for fear that she would break it, and hurt her fingers. Then I presented my hand, and willed her to give me the tumbler; she first put it to her lips, drank again two or three swallows, and *gave it back to me*.

These experiments, as well as the preceding, were declared satisfactory. * * *

A few moments having elapsed, I requested her to move from the rocking-chair, and sit on another chair, placed at about 12 feet distance. She got up, walked with a firm step, her eyes being perfectly closed, and sat on the chair which I presented to her.

Then Dr. Dewar told me, in a very low voice, that he was going to tickle her with a feather, and that I should cause her alternately to feel, and cease feeling, "by my will."

A bandage was set over her eyes. Mr. Clark stood behind her, with a pencil-case in his hand, in order to give the signal agreed upon. The first signal given, was, "not to feel." The feather was carried along her lips and nostrils; no effect was produced. The pencil-case, then, was placed in the vertical position, which indicated that I should cause the somnambulist to feel. Immediately she began to move her lips, raised her hands, and brushed the feather off. The contrary signal was given again, and she became as insensible as before. This experiment was declared satisfactory.

At my suggestion, a gentleman said that he should like to submit himself to the examination of the somnambulist, for the state of his health. In consequence, he seated himself by her, she took hold of his arm, and touched the pulse. After expressing herself about the state of the pulse, she added, "I don't think that this gentleman is very sick; I don't see any thing much out of order in him." "Look at me internally." "I was doing so." "How is my stomach?" "Pretty good; nothing ails it." "What is the size of my stomach—large?" Then she indicated with her hand the size and shape of the organ. "How does it look? what is its color?" "Red." "Is it very red?" "Not very; about like a blush-rose." "Look at the intestine, next to the stomach." "It is well." "How does it look internally—is it smooth or rough?" "It is rather rough; I see wrinkles, and a great many small edges, *as in a grater*." (This description of the intestine *duodenum*, coming from a person so entirely ignorant of anatomy, is certainly striking. Is it possible to use a more happy comparison, than that borrowed of a grater, to express the appearance of the numerous asperities, or villosities, that exist on the internal coat of the intestine?) "How are my lungs?" "They are sound; yet I see in them two or three small pipes, filled up with a *frothy, white, yellowish* matter, that ought to make you cough sometimes." "It is so in almost every body." "Oh, not in every body who is well." "How is my heart?" "Large." "How much does it weigh?" "I should think one pound." "Look at my liver; how is it?" "Your liver is dark-colored; it is darker than it ought to be; but I don't see any thing out of order in it, except *three or four white spots, like water blisters.*" "Are you sure of that?" "Certain; I see it." "I believe you are mistaken." "No, you may depend on my word; as there is a God in heaven, those white spots are on your liver." "On which part of the organ?" "On the lower edge; you must look out for that." "Why?" "Because they will keep spreading all around, if you don't take care." * * * The gentleman made some inquiries more, about his blood, &c.; but the somnambulist declared that she was very much fatigued. Then the gentleman got up, and said that he had been affected with a disease of the liver, some time past, but was getting rid of it.

This examination being finished, I announced that I was going to awake Miss Gleason. I approached her, and laying my hand on her forehead, I said, "You will awake in six minutes exactly." "I feel very much fatigued," said she, "but I will try to awake, as you want me to." Then I observed to the company, that I had noticed, on several occasions, that Miss Gleason could not "keep so good time, when her mind was fatigued, as when it felt easy and clear." Then I retired the length of about eight feet, and taking Dr. Jackson apart, I asked him, in his ear, to let me know which arm he wished that I should strike with palsy.

"The left," said he. Then, while a gentleman was holding a sheet of paper before the somnambulist's face, in order to prevent her seeing, (supposing that she *should feign*, which cannot be reasonably admitted, after so many trials,) I passed my hand two or three times over her left arm, from the shoulder down to the hand, and at the distance of several inches. First, a sudden convulsive motion of the head, neck, and chest, was manifested,—exactly like the effect produced by a shock of electricity. Soon after the left arm was seized with the same convulsion, and fell on the somnambulist's knees, insensible and motionless.

According to what I had announced, Miss Gleason awoke in a wrong time, viz. about two minutes after the prescribed time. She preserved no recollection of any kind of what had transpired. Dr. Jackson approached, and, in order to ascertain whether the left arm was really palsied, he passed his fingers, suddenly, and without speaking a word about it, towards the elbow, and pressed upon the *Cubital* nerve, in its passage along the head of the Cubitus bone. Every body knows how exceedingly sensitive this part is. Yet Miss Gleason gave no sign of sensibility. She was also pinched on her hand several times, and felt no sensation. The arm was lifted up and let drop suddenly; it fell down like a piece of wood. Several ladies and gentlemen were around Miss Gleason, in conversation with her.

Without mentioning it, I passed slowly behind her, made a sign to Drs. Jackson and Dewar, and in about one minute restored the arm, simply by pointing my fingers toward the shoulder, without touching it. This last experiment was considered to be the most surprising of all.

* * *

"A PRACTICAL MAGNETIZER"

[The Art of Magnetizing]†

The art of Magnetizing—All persons possess the power—Method of operating—The Magnetic state—Its leading features * * *

It is universally contended by Magnetizers that all persons possess the magnetic power—females as well as males, and even children—differing only in degree. It is also believed that all persons can be acted upon by magnetic influence, differing, of course, in the degree of their susceptibility.

In answer to the inquiry, "can every person be magnetized?" we answer—yes. But one individual cannot magnetize every body. The most powerful magnetizer in the whole world (if he could be found) might magnetize all the rest of his fellow beings. But until this man be found, we must be content with this simple principle of nature—a lesser power cannot overcome a greater.

The difference in magnetic power between any two individuals arises, of course, from the different amount of vital fluid in their systems; from the presence or absence of the intellectual and moral qualifications necessary to perform the operation; and from their knowledge or ignorance of the rules by which the art is governed. A man of powerful and well cultivated intellect, accustomed to mathematical abstraction, possessing a strong physical constitution full of vital fluid, will, of course, perform the operation of magnetizing better than a person in a low state of vitality, with a weak, uncultivated, or wandering mind. Thus it will be seen why some persons cannot magnetize every body. A lesser power cannot overcome a greater.

† From *History and Philosophy of Animal Magnetism with Practical Instructions for the Exercise of This Power: Being a Complete Compend of All the Information Now Existing upon This Important Subject* (Boston: J. N. Bradley & Co., 1843), pp. 10–13, 18–20.

The power of magnetizing is greatly increased by practice. The operator gains confidence—learns to economise his power, and to exert it to advantage—and acquires a certain knowledge, feeling, or "knack," which it is almost impossible to explain in language.

The usual method of magnetizing a "new subject," or one who has never been magnetized before, is this:

The magnetizer takes a seat in front of the person to be magnetized. * * * He first places the palms of his own hands upon the hands of the subject, and endeavors to establish an equal degree of warmth between them. He then places the balls of his thumbs against the balls of his subject's thumbs, holding the hands with a gentle pressure. Then abstracting his mind from all other thoughts and objects, and fixing his eyes upon the eyes of the subject, with earnest, determined, penetrating, but somewhat mild expression, he exerts an unremitted, unchanging effort of *will*, increasing in intensity the longer it continues, until the subject yield before his superior power, and closes his eyes in the magnetic sleep.

During all this operation the eyes of the magnetizer should not for an instant relax their hold upon the eyes of the subject, or move a hair's-breadth from their object, which is the very pupil of the eye. The magnetizer should not even wink from first to last, till the eyes of the subject close involuntarily as if made of lead. Incredible as it may seem, the eyes of a powerful magnetizer can be kept unwinking for half an hour, or even longer.

The act of magnetizing is now considered almost entirely a severe mental operation, very little physical exertion is believed to be required.

As soon as the eyes of the subject close, the magnetizer begins to make the "passes" as they are called, with both hands, from the crown of the head down the sides of the face and body, to the end of the fingers, throwing the hands outward and carrying them back again to the crown of the head in semi-circles. The fingers of the operator, at this time, should always be kept slightly separated. After making these passes two or three minutes, (or longer) the magnetizer should pass his hands lightly from the head, directly across the face to the pit of the subject's stomach (*always avoiding the nose and chin*) permitting them to rest upon the stomach for a moment, then throwing them outward as before. Let these passes be continued for a few minutes; then repeat the first passes; then make several long passes from the head down to the feet; and the work is finished. If many experiments should be tried with the subject, the short passes must be occasionally repeated.

The prevailing sentiment in the mind of the magnetizer, during this operation, should be strong determination of will, united with benevolence of feeling. The proper ingredients of the magnetic power, are happily illustrated by the magic circle on the last page of this work.

An experienced magnetizer can generally tell by his own feelings whether he is likely to be successful or not. If successful, he seems to fasten upon the eye of the subject, with a gathering fascinating power, of a peculiar nature—and when this has been accomplished, he should endeavor, by all means, to keep the "charm" unbroken. This is the feeling, or "knack," before alluded to.

A subject is awakened and brought out of the magnetic state, by making passes, at the distance of two inches from the body, upward from the stomach to the head, exerting the will in a moderate degree to produce the desired result. There is no difficulty in this, and extended directions are therefore unnecessary.

After the magnetic sympathy is established, between the magnetizer and his patient, by holding the thumbs, and exercising the *will*, the external senses of sight, hearing, feeling, tasting, and smelling, generally become blunted, one by one; the eyelids are irresistably drawn together; a tingling sensation is felt in the arms; cold currents of air seem to be passing around the body, in the direction of the magnetizer's hands; and a general torpor falls upon the limbs. The eye yields first to the slumbrous influence, but long after that organ has ceased to act, the hearing retains all its acuteness, and the patient is still able to indicate sounds. But at length the "porches of the ear" are closed, as well as the "curtain of the eye,"—the senses of feeling, taste, and smell, lose their external power and the patient, though still alive and breathing, is dead to every thing around him, save the magnetizer's voice.

This condition is not always, as has been supposed, a state of *perfect insensibility*. It is believed, however, that no power but magnetism can awaken a subject while in the perfect somnambulic state. You may call upon them, but unless you are placed in magnetic communication, they cannot hear you. You may make shrill noises in their ears, or discharge pistols over their heads, but you cannot start them. None of the subjects that we have operated upon, could be awakened by external injuries inflicted upon the body. Very strong ammonia applied to the nostrils, will sometimes cause them to move the head, and will bring tears from the eyes, but will not dispel the magnetic influence. So, if snuff, or red pepper, or hartshorn, should be thrust into the nostrils, with the end of a quill, until it reached the nerves of the eye, and affected the lungs, it would cause a sensation of pain, but would not arouse the patient, and he would know nothing of it, when brought back to his natural state. But what is very curious, although an arm or a leg might be amputated, without causing the patient to start, a slight dash of cold water thrown into the face will make him start more than any thing that can be done to him.

We know that many of the operations of the body go on as in ordinary life, and there is a living, palpitating substance beneath the paralyzed surface—but the avenues of external sensation seem to be generally closed—the patient loses control over his own thoughts and actions—and remembers nothing of what has passed, on being brought back to the natural state.

All persons, in the magnetic state, do not present the same phenomena.

Some persons are entirely rigid and insensible to pain, in every part of the body. You may pierce their flesh with knives, pull out their teeth, cauterize them with a hot iron, apply the most powerful caustic to their flesh, or give them an electric shock which would cause instant death in the natural state, but they appear totally unconscious of your attacks.

Others manifest a degree of sensation altogether unnatural, falling into fits of rage, or violent convulsions, if only touched by a spectator, or brought into contact with steel and other substances.

Some persons never speak while in the magnetic state; some speak with difficulty; others speak with the greatest elegance and fluency.

Some subjects possess the power of clairvoyance, and second-sight in a high degree, and can see things independently of the magnetizer, near their heads or at great distance, and describe them with astonishing accuracy. Others are never able to see or describe anything, near them or at a distance.

There is evidently no invariable rule with regard to the powers which may be elicited by magnetic influence, in different somnambulists. Nor are the same subjects always alike at different times.

* * *

The principal results of Magnetic power—Sympathy of Sensation—Spiritual Knowledge—Clairvoyance—Describing internal Diseases
* * *

The grand characteristic of the Magnetic state, is the general insensibility of the system, and the control exercised over the mind and body of the subject, by the will of the Magnetizer.

The principal results which have been produced, in different subjects, by this power, are the following.

Sympathy of Sensation. The great sympathy of sensation, established between the subject and the magnetizer, is one of the first results of the magnetic condition. Some subjects manifest a more feeble degree of sympathy than others; but in general they feel very acutely all the pains, pleasures, tastes, and other sensations which the magnetizer feels; read his thoughts, and the two, in this respect, become "one flesh." There is no doubt at all upon this point.

Spiritual Knowledge. The fact that a person in the magnetic state, possesses superior knowledge, and wonderfully increased capacity of mind, is also placed beyond dispute. Under the influence of this power, the ignorant become wise; the weak-minded become strong and intelligent; a person of no musical taste or cultivation, can sing and play with a skill surpassing the most experienced performers; the profane and the infidel, become devout; and the whole moral and intellectual character, becomes changed from the degraded condition of earth, to the exalted intelligence of a spiritual state. The external senses are all suspended, and the internal sense or spirit, acts with its natural power, as it will when entirely freed from the body after death.

No person, we think, can listen to the revelations of a subject in a magnetic state, respecting the mysteries of our nature, and continue to doubt the existence of a never-dying soul, and the existence of a future, or heavenly life.

Clairvoyance. We also believe in the reality of an independent power of second-sight, called Clairvoyance—the power of seeing through all space, and describing scenes as existing at the moment, in any part of the universe, without the aid of the Magnetizer. When the subject receives ideas of places and things through the mind of the Magnetizer, it is merely *thought-reading*, or sympathy of sensation, not true Clairvoyance. There has been much mistake upon this point, and we wish to convey a correct idea of the power.

When the subject is in the perfect somnambulic state, the whole universe appears to them, (so they invariably inform us,) as if filled with light. They see with an internal or spiritual sense of sight, through the magnetic medium. When the magnetizer directs his mind to a particular object or place in any part of the world, he acts us a guide to point out the place or object which he would have the subject look at, and the subject then actually sees, not only that particular object or place, but all other objects and places in the vicinity, *as they exist at the moment;* they can then see things which the magnetizer cannot see, and never has seen, with an independent power of sight. In true Clairvoyant experiments, the magnetizer only acts as a guide to the subject; the subject does not see objects as stamped upon his imagination, but by looking directly at the objects themselves. We are a full believer in this doctrine.

Describing Internal Diseases. The power of seeing and describing the internal organs of the human system, is another remarkable peculiarity of the magnetic state. There is no doubt in the minds of practical magnetizers on this subject. It is the result of the Clairvoyant power and spiritual knowledge. Magnetic subjects differ of course very much in their capacity of seeing, and power of describing diseases, but all of them describe the same diseases in the same way, as we have proved by hundreds of experiments. In general they can do little towards prescribing a cure, but their advice is often of a very valuable character. Whenever they do prescribe, it is some simple or natural medicine, as roots and herbs, or some directions as to diet, bathing, exercise, &c.

* * *

NATHANIEL HAWTHORNE

[An Intrusion into thy Holy of Holies][†]

Letter to Sophia Peabody, Boston, October 16, 1841

Most dear wife, I received thy letters and note, last night, and was much gladdened by them; for never has my soul so yearned for thee as now. But, belovedest, my spirit is moved to talk with thee to-day about these magnetic miracles, and to beseech thee to take no part in them. I am unwilling that a power should be exercised on thee, of which we know neither the origin nor consequence, and the phenomena of which seem rather calculated to bewilder us, than to teach us any truths about the present or future state of being. If I possessed such a power over thee, I should not dare to exercise it; nor can I consent to its being exercised by another. Supposing that this power arises from the transfusion of one spirit into another, it seems to me that the sacredness of an individual is violated by it; there would be an intrusion into thy holy of holies—and the intruder would not be thy husband! Canst thou think, without a shrinking of thy soul, of any human being coming into closer communion with thee than I may?—than either nature or my own sense of right would permit me? *I* cannot. And, dearest, thou must remember, too, that thou art now a part of me, and that by surrendering thyself to the influence of this magnetic lady, thou surrenderest more than thine own moral and spiritual being—allowing that the influence *is* a moral and spiritual one. And, sweetest, I really do not like the idea of being

† From *The Letters, 1813–1843*, ed. Thomas Woodson, L. Neal Smith, Norman Holmes Pearson (Columbus: Ohio State University Press, 1984), pp. 588–90. Reprinted by permission of The Ohio State University Press.

brought, through thy medium, into such an intimate relation with Mrs. Park![1]

Now, ownest wife, I have no faith whatever that people are raised to the seventh heaven, or to any heaven at all, or that they gain any insight into the mysteries of life beyond death, by means of this strange science. Without distrusting that the phenomena which thou tellest me of, and others as remarkable, have really occurred, I think that they are to be accounted for as the result of a physical and material, not of a spiritual, influence. *Opium* has produced many a brighter vision of heaven (and just as susceptible of proof) than those which thou recountest. They are dreams, my love—and such dreams as thy sweetest fancy, either waking or sleeping, could vastly improve upon. And what delusion can be more lamentable and mischievous, than to mistake the physical and material for the spiritual? What so miserable as to lose the soul's true, though hidden, knowledge and consciousness of heaven, in the mist of an earth-born vision? Thou shalt not do this. If thou wouldst know what heaven is, before thou comest thither hand in hand with thy husband, then retire into the depths of thine own spirit, and thou wilt find it there among holy thoughts and feelings; but do not degrade high Heaven and its inhabitants into any such symbols and forms as those which Miss Larned[2] describes—do not let an earthy effluence from Mrs. Park's corporeal system bewilder thee, and perhaps contaminate something spiritual and sacred. I should as soon think of seeking revelations of the future state in the rottenness of the grave—where so many do seek it.

Belovedest wife, I am sensible that these arguments of mine may appear to have little real weight; indeed, what I write does no sort of justice to what I think. But I care the less for this, because I know that my deep and earnest feeling upon the subject will weigh more with thee than all the arguments in the world. And thou wilt know that the view which I take of this matter is caused by no want of faith in mysteries, but from a deep reverence of the soul, and of the mysteries which it knows within itself, but never transmits to the earthly eye or ear. Keep thy imagination sane—that is one of the truest conditions of communion with Heaven.

Dearest, after these grave considerations, it seems hardly worth while to submit a merely external one; but as it occurs to me, I will write it. I cannot think, without invincible repugnance, of thy holy name being bruited abroad in connection with these magnetic phenomena. Some (horrible thought!) would pronounce my Dove an impostor; the great majority would deem thee crazed; and even the

1. Cornelia Hall Park, a Boston friend of Sophia Peabody, lived intermittently at Brook Farm and was thought to possess significant "magnetic" power.
2. "Miss Larned" has not been identified; Sophia Peabody's letters do mention a Mr. Larned as a friend of Mrs. Park.

few believers would feel a sort of interest in thee, which it would be anything but pleasant to excite. And what adequate motive can there be for exposing thyself to all this misconception? Thou wilt say, perhaps, that thy visions and experiences would never be known. But Miss Larned's are known to all who choose to listen. Thy sister Elizabeth would like nothing so much as to proclaim thy spiritual experiences, by sound of trumpet.

October [18th]. Monday.—Most beloved, what a preachment have I made to thee! I love thee, I love thee, I love thee, most infinitely. Love is the true magnetism. What carest thou for any other? Belovedest, it is probable that thou wilt see thy husband tomorrow. Art thou magnificent. God bless thee. What a bright day is here, but the woods are fading now. It is time I were in the city, for the winter.

Thine ownest.

Urban Observation

Though primarily located at an agricultural commune, *The Blithedale Romance* contains a number of significant excursions into nearby Boston, and all of its main characters are exiles from urban life. Coverdale, an urbane bachelor with highly developed powers of observation and a tendency toward voyeurism and the vicarious, has struck many readers of the novel as an early version of the *flâneur*, an emergent social type who attempts to master urban experience by treating the city as an arena of pleasurable observation (for an account of the significance of this figure in American literature, see Dana Brand, *The Spectator and the City*, listed in the "Selected Bibliography"). The selections provided here allow us to glimpse this new sensibility in action. The first is a brief definition of the *flâneur*, taken from Charles Baudelaire's *The Painter of Modern Life*. Baudelaire (1821–1867), was a French essayist and poet, and has become an exemplary instance of the emergence of a distinctly modern sensibility in Western culture. Though he was writing this essay in 1859, several years after *Blithedale*, Baudelaire's sense of this urbane figure was in part derived from the writings of Hawthorne's American contemporary Edgar Allan Poe. The second passage comes from a sketch of New York City street life by N. P. Willis (1806–1867), American editor, poet, and sketch writer, a popular early master of this spectatorial literary style. The final selection gives us some passages of urban observation from Hawthorne's *American Notebooks*, several of which found their way into the novel.

CHARLES BAUDELAIRE

[The Perfect *Flâneur*]†

* * *

The crowd is his element, as the air is that of birds and water of fishes. His passion and his profession are to become one flesh with the crowd. For the perfect *flâneur*, for the passionate spectator, it is an immense joy to set up house in the heart of the multitude, amid the ebb and flow of movement, in the midst of the fugitive and the infinite. To be away from home and yet to feel oneself everywhere at home; to see the world, to be at the centre of the world, and yet to remain hidden from the world—such are a few of the slightest pleasures of those independent, passionate, impartial natures which the tongue can but clumsily define. The spectator is a *prince* who everywhere rejoices in his incognito. The lover of life makes the whole world his family, just like the lover of the fair sex who builds up his family from all the beautiful women that he has ever found, or that are—or are not—to be found; or the lover of pictures who lives in a magical society of dreams painted on canvas. Thus the lover of universal life enters into the crowd as though it were an immense reservoir of electrical energy. Or we might liken him to a mirror as vast as the crowd itself; or to a kaleidoscope gifted with consciousness, responding to each one of its movements and reproducing the multiplicity of life and the flickering grace of all the elements of life. He is an 'I' with an insatiable appetite for the 'non-I', at every instant rendering and explaining it in pictures more living than life itself, which is always unstable and fugitive. 'Any man,' he said one day, in the course of one of those conversations which he illumines with burning glance and evocative gesture, 'any man who is not crushed by one of those griefs whose nature is too real not to monopolize all his capacities, and who can yet be *bored in the heart of the multitude*, is a blockhead! a blockhead! and I despise him!'

* * *

† From *The Painter of Modern Life and Other Essays*, translated and edited by Jonathan Mayne (London: Phaidon Press, 1964), pp. 9–10.

NATHANIEL PARKER WILLIS

Daguerreotype Sketches of New York[†]

March made an expiring effort to give us a spring day yesterday. The morning dawned mild and bright, and there was a voluptuous contralto in the cries of the milkmen and the sweeps, which satisfied me, before I was out of bed, that there was an arrival of a south wind.

* * *

I strolled up Broadway between nine and ten, and encountered the *morning tide down*; and if you never have studied the physiognomy of this great thoroughfare in its various fluxes and refluxes, the differences would amuse you. The clerks and workies have passed down an hour before the nine o'clock tide, and the sidewalk is filled at this time with bankers, brokers, and speculators, bound to Wall-street; old merchants and junior partners, bound to Pearl and Water; and lawyers, young and old, bound for Nassau and Pine. Ah, the faces of care! The day's operations are working out in their eyes; their hats are pitched forward at the angle of a stage-coach with all the load on the driver's seat, their shoulders are raised with the shrug of anxiety, their steps are hurried and short, and mortal face and gait could scarcely express a heavier burden of solicitude than every man seems to bear. They nod to you without a smile, and with a kind of unconscious recognition; and, if you are unaccustomed to walk out at that hour, you might fancy that, if there were not some great public calamity, your friends, at least, had done smiling on you. Walk as far as Niblo's, stop at the green-house there, and breathe an hour in the delicious atmosphere of flowering plants, and then return. There is no longer any particular current in Broadway. Foreigners coming out from the *cafes*, after their late breakfast, and idling up and down, for fresh air; country people shopping early; ladies going to their dress-makers in close veils and demi-toilettes; errand-boys, news-boys, duns, and doctors make up the throng. Towards twelve o'clock there is a sprinkling of mechanics going to dinner—a merry, short-jacketed, independent-looking troop, glancing gayly at the women as they pass, and disappearing around corners and up alleys.

[†] From *The New Mirror* (New York), 1.7 (20 May 1843): 104. Daguerreotypy was an early form of photography, pioneered by the Parisian Louis Daguerre (1789–1851) and brought to America in 1839. Willis's title suggests that his observations aspire to the immediacy of photographs.

And an hour later Broadway begins to brighten. The omnibuses go along empty, and at a slow pace, for people would rather walk than ride. The side streets are tributaries of silks and velvets, flowers and feathers, to the great thoroughfare; and ladies, whose proper mates (judging by the dress alone) should be lords and princes, and dandies, shoppers, and loungers of every description, take crowded possession of the *pave*. At nine o'clock you look into the troubled faces of men going to their business, and ask yourself "to what end is all this burden of care?" and at two, you gaze on the universal prodigality of exterior, and wonder what fills the multitude of pockets that pay for it! The faces are beautiful, the shops are thronged, the side-walks crowded for an hour, and then the full tide turns, and sets upward. The most of those who are out at three are bound to the upper part of the city to dine; and the merchants and lawyers, excited by collision and contest above the depression of care, join, smiling, in the throng. The physiognomy of the crowd is at its brightest. Dinner is the smile of the day to most people, and the hour approaches. Whatever has happened in stocks or politics, whoever is dead, whoever ruined since morning, Broadway is thronged with cheerful faces and good appetites at three! The world will probably dine with pleasure up to the last day—perhaps breakfast with worldly care for the future on doomsday morning! And here I must break off my Daguerreotype of yesterday's idling, for the wind came round easterly and raw at three o'clock, and I was driven in-doors to try industry as an opiate.

NATHANIEL HAWTHORNE

From The American Notebooks[†]

[*The Bar at Parker's*]

Tuesday, May 7, 1850

I did not go out yesterday afternoon, but after tea I went to Parker's.[1] The drinking and smoking shop is no bad place to see one kind of life. The front apartment is for drinking. The door opens into Court Square, and is denoted, usually, by some choice specimens of dainties

† From *The American Notebooks*, ed. Claude M. Simpson (Columbus: Ohio State University Press, 1972), pp. 494–97, 501–504. Reprinted by permission of The Ohio State University Press.

1. H. D. Parker's saloon-restaurant, located at 3 Court Street in Boston. Hawthorne used this notebook entry in describing the bar in chapter 21 of the novel (pp. 120–23) and in his depiction of old Moodie.

exhibited in the windows, or hanging beside the door-post; as, for instance, a pair of canvas-back ducks, distinguishable by their delicately mottled feathers; an admirable cut of raw beefsteak; a ham, ready boiled, and with curious figures traced in spices on its outward fat; a half, or perchance the whole, of a large salmon, when in season; a bunch of partridges, &c, &c. A screen stands directly before the door, so as to conceal the interior from an outside barbarian. At the counter stand, at almost all hours,—certainly at all hours when I have chanced to observe,—tipplers, either taking a solitary glass, or treating all round, veteran topers, flashy young men, visitors from the country, the various petty officers connected with the law, whom the vicinity of the Court-House brings hither. Chiefly, they drink plain liquors, gin, brandy, or whiskey, sometimes a Tom and Jerry, a gin cocktail (which the bar-tender makes artistically, tossing it in a large parabola from one tumbler to another, until fit for drinking), a brandy-smash, and numerous other concoctions. All this toping goes forward with little or no apparent exhilaration of spirits; nor does this seem to be the object sought,—it being either, I imagine, to create a titillation of the coats of the stomach and a general sense of invigoration, without affecting the brain. Very seldom does a man grow wild and unruly.

The inner room is hung round with pictures and engravings of various kinds,—a painting of a premium ox, a lithograph of a Turk and of a Turkish lady, [. . .] and various showily engraved tailors' advertisements, and other shop bills; among them all, a small painting of a drunken toper, sleeping on a bench beside the grog-shop,—a ragged, half-hatless, bloated, red-nosed, jolly, miserable-looking devil, very well done, and strangely suitable to the room in which it hangs. Round the walls are placed some half a dozen marble-topped tables, and a centre-table in the midst; most of them strewn with theatrical and other show-bills; and the large theatre bills, with their type of gigantic solidity and blackness, hung against the walls.

Last evening, when I entered, there was one guest somewhat overcome with liquor, and slumbering with his chair tipped against one of the marble tables. In the course of a quarter of an hour, he roused himself, a plain, middle-aged man, and went out, with rather an unsteady step, and a hot, red face. One or two others were smoking, and looking over the papers, or glancing at a play-bill. From the centre of the ceiling descended a branch with two gas-burners, which sufficiently illuminated every corner of the room. Nothing is so remarkable in these bar-rooms and drinking-places as the perfect order that prevails there; if a man gets drunk, it is no otherwise perceptible than by his going to sleep, or inability to walk.

Walking the side-walk, in front of this grog-shop of Parkers, (or, sometimes, in cold or rainy days, taking his station inside) there is generally to be observed an elderly ragamuffin, in a dingy and battered hat, an old surtout, and a more than shabby general aspect; a thin face and red-nose, a patch over one eye, and the other half-drowned in moisture; he leans in a slightly stooping posture on a stick, forlorn and silent, addressing nobody, but fixing his one moist eye on you with a certain intentness. He is a man who has been in decent circumstances at some former period of life, but, falling into decay, (perhaps by dint of too frequent visits at Parker's bar) he now haunts about the place, (as a ghost haunts the spot where he was murdered) to "collect his rents", as Parker says—that is, to catch an occasional ninepence from some charitable acquaintance, or a glass of liquor at the bar. The word "ragamuffin," which I have used above, does not accurately express the man; because there is a sort of shadow or delusion of respectability about him; and a sobriety, too, and kind of decency, in his groggy and red-nosed destitution.

* * *

[All the Nooks and Crannies of Cities]

I take an interest in all the nooks and crannies and every develope-ment of cities; so here I try to make a description of the view from the back windows of a house in the centre of Boston, at which I glance in the intervals of writing.[2] The view is bounded, at perhaps thirty yards distance (or perhaps not so much,) by a row of opposite brick dwellings, standing, I think, on Temple-place; houses of the better order, with tokens of genteel families visible in all the rooms betwixt the basements and the attic windows in the roof; plate-glass in the rear drawing-rooms, flower-pots in some of the windows of the upper stories; occasionally, a lady's figure, either seated, or appearing with a flitting grace, or dimly manifest farther within the obscurity of the room. A balcony with a wrought iron fence running along under the row of drawing-room windows above the basement. In the space betwixt this opposite row of dwellings, and that in which I am situ-ated, are the low out-houses of the above described dwellings, with flat-roofs; or solid brick walls, with walks on them, and high railings, for the convenience of the washerwomen in hanging out their clothes. In the intervals betwixt these ranges of out houses or walks, are grass-plots, already green, because so sheltered; and fruit-trees, now begin-ning to put forth their leaves, and one of them, a cherry tree, almost in full blossom. Birds flutter and sing among these trees. I should judge it a good site for the growth of delicate fruit; for quite enclosed on all sides by houses; the blighting winds cannot molest the trees; they have sunshine on them a good part of the day, though the shadow

2. Details from this passage appear in Coverdale's description of the view from his hotel window, chapter 17, pp. 103–06.

must come early; and I suppose there is a rich soil about their roots. I see grape vines clambering against one wall, and also peeping over another, where the main body of the vine is invisible to me. In another place, a frame is erected for a grape vine, and probably it will produce as rich clusters as the vines of Madeira, here in the heart of the city, in this little spot of fructifying earth, while the thunder of wheels rolls about it on every side. The trees are not all fruit-trees; one pretty well-grown buttonwood tree aspires upward above the roofs of the houses. In the full verdure of summer, there will be quite a mass or curtain of foliage, between the hither and the thither row of houses.

* * *

[A Scene of Life in the Rough]

Wednesday, May 8, 1850

I went, last night, to the National Theatre to see a pantomime; it was Jack the Giant Killer, and somewhat heavy and tedious. The audience was more noteworthy than the play. The theatre itself is for the middling and lower classes; and I had not taken my seat in the most aristocratic part of the house; so that I found myself surrounded chiefly by young sailors, Hanover-street shopmen, mechanics, and other people of that kidney. It is wonderful the difference that exists in the personal aspect and dress, and no less in the manners, of people in this quarter of the city, as compared with others. One would think that Oak Hall[3] should give a common garb and air to the great mass of the Boston population; but it seems not to be so; and perhaps what is most singular is, that the natural make of the men has a conformity and suitableness to their dress. Glazed caps and Palo-Alto hats[4] were much worn. It is a pity that this picturesque and comparatively graceful hat should not have been generally adopted, instead of falling to the exclusive use of a rowdy class.

In the next box to me were two young women, with an infant of perhaps three or four months old (if so much) but to which of them appertaining, I could not at first discover. One was a large, plump girl, with a heavy face, a snub nose, coarse looking, but good-natured, and with no traits of evil; save, indeed, that she had on the vilest gown—of dirty white cotton, so pervadingly dingy that it was white no longer, as it seemed to me—the sleeves short, and ragged at the borders—and an old faded shawl, which she took off on account

3. A large Boston clothing store selling men's ready-to-wear apparel at modest prices.
4. Wide-brimmed hats named for the battle of Palo Alto, which began the Mexican War; the hats became popular during the 1849 gold rush.

of the heat—the shabbiest and dirtiest dress, in a word, that I ever saw a woman wear. Yet she was plump, as aforesaid, and looked comfortable in body and mind. I imagine that she must have had a better dress at home, but had come to the theatre extemporaneously, and not going to the dress-circle, considered her ordinary gown good enough for the occasion. The other girl seemed as young, or younger than herself; she was small, with a particularly intelligent and pleasant face, not handsome, perhaps, but as good or better than if it were. It was mobile with whatever sentiment chanced to be in her mind; as quick and vivacious a face in its movements as I have ever seen; cheerful, too, and indicative of a sunny, though I should think it might be a hasty temper. She was dressed in a dark gown, (chintz, I suppose the women call it,) a good homely dress, proper enough for the fireside, but a strange one to appear at a theatre in. Both these girls appeared to enjoy themselves very much; the large and heavy one, in her own duller mode; the smaller manifesting her interest by gestures, pointing at the stage, and so vivid a talk of countenance that I could sympathize precisely as well as if she had spoken. She was not a brunette; and this made her vivacity of expression the more agreeable. Her companion, on the other hand, was so dark that I rather suspected her to have a tinge of African blood.

There were two men who seemed to have some connection with these girls; one an elderly, gray-headed personage, well stricken in liquor, talking loudly and foolishly, but good-humouredly; the other a young man, sober, and doing his best to keep his elder friend quiet. The girls seemed to give themselves no uneasiness about the matter. Both the men wore Palo Alto hats. I could not make out whether either of the men were the father of the child, or what was the nature of the union among them; though I was inclined to set it down as a family-party.

As the play went on, the house became crowded, and oppressively warm; and the poor little baby grew dark red, or purple almost, with the uncomfortable heat in its small body. It must have been accustomed to discomfort, and have concluded it to be the condition of mortal life; else it never would have remained so quiet. * * * Perhaps it had been quieted with a sleeping potion. The two young women were not negligent of it, but passed it to-and-fro between them, each willingly putting herself to inconvenience for the sake of tending it. But I really feared it might die in some kind of a fit; so hot was the theatre; so purple with heat, yet strangely quiet, was the child. I was glad to hear it cry, at last; but it did not cry with any great rage and vigor, as it should, but in a stupid kind of way. Hereupon, the smaller of the two girls, after a little inefficacious dandling, at once settled the question of maternity, by uncovering her bosom, and presenting it to the child, with so little care of concealment that I saw, and anybody might have seen, the whole breast, and the apex which the infant's little lips compressed. Yet there was nothing indecent in this; but a perfect naturalness. The child sucked a moment or two, and then became quiet, but still looked very purple. Children must be hard to kill, however injudicious the treatment. The two girls, and their cavaliers, remained till nearly the close of the play. I should like well to know who they are—of what condition in life—and whether reputable as members of the class to which they belong. My own judgement is, that they are so.

Throughout the evening, drunken young sailors kept stumbling into and out of the boxes, calling to one another from different parts of the house, shouting to the performers, and singing the burthens of songs. It was a scene of life in the rough.

CRITICISM

Contemporary Responses

The Blithedale Romance received a mixed response from its first readers. The novel sold quite well during its first year: its print run of 7,440 copies (in two impressions) surpassed the first-year figures for both *The Scarlet Letter* (6,000) and *The House of the Seven Gables* (6,710). These sales figures made it, by the standards of the time, a very successful book, though they did not put it in the new (and quite rare) category of the best seller; sales of such books, mostly by women writers, were measured in the tens of thousands. Hawthorne's income from these sales was $867 (about $25,000—by a very rough estimate—in today's dollars). Hawthorne's publisher sold the English rights to the novel for the notable sum of 200 pounds (about $1000 in 1852—or roughly $28,000 in today's dollars), testimony to Hawthorne's growing reputation. But unlike Hawthorne's first two novels, which sold steadily during the 1850s, subsequent sales of *The Blithedale Romance* were weak: there was a modest printing of 536 copies in 1855, and about 1,000 additional copies were printed before Hawthorne's death in 1864. (About 9,000 copies of *Blithedale* were printed during Hawthorne's life, compared to 13,500 of *The Scarlet Letter* and 11,550 of *The House of the Seven Gables*.)

This section begins with a set of informal thoughts about or responses to the book, contained in letters to and from Hawthorne himself. Five of nearly sixty known contemporary reviews follow; along with what they have to say about *The Blithedale Romance,* the reviews reveal a good deal about expectations for fiction in Hawthorne's time.

NATHANIEL HAWTHORNE

Letters on *The Blithedale Romance*

[*An Extra Touch of the Devil*]†

FROM LETTER TO HORATIO BRIDGE, JULY 22, 1851

[Horatio Bridge (1806–1893) was a Bowdoin College classmate of Hawthorne's who went on to a distinguished career as a naval officer. A close and supportive friend throughout Hawthorne's life, Bridge played an important role in the establishment of his career as a writer by secretly providing the financial guarantee that underwrote the first edition of *Twice-told Tales*. Hawthorne edited—and perhaps helped to write—Bridge's 1845 *Journal of an African Cruiser*, an account of Bridge's service on a vessel assigned to interdict the slave trade. In this letter, Hawthorne offers a first glimpse of the gestation of *The Blithedale Romance*.]

Dear Bridge,

* * *

Since the first of June, I have written a book of two or three hundred pages, for children; and I think it stands a chance of a wide circulation. The title, at all events, is an *ad captandum*[1] one—'A Wonder Book for Girls and Boys.' I don't know what I shall write next. Should it be a romance, I mean to put an extra touch of the devil into it; for I doubt whether the public will stand two quiet books in succession, without my losing ground. As long as people will buy, I shall keep at work; and I find that my facility of labor increases with the demand for it.

* * *

Your friend,
Nath[l] Hawthorne.

---

† From *The Letters, 1843–1853*, ed. Thomas Woodson, L. Neal Smith, Norman Holmes Pearson (Columbus: Ohio State University Press, 1985), pp. 461–62. Reprinted by permission of The Ohio State University Press.
1. *Ad captandum vulgus*: to take the fancy of the crowd (Latin).

[*A Huge Bundle of Scribble*]†

FROM LETTER TO E. P. WHIPPLE, MAY 2, 1852

[Edwin Percy Whipple (1819–1886), a well-known lecturer and critic and a friend of James T. Fields, Hawthorne's publisher, had reviewed *The Scarlet Letter* and *The House of the Seven Gables* favorably and thoughtfully. As this letter indicates, Hawthorne had considerable trust in his literary judgment. Indeed, Whipple returned the manuscript a few days later, expressing his admiration for it and making some suggestions that likely influenced Hawthorne to produce a more chastened and remorseful Hollingsworth in Chapter 28 of the novel. An enthusiastic letter from Whipple (now lost), based on this advance look at the manuscript, helped Fields get an excellent price for the English rights to the novel.]

Dear Whipple,

Behold a huge bundle of scribble, which you have thoughtlessly promised to look over! If you find it beyond your powers, hand it over to Ticknor at once, and let him send it to the Devil;[1] but before that happens, I should be glad to have it looked over by a keen, yet not unfriendly eye, like yours. Nobody has yet read it, except my wife; and her sympathy, though very gratifying, is a little too unreserved to afford me the advantages of criticism. After all, should you spy ever so many defects, I cannot promise to amend them; the metal hardens very soon after I pour it out of my melting-pot into the mould.

I wish, at least, you would help me to choose a name. I have put 'Hollingsworth,' on the title-page, but that is not irrevocable; although, I think, the best that has occurred to me—as presenting the original figure about which the rest of the book clustered itself.

Here are others—"Blithedale,"—well enough, but with no positive merit or suitability. "Miles Coverdale's Three Friends";—this title comprehends the book, but rather clumsily. "The Veiled Lady"—too melodramatic; and, besides, I do not wish to give prominence to that feature of the Romance. "Priscilla"—she is such a shrinking damsel that it seems hardly fair to thrust her into the vanguard and make her the standard-bearer. "The Blithedale Romance"—that would do, in lack of a better. "The Arcadian Summer"—not a taking title. "Zenobia"—Mr. Ware[2] has anticipated me in this. In short, I can think of

---

† From *The Letters, 1843–1853*, ed. Thomas Woodson, L. Neal Smith, Norman Holmes Pearson (Columbus: Ohio State University Press, 1985), pp. 536–37. Reprinted by permission of The Ohio State University Press.
1. A pun on "printer's devil," a term for a printer's apprentice.
2. A reference to the popular novel *Zenobia: or, The Fall of Palmyra: An Historical Romance*, published in 1837 by William Ware (1797–1852).

nothing that exactly suits the case. Perhaps just the thing will pop into your mind.

Now that the book is off my mind, I feel as if I were out of the body; but (like a great many other translated spirits, I fear) the sense of it does not exactly increase my happiness. I hope to get to Concord soon, and shall there set to work on a Second Wonder Book.[3]

Truly Yours,
Nath[l] Hawthorne.

P.S. Are you a Kossuthian?[4] I am about as enthusiastic as a lump of frozen mud, but am going to hear him at Charlestown, tomorrow, in hope of warming up a little.

[*Your Friend Stands Foremost*][†]

FROM LETTER TO HORATIO BRIDGE, OCTOBER 13, 1852

Dear Bridge,

I received your letter some time ago, and ought to have answered long since; but you know my habits of epistolary delinquency—so I make no apology. Besides, I have been busy with literary labor of more kinds than one. Perhaps you have seen Blithedale before this time. I doubt whether you will like it very well; but it has met with good success; and has brought me (besides its American circulation) a thousand dollars from England, whence likewise have come many favorable notices. Just at this time, I rather think, your friend stands foremost there, as an American fiction-monger. In a day or two, I intend to begin a new romance, which, if possible, I mean to make more genial than the last.[1]

* * *

Your friend,
Nath[l] Hawthorne.

3. A second volume of stories for children, released as *Tanglewood Tales* in 1853.
4. Louis [Lajos] Kossuth (1802–1894), the Hungarian revolutionary, was touring America seeking financial support for that country's attempts to gain independence from the Austrian Empire. Coverdale self-mockingly asserts his willingness to join Kossuth's cause in the last chapter of the novel.
† From *The Letters, 1843–1853*, ed. Thomas Woodson, L. Neal Smith, Norman Holmes Pearson (Columbus: Ohio State University Press, 1985), pp. 604–07. Reprinted by permission of The Ohio State University Press.
1. This "new romance" has not been definitively identified; Hawthorne's next romance, *The Marble Faun*, was not published until 1860.

HERMAN MELVILLE

[Who the Devel Ain't a Dreamer]†

From Letter to Hawthorne, July 17, [1852]

[Herman Melville (1819–1891) sent this lively but cryptic letter to Hawthorne the summer after the publication of *Moby Dick*, during a time of frequent contact and close friendship between the two writers.]

My Dear Hawthorne:—This name of *"Hawthorne"* seems to be ubiquitous. I have been on something of a tour lately, and it has saluted me vocally & typographically in all sorts of places & in all sorts of ways.—I was at the solitary Crusoeish island of Naushon (one of the Elizabeth group) and there, on a stately piazza, I saw it gilded on the back of a very new book, and in the hands of a clergyman.—I went to visit a gentleman in Brooklyne, and as we were sitting at our wine, in came the lady of the house, holding a beaming volume in her hand, from the city—"My Dear," to her husband, "I have brought you *Hawthorne's* new book." I entered the cars at Boston for this place. In came a lively boy *"Hawthorne's* new book!"—In good time I arrived home. Said my lady-wife "there is Mr *Hawthorne's* new book, come by mail" And this morning, lo! on my table a little note, subscribed *Hawthorne* again.—Well, the Hawthorne is a sweet flower; may it flourish in every hedge.

I am sorry, but I can not at present come to see you at Concord as you propose.—I am but just returned from a two weeks' absence; and for the last three months & more I have been an utter idler and a savage—out of doors all the time. So, the hour has come for me to sit down again.

Do send me a specimen of your sand-hill, and a sunbeam from the countenance of Mrs: Hawthorne, and a vine from the curly arbor of Master Julian.[1]

As I am only just home, I have not yet got far into the book but enough to see that you have most admirably employed materials which are richer than I had fancied them. Especially at this day, the

---

† From *Correspondence: The Writings of Herman Melville*, vol. 14, ed. Lynn Horth (Evanston: Northwestern University Press, 1993), pp. 230–31. Reprinted by permission of Northwestern University Press.
1. Hawthorne's son, six years old at the time of this letter.

volume is welcome, as an antidote to the mooniness of some dreamers—who are merely dreamers——Yet who the devel aint a dreamer?

H Melville.

WILLIAM B. PIKE

[Down Among the Questionings]†

From Letter to Hawthorne, July 18, 1852

[Hawthorne met William Baker Pike (1811–1876), whom he described as "a man of no letters, but of remarkable intellect" (*The Letters, 1843–1853* [1985], p. 430), when both men worked at the Boston Custom House, and Pike—lay preacher, customs official, and Democratic Party political operative—became one of his closest friends. Here Pike offers a vivid account of the psychological richness of Hawthorne's writing.]

Dear Hawthorne,— * * * I have read your "Blithedale Romance." It is more like "The Scarlet Letter" than "The House of the Seven Gables." In this book, as in "The Scarlet Letter," you probe deeply,—you go down among the moody silences of the heart, and open those depths whence come motives that give complexion to actions, and make in men what are called states of mind; being conditions of mind which cannot be removed either by our own reasoning or by the reasonings of others. Almost all the novel-writers I have read, although truthful to nature, go through only some of the strata; but you are the only one who breaks through the hard-pan,—who accounts for that class of actions and manifestations in men so inexplicable as to call forth the exclamation, "How strangely that man acts! what a fool he is!" and the like. You explain, also, why the utterers of such exclamations, when circumstances have brought them to do the very things they once wondered at in others, feel that they themselves are acting rationally and consistently. * * * In "Blithedale" you dig an Artesian well down among the questionings. I was reminded of an Artesian well opened by my neighbor,

† From Julian Hawthorne, *Nathaniel Hawthorne and His Wife*, vol. 1 (Boston: Houghton, Mifflin, and Company, 1897), pp. 444–47.

who, after boring through various strata of earth and several fresh springs, found clear, cold sea-water at the depth of two hundred feet, which came bubbling to the surface from beneath the whole. How little we on the upper crust imagined that, far in the depths, was a stream which received its origin, quality, and character from the mighty ocean,—or fancied that, ere the stream we saw pouring forth could be exhausted, the vast world of waters must be dried up! But so it is; and the motive powers, like pearls, shine far down in the deep waters, and we fail to see them. You show us that such depths exist, and how they operate through the different departments, till they reach the outward and become visible actions. Thus the strange acts of men are in perfect consistency with the individual self,—the profound self. How admirably you explore those lurking-places!

* * *

Your friend truly,
Wm. B. Pike.

GEORGE S. HILLARD

[A Drier and Handsomer Death]†

From Letter to Hawthorne, July 27, 1852

[George Stillman Hillard (1808–1879), a Boston lawyer, politician, and man of letters, was Hawthorne's friend and personal attorney.]

My dear Hawthorne,—You have written another book full of beauty and power, which I read with great interest and vivid excitement. I hate the habit of comparing one work of an author with another, and never do so in my own mind. Many of your readers go off in this impertinent way, at the first, and insist upon drawing parallels between "The Blithedale Romance" and "The Scarlet Letter" or "The House of the Seven Gables." I do not walk in that way. It is enough for me that you have put another rose into your chaplet, and I will not ask whether it outblooms or outswells its sister flowers.

† From Julian Hawthorne, *Nathaniel Hawthorne and His Wife*, vol. 1 (Boston: Houghton, Mifflin, and Company, 1897), p. 448.

Zenobia is a splendid creature, and I wish there were more such rich and ripe women about. I wish, too, you could have wound up your story without killing her, or that at least you had given her a drier and handsomer death. Priscilla is an exquisite sketch. I don't know whether you have quite explained Hollingsworth's power over two such diverse natures. Your views about reform and reformers and spiritual rappings are such as I heartily approve. Reformers need the enchantment of distance. Your sketches of things visible, detached observations, and style generally, are exquisite as ever. May you live a thousand years, and write a book every year!

Yours ever,
Geo. S. Hillard.

JAMES T. FIELDS

[No More Blithedales][†]

From Letter to Mary Russell Mitford, October 24, 1852

[James T. Fields (1817–1881) was the junior partner in the publishing firm of Ticknor & Fields, the editor of the *Atlantic Monthly* from 1861 to 1870, and Hawthorne's close friend. A brilliant and innovative promoter of books and creator of contemporary literary culture, Fields worked ingeniously to make Hawthorne the pre-eminent American writer of his time and to secure his later reputation. Here, in a frank letter to Mitford, a British writer published in the United States by his firm, Fields seems to lament *Blithedale's* unspectacular sales, especially when compared to the stunning success of Harriet Beecher Stowe's *Uncle Tom's Cabin*.]

My Dear Miss Mitford,

I regret so much not to have been at home when your kind letters were rec[eive]d in America. * * * Dr. Holmes has just been in and says when you write to Miss Mitford send my love to her. So said the excellent Hawthorne last week in Concord. He is at work on another Romance and from all I can gather from this silent genius it will be in the Scarlet Letter vein. I hope he will give us no more Blithedales.

---

† This item is reproduced by permission of the Huntington Library, San Marino, California.

The writer of Uncle Tom's Cabin is getting to be a millionaire. She has already bought a house and grounds with the proceeds of her work & is busy at the mill writing another book. * * *

Ever yours,
J. T. Fields

HENRY FOTHERGILL CHORLEY

[Eminently an American Book]†

[A prolific book reviewer and an important music journalist, Henry Fothergill Chorley (1808–1872) was one of Hawthorne's earliest admirers among English reviewers.]

* * *

Mr. Hawthorne's third tale, in our judgment, puts the seal on the reputation of its author as the highest, deepest, and finest imaginative writer whom America has yet produced. * * *

This 'Blithedale Romance' is eminently an American book;—not, however, a book showing the America of *Sam Slick* and *Leather-Stocking*,[1]—the home of the money-making droll rich in mother-wit, or of the dweller in the wilderness rich in mother-poetry.— Mr. Hawthorne's America is a vast new country, the inhabitants of which have neither materially nor intellectually as yet found their boundaries,—a land heaving with restless impatience, on the part of some among its best spirits, to exemplify new ideas in new forms of civilized life. But Mr. Hawthorne knows that in America, as well as in worlds worn more threadbare, poets, philosophers and philanthropists however vehemently seized on by such fever of vainlonging, are forced to break themselves against the barriers of Mortality and Time—to allow for inevitable exceptions—to abide unforeseen checks,—in short, to re-commence their dream and their work with each fresh generation, in a manner tantalizing to enthusiasts who would grasp perfection for themselves and mankind, and

---

† From *The Athenaeum* [London, England] (10 July 1852): 741–43.
1. Sam Slick is the shrewd Yankee clock peddler invented by the Nova Scotia writer Thomas C. Haliburton (1796–1865); Leather-Stocking is one of the nicknames of Natty Bumppo, the woodsman-hero of James Fenimore Cooper's Leatherstocking Tales, a set of five novels of the American frontier that appeared between 1823 and 1841.

that instantaneously.—The author's sermon is none the less a sermon because he did not mean it as such.

* * *

The reader is not, however, to imagine that 'The Blithedale Romance' is
a cold or prosy essay, done up after the fashion of a gilt pill, with a few
incidents enabling the reader to swallow its wisdom. Though rich in
thought and suggestion, the tale is full of mystery, suspense, and passion, exciting the strongest interest. Besides Zenobia, Hollingsworth,
and the Poet-narrator, the Blithedale Community included, as we have
said, the timid, pale girl Priscilla,—who appeared to have dropped into
the midst of it from the clouds, and who joined the company with no
idea higher or more general than that of satisfying her own heart's
yearning for shelter and escape. Stern and self-engrossed as was
Hollingsworth—nay, because of his stern earnestness,—he contrived
to fascinate both Zenobia and Priscilla: the former resolving to place
her wealth at his disposal,—the latter submitting her heart to him long
ere she guessed that it was gone from her. The two women were thus
brought into unconscious rivalry: and excellently true to nature is the
manner—as tender as it is real—in which Mr. Hawthorne manages to
maintain the individuality of each. We do not remember any study of
the passionate woman of genius, in which her whole heart-struggle is
so distinctly portrayed, without the impression of what is unfeminine
and repulsive being produced as this of Zenobia.

* * *

EDWIN PERCY WHIPPLE

[Through the Medium of an Imagined Mind][†]

[As noted above, Hawthorne placed a high value on Whipple's reviews
of his work, writing in a letter to his publisher James Fields that "Whipple's notices have done more than please me; for they have helped me to
see my book" (*The Letters, 1843–1853* [1985], p. 435.)]

* * *

"The Blithedale Romance," just published, seems to us the most perfect in execution of any of Hawthorne's works, and as a work of art,
hardly equaled by any thing else which the country has produced.
It is a real organism of the mind, with the strict unity of one of

† From *Graham's Magazine* 41 (September 1852): 333–34; this review was unsigned and
untitled, appearing in a section of the magazine called "Review of New Books."

Nature's own creations. It seems to have grown up in the author's nature, as a tree or plant grows from the earth, in obedience to the law of its germ. This unity cannot be made clear by analysis; it is felt in the oneness of impression it makes on the reader's imagination. The author's hold on the central principle is never relaxed; it never slips from his grasp; and yet every thing is developed with a victorious ease which adds a new charm to the interest of the materials. The romance, also, has more thought in it than either of its predecessors; it is literally crammed with the results of most delicate and searching observation of life, manners and character, and of the most piercing imaginative analysis of motives and tendencies; yet nothing seems labored, but the profoundest reflections glide unobtrusively into the free flow of the narration and description, equally valuable from their felicitous relation to the events and persons of the story, and for their detached depth and power. The work is not without a certain morbid tint in the general coloring of the mood whence it proceeds; but this peculiarity is fainter than is usual with Hawthorne.

The scene of the story is laid in Blithedale, an imaginary community on the model of the celebrated Brook Farm, of Roxbury, of which Hawthorne himself was a member. The practical difficulties in the way of combining intellectual and manual labor on socialist principles constitutes the humor of the book; but the interest centres in three characters, Hollingsworth, Zenobia, and Priscilla. These are represented as they appear through the medium of an imagined mind, that of Miles Coverdale, the narrator of the story, a person indolent of will, but of an apprehensive, penetrating, and inquisitive intellect. This discerner of spirits only tells us his own discoveries; and there is a wonderful originality and power displayed in thus representing the characters. What is lost by this mode, on definite views, is more than made up in the stimulus given both to our acuteness and curiosity, and its manifold suggestiveness. We are joint watchers with Miles himself, and sometimes find ourselves disagreeing with him in his interpretation of an act or expression of the persons he is observing. The events are purely mental, the changes and crises of moods of mind. Three persons of essentially different characters and purposes, are placed together; the law of spiritual influence, the magnetism of soul on soul begins to operate; and the processes of thought and emotion are then presented in perfect logical order to their inevitable catastrophe. These characters are Hollingsworth, a reformer, whose whole nature becomes ruthless under the dominion of one absorbing idea—Zenobia, a beautiful, imperious, impassioned, self-willed woman, superbly endowed in person and intellect, but with something provokingly equivocal in her character—and Priscilla, an embodiment of feminine affection in its simplest type. Westervelt, an elegant piece of earthliness, "not so much born as damned into the world," plays a Mephistophelian[1] part in this mental drama; and is so skillfully represented that the reader joins at the end, with the author, in praying that Heaven may annihilate him. "May his pernicious soul rot half a grain a day."

With all the delicate sharpness of insight into the most elusive movements of Consciousness, by which the romance is characterized, the drapery cast over the whole representation, is rich and flowing, and there is no parade of metaphysical acuteness. All the profound and penetrating observation seems the result of a certain careless felicity of aim, which hits the mark in the white without any preliminary posturing or elaborate preparation. The stronger, and harsher passions are represented with the same ease as the evanescent shades of thought and emotion. The humorous and descriptive scenes are in Hawthorne's best style. The peculiarities of New England life at the present day are admirably caught and permanently embodied; Silas Foster and Hollingsworth being both gennine Yankees and representative men. The great passage of the volume is Zenobia's death, which is not so much tragic as tragedy itself. In short, whether we consider "The Blithedale Romance" as a study in that philosophy of the human mind which peers into the inmost recesses and first principles of mind and character, or a highly colored and fascinating story, it does not yield in interest or value to any of Hawthorne's preceding works, while it is removed from a comparison with them by essential differences in its purpose and mode of treatment, and is perhaps their superior in affluence and fineness of thought, and masterly perception of the first remote workings of great and absorbing passions.

ANONYMOUS

[The Poetry of the Dissecting Room][†]

* * *

"The Blithedale Romance" will never attain the popularity which is vouchsafed (to borrow a pulpit vocable) to some of its contemporaries, but it is unmistakably the finest production of genius in either hemisphere, for this quarter at least—to keep our enthusiasm within limits so far. Of its literary merits we wish to speak, at the

---

1. Diabolical—after Mephistopheles, the devil in the *Faust* legend to whom Faust sold his soul.
† From an unsigned essay, "Contemporary Literature of America," *Westminster Review* [England] 58 (October 1852): 592–98. The review has been attributed—plausibly but inconclusively—to British novelist George Eliot.

outset, in the highest terms, inasmuch as we intend to take objection to it in other respects.

* * *

Hawthorne's *forte* is the analysis of character, and not the dramatic arrangement of events * * * for the ruling faculty is analytic. It is ever hunting out the anomalous; it discovers more points of repulsion than of attraction; and the creatures of its fancy are all morbid beings—all "wandering stars," plunging, orbitless, into the abyss of despair—confluent but not commingling streams, winding along to the ocean of disaster and death: for all have a wretched end—Zenobia and Priscilla, Hollingsworth and Coverdale—the whole go to wreck.

* * *

Hawthorne has a rich perception of the beautiful, but he is sadly deficient in moral depth and earnestness. His moral faculty is morbid as well as weak; all his characters partake of the same infirmity. Hollingsworth's project of a penitentiary at Blithedale is here carried out in imagination. Hawthorne walks abroad always at night, and at best it is a moonlight glimmering which you catch of reality. He lives in the region and shadow of death, and never sees the deep glow of moral health anywhere. He looks mechanically (it is a habit) at Nature and at man through a coloured glass, which imparts to the whole view a pallid, monotonous aspect, painful to behold. And it is only because Hawthorne can see beauty in everything, and will look at nothing but beauty in anything, that he can either endure the picture himself, or win for it the admiration of others. The object of art is the development of beauty—not merely sensuous beauty, but moral and spiritual beauty. Its ministry should be one of pleasure, not of pain; but our anatomist, who removes his subjects to Blithedale, that he may cut and hack at them without interference, clears out for himself a new path in art, by developing the beauty of deformity! He would give you the poetry of the hospital, or the poetry of the dissecting-room; but we would rather not have it. Art has a moral purpose to fulfil; its mission is one of mercy, not of misery. Reality should only be so far introduced as to give effect to the bright ideal which Hope pictures in the future. In fact, a poet is nothing unless also a prophet. Hawthorne is the former; but few poets could be less of the latter. He draws his inspiration from Fate, not from Faith. He is not even a Jeremiah, weeping amid the ruins of a fallen temple, and mourning over the miseries of a captive people. He is a Mephistophiles, doubtful whether to weep or laugh; but either way it would be in mockery. * * * That "Blithedale" itself should end in smoke, was, perhaps, fit matter for mirth; that

Hollingsworth's huge tower of selfishness should be shattered to pieces was poetically just; but that the imperial Zenobia should be vanquished, was to give the victory to Despair. Zenobia is the only one in the group worthy to be the Trustee of Human Right, and the Representative of Human Destiny; and she, at least, should have come out of all her struggles in regal triumph. But, after the first real trial of her strength with adversity, and when there was resolution yet left for a thousand conflicts, to throw her into that dirty pool, and not even to leave her there, but to send her base-hearted deceiver, and that lout of a fellow, Silas Foster, to haul her out, and to let the one poke up the corpse with a boat-hook, and the other tumble it about in the simplicity of his desire to make it look more decent—these, and many other things in the closing scene, are an outrage upon the decorum of art, as well as a violation of its purpose. That such things do happen, is no reason why they should be idealized; for the Ideal seeks not to imitate Reality, but to perfect it. The use it makes of that which *is* true, is to develope that which *ought* to be true; and it ought *never* to be true that the strong should be conquered by the weak, as Zenobia was by Priscilla; or, that the most buoyant spirit should sink soonest in the struggle of life, as did Zenobia, who was the first that found a grave in "Blithedale;" or, that *all* should be wrecked that sail on troubled waters, as were all who figure in this romance. It is a hard saying to proclaim to a fallen world, that the first false step is a fatal one. There was more truth in the words, and more beauty in the picture, of the man standing by the outcast, telling her to go and sin no more. From thence let Hawthorne draw his inspiration. Let him study that benignant attitude, and endeavour to realize it in himself toward a similar subject, and he might yet write with a prophet's power, and accomplish a saviour's mission.

* * *

A poetic soul sees more in history than it can reproduce in a historical form, and must, therefore, create a symbolism for itself, less inexorable in its conditions, and more expressive of his latest thought. The historical result of the experiment at Brook Farm, and its direct didactic value, may have been inconsiderable enough, but its reproductive capacity in a fruitful mind might have issued in a work which would have rendered that bubble a permanent landmark in the progress of humanity.

But here, again, Hawthorne disappoints us, and again through his lack of moral earnestness. Everybody will naturally regard this story, whether fact or fiction, as a socialistic drama, and will expect its chief interest as such to be of a moral kind. "Blithedale," whatever may be its relation to Brook Farm, is itself a socialistic settlement, with its corresponding phases of life, and therefore involves points both of moral and material interest, the practical operation of which should have been exhibited so as to bring out the good and evil of the system. But this task Hawthorne declines, and does not "put forward the slightest pretensions to illustrate a theory, or elicit a conclusion favourable or otherwise to Socialism." He confines himself to the delineation of its picturesque phases, as a "thing of beauty," and either has no particular convictions respecting its deeper relations, or hesitates to express them. It was not necessary for him to pass judgment upon the theories of Fourier or Robert Owen. He had nothing to do with it as a theory; but as a phase of life it demanded appropriate colouring. Would he paint an ideal slave-plantation merely for the beauty of the thing, without pretending to "elicit a conclusion favourable or otherwise" to slavery? Could he forget the moral relations of this system, or drop them out of his picture, "merely to establish a theatre a little removed from the highway of ordinary travel, where the creatures of his brain may play their phantasmagorical antics without exposing them to too close a comparison with the actual events of real life?" In respect of involving moral relations, the two cases are analogous, and the one may be rendered morally colourless with no more propriety than the other. "Blithedale," then, as a socialistic community, is merely used here as a scaffolding—a very huge one—in the construction of an edifice considerably smaller than itself! And then, the artist leaves the scaffolding standing! Socialism, in this romance, is prominent enough to fill the book, but it has so little business in it, that it does not even grow into an organic part of the story, and contributes nothing whatever toward the final catastrophe. It is a theatre—and, as such, it should have a neutral tint; but it should also be made of neutral stuff; and its erection, moreover, should not be contemporaneous with the performance of the play. But the incongruity becomes more apparent when we consider the kind of play acted in it. Take the moral of Zenobia's history, and you will find that Socialism is apparently made responsible for consequences which it utterly condemned, and tried, at least, to remedy. We say, apparently, for it is really not made responsible for anything, good, bad, or indifferent. It forms a circumference of circumstances, which neither mould the characters, nor influence the destinies, of the individuals so equivocally situated,—forms, in short, not an essential part of the picture, but an enormous fancy border, not very suitable for the purpose for which it was designed. Zenobia's life would have been exhibited with more propriety, and its moral brought home with more effect, in the "theatre" of the world, out of which it really grew, and of which it would have formed a vital and harmonious part. Zenobia and Socialism should have been acted in the ready-made theatre of ordinary humanity, to see how it would fare with them there. Having occupied the ground, Hawthorne owed it to truth, and to a fit opportunity, so to dramatize his experience and observation of Communistic life, as to make them of practical value for the world at large.

ANONYMOUS

[No Genius for Realities]†

* * *

We believe that if Mr. Hawthorne had intended to give a faithful portrait of Brook Farm and its inmates, he would have signally failed. He has no genius for realities, save in inanimate nature. Between his characters and the reader falls a gauze-like veil of imagination, on which their shadows flit and move, and play strange dramas replete with second-hand life. An air of unreality enshrouds all his creations. They are either dead, or have never lived, and when they pass away they leave behind them an oppressive and unwholesome chill.

* * *

But we question much, if we strip Mr. Hawthorne's works of a certain beauty and originality of style which they are always sure to possess, whether the path which he has chosen is a healthy one. To us it does not seem as if the fresh wind of morning blew across his track; we do not feel the strong pulse of nature throbbing beneath the turf he treads upon. * * * The soul of beauty is Truth, and Truth is ever progressive. The true artist therefore endeavors to make the world better. He does not look behind him, and dig out of the graves of past centuries skeletons to serve as models for his pictures; but looks onward for more perfect shapes, and though sometimes obliged to design from the defective forms around him, he infuses, as it were, some of the divine spirit of the future into them, and lo! we love them with all their faults. But Mr. Hawthorne discards all idea of successful human progress. All his characters seem so weighed down with their own evilness of nature, that they can scarcely keep their balance, much less take their places in the universal march. Like the lord mentioned in Scripture, he issues an invitation to the halt, the blind, and the lame of soul, to gather around his board, and then asks us to feast at the same table. It is a pity that Mr. Hawthorne should

† From "*The Blithedale Romance*," *American Whig Review* 16 (November 1852): 417–24.

not have been originally imbued with more universal tenderness. It is a pity that he displays nature to us so shrouded and secluded, and that he should be afflicted with such a melancholy craving for human curiosities. His men are either vicious, crazed, or misanthropical, and his women are either unwomanly, unearthly, or unhappy. His books have no sunny side to them. They are unripe to the very core.

We are more struck with the want of this living tenderness in the Blithedale Romance than in any of Mr. Hawthorne's previous novels.

* * *

ANDREW PRESTON PEABODY

[Utter Homelessness]†

[Andrew Preston Peabody (1811–1893) was a Unitarian minister who became the Plummer Professor of Christian Morals at Harvard and preacher to the University. He had broad interests in social and political questions and wrote frequently for the *Whig Review* and the *North American Review*, which he edited from 1854 to 1863.]

* * *

[T]he Blithedale Romance is a work of no ordinary power, and indicative of all its author's mental affluence. In character-painting, he has overtaken his highest previous skill in Hollingsworth, and exceeded it in Zenobia. Then, of lesser personages, who could fail to recognize, in Silas Foster, the agricultural foreman of the farm, a marvellously accurate type of the New England yeoman of the generation just now passing the meridian of manhood? The descriptions of the kitchen, the table, the style of dress, the manner of labor, and the Sunday habits of the Blithedale community, attractive as they are in themselves, are doubly so, as being beyond a question the portions in which observation and experience, rather than fancy, furnished the material for the narrative.

* * *

[Y]et we may not unaptly crave a moment's heed for reflections which this book forces upon us. Blithedale has left upon our memory only

† From "*The House of the Seven Gables* and *The Blithedale Romance*," *North American Review* 76 (January 1853): 227–48.

associations of sadness and desolation, and that not alone on account of the tragedy consummated within its domain, but from the utter homelessness of its inmates. The shades wandering on the hither side of the Styx hardly offer a more dreary image to the fancy, than these inmates of the phalanstery on their holidays. We can, indeed, conceive of the relations and affections of life as subsisting in some sort independently of separate homes. The conjugal relation, though fearfully imperilled, might be kept sacred, and the parental tie, if loosened, not wholly dissolved, in the gregarious life which the socialist reformer would have us lead. It has also been pretty fairly demonstrated that there would be not only a more equal diffusion, but a more profuse creation, of the elements of material comfort and enjoyment, did men, women, and children herd together in organized groups, by fifties, hundreds, and thousands. But, after all, there is in human nature an irresistible tendency to the erection of a distinct abode for every household. There are chords of sentiment in every heart, which can respond only to the word HOME. There are profound and almost universal wants which could be met, there are joys which could be experienced, under no other condition of things.

* * *

Selections from Classic Studies

This section begins with reflections on *The Blithedale Romance* by several of Hawthorne's fellow novelists. Brief excerpts from some key academic studies of the novel, from the 1940s through the early 1980s, follow.

HENRY JAMES

[*The Blithedale Romance*]†

[The following passages are taken from a book on Hawthorne's life and work written by the American novelist Henry James (1843–1916) for *English Men of Letters*, a series of short books on significant English writers; Hawthorne was the only American included. For James, Hawthorne exemplified the predicament of a literary genius who could draw only on the thin materials a provincial American culture supplied him—and who was thus driven toward the abstract, the allegorical, and the psychological.]

* * *

The story is told from a more joyous point of view—from a point of view comparatively humorous—and a number of objects and incidents touched with the light of the profane world—the vulgar, many-coloured world of actuality, as distinguished from the crepuscular realm of the writer's own reveries—are mingled with its course. The book, indeed, is a mixture of elements, and it leaves in the memory an impression analogous to that of an April day—an alternation of brightness and shadow, of broken sun-patches and sprinkling clouds. Its *dénoûment* is tragical—there is, indeed, nothing so tragical in all Hawthorne, unless it be the murder of Miriam's persecutor by Donatello, in *Transformation*, as the suicide of Zenobia; and yet, on the whole, the effect of the novel is to make one think more agreeably

---

† From *Hawthorne* (London: Macmillan, 1879), pp. 128–29, 130–31, 132.

of life. The standpoint of the narrator has the advantage of being a concrete one; he is no longer, as in the preceding tales, a disembodied spirit, imprisoned in the haunted chamber of his own contemplations, but a particular man, with a certain human grossness.

* * * Coverdale is a picture of the contemplative, observant, analytic nature, nursing its fancies, and yet, thanks to an element of strong good sense, not bringing them up to be spoiled children; having little at stake in life, at any given moment, and yet indulging, in imagination, in a good many adventures; a portrait of a man, in a word, whose passions are slender, whose imagination is active, and whose happiness lies, not in doing, but in perceiving—half a poet, half a critic, and all a spectator. He is contrasted excellently with the figure of Hollingsworth, the heavily treading Reformer, whose attitude with regard to the world is that of the hammer to the anvil, and who has no patience with his friend's indifferences and neutralities. * * *

The finest thing in *The Blithedale Romance* is the character of Zenobia, * * * which strikes me as the nearest approach that Hawthorne has made to the complete creation of a *person*. She is more concrete than Hester or Miriam, or Hilda or Phœbe; she is a more definite image, produced by a greater multiplicity of touches. It is idle to inquire too closely whether Hawthorne had Margaret Fuller in his mind in constructing the figure of this brilliant specimen of the strong-minded class, and endowing her with the genius of conversation; or, on the assumption that such was the case, to compare the image at all strictly with the model. There is no strictness in the representation by novelists of persons who have struck them in life, and there can in the nature of things be none. From the moment the imagination takes a hand in the game, the inevitable tendency is to divergence, to following what may be called new scents. The original gives hints, but the writer does what he likes with them, and imports new elements into the picture. If there is this amount of reason for referring the wayward heroine of Blithedale to Hawthorne's impression of the most distinguished woman of her day in Boston; that Margaret Fuller was the only literary lady of eminence whom there is any sign of his having known; that she was proud, passionate, and eloquent; that she was much connected with the little world of Transcendentalism out of which the experiment of Brook Farm sprung; and that she had a miserable end and a watery grave—if these are facts to be noted on one side, I say; on the other, the beautiful and sumptuous Zenobia, with her rich and picturesque temperament and physical aspects, offers many points of divergence from the plain and strenuous invalid who represented feminine culture in the suburbs of the New England metropolis. This picturesqueness of Zenobia is very happily indicated and maintained; she is a woman in all the force of the term, and there is something very vivid and powerful in her large expression of womanly gifts and weaknesses. Hollingsworth is, I think, less successful, though there is much reality in the conception of the type to which he belongs—the strong-willed, narrow-hearted apostle of a special form of redemption for society. There is nothing better in all Hawthorne than the scene between him and Coverdale, when the two men are at work together in the field (piling stones on a dyke), and he gives it to his companion to choose whether he will be with him or against him.[1] * * *

The most touching element in the novel is the history of the grasp that this barbarous fanatic[2] has laid upon the fastidious and high-tempered Zenobia, who, disliking him and shrinking from him at a hundred points, is drawn into the gulf of his omnivorous egotism. The portion of the story that strikes me as least felicitous is that which deals with Priscilla, and with her mysterious relation to Zenobia—with her mesmeric gifts, her clairvoyance, her identity with the Veiled Lady, her divided subjection to Hollingsworth and Westervelt, and her numerous other graceful but fantastic properties—her Sibylline attributes, as the author calls them. Hawthorne is rather too fond of Sibylline attributes—a taste of the same order as his disposition, to which I have already alluded, to talk about spheres and sympathies. As the action advances, in *The Blithedale Romance*, we get too much out of reality, and cease to feel beneath our feet the firm ground of an appeal to our own vision of the world—our observation. I should have liked to see the story concern itself more with the little community in which its earlier scenes are laid, and avail itself of so excellent an opportunity for describing unhackneyed specimens of human nature. * * * But when all is said about a certain want of substance and cohesion in the latter portions of *The Blithedale Romance*, the book is still a delightful and beautiful one. Zenobia and Hollingsworth live in the memory; and even Priscilla and Coverdale, who linger there less importunately, have a great deal that touches us and that we believe in.

* * *

1. See Chapter XV.
2. I.e., Hollingsworth.

272

WILLIAM DEAN HOWELLS

[Pity Almost to Heart-break]†

[On an 1860 pilgrimage to New England to visit some of his literary heroes, the young, Ohio-born Howells (1837–1920)—who would become the author of such distinguished novels as *The Rise of Silas Lapham* (1885) and *A Hazard of New Fortunes* (1890) and, as editor of *Atlantic Monthly* and *Harper's Magazine*, an influential arbiter of literary taste and supporter of younger novelists—delighted Hawthorne by naming *The Blithedale Romance* as his favorite among the older writer's novels. Readers will notice that Howells's praise for the novel simultaneously argues on behalf of his own "realistic" narrative practice.]

Hester Prynne in "The Scarlet Letter" is studied in the round, with an effect of life which is wanting to heroines in the flat, whatever their charm of color and drawing may be; and Zenobia and Priscilla— especially Zenobia—are still more vitalized by the same method of handling, in "The Blithedale Romance." That romance * * * is nearer a novel than any other fiction of the author. At times we find ourselves confronted there, in spite of the author, with a very palpitant piece of naturalism. This is not more the fact in the case of the brawny, tobacco-chewing Silas Foster, who instructs the town-bred communists at Blithedale in farming, than in the sumptuous personality of Zenobia, the woman with a mysterious past, who glows upon us in tropical splendor from the first chapters of the romance, and illumines it throughout with the rich ardor of her impassioned presence.

Never could a writer have had material more to his mind than Hawthorne found in the conditions at Brook Farm, which he transmuted for his purposes to the imaginary situation at Blithedale, with the restricted scene, sparingly and fitfully contrasted at times with the town life which the visionary reformers, the poets, artists, philanthropists, and mystics, had left behind them in Boston. The small group of characters; the play of interests freed from the sordid alloy of the world; the psychological and emotional possibilities of an ideal action strongly backgrounded by fact hardly less ideal—these are the materials of a story so slight that one marvels at the treasure of motive

† From *Heroines of Fiction*, 2 vols. (New York: Harper & Brothers, 1901), 1: 175–79.

and event which it is made to hold. The pages are few in which Hollingsworth, the gloomy friend and potential reformer of criminals, has his being with Zenobia, whose strong heart he breaks, and Priscilla, the pale maiden on whose weakness his misery relies, and Miles Coverdale, the minor poet, and self-conscious historian of a tragedy which he observes with a cynical curiosity rather than a human sympathy. Yet no other book in the whole range of Anglo-Saxon fiction says so much to certain important moods in the reader. There is, of course, some such mechanical toy[1] in "The Blithedale Romance" as is central in every romance, but in this case the toy has a mainspring of reality, a scientific authority, and the story pulsates from it like a living organism. Zenobia and Priscilla are half-sisters; the one, daughter of the father's past opulence and luxury; the other, child of his blighted and ruined present; and in their temperaments they consistently express the qualities of his different fortunes. They express them only too consistently, and with too great constancy to their appointed functions. They are lifelike, but if they were alive they would be more convertible; and in this difference exists the essential and eternal inferiority of the ideal to the real in fiction: the one must keep to its *parti pris*;[2] the other may avail itself of every caprice and vacillation and mutability known to observation and experience, and be only more faithful to nature, its supreme and sole exemplar.

All this is not saying that Hawthorne does not handle his mechanism like the consummate artist he was. There are long times when he makes you or lets you forget it; he never intrudes it; and it is chiefly in the perfunctory appearances of the father upon the scene that one is aware of Zenobia and Priscilla being operated by it. Priscilla, indeed, is operated throughout, but not by the activity of this principle of heredity so much as by the passions of those about her. She is not so merely a spectator as Coverdale, but she is almost more negative, and her elusive personality is ascertained with exquisite delicacy and a succession of shadowy approaches on the part of the author which enlist the tremulous sympathy of the reader rather than reward it. After all, there does not seem to be very much of Priscilla. Objectively she is a pale, sickly little seamstress, whom Hollingsworth brings to the nascent community at Blithedale by her father's wish, and in unconscious fulfilment of old Fauntleroy's hope that she may there somehow commend herself to the favor of her half-sister Zenobia. Subjectively, she is a capacity for clinging to any strength about her, and attaching it to herself through compassion. With the rude force of a prepotent philanthropist like Hollingsworth this compassion

---

1. Plot contrivance.
2. Adopted position, bias; here, its already established function.

becomes passion, in compliance with the ironical pleasure of nature, while the proud and beautiful Zenobia is offering him her love in vain.

Zenobia is the great personality in the book, and she is substantiated with the conscience of a realist to the material as well as the spiritual vision. * * *

Zenobia is more and more compassed about by the tragical shadows which the effulgence of her own passion casts, till her despair ends with the defeat of her last vanity in the ugliness of her self-sought death. The history is always without the concealment of the fact that from first to last her fineness was intellectual, and that emotionally, spiritually, she was of a coarse fibre, with even a strain of vulgarity. A certain kind of New England woman, to specialize a little more than to say American woman, has never been so clearly seen or boldly shown as in Zenobia; and in her phase of tragedy she stands as impressively for the nineteenth century as Hester Prynne for the seventeenth in hers. It is with pity almost to heart-break that one witnesses her sacrifice of her belief in the cause of women to Hollingsworth's greedy and relentless philanthropy, and her meek abeyance before his savage proclamation of man's superiority, his brute avowal of contempt for women except as the helpers and comforters of men.

* * *

D. H. LAWRENCE

[The Disintegration of the Psyche][†]

[The English writer David Herbert Lawrence (1885–1930), best known as the author of such novels as *Sons and Lovers* (1913), *Women in Love* (1920), and the scandalous *Lady Chatterley's Lover* (1928), published the brilliant and idiosyncratic *Studies in Classic American Literature*—a book that profoundly shaped the emerging field of American literature and continues to provoke and surprise its readers—in 1923. Lawrence sought to rescue American writers from the category of children's literature by revealing the emotional extremity and psychological darkness of their writing. The book includes chapters on *The Scarlet Letter* and *The Blithedale Romance*, as well as influential treatments of Cooper, Melville, Poe, and Whitman.]

† From *Studies in Classic American Literature* (1923; rpt. New York: Penguin, 1977), pp. 112–17. Reproduced by permission of Pollinger Limited and the Estate of Frieda Lawrence Ravaglia.

* * *

Hawthorne came nearest to actuality in the *Blithedale Romance*. This novel is a sort of picture of the notorious Brook Farm experiment. There the famous idealists and transcendentalists of America met to till the soil and hew the timber in the sweat of their own brows, thinking high thoughts the while, and breathing an atmosphere of communal love, and tingling in tune with the Oversoul, like so many strings of a super-celestial harp. An old twang of the Crèvecœur instrument.[1]

Of course they fell out like cats and dogs. Couldn't stand one another. And all the music they made was the music of their quarrelling.

You *can't* idealize hard work. Which is why America invents so many machines and contrivances of all sort: so that they need do no physical work.

And that's why the idealists left off brookfarming, and took to bookfarming.

You *can't* idealize the essential brute blood-activity, the brute blood desires, the basic, sardonic blood-knowledge.

That you *can't* idealize.

And you can't eliminate it.

So there's the end of ideal man.

Man is made up of a dual consciousness, of which the two halves are most of the time in opposition to one another—and will be so as long as time lasts.

You've got to learn to change from one consciousness to the other, turn and about. Not to try to make either absolute, or dominant. The Holy Ghost tells you the how and when.

Never did Nathaniel feel himself more spectral—of course he went brookfarming—than when he was winding the horn in the morning to summon the transcendental labourers to their tasks, or than when marching off with a hoe ideally to hoe the turnips, 'Never did I feel more spectral,' says Nathaniel.

Never did I feel such a fool, would have been more to the point.

Farcical fools, trying to idealize labour. You'll never succeed in idealizing hard work. Before you can dig mother earth you've got to take off your ideal jacket. The harder a man works, at brute labour, the thinner becomes his idealism, the darker his mind. And the harder a man works, at mental labour, at idealism, at transcendental occupations, the thinner becomes his blood, and the more brittle his nerves.

Oh, the brittle-nerved brookfarmers!

1. Lawrence makes fun of two ideas associated with American writers; Emerson coined the term "Over-soul" to refer to the supreme spirit that animates the universe, of which all individual souls are part; Lawrence sees this conception as derived from the idealized and unconvincing view of nature he finds in the writings of J. Hector St. John de Crèvecoeur (1735–1813), a French immigrant whose *Letters of an American Farmer* (1782) offered European readers an optimistic view of life in the new republic.

You've got to be able to do both: the mental work, and the brute work. But be prepared to step from one pair of shoes into another. Don't try and make it all one pair of shoes.

The attempt to idealize the blood!

Nathaniel knew he was a fool, attempting it.

He went home to his amiable spouse and his sanctum sanctorum of a study.

Nathaniel!

But the *Blithedale Romance*. It has a beautiful, wintry-evening farm-kitchen sort of opening.

Dramatis Personae:

1. *I.* The narrator: whom we will call Nathaniel.[2] A wisp of a sensitive, withal deep, literary young man no longer so very young.
2. *Zenobia:* a dark, proudly voluptuous clever woman with a tropical flower in her hair. Said to be sketched from Margaret Fuller, in whom Hawthorne saw some 'evil nature'. Nathaniel was more aware of Zenobia's voluptuousness than of her 'mind'.
3. *Hollingsworth:* a black-bearded blacksmith with a deep-voiced lust for saving criminals. Wants to build a great Home for these unfortunates.
4. *Priscilla:* a sort of White Lily, a clinging little mediumistic sempstress who has been made use of in public seances. A sort of prostitute soul.
5. *Zenobia's Husband:* an unpleasant decayed person with magnetic powers and teeth full of gold—or set in gold. It is he who has given public spiritualist demonstrations, with Priscilla for the medium. He is of the dark, sensual, decayed-handsome sort, and comes in unexpectedly by the back door.

PLOT I.—I, Nathaniel, at once catch cold, and have to be put to bed. Am nursed with inordinate tenderness by the blacksmith, whose great hands are gentler than a woman's, etc.

The two men love one another with a love surpassing the love of women, so long as the healing-and-salvation business lasts. When Nathaniel wants to get well and have a soul of his own, he turns with hate to the black-bearded, booming salvationist, Hephaestos of the underworld. Hates him for tyrannous monomania.

PLOT II.—Zenobia, that clever lustrous woman, is fascinated by the criminal-saving blacksmith, and would have him at any price. Meanwhile she has the subtlest current of understanding with the frail but deep Nathaniel. And she takes the White Lily half-pityingly, half contemptuously under a rich and glossy dark wing.

---

2. Lawrence renames Coverdale "Nathaniel," perhaps so as to suggest a close link to Hawthorne himself.

PLOT III.—The blacksmith is after Zenobia, to get her money for his criminal asylum: of which, of course, he will be the first inmate.

PLOT IV.—Nathaniel also feels his mouth watering for the dark-luscious Zenobia.

PLOT V.—The White Lily, Priscilla, vaporously festering, turns out to be the famous Veiled Lady of public spiritualist shows: she whom the undesirable Husband, called the Professor, has used as a medium. Also she is Zenobia's half-sister.

Débâcle

Nobody wants Zenobia in the end. She goes off without her flower. The blacksmith marries Priscilla. Nathaniel dribblingly confesses that he, too, has loved Prissy all the while. Boo-hoo!

Conclusion

A few years after, Nathaniel meets the blacksmith in a country lane near a humble cottage, leaning totteringly on the arm of the frail but fervent Priscilla. Gone are all dreams of asylums, and the saviour of criminals can't even save himself from his own Veiled Lady.

There you have a nice little bunch of idealists, transcentalists, brookfarmers, and disintegrated gentry. All going slightly rotten.

Two Pearls: a white Pearl and a black Pearl: the latter more expensive, lurid with money.

The white Pearl, the little medium, Priscilla, the imitation pearl, has truly some 'supernormal' powers. She could drain the blacksmith of his blackness and his smith-strength.

Priscilla, the little psychic prostitute. The degenerate descendant of Ligeia.[3] The absolutely yielding, 'loving' woman, who abandons herself utterly to her lover. Or even to a gold-toothed 'professor' of spiritualism.

Is it all bunkum, this spiritualism? Is it just rot, this Veiled Lady?

* * *

Vibrations of subtlest matter. Concatenations of vibrations and shocks! Spiritualism.

And what then? It is all just materialistic, and a good deal is, and always will be, charlatanry.

Because the real human soul, the Holy Ghost, has its own deep prescience, which will not be put into figures, but flows on dark, a stream of prescience.

---

3. The fantastically devoted, strangely powerful wife in a story by Poe, who returns from death by repossessing the body of her successor.

And the real human soul is too proud, and too sincere in its belief in the Holy Ghost that is within, to stoop to the practices of these spiritualist and other psychic tricks of material vibrations.

Because the first part of reverence is the acceptance of the fact that the Holy Ghost will never materialize: will never be anything but a ghost.

And the second part of reverence is the watchful observance of the motions, the comings and goings within us, of the Holy Ghost, and of the many gods that make up the Holy Ghost.

The Father had his day, and fell.

The Son has had his day, and fell.

It is the day of the Holy Ghost.

But when souls fall corrupt, into disintegration, they have no more day. They have sinned against the Holy Ghost.

These people in *Blithedale Romance* have sinned against the Holy Ghost, and corruption has set in.

All, perhaps, except the I, Nathaniel. He is still a sad, integral consciousness.

But not excepting Zenobia. The Black Pearl is rotting down. Fast. The cleverer she is, the faster she rots.

And they are all disintegrating, so they take to psychic tricks. It is a certain sign of the disintegration of the psyche in a man, and much more so in a woman, when she takes to spiritualism, and table-rapping, and occult messages, or witchcraft and supernatural powers of that sort. When men want to be supernatural, be sure that something has gone wrong in their natural stuff. More so, even, with a woman.

* * *

PHILIP RAHV

[The Dark Lady]†

* * *

[Hawthorne's] tales and romances * * * bring to life * * * possibly the most resplendent and erotically forceful woman in American fiction. She dominates all the other characters because she alone personifies the contrary values that her author attached to experience. Drawn on a scale larger than reality, she is essentially a mythic being, the incarnation of hidden longings and desires, as beautiful, we are repeatedly told, as she is "inexpressibly terrible," a temptress offering the ascetic sons of the puritans the "treasure-trove of a great sin."

† From "The Dark Lady of Salem," *Partisan Review* 8 (1941): 362–81.

We come to know this dark lady under four different names—as Beatrice in the story *Rappaccini's Daughter*, Hester in *The Scarlet Letter*, Zenobia in *The Blithedale Romance*, and Miriam in *The Marble Faun*. Her unity as a character is established by the fact that in each of her four appearances she exhibits the same physical and mental qualities and plays substantially the same role. Hawthorne's description of her is wonderfully expressive in the fullness of its sensual imaginings. He is ingenious in devising occasions for celebrating her beauty, and conversely, for denigrating, albeit in equivocal language, her blonde rival—the dove-like, virginal, snow-white maiden of New England. But the two women stand to each other in the relation of the damned to the saved, so that inevitably the dark lady comes to a bad end while the blonde is awarded all the prizes—husband, love, and absolute exemption from moral guilt.

* * *

IRVING HOWE

[Coverdale's Politics][†]

* * *

Coverdale is a self-portrait of Hawthorne, but a highly distorted and mocking self-portrait, as if Hawthorne were trying to isolate and thereby exorcise everything within him that impedes full participation in life. The tendency to withdrawal that is so noticeable in Coverdale represents not merely a New Englander's fear of involvement in the dangers of society; it is also a moony narcissism by means of which an habitual observer, unable to validate his sense of the external world, tries magically to deny its reality.

* * *

Coverdale's relation to the utopian community is one of the first but still among the best treatments in American writing of what happens when a hesitant intellectual attaches himself to a political enterprise. Looking back from his withered bachelorhood Coverdale is proud that at least once in his life he dared to plunge: "Whatever else I repent of, let it be reckoned neither among my sins nor my follies that I once had force and faith enough to form generous hopes of the world's destiny. . . ." And throughout the book Hawthorne retains a

† From "Hawthorne: Pastoral and Politics," in *Politics and the Novel* (New York: Horizon Press, 1957), pp. 163–75.

qualified affection for that side of New England utopianism which would later prompt Parrington to speak of Brook Farm as "a social poem fashioned out of Yankee homespun."[1]

When Coverdale finally leaves Blithedale, he does so from a feeling—it will reappear in many American novels—that he is inadequate to public life, incapable of the monolithic enthusiasms a utopian politics demands. ("The greatest obstacle to being heroic," he shrewdly notes, "is the doubt whether one may not be going to prove one's self a fool.") Partly, too, he "sees through" the utopian impulse, discovering what would hardly surprise or shock a more realistic and experienced man: that behind its ideal claims it often shelters personal inadequacy and ideological fanaticism. And finally he grows weary of that constant depreciation of the present in the name of an ideal future which seems so necessary to utopian radicalism: "I was beginning to lose the sense of what kind of world it was, among innumerable schemes of what it might or ought to be."

Yet all of this, though pointed enough, is not very far from the usual criticism of utopian politics or, for that matter, from the usual attack upon 19th century ideas of progress; and what really distinguishes *The Blithedale Romance* is another kind of criticism double-edged, subtle and generally unnoticed. Hawthorne saw that, motives apart, the formation of isolated utopian communities is seldom a threat to society; he understood that no matter how pure its inner moral aspirations might be, the utopian community could not avoid functioning as part of the materialistic world it detested.

> I very soon became sensible [says Coverdale] that, as regarded society at large, we stood in a position of new hostility, rather than new brotherhood . . . Constituting so pitiful a minority as now, we were inevitably estranged from the rest of mankind in pretty fair proportion with the strictness of our mutual bond among ourselves.

And at another point:

> The peril of our new way of life was not lest we should fail to become practical agriculturists, but that we should probably cease to be anything else.

It is interesting, and a little amusing, to note how closely these caustic observations approach the Marxist criticism of utopian communities. For if Hawthorne's sentences are transposed into economic terms, what he is saying is that by virtue of being subject to the demands and pressures of the market, the utopian community becomes a competitive unit in a competitive society ("we stood in a

1. Vernon Louis Parrington (1871–1929) was the author of *Main Currents of American Thought: An Interpretation of American Literature from the Beginning to 1920*; the first two volumes of this influential intellectual history, which appeared in 1927, won the Pulitzer Prize [*Editor's note*].

position of new hostility") and must therefore be infected with its mores. The utopian who would cut himself off from the ugly world must, to preserve his utopia, become a "practical agriculturist"— which means to model his utopia upon the society he rejects.

This criticism,[2] which strikes so hard a blow at the political fancies of many 19th century American intellectuals, is advanced by Hawthorne with a cruel and almost joyous insistence, but that does not make it any the less true. Hawthorne, of course, was as far from the Marxist imagination as anyone could be, but almost any criticism of utopian politics from a point of view committed to struggle within the world would have to render a similar judgment.

If Hawthorne criticizes the utopian impulse on the ground that it does not really succeed in avoiding the evil of the great world, he also implies that another trouble with utopianism is that it does not bring its followers into a sufficiently close relation with the evil of the great world.

* * *

LEO B. LEVY

[A Sociology of the City]†

* * *

The Blithedale Romance is not a tract on the evils of the factory system or an essay on the decline of a rural society; it proceeds by way of modest observations of large inferential value, as in the notation of Coverdale's view from his hotel room of the people below, "cut out on one identical pattern, like little wooden toy-people of German manufacture." From his window, the roofs of all the buildings appear as one. Perplexed and annoyed, he regrets that he cannot "resolve this combination of human interests into well-defined elements." A sociology of the city, of which Coverdale here perceives the need, awaited *The Bostonians*,[1] but *The Blithedale Romance* is a step in this direction. For

2. Nor was Hawthorne alone in making it. His sister-in-law Elizabeth Peabody wrote in the 1840's that Brook Farm proved little beyond the fact that "gentlemen, if they will work as many hours as boors, will succeed even better in cultivating a farm." And Emerson, who understood very well the precarious relation between intellectuals and society, wrote in his journal that he refused to join Brook Farm because to do so would be "to hide my impotency in the thick of a crowd." [*Howe's note*].

† From "*The Blithedale Romance*: Hawthorne's 'Voyage Through Chaos,'" *Studies in Romanticism* 8 (1968): 1–15. Reprinted by permission of Taylor and Francis.

1. A novel (1886) by Henry James set in post–Civil War Boston; it shares some key narrative interests—New England reform culture, mesmerism, urban life—with *The Blithedale Romance* [*Editor's note*].

such a purpose, Hawthorne saw the value of an internal narrator whose integrity could be doubted precisely because he was as damaged by the conditions he describes as any of the other characters. * * * Coverdale's voyeurism is the pathological expression of his acknowledged emptiness and his need to enter into the lives of others through an act of sympathy. His empathic gifts are in inverse ratio to his sense of exclusion. The quickened rhythms of the prose that conveys the quality of his consciousness, the swift transitions from keen perceptions to defensive or malicious reactions, the alternations of genuine involvement and frightened withdrawal, and the conscious triviality of his own emotions—all these shape the recollections of a man who has tried with his friends to cross the bridge from an America they find lacking to a land of dreams. The utopian vision is universal, but in the United States, as this romance demonstrates, it found itself compromised by the difficulty of adapting the values of agrarian life to an advancing industrial order whose outlines Hawthorne perceived with remarkable prescience.

JAMES McINTOSH

[The Modernity of *The Blithedale Romance*]†

* * *

Zenobia * * * is an example of a soul at odds with itself, a person enormously gifted and yet unable to give direction to her gifts. She has not enough moral presence of direction to be the tragedy-queen she imagines herself. Like Coverdale, she has a contemporary sensibility; she exists—detached, astute, and enigmatic—within her sole self, and is thus hardly capable of the believing commitment necessary for a tragic relationship. But though she appeals to us in no simple or traditional way, her unpredictable capriciousness fascinates Coverdale and, through him, the reader. When he implies later that her "human spirit" is "inestimable," we may think back scenes * * * in which she has revealed the enigmatic variety and power of her personality—*this* is part of what is beyond estimation. And Coverdale's peculiar open-mindedness, his combination of prying sympathy with her grief and uncommitted, ironic acceptance of her foibles, allows him to convey that variety. Moreover, he has a kind of hidden fraternity with her. Both are experts at mockery and compulsive fondlers of their own

† From "The Instability of Belief in *The Blithedale Romance*," *Prospects* 9 (1984): 71–114. Reprinted by permission of Cambridge University Press.

anguish. Insofar as they accept themselves they accept each other, and pass beyond judgment to mutual, if still guarded, appreciation.

Coverdale, in such a scene, is a mediator of a flexible morality and is subject himself to no rigid or traditional moral standards. Since Hawthorne invests himself in Coverdale and uses him often as his own vehicle, he at times makes his own more settled moral criteria seem irrelevant to the action he records. Thus, almost despite himself, he conveys a sense of the possibilities of untethered human nature in the course of *Blithedale*. The gist of his surreptitious thought on the subject is, "If the modern world is a chaos, at least we have ourselves for entertainment; our mutual strangeness is a sop to our appetite for mystery." Yet this is hardly an encouraging thought. It is an intellectual form of "maniac levity," a temporary expedient that resolves nothing. It makes no effective connections in a disoriented world. It does not suggest that each human being truly has the inner resources to deal with his disorientation and review his faith, as Emerson urges and as Hawthorne himself grants on his own terms elsewhere. But *Blithedale* is not about the peace to be found deep within the cavern of the heart. The very name of "*Cover*dale" signifies that the depths of the heart are covered and obscure to the narrator. The "gloom and terror" in Coverdale are off-set not by the deep inner light of eternal beauty, but by flickering fires of transient entertainment.

Thus the new possibilities of men and women who sever themselves from their traditions—however appealing these human beings are—come to nothing. The book remains fundamentally desperate. Nevertheless, a strange sense of freedom accompanies its despair. When Hawthorne's inherited beliefs fall away from him, his stance of casual, baffled responsiveness toward the new suggests that his mind is not finally closed to it. He judges it assiduously throughout, but his judgments are never pontifical or final. This freedom, this irresolute-ness, and this judging concern recur together in other writings in which Hawthorne considers the contemporary scene (I am thinking especially of "The Old Manse" and "Chiefly about War Matters").[1] None of these writings suggest that he is at ease with himself in Zion, yet his divided stance in them, as in *The Blithedale Romance*, makes it foolish to consider him as merely a conservative, a Christian, an ironic pessimist, or even an anti-Emersonian. His voice is asking that we listen to him whole in all his intelligent tentativeness.

---

1. Two essays, or "sketches," by Hawthorne. "The Old Manse," an account of his daily life in Concord, Massachusetts, introduces *Mosses from an Old Manse* (1846), a collection of his stories and sketches; "Chiefly About War Matters," based on a visit in the spring of 1862 to Washington, D.C. and nearby battlefields and encampments, appeared in the *Atlantic Monthly* in July 1862 [*Editor's note*].

Recent Criticism

Recent criticism of *The Blithedale Romance* has been engaged in answering the following question: how does the novel itself write—or enable its critics to write—the complex history of its era. The array of essays presented here begins with the work of Nina Baym, whose 1976 book *The Shape of Hawthorne's Career* gave us a new Hawthorne, bracingly critical of the orthodoxies and pieties of his culture—and, in effect, inaugurated the current "generation" of Hawthorne criticism. Her chapter reads the novel as profoundly sympathetic to Zenobia, its female rebel, and as mounting a radical challenge to patriarchal authority. The essays that follow each explore a facet of the novel's exploration or illumination of a complex, conflicted American culture. Joel Pfister joins Baym in exploring questions of gender, power, and resistance in *The Blithedale Romance*, while the essays by Millington and Brodhead see the novel as, in different ways, exploring the impact on the individual consciousness of an emergent American modernity; for Berlant, Castronovo, and Levine, *Blithedale* exposes or addresses key political and ethical questions—the demands of political action, the nature of citizenship, and the morality of sympathetic identification, respectively. In arranging the essays, I have departed slightly from chronological order to register a difference in critical method, moving from essays that derive their insights mainly from close attention to features of the text of the novel to those more driven by the generative juxtaposition of that text with a striking array of historical materials.

NINA BAYM

[Passion and Oppression in *The Blithedale Romance*]†

* * *

The House of the Seven Gables concluded with the overthrow of a tyrant that turned out to be a Pyrrhic victory; the act of overthrow encumbered the free imagination with guilt, and the radical who entered the house left it a conservative.[1] If such an event is inevitable, it was nevertheless managed in the romance so rapidly and with such ambivalence that the reader who feels uncertain about Hawthorne's intentions at the conclusion is quite justified. In *The Blithedale Romance* Hawthorne returns to a point before that of the ending of *The House of the Seven Gables* and repeats the event. Giving the other side every benefit of the doubt, Hawthorne imagines a group of people who assert that they are not slaves to an oppressive personal history but are oppressed entirely by social institutions, which can be discarded at will because they have no organic relation to the self. These people leave society, as Holgrave left the house of the seven gables, but without his debilitating sense of complicity in the evils that inform the structures they are abandoning. They withdraw to construct their own expressive forms, free in theory of bias or entanglement. Like Holgrave, they move away from the city into the country, but they are more evidently attempting to reproduce the situation of the original Maule, by finding some plot of ground still in a natural state and working it into organic representations of their own ideals.

With this opportunity to live in freedom, what happens to these people? The answer is, of course, that they re-create the oppression they left behind, because they are not free. Hawthorne devotes the whole of *The Blithedale Romance*, then, to making the point reserved for the last two chapters of *The House of the Seven Gables*. People are civilized, which means that they bring with them,

---

† From *The Shape of Hawthorne's Career*, pp. 184–203. Copyright 1976. Reprinted with permission of Cornell University Press. Except where indicated, the notes are Baym's.
1. Baym makes a number of comparisons to *The House of the Seven Gables* (1851), the novel Hawthorne wrote before *The Blithedale Romance*. In that work, the theft of the Maule family property by the oppressive, acquisitive Pyncheons is repaired via the marriage of the artist Holgrave, a descendant of the Maules, to Phoebe Pyncheon—and by the death and exorcism of Jaffrey Pyncheon, who embodies the exploitative Pyncheon legacy [*Editor's note*].

because they have within them, attitudes that they thought were purely external. If repression and oppression are not original nature, they have become, in a long course of socialized life, second nature.

Because in *The Blithedale Romance* a Utopian ideal falls victim to human weakness and depravity, the work is read over and over again—with virtual critical unanimity until fairly recently—as Hawthorne's text on original sin. For this reason it cannot be too much emphasized that the "sin" is not one of disobedience, but of tyrannizing and repressing. The snake in this Eden, as well as its greatest sinner, is Hollingsworth, the authoritarian fatherly figure who stands against everything the Blithedale people believe in. The sin is the father's against the children, and not the children's against the father. Hollingsworth literally subverts the Blithedale enterprise, joining the community merely in order to gain access to its property and approach Zenobia for financial gain. His motives may seem exalted, but his relation to the property and the people who live on it is no less materialistic or ruthless than Pyncheon's.

As in *The House of the Seven Gables*, there is a basic territorial symbolism, in which a plot of land is identified with the self's body, and the self's potential is represented in the relation between the human being and land. As Hollingsworth takes over the role of Pyncheon, so the Maule-figure in *The Blithedale Romance* is Coverdale, its narrator. An artist, like Holgrave, Coverdale differs from his predecessor because he is not socially alienated and he has not preserved a radical self free from institutional influence. But he retains enough spark to wish to achieve freedom; *The Blithedale Romance* is the story of his quest and his failure. The world of Blithedale is the realization of his story, and all the events and characters take their fundamental meanings from their pertinence to his goal. Since it is Coverdale's story that we are following, the innumerable critical analyses of his character as detached voyeur are very much beside the point; but Coverdale's passivity is much to the point. Not only is Coverdale represented in the romance to some extent as the dreaming mind passively observing the images of its own creating * * * ; his passivity indicates his oppression and inhibition.

He is the product of a middle-class cosmopolitan way of life that sees no goals beyond comfort and pleasure and has confused the necessary material means of human existence with its ends. He thinks that by leaving behind his bachelor apartment, his sherry, and his urban entertainments, he will become a strong free man. But of course he is wrong. The characters and their interrelations tell the story of his error. The gradual drift from harmonious relations toward polarization and eventual violent antagonism represents the fragmentation of a personality. Imagery of masks and veils, much noted in the criticism, contributes to the dreamlike atmosphere of uncertain identities and reminds one of the indirect, misleading, and elusive ways in which truth is both asserted and disguised in fantasy. The carnival, or pageant, during which Zenobia is repudiated by Hollingsworth is not play-acting at all, but the moment of revelation when the characters cease to pose as people and appear in their symbolic meanings for Coverdale. Zenobia is the repudiated queen of the soul, Hollingsworth its wrathful judge. Recalling the mythology of "Main-street,"[2] we might see in Zenobia the great Squaw Sachem dispossessed and obliterated from memory by the Puritan patriarchy that Hollingsworth, cast as a Puritan judge, suddenly comes to represent. The event echoes Pyncheon's strategy of labeling his opponent a wizard; and when we remember the Salem persecutions we find a role for Priscilla in this transaction as well, as Zenobia's accuser. The catastrophic conclusion leaves Coverdale a permanently passive character. The spark that drove him to Blithedale has been altogether extinguished. He withdraws his allegiance from Zenobia and bestows it on Priscilla.

In the opening chapters Coverdale takes the familiar literary journey of the self into its own depths, hoping to make contact with the sources of energy and life within and to return to the surface a new man. In Boston he has enjoyed the "sweet, bewitching, enervating indolence"[3] of a genteel bachelorhood, parceling out his social days: "My pleasant bachelor-parlor, sunny and shadowy . . . [with] centre-table, strewn with books and periodicals . . . writing-desk, with a half-finished poem in a stanza of my own contrivance; my morning lounge at the reading-room or picture gallery; my noontide walk along the cheery pavement, with the suggestive succession of human faces, and the brisk throb of human life, in which I shared; my dinner at the Albion . . . my evening at the billiard-club, the concert, the theatre, or at somebody's party, if I pleased" (p. 40). This life is pleasant indeed, but effete; in its tepidly hedonistic atmosphere, art is but another languid pastime. Coverdale leaves it behind to liberate and test his talent. He wants to become a true poet, "to produce something that shall really deserve to be called poetry—true, strong, natural, and sweet" (p. 14). Presiding over the decadent life of the city is a mysterious idol, the Veiled Lady, who represents a decadent exploitation of spirituality; at the farm, Zenobia is the goddess in residence.

The movement from Boston to Blithedale represents a personal liberation, Coverdale's turning within himself, his abandonment of

---

2. In Hawthorne's "Main-street" (1849), an itinerant showman presents a diorama of Salem's history to its present-day inhabitants [*Editor's note*].

3. *The Blithedale Romance*, Centenary Edition of the Works of Nathaniel Hawthorne, vol. 3, ed. William Charvat *et al.*, (Columbus: Ohio State University Press, 1965), p. 19. Subsequent references given parenthetically in the text [*Editor's note*].

artificial forms in search of natural expression. As in the other romances of Hawthorne's major period, there is behind this personal story the question of the possibility of reconstructing society on larger and more generous principles than a narrow and repressive materialism. Boston is an institutional prison. Leaving the city with others about to join the community, Coverdale notes: "The buildings, on either side, seemed to press too closely upon us, insomuch that our mighty hearts found barely enough room to throb between them. The snow-fall, too, looked inexpressibly dreary, (I had almost called it dingy,) coming down through an atmosphere of city-smoke, and alighting on the sidewalk only to be moulded into the impress of somebody's patched boot or overshoe." And he draws a transcendental moral: "Thus, the track of an old conventionalism was visible on what was freshest from the sky" (p. 11).

In contrast, Blithedale aims to establish forms of labor and love that will permit the expression of the human spirit instead of inhibiting and distorting it. In an atmosphere of informality and innovation, it hopes to restructure human relations on the principle of "familiar love" and to "lessen the laboring man's great burthen of toil." Life will be "governed by other than the false and cruel principles on which human society has all along been based" (p. 19). But the community's economic aims have no deep interest for Coverdale, and the romance does not pursue the socialist dimension of the experiment, restricting itself to the drama of the inner life.

The springtime in which Coverdale leaves for Blithedale symbolizes (as has often been noted in the criticism) the rejuvenating purposes of his social withdrawal as well as his initial optimism. The severe snow that he encounters represents the necessary death of the social self prior to spiritual rebirth. Coverdale attributes the severity of his illness directly to the "hot-house warmth of a town-residence and the luxurious life" in which he indulged (p. 40). Recovered, he joins the community officially on May Day, confident that he is a new man and that his trials are all behind him:

> My fit of illness had been an avenue between two existences; the low-arched and darksome doorway, through which I crept out of a life of old conventionalisms, on my hands and knees, as it were, and gained admittance into the freer region that lay beyond. In this respect, it was like death. And, as with death, too, it was good to have gone through it. No otherwise could I have rid myself of a thousand follies, fripperies, prejudices, habits, and other such worldly dust as inevitably settles upon the crowd along the broad highway, giving them all one sordid aspect, before noon-time, however freshly they may have begun their pilgrimage, in the dewy morning. The very substance upon my bones had not been fit to live with, in any better, truer, or

more energetic mode than that to which I was accustomed. So it was taken off me and flung aside, like any other worn out or unseasonable garment; and, after shivering a little while in my skeleton, I began to be clothed anew, and much more satisfactorily than in my previous suit. In literal and physical truth, I was quite another man. [P. 61]

In fact, Coverdale's serious struggle is about to begin. He has replaced the flesh upon his bones, to be sure, but the attitudes that are wrought in the bone have yet to reveal themselves. The outer man has been renewed, but the inner man persists the same.

Coverdale's intention of tapping the soul's reservoir of energy, of contacting its passionate, creative, active principle, requires a representation in the romance of that underlying principle. Zenobia, who unites sex, art, and nature in one image, is that symbol. As the true aim of Coverdale's quest, she is waiting to greet him at Blithedale; and again Hawthorne creates the illusion, soon to be dispelled, that Coverdale's aims are easily and quickly realized. More than the community, Zenobia is the reality Coverdale seeks, and that is why in comparison with her the rest of the enterprise pales and looks unreal, becomes "a masquerade, a pastoral, a counterfeit Arcadia" (p. 21). The opposition between her and the rest of the community recalls the contrast, in "The Custom-House," between the transcendentalists, who represent an unerotic cloudland idealism, and Hester, who combines imagination and Eros in one figure. Sexual and poetic energy are varying forms of the same drive. In her symbolic function Zenobia stands for the creative energy of both nature and the self, equivalent in this romance to the fountain in *The House of the Seven Gables*.

In using a woman for this symbolism, Hawthorne returns to an important concept in *The Scarlet Letter* that he had put aside in *The House of the Seven Gables*: the idea that a man's liberation and fulfillment require his accepting a more fully sexual image of woman than the culture allows. The woman's sexuality (she is a secondary being in a patriarchal system) is suppressed in society as a means of inhibiting the male; both sexes suffer. Zenobia is described in unambiguously admiring physical images of softness, radiance, warmth, and health. She has a "fine, frank, mellow" voice, a "very soft and warm hand," and her smile "beamed warmth upon us all." Her laugh is "mellow, almost broad," her modes of expression "free, careless, generous" (pp. 14–16). Observing her, Coverdale thinks: "We seldom meet with women, now-a-days, and in this country, who impress us as being women at all; their sex fades away and goes for nothing, in ordinary intercourse. Not so with Zenobia" (p. 17). Later he rhapsodizes over "the native glow of coloring in her cheeks . . . the flesh-warmth over her round arms, and what was visible of her full bust" (p. 44). One astute critic of *The Blithedale Romance* has observed that Zenobia is linked to Phoebe through frequent sun images,[4] and the point is certainly valid; but Phoebe's is a capacity for decorating the surface, while Zenobia can radiate from within.

Coverdale understands much better than many modern readers of the romance that his morbid and oversensitive shrinking from the force and energy of Zenobia's personality indicates his own "illness and exhaustion" and not a flaw in Zenobia (p. 44). Many critics interpret the hothouse flower that she always wears as Hawthorne's sign of her sensual evil. But when one reads that the flower was "so fit, indeed, that Nature had evidently created this floral gem, in a happy exuberance, for the one purpose of worthily adorning Zenobia's head" (p. 45), one must abandon the idea that the bloom is either unnatural or evil, although it is certainly sexual. To impose the idea of evil on sexuality is in fact to fall into the cultural trap that Coverdale hopes to escape. He will be recovered, he realizes, when Zenobia no longer embarrasses him. His energies are blocked because he cannot accept the passionate foundation of the human character and the inextricable union of art and Eros. Zenobia should be his poetic inspiration and subject. Until she becomes so, Coverdale will remain a childish man and (to borrow Whitman's term) a mere "poetling."

The relationship between Zenobia and Coverdale begins auspiciously as the two sit comfortably together before the blazing kitchen fire. But the fire is only brush; it will not endure, nor will Coverdale's easy frame of mind. Their companionable solitude is broken by the knock on the door that announces the arrival of Hollingsworth and Priscilla, whose destruction of Zenobia will put out the fires of Blithedale permanently for Coverdale. Zenobia soon laughingly forecasts her own death and even the manner of her dying when she calls Hollingsworth the "sable knight" and Priscilla the "shadowy snow maiden who . . . shall melt away at my feet, in a pool of ice-cold water and give me my death with a pair of wet slippers" (p. 33).

From the beginning, Hollingsworth is imaged in terms of fire, ice, animals, and iron. In his great snow-covered coat he looks like a polar bear. The imagery of cold is clear enough, and the experienced reader of Hawthorne will know by the iron metaphors that another Puritan has entered the scene. To Priscilla, the docile maiden, he displays a face that "looked really beautiful with its expression of thoughtful benevolence" (p. 30), but to the unconventional Zenobia his aspect is "stern and reproachful"; so he enters at once into the

4. Rudolph Von Abele, *The Death of the Artist* (The Hague: Martinus Nijhoff, 1957), p. 78.

business of judging and reproving. "It was with that inauspicious meaning in his glance," Coverdale remarks, "that Hollingsworth first met Zenobia's eyes, and began his influence upon her life" (pp. 28–29). The outcome of the story is implicit in this first meeting, but Coverdale is long reluctant to believe what he has seen because he wants to believe that Hollingsworth is a benign and loving person.

And why does this matter to him? Because Hollingsworth is a figure of authority, and Coverdale wants to believe in the goodness of authority. This is the other side of his weakness: he denies passion, he respects authority. Thus, he wants authority to give its blessing to his Blithedale venture, and until it does he hesitates to commit himself. It is completely unrealistic of him to imagine that authority might countenance his radical aims, of course, and he finds this out. He understands at last that Hollingsworth desires nothing from individuals but their submission, that his high morality conceals and serves his wish to dominate others. The apex of Coverdale's development occurs when he refuses to join Hollingsworth in the scheme to betray the Blithedale community and thereby loses the friendship that is so valuable to him.

From the first he has known that Hollingsworth's heart "was never really interested in our socialist scheme, but was forever busy with his . . . plan" (p. 36). Coverdale thinks that Hollingsworth has joined the community because as an outcast he feels more at home with other outcasts (p. 55). But this is a sentimental view. Hollingsworth has come, as one critic puts it, to "bore from within."[5] He is the counter-revolution. His purpose is to acquire the Blithedale property for himself, as the site of his reform school. This school could not be in greater contrast to the Blithedale community and appropriately requires dispossessing the Blithedalers as a first step. Far from envisioning a free relation between man and nature, Hollingsworth would shut people away from nature in an institution, a building, which conforms not to the spirit of the individuals within it but to *his* spirit.

Forever busy planning his structure to the last detail, Hollingsworth allows absolutely no freedom to those whom he proposes to reform. His solid material edifice negates the organic ideal of the Blithedale group, who wish institutions to take shape from inner motives and to remain sensitive to inner flux. Once again Maule is to be supplanted by Pyncheon. While the Blithedalers are programmatic nonconformists, Hollingsworth's plan imposes sameness on all. People may not grow their ways, but must grow his way. Starting with the premise that men are criminals, Hollingsworth denies the basic

5. Irving Howe, *Politics and the Novel* (New York: Horizon Press, 1957), p. 167.

transcendental belief in the inherent divinity of the human being; setting himself apart from his criminals, he rejects human brother-hood. Perhaps most important, in accepting the social judgments that define some as criminals and others not, Hollingsworth's scheme rests on the social and institutional perceptions of human nature that the romantic soul rejects. In sum, Hollingsworth is not a romantic extremist but a representative of the authoritarian prin-ciple. To confuse his kind of reform with the goals of Blithedale is to miss the entire point of *The Blithedale Romance*.

His attachment to Zenobia, based wholly on his interest in her money, reveals his materialistic approach to human beings more clearly than anything else. When the fortune shifts from Zenobia's to Priscilla's possession, so does Hollingsworth's allegiance, and he rescues Priscilla from the clutches of the villain only a few days after he had agreed that she might be delivered to him. Despite his rheto-ric, Hollingsworth is a man of things, power, money, and material. The disparity between his self-righteous dismissal of Zenobia and the nature of his own motives shows his sanctimonious morality to be sheer, if unconscious, hypocrisy.

The rerouting of the fortune is more than a device to expose Hollingsworth's depravity and disloyalty. Although throughout most of the romance Zenobia is wealthy, she operates in a frame indepen-dent of money. Her wealth is in the abundance of her natural gifts. Priscilla, on the other hand, is very much a creature of money or the absence of it. Whether one thinks of her as a seamstress or as the Veiled Lady, one finds her characterization intimately bound up with economic questions, for she serves an environment that demands artifice and exploits its suppliers. As seamstress, she makes one highly specialized luxury item—a finely wrought silk purse. This object, whether interpreted sartorially or sexually, appeals to a jaded taste. As the Veiled Lady, Priscilla herself is an artificial construct appealing to sated appetites.

The contrast between the one sister's naturalness and the other's artificiality is brought out ironically in the Boston interlude of the romance (chapters 17–20). Zenobia, beautiful as ever, seems curi-ously artificial and dead despite the astonishing luxury of her cos-tume, indeed because of it. The hothouse flower has been replaced by a jewel. The metamorphosis signifies that her attractions appear unnatural in an urban setting. Coverdale, while talking to her, feels that she is playing a part (p. 165).

But Priscilla comes to life. The city is her element. Although Coverdale opines that her beauty is of the delicate sort that would be falsified by the art of dress, he declares almost in the same breath that her perfection in the city is due to consummate art: "I wondered what Zenobia meant by evolving so much loveliness out of this poor girl." Art or artifice has turned Priscilla into a symbol of purity and innocence, but this meaning is inseparable from her situation in the city. "Ever since she came among us, I have been dimly sensible of just this charm which you have brought out. But it was never absolutely visible till now." And then Coverdale expresses one of the romance's bitter insights: "She is as lovely," he rhapsodizes, "as a flower" (p. 169). In other words, Priscilla is the story's true artificial flower, the bloom that seems natural in the city domain of repression and unnatural pleasure. In the distorting glass of civilization Zenobia's flower looks fake. She does not belong here. It is right that the fortune be taken from her and given to Priscilla.

As Zenobia is the natural or precivilized woman, or the future possibility of woman, Priscilla is the woman in history, distorted by her social role and misrepresented by the ideals derived from her. She is considered an inferior being and is subjugated and exploited; at the same time she is idealized. The ideal is obviously pernicious because it derives from woman's subject status and ultimately ennobles an enslaved condition. As a seamstress Priscilla represents the whole range of exploited female roles in society, and particularly the fact of female labor in an age that pretended women were too feeble to work. She may or may not have been a prostitute, but the possibility is forcefully suggested.[6]

Her economic servitude is recapitulated on a psychosexual level in the murky symbol of the Veiled Lady. When Priscilla is not making purses to support her father, Old Moodie, she performs onstage as the subject of Westervelt's mesmeric powers, hidden behind a many-layered, gauzy white veil. The Veiled Lady is an idea of womanhood as noncorporeal and hence spiritual. The idea is carried to an extreme and implicates in its extremity some very base human emotions. Though she is proclaimed a spiritual being, she is really a possessed creature, owned and exploited by Westervelt. Her condition denies her spiritual nature even while pretending to demonstrate it. The particular being in whose service she performs is a cosmopolitan devil. Like Moodie, another urban figure, Westervelt lives from the proceeds of his exploitation, but, because his is a spiritual violation of the woman, his behavior is much worse than Moodie's. Westervelt caters to prurient and voyeuristic tastes in an audience that pays to see purity violated and modesty exhibited. On the one hand, talk of purity "veils" what is actually taking place; on the other, purity itself contributes to the prurient excitement of the display.

The veil, along with references to Priscilla's insubstantial frame, and metaphors of shadows and melting snows, and contrasts to

6. See Alan and Barbara Lefcowitz, "Some Rents in the Veil: New Light on Priscilla and Zenobia in *The Blithedale Romance*," *Nineteenth-Century Fiction*, 21 (1966), 263–76.

Zenobia's rich physicality and assertiveness, suggests that in this spiritual ideal a crude equation has been made between spirit and lack of body. The more body, the less spirit. To deny the flesh is to deny the emotions flesh arouses, and hence the normality of sex. The result is an abnormal sex indeed, in which young, frail, immature girls become objects of sexual interest while fully sexed adult women are experienced as frightening, corrupt, or repellent. The ideal is diabolic, for it thoroughly corrupts the natural growth of a strong human personality. It promises a fulfillment that is in fact an incompleteness. So Zenobia implies in her "Legend of the Silvery Veil," which she recites in chapter 12.

Theodore, sneaking into the Veiled Lady's dressing room for a peek at the hidden lady, is asked for a kiss by the shrouded figure. The idea repels him. He imagines all kinds of horrors beneath the evil and refuses indignantly. This failure to accept the physical aspect of the relation between the sexes dooms him and the lady to subjection and separation. She sorrowfully disappears, but not before Theodore has seen her lovely face, the memory of which is to haunt him for the rest of his life, and mock him with his empty and insubstantial existence. Priscilla, then, is both a real person and an image: imprisoned in the image of the Veiled Lady is a girl, or woman, who needs to be rescued, to be made into a being of flesh and blood.

But who will rescue Priscilla? Certainly not Coverdale, who likes her as she is, in all her frailty and vulnerability and in the very insubstantiality of her presence. His imagination is much preoccupied with her feebleness, but, as he admits, he mostly uses her vagueness as the ground for his own fantasies. What she really "is" does not matter to him; he would rather not know. Precisely to the extent that she is unassertive, his imagination can expand. Celebrating the feeble and victimized woman, Coverdale makes no effort to rescue the woman from the image; he locks her more firmly into it. Nor will Hollingsworth allow her out of the prison; he merely wrests the image away from Westervelt's possession. Finally, and perhaps most tragically, Zenobia will not make the effort. As the conclusion to her legend shows, Zenobia, who wants—quite legitimately—to eradicate the image from men's minds, has made the mistake of equating the real human being with its symbolic role. When she throws the veil over Priscilla she plays the role of jailor herself.

Priscilla at Blithedale is the perpetual reminder of ideals that the community has presumably tried to reject. Sensing this, Zenobia attempts to destroy her rival, and in these attempts she shows how much she herself, as a woman, is a victim of the patriarchal system she aspires to overturn. Her strategy of denigrating Priscilla is of course self-defeating, for it summons up all the chivalric impulses of the men, who will fight to the death to preserve Priscilla as a pathetic creature. Increasingly, Zenobia's tactics only define the polarity of pit and pedestal and put Zenobia herself in the pit. Coverdale becomes more and more uncomfortable and hostile as she ridicules his genteel attachments; and as for Hollingsworth, Zenobia's views have never held any attraction for him.

Yet, in this segment of the story, it is less important that Zenobia's strategy fails to engage the affection of the men than that it fails to recognize Priscilla as her sister, which she is, literally. Zenobia thus shows a fatal man-centeredness; the victimized woman in Priscilla, the possible development of Priscilla as a free human being: these issues do not interest her. She is a bad advocate for feminism because she has no sense of sisterhood. Hawthorne points up her frequent cruelties to the young girl, who wants above everything else to be accepted and loved by the older woman. Priscilla goes to Hollingsworth at the end only when Zenobia will not have her. Here is an opportunity wasted, a challenge not responded to. And here is a criticism of Zenobia, not because she is a feminist, but because she is not feminist enough.[7] After all, despite her talent and brilliance, Zenobia as a social creature cannot imagine any function in life other than adhering to some man whose superiority will enhance her own status.

Choosing Hollingsworth as the man she fancies, Zenobia shows that her male ideal is the cultural stereotype of masculinity. There is the shaggy aggressiveness, the scarcely concealed brutality, the obsession with mastery and domination, the sexual coldness (taken as a sign of devotion to "higher" things), the preference for abstractions to human particulars, the lack of sensitivity and subtlety masquerading as forceful logic. Hollingsworth is masculine precisely to the extent that he is a human failure. As Jaffrey Pyncheon represents Hawthorne's severely critical embodiment of the patriarchal system, so Hollingsworth is an attack on the patriarchal ideal of manhood. Enslaved by this ideal, Zenobia seriously undervalues herself and has little but contempt for other women. Coverdale is right to be appalled when she weakly acquiesces in Hollingsworth's ferocious diatribe against liberated women: "Her place is at man's side. Her office, that of the Sympathizer, the unreserved, unquestioning Believer. . . . Woman is a monster . . . without man, as her acknowledged principal" (pp. 122–23). "Let man be but manly and godlike," she responds, "and woman is only too ready to become to him what you say" (p. 124).

7. The critical treatment of Hawthorne's feminism is very murky, having been mostly carried out by critics who themselves are strongly antifeminist. Hawthorne's dislike for Margaret Fuller has been confused with a general dislike for the feminist movement; but his response to Fuller was a personal reaction that had nothing to do with her views and a good deal to do with his suspicion (perhaps right, perhaps wrong) that she was not sincere in them. Hawthorne's prevailing attitude toward feminist ideas, in all four major romances, is strongly sympathetic.

Later, when Hollingsworth casts her off, she takes refuge in a litany of her feminine imperfections:

> A woman—with every fault . . . that a woman ever had, weak, vain, unprincipled, (like most of my sex; for our virtues, when we have any, are merely impulsive and intuitive,) passionate, too, and pursuing my foolish and unattainable ends, by indirect and cunning, though absurdly chosen means, as an hereditary bond-slave must—false, moreover, to the whole circle of good, in my reckless truth to the little good I saw before me—but still a woman! A creature, whom only a little change of earthly fortune, a little kinder smile of Him who sent me hither, and one true heart to encourage and direct me, might have made all that a woman can be! [Pp. 217–18]

To perceive Hollingsworth as a "cold, heartless, self-beginning and self-ending piece of mechanism" is evidently not, for Zenobia, to be free of his myths of female nature. So Zenobia, like Coverdale, wants the blessing of male authority.

Her desire to be subject to authority derives not only from her place in the book's scheme as a part of Coverdale. It arises also because, in the modern world in which Zenobia must function as both Eros and Woman, the sole permitted expression is in Romantic Love. After her death, when the cynical Westervelt refuses to be moved by her sentimental tragedy, asserting instead that "it was an idle thing—a foolish thing—for Zenobia to do. . . . She had life's summer all before her, and a hundred varieties of brilliant success!" (pp. 239–40), Coverdale cannot help but partly agree. "It is nonsense, and a miserable wrong—the result, like so many others, of masculine egotism—that the success or failure of a woman's existence should be made to depend wholly on the affections, and on one species of affection; while man has such a multitude of other chances" (p. 241). Zenobia's perversities represent, like the perversities of the wizard Maules, the distortions of Eros in civilized life.

For Coverdale to imagine, then, that his creative energies could rescue him is naive folly. It is he who must rescue them. But to articulate the matter in this way is to realize the impossible situation. This stunted man cannot make himself whole. *The Blithedale Romance* is indeed a criticism of social optimism, but hardly because it warns against the dangers of untrammeled self-expression. It points out, rather, how naive is the assumption that such freedom might ever come to pass in the modern world. The dangers it exposes are of the repressive and punishing forces that will permanently damage the personality if given the opportunity. Such dangers threaten not only the individual personality but society as a whole. Hollingsworth finally becomes his own victim; his repudiation of Zenobia is suicidal.

There are no people without passion, and no societies without people. To extinguish passion is to extinguish life. In the civilized man, passion is already more than adequately controlled. It is control itself that needs boundaries.

Thus, although greatly moved by the romantic ideal, Hawthorne in *The Blithedale Romance* expresses no faith in it. But because he is moved by it, he portrays its collapse—a collapse he apparently thinks is inevitable—as a social and personal tragedy. Of course, this collapse is pertinent to the artist. Coverdale's *Blithedale Romance* is the confession of a failed artist, who has abandoned his ideal of writing something strong and true and returned to producing the only sort of art that appears to be possible in his society: genteel art. Having worked through to a conception of imaginative activity that was weighty and significant enough to justify the dedication of a lifetime, Hawthorne now appears to see that the art resulting from such activity is unattainable or forbidden in contemporary America. This was implied, to some extent, in Hester's removal of Pearl to the Old World, where—it was imagined—a more generous society would permit a freer personal development. Coverdale's story shows the American artist in a double bind, prevented on the one hand from developing a serious and worthy art, disparaged on the other for the genteel art he is expected to produce.

Coverdale may be understood as a typical American artist, but it would be a serious mistake to equate him with Hawthorne himself, as so many critics have done.[8] Hawthorne is not Coverdale but his creator, and the imagination that can create such a character and use it as Hawthorne did in *The Blithedale Romance* has clearly transcended the limits that confine the character. Through Coverdale, Hawthorne puts forward an explanation for the prevalence of genteel art in America by demonstrating how one artist of the genteel is produced. The effect of the critical evaluation of the character is to separate Hawthorne from the kind of art that Coverdale exemplifies.

One may compare Coverdale's literary situation with Hawthorne's as the latter is expressed in the preface to *The Blithedale Romance*. Hawthorne has the problem not of works that he cannot write, but of works that his audience cannot understand.

* * *

8. Mistakes are compounded when, to an identification of Coverdale and Hawthorne, the critics add an interpretation of Coverdale as a cold and heartless observer. From the resulting syllogism (along with the evidence of one fragment of a sentence from "Sights from a Steeple" in which the narrator speculates briefly on the pleasures of being a "spiritual Paul Pry") some critics have constructed an elaborate reading of Hawthorne as an aloof artist filled with guilt by his inability to connect with fellow mortals. This is quite ingenious, but entirely unsupported by the writings or by the biographical facts.

RICHARD H. MILLINGTON

American Anxiousness: Selfhood and Culture in *The Blithedale Romance*†

Nothing else; nothing but self, self, self!
—Zenobia on Hollingsworth

But what, after all, have I to tell? Nothing, nothing, nothing!
—Coverdale on himself

At the center of Hawthorne's depiction of character and culture in *The Blithedale Romance* is the suspicion that middle-class existence has been reduced to the self's absorbing effort to disguise its own emptiness. Within the novel, personal and communal anxiety is expressed in various forms of uneasiness about the authenticity of the self and in the fantasies of power and acts of domination that assuage that uneasiness: in Coverdale's fear of exposure, in the attraction of veiling and masquerading, in the fascination with occult access to the secrets—and thus to the selves—of others. The book's combination of interests—in the elaborately defended psyches of its characters, in the forms of cultural expression that manifest the shared anxieties of the community, and in the new emotions and experiences that belong to life in the city—reveals that in this romance Hawthorne is engaged in a striking act of cultural diagnosis. He is identifying what Raymond Williams calls a "structure of feeling": a specific historical moment—here, the emergence of a careening market economy in the middle years of the nineteenth century—as it expresses itself in private feel-ing and in the cultural forms a community produces.[1]

Because of their extraordinary power to entrap character and stul-tify experience within the world of the novel, the anxieties and fan-tasies of *The Blithedale Romance* call into being a newly aggressive fictive strategy involving complex connections between the book's depiction of the logic of identity, its account of social psychology, and its way of engaging its reader.[2] In a sustained and specific way *The*

† From *The New England Quarterly* 63.4 (Dec. 1990): 558–83. Copyright 1990 by The University of New England Quarterly, Inc. All notes are Millington's and have been renumbered; some notes have been condensed or eliminated for this Norton Critical Edition.

1. Raymond Williams, *Marxism and Literature* (Oxford: Oxford University Press, 1977), pp. 131–33. For a lucid account of the social changes that attended this economic trans-formation and of the anxieties it produced, see Karen Halttunen, *Confidence Men and Painted Women* (New Haven: Yale University Press, 1982), chaps. 1 and 2.
2. Gordon Hutner has published an admirable reading of the novel (*Secrets and Sympathy: Forms of Disclosure in Hawthorne's Novels* [Athens: University of Georgia Press, 1988], chap. 3) that makes two points crucial to my argument: that Coverdale is engaged,

Blithedale Romance is a counter-novel to *The House of the Seven Gables*. The forms of feeling and behavior that had seemed the resources of middle-class culture in the earlier book—sympathetic attachment, one person's capacity to "influence" another, the vision of reform, the shared stories that hold a community together—all become in *Blithedale* either masks for acts of self-aggrandizement and predation or defenses against awareness. It is as though in writing *Blithedale*, Hawthorne had come to recognize that beneath the surface of the middle-class culture he sought to celebrate and renovate in *The House* lurked certain ills and, acting on that recognition, set out to administer the shock treatment that might dispel them.

I

In inventing Miles Coverdale Hawthorne engaged in his most complex investigation of the vicissitudes of identity. Coverdale's writing of his memoir is in essence his attempt to compose a self, to locate in retrospect an authenticity that continues to elude him. Coverdale discovers, as he writes, a self built upon a principle of displacement, structured by

> that quality of the intellect and the heart, which impelled me (often against my own will, and to the detriment of my comfort) to live in other lives, and to endeavor—by generous sympathies, by delicate intuitions, by taking note of things too slight for record, and by bringing my human spirit into manifold accordance with the companions whom God assigned me—to learn the secret which was hidden even from themselves. [P. 160][3]

Apparent in this passage is Coverdale's characteristic combination of perspicacity and blindness to the implications of what he notices. He precisely identifies the logic of vicariousness upon which he constructs a self: a sustained act of observation will yield him not an interiority of his own but something he finds more compelling—possession of the "secret" that constitutes the selfhood of another. Coverdale's ceaseless attempts to penetrate the mysteries that experience presents him—Zenobia's sexual history, Priscilla's "maidenly mystery," Hollingsworth's romantic transactions with each of them—constitute his way of "living," of having a self. What needs to be uncovered in *The Blithedale Romance*, then, is not simply the

---

through his voyeurism, in an elaborate defense of his individuality; and that his personal psychology is symptomatic of a larger cultural condition.

3. Quotations from *The Blithedale Romance* are from vol. 3 of *The Centenary Edition of the Works of Nathaniel Hawthorne*, ed. William Charvat et al. (Columbus: Ohio State University Press, 1964).

process of Coverdale's voyeurism but a full description of the nature of the need that induces it.[4]

We might begin such a description by looking at the language Coverdale chooses to depict the dynamics of mind. As an apology for the intensity of his speculations about Zenobia's sexual past, he offers this description of the physics of fever:

> Vapors then rise up to the brain, and take shapes that often image falsehood, but sometimes truth. The spheres of our companions have, at such periods, a vastly greater influence upon our own than when robust health gives us a repellent and self-defensive energy. Zenobia's sphere, I imagine, impressed itself powerfully on mine, and transformed me, during this period of my weakness, into something like a mesmerical clairvoyant. [Pp. 46–47]

The passage suggests that Coverdale defines the usual interactions between people as a state of perpetual warfare. Each self, at risk of being overcome by the "sphere" of another unless it summon "repellent" energy sufficient for self-defense, is doomed to constant, anxious vigilance. Coverdale's portrayal of himself as entrapped by his relation to Zenobia, Hollingsworth, and Priscilla employs a similarly revealing range of metaphor:

> There seemed something fatal in the coincidence that had borne me to this one spot, of all others in a great city, and transfixed me there, and compelled me again to waste my already wearied sympathies on affairs which were none of mine, and persons who cared little for me. It irritated my nerves; it affected me with a kind of heart-sickness. After the effort which it cost me to fling them off—after consummating my escape, as I thought, from these goblins of flesh and blood, and pausing to revive myself with a breath or two of an atmosphere in which they should have no share—it was a positive despair, to find the same figures arraying themselves before me, and presenting their old problem in a shape that made it more insoluble than ever. . . . As for me, . . . I would pass onward with my poor individual life, which was now attenuated of much of its proper substance, and diffused among many alien interests. [P. 157]

Coverdale's use of the language of enchantment—he has been "transfixed," "compelled"—registers, like the fever passage, his frustration at this own passivity and his sense of the power latent in

---

4. See also the interesting discussion of Coverdale's voyeurism, which connects it to Hawthorne's ambivalence about self-revelation, in Edgar A. Dryden's *Nathaniel Hawthorne: The Poetics of Enchantment* (Ithaca: Cornell University Press, 1977), pp. 71–80.

others. Allied to his fear of being controlled is a deeper anxiety: a fear of being consumed. He is forced to "waste" his store of sympathies; the "goblins" infect the atmosphere he sought to preserve as his own; he envisions his connection to them, even as an observer, leaving his life "attenuated" of "substance" and "diffused." Coverdale's refuge in vicariousness—a refuge that itself threatens in this passage to entrap him—is provoked, his science of mind suggests, by a sense of the self as dangerously permeable and frighteningly depletable and of the other as voracious and in possession of a power Coverdale knows only by its absence in himself.

What sends Coverdale to the woods is a self-protective impulse, a worry that his self has been dissipated by too much community: "Unless renewed by a yet farther withdrawal towards the inner circle of self-communion, I lost the better part of my individuality" (p. 89). A curious principle, however, governs his choice of the place of rescue: "I . . . looked about me for some side-aisle, that should admit me into the innermost sanctuary of this green cathedral; just as, in human acquaintanceship, a casual opening sometimes lets us, all of a sudden, into the long-sought intimacy of a mysterious heart" (pp. 89–90). Coverdale's fear and desire are inextricably linked: his hunger for access to the mystery of another is most strongly revealed in the image he chooses to embody his flight from the danger his tenuous self experiences in actual contact with others.

The iconography of his hermitage reflects more fully the intricate logic of anxiety's usurpation of desire. Coverdale describes his dwelling as

> a kind of leafy cave, high upward into the air, among the midmost branches of a white-pine tree. A wild grapevine, of unusual size and luxuriance, had twined and twisted itself up into the tree, and, after wreathing the entanglement of its tendrils almost around every bough, had caught hold of three or four neighboring trees, and married the whole clump with a perfectly inextricable knot of polygamy. . . . A hollow chamber, of rare seclusion, had been formed by the decay of some of the pine-branches, which the vine had lovingly strangled with its embrace, burying them from the light of day in an aerial sepulchre of its own leaves. It cost me but little ingenuity to enlarge the interior, and open loop-holes through the verdant walls. Had it ever been my fortune to spend a honey-moon, I should have thought seriously of inviting my bride up thither, where our next neighbors would have been two orioles in another part of the clump.
>
> This hermitage was my one exclusive possession, while I counted myself a brother of the socialists. It symbolized my individuality, and aided me in keeping it inviolate. [Pp. 98–99]

Miles Coverdale has marriage on his mind. He finds in his hermitage representations of his fears about the customary route to the intimacy he so desires. Sexuality appears as a form of murder; the pine branches become the victims of the vine's loving strangulation, present only as the absent possessors of the "aerial sepulchre" their depletion leaves behind. Coverdale finds himself quite at home in this emptiness excavated by the dangers of love; the creation of some loopholes—the transformation of the bower from a place of love to a place of watching—redeems it for him. Coverdale goes to the hermitage literally to watch out for himself; his looking is not simply a perversion of desire but an act of self-defense.[5]

The hermitage "aids" in keeping a fragile self, paradoxically conceived as both empty and endangered, "inviolate" by representing the danger of intimacy and inviting the compensations of fantasy. Worth noticing as well is the habit of mind that induces the discovery of this iconic refuge: as striking as the *way* in which the hermitage symbolizes Coverdale's selfhood is his sense that the self *needs* symbolizing in order to maintain its wholeness. To be so on the lookout for external representations of the self is to testify to its internal attenuation, and all of Coverdale's symbols, all the details of setting that most fascinate him, seem to play out his dramas of endangered selfhood. Thus, to take a single example, the silk purses Priscilla manufactures, whose "peculiar excellence . . . lay in the almost impossibility that any uninitiated person should discover the aperture" (p. 35), capture Coverdale's desire to penetrate and possess her mystery, his sense that he in particular lacks the sexual initiation to do so, and his interest in the secretive purse as an ideal image of the adequately guarded self.

I think it is safe to posit that in his headlong flight toward vicariousness and away from himself, Coverdale seeks to evade some unspoken knowledge. The nature of that knowledge, I believe, can be inferred from Coverdale's reaction to Professor Westervelt, to whom, as a number of readers have noticed, he responds with the kind of incommensurate repulsion that indicates self-recognition. Two aspects of Westervelt's character engender particular loathing in Coverdale. The first is apparent in this portrait.

> He was still young, seemingly a little under thirty, of a tall and well-developed figure, and as handsome a man as ever I beheld. The style of his beauty, however, though a masculine style, did not at all commend itself to my taste. His countenance—I hardly know how to describe the peculiarity—had an indecorum

---

5. On observing as a form of defense against the threats the world poses to a shakily established self, see Helen Block Lewis, "A Case of Watching as a Defense against an Oral Incorporation Fantasy," *The Psychoanalytic Review* 50 (1963): 68–80.

in it, a kind of rudeness, a hard, coarse, forth-putting freedom of expression, which no degree of external polish could have abated, one single jot. Not that it was vulgar. But he had no fineness of nature; there was in his eyes (although they might have artifice enough of another sort) the naked exposure of something that ought not to be left prominent. With these vague allusions to what I have seen in other faces, as well as his, I leave the quality to be comprehended best—because with an intuitive repugnance—by those who possess least of it. [Pp. 91–92]

We all seem to share—even if we recognize it only by the repugnance it induces—this quality which Westervelt so rudely, hardly, and coarsely puts forth and which Coverdale will not name. Lurking in the language of erection that Coverdale chooses here is not simply, despite his protestations, an awareness of the aggressiveness he shares with Westervelt but the suspicion that for him, as in the murderous embrace of the grapevine in his hermitage, sexuality and aggression are disturbingly linked.[6]

Coverdale finds Westervelt loathsome, then, for mirroring an aspect of selfhood that might need suppressing, the permeation of desire by aggression. But the moment of identification that follows this one is deeper and more unsettling.

Here the stranger seemed to be so much amused with his sketch of Hollingsworth's character and purposes, that he burst into a fit of merriment, of the same nature as the brief, metallic laugh already alluded to, but immensely prolonged and enlarged. In the excess of his delight, he opened his mouth wide, and disclosed a gold band around the upper part of his teeth; thereby making it apparent that every one of his brilliant grinders and incisors was a sham. This discovery affected me very oddly. I felt as if the whole man were a moral and physical humbug; his wonderful beauty of face, for aught I knew, might be removeable like a mask; and, tall and comely as his figure looked, he was perhaps but a wizened little elf, gray and decrepit, with nothing genuine about him, save the wicked expression of his grin. The fantasy of his spectral character so wrought upon me, together with the contagion of his strange mirth on my sympathies, that I soon began to laugh as loudly as himself. [Pp. 94–95]

Westervelt presents Coverdale with a vision of the self as mere mechanism. This "discovery," as Coverdale notes, draws from him

6. The sexual self-disgust that seems to fuel Coverdale's loathing for Westervelt is confirmed in a later passage. "My dislike for this man was infinite. At that moment, it amounted to nothing less than a creeping of the flesh, as when, feeling about in a dark place, one touches something cold and slimy, and questions what the secret hatefulness may be" (p. 172).

an automatic acknowledgment, an act of "sympathy" reduced to "contagion," a moment of unconscious mimicry. This intense, unconscious recognition of his affiliation with Westervelt's embodiment of the falseness of the self suggests that, for Coverdale, the self-loathing provoked by what he does—by his predatory, voyeuristic form of love—is less extreme than that engendered by his sense of what he lacks. He evades the guilt that attaches to his voyeuristic raids on the secrets of others so easily because that guilt assuages a deeper one, the guilt of the absence of a self to generate even so oblique a form of desire.[7] Images of a mechanistic self, here tinged with black humor, veer into images touched with horror and pity as Westervelt occasions a meditation by Coverdale on men who cannot love.

> Externally, they bear a close resemblance to other men, and have perhaps all save the finest grace; but when a woman wrecks herself on such a being, she ultimately finds that the real womanhood within her has no corresponding part in him. Her deepest voice lacks a response; the deeper her cry, the more dead his silence. The fault may be none of his; he cannot give her what never lived within his soul. But the wretchedness on her side, and the moral deterioration attendant on a false and shallow life, without strength enough to keep itself sweet, are among the most pitiable wrongs that mortals suffer. [P. 103]

Coverdale is particularly prone to moments, like this one, when he suddenly perceives the deadness of things. On his first evening at Blithedale, he records this vision: "Starting up in bed, at length, I saw that the storm was past, and the moon was shining on the snowy landscape, which looked like a lifeless copy of the world in marble" (p. 38). What so horrifies Coverdale about Zenobia's body when they pull it from the water is its rigidity, its "terrible inflexibility" (p. 235). A principle of recognition seems to govern such insights. Coverdale's horror of rigidity, his sense of the ease with which the animate becomes empty, the authentic a copy, all testify to his ever abiding fear for his own actuality.

The double self-loathing implicit in Coverdale's reaction to Westervelt—the sense that a shamefully aggressive sexuality covertly organizes his behavior, the suspicion that even that manifestation of selfhood is illusory—accounts for some of Coverdale's most interesting traits. His affinity for embarrassing situations and enjoyment of moments of abasement—he finds Priscilla's imperious dismissal of him after one of his verbal attacks upon her, for example, "bewitching"

---

7. I am indebted to R. D. Laing for the distinction he makes between true and false guilt in a schizophrenic, *The Divided Self: An Existential Study in Sanity and Madness* (1959; reprinted, Harmondsworth, England: Penguin, 1965), pp. 129 ff.

(p. 126)—seem to offer the relief of simultaneously punishing and demonstrating the sexual aggression that he both repudiates and treasures as a sign of selfhood. His tribute to the beauty of Priscilla's absolute, passive adoration of Zenobia suggests his hunger for so safe and self-guaranteeing a form of love. More crucially, his attachment to the Blithedale project is generated by the fantasy (which he shares with his fellow utopians) that the self is utterly reformable—exactly the wish that would most appeal to someone convinced of its present inauthenticity: "My fit of illness had been an avenue between two existences; the low-arched and darksome doorway, through which I crept out of a life of old conventionalisms, on my hands and knees, as it were, and gained admittance to the freer region that lay beyond. . . . In literal and physical truth I was quite another man" (p. 61).

Hawthorne makes understanding a character in *The Blithedale Romance* a matter of understanding a particular strategy of self-construction; what constitutes character, that is, is one's share of and response to the anxiety about selfhood that Coverdale so complexly exemplifies. The most economical summation of the connection between the logic of identity and the relations between the four central characters occurs in one of Coverdale's dreams.

> It was not till I had quitted my three friends that they first began to encroach upon my dreams. In those of the last night, Hollingsworth and Zenobia, standing on either side of my bed, had bent across it to exchange a kiss of passion. Priscilla, beholding this—for she seemed to be peeping in at the chamber-window—had melted gradually away, and left only the sadness of her expression in my heart. There it still lingered, after I awoke; one of those unreasonable sadnesses that you know not how to deal with, because it involves nothing for common-sense to clutch. [P. 153]

The parts the characters play in Coverdale's dream correspond precisely to the logic of selfhood each of them embodies. He and Priscilla are miniature, infantile, while Hollingsworth and Zenobia loom over them, sexual and substantial.

Throughout the novel Priscilla manifests an insubstantiality analogous to Coverdale's. She lives out what Coverdale experiences as one of his chief anxieties: the self's permeability to others. Thus she begins to resemble Margaret Fuller as she hands Coverdale a letter from her (p. 52). The clairvoyance that makes her marketable as the Veiled Lady originates in her near absence of personality: "There was a lack of human substance in her; it seemed as if, were she to stand up in a sunbeam, it would pass right through her figure, and trace out the cracked and dusty window-panes upon the naked floor" (pp. 185–86). Coverdale possesses as a manifestation of selfhood only a pallid hybrid of aggression and desire; Priscilla, more fortunate, has inherited "a profound and still capacity of affection" (p. 186). She uses this capacity to love, however, the way Coverdale uses his powers of observation: as a defense against disappearance. Her unshakeable love for Hollingsworth successfully provides her with what she lacks, a presence, a gravitational force that will hold her translucent selfhood in configuration. Thus Coverdale is struck by the ease with which she sheds her attachment to Zenobia: "Her engrossing love made it all clear. Hollingsworth could have no fault. That was the one principle at the centre of the universe" (p. 220). Like Coverdale, Priscilla sets out to achieve an identity by displacing herself, by colonizing the selfhood of another.

As Hollingsworth's final collapse into regression indicates—"the powerfully built man showed a self-distrustful weakness, and a childlike, or childish, tendency to press close, and closer still, to the side of the slender woman whose arm was within his" (p. 242)—his seeming substantiality is the product of a kind of intrapsychic con game. Hollingsworth generates the magnetism that enables Priscilla to build a selfhood upon him, Coverdale to revere him, and Zenobia to love him only by an elaborate act of self-containment. Zenobia charges that Hollingsworth is a "self-beginning and self-ending piece of mechanism," that he is Blithedale's best masquerader because his "disguise is a self-deception" (p. 218). The logic of her accusation, which claims that Hollingsworth's apparent generosity is merely the manifestation of his self-enclosure, is unfolded in Coverdale's sermon on the philanthropist.

> They have an idol to which they consecrate themselves highpriest, and deem it holy work to offer sacrifices of whatever is most precious, and never once seem to suspect—so cunning has the Devil been with them—that this false deity, in whose iron features, immitigable to all the rest of mankind, they see only benignity and love, is but a spectrum of the very priest himself, projected upon the surrounding darkness. And the higher and purer the original object, and the more unselfishly it may have been taken up, the slighter is the probability that they can be led to recognize the process, by which godlike benevolence has been debased into all-devouring egotism. [Pp. 70–71]

Hollingsworth's apparently compelling presence is generated by mere duplication: it consists of two images of self, one worshipping the other. That this sustained self-mirroring passes so compellingly for selfhood, taking in, for a time, even Zenobia, seems to testify to an endemic thinness of identity in the world of *The Blithedale Romance*. Indeed, the attenuated form Hollingsworth's love takes—the recruitment of adjuncts to his project of self-adoration—is but the flip side of the identity by substitution Priscilla and Coverdale both practice. Thus Hollingsworth describes for Priscilla a vision of womanhood as idealized vicariousness: "Her place is at man's side. Her office, that of Sympathizer; the unreserved, unquestioning Believer" (p. 122). And the offer of discipleship that so tempts Coverdale suggests a dark version of the Oedipal bargain, the paternal Hollingsworth conferring substantiality and potency in return for complete submission: "Strike hands with me; and, from this moment you shall never again feel the languor and vague wretchedness of an indolent or half-occupied man! . . . there shall be strength, courage, immitigable will—everything that a manly and generous nature should desire!" (p. 133).

It is a measure of the bitterness of *The Blithedale Romance* that the only character who possesses an identity not constructed as a defense against selflessness commits suicide. Zenobia simply has what the other characters lack. Because her selfhood is *there* it becomes impossible to describe the strategy of its manufacture, and Coverdale's language finds a different metaphoric register when he describes her. Unlike the translucent Priscilla, the artificial Westervelt, the self-inflated Hollingsworth, and the embarrassed Coverdale, Zenobia is in full possession of her body. Coverdale's interesting reaction to this "womanliness incarnated" is to wish for its "multiplication" all over the earth in the form of painted and sculpted images, which seems to reflect both a hope that such unique substantiality might be possessed by replication and a desire to defuse her power by returning her to the realm of the manufactured. He notes that she possesses the rare gift of "natural movement," exclusively "the result and expression of the whole being" (p. 155). So substantial is her presence that, when she leaves him after her final display of grief, "It was as if the vivid coloring of her character had left a brilliant stain upon the air" (p. 228). In his invention of the passionately theatrical Zenobia, Hawthorne anticipates the ethical discovery that informs the late novels of Henry James: there is a form of self-conscious performance that leads not to inauthenticity but to existence.

Coverdale's dream, then, unconsciously posits the nature of the relationship among the four central characters, a relation between the realized and the fugitive self. In order to interpret the dream, we need first to notice how completely Coverdale identifies himself with Priscilla. In the chameleon logic of dreams, Coverdale is both himself and Priscilla; he *sees* the kiss of passion directly but feels it by observing its effect on her. Thus the dream elides the distinction between their reactions: when she melts away, he finds the sadness of her expression in his heart. This identification reveals the theory of causality that informs the dream; the passionate kiss exchanged by Hollingsworth and Zenobia does not simply exclude Coverdale but causes his dissolution. Already marginal and merely observatory in his relation to the others—lying unnoticed in bed and, as Priscilla, "peeping in at the chamber-window"—he sees himself in the act of disappearing. Implicit in the dream's causality is the chief emotion of the attenuated self; the reality of others, expressed here as sexual passion, is felt as a form of attack. Coverdale's dream possesses the obvious lineaments of a primal scene, but it is a primal scene performed under the aspect of anxiety about the very existence of the self. The "unreasonable sadness" that Coverdale feels in the wake of the dream is not simply grief for the wound of sexual exclusion but a moment of mourning for a selfhood that will not take shape.[8]

Condensed in Coverdale's dream is the dominant logic of identity in *The Blithedale Romance:* a suspicion that the self is absent. This sense of emptiness, which flickers at the edge of consciousness, engenders an anxiety strong enough to twist desire to its own shape; in every case but Zenobia's, both love and aggression are reducible either to defenses against the suspicion of emptiness or to fantasies of self-possession. The self is a fugitive, seeking protection, by acts of stealth and watching, from the dissolution that exposure to others threatens.

II

Hawthorne's complex articulation of the anxiety that produces Coverdale's oblique strategies of identity is matched by an extensive and wide-ranging cultural portraiture that alerts us to a corresponding unease in the urbanizing culture *The Blithedale Romance* reflects.[9] Hawthorne's enfolds his fullest account of the psychology of this culture of anxiousness in the stories told within the world of the novel, particularly as they find expression as forms of popular legend.

8. John Carlos Rowe offers a similar reading of the dream (*Through the Custom House: Nineteenth-Century American Fiction and Modern Theory* [Baltimore: Johns Hopkins University Press, 1982], pp. 82–83), noting that Priscilla is "a displaced image of Coverdale's own exclusion" and that the dream suggests that both he and Priscilla are "dominated or enchanted by the passion of others." Rowe, however, reads the dream as an important moment in Coverdale's education in the nature of the imagination.
9. Compare James McIntosh's suggestion that Hawthorne "pictures Coverdale as a key representative of the [cultural] disintegration he reveals, as the self-erasing center of a chaotic world" in his excellent essay on the book, "The Instability of Belief in *The Blithedale Romance," Prospects* 9 (1984): 81. Irving Howe (*Politics and the Novel* [New York: Horizon Press, 1957], p. 168), has argued that Hawthorne understood that "the utopian community becomes a competitive unit in a competitive society . . . and must therefore be infected with its mores." The predatory and exploitative quality of the relations between characters in the novel especially bears out this suggestion.

A set of symptomatic ghost stories haunts the middle-class culture Hawthorne depicts. The most prominent of these is the legend of the Veiled Lady, which Zenobia dramatizes in "The Silvery Veil." The ability of the Veiled Lady to attract so much attention derives, I suggest, from her representation of the kind of speculations about selfhood that obsess the inhabitants of *The Blithedale Romance*. On the one hand in the access her veiling offers to the occult, in particular to the secrets of other selves, lies confirmation of the hope that power is latent in the self, that it is capable of being generated by an act of sequestration. On the other hand, however, her power is accompanied by all the trappings of subordination; the Veiled Lady is enslaved by a magician whose own power is rumored to derive from the sale of his soul to the devil. As in the passages that envision the vulnerability of the self to an engulfing outer world, power is imagined to reside outside of the self, available only at the cost of the identity such power is sought to guarantee. The speculations Zenobia cites about what lies beneath the veil amount to a catalog of anxieties and fantasies about the nature of one's own inner life and the hidden selves of others:

> Some upheld, that the veil covered the most beautiful countenance in the world; others—and certainly with more reason, considering the sex of the Veiled Lady—that the face was the most hideous and horrible, and that this was her sole motive for hiding it. It was the face of a corpse; it was the head of a skeleton; it was a monstrous visage, with snaky locks, like Medusa's, and one great red eye in the centre of the forehead. Again, it was affirmed, that there was no single and unchangeable set of features, beneath the veil, but that whosoever should be bold enough to lift it, would behold the features of that person, in all the world, who was destined to be his fate. [P. 110]

The popular imagination oscillates between images of the deadness of the unveiled self (or the Medusa-like power of the other to confer such rigidity by gazing) and this anxiety's obverse, the notion that identity is fluid, literally unidentifiable.

The skeptical Theodore, on a dare, sets out to solve the mystery of the Veiled Lady's identity. His errand brings him more than he bargained for: the lady agrees to the lifting of the veil, but with a condition. He must kiss her before he lifts the veil, an act of faith that, she informs him, will confer a blissful reward: "thou shalt be mine, and I thine, with never more a veil between us! And all the felicity of earth and of the future world shall be thine and mine together." The other option: to lift the veil "in scornful scepticism and idle curiosity," which will transform her into his "evil fate," destroying his future happiness (p. 113). Theodore, a wary consumer, decides to inspect before kissing; he gets a glimpse of her beautiful face as the lady disappears and in that moment is doomed "to pine, forever and ever, for another sight of that dim, mournful face . . . to desire, and waste life in a feverish quest, and never meet it more" (p. 114). What the Veiled Lady offers Theodore is the self-risking interchange that Hawthorne—implicitly in his fiction, explicitly in his letters to his wife—defines as love. This mutual lifting of the veil of selfhood, we should notice, is precisely the act that the novel establishes as most threatening even while most necessary. Theodore's refusal to risk himself paradoxically robs him of the chance for self-completion that love, for Hawthorne, promises and instead engenders a form of desire that effects the depletion of the self, the "waste" of life.

The auditors of this cautionary tale elude its meaning by treating it as an amusement. Indeed, the successful forms of art we encounter in *The Blithedale Romance* offer gratifications more immediate than those of interpretation.[1] In "The Village Hall" chapter, Coverdale catalogs the kinds of popular entertainment his culture makes available, including some encountered second-hand.

> I heard, from a pale man in blue spectacles, some stranger stories than ever were written in a romance; told, too, with a simple, unimaginative steadfastness, which was terribly efficacious in compelling the auditor to receive them into the category of established facts. He cited instances of the miraculous power of one human being over the will and passions of another; insomuch that settled grief was but a shadow, beneath the influence of a man possessing this potency, and the strong love of years melted away like a vapor. At the bidding of one of these wizards, the maiden, with her lover's kiss still burning on her lips, would turn from him with icy indifference; the newly made widow would dig up her buried heart out of her young husband's grave, before the sods had taken root upon it; a mother, with her babe's milk in her bosom, would thrust away her child. Human character was but soft wax in his hands; and guilt, or virtue, only the forms into which he should see fit to mould it. The religious sentiment was a flame which he could blow up with his breath, or a spark that he could utterly extinguish. It is unutterable, the horror and disgust with which I listened, and saw, that, if these things were to be believed, the individual soul was virtually annihilated, and all that is sweet and pure, in our present life, debased, and that the idea of man's eternal responsibility was made ridiculous, and

1. See the interesting discussion of art in the barroom Coverdale visits in chapter 21 in Joel Porte's *The Romance in America: Studies in Cooper, Poe, Hawthorne, Melville, and James* (Middletown: Wesleyan University Press, 1969), pp. 130–33.

immortality rendered, at once, impossible, and not worth acceptance. But I would have perished on the spot sooner than believe it. [P. 198]

Coverdale's reaction, though intriguingly overheated, seems logically correct. The wizard's mysterious powers place him in the position that Coverdale's yearnings identify as ideal: himself invulnerable, he has complete access to the inner lives of others. The uses the teller finds for the enchanter's potency, moreover, bear a high libidinal charge: he adjusts women's affections, presumably for his own bene-fit, and he can also be seen as engaged, more covertly, in an act of revenge against women for their apparently privileged access to the kinds of deep emotional ties—love, grief, mothering—that verify the existence of a self which does the feeling. In a deeper sense, however, these tales of the violation of the self contain the oblique cry of a psy-che overburdened by the responsibilities that have customarily belonged to a being of a substantiality it now finds itself unable to sustain. Love and grief, guilt and virtue *have* become merely "forms" in the world of the novel, and the storyteller's attribution of power to a figure external to the self conceals an offer of forgiveness intended to relieve the burden of feeling. Coverdale's horrified reaction to these tales seems to me a submerged acknowledgment of their accuracy; hearing them raises for him not a question of truth but a problem of volition: will he have the strength *not* to believe this tran-scription of his own anxieties?

The stories of the man with the blue spectacles, pieces of the mythology of his cultural moment, work like the horror movies of our own: they locate widely-shared anxieties and, offering fan-tasies of inordinate potency or the comforting illusion that what they are portraying is alien to the self, turn themselves into a source of pleasure. We need to notice, too, how Hawthorne is using these brief vignettes to forecast or warn against the disinte-gration, under the pressure of the anxiousness he diagnoses, of the cultural consensus he had celebrated in *The House of the Seven Gables*. The character-erasing power of the mesmerist-magus is a sustained inversion of the "influence" customarily proclaimed as the key to the formation of a stable, moral character when exer-cised by a properly domestic "magician" like Phoebe Pyncheon or by the figure of the mother so widely invoked in antebellum writing about the middle-class home. The notion of the self's per-meability to others—the central tenet of sentimental ideology—is simply becoming too frightening for the vulnerable, defensive inhabitants of *The Blithedale Romance*.

In the last spectral legend, "Fauntleroy," Hawthorne explores the relation between the marketplace and the economy of self-construction. "Fauntleroy" chronicles the earlier career of Old Moodie, the progenitor of both Priscilla and Zenobia. In his present incarnation, Moodie represents the insubstantial self in pantomime: "His very gait demonstrated that he would gladly have faded out of view, and have crept about invisibly, for the sake of sheltering himself from the irksomeness of a human glance" (pp. 184–85). We first encounter Fauntleroy as a financial success, his form of selfhood the product of his wealth: "His whole being seemed to have crystallized itself into an external splendor . . . and had no other life than upon this gaudy surface" (p. 182). When Fauntleroy, "conscious of no innate worth to fall back on," loses his money, he utterly loses himself. Disgraced and impoverished, "being a mere image, an optical delusion, created by the sunshine of prosperity" (p. 183), he fades from sight and memory, eventually reappearing in Boston as Old Moodie.

The legend adds to our understanding of the anxious culture of *The Blithedale Romance* a sustained analogy between the condition of character and economic activity.[2] Identity for Fauntleroy/Moodie is not a stable quantity; like an inflated currency or a stock under speculation, the self possesses negligible intrinsic value, its worth instead determined by the vagaries of the market. In an attempt to avert bankruptcy, Fauntleroy has committed an offense: "it was just the sort of crime, growing out of its artificial state, which society (unless it should change its entire constitution for this man's unworthy sake) neither could nor ought to pardon. More safely might it pardon murder." This crime, apparently forgery, bespeaks an economy in which the authenticity of financial documents is paramount and persons are quite expendable. Fauntleroy's association with sudden, unpredictable fluctuations in value; with the paper instruments that newly, mysteriously, and not necessarily reliably represented wealth; and with secretive forms of transaction conducted in the interstices of urban life reveal him to be an embodiment of the manifold queasiness of antebellum economic life. Even the product by which Moodie earns his living, Priscilla's hermetic purses, links monetary value to the strategies of concealment and mystification that produce identity in the world of the novel. Taken together, these analogies between Fauntleroy's economic behavior and the

---

2. For a discussion of the impact of this economic transformation on Hawthorne's work, see Michael T. Gilmore's *American Romanticism and the Marketplace* (Chicago: University of Chicago Press, 1986), chaps. 3, 4, and 5. Gilmore reads "Rappaccini's Daughter," *The Scarlet Letter*, and *The House of the Seven Gables* as allegorizations of Hawthorne's encounters with the literary marketplace. I am arguing here that Hawthorne explores in *The Blithedale Romance* the way a culture internalizes the marketplace and that his relation to this issue is analytic, not irresolvably ambivalent or defensive.

emptiness of his character hint at an economic cause for the anxiety that permeates the novel.[3]

"The Silvery Veil" and "Fauntleroy" are linked within the book by their status as freestanding tales and thus call our attention to the relation between them. Each offers a theory that can be taken to account for the anxiousness that pervades *Blithedale*. In the legend of the Veiled Lady the etiology proposed is psychological: an inner lack—an inherent or characteristic fragility in the constitution of the human self—generates a private defensiveness that unfolds in its culture's predatory fantasies and forms of behavior. In "Fauntleroy" an inexplicable, unstable market world infects the self, putting it continually at risk and constantly on guard. The book does not equip us to choose between or rank these diagnoses. Their equal authority within the text suggests, rather, that it is the mutual permeation of the economic and the psychological that makes the anxiety the book depicts so powerful: private emotion and communal connection are alike endangered by a peculiar, unhappy synergy between the constitution of the self and the experiences that belong to a new economic and social life.[4]

III

"I agree with you in your detestation of Hawthorne," wrote Sarah Hale to her son, Edward Everett Hale, upon completing *The Blithedale Romance;* "the more I think of his book the more the disagreeable preponderated." Hale's response provides a useful starting point for a fuller discussion of the way the book constructs its interchange with the reader, its way of performing the work of romance, for in several ways anger and aggression are at the center of the

---

3. In her notes to the Penguin edition of *The Blithedale Romance*, Annette Kolodny—relying on work by Charles Swann—suggests the London banker Henry Fauntleroy, whose conviction and hanging for forgery was widely reported in the U.S., as a source for Fauntleroy. The fascinating connections suggested in Halttunen's *Confidence Men and Painted Women* (pp. 16–20) between the anxieties generated by the development of a market economy and the fears about the integrity and substantiality of the self apparent in the mythology of the Confidence Man (as well as other rituals and practices of middle-class culture) have shaped my view of Old Moodie and helped me recognize the economic aspect of the anxiety Hawthorne analyzes in *The Blithedale Romance*. Halttunen's account of the figure of the "liminal" young man—culturally dislocated, internally unstable, at sea in the city's slippery world of signs and vulnerable to the manipulation of its erotic and economic predators—derived from the advice literature of the time, is especially helpful in recovering the force of Hawthorne's urban portraiture.

4. For a striking analysis of the way in which the figure of the Veiled Lady represents important trends in antebellum culture and for an alternative account of the way in which Hawthorne is writing the cultural history of his time in *The Blithedale Romance*, see Richard H. Brodhead's "Veiled Ladies: Toward a History of Antebellum Entertainment," *American Literary History* 1 (Summer 1989): 273–94.

book's engagement with its culture.[5] As in *The Scarlet Letter*, our best access to the book's designs upon us comes by examining its depictions of interpretation.

Let us begin with the novel's most curious and controversial moment, Coverdale's confession. This is *The Blithedale Romance's* moment of interpretive demand, where Hawthorne leaves us on our own, submitting his work most radically to the risk of reading. This brief chapter, containing his attempt to "say a few words about myself," records Coverdale's interpretation of his own memoir: "I have made but a poor and dim figure in my own narrative, establishing no separate interest, and suffering my colorless life to take its hue from other lives. . . . But what, after all, have I to tell? Nothing, nothing, nothing!" (p. 245). Coverdale's solution to the problem of his absence is a second confession: "As I write it, [the reader] will charitably suppose me to blush, and turn away my face:—I—I myself—was in love—with—Priscilla!" (p. 247). More significant than the question of the truth or falsehood of his statement—Coverdale is in love with everybody and able to love no one—is the *way* he makes it. This moment of revelation, which claims that his behavior has all along been governed by a principle known only to him, is itself tinged by his customarily oblique aggression: he seeks to put the reader in his own accustomed position—adrift in the wake of mystery—and to place himself among those who possess selves and secrets. But there is a more deeply revealing logic at work here as well. Our understanding of Coverdale's anxiety suggests that the success of his confession is vital; it is his last, best hope for self-hood. But, as all the bogus apparatus that accompanies it—the blush, the melodramatic punctuation—makes clear, Coverdale can only make such a confession in a way that announces its own inauthenticity. And it acknowledges as well the depth of his anxiousness and guilt about having nothing to confess, nothing to say, because he has succeeded in being nothing. Embedded within the failure of his confession is the failure of his artistic project, too: his act of telling succeeds not in enacting the selfhood that has eluded him in the original experiencing but only in representing, through an act of aggression directed against both the reader and himself, his emptiness. In Coverdale's art, as in his life, nothing will come of nothing.

---

5. The letter of 30 July 1852 can be found in the Hale Family Papers, Sophia Smith Collection, Smith College, and is cited by permission. Hale often comments on novels in her letters and might be taken as a particularly intelligent, well-informed but still representative middle-class reader. (This is not the Sarah Hale who edits *Godey's Lady's Book*, though she was involved in the contemporary literary scene through her substantial work on her husband's newspaper, *The Boston Daily Advertiser*.) The most striking and articulate published expression of this readerly anger occurs in an anonymous review of the book in the *Westminister Review* of October 1852, [see above, p. 263, *Editor's note*].

As the reader of his own tale, Coverdale has missed the possibility that defines Hawthornian romance: the chance to recognize and revise the self. He habitually justifies his voyeurism by presenting himself as a model interpreter, an adept at the detection of "the final fitness of incident to character" and the distillation of "the whole morality of the performance" (p. 97). The problem with Coverdale's reading of his experience, which Hawthorne has him demonstrate again and again, is not a lack of acuity or even sympathy but an impenetrable defense against applying anything he notices about the latent motivations of others to his own case. His frequent comments on the dangers of an analytic relation to others—"It is not, I apprehend, a healthy kind of mental occupation, to devote ourselves too exclusively to the study of individual men and women" (p. 69)—never yield an attempt to change the form his friendship takes. Analysis, for Coverdale, is not a prologue to action but a completely adequate substitute for it.

Coverdale is not alone, however, in his ability to elude the implications of experience, whether real-life or artistic. Every audience we witness in *The Blithedale Romance* is either escapist in its choice of art—like those who attend the Veiled Lady's performance at the Village Hall, hungry for fantasies of power or guiltlessness—or dysfunctional in its reception of it. Such an unreachable reader, if encountered in the world at large, threatens to destroy the exchange at the center of romance and to turn Hawthorne, despite himself, into a version of Coverdale, condemned to write out a covert testimony to his own isolation and impotence.

Hawthorne's attack on the self-protective reader performs, it seems to me, a curious alchemy in transforming the actual reader's hostile relation to the book's narrator into an alliance with its author. By so compellingly defining the personal and cultural costs of failing to read the self, Hawthorne in effect dares one to risk being part of the portrait. Encoded in *The Blithedale Romance* is a relation between writer and reader based on shared anger: anger against Coverdale's evasions and self-evasions, against the constricting culture that endorses them—against what the book represents and the defensive form that representation takes. We feel Coverdale's narration, I am suggesting, as alienating both us and the Hawthorne he has displaced. The reader imagined by this novel is not, as in *The House of the Seven Gables*, on the threshold of community, a voice to be transformed, with like-minded others, into a "we." *The Blithedale Romance* seems to aim, rather, at a kind of joint apostasy, a salutary mutual rage.

The moral logic of the novel leads us, it seems to me, to a critical distinction. Cruelty is generated in *The Blithedale Romance* when anxiety displaces emotion: thus love appears in the novel only as infiltrated by aggression or deployed by narcissism or greed. Unlike Coverdale's voyeurism or the fantasies that emerge as popular entertainment, the anger shared by writer and reader is not a defense against emotion but an expression of it, not a displacement of selfhood but its exercise. Our angry reading of the novel places us, along with Hawthorne, in an aggressive relation to communal life, speaking what the community cannot bear to hear. But our anger may save us from Coverdale's perennial observorship, his empty relation to himself and others. This, then, is the hope implicit in the way *The Blithedale Romance* engages its audience: that the anger Hawthorne risks calling forth in his reader—an anger easily directed against the writer, as Hale's response indicates—might induce the clarity of mind and generosity of purpose needed to break the hold of the culture of anxiousness he depicts. He sets out, in his own chastened version of reform, to renovate his community of readers from the inside out.

Yet some of the uneasiness created by the paradox of a regenerative hostility remains intractable, the consequence of the novel's own account of the culture of anxiousness arrayed against its humane purposes. The failure of the Blithedale community suggests that there exists no safe margin of culture, no "outside" from which to work the needed transformation. Even the curative "neutral territory" of romance—the place of freeing revision of mind called into being in Hawthorne's writings—may, in the face of our elaborate defenses against self-recognition, be only a wish, a compensatory fantasy. The residual uneasiness is Hawthorne's acknowledgment of the problematic nature of a writer's cultural power, a statement, as it were, of the long odds against romance. If it is to do more than replicate the pattern of attack and withdrawal it reveals, the book must free the anxious reader it describes. But Hawthorne must rest his hopes for cure on a support undermined by his own analysis: the unverifiable capacity of fiction to change its readers' minds. Haunted by the spectre of the unreachable reader, Hawthorne engages and resists in *The Blithedale Romance* his own version of the anxiety he discovers in the world of the novel: an anxiety induced by the suspicion of one's powerlessness, by an intuition of the emptiness of one's form.

JOEL PFISTER

From Plotting Womanhood: Feminine Evolution and Narrative Feminization in *Blithedale*†

During the past two decades literary critics, historians, and sociologists have begun to theorize gender as a social, historical, and ideological construction. Thus, in her study of the signification of the "feminine" in the works of Henry James, Elizabeth Allen defines the "feminine" as "the whole range of potential meanings for woman which are seen as natural but are in fact socially constructed."[1] The social category of the "feminine," notes historian Mary Ryan, "conspires to dichotomize the human personality according to sex."[2] In the first section of this [essay] I will establish that Hawthorne was thinking along these lines and developed a mid-nineteenth-century understanding of the social construction of gender in his works, most elaborately in *The Blithedale Romance* (1852). The second section of this [essay] proposes that Hawthorne in *Blithedale* had Zenobia resist her narrator's effort to feminize the way in which we read her death. Zenobia's resistance to Miles Coverdale's narration of her as an Ophelia clarifies the role that Hawthorne saw literature and his own writing playing in the ideological process of feminization.

Hawthorne on the Social Construction of Femininity

Hawthorne's thematic interest in the cultural "making" of women took some seemingly oddball twists and turns, especially in his concept of their evolution. Hence the "not unsubstantial persons" of the women who throng around the scaffold in the opening scene of *The Scarlet Letter* display, in the narrator's mind, specific seventeenth-century characteristics. These substantial women have no compunction about indecorously flaunting their unrefined "persons" in public. "Morally, as well as materially," we are told, "there was a coarser fiber in those wives and maidens of old English birth and breeding, than in their fair descendants, separated from them by a series of six or seven generations; for, throughout that chain of ancestry, every successive mother has transmitted to her child a

† From *The Production of Personal Life: Class, Gender, and the Psychological in Hawthorne's Fiction*, pp. 80–103. Copyright 1991 by the Board of Trustees of the Leland Stanford Junior University. Used with permission of Stanford University Press. Except where indicated, all notes are Pfister's.

1. Elizabeth Allen, *A Woman's Place in the Novels of Henry James* (London: Macmillan, 1984), p. 5.
2. Mary P. Ryan, "Femininity and Capitalism in Antebellum America," in Zillah Eisenstein, ed., *Capitalist Patriarchy and the Case for Socialist Feminism* (New York: New Viewpoints, 1977), p. 151.

fainter bloom, a more delicate and briefer beauty, and a slighter physical frame, if not a character of less force and solidity, than her own." These women, still showing evidence of the "beef and ale of their native land," congregated "within less than half a century of the period when the man-like Elizabeth had been the not altogether unsuitable representative of her sex" (1: 50).[3]

Hawthorne then hints at a transformation of puritan women well underway in his own times. These puritan matrons, with "broad shoulders," "well-developed busts," and "round and ruddy cheeks" had "hardly yet grown pale or thinner in the atmosphere of New England" (1: 50–51). This paleness betokens not just a physical alteration, but a different discourse and behavior. The "boldness and rotundity of speech among these matrons" would "startle" the nineteenth-century observer "whether in respect to its purport or its volume of tone" (1: 51). Such public activity is both aesthetically and socially taboo by the nineteenth century. By contemporary standards this "man-like" look and behavior are unfeminine. Hawthorne does believe that femininity existed in the seventeenth century but that it was different from what he knows in the nineteenth. On the scaffold Hester "was lady-like, too, after the manner of the feminine gentility of those days; characterized by a certain state and dignity, rather than by the delicate, evanescent, and indescribable grace, which is now recognized as its indication" (1: 53).

The distinction that Hawthorne makes between rotund English-women and their nineteenth-century New England counterparts is one that he also thinks valid in his own era. This is evident in the passage from Hawthorne's *English Notebooks* in which he eviscerates the "red-faced monsters" who, "unconscious of the wrong they are doing to one's idea of womanhood," accompany their husbands to a meeting of a British scientific association. "American women, of all ranks, when past their prime, generally look thin, worn, care-begone, as if they may have led a life of much trouble and few enjoyments; but English women look as if they had fed upon the fat of meat, and made them-selves earthy in all sorts of ways." Hawthorne laments that men are constrained to "choose between a greasy animal and an anxious skele-ton"; but, as "a point of taste," he prefers his "own countrywomen."[4] The "delicate, evanescent, and indescribable grace" ascribed to his "countrywomen" in *The Scarlet Letter* is viewed here in a less sanguine light: the American female is "thin, worn, care-begone."

---

3. All references to Hawthorne's works are to *The Centenary Edition of the Works of Nathaniel Hawthorne*, ed. William Charvat *et al.*, 23 volumes (Columbus: Ohio State University Press, 1963–1996), and are indicated parenthetically within the text by vol-ume and page number [*Editor's note*].
4. Nathaniel Hawthorne, *The English Notebooks by Nathaniel Hawthorne*, ed. Randall Stew-art (New York: Modern Language Association of America, 1941), p. 89.

The notion that the American woman has become a cold, passionless skeleton is present even in Hawthorne's final works.[5] In *The Marble Faun* (1860) Hawthorne describes Kenyon's statue of Cleopatra as "the fossil woman of an age that produced statelier, stronger, and more passionate creatures, than our own" (4: 377). Even *Septimius Felton*, the rough fragments of Hawthorne's last effort to write a novel, depicts a Revolutionary War character, Rose Garfield, who tells us that her grandfather has observed the women of present times to have grown "slighter still; so that we are dwindling away" (8: 6).

These representations mystify historically specific shifts in the category of femininity. Comparing gender roles in colonial times and the nineteenth century, Stephanie Coontz notes that seventeenth-century "femininity was often seen as weaker or more prone to evil than masculinity but it was not yet equated with a qualitatively different set of capacities." It was only after the American Revolution that special characteristics were assigned to female nature.[6] Since republican ideology removed many of the limits imposed on character and behavior by the colonial hierarchy, republican wives and mothers were viewed as *naturally* qualified—in the setting of the home—to place moral constraints on males who competed in the marketplace. Rather than rooting changes in the definitions of femininity in the specific contexts of colonial hierarchical relations, republican ideology, and nascent industrial capitalism, the evolutionary description outlined in some of Hawthorne's fictions *biologizes* the historical process.

Hawthorne's idea of feminine evolution (more like a progressive atrophy of women's bodies) is developed most fully in *The Blithedale Romance*. Zenobia's active intelligence, robust sexuality, full body, and "noble earthliness" (3: 101) make her stand out. The "peculiarity" Coverdale refers to in his profile appears to be nothing other than her unemaciated womanhood:

> There was another peculiarity about her. We seldom meet with women now-a-days, and in this country, who impress us as being women at all,—their sex fades away and goes for nothing, in ordinary intercourse. Not so with Zenobia. One felt an influence breathing out of her, such as we might suppose to come from Eve, when she was just made, and her Creator brought her to Adam, saying 'Behold! here is a woman!' Not that I would convey the idea of especial gentleness, grace, modesty, and shyness, but of a certain warm and rich characteristic, which seems, for the most part, to have been refined away out of the feminine system. (3: 17)

5. See Nancy F. Cott, "Passionless: An Interpretation of Victorian Sexual Ideology, 1790–1850," in Nancy F. Cott and Elizabeth H. Pleck, eds., *A Heritage of Her Own: Toward a New Social History of American Women* (New York: Simon and Schuster, 1979); Barbara Berg, *The Remembered Gate: Origins of American Feminism: The Woman and the City, 1800–1860* (New York: Oxford University Press, 1978).
6. Stephanie Coontz, *The Social Origins of Private Life: A History of American Families, 1600–1900* (London: Verso, 1988), p. 98.

Coverdale imagines the sexy Zenobia as a female original unmutated by the cultural alchemy of successive "feminine systems."

Zenobia is contrasted to Priscilla, who seems to be the ideal of the nineteenth-century feminine woman. Westervelt, however, views this spurious ideal as a cultural aberration and echoes the sentiments of some mid-century health reformers:

> She is one of those delicate, nervous young creatures, not uncom- mon in New England, and whom I suppose to have become what we find them by the gradual refining away of the physical system, among your women. Some philosophers choose to glorify this habit of body by terming it spiritual; but, in my opinion, it is rather the effect of unwholesome food, bad air, lack of out-door exercise, and neglect of bathing, on the part of these damsels and their female progenitors, all resulting in a kind of hereditary dyspepsia. (3: 95)

Thus he praises Zenobia, in spite of "her uncomfortable surplus of vital- ity," as "far the better model of womanhood" (3: 95–96). Priscilla's half- starved grace "lay so singularly between disease and beauty" (3: 101).[7]

Hawthorne was not alone in his perception of "anxious skeletons." Sections of mid-nineteenth-century medical texts, even those that stereotype women, criticize the narrowing of woman's sphere and comment upon the appearance of feminine palefaces.[8] Some physi- cians suggested that women were undergoing a radical transmutation at the hands of the culture: the Georgianas of America were being confined and whitewashed.[9] By 1875 Dr. Edward H. Clarke, who dis- paraged the idea that women were physiologically capable of pursuing higher education, also despaired that "pale, bloodless female faces" prevailed in American "factories, workshops, and homes." Thus he quipped inanely that men who desired women who had not lost their bloom would soon have to consider importing mothers of the republic from Europe.[1] "Travellers to America during the first half of the

---

7. Reviewers in the 1850's saw Priscilla as, in the words of one critic, "one of those pretty phantoms with which Mr. Hawthorne occasionally adorns his romances," a "pretty-looking ghost." This critic goes on to chide Hawthorne for failing to make the effort to embody Priscilla: "A very few lines will indicate a spectre, when it would take an entire month to paint a woman." If Hawthorne continues to give his readers "shadows," soon his "imita- tors will inundate their books with skeletons" (anonymous review of *The Blithedale Romance* in *The American Whig Review* 16 (Nov. 1852): 417–24; the quote is on p. 421.

8. Caroll Smith-Rosenberg, "Puberty to Menopause: The Cycle of Femininity in Nineteenth- Century America," in Mary Hartman and Lois Banner, eds., *Clio's Consciousness Raised: New Perspectives in the History of Women* (New York: Octagon, 1976), p. 27; also G. J. Barker-Benfield, "The Spermatic Economy: A Nineteenth-Century View of Sexuality," in Michael Gordon, ed., *The American Family in Social Historical-Perspective* (New York: St. Martin's, 1978).

9. Georgiana is a central character in Hawthorne's story "The Birth-mark" (1843), and is the victim of her husband's scientific experiments. [*Editor's Note*]

1. Edward H. Clarke, *Sex in Education* (Boston: Osgood, 1875), pp. 62, 63. On pale women also see William Buchan, *Domestic Medicine: or, a Treatise on the Prevention and Cure of Diseases by Regimen and Simple Medicine* (Charleston, S.C.: John Hoff, 1807), p. 330. (quoted in Frances B. Cogan, *All American Girl: The Ideal of Real Womanhood in Mid- Nineteenth Century America* [Athens: University of Georgia Press, 1989], p. 7).

nineteenth century usually praised the delicate beauty and high-spirits of the American girl," observes historian Barbara Welter, "but they regretted that she was abnormally pale, collapsed under maternal responsibilities, and was likely to be a faded invalid by thirty."[2]

Zenobia, in what is surely the most provocative statement in Hawthorne's novel, recognizes Priscilla and her kind as cultural *inventions*: "She is the type of womanhood such as man has spent centuries in making it" (3: 122). This awareness appears to have been rare in the mid-nineteenth century, although it can be found in the writings of Sarah Grimké and Margaret Fuller and in the works of female authors who wrote later in the century. In 1838 Grimké held that "intellect is not sexed" and discarded the notion of sexual difference as a pernicious cultural mystification. "We approach each other, and mingle with each other, under the constant pressure of a feeling that we are of different sexes; and, instead of regarding each other only in the light of immortal creatures, the mind is fettered by the idea which is early and industriously infused into it, that we must never forget the distinction between male and female." The "true dignity of woman" is damaged because "she is approached by man in the character of a female" rather than as a social and intellectual equal.[3]

Two anonymous contributors to *The Lily* in 1851, who were writing in the tradition of Grimké, published their view of the debate between Sydney Smith, the outspoken English theologian, and T. S. Arthur, a sentimental writer and upholder of "true" womanhood. They quote Smith approvingly: "As long as boys and girls run about in the dirt, and trundle hoops together, they are both precisely alike. If you catch up one-half of these creatures, and train them to a particular set of actions and opinions, and the other half to a perfectly opposite set, of course their understanding will differ."[4]

Like Hawthorne and contemporary physicians, Margaret Fuller worried about whether America's "bodiless ideas," the "ladies," were fit to be "mothers of a mighty race." Unlike Hawthorne and the physicians, the shocking implications she drew were feminist: "There are no American women, only overgrown children." For that reason perhaps Fuller refused to write for *Godey's*, which she dismissed as an "opiate."[5] Elizabeth Stuart Phelps [Ward], in her essay on "The True Woman" (1871), demystifies the "true" woman as patently false, an ideological

2. Barbara Welter, *Dimity Convictions: The American Woman in the Nineteenth Century* (Columbus: Ohio State University Press, 1976), p. 57.
3. Sarah Grimke, *Letters on the Equality of the Sexes and the Condition of Women* (New York: Burt Franklin, 1970 [1838]), pp. 33, 22.
4. "Sydney Smith vs T. S. Arthur," *The Lily* 3 (Aug. 1851): 62.
5. Fuller's remark on overgrown children is quoted by Welter, "Coming of Age in America: The American Girl in the Nineteenth Century," in *Dimity Convictions*, p. 12. For Fuller's view of *Godey's* see Ann Douglas, *The Feminization of American Culture*, (New York: Avon, 1977) p. 323.

fiction. Phelps's profile of the "true" woman evokes the image of Pyg-malion's silent partner: she is an "empty and powerful figure" who "is patched up by men, and by those women who have no sense of charac-ter but such as they reflect from men." In remarks that bring to mind "The Birthmark," she argues that this "sad Sphinx" "has been always experimented upon" and "manufactured . . . to man's convenience."[6]

Hawthorne's occasional mystification of this socializing process as female evolution is interwined with his understanding of nineteenth-century femininity as a construction. We can describe this evolution, culminating in the wax angels and bloodless "skeletons" of the mid-century, as a process of feminization. Judith Fetterley, in a clever read-ing of "The Birth-mark," has argued that the story is about "how to murder your wife." I would argue that the tale is about a cultural and discursive process that is more subtle and insidious: the feminization of a colorful and perhaps creative wife. Feminization is the cultural process that contextualizes the psychological disturbance in Aylmer. The story emerges from a culture in which middle-class sex roles, in their stereotyped forms, must remain distinct.[7] Its conflict centers on the removal of a woman's distinguishing mark, a sign of life that might blur that distinction. If the "bloody hand" can be associated with a physiological process that signifies a female's biological maturation from girlhood to womanhood, then its papering over is an infantaliza-tion, a feminization that bears out Fuller's remark about American women as "overgrown children."

It is Zenobia who persistently stresses that literature plays a key role in this feminizing "alchemy." She jests that since Priscilla has "hardly any physique," "a poet, like Mr. Miles Coverdale, may be allowed to think her spiritual!" (3: 34). To Coverdale's (mis)repre-sentation of Priscilla, "She is as lovely as a flower!" (3: 169), Zenobia retorts: "Well; say so, if you like. . . . You are a poet—at least as poets go now-a-days—and must be allowed to make an opera-glass of your imagination, when you look at women" (3: 170).

Priscilla herself, albeit far less critically aware than Zenobia, calls into question the optic distortions of Coverdale's "opera glass." "You, especially, have always seemed like a figure in a dream—and now more than ever" (3: 168), he confesses. In a rejoinder that

6. Elizabeth Stuart Phelps Ward, "The True Woman," reprinted in *The Story of Avis*, ed. Eliz-abeth Hardwick (New Brunswick, N.J.: Rutgers University Press, 1985); see pp. 269–72.
7. Fetterley, *The Resisting Reader, A Feminist Approach to American Fiction* (Bloomington: Indiana University Press, 1978) p. 22. Also see M. P. Ryan: "Significant sex segregation cut an especially deep rift through American life in the nineteenth-century, dividing cul-ture, society, and even human emotions into male and female domains" (*The Cradle of the Middle Class: The Family in Oneida County, New York, 1790–1865* [Cambridge: Cam-bridge University Press, 1981] p. 191).

would no doubt please the anonymous *Godey's* critic of shrinking hands, Priscilla reminds him that "there is substance in these fingers of mine! . . . Why do you call me a dream?" (3: 169). Priscilla is in truth not quite so "impressible as wax" as "she seemed" (3: 78) to Coverdale and Westervelt. Coverdale, however, sounding like Pygmalion, himself acknowledges that Priscilla excites him not "for her realities—poor little seamstress, as Zenobia rightly called her!—but for the fancywork with which I have idly decked her out!" (3: 100).

Not long after Priscilla's dramatic entrance at Blithedale, Zenobia recognizes that both she and Priscilla are being transformed by Coverdale's "poetical" "light" (3: 33). This "poetical" "light" colors what *we* read. Coverdale, for example, supposes that Priscilla "had read some of Zenobia's stories, (as such literature goes everywhere,) or her tracts in defence of the sex, and had come hither with the one purpose of being her slave" (3: 33). He elects to depict her as a literary "slave" rather than as disciple or student or friend. There is also the fear * * * that powerful women infect or even impregnate other women with their heresies (thus making them "slaves"). In response to these speculations Zenobia satirically invites Coverdale to do what she knows he is already in the process of doing: "you had better turn the affair into a ballad. It is a grand subject, and worthy of supernatural machinery" (3: 33). This "supernatural machinery" is a male narrative experiment that reconstructs women.

Feminization is a social process that too easily appears to be invisible; thus, nineteenth-century "female complaints" seem to be the consequence of female "nature" rather than feminine roles. Psychoanalysis often tends to foreclose our consideration of social and historical processes, such as feminization, of which its own mode of thinking is an outgrowth. The use of psychoanalytic labels for psychological processes can provide insight into feminization while simultaneously contributing to its invisibility as a social and historical development. Anna Freud, as I have already noted, helps us see that Georgiana's response to Aylmer's succession of experiments is "altruistic projection," and so it is. Yet there is another way of reading Georgiana's positioning that accounts for this tendency to be obsessively altruistic. The feminizing ideology that Georgiana has internalized is obsession with beauty. John Berger describes this *social* process:

> Men survey women before treating them. . . . How a woman appears to a man can determine how she will be treated. To acquire some control over this process, women must contain it and interiorize it. . . . The surveyor of woman in herself is male:

the surveyed female. Thus she turns herself into an object—
and most particularly an object of vision: a sight.[8]

It is feminization that allegorizes a woman's apparent physical defect
as a moral and spiritual blemish and transforms women into allegorical problems for men and for one another.

Conventions of beauty constitute one mode of this historical process of feminization. Feminine beauty acquired obsessive significance for middle-class women as a substitute for social power and
public participation. The *Godey's Lady's Book* line was that beauty
should be regarded as more than ornament: it was "woman's *business*." Yet no one could really succeed in this "business." In 1868
Harriet Beecher Stowe complained that the American ideal of
beauty had narrowed the concept of "womanhood" quite literally,
disqualifying women with "vigor of outline": "When we see a woman
made as a woman ought to be, she strikes us as a monster." Women
consumed arsenic (perhaps Aylmer's "solution," Giovanni's "antidote")
to achieve delicate, translucent complexions. By the 1850's women
even painted their faces white to look like the American "angels"
that Hawthorne in the 1860's would contrast to the "beefy" English-
woman.[9] Aylmer's refusal to accept what he allegorizes as Georgiana's mortality is one important index of how unreal the "true"
woman had become.

Alice James once described herself as "absorbing into the bone
that the better part is to clothe oneself in neutral tints."[1] Wearing no
such "neutral tints," Zenobia had instead "a rich, though varying
color" and "was alive with a passionate intensity" (3: 102). By contrast, Coverdale describes himself as a parasite "suffering my colorless life to take its hue from other lives" (3: 245). Zenobia can resist
his "eye-shot" with her own powerful vision: her "eyes glowed" (3:
102) on one occasion, and on another they "were shooting bright
arrows, barbed with scorn, across the intervening space" (3: 158).
She is a woman who sees and sees through others and who refuses,
in Berger's words, to be a mere "object of sight" or a mere face. Georgiana is killed because of the way she is looked at, whereas Zenobia is
done in because of the way she sees. Thus it is worth challenging how
Coverdale represents Zenobia's response to the fond looks
Hollingsworth gives to Priscilla: Zenobia "would have given her eyes,
bright as they were, for such a look" (3: 72). As I shall make evident
below, I harbor doubts that she would have engaged in this feminine
romance of dismemberment.

8. John Berger et al., *Ways of Seeing* (Harmondsworth, Middlesex: Penguin, 1979), pp. 46–47.
9. See Lois Banner, *American Beauty* (New York: Knopf, 1983): she comments on social powerlessness and beauty on pp. 13–14; quotes the 1852 *Godey's* on p. 10; quotes Stowe on p.
   47; reports on arsenic and painting faces on pp. 41, 4; quotes Hawthorne on pp. 57, 305.
1. Alice James, *The Diary of Alice James*, ed. Leon Edel (New York: Penguin, 1973), p. 95.

The Death of Ophelia as the Birth of Medusa

Throughout Coverdale's narrative Hawthorne uses Zenobia to under-
score how she and others are (mis)represented by the "minor" (3: 246)
poet. Near the end of the novel she has *ostensibly* outlived her narrative usefulness. Zenobia is written off all too blithely by Coverdale,
who entombs her in the literary grave of Ophelia, Shakespeare's
lovesick maiden who drowns herself when rejected by her Hamlet:

> She had seen pictures, I suppose, of drowned persons in lithe and
> graceful attitudes. And she deemed it well and decorous to die as
> so many village maidens have, wronged in their first-love, and
> seeking peace in the bosom of the old familiar stream—so famil-
> iar that they could not dread it. . . . But, in Zenobia's case, there
> was some tint of the Arcadian affectation that had been visible
> enough in all our lives, for a few months past. (3: 236—37)

Coverdale would have us believe that Zenobia's death represents
nothing other than a girlish imitation of Ophelia. But for Coverdale
this effort to imitate a "decorous," poetic death has miscarried:
"Being the woman that she was, could Zenobia have foreseen all the
ugly circumstances of her death, how ill it would become her, the
altogether unseemly aspect which she must put on . . . she would no
more have committed the dreadful act, than have exhibited herself
to a public assembly in a badly-fitting garment!" The brilliant Zenobia, now ugly, has blundered: "Six hours before, how beautiful! At
midnight, what a horror!" (3: 236).

Zenobia is, nevertheless, a rather rebellious "horror." The description we get is the opposite of the "quiet, gradual, graceful" and "deco-
rative" death that Ann Douglas identifies as an established convention
of women's sentimental fiction.[2] Georgiana's genteel death, which followed the erasure of her "hand," was within the confines of this convention. The most noticeable feature of Zenobia's dead body, by
contrast, is her hands. Coverdale is unsure whether her unfeminine
hands are "clenched" in "the attitude of prayer," or "in immitigable
defiance." Her posture might be termed an anti-pose, a position which
offers nothing for the voyeur.[3] It is quite the contrary of what
Coverdale, earlier on, would like to see her do: "sit endlessly to painters
and sculptors, and preferably the latter; because the cold decorum of
the marble would consist with the utmost scantiness of drapery, so
that the eye might chastely be gladdened with her material perfection"

2. Douglas, *Feminization of American Culture*, pp. 153, 2. Poe also writes of female death as
   a romantic ideal: "The death, then, of a beautiful woman is unquestionably, the most
   poetical topic in the world" (*The Letters of Edgar Allan Poe,* ed. John Ward Ostrom [Cam-
   bridge: Harvard University Press, 1948] p. 38).
3. See Craig Owens, "Posing," in Craig Owens et al., *Difference: On Representation and Sexuality* (New York: The New Museum of Contemporary Art, 1985), p. 7.

(3: 44). Positioned thus, Zenobia's role in life would be to serve as raw material for male images of her.

Silas Foster, struck by the rigidity of her arms which "bade him defiance" (3: 236), struggles to straighten her out, but she is eternally bent. During their debate over women's rights at Eliot's pulpit, Hollingsworth invoked man's "physical force" as that "unmistakable evidence of sovereignty" (3: 123) over women. But here Hawthorne makes Zenobia, though dead, refuse to bend to male "force." * * * The description of her arms resembles the "crooked and unmanageable boughs" found at Blithedale, which "could never be measured into merchantable cords for the market" (3: 13). And these "cords" resemble the "variety of grotesque shapes" of the trees in Hawthorne's "orchard" at the "Old Manse." By "Why, man, it's not decent!" (3: 236), Foster really means that her posture, rigidly phallic, is unfeminine. Coverdale applies literary mythology, a cultural force, to do what Foster cannot do: straighten out Zenobia. He rechristens her Ophelia.

Coverdale, himself besotted with Hollingsworth, has little problem imagining that Zenobia would kill herself once rejected by the "iron"-willed reformer. But some mid-nineteenth-century critics had difficulty swallowing this ending (this "antidote" or "solution"). "We do not believe in Zenobia drowning herself," Mrs. Oliphant protested in 1855. "It is a piece of sham entirely, and never impresses us with the slightest idea of reality."[4] Of course, *Blithedale* is not "reality"; it is a "romance," a narrative experiment in "cloud-land." Another critic in 1853 charged that Zenobia's suicide was gratuitous, "and positively conflicts with the moral of her portrait as well as of the story." An appropriately conventional ending would have straightened her out in a more didactic manner: "marry her off"—make her a merchantable cord for market.[5]

Perhaps Hawthorne would not have been entirely comfortable emplotting his feminist in this conventional way. He prefers instead to draw our attention to the way, the literary way, that Coverdale tries to stereotype her. In several instances Hawthorne encourages his reader to develop a critical distance from Coverdale in order to problematize the politics and strategies of his narrative prestidigitations.

I shall argue that Hawthorne's Zenobia, as opposed to Coverdale's Zenobia, sends signals that her drowning *should* be read as "a piece of sham entirely." Her botched Ophelia-death is not simply a lovesick suicide but a parody of the way her culture stereotyped women. Some mid-century critics, for example, regarded her narrative submersion as poetic justice: such "unwomanly" women, wrote one,

4. Margaret Oliphant, "Modern Novelists—Great and Small," *Blackwood's Edinburgh Magazine* 77 (May 1855): 554–68.

5. R. H. N., "American Authorship—Hawthorne," *Southern Quarterly Review* 7 (Apr. 1853), p. 506. George Eliot felt that Hawthorne's narrative decision not to let Zenobia "come out of her struggle in regal triumph" exhibited his "lack of moral earnestness" (quoted in Arlin Turner, *Hawthorne: A Biography* [New York: Oxford University Press, 1980], p. 241).

"blaspheme God by stepping beyond the limits he assigned to them through all the ages." Her monstrosity makes this critic "shrink closer every moment from the contact."[6] Zenobia's gestures suggest that her culture, which speaks through Hollingsworth and some of the reviewers of *Blithedale*, had already tried to drown her out and shut her up when she was alive. "With the last, choking conscious-ness, her soul, bubbling out through her lips, it may be had given itself up to the Father, reconciled and penitent" (3: 235). Judging from the iconography of her body, Zenobia's "choking conscious-ness" or consciousness of having *been choked* may well have been her motive for refusing in the end to bend to "the Father."

The message her form of death sends is a distinctively literary one, which should be read in the context of her objections to Coverdale's literary alchemy. When bidding farewell to Coverdale, she alludes indirectly to the image that her narrator will later deploy: "I intend to become a Catholic, for the sake of going to a nunnery" (3: 227). Hamlet taunts Ophelia, "Get thee to a nunnery."[7] Plotting her through the grid of the Ophelia narrative, Coverdale reads Zenobia as a failed copyist; but her message, on the contrary, is original.

Zenobia's commentary on Ophelia is clarified when put in the context of remarks by another female critic of Shakespeare. Mrs. Jameson's *Characteristics of Women* (1833), which Hawthorne had borrowed from the Salem Atheneum on two occasions in 1835,[8] offers profiles of Shakespeare's heroines as plotted on a properly domestic grid. She sketches a sentimental portrait of Ophelia that is antithetical to the proud Zenobia—charmingly helpless and unearthly, "far too soft, too good, too fair, to be cast among the working-day world, and fall and bleed upon the thorns of life!" She is capable of evaporating on contact, "like the snow-flake dissolved in air before it has caught the stain of earth." Ophelia's incapacity to resist is the essence of her charm. Her demise is likened to that of a dove who "flitted . . . hither and thither, with its silver pinions shining against the black thunder-cloud, till, after a few giddy whirls, it fell blinded, affrighted, and bewildered, into the turbid wave beneath, and was swallowed up forever."[9] Mrs. Jameson sentimentalizes Ophelia's death as an aesthet-ically pleasing event.

From reading Mrs. Jameson it becomes apparent that Coverdale has impressed qualities on Zenobia that he either found in or

---

6. Review of *The Blithedale Romance, American Whig Review* 16 (Nov. 1852): 417–424; see p. 419.
7. *Hamlet* 3.1.142.
8. Marion Kesselring, "Hawthorne's Reading," *Bulletin of the New York Public Library* 53 (Apr. 1949), p. 184.
9. Anna Jameson, *The Characteristics of Women, Moral, Poetical, and Historical* (New York: John Wiley, 1833), pp. 130–33.

projected on Priscilla. Mrs. Jameson's Ophelia is closer to a profile of Priscilla than Zenobia: she is "a young girl who, at an early age, is brought from a life of privacy into the circle of a court. . . . She is placed immediately about the person of the queen, and is apparently her favorite attendant." Coverdale, of course, earlier sees Zenobia as the "Queen." Zenobia is far more akin to Mrs. Jameson's portrait of Shakespeare's Beatrice, who displays "high intellectual and animal spirits," "a touch of insolence," and a "satirical humour."[1] Coverdale miscasts Zenobia as Ophelia rather than a Beatrice who fights back. In doing so, Coverdale, like Aylmer, attempts to reconstruct the properly feminine body. But Hawthorne has Zenobia refuse to cooperate.

Thus the intractable Zenobia was not only "fond of giving us readings from Shakespeare" (3: 106) but also of giving us readings *of* Shakespeare. Elaine Showalter, in her provocative historical study of women and madness, has noted the appearance of an Ophelia complex in mid- and late-nineteenth-century English asylums for women. Medical books routinely printed photographs of women decked out as Ophelia. Showalter analyzes the phenomenon as one that can be explained by understanding how "madness expressed conflicts in the feminine role itself." The lovesick Ophelia became a logical stereotype for women who experienced such conflicts to adopt. But the Ophelia photographs also suggest how Victorian physicians, not unlike Coverdale, actively "imposed cultural stereotypes of femininity and female insanity on women who defied their gender roles." Showalter examines the "moral management" of these domesticated asylums as one that institutionalized "the discipline of femininity" ("ladylike values of silence, decorum, taste, service, piety, and gratitude"). Ophelia surfaced as more than a mid-nineteenth-century literary convention; she was a stereotype for how the culture was fashioning femininity and representing women and their "problems" to women.[2]

Zenobia's own narrative of Theodore and the Veiled Lady opens up another reading of her death that conflicts with Coverdale's rendition. The Veiled Lady, a mute theatrical spectacle, pledges herself to young Theodore if he agrees to kiss her no matter what face he discovers beneath her veil. It is her utmost wish to be unveiled and accepted for who she is. Although she most resembles Priscilla, one cannot help but hear the voice of Zenobia in her plea to Theodore: "thou canst lift this mysterious veil, beneath which I am a sad and lonely prisoner, in a

1. A. Jameson, *Characteristics of Women*, pp. 131, 72, 74.
2. Elaine Showalter, *The Female Malady: Women, Madness, and Culture in England, 1830–1980* (New York: Pantheon, 1986), pp. 60, 86, 81, 79. Also see Showalter's "Representing Ophelia: Women, Madness, and the Responsibility of Feminist Criticism," in Patricia Parker and Geoffrey Hartman, eds., *Shakespeare and the Question of Theory* (New York: Methuen, 1985).

bondage which is worse to me than death" (3: 112). She invites both trust and reciprocity, "thou shalt be mine, and I thine, with never more a veil between us" (3: 113). The veil invites multiple readings; but it had specific cultural significance for Elizabeth Stuart Phelps [Ward], who read the nineteenth-century "veil" as the sign of the so-called "true" woman who has been falsified by her culture. When sexual difference is acknowledged as a mystification, she wrote, "only then can we draw the veil from the brows of the true woman."[3]

Priscilla's paper-like veil, Westervelt's "enchantment," seems to have been conjured in the literary laboratory of cloud-land. "It was white . . . like the sunny side of a cloud; and falling over the wearer, from head to foot, was supposed to insulate her from the material world, from time and space, and to endow her with many of the privileges of a disembodied spirit" (3: 6). Her veil bears striking similarities to a domestic ideology that promises to "insulate" woman "from the natural world" and to elevate her as a "disembodied spirit." This paper lady seems very like the feminized woman fetishized by Hollingsworth: she serves as a blank envelope for male messages. The paper veil also may be a symbol for a feminine narrative, a veiled discourse that screens what a woman can explain to a man: "So much may a maiden say behind the veil!" (3: 113) she tells Theodore.

If the veil is a sign of a culturally draped femininity, a paper *shroud*, this discursive femininity also goes hand in hand with myths that figure the female body as dangerous and decayed (as in "The Birthmark," the body that wrote "mortality"). Thus young Theodore balks at the unveiling: suppose "he should salute the lips of a dead girl, or the jaws of a skeleton, or the grinning cavity of a monster's mouth!" (3: 113). Zenobia herself becomes a "dead girl" who, by Hollingsworth's definition of a feminist, has a "monster's mouth." Earlier in her narrative Theodore and his friends speculate that behind the veil one would find "the face of a corpse . . . the head of a skeleton . . . a monstrous visage, with snaky locks, like Medusa's, and one great red eye in the centre of the forehead" (3: 110).

This Medusa image is crucial. Medusa is the quintessential image of the powerful female stereotyped as horribly corporeal and grotesque. Hawthorne wants us to see that Coverdale misses this connection in his final gaze at Zenobia. Zenobia has made a grievous blunder, he thinks, because she does not resemble poetic images of Ophelia. But the dead Zenobia, when ugly, looks more like Medusa. From another perspective she appears like a petrified victim of some Medusa: "Ah, that rigidity! It is impossible to bear the terror of it" (3: 235). Ophelia is Coverdale's "antidote" for the "terror." Hawthorne wants the rigidified Zenobia to tell us not that she is a lovesick Ophelia

---

3. Ward, "The True Woman," p. 272. And see Richard Brodhead, "Veiled Ladies: Toward a History of Antebellum Entertainment," *American Literary History* 1 (1989): 273–94.

but that she has been turned to stone ("cold as moonshine") by an inflexible society and the sentimental literary discourse that ideologically upholds it.

* * *

RICHARD H. BRODHEAD

Veiled Ladies: Toward a History of Antebellum Entertainment[†]

When she is not at Blithedale, the Priscilla of Hawthorne's *The Blithedale Romance* has a career. She makes public appearances as the Veiled Lady: clothed in a silvery white veil, which purportedly insulates her from terrestrial reality, she goes onstage as a human conduit to occult knowledge, giving sibylline answers to the questions her audience puts. Hawthorne, we know, felt a final dissatisfaction with this figure of his creation. When *Blithedale* was finished but unnamed he considered "The Veiled Lady" as a possible title for the book but ruled that "I do not wish to give prominence to that feature of the Romance."[1] But would he or no, prominence is just what *Blithedale* gives the Veiled Lady. The book begins with Miles Coverdale "returning to my bachelor-apartments" from "the wonderful exhibition of the Veiled Lady" (5). Its plot machinations—unusually intricate for a Hawthorne novel—all turn on moves to rescue Priscilla from or to reimprison her in her onstage role. And if any figure in *Blithedale* might be said to be figurally belabored, it is the Veiled Lady, this book's prime site of symbolic overdevelopment. The question I want to put in this essay is what, historically, is on Hawthorne's mind when he writes *Blithedale* in 1851–52, and by extension, what cultural situation a novelist would have had to address at this moment of American literary history. If I begin with the Veiled Lady, it is on the assumption that she embodies answers to questions of this sort.

What cultural history could Hawthorne's Veiled Lady stand for? She is "a phenomenon in the mesmeric line" (5), and she has as her most obvious referent the "magnetized" subjects used by the

† From *American Literary History* 1.2 (Summer 1989): 273–94. Copyright Oxford University Press. Reprinted with permission of Oxford University Press. All notes are Brodhead's and are renumbered.
1. Hawthorne to E. P. Whipple, 2 May 1852 (*Letters* 536).

importers of mesmeric lore—Charles Poyen and his many imitators—
to demonstrate theories of animal magnetism to American publics
after 1836. (In her clairvoyance the Veiled Lady is meant specifically
to demonstrate the supermagnetized state that Mesmer's follower the
Marquis de Puysegur termed "extraordinary lucity."[2]) More generally
the Veiled Lady images, as a salience of contemporary life, the cultural
attraction of what *Blithedale* calls "new science[s]" (5), that congeries
of systems—Swedenborgianism, phrenology, utopian socialism,
and Grahamite dietary lore are other examples—that developed into
something between fad philosophies and surrogate religions in the
American 1840s. Grouped as she is with Hollingsworth, Zenobia, and
the Blithedalers, Priscilla shows such new sciences as literally living
together with many other social movements of comparably recent
birth: penal reform, the women's rights movement, communitarianism, and so on. In this sense, this exhibit of the "new truths" of
mesmerism appears as one manifestation of the variously directed
energy of social and intellectual reconstruction that touched almost
all aspects of American culture in the 1840s, known by the generic
label "reform."

But history teaches us that the hectic innovations of antebellum
reform developed alongside the establishment of new forms of social
normality in America, in particular the normalization of the nineteenth-
century model of middle-class domestic life; and Hawthorne's Veiled
Lady is figuratively implicated in this development quite as much as in
the history of reform.[3] Priscilla is a woman, but the Veiled Lady is a
presentation or representation of a woman; and the representation that
the Veiled Lady embodies intricately reflects the representation of
"woman" in the domestic ideology of Hawthorne's time. The Veiled
Lady is a lady, but in being *veiled* she is made into a lady who does not
appear in public. As such she images woman being publicly created
into a creature of private space, native of that separate nonpublic, non-
productive zone marked off in nineteenth-century ideology as the
home or woman's sphere. Bred in a "little room," her existence has
been circumscribed in such a way that extradomestic space has
become terrifyingly alien to her: "The sense of vast, undefined space,
pressing from the outside against the black panes of our uncurtained
windows, was fearful to the poor girl, heretofore accustomed to the

2. On the American history of mesmerism see Fuller, esp. 16–47. Puysegur and the concept
of a clairvoyance-yielding "lucity" are discussed on 10–11.
3. Among the many works on nineteenth-century domesticity as an ideological construct
and social reality see particularly Douglas, Cott, Ryan, and my "Sparing the Rod." The
last two works deal extensively with the symbiotic relations between domestic enclosure
and public reform movements.

narrowness of human limits" (36), Hawthorne writes, in a perfect description of the agoraphobia that Gillian Brown has presented as the psychological equivalent of middle-class women's domestic enclosure.[4]

As it erases her as a public figure, the Veiled Lady's veil specifically puts her body out of sight, or paradoxically makes her appear without a body; and in this sense the Veiled Lady might be called a figure for the disembodiment of women in nineteenth-century domesticity, that is, for the construction of "woman" as something separate from or opposed to bodily life and force. "Wan, almost sickly" of complexion, her brown hair falling "not in curls but with only a slight wave" (27), possessed (in the emphatically undisembodied Zenobia's contemptuous term) of "hardly any physique" (34), Priscilla's carefully noted body type minutely reflects the one that (as Lois Banner has shown) was normalized as a feminine ideal in America in the antebellum decades, that pallid, fragile-appearing, unvoluptuous, unrobust physical type that realized, at the bodily level, a social model of domestic leisure and feminine unproductiveness.[5] In Priscilla's "tremulous nerves"—a sensitivity so overdeveloped as to render her liable to regular collapses of spirits and strength—Hawthorne describes the neurasthenia that is the medical signature of this social type.

When she is veiled, this woman, already strongly repressed at the level of physical life, loses her physicality altogether and becomes what woman most essentially is in the nineteenth-century domestic conception: the embodiment of spiritual forces. Augustine St. Clare's mother in *Uncle Tom's Cabin*, the ideal woman as the cult of domesticity dreams that ideal (Little Eva is her reincarnation), is so fully identified with spirit that St. Clare can say of her: "*She* was *divine!* She was a direct embodiment and personification of the New Testament" (*Uncle Tom's Cabin* 333). Produced as she is, the Veiled Lady too can be said to be "in communion with the spiritual world," indeed to "behold the Absolute!" (201). The "tremulous nerves" that are the sign of her physical devitalization confer on her at least the appearance of spiritual privilege, or in the book's locution, "endow her with Sibylline attributes" (2). So too the veil that bounds her off from public and physical life is (or is at least said to be) what *creates* her as spiritual being: by "insulat[ing] her from the material world," this mark of delimitation "endow[s] her with many of the privileges of a disembodied spirit" (6).

---

4. See Brown. For another discussion of the cultural history of privacy and of the highly charged bounding off of public and private space in the antebellum decades, see Haltunnen, esp. 102–12.
5. Banner discusses the cultural authority of what she calls "the steel-engraving lady" (45–65).

The figure of the Veiled Lady may originate in the history of American cult movements and pseudosciences, I am suggesting, but this figure is not readable wholly in terms of such movements. In the terms of her constitution she precisely reflects another development just as much a part of *Blithedale*'s historical moment as mesmeric exhibits or communitarian experiments: the cultural construction of a certain version of "woman," and of the whole set of social arrangements built upon this figure of domestic life. This, much more than mesmerism or even reform, is the real subject of historical meditation in the Veiled Lady portions of *Blithedale*. Yet what is most interesting about the Veiled Lady is that this personification of woman domestically defined is in no sense domestic. Produced as a creature of physical invisibility, the Veiled Lady nevertheless leads a life of pure exhibitionism. Rendered an insular or private spirit, her sphere is nevertheless always the public sphere, and her work is not to make a home but to "come before the public" on the most spectacular of terms. In this respect she challenges us to find a rather different historical meaning for her than any we have established thus far.

What the Veiled Lady is most essentially is an image of woman as public performer; and if we insisted on reading this image as historically based, she could help us to the realization that the same period already known to us as the decade of reform and of the establishment of a more privatized and leisured model of middle-class domesticity could also be described as the time of the emergence of some women—specifically women in the entertainment sector—to an exaggeratedly public life.[6] Behind the Veiled Lady we could see arrayed the new female celebrities who, first in the 1840s, then more decisively around 1850, began to appear before audiences newly huge in scale, and to be *known* to publics much greater yet. Mesmerism did not produce a female celebrity of this order. But as a "name" attraction the Veiled Lady could find her likeness in Fanny Elssler, the Viennese dancer who made a triumphal tour of America in 1841. Or she could find her likeness in

6. To be fully understood, the quite spectacular emergence of women into public artistic celebrity around 1850 would have to be grasped together with the much more heavily obstructed movement of women into other forms of public life at the same time. Priscilla is partly defined in opposition to Zenobia, who contemplates a countercareer as a feminist political orator. Zenobia's historical correlatives are the women who asserted themselves as speakers in the antislavery and women's rights causes in the late 1830s and 1840s, who found their ways barred by the still strongly enforced social insistence that women not speak in public before mixed male-female audiences. O'Connor's useful volume reminds us that women were enrolled as students at the coeducational Oberlin College, but were not allowed to perform the public-speaking exercises in oratory classes; and that many women publicly prominent in education had male spokesmen read their messages aloud when called on to speak in mixed company (22–40). Calvin Stowe read Harriet Beecher Stowe's responses to the crowds she drew on her English tour (Wilson 349).

Jenny Lind, whose American tour exactly at *Blithedale*'s moment—
Lind concluded her eighteen months of concerts in May 1852, the
month *Blithedale* was completed—consolidated enduring patterns
of American mass-cultural stardom: the road tour with entourage,
the mobbing of the star's vehicle and the surrounding of her hotel,
the conversion of ticket acquisition into a high public drama (tick-
ets to Jenny Lind's concerts were auctioned off at newsworthy
prices), the exposure of the well-guarded star in carefully arranged
public appearances. (When she came before the public Lind too
was dressed in white.)[7]

Or the Veiled Lady could find her likeness in another group of
entertainers who emerged into mass visibility at just the same time:
the women novelists who attained to a new degree of popularity right
at *The Blithedale Romance*'s moment. The scale of the American
market for literary goods, we know, expanded abruptly at this time.
Where a "decided hit" might have sold five or six thousand copies in
America heretofore, around 1850 books like Susan Warner's *The
Wide, Wide World* and Maria Cummins's *The Lamplighter* began to
sell tens (and in the case of *Uncle Tom's Cabin* hundreds) of thousands of copies. Born together with this new scale of circulation was
a new kind of publicity broadcasting such authors' wares *as* popular,
indeed proclaiming them the object of insatiable and universal
demand: the literary publicity campaign that seized on the mass
medium of journalism to announce the staggering sales record of a
newly published book was pioneered by the printer of *Uncle Tom's
Cabin* in *Blithedale*'s year, and became industry standard almost at
once.[8] As the focus of these developments, the new best-selling
writers of the early 1850s found audiences and became names on
terms quite similar to Jenny Lind's. Ruth Hall, the successful author-
hero of Fanny Fern's book of that name (1855), has a steamship
named after her, as a suitable tribute to (and advertisement of) her
popular fame (176). Fanny Fern herself had a railroad parlor car
named in her honor, among other trumpetings of her name. When
Uncle Tom's Cabin was published in 1852 Stowe became, exactly, a
celebrity. Visiting New York after completing the novel, Stowe got
into one of Jenny Lind's last concerts—long since sold out—*as* a
celebrity, by being recognized as the famous Harriet Beecher Stowe.
Her English tour of 1853 recapitulated the Jenny Lind tour with a
writer in the singer's place. Stowe drew her own dockside crowds,

---

7. Banner discusses Fanny Elssler's tour, 63–64. On Jenny Lind's American concert tour see
    Barnum, esp. chapters 17–19, and Harris 111–42.
8. The most comprehensive treatment of 1850s literary promotion and the expansion of the
    American book market is Geary. See also the discussion of publication and promotion in
    Kelley's comprehensive history of antebellum best-seller writers (3–27).

had her own travel plans publicly announced, packed her own halls, appeared before audience after audience as her celebrated self: found a career, like Lind or like the Veiled Lady, as a famous object of public attention.[9]

Such likenesses suggest that what lies behind *Blithedale* is a development specific to the history of entertainment quite as much as any development in general social life. What the Veiled Lady registers, we might say, is the historical emergence, at midcentury, of a more massively *publicized* order of entertainment in America. She images a remaking of the social organization of entertainment by which artistic performance (broadly understood) came to reach larger and more stabilized mass publics, and by which participation *in* performance came to yield enlarged public visibility, to women above all. Or, to draw the many sides of this figure together, we might say that the Veiled Lady registers the creation of a newly publicized world of popular entertainment taking place simultaneously with the creation of a newly privatized world of woman's domestic life. She embodies the suggestion that the same contemporary cultural processes that worked in one direction to delimit women to dephysicalized and deactivated domestic privacy also helped open up an enlarged publicity women could inhabit, in the entertainment field—a suggestion rich in historical implication.

After all, the steep escalation of literary sales figures around 1850 must be understood to have reflected not only improved production factors like cheaper printing technologies or more active marketing campaigns, but quite as essentially the historical creation of a new social *place* or *need* for literary entertainment to fill. The mass-market novels of the 1850s point to middle-class domesticity as the scene they address because it was above all the institution of this social formation that created literature its new mid-nineteenth-century place. As I have shown elsewhere, the canons of domestic instruction that defined the home as a private, leisured, nonmaterialistic, feminine space in the antebellum decades also and with almost comparable insistence defined reading as a preferred domestic activity ("Sparing" 88–92).[1] In consequence of this linkage, the implementation of this social model in the decades after 1830 had the secondary effect of enlarging demand for reading for the

---

9. Kelley 3, Wilson 291 and 344–86. Stowe was assured of an English "reception as enthusiastic as that of Jenny Lind" (Wilson 334). An important related discussion of "the modelling of a highly visible identity under . . . new circumstances of conspicuous performance" (164) is Fisher's. But Fisher locates in the 1890s the developments I see beginning in the late 1840s.

1. All discussions of the joint birth of mass-market fiction and middle-class privacy must acknowledge their debt to Ann Douglas, whose *Feminization of American Culture* first suggested the American version of this linkage, and to the still important chapter "Private Experience and the Novel" in Watt (174–207).

home—and so too of creating public roles for literary producers and public attention for literary works.

The new, popular women novelists whom the Veiled Lady images in part are the figures who most fully seized the public life that domestic privacy helped construct. As Mary Kelley has shown, by using their own feminine domestic competences to address the domestic concerns that identified the new mass audience, these women were able to escape from domestic confinement and capture a new public role: the role of author. (But as Kelley also notes, winning a transdomestic social place did not help such authors escape from domestic self-conceptions. Among other manifestations of this entrapment, they typically attained to public identities without feeling entitled to assert themselves as public creatures: hence their regular use of pseudonyms, the literary equivalent of that highly public erasure of oneself in public embodied in the Veiled Lady's veil. "I have a perfect horror of appearing in print," Catharine Sedgwick wrote before the publication of her first novel, echoing the Veiled Lady's terror of the public or published domain. "We all concur in thinking that a lady should be veiled in her first appearance before the public" (qtd. in Kelley 129–30), Sedgwick's brother wrote at this time, a sentiment Professor Westervelt would share.[2]). The historical situation that writers like Elizabeth Wetherell, Fanny Fern, and Marion Harland—behind the veil, Susan Warner, Sara Willis Eldridge Parton, and Mary Virginia Terhune—capitalized on was, we need to remember, not theirs alone. They were only the most successful exploiters of a cultural restructuring that affected the whole field of literary writing, and adjacent entertainment fields as well. Accordingly, if we find Hawthorne meditating on such public-private figures in the Veiled Lady of *Blithedale*, we need to understand that they embody for him not just new literary competition but the new social conditions of literary production that he too finds himself working under at this time: a situation in which artistic creation has had a potentially massive new public life created for it on the condition that it align itself with a certain structure of private life.

At this point it is important to acknowledge that the historical situation of the literary that *Blithedale* addresses cannot be understood from *Blithedale* alone. Most glaringly, Hawthorne shows no grasp of the enabling side of the publicity that he knows as new at this time. The Veiled Lady is a victim of her display; in celebrity she is only exploited. Her real historical sisters-in-celebrity won wealth, power, prestige, and a measure of independence from their performers' careers. The saucy and independent-minded Fanny Fern—to cite the

---

2. Kelley's discussion of female literary pseudonyms (124–37) is a crucial contribution to the historical meaning of women's veiling in the mid-nineteenth century.

figure most antithetical to the droopy, dependent Priscilla—entered into a prenuptial contract giving her sole control of the property her royalties had amassed: a Priscilla who struck for such a deal would represent a revision indeed (Kelley 158).[3] The successful author's gloating over the bank stock she now owns at the end of *Ruth Hall* suggests a second possible attainment newly open to the woman-celebrity of this time: not just wealth but the pleasure wealth brings as a mark of achievement and entitlement. (A Priscilla who took pleasure in performance or its rewards would be someone else.) The Veiled Lady displays no talent, her "performance" is a hoax of some-one else's devising. But Lind sang, Elssler danced, Southworth and Stowe and Warner wrote, Fanny Fern spoke her piece: the opening that brought them publicity also expanded their field of *expression*, certainly not the least of their gains. Hawthorne is in no position to see this side of the contemporary picture, which we must learn of from other accounts. But partial though it is, *Blithedale* makes its most interesting sense as a reading of the new literary situation of its moment; and *Blithedale* has things to teach about this newly emerg-ing order not easily learned from other sources.

To name a first: *Blithedale* reflects a world in which artistic per-formers, and preferentially women, have won a new capacity to amass large audiences for themselves. But it also suggests that the development that puts performance in this new relation to popularity installs it in other relations at the same time. The Veiled Lady wins celebrity not by herself but through her bond to Professor Westervelt. This "attraction" is one half of an entertainment partnership the other member of which is her manager. As such this figure brings back to our attention the mid-nineteenth-century female celebrity's typical dependence on a male handler to achieve her public "life." P. T. Barnum was Jenny Lind's Westervelt. Chevalier Wyckoff, who Barnum beat out for the right to manage Jenny Lind, was Fanny Elssler's manager, or in Barnum's phrase the "speculator" who had Elssler "in charge" (Barnum 173).[4] Fanny Fern and Mrs. E.D.E.N. Southworth found the eventual sustainer of their long-lived popular success in Robert Bonner, publicist-publisher of the *New York Ledger*. At the bittersweet close of *Ruth Hall* the popular author Ruth

---

3. Barnum's Jenny Lind chapters make clear that she profited from her performance career quite as much as he did.
4. On Bonner, see Kelley 3–6, 21–24, and 161–63. Kelley's evidence suggests how much generosity such a manager might be capable of, and what benefits a woman might gain through her dealings with him, facts that must not be underrated. (In *Ruth Hall* Ruth thinks of her manager as a real brother, unlike her miserable actual brother Hyacinth.) But it is a tendency of Kelley's argument to slip over the market relation that a bond *to* a publicist-promoter necessarily involved: Kelley thus treats this relation as background or introductory information, instead of as a relation that helps *constitute* the female literary "success."

stands at her husband's grave with her daughter and the man in her new public/literary life, her publisher-agent John Walter.

More than a manager, Westervelt is in the full sense of the term the Veiled Lady's *producer*. Having contracted for the rights to Priscilla as an entertainment property, he has made her *into* the Veiled Lady, has created a public identity for her and created public attraction *to* this identity—and he has done so not disinterestedly but as a way to increase the take. In this respect *Blithedale* reminds us that the handlers newly prominent in the popular entertainment of its time are really the sign of such entertainment's entrance into new relations to market forces. The Jenny Lind chapter in P. T. Barnum's autobiography *Struggles and Triumphs*—which spells out the terms of the performer-manager contract that *Blithedale*'s "Fauntleroy" chapter left vague—is fitly called "The Jenny Lind Enterprise."[5] In herself a woman, in Barnum's hands Jenny Lind became a business venture, a singer made *into* Jenny Lind the musical wonder by Barnum's incessant promotional activities, to the end of enriching them both. Similarly the literary-historical meaning of the new mass-market novels of the 1850s is not just that they were more popular than earlier books but that they mark a historical change in the meaning of the word "popular," a term that now comes to denote not just "well-liked" or "widely read" but specifically production *into* a certain market status through commercial management of a book's public life. The new promotional campaigns mounted by the publishers of such works to an altogether new extent *produced* public demand for them, demand which was then republicized as a way of creating further demand. Jewett's early ad for *Uncle Tom's Cabin* "TEN THOUSAND COPIES SOLD IN TWO WEEKS!" or James Cephas Derby's hyping of *Fern Leaves from Fanny's Portfolio* (1853) "FANNY FERN'S BOOK, 6,000 Copies Ordered in Advance of Publication!" promoted these books *as popular*, made their popularity the basis of their market identity (Geary 378, 382). And of course the publicity that made these books known to the public also made them wares marketed to the public: it is not for nothing that we establish the popularity of such works by enumerating their sales.

In *Blithedale* the Veiled Lady's public life is managed toward commercial ends, but it is the particular nature of this management to be hard to see. A curious but persistent feature of narration in this book is that the many dramatically crucial scenes in which Priscilla's deployment as Veiled Lady is arranged or contested all take place off the narrative record. The Veiled Lady's performance thus opens the

---

5. In the same vein Barnum calls Lind's tour "an enterprise never before or since equalled in managerial annals" and gloats: "I had marked the 'divine Jenny' as a sure card," and so on (170–72).

novel, except that it is finished just before Coverdale begins his tale. The scene in which Old Moodie then intercedes with Hollingsworth to take Priscilla to Blithedale occurs between chapters, so that we never learn what understanding he reached with Hollingsworth or what relation his act had to her career of display—though there is a later hint that her contract with Westervelt has just run out. The subsequent interview in which Westervelt by some means (black-mail?) talks Zenobia into returning Priscilla to his charge occurs before Coverdale's eyes, but out of his earshot. The scene of the Veiled Lady's recapture—the scene in which Zenobia lowers the veil back over Priscilla—is seen and heard but wholly misunderstood: "we thought it a very bright idea of Zenobia's, to bring her legend to so effective a conclusion" (116), Coverdale says of this reveiling, with even greater than usual obtuseness. A presumably contempora-neous scene in which Hollingsworth agrees to the plan of turning Priscilla over to Westervelt ("he bade me come" [171], Priscilla later states—but in consideration of what? of Zenobia's offer of her fortune?) is missing altogether. Later, Coverdale sees Priscilla through his hotel window in the city, but he fails to see how she got there or where she is taken next. In "The Village-Hall" he sees her exhibited again, but she is again produced out of nowhere; when Hollingsworth now intervenes to rescue her from onstage life—for reasons we never see him arrive at—he too takes her we know not where. Finally, when Hollingsworth rejects Zenobia's schemes for Priscilla's and his life, our man on the scene arrives a little late, and so succeeds in missing this decisive exchange.

Did ever a book miss so much of the story it purports to tell? But this insistent narrative *missing*, usually thought merely inept, is itself deeply interesting in the context I am considering. In its narrative organization *Blithedale* constructs a zone in which highly interested arrangements are made and remade around the figure of a female entertainer, and it renders that zone at once controlling of the apparent action and yet imperfectly available to knowledge. In this respect the book might be said to image not just the management of high-visibility performance as commercial attraction but the simul-taneous effacement, in such entertainment, of the interests and deals through which its public life is contrived. The new popular entertainment of the mid-nineteenth-century works, in part, through just this cloaking of its business end. Barnum, an apparent exception to this statement, made no secret either of his role in Jenny Lind's tour or of the terms of their commercial engagement. But even this most exhibitionistic or least *veiled* of publicists erased a portion of his act. His publicity for Lind works by creating the fascinating sense that she both is and is not his creation, that she is both the object of his shameless exploitation and at the same time a self-directing agent beyond the reach of his consumeristic wiles. But through its apparent frankness about its own motives such publicity conceals the extent to which Barnum both manufactured the appearance of the "untouched" Jenny and exploited that appearance as a marketing resource. The divineness of "the divine Jenny" was essential to her appeal; but Barnum helped establish her appearance of divineness, for example by arranging for her to sing Handel oratorios. When Jenny Lind gave her concert proceeds to public charities, Barnum publicized her charitableness and so made her yet more commercially valuable; in other words, he arranged a commercial payoff by advertising her separation from commercial ends. Fanny Fern's *Ruth Hall* provides a much more overt instance of a popular entertainment that hides the commercial ground of its generation. *Ruth Hall* tells of a contentedly domestic woman left destitute by her husband's death and threatened with the loss of her child until, in her darkest hour, she finds her way to the work of writing. Against all odds, by dint of unforeseen talent and strength of maternal will, Ruth establishes herself as a best-selling author and literary celebrity (Fern prints sample fan mail), and is at last able to reconstitute her broken family with the proceeds of her literary success. This book tells one story of the relation of women to writing; but that story keeps us from suspecting another story quite different in character—the story of how Fern's own book came to be written. Susan Geary has recently established that the writing of *Ruth Hall* was first proposed not by Fern but a publisher—Mason Brothers— eager to add this profitable author to its fold; that so far from winning its way to popularity by its irresistible strengths, the book was made popular through a highly premeditated and unprecedentedly intricate advertising campaign; and that so far from merely earning, after publication, the reward her book deserved, Fern was moved to write the book by the terms Mason Brothers offered "up front," not least their pledging, in the language of their contract, "to use extraordinary exertions to promote the sale thereof, so as, if possible, to make it exceed the sale of any previous work" (Geary 383–89).

Performance with this backstage: a veiled zone of contrivance in which potential popular entertainments are dreamed up and contracted for with an eye to their commercial profit; a zone in which strategies are contrived to *make* the mass popularity no longer allowed to just happen; a zone that allows itself to be known to exist, indeed that shows its commercialism a little as part of the glamorization of its product; but a zone that shuts the public out from detailed knowledge of its motives or arts of contrivance: *this* is show business as show business begins to exist in America at *Blithedale*'s historical moment. This recognition would help us to the further perception that the entertainment industry that is one of the most decisive identifying marks of the modern cultural order has its inception in America not *in* modernity but in the age of the so-called cult of domesticity, taking the literature produced for domestic consumption as one of its first sites of industrial development. But if it helps bring this little-recognized fact into sharpened focus, *Blithedale's* most interesting historical suggestion is that the same restructuring of entertainment that produced these arrangements in the sphere of cultural production around 1850 produced corresponding novelties in the sphere of consumption: changes figured, I would suggest, in Miles Coverdale.

Coverdale and Priscilla are incongruous as lovers, but they constitute a couple in several related senses. Coverdale is, the book repeatedly suggests, the "man" who corresponds to Priscilla's version of the term "woman." Imaged as Theodore in Zenobia's tale "The Silvery Veil," his prurient interests in yet insurmountable terror of female sexuality are read as the masculine by-products of the cultural construction that disacknowledges or requires the veiling of woman's erotic embodiedness. But in no less important a sense Coverdale is also the spectator constituted by the Veiled Lady's version of spectacle. Passive in person, Priscilla only acts when she goes onstage, into a separate zone of spectacle marked off from its seated audience. Such a construction of *acting* finds its complement in someone else's passive, nonperforming *watching*, in short in the Coverdalean habit of mind. The language of *Blithedale* urges us to give the word "observer," as a term for Coverdale, the intensified sense of he who exists only in and as a watcher. "As if such were the proper barrier to be interposed between a character like hers, and a perceptive faculty like mine" (160), Coverdale huffs when Zenobia lowers the curtain on his peeping, his words baring his assumption that others are full persons and performers, but he a mental faculty only equipped to register their performances. "You are a poet—at least, as poets go, now-a-days—and must be allowed to make an opera-glass of your imagination, when you look at women" (170), Zenobia later mockingly retorts, correctly identifying Coverdale's relation as self or mind to the instrument used by spectators of nineteenth-century mass entertainments to enable them (just) to *see*.[6]

"Men of cold passions have quick eyes" Hawthorne writes in a remarkable notebook entry, by which I take him to mean: people who systematically deaden themselves at the level of primary drives arrange a surrogate life—contrive to be quick, not dead—in their sense of sight

6. On actor and spectator in nineteenth-century European culture see for instance Richard Sennett's discussion of Pagliaccian virtuosity and the new etiquette of audience silence (195–218).

(*American Notebooks* 169). What makes Coverdale powerful as a description of the spectator is not just his self-delimitation to a visual self but the book's sense that eye-life has become his way of *having* life. In a moving passage Coverdale speaks of "that quality of the intellect and heart, that impelled me (often against my will, and to the deteriment of my comfort) to live in other lives" (160), and these words well explain what makes watching a compulsive or compulsory activity for him. Life as Coverdale understands it is not what he has or does but something presumed to be lodged in someone else. Watching that someone, inhabiting that other through spectatorial self-projection and consuming it through visual appropriation, becomes accordingly a means to "live" *into his* life some part of that vitality that always first appears as "other life."

What the entertainments of the mid-nineteenth century *did* to the mass publics that consumed them, like all questions about the real history of literary reception, is something we cannot know without considerable aid from speculation. But there is good evidence to support *Blithedale*'s surmise that the formation of entertainment new in America at its time sponsored a Coverdalean mode of participation. All of the spectacles we have considered strongly reinforce the habit of motionlessly seeing. When Jenny Lind was touring America, Barnum had another crew scouring Ceylon for elephants and other natural wonders which, reimported and publicly displayed, became his other great enterprise of 1851, Barnum's Great Asiatic Caravan, Museum, and Menagerie—a show that opened a wonderworld to audiences willing to experience wonders in the passive or spectatorial mode (Barnum 213–14). (Barnum arranged for Jenny Lind to review the circus parade in New York City; in other words, to appear in public as an exemplary watcher.) The crowds that mobbed Stowe on her arrival in England were, in her words, "very much determined to look" at her: on this tour Stowe became at once a figure of fame and an object of visual consumption (qtd. in Wilson 345). And what could the proliferation of novel reading at this time reflect if not a mass extension of habits of bodily deactivation and of the reconcentration of self into sight? The reader of every nineteenth-century novel made him- or, more likely, herself a Coverdale to the extent that she conferred the status of "characters" on performatively generated others (Little Eva, Zenobia, Ruth Hall), while consigning herself to the category of perceptual faculty or *reader*, enterer into others through an action of the eye. Ellen Montgomery, the heroine of Susan Warner's *The Wide, Wide World* (1851), begins the novel Coverdale-fashion, looking out the window: shut into a world of enclosed domestic idleness, she scans the space across its boundary for something for her eye to inhabit. When she enters the ideally constructed domesticity of the

Humphreys household she finds an object for this visual appetite in reading: in Warner's account, novels offer the residents of immobilized private space adventure through the eye.

Quite as interestingly, there is abundant evidence that the form of mass entertainment new in America around 1850 held its audience in the position *of* audience by seeming to embody consumable "life." N. P. Willis's further-information-for-the-curious *Memoranda of the Life of Jenny Lind* (1851)—a book built on press releases supplied by Barnum, and so aimed to create the interest it pretended only to address—treats Lind as a public figure whose celebrity invites inescapable curiosity about her personal life. "The private life of Jenny Lind is a matter of universal inquisitiveness" (163), Willis informs the reader in a chapter on her "Private Habits and Manners" (166); then, instructing us in how such inquisitiveness might be mounted and targeted, he himself muses on the love life of this great singer: "One wonders, as one looks upon her soft eyes, and her affectionate profusion of sunny hair, what Jenny's heart can be doing all this time. Is fame a substitute for the tender passion? She must have been desperately loved in her varied and bright path" (159).[7] (The relation to Coverdale's speculations on Zenobia's sexual history or his urge to peep behind the petals of Priscilla's erotic bud will be clear at once.) Through such promotion Lind is made into a public embodiment of a fascinating private life, and her audience is invited to try to get some fascination into its own life by consuming the public spectacle of hers: no wonder interested spectators actually invade this female performer's private dressing room in a Willis incident uncannily like *Blithedale*'s tale of Theodore (Willis 163–65).[8] *Ruth Hall* is as personal a work as the 1850s produced. It tells Fern/Parton's personal history of struggles and triumphs with hot display of her personal loves and resentments (resentments above all against her brother N. P. Willis, the villain of the piece.) But this book's intimacy of record was inseparable from its public or market life. What *Ruth Hall* offered its readers was the chance to "live" a public figure's "hidden" private life by buying and reading a book—and lest the public not be in on the opportunity for vicariousness the book embodied, Mason Brothers publicized its "obscure" personalness, running ads that tantalizingly asked: "IS RUTH HALL

7. Willis's reverie continues, in a locution truly astonishing: "To see such a heaven as her heart untenanted, one longs to write its advertisement of 'To Let'" (160). Readers of the Willis *Memoranda* will be struck by the close analogies to Priscilla in Lind's "white garb of purity" (132), her pallid and "insensuous" appearance (140–41), her upbringing as a "poor and plain little girl" locked "in a little room" (5), and so on.
8. "Your uninvited presence here is an intrusion," Lind tells the invaders of what *Blithedale* would call her "private withdrawing room" (110–11); but the celebrity privacy that brands public entrance intrusion in fact invites just such intrusion, as Willis virtually says.

AUTOBIOGRAPHICAL?"[9] So it is that a buried, commercial publicity operation, by producing the sense that a rare "life" lies veiled
inside the most public of performances, could further its audience's
disposition to seek "life" through the consumption of such performances, and so convert private men and women into a huge paying
public: in other parlance, a Westervelt creates a Veiled Lady and
thereby produces a Coverdale, and by extension a literary mass market as well.

The strategies by which "life" is made to seem available in consumable objects and experiences and the appetite *for* "life" used to draw
publics into stabilized bodies of consumer demand are as familiar as
daily life itself in modern consumer culture. The products or produc-
tions that draw Coverdale by their apparent "surplus of vitality" (96)
have their successors (to name no more) in the mass-circulation
magazine that sold itself not as pictures to look at but as *Life*; or the
soft drink that has offered not to quench our thirst but to help us
"Come Alive"; or the car that, at this writing, is inviting us to buy it as
a way to discharge our obligation (the ads quote James) to "Live all
you can; it's a mistake not to."[1] One historical use of *The Blithedale
Romance* is to take us back, if not to the origins, then at least to the
early history of a social system held together by the public simulation
of "life" as a marketing art and a private imperative to remedy defi-
ciencies of "life" in one's life—a system, *Blithedale* tells us, that has
its first large-scale social manifestation in the 1840s and 1850s, and
that begins its operations in the entertainment sphere. But if the
hunger for a "life" felt as alienated into other lives drives the man or
woman of this time into spectatorial dependence on commercial
entertainment, we might ask at this point, what gives rise to this
driving sense of lack? *Blithedale*'s answer, I take it, is privacy: that this
need is a product *in* the self of a social-historical construction of privacy as the self's living "world."

Quite as much as he is an observer, Coverdale is a figure of private
life. The spaces he seeks out are always strongly bound off from the
public or collective realm: an apartment (the name itself equates
dwelling space with separation); a hermitage; the single-family
dwelling "just a little withdrawn" (80) that is this communitarian's
dream of a utopian social space. At home in the private, Coverdale
also carries the private within him as a structure of habitual understanding. The self, this character assumes, is "inviolate" only in the
world of its "exclusive possession" (99): to live in the communal, by

9. See Geary, 388–89. As Geary notes, the really fascinating question this publicity raises—
   whether Fern wrote up her life in the knowledge that it would be marketed in this way—is
   impossible now to answer.
1. Rolls Royce ran this advertisement in the April 1988 issue of *Gourmet*.

parallel assumption, is to have one's "individuality" (99) in continual danger of violation. Other characters claim the public—or the public *too*—as their proper theater of action; but when they do so Coverdale's privatizing mind instinctively reads back from their public assertion to the state of private or "individual affections" alleged to "cause" such assertion: "I could measure Zenobia's inward trouble, by the animosity with which she now took up the general quarrel of woman against man" (121), is Coverdale's understanding of Zenobia's feminism. A privatized and privatizing mind, the privacy Coverdale embodies is defined not just through its cult of confinement within the "safe" private sphere but also through its attenuation of the erotic in private life—Coverdale's "apartment" is a "bachelor apartment"—and its exclusion of active, productive labor from the private world: Coverdale is the "idle" or "half-occupied" man (247, 133), his apartment the scene of "bewitching, enervating indolence" (19). This is to say that Coverdale represents a human self constructed upon the same social plan that we have seen imaged in the Veiled Lady: the nineteenth-century middle-class construction that locates the self's home or fulfilled state in the enclosed, physically attenuated, leisured, *private* world of domestic life.

But as the veil imprisons the lady condemned to wear it, so the social construction of the private that Coverdale embodies has the peculiarity of being at once desperately clung to and deeply self-impoverishing. Safe at home, his adventures in communitarianism now long behind him, Coverdale finds the private home a sheer emptiness: "Nothing, nothing, nothing" (245) is the weary tale his private life has been able to generate. And it would be easy to guess that what has established this home as a space of deficiency are the very acts of exclusion that established it in the first place. Having shut out the collective world, Coverdalean privacy has *made* itself the place of "loneliness" (70); having sealed itself in from the public, the overtly erotic, the productive, and the active, it has made those modes of life into an "other life" apart from itself and has replaced them, within itself, with a positive sense of their lack. Life in certain of its primary and potent forms, *Blithedale* says, is what the nineteenth-century cult of domesticity insists on not having *in* its life *and what it therefore also* hungers to repossess. At least as *Blithedale* figures it, this is why the contemporary structure of privacy imaged in Coverdale at once closes in on itself and builds, at the heart of private space, means for a surrogate, spectatorial relation to the life it has put outside. Coverdale's hermitage functions at once to protect a self that feels inviolate only in private and to make that self a watcher, a spectatorial participant in Zenobia and Westervelt's richer intimacies. The private bedroom that shields Coverdale at Blithedale becomes, in its enclosure, an auditorium, a place to listen in on the "awful privacy" (39) of Hollingsworth's adjacent intimacy. The city apartment that guards Coverdale's privacy also drives him to seek entertainment by converting the world of others into a domestically viewable visual field—and so leads him to become, at the moment when he is most fully *at home* in the book, first a reader of novels, then a viewer of the Veiled Lady being readied for the stage.[2]

The Veiled Lady, I began by saying, images the constructions of a certain version of private life and a certain version of public spectacle as two sides of a single process. We are now in a position to say what the logic is that holds these two historical developments together. We could now speculate that a more publicized and spectatorial entertainment order and a more leisured, privatized domestic model arose at the same time in America because it was the nature of that domestic model to create a *need for* such entertainment: a need for a now foregone life to be made repossessible in a form compatible with the deactivations this new order prescribed. By learning how to aim its products toward this life-hunger a new entertainment industry was able to mobilize domestic privacy as a mass entertainment market. But that industry could insert itself in the domestic realm because it met needs produced by that realm: chief among them the need to acquire extradomestic life in the spectatorially consumable form of *other* or *represented* life.[3]

What I have been speculatively reconstructing here—with *Blithedale*'s aid because this history has not proved fully knowable *without* its aid—is the situation of literature in antebellum America: a matter that includes the histories of literary production and consumption but that is not wholly external to literature itself. Literary works, it might be worth insisting, do not produce their own occasions. They are always produced within some cultural situation of the literary, within the particular set of relations in which literature's place is at any moment socially determined. Literature's situation in America in the late 1840s and early 1850s was that it was being resituated: placed into the entangled new relations to publicity, to domestic privacy, to the commercial and the promotional, and to vicarious consumption that I have described here. When this change took place, writers could exploit its new structure of literary

2. Does my phrasing sufficiently suggest that I see *Blithedale* as prophetically describing the "living room" of the modern private home, focused on the sound system, television, and VCR? That the average American watches television seven or more hours a day *in* such enclosures is the social fact *Blithedale* helps foresee. On the American tradition of opposition to privacy as a spatial and social construct see Hayden.

3. My understanding that mass-cultural instruments can build social groups into markets because they also meet those groups' socially created needs has been influenced by Ohmann. Like Fisher, Ohmann focuses these developments in the 1890s.

opportunity in various ways. What they could not do was to ignore the cultural conjunction it produced: could not ignore it because it set the terms for their work's public life.

If we ask the long-postponed question why this set of relations should be so much on Hawthorne's mind in *Blithedale*, then, the most forcible answer would be that they preoccupy him at this time because they define his own new literary situation. Hawthorne himself, after all, found a newly enlarged public for his work around 1850, after more than twenty years of writing in obscurity. Hawthorne too acquired augmented public life at this time at least in part by being taken in charge by his own producer-promoter, the publisher James T. Fields. Hawthorne too began to have his "private life" advertised at this time as part of the creation of his allure: literary mythologizings of Hawthorne's "reclusive" personality and tours-in-print past Hawthorne's private home began in the early 1850s, with full cooperation from Hawthorne's promoters. And Hawthorne too entered into the predicaments of high visibility at this moment: how, in coming before a large, impersonal audience, still to keep "the inmost Me behind its veil" (*SL* 4) becomes this privacy-loving public figure's problem in 1850 just as much as it is Catharine Sedgwick's or The Veiled Lady's.[4]

The Blithedale Romance, accordingly, needs to be understood not just as a depiction of self-evident cultural realities but more specifically as an act of reconnaissance into an emerging cultural form. In writing this book Hawthorne uses his work to *work out* the shape of the field writing has now been placed in, and to measure the meaning of his work's new situation. But the novelists of this time all face the same situation, which they explore in works of their own. *The Wide, Wide World* is in one aspect a fictional history of this same entertainment revolution. In a central scene Warner memorably contrasts the bee characteristic of an older social order—an entertainment in which the private is not split from the communal, pleasure not split from productive labor, and the performers not other people than the enjoyers—with the passive, leisured, privatized entertainment form (reading) characteristic of modern domesticity, the scene of its own consumption. Melville, who repositioned himself as an antipopular author in face of the same emerging situation that Hawthorne and Warner embraced on other terms, wrote his history of this development in *Pierre* (also 1852), a book that finds its threefold adversary in

---

4. Further evidence that the issue of Hawthorne's writing around 1850 is the issue of enlarged publicity would be found in the 1851 preface to *Twice-Told Tales* and in his other novels of 1850–52, which both open with a crisis of public exposure: Hester's exposure on the Puritan scaffold in *The Scarlet Letter* and the "going visible" that accompanies Hepzibah's opening of her shop in *The House of the Seven Gables*. On the promotion or public creation of Hawthorne in the 1850s and after, see my *School of Hawthorne*, 48–66.

the cultural organization that encloses sympathy within domestic confinements; a literary market that hypes talent into literary celebrity; and a cultural ordering that sets the literary in opposition to unrepressed bodily life.[5] Fanny Fern, unlike Melville a courter of popularity and unlike Warner an enjoyer of fame, made a different accommodation to the literary situation she too found around her. She takes her more sanguine measure of the same ground in *Ruth Hall*, a book that plots the birth of the popular writer at the junction of a business of literary production and a domesticity in need of its wares. Ruth's fan mail—the proof of her celebrity status—makes clear that a home audience consumes her work to help satisfy cravings domestic life has not allayed.

Not long after this moment, American literature had other situations socially created for it. The Beadle's Dime Novels already in full commercial flower by 1860 embody a quite different world of popular writing, organizing a mass audience on other terms than a domestic one. By that year a nonpopular "serious" literary zone was successfully institutionalized as part of the establishment of a self-consciously high culture in America, a development that laid the ground for a quite different figure of the author to emerge later on. But those structures were not yet in place a decade before. The dominant world of writing in mid-nineteenth-century America was the highly vicarious, highly managed, privacy-addressing, mass-public one that came together around 1850; and the central fact of literary life then was that a writer who hoped to reach a significant public would have to engage a communication system structured on those terms. Small wonder that the author's *work* at this time is to figure out what this situation means: a work performed, among other ways, through the writing of the story of The Veiled Lady.

---

5. For Melville's struggle to describe "life" and its alienation in contemporary writing see for instance this remarkable passage:

> Pierre is young; heaven gave him the divinest, freshest form of a man; put light into his eye, and fire into his blood, and brawn into his arm, and a joyous, jubilant, overflowing, upbubbling, universal life in him everywhere. Now look around in that most miserable room, and at that most miserable pursuit of man, and say if here be the place, and this be the trade, that God intended for him. A rickety chair, two hollow barrels, a plank, paper, pens, and infernally black ink, four leprously dingy white walls, no carpet, a cup of water, and a dry biscuit or two. Oh, I hear the leap of the Texan Camanche, as at this moment he goes crashing like a wild deer through the green underbrush; I hear his glorious whoop of savage and untamable health; and then I look in at Pierre. If physical, practical unreason make the savage, which is he? (*Pierre* 302)

Works Cited

Banner, Lois W. *American Beauty*. New York: Knopf, 1982.

Barnum, P. T. *Struggles and Triumphs*. New York: Penguin American Library, 1981.

Brodhead, Richard H. *School of Hawthorne*. New York: Oxford UP, 1986.

———. "Sparing the Rod: Discipline and Fiction in Antebellum America." *Representations* 21 (1988): 67–96.

Brown, Gillian. "The Empire of Agoraphobia." *Representations* 20 (1987): 134–57.

Cott, Nancy. *The Bonds of Womanhood: "Woman's Sphere" in New England, 1780–1835*. New Haven: Yale UP, 1977.

Douglas, Ann. *The Feminization of American Culture*. New York: Knopf, 1977.

Fern, Fanny. *Ruth Hall and Other Writings by Fanny Fern*. Ed. Joyce W. Warren. New Brunswick: Rutgers UP, 1986.

Fisher, Philip. "Appearing and Disappearing in Public: Social Space in Late-Nineteenth-Century Literature and Culture." *Reconstructing American Literary History*. Ed. Sacvan Bercovitch. Cambridge: Harvard UP, 1986.

Fuller, Robert C. *Mesmerism and the American Cure of Souls*. Philadelphia: U of Pennsylvania P, 1982.

Geary, Susan. "The Domestic Novel as a Commercial Commodity: Making a Best Seller in the 1850s." *Papers of the Bibliographical Society of America* 70 (1976): 365–93.

Haltunnen, Karen. *Confidence Men and Painted Women: A Study of Middle-Class Culture in America, 1830–1870*. New Haven: Yale UP, 1982.

Harris, Neil. *Humbug: The Art of P. T. Barnum*. Chicago: U of Chicago P, 1973.

Hawthorne, Nathaniel. *The American Notebooks*. Vol. 8 of *Centenary Edition of the Works of Nathaniel Hawthorne*. Columbus: Ohio State UP, 1962–.

———. *The Blithedale Romance*. Vol. 3 of *Centenary Edition of the Works of Nathaniel Hawthorne*.

———. *The Letters, 1843–1853*. Vol. 14 of *Centenary Edition of the Works of Nathaniel Hawthorne*.

———. *The Scarlet Letter*. Vol. 1 of *Centenary Edition of the Works of Nathaniel Hawthorne*.

Hayden, Dolores. *The Grand Domestic Revolution: A History of Feminist Designs of American Homes, Neighborhoods, and Cities*. Cambridge: MIT P, 1981.

Kelley, Mary. *Private Woman, Public Stage: Literary Domesticity in Nineteenth-Century America*. New York: Oxford UP, 1984.

Melville, Herman. *Pierre; or, the Ambiguities*. Evanston: Northwestern UP and the Newberry Library, 1971.

O'Connor, Lillian. *Pioneer Women Orators*. New York: Columbia UP, 1954.

Ohmann, Richard. "Where Did Mass Culture Come From? The Case of Magazines." *Politics of Letters*. Middletown: Wesleyan UP, 1987. 135–51.

Ryan, Mary. *Cradle of the Middle Class: The Family in Oneida County, New York 1790–1865*. Cambridge, Eng.: Cambridge UP, 1981.

Sennett, Richard. *The Fall of Public Man*. New York: Knopf, 1977.

Stowe, Harriet Beecher. *Uncle Tom's Cabin*. New York: New American Library, 1981.

Watt, Ian. *The Rise of the Novel*. London: Chatto and Windus, 1957.

Willis, N[athaniel] Parker. *Memoranda of the Life of Jenny Lind*. Philadelphia: Robert E. Peterson, 1851.

Wilson, Forest. *Crusader in Crinoline: The Life of Harriet Beecher Stowe*. Philadelphia: Lippincott, 1941.

LAUREN BERLANT

[History's Burial in *The Blithedale Romance*: Rethinking Hollingsworth]†

* * *

More than a satire and repudiation of contemporary social reform is struck out in the blacksmith's characterization. Hollingsworth is also the reformer in history, an embodiment not only of the contemporaneous project of American utopianism, but also of the utopianism that since the Puritans has constituted the mythos and the politics of American national identity. Hollingsworth's characterization by Coverdale hinges on his inheritance of the voice of the utopian past. Eliot's Pulpit, where Hollingsworth "preaches" to his own brethren two centuries after John Eliot preached to some Native Americans, is thus simultaneously a gloss on the history and politics of missionary/philanthropic activity in America and an evaluation of the crisis of national-utopian politics contemporary to the Blithedale experiment. At no time is Eliot's Pulpit characterized by the kind of democratic love ethos characteristic of radical nineteenth-century social theories—although, as I will suggest, nineteenth-century interpretations of Eliot insist on his exemplary treatment of the Indians. Instead, this utopian heritage is distinguished by the enlightened man's covenantal duty to educate and convert the "proselytes," or natives.

* * *

However much legitimacy one gives to Zenobia and Coverdale's claim that Hollingsworth is a moral monster, it must also be said that Coverdale recognizes a greatness of spirit in Hollingsworth as well. Through the thin walls of the common house, Coverdale hears Hollingsworth fervently pouring out his soul to God: a man this pious, in Coverdale's eyes, is "marked out by a light of transfiguration, shed upon him in the divine interview from which he passes into his daily life" (III: 40). Hollingsworth's transfiguration is clearly not physical—as Coverdale's has been, through his illness and subsequent muscular development—it is spiritual, otherworldly, the biblical veil that hides nothing but signifies the man's relation to

† From "Fantasies of Utopia in *The Blithedale Romance*," *American Literary History* 1.1 (1989): 30–62. Copyright Oxford University Press. Reprinted by permission of Oxford University Press. All parenthetical volume or page references are to the *Centenary Edition of the Works of Nathaniel Hawthorne*; all notes are Berlant's and are renumbered.

heavenly spirit. It is in this holy light that Hollingsworth first assumes the form of Apostle Eliot.[1]

John Eliot does not figure actively in this narrative—not in the way, for example, Reverend Wilson does in *The Scarlet Letter*—and the characters' collective consciousness of him seems limited to "a tradition that the venerable Apostle Eliot had preached" at "a certain rock," "two centuries gone by, to an Indian auditory" (III: 118). But the Apostle is active in Coverdale's fantasy life. Seated at Eliot's Pulpit, Coverdale "sees" the Apostle: "I used to see the holy Apostle of the Indians, with the sunlight flickering down upon him through the leaves, and glorifying his figure as with the half-perceptible glow of a transfiguration" (III: 119). Eliot's Pulpit is to *Blithedale* what the scaffold is to *The Scarlet Letter*: the place of sexual, juridical, and theological confrontation.[2] It is also Coverdale's personal touchstone. Both during his tenure at Blithedale and after he leaves, he returns in memory and refers to this rock, anointing it the omphalos of his experience, the place that contains the tangle of memory and desire his narration attempts to unravel (or reconstruct).

Hollingsworth becomes Eliot there, and Priscilla, Zenobia, and Coverdale by analogy become Eliot's Indians, neophytes who try to learn the language of the spirit and the necessity of commitment. But Hollingsworth's exhortations are valuable less for what they contain—Coverdale never reports their content to us—than for what they sound like. As with Dimmesdale, Hollingsworth's seductive pulpit moves listeners not by the light of reason but by the attraction of emotions transmitted by rhetoric—even while Hollingsworth is emphatically against theories of the passional basis of social reform.

> . . . Hollingsworth, at our solicitation, often ascended Eliot's pulpit, and—not exactly preached—but talked to us, his few disciples, in a strain that rose and fell as naturally as the wind's breath among the leaves of the birch-tree. No other speech of man has ever moved me like some of these discourses. It seemed most pitiful—a positive calamity to the world—that a treasury of golden thoughts should thus be scattered, by the liberal handful, down among us three, when a thousand hearers

---

1. Mather writes of Eliot that he (like Hollingsworth) "made it his daily practice 'to enter into that Closet, and shut his Door, and pray to his Father in secret'" (I: 531).
2. This particular rock or "Pulpit" does not figure centrally in histories of Eliot and his work with the Indians. In addition, Eliot did not usually preach to the Indians at Roxbury (his first church assignment in New England was at Roxbury, but his missionary work was initiated at Concord, and then on his lands at Natick). Only on one occasion did the Indians gather for purposes of worship there (see Eliot 1834). For a more limited, "symbolic" reading of Eliot's Pulpit in *Blithedale*, see Stay.

might have been the richer for them; and Hollingsworth the richer, likewise, by the sympathy of multitudes. (III: 119)

Coverdale here expresses the values of sentimental religion. Hollingsworth ought to become "rich" by "enriching" the masses with his "golden thoughts": rather than take to heart what Hollingsworth says (it is the following chapter, "The Crisis," where Hollingsworth proposes to and is rejected by Coverdale), Coverdale covets his *discourse*, his style, his golden "language." In this respect Coverdale is very much like an Indian listening to John Eliot: he may or may not actually comprehend the content of what he hears, but he thinks he knows the *sense* of the language itself, and thinks he knows that the act of translation from one system (English; Hollingsworth's philosophy) to another (Indian; the proselytes' combined ignorance and resistance) is an act of love. But aside from structural analogies perfectly clear to Coverdale, what does it mean—to *The Blithedale Romance*—that Hollingsworth repeats Eliot?

Coverdale brings the collective and the individual together by giving priority to individual history: he cannot see Blithedale as a significant mass of people, but can only see the psychodrama of a limited few on the dramatic stage of his own consciousness. Elevating the fulfillment of the individual's passions to the place of the utopian principle, he sees Hollingsworth as a monster because he acknowledges no body, and sees his philanthropy as a deformed and distorted approach to the human subject, because Hollingsworth is committed to reclaiming a group of nameless and placeless people, people so marginalized that they are unimaginable within the complacent and class-divided system of Blithedale.

The ideational split between these two men suggests that, in *The Blithedale Romance*, a philosopher's relation to his libidinal desire can be predicted by the centrality to his social theory of the individual subject. Coverdale's Blithedale works on the star system; Hollingsworth's vision, influenced largely by his own working-class background, assumes a postlapsarian inevitability to the criminality he wants to reform in others. Coverdale valorizes his own passions, and so his social theory relies on a collective egotism, a mass commitment to subjectivity. Hollingsworth is a more complex case. For him, the libidinal impulses of the self must be subordinated to the regulation of social behavior, and so he attempts to reformulate the criminal subject by transforming the sphere of the social.

Yet Hollingsworth, according to Coverdale, also wants to use the force of his individual will to redeem the collectivity. Hollingsworth's system is insidious because the anonymity of his potential subjects contrasts with his personal power so much that his personality (the key to the project) looks like the monstrous egotism of which he has been justly accused by characters and critics alike. This distortion of personality may be a failure on Hollingsworth's part. But it may also signify a symptomatic contradiction for a certain kind of utopian thinker; it is this contradiction that informs Apostle John Eliot's place in the text.

The project of historical archaeology that takes us from Blithedale to Natick, Eliot's first missionary settlement, suggests that Eliot's function as a pre-text for Hollingsworth extends to the way his missionary work precedes Blithedale. Eliot is the originary American reformer, and his "praying towns" are among the originary American utopian experiments. One can see in the fate of that movement some kind of analogy to the present case. The Apostle "transfigures" Hollingsworth in two ways. First, Eliot's approach to social reform anticipates Hollingsworth's own theories about how to reform a particular marginal group (Indians, criminals) by seeing them as individuals to be reformed but also as functions in an ongoing social economy. They do not want to transform the world—both are conservatives, in that sense—but to transform problematic individuals in it. Second, both Eliot and Hollingsworth are said to project powerful personalities that rouse suspicions about the motives behind their visionary social schemes. The cultural reception of this kind of utopian thinker turns out often to substitute for a rigorous analysis of his project; that this is so, and why this is so, not only figures heavily in the historical status of Eliot, but also translates into Coverdale's representation of Hollingsworth as well.

"We had a tradition among us, 'That the country could never perish so long as Eliot was alive'," writes Cotton Mather (I: 578). Writing a biography of Eliot, then, would be coterminous with writing the life of America, and so too the "meaning" of John Eliot would also, somehow, provide a meaning for his country. Mather's *Life of Eliot* is, like many of Mather's major biographies, careful to establish a particular paradigm for his subject that would contain at once the history of the man, its effect on the formation of America, and its place in Puritan eschatology: "The world would now count me very absurd, if, after this, I should say that I had found the SEPULCHRE of MOSES in America: but I have certainly here found Moses himself; we have had among us one appearing in the Spirit of a Moses; and it is not the *grave*, but the *life* of such a Moses, that we value ourselves upon being the owners of" (I: 528).

Mather identifies John Eliot as Moses not because he led his people on an exodus into exile, but because through his missionary work he brought the Algonquin Indians of New England from their spiritual exile into a new regenerate community. This interpretation of Eliot's work is complicated by the fact that the English immigrants to New England were simultaneously pushing the Indians off of their tribal property. But for those who, sympathetic to the Puritan cause, believed in the missionary project that was an original motivation for the Massachusetts Bay Colony—the seal of the colony contains in its center a picture of an Indian saying "Come over and help us" (Jennings 229)—the displacement of the Indians reveals "a law of human progress, that civilization must overtop and displace uncivilized man."[3]

Eliot is typologically Moses because he institutes a civil and ecclesiastical government for the Indians according to the rules laid out in Exodus 18; he does this by envisioning and then actually instituting "praying towns" for willing tribes of Indians.[4] These towns, instituted in 1650 and growing to twelve in number, sprung from Eliot's assumption that a change in the spirit of an Indian would be insufficient conversion; rather, a full conversion to the ways of civility was needed in order to assure that the Indians' feelings of regeneration would be accompanied by appropriate practice (Francis 161). Eliot himself purchased the land at Natick; he also purchased the materials the Indians would need to become self-governing and self-sufficient in these regenerate towns.

The parallels between Eliot's and Hollingsworth's utopian plans are clear: Hollingsworth's criminal, the nineteenth-century version of Eliot's Indian—whose practice of Indian religious ritual was actually outlawed on pain of death in 1646—would be set up in a community with other criminals, and only a few outsiders would participate in the material and spiritual self-improvement of the participants (Jennings 241). Each enterprise has as its goal the eventual assimilation of its members into mainstream society. In this sense utopian thought is being employed for local, not millennial ends— although, as James Holstun points out, Puritan consciousness demonstrated a strong tendency to confuse or to obliterate the distinction between the two. Moreover, each enterprise claims pure motives for its philanthropy, because the missionary apparently gets nothing but good feeling from his efforts: repeatedly in Eliot's own representations of his project as well as others' redactions of it, Eliot's labor of "love" manifests itself not in wages he earns, but in his "love" for the Indians as brethren under the skin, so that "love"

3. Francis 298–305. Francis's *John Eliot* provided Hawthorne with much of the source material as well as the tone of the *Grandfather's Chair* section on Eliot.
4. James Holstun suggests that Exodus 18—where Moses learns to govern by delegating power within the community, creating variously "rulers of thousands, and rulers of hundreds, rulers of fifties, and rulers of tens" (Exodus 18:21)—is a strange text for an enterprise such as Eliot's, since it aims at instituting utopian "procedures which will make [Eliot's] own authority unnecessary." Holstun suggestively situates Eliot's utopianism in the context of other textual utopias, such as More's *Utopia*, in order to describe the way his praying towns raised "the possibility of an unprecedented integration of religious and political life" (122).

becomes both the motivating factor of the difficult labor and the payment-in-kind the labor generates.[5]

This unambivalent interpretation of Eliot's mode of utopian thought and practice is evident in many histories of Hawthorne's day, especially that of Convers Francis.[6] In the tradition of many of Eliot's contemporaries, and reinforced by Cotton Mather's hagiographic biography of Eliot, Hawthorne himself, in *Grandfather's Chair*, a history book for children, fashions Eliot's humanitarian and visionary benevolence as an ideal type of American social consciousness and practice.[7] "Grandfather," who "was a great admirer of the Apostle Eliot" (VI: 45), distinguishes Eliot from the mass of Puritan magistrates and ministers because he had faith in the reformability of the Indians: "[The Puritan rulers] felt no faith in the success of any such attempts, because they had no love for the poor Indians. Now Eliot was full of love for them, and therefore so full of faith and hope, that he spent the labor of a lifetime in their behalf" (VI: 43). Eliot, Grandfather says, viewed the Indians as "his brethren"; he "persuaded" them "to leave off their idle and wandering habits," and to live like the English: building houses, farming, going to school, praying (VI: 44). The Indian Bible was perhaps Eliot's greatest achievement, says Grandfather, because Eliot, like Grandfather himself, gave the Indians (who were the "long lost descendants of the ten tribes of Israel," according to some theories) access to "the history of their forefathers" (VI: 48).

But young Laurence, who identifies mightily with the spirit of the Apostle, brings a dark cloud to Grandfather's proceedings: he wonders whether Eliot's labors were for naught, since there are no Indians left to read the language of which Eliot's work is now a "relic." The moral of the story, says Grandfather, is not that utopian gestures such as Eliot's fail, but that "man is capable of disinterested zeal for his brother's good" so that "if you should ever feel

---

5. Bancroft's reading of Eliot's project is typical: "Foremost among these early missionaries— the morning star of missionary enterprise—was John Eliot. . . . His actions, his thoughts, his desires, all wore the hues of disinterested love. His uncontrollable charity welled out in a perpetual fountain" (Bancroft 94–95).

6. The first half of the nineteenth century witnessed a strong interest in Eliot. For example, not too long before the writing of *Blithedale*, a monument to Eliot was erected. Hawthorne might have seen Henry Dearborn's widely distributed "A Sketch of the Life of the Apostle Eliot Prefatory to a Subscription for Erecting a Monument to his Memory." Dearborn specifically includes Eliot in a history of important translators of the Bible that includes Miles Coverdale (19). See also Jacobs and Winslow for other typical contemporary enshrinements of Eliot. I isolate Francis's influence on Hawthorne's reading of Eliot because in *Grandfather's Chair*, "Grandfather now observed, that Dr. Francis had written a very beautiful Life of Eliot, which he advised Laurence to peruse" (VI: 49–50).

7. The Massachusetts Historical Society publication of "Tracts Relating to the Attempts to Convert to Christianity the Indians of New England" contains glowing self-interpretation from Eliot himself, along with supporting letters by the Reverends Shepard, Whitfield, Mayhew, and Winslow. It is important to note that these letters were public documents used mainly to raise funds for the Colony's, and especially Eliot's, missionary work.

your own self-interest pressing upon your heart too closely, then think of Eliot's Indian Bible. It is good for the world that such a man has lived, and left this emblem of his life" (VI: 49).

Grandfather, in contrast to Hawthorne, identifies himself as a Harvard man (VI: 32), and this locates him squarely within liberal, Unitarian ideology and tells us something about the purpose of Grandfather's storytelling: to reproduce American history in its full and inevitable providential glory, and to reveal along the way the "capability" of (especially American) man to perform truly and purely good acts. We must read this strain of thought into Hawthorne's reading of Eliot, and into Coverdale's idolization of the Apostle in *Blithedale*. Hollingsworth and Eliot are both characterized as central to the reproduction of the American utopian project: each embodies the national commitment to reading human nature as capable of thinking utopian thoughts and of trying to enact them in good faith.

But Eliot, like Hollingsworth, was also subject to much criticism for these same acts.[8] The missionary was criticized for being both hypocritical and obstinate in his opinions; at once ascetic and yet luxuriantly egocentric in his practice (Francis; Bancroft; Mather). In addition, "Great opposition was made to the collection [of funds for missionary work with the Indians] in England; and the conversion of the Indians was represented as a mere pretence to draw money from men of pious minds" (Hutchinson I: 141). Francis Jennings writes that some of the money Eliot received disappeared; moreover, he documents that Eliot took credit for missionary work done by others, especially Thomas Mayhew, Jr., "the man who had worked in lonely isolation with never a penny of encouragement from Massachusetts" (245). Like Hollingsworth, Eliot was accused of accumulating capital (and sacrificing people) for the advancement of his own cause—some people thought that his cause was himself.

What do these various charges of corruption say about the mutual glossing of Eliot and Hollingsworth? That visionary thinkers are, as Hollingsworth says, "by necessity" obstinate and egocentric. But this is not because every act hides a secret will to power (although this might always be the case) but because it takes power to articulate and hold a theoretical position, and even more (in the logic of this novel) to resist the encroachments of the "world," the "hitherto unwedded bride," who would distract you from or annihilate your theory and your practice in the name of the claim of that which already is. Both of these thinkers operated on a principle of "love" with respect to the objects of their philanthropy, but their love fuels

---

8. Hawthorne would have read of the resistance to Eliot in Mather and Francis (both of whom are unsympathetic to Eliot's critics) and in Hutchinson's *Massachusetts-Bay* (which reports the criticism of Eliot without comment).

a private, personal commitment that preexists the implementation of their project as well as its public expression.

Thus both men are "transfigured" by their theoretical and practical zeal, because they do not need to think personal and collective history "alternately," but instead try to think them together, as one. This very act of will (the force that most frightens Coverdale and attracts the women) makes the utopian theorist look like a monster of self, a master totalizer who refuses to honor the differences between the individual and the collective, public and private, spirit and politics. The "world's" fundamental lack of sympathy with the utopian thinker is masked by a cult of personality that forms in homage to the thinker's personal power; along with it grows the "tragic" trajectory of history that relies fully on the personal story; the utopian as a category of possible political and philosophical thought is then entirely repudiated as too frightening and *self*-consuming a project.

The "deluded generations," whose histories would be otherwise articulated by the utopian course of history, are buried under the "dust" of nationalist-romantic historiography. If Coverdale is any example, the clichés of Puritan history are a part of our national consciousness and our individual personalities—we all can *identify with* the Pilgrims, as the Blithedalers do, but we cannot *identify* John Winthrop's "city on a hill" speech when Hollingsworth gives his version of it—but much about the Puritan settlers (both events and ideology) is buried under this dust; and along with those are buried generations of Indians whose histories are entirely unknown to us.[9] In Hawthorne's romances too, Native Americans are always at the farthest margins of representation—of the crowd (in *The Scarlet Letter*), of property (land and the map in *Seven Gables*), and in parentheses, in *Blithedale*: " . . . it was still as wild a tract of woodland as the great-great-great-great grandson of one of Eliot's Indians (had any such posterity been in existence) could have desired, for the site and shelter of his wigwam" (III: 118).

Eliot's project of constructing villages in which the Indians would learn to live exemplary lives was crushed by King Philip's War (1673–75). The "praying Indians" were annihilated, because they were caught between the interests of the white population (who did not entirely trust them) and the hostile Indian population (who felt that their conversion to Christianity signified their allegiance to the Englishmen). The history of these utopian experiments therefore cannot be usefully integrated into American self-mythologizing; instead, the one figure whose life might in

9. Hollingsworth says, "But I offer my edifice as a spectacle to the world that it may take example and build many another like it. Therefore I . . . mean to set it on the open hillside"; Coverdale's response is to wonder why "Hollingsworth should care about educating the public taste in the department of cottage-architecture, desirable as such improvement certainly was" (III: 80).

part redeem our national treatment of the Indians, John Eliot, is valorized and apotheosized.

Thus the burial of Indian history beneath the dust of other American delusions is both enacted and alluded to in this novel by an allusion to one man, Apostle Eliot. Instead of a truly collective history, one that would take into account the complete story of American culture, Coverdale symptomatically provides for us a romance of history marked by great figures; character, rendered allusively, parodically, or stereotypically substitutes for the exposition and explanation of plot, and also for the social configurations on which the plotting hinges.

Characters in his *Blithedale* are the site of history's burial: the "unwedded bride" is the analogy for that which we do not know, and—given Coverdale's particular feelings about Zenobia—that which we, as readers and citizens, do not want to know. The veil is a powerful object because, as Zenobia's story of Theodore and "The Silver Veil" tells us, it hides that which we do not want to uncover.

* * *

To write the complete American history on its utopian trajectory would be to write the history of scandal (mass killing) and to read a series of failures; thus what we get instead is a record of the obsessions of a failed (his) storyteller and a bachelor to boot (Coverdale), who writes about a failed world-historical figure (Hollingsworth), a dead "unwedded bride" (Zenobia), and a pallid and yet self-satisfied audience (Priscilla), the single-minded reader who gets what she wants—a "great man" whose authority she never questions.

* * *

Works Cited

Bancroft, George. *History of the Colonization of the United States.* Vol. 2. Boston, 1837.

Dearborn, Henry A. S. "A Sketch of the Life of the Apostle Eliot Prefatory to a Subscription for Erecting a Monument to his Memory." Roxbury, 1850.

Eliot, John. "The Examination of the Indians at Roxbury, The 13th Day of the 4th Month, 1654." *Collections of the Massachusetts Historical Society.* 3rd ser. 4 (1834): 269–87.

———. *The Christian Commonwealth: Or, The Civil Policy of the Rising Kingdom of Jesus Christ. Written Before the Interruption of the Government. 1659. Collections of the Massachusetts Historical Society.* 3rd ser. 9 (1846): 127–64.

Francis, Convers. *Life of John Eliot, The Apostle to the Indians. The Library of American Biography* 5. Boston, 1836.

Hawthorne, Nathaniel. *The Centenary Edition of the Works of Nathaniel Hawthorne.* 20 vols. Columbus: Ohio State UP, 1963–.

———. *The Blithedale Romance.* Vol. 3 of *The Centenary Edition of the Works of Nathaniel Hawthorne.*

———. *The Whole History of Grandfather's Chair.* Vol. 6 of *The Centenary Edition of the Works of Nathaniel Hawthorne.*

Holstun, James. *A Rational Millennium: Puritan Utopias of Seventeenth-Century England and America.* New York: Oxford UP, 1987.

Hutchinson, Thomas. *The History of the Colony of Massachusetts-Bay.* 2nd ed. 2 vols. London, 1760.

Jacobs, Sarah S. *Nonantum and Natick*. Boston: Massachusetts Sabbath School Society, 1853.

Jennings, Francis. *The Invasion of America*. Chapel Hill: U of North Carolina P, 1975.

Massachusetts Historical Society, Collection of. 3rd ser., IV (1834): 1–287.

Mather, Cotton. *Magnalia Christi Americana; or, The Ecclesiastical History of New England*. 2 vols. 1852. New York: Russell and Russell, 1967.

Salisbury, Neal. "Red Puritans: The 'Praying Indians' of Massachusetts Bay and John Eliot." *William and Mary Quarterly* 3rd ser. 31 (Jan. 1974): 27–54.

Stay, Byron L. "Hawthorne's Fallen Puritans: Eliot's Pulpit in *The Blithedale Romance*." *Studies in the Novel* 18 (Fall 1986): 283–90.

Winslow, Ola Elizabeth. *John Eliot: "Apostle to the Indians."* Boston: Houghton Mifflin, 1968.

RUSS CASTRONOVO

The Half-Living Corpse: Female Mediums, Seances, and the Occult[†]

* * *

Séances, ghostly mediums, animal magnetism, spirit rappings—in short, an assortment of occult practices for staging interiority in the U.S. public—are also political practices that engender an ideal of citizenship supposedly free of material considerations. Rather than add to doubts about the credibility of mediumship and other paranormal demonstrations from this era, I suggest that *Blithedale*, in conjunction with mesmerist and spiritualist texts, reflects an occult sphere of citizenship that popularized the suspension of historical awareness. Trance and sleepwalking doubled as political perception; hypnosis and animal magnetism outstripped democratic attention to social issues; clairvoyance and mediumship saw past civic engagement: in each case, a mystic sense of the unconscious overshadowed a type of republican consciousness associated with the public sphere. Enraptured by psychological investigations and otherworldly knowledge that by the 1850s had become a "national phenomenon," the citizen found it easy to forget the inequities and hierarchies that made his or her privileged ignorance possible.[1]

As mesmerism and spirit rapping came into vogue amid an era described by historians as a "spiritual hothouse" and "nationwide spiritual ferment," religious, early psychological, and occult interests

---

† From "'That Half-Living Corpse': Female Mediums, Seances, and the Occult Public Sphere," in *Necro Citizenship: Death, Eroticism, and the Public Sphere in the Nineteenth-Century United States*, pp.101–50. Copyright 2001 by Duke University Press. All rights reserved. Used by permission of the publisher. Except where indicated, all notes are Castronovo's and have been renumbered; some notes have been condensed for this Norton Critical Edition.

1. Jon Butler, *Awash in a Sea of Faith: Christianizing the American People* (Cambridge, Mass.: Harvard University Press, 1990), 255.

combined in an "interdisciplinary" focus on the individual soul as a means of thinking about—and also screening—the body politic.[2] This psychic nation is more than an artifact of transcendence or sublimation: the public sphere's spiritual dimension lodges the most intimate revelation of self—the soul—at the center of public life. Intimacy stands at the center of public life since it is the coming together of private persons that constitutes the public sphere.[3] Not that bourgeois society need apologize for its private origins: rather, the problem is that the public sphere returns obsessively to its origins, privatizing the politics that transpire when persons come together as a public.

Hawthorne's novel reveals the interplay of public sphere and private affair as the ascendancy of privatization as a political mode. Joining an experiment in collective living, the book's narrator, Miles Coverdale, quickly confuses the fate of socialism with his own failure to seduce the commune's women, Zenobia, a passionate feminist, and her protégé Priscilla, a girl of reputed psychic prowess. The dystopic unraveling of this idealized community once blessed with emancipatory potential animates Coverdale's confession, the last words of Blithedale: "I—I myself was in love—with—Priscilla!"[4]. The resolution to turn away from the pleasures and challenges of associative life and look inward at the libidinal investments that drive his narrative amounts to a decision to make emancipation a personal quest. Such interiorization seems, both to Blithedale's liberal reformers and Habermas, laden with freedoms, specifically the freedom to be unconscious of material inequality. This desire to cloak material conditions beneath heartfelt emotion represents a sublime moment in the psychological privatization of political life.

Disclosure of one last secret, coming long after Coverdale has pried open the histories and hearts of a band of utopian schemers, hardly smacks of political import. After poking into the earthly passions of a prison reformer, a women's rights activist, and a spiritual medium, Coverdale stumbles across his own frustrated erotic devotion to a teenage girl. This personal announcement seemingly represents nothing more than an ironic and pathetic urge to understand the hidden motivations and innermost sympathies that disrupt community. Public presentation of this desire is a very different story—one that politicizes Hawthorne's tale of community. As a narrative that begins with a group of reformers and soon focuses on four of its residents only to end with the confession of just one, the narrator himself, Blithedale tells an important story about the death of political life.

2. See ibid., 225–56; and Paul E. Johnson and Sean Wilentz, The Kingdom of Matthias (New York: Oxford University Press, 1994), 6.
3. See Habermas, Structural Transformation, 25–30.
4. The Blithedale Romance, The Centenary Edition of the Works of Nathaniel Hawthorne, vol. 3, ed. William Charvat et al., (Columbus: Ohio State University Press, 1965), p. 247. Subsequent references given parenthetically in the text [Editor's note].

Hawthorne's romance, in effect, reduces the republican conscious-ness associated with the public sphere to private desire.[5]

Privatization is what Coverdale loves about Priscilla: she offers him reassuring experiences of substituting individual but still universal feelings of love for materially specific (and often messy) understand-ings of the world. Love is among the many splendored things ahistori-cal enough to allow interiority to seem equally and generally shared. The citizen's infatuation with private bodies and privacy is an age-old intrigue. Fear of the public sphere stands as a pillar in traditions of Anglo-American citizenship theory, according to Margaret Somers.[6] In her historical sociology of citizenship, Somers shows how liberal democratic societies privilege a metanarrative that overreacts to threats of state tyranny by demonizing forms of associative life. In turn, freedom and politics are elevated—and constricted—to intimate experience, a private affair. Privatization is thus also what Priscilla offers audiences in her mesmeric performances as a psychic prodigy known by her stage name, the "Veiled Lady": she holds out to citizens earthly glimpses of a spiritual realm impenetrable to the clamors of the socius. Coverdale's admission of love for a waif seems unre-hearsed and sudden, especially since so much of *Blithedale* concerns his erotic musings about Zenobia's mature body and his homoerotic ties to Hollingsworth. By the book's final chapter, however, Coverdale behaves like so many nineteenth-century reformers, philanthropists, and liberal critics preferring disembodied forms to embodied sub-jects, desiring hermeticism and not the egalitarian possibilities of homosociality, and privileging individual feeling over public life.

This fascination with Priscilla, her body repeatedly described as having "hardly any physique" and "a lack of human substance," betrays the *immaterial* conditions that popularize, idealize, and finally privatize democratic possibility in the United States (34, 185). While critics at least since Marx have rightly emphasized the necessity of

5. As a type of political discourse that stages the public admission of private desire, Coverdale's confession is much more than an anticipation of the confessional mode cur-rent in contemporary U.S. public life, made popular, if not mandatory, by the personal interview, press conference, and ubiquity of the television talk show. Bill Clinton admits to his carryings-on with a White House intern, evangelist Jimmy Swaggart claims his sin, Jimmy Carter makes what he thought would be an innocuous comment about the lust in his heart: immortalized by flashbulbs and sound bites only to fade, these moments stand as sensational echoes of a banal obsession with airing indiscretion whose origins date back at least as far the democratic experiments of the nineteenth century. Hawthorne's novel suggests that such invasively public moments are not really about the loss of privacy; rather, they are about the articulation of citizenship as a private affair. On the confused identification of privacy with politics, see Mark Seltzer's reversal of the 1960s' epigram: "The notion that 'the personal is the political' has been reversed, turned round to the notion that the 'political is the personal'" (*Serial Killers*, 258). See also Lauren Berlant and Michael Warner, "Sex in Public," *Critical Inquiry* (winter 1998): 547–66.

6. Margaret R. Somers, "The Privatization of Citizenship: How to Unthink a Knowledge Culture," in *Beyond the Cultural Turn: New Directions in the Study of Society and Culture*, ed. Victoria E. Bonnell and Lynn Hunt (Berkeley: University of California Press, 1999), 121–61.

attending to material relations, *Blithedale* suggests that equality, especially in its failed U.S. mode, originates in the public sphere's "criteria for generality and abstractness."[7] Generic existence and dis-embodiment became public spectacle in midcentury culture as the wispy female forms of somnambulists, teenage trance speakers, and hypersensitive mediums took the stage at village lyceums, women's rights conventions, and antislavery fairs. Occult practices popular-ized mystical experiences of citizenship that pretend to have no debts to material circumstances of privilege or empowerment. At the end of this process of spiritual refinement, citizenship stands transcendent and depoliticized. Erotic energy in the novel turns on references to "magnetism" (134), clairvoyance (47), and "disembodied" presence (6); these shadowy contexts of mesmerism and spiritualism, two related occult "sciences" concerned with the political possibilities of death, advertise young girls like Priscilla as the ideal type of citizen. Clearly, only white men qualified as full citizens until ratification of the Fourteenth Amendment in 1868, but in a paradoxical privatiza-tion of public citizenship, liberal white men desired civic identities modeled on the female medium's disconnection from context and contingency. A popular taxonomy of citizenship emanates from the necromantic, ill-defined, and ahistorical conditions of a girlhood that kept company with spirits.

To tame radicals "miscarried by the wild speculations of material-ism," as an early nineteenth-century psychic researcher put it, liberal reformers often acted as Coverdale, becoming enamored of bodies that had no substance within the body politic.[8] Bodies that provided the best medium for citizenship turned out to be the most private—namely, persons caught in the deathlike trance of mesmerism and, later, persons with spiritual affinity for the "electrical" vibrations of the departed. Coverdale's offer of "a slim and unsubstantial girl" (26) as the key to his narrative echoes popular occult discourses that explained the dark facts of inequality by turning to the immaterial conditions forecast by the young women who occupied the center stages of mesmerism and spiritualism. "Wild speculations" about class inequity or racial injustice paled before more intangible and thus less actionable visions of social conditions. Refracted through the pro-topsychological interest in the unconscious, sociopolitical discourse became caught in a mystic trance, as it were, enraptured with the idea that the hierarchies governing U.S. life transcended worldly causes.

7. Habermas, *Structural Transformation*, 54.
8. Charles Poyen, introduction to *Report on the Magnetical Experiments Made by the Commission of the Royal Academy of Medicine, of Paris, Read in the Meetings of June 21 and 28, 1831*, by Henri Marie Husson (Boston: D. K. Hitchcock, 1836), xxxix. The political valence of spiritual and early psychological discourses in non-U.S. contexts has been noted as well. See Robert Darnton for a discussion of "political somnambulism" (*Mesmerism and the End of the Enlightenment in France* [Cambridge, Mass.: Harvard University Press, 1968], 108).

What structured a discourse on equality were not simply marketplace realities or the undeniable presence of lower-class and enslaved bodies; what authorized a fantasy of equality were the revelations of trance speakers, the insensible bodies of mesmerized subjects, and the passive wills of spirit mediums. So receptive were citizens to the wonders of the occult that the facticity and grittiness of sociopolitical discourse became sublimated as sociocelestial discourse.

Mesmerized Citizens and Spiritualist Politics

> Seek . . . the angel-world for the types of a true, social,
> affectional life.   —*Plain Guide to Spiritualism* (1863)

New technologies of apperception and communication such as clairvoyance, the "spiritual telegraph," "animal magnetism," and séances attracted popular interest in epistemologies that claimed to render knowledge in utopian and nonhierarchical fashion. "The movement is essentially indigenous and American," opined the *New York Herald* of spiritualism, "bearing the most absolute marks of its democratic and popular origin."[9] By 1857, the preface to the anonymous *Zillah, the Child Medium*, a novel of erotic clairvoyance and necromancy, could aver that "there are not many families in the Union that do not boast a 'medium' among their members."[1] While such estimates are

9. Quoted in Uriah Clark, *Plain Guide to Spiritualism: A Hand-Book for Skeptics, Inquirers, Clergymen, Believers, Lecturers, Mediums, Editors, and All Who Need a Thorough Guide to the Phenomena, Science, Philosophy, Religion, and Reforms of Modern Spiritualism*, 4th ed. (Boston: William White and Co., 1863), 31. Aware that these new movements lacked institutional authority, most supporters were careful to include testimony of each movement's broad-based appeal as a way of claiming democratic authority. Contemporary critics and historians have agreed with what spiritualists and mesmerists had to say about their wide popularity; see Daniel Cottom, *Abyss of Reason: Cultural Movements, Revelations, and Betrayals* (New York: Oxford University Press, 1991), 5, 27, 41; Fuller, *Mesmerism*, 15; R. Laurence Moore, *In Search of White Crows: Spiritualism, Parapsychology, and American Culture* (New York: Oxford University Press, 1977), 3–4; Howard Kerr, *Mediums, Spirit-Rappers, and Roaring Radicals: Spiritualism in American Literature, 1850–1900* (Urbana: University of Illinois Press, 1972), 3–9; Ruth Brandon, *The Spiritualists: The Passion for the Occult in the Nineteenth and Twentieth Centuries* (Buffalo, N.Y.: Prometheus Books, 1984), 40; Russell M. Goldfarb and Clare R. Goldfarb, *Spiritualism and Nineteenth-Century Letters* (Cranbury, N.J.: Associated University Presses, 1978), 26, 38; and Gary Laderman, *The Sacred Remains: American Attitudes toward Death, 1799–1883* (New Haven, Conn.: Yale University Press, 1996), 55, 61.
1. *Zillah, the Child Medium; a Tale of Spiritualism* (New York: Dix, Edwards, and Co., 1857), iii. Throughout this [essay] I discuss mesmerism and spiritualism in the same breath even though many differences exist between the two movements/pseudosciences. Yet mesmerism and spiritualism are part of an overlapping cultural continuum in which spiritualism incorporates mesmerist theories of magnetism and the unconscious. For many reformers, spiritualism was the final development of mesmerism's utopian possibilities. Thus Uriah Clark's *Plain Guide to Spiritualism* averred, "Most of those who were at first mesmeric subjects are now acknowledged as spirit mediums" (112). Edgar Allan Poe's "Mesmeric Revelation" also suggests how quickly animal magnetism could bleed into a type of spiritual practice, and Simon C. Hewitt cited spiritualist healing's reliance on "Electricity and Magnetism" as an inheritance of "the old Mesmeric way" (*Messages from the Superior State; Communicated by John Murray, through John M. Spear in the Summer of 1852: Containing Important Instruction to the Inhabitants of the Earth, Carefully Prepared for Publication, with a Sketch of the Author's Early Life, and a Brief Description of the Spiritual Experience of the Medium* [Boston: Bela Marsh, 1853], 19, 41).

no doubt inflated, animal magnetizers and clairvoyants boasted of the occult's democratic popularity, and persons awaiting the advent of equality seemed easily convinced that the afterlife provided a missing piece to the puzzle of universal emancipation. Members and associates of Hawthorne's own family dabbled in this psychopolitical sphere. His fiancée, Sophia Peabody, sought relief from headaches in the mystic passes of a mesmerist, much to the novelist's consternation, who feared that this little understood practice would expose his future wife to psychological violation. Years later, his children's governess announced herself a writing medium capable of transcribing messages sent from beyond the grave.[2]

Although Hawthorne viewed such activities with distrust, many of his fellow cultural critics—including those he joined at Brook Farm—looked to mesmerism, especially as it was later incorporated into spiritualist practices, as a means of realizing "the Jacksonian era's belief in the ultimate perfectibility of society through the progressive improvements of its citizens."[3] As clairvoyants and sleep-walkers proved receptive to vibrations from the "other side," more and more whites in the United States doubled as mediums between the public and heavenly spheres: by 1863, not uncoincidentally a point during the Civil War when families increasingly saw brothers, fathers, sons, and husbands enter the spirit realm, one promoter of supernatural activity estimated that "at this date 2,500,000 [persons] . . . have arrived at their convictions of spiritual communication, from personal experience."[4] *Blithedale* both anticipates and documents this fascination with ghostly disembodiment. Like the novel's self-confessed minor poet and ardent philanthropist whose sexual interests ultimately settle on the undeveloped body of Priscilla rather than the voluptuous corporeality of Zenobia, at the nexus of animal magnetism and spiritualism, abolitionists, women's rights activists, and other liberal critics of the nation privileged a virginal history unburdened by contradiction or complexity.

2. On Sophia Peabody's consultations with a mesmerist and governess Ada Shephard's writing mediumship, see Gordon Hutner, *Secrets and Sympathy: Forms of Disclosure in Hawthorne's Novels* (Athens: University of Georgia Press, 1988), 130; Taylor Stoehr, *Hawthorne's Mad Scientists: Pseudoscience and Social Science in Nineteenth-Century Life and Letters* (Hamden, Conn.: Archon Books, 1978), 40; and Maria M. Tatar, *Spellbound: Studies on Mesmerism and Literature* (Princeton, N.J.: Princeton University Press, 1978), 205.
3. Fuller, *Mesmerism*, 21. Mesmerism "was intimately bound up with the life of popular culture," writes Fuller (15).
4. Quoted in William Howitt, *The History of the Supernatural in All Ages and Nations and in All Churches Christian and Pagan Demonstrating a Universal Faith* (Philadelphia, Pa.: J. B. Lippincott, 1863), 2:196. Even more reckless estimates of the number of spiritualist followers had ranged as high as eleven million in the previous decade, the 1850s (Moore, *In Search of White Crows*, 14).

As somnambulic trances increased in frequency and popularity, the dead outlined an occult public sphere for U.S. democracy. Mediums spoke with key political leaders of the national past and received descriptions of everlasting liberty. Encouraged perhaps by the efforts of the Franklin Pierce first family to contact a son who had died in a railroad accident, one senator in 1854 introduced a petition signed by 15,000 constituents asking Congress to investigate otherworldly communication. The president's ghost son was successfully married in a spirit ceremony to the infant soul of Katie Eaton, who died at the age of three weeks, but senators laughed at the idea of asking the Committee on Foreign Relations to establish contact with emissaries from the other side.[5] Despite congressional mockery of spiritual suggestions, the occult continued to influence and structure politics. In ghostly chats with departed figures such as Franklin, Jefferson, and Webster on concrete topics such as labor laws, temperance, tariffs, antislavery fairs, and the Fugitive Slave Law, sleepwalking subjects never failed to speak in an idiom that was at core ahistorical, abstracted, and universalized. Issues inviting debate and conflict were easily resolved once divested of substance and specificity: politics became spectral in an occult public sphere.[6] But as it spiritualizes sociopolitical arenas, the occult frames a civic demeanor that exalts passivity and disconnection. While mesmerism and spiritualism often intersected with pressing issues of race, class, gender, and national destiny, their structure and style blocked democratic critique by displacing sociopolitical agitation to a psychospiritual realm of eternal consensus. The occult public sphere works by contradiction, engaging politics and social conflicts only to disencumber citizens of sociopolitical consciousness.

Because an occult public sphere orients inquiry around invisible psychological matters, Jacksonian democracy might be rethought to question how active and democratic its democratic activity was. Impassioned rhetoric about slavery as literal Southern bondage and metaphoric intemperance, white industrial labor, and physiological vice suggests the era's political vibrancy. If ever a golden age of the U.S. public sphere existed, according to Michael Schudson, it appeared at these moments. These nineteenth-century instances, as Mary Ryan adds, were characterized by a "raucous, contentious, and

5. See Brandon, *Spiritualists*, 39.
6. Political and social issues were clustered about the occult. Mesmerism brought with it fears of foreign conspiracy, and spirit rapping had strong connections to women's rights, as Robert Levine and Ann Braude respectively show. See Robert S. Levine, *Conspiracy and Romance: Studies in Brockden Brown, Cooper, Hawthorne, and Melville* (Cambridge, U.K.: Cambridge University Press, 1989), 148; and Ann Braude, *Radical Spirits: Spiritualism and Women's Rights in Nineteenth-Century America* (Boston: Beacon Press, 1989).

unbounded style of debate" that makes the public sphere in U.S. incarnations seem a far cry from an enlightened zone of rational consensus.[7] Amid the improbability of distilling an ideal bourgeois public from the unruly stir of civic life, the public sphere seems less a historical fact and more a political effect that turns private bodies into public members. As a political operation, then, the public sphere outstrips incrustations attached to specific persons by privileging *"human beings pure and simple,"* to return to Habermas's phrase. Mesmerism and spiritualism advance this dematerializing agenda in ways that represent not a historical deviation to the public sphere but its theoretical fulfillment. By valuing (un)consciousness over corpo-reality and prioritizing psychic interiority over sociopolitical aware-ness, the occult represses material conditions and national divisions in search of inward truths and higher spiritual unity. Clairvoyance and somnambulism model citizenship. A psychosocial discourse of passivity and abstraction disputes the historical narrative of Jackson-ian activism. If citizens were active, they were active in producing political passivity. The occult, like the bourgeois public sphere under Oskar Negt and Alexander Kluge's critique, excluded "substantial life interests." Following the cues of mesmerism and spiritualism, a more perfect democracy lay not in redressing material inequities but in explaining hierarchy as an effect of an immaterial set of conditions.

Social and literary activists such as Harriet Martineau, Harriet Beecher Stowe, William Lloyd Garrison, Amy and Isaac Post, and Lydia Maria Child underwent mesmeric therapy or attended séances as part of a political faith that sought to transcend politics itself.[8] Discovery of a spiritual telegraph uniting this world to the other side augured the cessation of striving with material conditions of embodi-ment, racial oppression, marketplace anxiety, and gender inequality. The heroine of T. S. Arthur's *Agnes; or, the Possessed, a Revelation of Mesmerism* (1848) happily triumphs over the material world once she is magnetized. Pained by a decaying tooth, yet too squeamish to face extraction of her molar, Agnes undergoes hypnosis and placidly submits to treatment. "Not a muscle stirred! . . . [T]he expression of her face was all unchanged," reports an excited and no longer dubious

---

7. Ryan, "Gender and Public Access," 264. See Michael Schudson, "Was There Ever a Pub-lic Sphere? If So, When? Reflections on the American Case," in *Habermas and the Public Sphere,* ed. Craig Calhoun (Cambridge, Mass.: MIT Press, 1992), 147. Schudson identi-fies 1840–1900 as the time span of what could best qualify as a public sphere in the United States.

8. On the interests of liberal reformers in mesmerism and spiritualism, see Lewis Perry, *Radi-cal Abolitionism: Anarchy and the Government of God in Antislavery Thought, with a New Preface* (1973; reprint, Knoxville: University of Tennessee Press, 1995), 188; Moore, *In Search of White Crows,* 3; Goldfarb and Goldfarb, *Spiritualism,* 61; and Lynn Wardley, "Relic, Fetish, Femmage: The Aesthetics of Sentiment in the Work of Stowe," in *The Culture of Sentiment: Race, Gender, and Sentimentality in Nineteenth-Century America,* ed. Shirley Samuels (New York: Oxford University Press, 1992), 205–8. I will examine the spe-cific intersections of spiritualism, slavery, and abolition in chapter 4 [of *Necro Citizenship*].

witness of the mesmerist's skill.[9] Modeled probably on an 1836 account in the *Boston Medical and Surgical Journal* in which a French immigrant named Charles Poyen hypnotized a twelve-year-old girl prior to dental surgery, Agnes's experience produces a fantasy that is at once psychological and political: bodies (and bodies politic) can become so enthralled with immaterial conditions that trauma and disturbance pass unnoticed.

In a story every bit as erotically charged as Arthur's exposé of spellbound maidens, Hawthorne's *Blithedale* expresses similar distrust of the mystical power that surmounts the free will of another innocent New England girl. Mediums, mesmerists, and enslaving spiritualists sinisterly flit through the utopian undertaking at the novel's center. Psychological mysteries/frauds are not limited to the pandering of the Veiled Lady in exhibitions that polite society would no doubt view as promiscuous. Coverdale imagines that his illness transforms him "into something like a mesmerical clairvoyant" (47); Zenobia reveals that Coverdale's verses have "stolen into my memory, without my exercising any choice or volition about the matter" (15); Priscilla's artless gambols captivate Hollingsworth; Zenobia's artful legend of the Veiled Lady transfixes Priscilla; and Hollingsworth's effort to galvanize adherents to his reformist scheme causes him to appear a willful magnetizer. Each suggestion of spiritual phenomena and magnetic influence is laden with malignant sympathy, prompting the critical observation that Hawthorne found an uncanny resemblance between the mesmerist and the novelist who seeks to captivate readers.

Analogies between novelist and mesmerist, however, only repeat the privatizing impulse of Coverdale's belated confession of love. Like the mesmerized subject who sits insensible of worldly stimuli and circumstances, the critical focus on psychological events in Hawthorne's novel excludes the material political world portrayed in his art. Thus, for one critic, to appreciate the hypnotic effects of Hawthorne's psychological drama readers must eschew a "social and political perspective" so as to become receptive to "Hawthorne's understanding of the compulsion hidden in the human psyche."[1] This evaluation misses the point that attention to intimate relations rests on privileges of privacy. Like the magnetized patient immune to external influence—even a dentist's scalpel—and like the medium who becomes somnolent in order to receive messages from the dead, critical readings that personalize politics do so at the risk of eclipsing history, especially embodied histories. Discussions of

9. T. S. Arthur, *Agnes; or, the Possessed, a Revelation of Mesmerism* (Philadelphia, Pa.: T. B. Peterson, 1848), 16.
1. Samuel Coale, "The Romance of Mesmerism: Hawthorne's Medium of Romance," in *Studies in the American Renaissance, 1994*, ed. Joel Myerson (Charlottesville: University Press of Virginia, 1994), 284. See also Samuel Coale, *Mesmerism and Hawthorne: Mediums of American Romance* (Tuscaloosa: University of Alabama Press, 1998).

Blithedale address how designs of the would-be utopians harm the psychological *self*, in the process ignoring how *bodies* at Blithedale farm have a political substantiality that extends beyond self to impinge on other social actors all the while being shaped by antecedent histories of forgery, poverty, and sex. The problem of such readings is the same as that of Coverdale's narrative: as Lauren Berlant argues, Coverdale gives "priority to individual history," thereby obscuring and deanimating the contentiousness that textures a complex communal (or national) history.[2]

Whether the explanation is love (as with Coverdale), the presence of disembodied spirits (as with citizen-mediums), or inner psychological workings (as with a literary critical focus on the "human psyche"), each interpretation bears witness to the enduring sway of nonsocial thinking. Unrequited love neatly explains away tension and distrust within a community like Blithedale. Loving an insubstantial girl over a socially critical woman like Zenobia proves easier than grappling with gender inequality and economic disparity. How better to ignore political antagonism than to become enraptured with a young girl's messages from the dead so that citizens can ignore the inarticulate protests of the living? As the disembodied soul of William Penn, speaking through a medium, revealed the same year as *Blithedale*'s publication,

> In the spirit life all contention ceases; even those who were undeveloped, when they enter, feel no disposition to contend; and those who progress have far nobler attainments in prospect, than contending either about imaginary or real differences; and, I advise all who are clothed with bodies, to abstain from doubtful disputations. . . . I see no better way, than for the friends of progress to become as passive as possible, and quietly wait.[3]

Political lessons emerge from the other side: brotherly love is secured by "passive" citizenship. Democracy becomes ideal precisely when it can no longer be called democratic, when it no longer derives from dialogue and difference.

Along with the confluences of the unconscious and otherworldly revelation, an occult public sphere makes literal Marx's early critique

2. Lauren Berlant, "Fantasies of Utopia in *The Blithedale Romance*," in *The American Literary History Reader*, ed. Gordon Hutner (New York: Oxford University Press, 1995), 17. For discussions of abstract, noncontingent selfhood in *Blithedale*, see Hutner, *Secrets and Sympathy*, 102–35; and Richard H. Millington, "American Anxiousness: Selfhood and Culture in Hawthorne's *The Blithedale Romance*," *New England Quarterly* 63 (December 1990): 558–83. Joel Pfister's work offers an important exception by asserting that an academic concern with "subjectivity and personal life" stems from "a distinctly individualistic and often ahistorical vision" (*The Production of Personal Life: Class, Gender, and the Psychological in Hawthorne's Fiction* [Stanford, Calif.: Stanford University Press, 1991], 1).

3. Isaac Post, *Voices from the Spirit World, Being Communications from Many Spirits. By the Hand of Isaac Post, Medium* (Rochester, N.Y.: Charles H. McDonnell, 1852), 222.

of bourgeois democracy as "spiritualist." The person interpellated by democracy seems a ghost of the embodied historical subject; the *"modern spiritualist democratic representative state"* mobilizes a brand of citizenship that discards nonpolitical aspects of identity.[4] Much as the public sphere minimizes Negt and Kluge's "substantial life interests" and other palpable historical conditions, citizenship depends on a democratic will-to-amnesia that overlooks specific differences by pointing to larger psychospiritual affinities. "For the nineteenth-century state, the public sphere corresponds to this heaven of ideas," they write.[5] The private workings of community, whether as utopian farm or nineteenth-century state, collapse the stark oppositions between heavenly and historical spheres. But rather than abject the private as nonpolitical, U.S. democracy celebrates privacy as an ideal political posture. In order for this spectral, publicly dead person to appear, the embodied subject must lose a good deal of historical weight.

Ahistorical Performances of Utopia

BROOK FARM AND BLITHEDALE

> Why deny the soul the faculty of recognizing external objects through unusual ways, without the help of the senses, and of annihilating time and space?
> —*Letter to Doctor A. Brigham, on Animal Magnetism* (1837)

Integral to mesmerism and idealized by spiritualism, abstracted bodies redefined public culture as a vaporous sphere of insensibility. Not that animal magnetizers, trance speakers, charlatans, and séance leaders offered a compact or consistent theory as they toured lecture halls and gave public demonstrations. Inegalitarianism and skewed hierarchies did not evaporate in an arena of disencumbered souls, although the assurance that "government is patriarchal" in the spirit sphere no doubt implied that ethereal institutions, like earthbound domestic ones, were on the right track.[6] As séances allowed the dead to contact

---

4. Karl Marx and Friedrich Engels, *The Holy Family or Critique of Critical Critique,* trans. R. Dixon (1845; reprint, Moscow: Foreign Languages Publishing House, 1956), 164. Emphasis in original. Michael Walzer references Marx's language here as one realization that under modernity, citizenship is an often thin, formalistic experience that does not involve the fullness of human experience ("Citizenship," in *Political Innovation and Conceptual Change,* ed. Terence Hall, James Farr, and Russell L. Hanson [Cambridge, U.K.: Cambridge University Press, 1989], 217–18).
5. Negt and Kluge, *Public Sphere and Experience,* 2 n. 3.
6. John W. Edmonds and George T. Dexter, *Spiritualism, with an Appendix by Nathaniel P. Tallmadge,* 4th ed. (New York: Partridge and Brittan, 1853), 279. Edmonds's conversion to spiritualism after his wife's death lent credibility and authority to the movement. His reputation as an astute jurist also seemed to argue that no fraud could be involved in spiritual demonstrations.

departed family members, and mediums learned of postmortem accords between rivals such as Calhoun and Clay, traces of political antagonism seemed to vanish. The mediumistic endeavors of citizens belabored a disembodied subject generic enough to reconcile all sorts of diverse interests—evangelical, feminist, sentimental, abolitionist, or erotic. Bodies like those of twelve-year-old Katherine Fox, who received antislavery messages from the dead, or even the more mature Harriet Martineau, who averred that "mesmeric treatment alone" cured debilitating illness, represented the unconscious as a new half-understood frontier in human progress.[7] One thing, however, was certain at these mystical limits: psychological demonstrations and spiritual manifestations that ranged from faddish public entertainment to intimate séances were inexplicable in concrete historical terms.

This impenetrability upholds the image of a national community whose structures of governance are beyond explanation or change. Psychological experiments in animal magnetism, spirit séances, and clairvoyance conjured immaterial conditions that had real effects in sustaining hierarchy and privilege. Virginal yet enslaved to another's will, blindfolded yet able to see and locate objects, alive yet an associate of the dead, mesmerized and spiritualized bodies validated a governing paradox of U.S. public life. Citizens learned to associate passivity and unresponsiveness with democratic virtue; popular psychic rituals taught that privatization best conditioned one to public life. Akin to the antislavery equations of liberty and death, . . . the occult asked individuals to seek an identity "annihilating time and space," to yearn for a tranquil repose in which disconnection masqueraded as self-control. Among the Blithedalers, this yearning manifests itself in desires for "Priscilla's lack of earthly substance" (188): Coverdale, Hollingsworth, Zenobia, and the charlatan mesmerist Westervelt, despite their difference in humanitarian commitment and social position, seek contentment in a maiden body saturated with impressions of death. Priscilla's rigid, unresponsive body excites and temporarily unifies reformers and opportunists by suppressing the material differences between them. Her public performance as a corpse dramatizes citizenship as an act of political necrophilia. Ghostly attractions deactivate membership in democratic community.

Priscilla's insubstantiality is most palpably felt in the village hall, the public space where high and low cultures meet. With entertainment ranging from "the itinerant professor [who] instructs separate classes of ladies and gentlemen," a reference to health reformers like Mary

---

7. Harriet Martineau, "Miss Martineau on Mesmerism" (8 February 1845), quoted in Nathaniel Hawthorne, *The Blithedale Romance*, ed. William E. Cain (Boston: St. Martin's Press, 1996), 302.

Gove and Sylvester Graham, to an edifying "choir of Ethiopian melodists," the lyceum both constructs and reflects popular interests (196). On this stage before an economically diverse audience, Priscilla surfaces as the Veiled Lady—only to remain impervious to its democratic "clamor." As proof of her resistance to all material tarnish,

> several deep-lunged country-fellows, who looked as if they might have blown the apparition away with a breath, ascended the platform. Mutually encouraging one another, they shouted so close to her ear, that the veil stirred like a wreath of vanishing mist; they smote upon the floor with bludgeons; they perpetrated so hideous a clamor, that methought it might have reached, at least a little way, into the eternal sphere. Finally, with the assent of the Professor [Westervelt], they laid hold of the great chair, and were startled, apparently, to find it soar upward, as if lighter than the air through which it rose. But the Veiled Lady remained seated and motionless, with a composure that was hardly less than awful, because implying so immeasurable a distance betwixt her and these rude persecutors. (202)

Priscilla transcends the hardy specimens of New England independence; insensibility tokens freedom from discordant accents of lower-class life. The "distance" expressed by her nonresponsiveness reveals a social ladder with her own squalid history as a motherless seamstress surely among the bottom rungs. Now, however, lack of bodily response and mimicry of death open a breach between her and her past as well as the overembodied rural folk come to town for a night's entertainment. As the Veiled Lady, her virtue is that she belongs neither to a past nor people. Her reaction is invisibly psychological, and as such, it spiritualizes "bludgeons" and other material emblems of class consciousness, making the base purposes of Westervelt's spectacle seem incidental to the airy insubstantiality of an adolescent girl. The Veiled Lady performs what Habermas calls "audience-oriented privacy," unfolding her interiority in public as she conveys the lesson that private bodies can appear in public, not if they abide by "general and abstract laws" but if they themselves are generic and abstracted.[8]

Coverdale obsesses about Priscilla's unattainable body because sexuality—even if hers is a sexuality he will never know intimately—occludes complex social conditions. "Sexuality provides for him an

---

8. Habermas, *Structural Transformation,* 51, 54.

epistemology, a conventional and stabilizing structure of interpretation," writes Berlant of Coverdale.[9] Much as the Veiled Lady withstands "rude" intrusions of the folk, Coverdale, by virtue of his not-so-virtuous fascination with Blithedale's women and their sexual histories, withstands class-based associations that would force him to confess that the storied egalitarianism of Blithedale is just that—a story of democracy that conceals inequality. In her trance, the Veiled Lady discerns a region where particularity and difference fade. "She beholds the Absolute!" says Westervelt in a bit of staged enthusiasm (201). Although his report of what the Veiled Lady sees in her "communion with the spirit world" (201) lacks the exhaustiveness of out-of-body visions found in volumes such as *Dealings with the Dead* (1861–1862) or *Voices from the Spirit World* (1852), Westervelt's brief description does contain information—or better still, a lack of information—that mystifies the public sphere. For the subject beneath the veil, "the limitations of time and space have no existence" (201); consciousness becomes ahistorical and abstracted. The mesmerist proclaims "an era that would link soul to soul . . . into one great, mutually conscious brotherhood" (200). Surely an egalitarian thought of utopian dimension—but Coverdale can no more forget his social superiority over someone like the pretender Westervelt any more than he can relinquish hierarchical tendencies while sequestered at Blithedale. Coverdale fails to understand that the earthly presence of the mesmerist is indispensable to Priscilla's sublime show. Coverdale's awareness of "a cold and dead materialism" heightens the Veiled Lady's disembodiment; the poet is duped by his own distaste for Westervelt into idealizing Priscilla's estrangement. Westervelt traffics a teenage femininity that he intentionally links to his own dandified masculinity. In the pairing of mesmerist and medium, the audience grasps the contradiction of "the actual presence of a disembodied spirit as anything that stagecraft could devise" (201), an animation of the deathlike conditions that render context, history, and contingency meaningless.

The Veiled Lady embodies—or more accurately, disembodies—Habermas's assertion that the "bourgeois public sphere may be conceived above all as the sphere of private people come together as a public."[1] Yet the public that gathers is made up of political zombies who are alive as an audience though dead as historical actors invested with the particularity of memory and subjectivity. Priscilla enacts this death for a fee: her sublime disconnection signals how citizens who enter the public transcend and forget the sources of

9. Berlant, "Fantasies of Utopia," 6. Also see Levine, *Conspiracy and Romance,* which argues that Coverdale's final declaration "should perhaps be taken as a confession of his love not for Priscilla but for her situation" (156). What Coverdale loves about her situation is that it lacks context.
1. Habermas, *Structural Transformation,* 27.

privilege that allow their abstraction as a public in the first place. The Veiled Lady theatricalizes historical consciousness so that it loses substance. Her spellbound body suggests that the most desirable way to appear in public is as a private body. In her isolated insensibility, she reenacts a social drama that the communitarians at Blithedale have been playing all spring and summer: as Coverdale remarks, the utopian scheme sets out to give voice to "blithe tones of brotherhood" by breaking with "the weary tread-mill of the established system" (12, 19). Not that "brotherhood" is a nefarious goal, but Coverdale's catachrestic use of a "tread-mill" to substitute for society turns on a mandarin aversion to work and labor. The reformers seek "brotherhood" by forgetting, rather than addressing, the material accents that clash with idealistic "tones." They pretend that class differences do not exist even though the first common meal that seats dandies from town next to laborers from the field creates an "oppressive" awkwardness (25). Like Priscilla, they feign unconsciousness and sleepwalk past historical conditions that create social division.

Affected annihilations of class consciousness surface in the history of Brook Farm, the utopian community that Hawthorne joined and later used as a model for Blithedale. In an invitation to Emerson to buy into the Fourierist project, Brook Farm's founder, George Ripley, drew attention to inequities of labor only to resolve these inequities by subtly forgetting them:

> Our objects, as you know, are to insure a more natural union between intellectual and manual labor than now exists; to combine the thinker and the worker, as far as possible, in the same individual; to guarantee the highest mental freedom, adapted to their tastes and talents . . . to do away with the necessity of menial services. . . . Thought would preside over the operations of labor, and labor would contribute to the expansion of thought; we should have industry without drudgery, and true equality without vulgarity.[2]

Although Ripley desires to bridge a social gulf, his language remains elitist, suspicious of the physicality of labor cast as "drudgery" and "vulgarity." Couched in terms that reify humans on the basis of work, Ripley's vision adheres to typical assumptions about workers who do not think and intellectuals who do not work. Citizens tethered to a treadmill have no time to meditate on "brotherhood." When Brook Farm drafted a constitution in 1844, the language of universalism made the forgetting of class consciousness and economic grievances

2. George Ripley to Ralph Waldo Emerson, 9 November 1840, *Autobiography of Brook Farm*, ed. Henry W. Sams (Englewood Cliffs, N.J.: Prentice-Hall, 1958), 6. On Ripley's spiritualist leanings, see Moore, *In Search of White Crows*, 3; and Coale, *Mesmerism and Hawthorne*, 106).

complete: "From this document . . . we propose a radical and universal reform, rather to redress any particular wrong or remove the sufferings of any single class of human beings."[3] Declaring inconsequential the "particulars" of oppressed groups, the associationists overlooked historically based inequities that cause a "single class" to be singled out as the slighted recipient in the circulation of goods, resources, and justice. Spiritual unity silences concerns about material inequity. In gauging the effects of mediumistic revelation, *Modern Spiritualism* (1855) echoed the logic of Brook Farm's constitution: "It [spiritualism] has, undoubtedly, a tendency to liberalize and enlighten, and to bring together all minds on the one point of immortality. Thus united on one subject . . . it will, almost of necessity, produce, ultimately, more harmony than has heretofore existed in the liberal world."[4] Liberalism in its occult mode encourages a final estrangement of private persons from public conflict. Within this inert consensus, the necessary antagonism of democratic life ceases: spiritualized citizens do not advert death but rather, in a necrophilic impulse, court an identity that is as posthumous as it is postpolitical.

The spectral opposes embodiments of history by etherealizing utopia's material conditions. Hawthorne, for one, dematerialized his own work at Brook Farm. The laborer that milked cows and hoed potatoes, he wrote to Sophia Peabody in September 1841, was a "Spectre" and "not thy husband."[5] No wonder, then, that the Blithedalers play at scenes of transcendence, recasting farmwork as "the spiritualization of labor" (65). It is Priscilla who best performs the spectral, however. As a medium in Westervelt's séance, she dramatizes the evacuation of history at the center of the public sphere. Her past a mystery and her body evanescent, the Veiled Lady acquires "many of the privileges of a disembodied spirit" (6). The precise nature of these "privileges" Coverdale does not specify, although his declaration of love speaks volumes about just how attractive he finds her ability to linger in forgetfulness of the village hall's lower-class accents and other social contexts.

3. *Constitution of the Brook Farm Association, for Industry and Education, West Roxbury, Mass., with an Introductory Statement,* in *Autobiography of Brook Farm,* ed. Henry W. Sams (Englewood Cliffs, N.J.: Prentice-Hall, 1958), 96. The ethos of the association also worked to harmonize racial oppression and universal reform: as one member of Brook Farm wrote in December 1844, "I feel that the Association is doing and will do more for Antislavery than anything else can" (quoted in Lindsay Swift, *Brook Farm: Its Members, Scholars, and Visitors* [1900; reprint, Seacaucus, N.J.: Citadel Press, 1961], 122).
4. Eliab Wilkinson Capron, *Modern Spiritualism: Its Facts and Fanaticisms, Its Consistencies and Contradictions, with an Appendix* (1855; reprint, New York: Arno Press, 1976), 379.
5. Nathaniel Hawthorne to Sophia Peabody, 3 September 1841, quoted in Henry W. Sams, ed., *Autobiography of Brook Farm* (Englewood Cliffs, N.J.: Prentice-Hall, 1958), 34. Coverdale shares Hawthorne's tendency to romanticize labor. On this point, see Gillian Brown (*Domestic Individualism: Imagining Self in Nineteenth-Century America* [Berkeley: University of California Press, 1990], 107–10), and D. H. Lawrence's commentary on Hawthorne's negotiation of the contrast between "brookfarming" and "spectral" existence (*Studies in Classic American Literature* [New York: Viking, 1971], 105).

The occult—as the airy stuff of public spectacle—enacts Marx's famous formulation in 1852, the same year as the publication of *Blithedale*, that "the spirits of the past" shroud historical conscious-ness by forgetting the material conditions that structure the past. But whereas Marx toys with spectral allusions to argue for the inescapability of historical conditions, Coverdale looks to Priscilla's disembodiment to prevent recognition of any such contingency. "Men [sic] make their own history," as Marx reminds us, but "they do not make it just as they please; they do not make it under circum-stances chosen by themselves, but under circumstances directly encountered, given, and transmitted from the past."[6] Priscilla per-mits Coverdale and the rest of the lyceum audience to admit the first part of Marx's dictum only to reject the latter: citizens certainly make their own history, but they believe themselves freed of boister-ous shouts and other material circumstances. The Veiled Lady sits on stage as the disembodiment of history, placid and unmoving, her wispy transparency the very stuff of an ideology that mystifies hierar-chical social structures by turning to the spiritual.

* * *

Veiled Labor

As the somnambulist of Edgar Allan Poe's "Mesmeric Revelation" (1844) states, "The senses of my rudimental life are in abeyance, and I perceive external things directly, without organs."[7] Mesmerist practice and spiritualist phenomena induce a subjectivity that liter-alizes Gilles Deleuze and Félix Guattari's portrait of a body impervi-ous to social contexts and material relations—the body without organs. For the authors of *Anti-Oedipus*, the body without organs describes an organism immune to the stimuli that shape subjectivity in accordance with strata of alienation and dominance. It is not that the body without organs is hollow inside; rather, the lifeless body is hollow outside because its "smooth, slippery, opaque, taut surface" does not react to an external sociopolitical universe.[8] The body with-out organs resists stratifications of the socius; neither hierarchies of selfhood nor fictions of individuality glom onto this quiescent organ-ism that precedes the cultural formation of the subject.

6. Karl Marx, *The Eighteenth Brumaire of Louis Bonaparte* (1852; reprint, New York: International Publishers, 1963), 15. My attention to the connections between Marx and spiritualism was first drawn by Cottom's argument in *Abyss of Reason* (5). And see, generally, Jacques Derrida, *Specters of Marx: The State of the Debt, the Work of Mourn-ing, and the New International*, trans. Peggy Kamuf (New York: Routledge, 1994).
7. Edgar Allan Poe, "Mesmeric Revelation," in *The Complete Works of Edgar Allan Poe*, ed. James A. Harrison (New York: AMS Press, 1965), 250.
8. Gilles Deleuze and Félix Guattari, *Anti-Oedipus: Capitalism and Schizophrenia*, trans. Robert Hurley, Mark Seem, and Helen R. Lane (New York: Viking Press, 1972), 9.

Seemingly independent of social apparatuses, the body without organs lives as an unmarked subject: "*Alone it stands. And in no need of skin, flesh, face or fluid.* . . . The subject is what remains when the body is taken away; it is literally *in*human (I am—dead)."[9] So also reads the fatal pronouncement of the speaker in Poe's "The Facts in the Case of M. Valdemar" (1845) who uses animal magnetism to withstand physiological decay: "*I say to you that I am dead.*"[1] Biological stasis analogizes the inert political consciousness of the modern citizen who lives beyond history. The dead have the luxury of ignoring the cultural production of something as "natural" as the body, and instead live in an ahistorical fantasy that misrecognizes, among other things, capitalism's impact on subjectivity. This fiction is what Deleuze and Guattari call "antiproduction."[2] Their argument recapitulates the scornful deconstruction of Priscilla's idealized femininity as the anti-product of ages of male privilege, exposing innocent girlhood and true womanhood as always enmeshed in economic, historical, and political pathologies. The traditional subject of girlhood, Zenobia maintains, cannot be aroused to respond to this embeddedness. Her ghostly and culturally transcendent body completes the citizen's necrophilic fantasy of a socially dead identity. Zenobia, like Deleuze and Guattari after her, restores context to this subject, remarking on the constructed body that stands prior to the natural one, documenting the loss of history that perfects an amnesiac subject.

But Zenobia's analysis is lost on the men of Blithedale. Coverdale, for one, ends up enamored of Priscilla even though he has devoted his bachelor reveries to Zenobia's bodily organs. As opposed to Zenobia's "not exactly maidenlike" form (47), Priscilla's unstudied innocence promises social harmony. She partakes of a "universally pervasive fluid" (200), as Westervelt puts it in anticipation of Deleuze and Guattari's "amorphous, undifferentiated fluid" that flows against repressive social linkages.[3] To ensure her social chastity, Hollingsworth discourages questions about Priscilla's past, audiences validate her unfathomable performance as the Veiled Lady, and Coverdale proclaims an unrealizable love for her. Yet a material politics brusquely intrudes on the supposedly transcendent and disconnected sphere of an occult public. Priscilla's public display of privacy and disembodiment is not the only model of

9. Marcus Doel, "Bodies without Organs: Schizoanalysis and Deconstruction," in *Mapping the Subject: Geographies of Cultural Transformation*, ed. Steve Pile and Nigel Thrift (New York: Routledge, 1995), 230. Emphasis in original.
1. Edgar Allan Poe, "The Facts in the Case of M. Valdemar," in *Great Short Works of Edgar Allan Poe*, ed. G. R. Thompson (New York: Harper and Row, 1970), 490. Emphasis in original.
2. Deleuze and Guattari, *Anti-Oedipus*, 15.
3. Ibid., 9.

citizenship presented in *Blithedale*. Coverdale comes down to earth when he spitefully allegorizes his acquaintances as the farm's hogs, calling them "greasy citizens," overflowing with "sensual comfort" and "corporeal substance" (144, 143). He naturalizes what he takes to be his moral ascendancy over his fellow utopians by castigating them with animalistic embodiment. Everything is not ideal in an ideal community; the privilege of demeaning others remains intrinsic to Coverdale's exercise of democratic citizenship. Bodies laden with organs, the "four huge black grunters" are irredeemably creatures of production destined for consumption (143). A poet and a reformer, Coverdale attempts to clean up, to spiritualize, these citizens: watching their heavy-lidded sleep, he interprets the pigs as mediums, as shuttles "betwixt dream and reality," flitting in and out of spheres of consciousness and unconsciousness (144). A voice from the working class disrupts his trancelike reverie as Silas Foster, Blithedale's agricultural laborer, reminds him that the swine will soon be slaughtered, transformed into spareribs and other choice cuts of pork. "Oh, cruel Silas, what a horrible idea!" responds Coverdale, dismayed not so much by the prospect of butchery as the recognition that "natural" bodies are indeed produced, their existence but a function of the demands of consumption (144).

Insistent on unsublimated activities such as eating and husbandry, Silas is one of the novel's most politically significant characters and also one of the most overlooked. In preening over "the little child" as the "true democrat," St. Clare, Coverdale, and other devotees of political necrophilia project a frozen, motionless social order all the while forgetting less well-mannered bodies whose work makes stasis possible. Coverdale's impatience with Silas, matched by literary critics' inattention to Silas's character, reveals a tendency to focus on persons for whom democracy is a leisure while slighting others for whom democracy is something to work at, both a labor and a pleasure. In the same vein as his spiritualization of swine, Coverdale dematerializes the farmer: "The steam arose from his soaked garments, so that the stout yeoman looked vaprous and spectre-like" (18). Echoing the evasion of "manual labor" in George Ripley's *Constitution of the Brook Farm Association*, Blithedale's resident poet performs his own Westervelt-like sleight of hand in an effort to make work a ghostly presence. Not the Veiled Lady but the Veiled Laborer inspires faith in a perfected social order where citizens are, according to *Modern Spiritualism*, "freed from all admixture with earth."[4] Priscilla is also a Veiled Laborer, her public

---

4. Capron, *Modern Spiritualism*, 354. Or, see Isaac Post's *Voices from the Spirit World*, which describes a realm free from material cares: "The spirit . . . is freed from that cumbrous body and its requirements and hindrances—no house to be built for it, no bread to prepare to sustain it, no clothes to provide, and therefore, all anxiety for these ceases" (136).

performance hiding her manufacture and sale of erotically charged purses. Under the fantasy that production and consumption do not encumber identity, the evasion of materiality pays sociopolitical dividends by cleaning up any traces of exploitation. Within this version of the public sphere re-created as a zone of antiproduction, Priscilla and Silas seem ideal citizens forgetful of social tensions and historical inequities.

Or, at least, that's how Coverdale wishes them to be. Once more dispelling Coverdale's fantasy of bodies under erasure, Silas jarringly recalls the liberal utopians to the different and unequal positions that underlie the community's fantasy of antiproduction. He makes this appeal without words, instead using bodily stimuli as insistent reminders of the class consciousness sublimated by spiritual democracy. Silas draws attention to the materiality of production and consumption with a brawny literalness that embarrasses Coverdale; that is, the laborer eats:

> Grim Silas Foster . . . had been busy at the supper-table, pouring out his own tea, and gulping it down with no more sense of its exquisiteness than if it were a decoction of catnip; helping himself to pieces of dipt toast on the flat of his knife-blade, and dropping half of it on the table-cloth; using the same serviceable implement to cut slice after slice of ham; perpetrating terrible enormities with the butter-plate, and in all other respects, behaving less like a civilized Christian than the worst kind of ogre. Being, by this time, fully gorged, he crowned his amiable exploits with a draught from the water-pitcher. (30)

As he satisfies his wants and makes known his irrepressible embodiment, Silas acts democratically, not by participating in a privatized illusion of the public sphere but by recognizing that people's needs and desires take up space in the social hierarchy. While the rest of the company wonder how to deal with a sickly seamstress Priscilla, cast down on the community's doorstep, Silas treats her as he treats himself—as a body with organs. "Give the girl a hot cup of tea, and a thick slice of this first-rate bacon," he says, enmeshing Priscilla in, and so vitally reconnecting her to relations of production and consumption (31). Never one to dematerialize his fellows as Coverdale does, Silas attends to her physical being as a means of confirming her belonging to the community: "In a week or two, she'll begin to look like a creature of this world!" (31). Unlike the sociocelestial views of the Blithedalers and the lyceum crowd, his politics promote imbrication not disconnection. With this perspective that gives Priscilla substance, a community might begin to substantiate the specific conditions—her genealogy, economic history, labors with the needle, and gender—that have brought her to Blithedale.

Not a true democrat in the sense that his insistent corporeality cannot represent abstract virtue as does the virgin reserve of Priscilla or Eva, Silas is rather a radical democrat. What distinguishes radical from true democracy is the configuration of freedom: a citizen such as Stowe's half-living corpse or Hawthorne's Veiled Lady rejects all earthly dross, imagining freedom as freedom *from* the socius, whereas a citizen such as Silas grapples with social conditions, experiencing freedom as a freedom *to* participate in the daily forms and activities that constitute community. "Let her stay with us . . . and help in the kitchen, and take the cow-breath at milking time," he says of Priscilla, according her the opportunity to add to their joint-stock company in substantial ways. The radical democrat acknowledges contingency, in contrast to the true democrat who constructs subjects freed from cultural influence. As he speaks of Priscilla, dependent clauses signal awareness of contingency: "Let her" perform these mild labors, Silas says, so that she will soon become a "creature of *this* world," as opposed to an occult sphere of antiproduction that veils conflict and antagonism. He does not issue an ultimatum but does make work a condition of belonging. Unlike the true democrat who adopts a transcendent perspective that abstracts a body without organs from material conditions, the radical democrat contextualizes citizenship, creating dialogue between people, production, and consumption.

Zenobia's Corpse

> Her free, careless, generous modes of expression often had this effect of creating images which, though pure, are hardly felt to be quite decorous.
> —Nathaniel Hawthorne, *The Blithedale Romance*

Although gender and class separate her from Silas, Zenobia also practices radical democracy. Both remind the community of tangible histories that Coverdale's poetic tendency and Hollingsworth's reformist consciousness would soon forget. Silas gives commonsense demonstration that all nourishment is not spiritual, and Zenobia insists that the dead need not sublimate earthly oppression by becoming departed spirits. Zenobia is emphatic about the materiality of death, counteracting the occult's central tenet. Like Silas at the supper table, she does not voice her protest so much as she renders it intelligible with a series of unappeasable gestures. She expresses herself via rigor mortis, an unyielding posture that raises questions about the capacity to move effortlessly between sociocelestial (and sociopolitical) spheres. Her corpse neutralizes political fantasies of girlhood as a noncontingent state in which restrictive differences melt away to reveal a historyless body as the perfected citizen.

Coverdale has so fallen in love with this sort of deanimation that he makes Zenobia emblematic, nullifying the specificity that lends depth to her grievances and betrayals. "She is reduced by Coverdale to a disembodied idea—woman incarnate, the enigma of femininity," writes Elisabeth Bronfen.[5] Coverdale wants to see this woman humbled, attending to her soul's enfranchisement rather than her body's empowerment. When he and the other men of Blithedale pull her drowned corpse from the river, he quickly interprets her expression, musculature, and posture as proof that even a person committed to women's rights and sexual equality will abandon social agitation, and so at last find repose. Coverdale hopes that in death, Zenobia transcends the need to act politically, and to convince himself of her transcendence he puts into effect Emerson's famous formula in *Nature* that "particular natural facts are symbols of particular spiritual facts."[6] He looks at her corpse and does not see it; in place of her material body, he creates a spiritual symbol that outstrips her deconstruction of womanhood. Like the mesmerized subjects of Poe and Poyen, he sees beyond her organs to uncover the lifeless bliss of biological as well as political stasis. In life, Zenobia protests women's circumscribed roles, but as the half-living corpse of Coverdale's imagination, she counsels the living about the wisdom of complacence and submission:

> Her arms had grown rigid in the act of struggling, and were bent before her, with clenched hands; her knees, too, were bent, and—thank God for it!—in the attitude of prayer. Ah, that rigidity! It is impossible to bear the terror of it. . . . She knelt, as if in prayer. With the last, choking consciousness, her soul, bubbling out through her lips, it may be, had given itself up to the Father, reconciled and penitent. (235)

No longer "struggling" against the social current, she submits to an ultimate patriarchal power. The poet's necrophilia calms her: Coverdale's words make Zenobia politically somnolent and reveal him to be as much a mesmerist as Poyen or Westervelt. Thrown into a trance and released from "nervous" meditations on gender inequality, Zenobia reaffirms earthly hierarchy as a higher truth. In Coverdale's mind, this feminist knows her place.

Mesmerized by Coverdale's description, Zenobia's body-as-spirit finds peace. His narrative represses the discontent that gave her conversation and actions an unremitting critical edge. Yet the repressed returns: historical traces of her resistance to being an

---

5. Bronfen, *Over Her Dead Body*, 247.
6. Ralph Waldo Emerson, *Nature*, in *Essays and Lectures* (New York: Library of America, 1983), 20.

ideal citizen, a good girl like Priscilla, or a true democrat like Evangeline erupt from the very posture Coverdale at first represents as so allaying. Her body accepts death but not dematerialization. As Coverdale is forced to acknowledge:

> But her arms! They were bent before her, as if she [struggled] against Providence in never-ending hostility. Her hands! They were clenched in immitigable defiance. Away with the hideous thought! (235)

Zenobia's recalcitrant materiality overcomes Coverdale's desire for a passive female subject, for a body forgetful of its opposition to prevailing social conditions. * * *

His effort to render public citizenship as a psychopolitical affect modeled on privacy and acquiescence fails, however. Zenobia's motionless, statuesque body expresses history if not accusation. The use of a hooked pole to retrieve the drowned woman wounds her breast, its disfigurement becoming a memento mori to the crass speculations about her sexuality and fortune. Zenobia is the citizen who will not suffer amnesia; her corpse chooses the ghastly over the sentimental, memory over transcendence. Her combative body becomes a gruesome memorial to a quasi socialist community that, whatever its claim to equality, insists on women's docility. Coverdale loves this corpse because his only other option is to fear it. Political necrophilia seeks to regulate unruly bodies, such as Zenobia's, that awkwardly inhabit the designation of citizen, their maladjustment to citizenship inciting panic that citizenship is an internally divided category invested with oppositional force. Erotic desire for the dead citizen results from a horror of socially alive and politically animated actors who engage with the public sphere in particularistic and materially untranscendent ways. Necrophilia is an incomplete turn away from a phobia of democratic contention and unpredictability; the dead citizen remains haunted by the politically living actor. This fault line marks the perpetually unsettled ground of radical democracy.

* * *

"Unwarrantable liberties" arise when Silas joins Hollingsworth and Coverdale's all-male ideological assault on a dead woman's corpse. The laborer notices Zenobia's unseemly position, and endeavors to sentimentalize her defiant stance by forcing her arms to hang complacently at her side. His efforts meet with no success, however, and Coverdale, always one to help out in a communal crisis, upbraids the impromptu undertaker, "In God's name, Silas Foster . . . let that dead woman alone" (236). It no doubt seems odd that this yeoman farmer (who I earlier distinguished as a radical

democrat in contrast to Stowe's dying child as a true democrat)
essays to erase the historicity of Zenobia's final gesture. Being a radical democrat does not mean that he will be a perfect citizen but it
does mean that he will touch, interact, and struggle with his compa-
triots. Silas vies with Zenobia's corpse over issues of feminine propriety and his actions reject Coverdale's notion that contexts of labor
should not touch women's bodies. Lower-class hands may produce
stimuli and sensations that will sexualize, not spiritualize, the social
corpse of the citizen. Necrophilia is only for those liberals who, like
Coverdale, privilege privacy above all else. Political motive is, of
course, bound up with Coverdale's respect for the dead: noninter-
course with her corpse ensures that her unbecoming resistance will
make no tangible impression on any member of utopia.[7]

Coverdale's outrage is surprising, given his predilection for young
girls caught in the deathlike trance of mesmerism and his participation in a full-blown cultural necrophilia hostile to embodied historical citizenship. But Zenobia is not a proper necrophilic subject. In
contrast to departed spirits who convey messages of serene social
organization, this dead woman does not glory in an occult public
sphere without strife. In contrast to the medium as half-living
corpse who closes herself off to external stimuli, Zenobia remains
entrenched in the struggles of this world. Her dead body bears the
eloquent memory of discord in a community that was supposed to
have none. Efforts to make her body appear decent only exacerbate
her contentiousness since she so earnestly critiqued notions of
decency and other gender expectations in the first place. Coverdale
attempts to smooth over this ongoing conflict by encouraging amnesia, by banishing "the hideous thought" of a body animated by social
opposition. His respect for Zenobia's privacy originates in a desire to
privatize the political actor. His narrative eulogizes her domesticated
identity—despite the fact that throughout the novel, she is only
known by the "magazine-signature" of her public persona (13):

> Being the woman that she was, could Zenobia have foreseen
> all these ugly circumstances of death, how ill it would become
> her, the altogether unseemly aspect which she must put on,
> and, especially, old Silas Foster's efforts to improve the matter,
> she would no more have committed the dreadful act, than
> have exhibited herself to a public assembly in a badly-fitting
> garment! (236)

7. Coverdale's rebuke of Silas echoes warnings that receptive female mediums take pains
not to grant "access to persons from whose society they would otherwise be excluded," as
Uriah Clark's *Plain Guide to Spiritualism* put it (233). Not all Veiled Ladies could be
depended on to display Priscilla's extreme disengagement and remain unmoved by the
lower-class contexts of the village hall lyceum described in *Blithedale*. The public
medium needs to take "solemn caution against all undue freedom" (Clark, *Plain Guide to
Spiritualism*, 233). "Undue freedom" materializes amid séances when bodies, too
weighted down by socioeconomic organs, join a spiritual bourgeois communion.

Perhaps in this fantasy of embarrassment, Zenobia will be so mortified as to return home to the grave's intimate seclusion. This collapse of public and private spheres trivializes her death as a fashion
mistake even as it equates public appearance to a type of death.

* * *

To die a proper death is to live as a public body without organs.
Rigid and immobile, the corpse cherishes alienation. As Deleuze and
Guattari explain, bodies without organs, bodies without the sensibility to experience culture, are "catatonic bodies [that] have fallen
into the river like lead weights, immense transfixed hippopotamuses
who will not come back up to the surface."[8] So too, in her suicide by
drowning, Zenobia has fallen into the river, but she resurfaces and is
borne back to the community. Using a makeshift bier, the men
struggle "slowly, slowly, with many a dreary pause" to carry her
waterlogged corpse (237). In her afterlife, Zenobia demands that the
representatives of utopia perform labor, that its necrophilic imagination experience her identity as a material condition.

Perhaps Poe best appreciated women's death as an occasion of
male cathexis in his 1846 remark that "the death, then, of a beautiful woman is, unquestionably the most *poetical* topic in the world."[9]
Poe is only about half right, however. The image of a dead woman is
one of the most *political* topics in a U.S. world of protopsychological
discourses. But it is a politics that ultimately disengages the socio-
historical world in a movement patterned after the somnambulist's
trance. As both spectacle and specter, public womanhood deadens
citizenship. The half-living corpse that offers a site of political
(mis)recognition, first and foremost provides erotic material for liberal male imaginations such as Coverdale's. Against a commonsense
view of nineteenth-century whites in the United States as caught up
in intense democratic debate and vibrant social reforms, the occult
suggests a history haunted by inactivity and a rigid commitment to
the political status quo. We might think of this history as a cultural
history of eroticism that explains the citizen's desire to privatize public life as the normative longing of deathly citizenship.

Epitaph

It is difficult to learn anything from the dead woman's corpse without also occupying Coverdale's position of intellectual voyeur. One
way to avoid this position is to read against a necro ideology that
reduces referentiality and to instead interpret the dead as making an

---

8. Deleuze and Guattari, *Anti-Oedipus,* 135.
9. Edgar Allan Poe, "The Philosophy of Composition," in *Great Short Works of Edgar Allan
   Poe,* ed. G. R. Thompson (New York: Harper and Row, 1970), 535. Emphasis added.

active commentary on life in the U.S. public sphere. The dead speak: the question is whether the living will hear a story about the ways in which belonging, incorporation, and other processes of democratic community produce social corpses. The dead tell an alternative tale of the citizen-subject as haunted, as an internally divided category unable to resolve an ambivalence between abstraction and political engagement, generic being and specific embodiment, and tranquil consensus and spirited conflict.

In its golden moments when rationality and abstraction reigned supreme, the public sphere seemed flush with emancipatory potential. "The clichés of 'equality' and 'liberty,' not yet ossified into revolutionary bourgeois propaganda formulae, were still imbued with life," writes Habermas of this storied time.[1] Zenobia's living corpse argues, however, that as equality and liberty appear in public, they are already imbued with death because exclusion and forgotten privilege precede—and enable—the human actor's entrance into the public sphere and underwrite his or her freedom. In this context, the citizen's confession is not that he or she was in love with radical democracy but rather is that the citizen—was in love—with—Priscilla and the depoliticized specter of democracy.

ROBERT S. LEVINE

Sympathy and Reform in *The Blithedale Romance*[†]

For a participant in a reform association that aspires to regenerate society, Miles Coverdale, the first-person narrator of Hawthorne's third novel, *The Blithedale Romance* (1852), spends very little time actually doing the work of social reform. Instead, he seems content simply to look at people, imagine their private circumstances, and fantasize about their sexual proclivities and histories. Does this mean that the narrator of Hawthorne's novel of social reform is merely a voyeur whose only true commitment is to the pleasures of his private imagination? In a key moment about two-thirds into the novel, Coverdale offers his own reflections on his moral imagination just after dreaming that Hollingsworth and Zenobia are kissing over his bed while Priscilla shrinks away, and just before he peers

1. Habermas, *Structural Transformation*, 54.
† From *The Cambridge Companion to Nathaniel Hawthorne*, ed. Richard H. Millington (New York and Cambridge: Cambridge University Press, 2004), pp. 207–29. Reprinted with the permission of Cambridge University Press. All parenthetical volume/page references are to the *Centenary Edition of the Works of Nathaniel Hawthorne*; all notes are Levine's and have been renumbered.

through the boarding-house window where he discovers Zenobia, Priscilla, and Westervelt together for some mysterious purpose. Initially he judges his imagination in negative terms, proclaiming, "That cold tendency, between instinct and intellect, which made me pry with a speculative interest into people's passions and impulses, appeared to have gone far towards unhumanizing my heart." But then he rejects that negative assessment, declaring that his voyeuristic tendencies have everything to do with what he regards as the excess of his sympathetic imagination: "But a man cannot always decide for himself whether his own heart is cold or warm. It now impresses me, that, if I erred at all, in regard to Hollingsworth, Zenobia, and Priscilla, it was through too much sympathy, rather than too little" (111: 154). Sympathy is the key word here. As a number of critics have emphasized, sympathy is a crucial thematic in Hawthorne's fiction, imparting "a romantic ideal of communication . . . an understanding that passes beyond words."[1] There are several moments in *Blithedale* when Coverdale appears to possess this sort of exquisite sympathetic understanding of others, such as when he drinks with Moodie in the tavern, and even during some of his interactions with Zenobia and Hollingsworth. But there are many other moments when Coverdale's expressions of sympathy suggest a failure of communication and understanding, and point to his distance from those impulses that might help to bring about social reform. One of the large questions raised by Hawthorne's first-person narrator, then, is this: does sympathy help to connect the self to the other (and in this way contribute to social reform) or does sympathy create barriers between the self and other (and in this way thwart social reform)?

In putting the sympathetic imagination at the center of his novel about a community of social reformers, Hawthorne chose to interrogate a basic tenet of 1850s sentimental culture, particularly as expressed in reformist discourse of the time, which celebrated the power of sympathy to link the self to unfortunate others. This belief had important sources in eighteenth-century Scottish moral philosophy, particularly writers such as Francis Hutchinson and Adam Smith, who argued that the human predilection to sympathize provided a crucial foundation for the virtuous society. Hawthorne was familiar with those philosophers, and in many of his writings, particularly the sketches and *The House of the Seven Gables*, he drew on and engaged the Scottish sentimental tradition of moral

---

1. Gordon Hutner, *Secrets and Sympathy: Forms of Disclosure in Hawthorne's Novels* (Athens: University of Georgia Press, 1988), p. 8. See also Roy R. Male, "Hawthorne and the Concept of Sympathy," *PMLA* 68 (1953): 138–49; and John Stafford, "Sympathy Comes to America," in *Themes and Directions in American Literature: Essays in Honor of Ray B. Browne and Donald Pizer* (Lafayette, IN: Purdue University Studies, 1969), pp. 24–37.

and social thought.[2] In this respect, he shared much with the popular sentimental and reformist writers of the American 1850s. This
[essay] will examine *Blithedale* in relation to antebellum constructions of sympathy and reform and will be arguing that, despite its
apparently satirical perspective on reform, *Blithedale* is not so dis-
dainful of reform (or sympathy) as it might initially seem, and that in
certain respects *Blithedale* offers a more capacious perspective on
the possibilities of social change than many of the more explicitly
reformist sentimental novels of the period.

In considering novels of social reform of the 1850s, it would be
difficult not to regard Harriet Beecher Stowe's *Uncle Tom's Cabin*
and Hawthorne's *Blithedale Romance*, both published in 1852, as
works that develop completely different perspectives on the power
of sympathy to affect social reform. Whereas Hawthorne seems to
urge readers of *Blithedale* to recognize the impossibility of achieving
any sort of meaningful identification with those whom social reform
might benefit, Stowe deploys rhetorical strategies intended to get
her middle-class readers to identify emotionally with the specific
objects of her reformist novel: the nation's slaves. Like many senti-
mentalists of the 1850s, Stowe was indebted to Adam Smith's belief
that a constituent part of being human was the ability to empathize
with and even apprehend the pain of others through the workings of
the moral imagination. In a passage that has become the *locus classi-
cus* of current critical debate on the promise and limits of sympathy,
Smith writes in his 1759 *The Theory of Moral Sentiments*:

> Though our brother is upon the rack, as long as we ourselves
> are at our ease, our senses will never inform us of what he suf-
> fers. They never did, and never can, carry us beyond our own
> person, and it is by the imagination only that we can form any
> conception of what are his sensations . . . By the imagination
> we place ourselves in his situation, we conceive ourselves
> enduring all the same torments, we enter as it were into his
> body, and become in some measure the same person with him,

2. On Hawthorne and Adam Smith, see Lester H. Hunt, "*The Scarlet Letter*: Hawthorne's
Theory of Moral Sentiments," *Philosophy and Literature* 8 (1984): 75–88; and Lori
Merish, *Sentimental Materialism: Gender, Commodity Culture, and Nineteenth-Century
American Literature* (Durham, NC: Duke University Press, 2000), ch. 3. According to
Marion L. Kesselring, *Hawthorne's Reading, 1828–1850: A Transcription and Identification of Titles Recorded in the Charge-Books of the Salem Athenaeum* (1949; rpt. New York:
Haskell Books, 1975), p. 61, Hawthorne borrowed Smith's *Theory of Moral Sentiments*
from the Salem Athenaeum in 1827. My argument on connections between antebellum
sentimental culture and eighteenth-century notions of sympathy and sensibility is
indebted to June Howard, "What is Sentimentality?," *American Literary History* 11 (1999):
63–81. See also Julia Stern, *The Plight of Feeling: Sympathy and Dissent in the Early
American Novel* (Chicago: University of Chicago Press, 1997); Elizabeth Barnes, *States
of Sympathy: Seduction and Democracy in the American Novel* (New York: Columbia
University Press, 1997); and Julie Ellison, *Cato's Tears and the Making of Anglo-American
Emotion* (Chicago: University of Chicago Press, 1999).

and then form some idea of his sensations, and even feel something which, though weaker in degree, is not altogether unlike them.[3]

Now, Smith does go on to allow that these sentimental identifications are always imperfect and can be elicited as much by theatricalized as authentic suffering. But it is the promise of emotional communion that has led Jane Tompkins and many other critics to celebrate Stowe's sentimentalism for having stimulated antislavery action along humanitarian lines by creating in the reader (particularly the white middle-class female reader) a sense of commonality with the black slave—an emotional connection that was often gendered in terms of domestic ideals of motherhood and family.[4]

Some recent criticism on sentimentalism in Stowe and reform discourses of the 1850s, however, has emphasized the more problematical nature of that sympathetic identification. For Karen Sánchez-Eppler, social reform as practiced by white middle-class women, who lamented their own "enslavement" in patriarchal culture, was less about the suffering other than about the suffering self. As Marianne Noble trenchantly puts the case in *The Masochistic Pleasures of Sentimental Literature*:

> In the sentimental ideal . . . [o]ne does unto one's neighbor as unto oneself, because one's neighbor *is*, in a sense, oneself. But the physical gratification associated with that experience does not necessarily extend the observer outward to a communion with the sufferer; it may turn the observer inward, compensating with a self-satisfying *illusion* of humanitarian altruism that may well not be acted upon at all.

In response to Noble, Glenn Hendler defends Stowe by arguing that, however fragile the connections between subject and object may have been, sentimentalism worked in the nineteenth century to create fictions of "experiential equivalence" that resonated emotionally and prompted the cultural work of antislavery and other social reforms. Noble comes close to conceding that point, but ultimately regards what she terms "masochistic fantasies" of identification as

---

3. Adam Smith, *The Theory of Moral Sentiments*, ed. D. D. Raphael and A. L. Macfie (London: Oxford University Press, 1976), p. 9. For a useful discussion of the theatrical dynamics of Smith's notion of sympathy, see David Marshall, *The Surprising Effects of Sympathy: Marivaux, Diderot, Rousseau, and Mary Shelley* (Chicago: University of Chicago Press, 1988), esp. pp. 4–7.

4. See Jane Tompkins, *Sensational Designs: The Cultural Work of American Fiction, 1790–1860* (New York: Oxford University Press, 1985), ch. 5. On sentimentalism and reform, see also Shirley Samuels, "Introduction," in Samuels, ed., *The Culture of Sentiment: Race, Gender, and Sentimentality in Nineteenth-Century America* (New York: Oxford University Press, 1992); and Joanne Dobson, "Reclaiming Sentimental Literature," *American Literature* 69 (1997): 263–88.

"efforts to find power and wield it—with mixed benefits and mixed political ramifications."[5]

Drawing on what can be regarded as the dialectic enacted by the current critical debate on sympathy and reform in Stowe, I would agree with sympathy's advocates that it was precisely the illusory sense of becoming and understanding the other that gave such a rich emotional resonance to sentimental fictions of the time, and that those fictions probably did work to inspire some reform efforts. But I would also agree with sympathy's dissenters that the efforts of white middle-class readers to project themselves into the situations of others (by viewing the other through the lens of evangelical Christianity or the discourses that portrayed slaves in the middle-class terms of domestic culture as suffering mothers, fathers, sisters, brothers, daughters, sons, and so on) could sometimes work to elide differences between black and white, slave and free, rich and poor, and thus may have forestalled social reforms that would have truly attended to difference. In this respect, sentimentalism may have undermined readers' abilities to apprehend the other as truly other, encouraging readers instead to take stock in narcissistic fantasies of communion. Such identificatory fantasies, which are not all that different from Coverdale's modus operandi in *Blithedale*, ultimately work to uphold rather than break down distance and difference. Our recognition of the limits of Coverdale's sentimental efforts to make connections to others—the recognition, that is to say, that the other in *Blithedale* is to a certain extent a projection of Coverdale's self—points to the limits of Stowe's sentimental strategies as well.

The argument that I want to develop in this [essay], then, is that *Blithedale* is participating in the sentimental project of the 1850s of imagining the other in terms of the self, while at the same time developing a critique of that project. In crucial ways, *Blithedale* looks forward to, indeed anticipates, recent critiques of sentimental reformism by Noble and others. Though *Blithedale* does not address the debate on slavery, except implicitly in its portrayal of mesmerism as a form of enslaving patriarchal power, it does address a number of the central concerns of antebellum reform. Reading with and against the grain of Coverdale's scopic, narcissistic narrative, we confront the

5. Marianne Noble, *The Masochistic Pleasures of Sentimental Literature* (Princeton: Princeton University Press, 2000), p. 144; Glenn Hendler, "The Structure of Sentimental Experience," *Yale Journal of Criticism* 12 (1999): 147; Noble, "Response to the Responses," *Yale Journal of Criticism* 12 (1999): 167. (Hendler had responded to Noble's chapter on Stowe, "The Sentimental Ecstasies of Sentimental Wounding in *Uncle Tom's Cabin*," which was first printed in *Yale Journal of Criticism* 10 [1997]: 295–320.) Karen Sánchez-Eppler writes: "At stake in the feminists' likening of women to slaves is the recognition that personhood can be annihilated and a person owned, absorbed, and unnamed . . . The difficulty of preventing moments of identification from becoming acts of appropriation constitutes the essential dilemma of feminist-abolitionist rhetoric" (*Touching Liberty: Abolition, Feminism, and the Politics of the Body* [Berkeley: University of California Press, 1993], pp. 19–20).

problem of class inequalities and tensions, as we learn about and imagine Priscilla's and Moodie's personal histories, and of gender inequities, as we imagine Zenobia's resistant feminist perspective. But because Hawthorne does not give readers full access to those perspectives, he does not allow alterity to be short-circuited. Pushing the reader to imagine the other by resisting Coverdale's voyeuristic fantasies, Hawthorne, through Coverdale, pushes us as well to recognize that people have secret and individual histories, histories that could be very different from those imagined by privileged sympathizing reformers. Although recent commentators on *Blithedale* have been emphasizing the novel's satirical tone and conservative politics, I will be arguing that the overall novel presents us with a potentially promising reform culture consisting of myriad individuals with complex, hidden, and not so easily appropriated lives that all too often elude Coverdale's grasp. Moreover, there are suggestions that, despite his satirical aims, Coverdale may be covering up the very commitment to reform that he affirms at the opening of his narrative: "Whatever else I may repent of, therefore, let it be reckoned neither among my sins nor follies, that I once had faith and force enough to form generous hopes of the world's destiny" (III: 11).

Coverdale's declaration of his hopes and aspirations ought to be taken seriously, for it speaks to Hawthorne's own attraction to the possibilities of reform. Though Hawthorne in an 1835 notebook entry compared the "modern reformer" to an escaped lunatic, he nevertheless chose to join the socialistic Brook Farm community in West Roxbury, Massachusetts, for seven months in 1841 (VIII: 10). Founded by a group of Transcendentalist reformers who would become increasingly swayed by the socialistic theories of the French political theorist Charles Fourier, Brook Farm was one of a number of fairly vital communitarian groups in antebellum America during the 1840s that hoped to restructure social and economic relationships. (The group disbanded in 1846 after a fire destroyed its buildings.) Hawthorne's motivation for participating in the project is not completely clear. His letters from Brook Farm to his future wife, Sophia Peabody, suggest that he may have joined the community with the hope that it would provide him with the quiet and repose of a writers' community; hence his subsequent disillusionment with the "drudgery" of the "manual labor" that was required of him.[6] But

6. Hawthorne to David Mack, letter of 18 July 1841, in *Letters*, XV: 552. As he wrote Sophia Peabody from Brook Farm on 1 June 1841: "It is my opinion, dearest, that a man's soul may be buried and perish under a dung-heap or in a furrow of the field, just as well as under a pile of money" (XV: 545). For background on Brook Farm, see Henry W. Sams, ed., *Autobiography of Brook Farm* (Englewood Cliffs, NJ: Prentice-Hall, 1958); Richard Francis, "The Ideology of Brook Farm," in *Studies in the American Renaissance* (Boston: Twayne, 1977); Joel Myerson, ed., *The Brook Farm Book: A Collection of First-Hand Accounts of the Community* (New York: Garland Publishing, Inc., 1987); and the materials in the Bedford Cultural Edition of Nathaniel Hawthorne, *The Blithedale Romance*, ed. William E. Cain (Boston: Bedford Books, 1996).

given his short-term commitment to the community, one imagines that he was not entirely cynical about the possibility that the Brook Farmers, by posing a challenge to the competitive practices of market culture, could help to make New England into a better place. In his Preface to *Blithedale*, Hawthorne for the most part affirms his earlier commitment to Brook Farm, remarking that he had "the good fortune, for a time, to be personally connected" (III: 1) with the communitarians, and that he regards his participation as "the most romantic episode of his own life" (III: 2). To be sure, Hawthorne is notoriously unreliable in his prefaces, regularly insisting as a romancer on his fiction's disconnection from the "reality" (III: 2) that he nonetheless invokes. But perhaps we should take at face value his generally positive statements about his participation in Brook Farm, and his statement as well that in writing about the associative community he does not wish to "put forward the slightest pretensions to illustrate a theory, or elicit a conclusion, favorable or otherwise, in respect to Socialism" (III: 2). Rather than praise or damn the reform impulse, Hawthorne in his retrospective *Blithedale* reveals his conflicted attitudes toward the aspirations that he himself had once embraced.[7]

And yet satire and skepticism, at first glance, would appear to outweigh any sort of commitment to reform. According to Coverdale, the participants at Blithedale tend to be self-important, elitist, and just plain selfish, generally regarding those outside the community from "a position of new hostility, rather than new brotherhood" (III: 20). Despite his recurrent gestures of solidarity, Coverdale takes pains to suggest that hostility, rather than fellow-feeling (or sympathetic communion), governs the actions of virtually all of the reformers in the book: Hollingsworth seeks to undermine the Blithedale community so that he might gain the community's land for his prison-reform project; the feminist reformer Zenobia, partly modeled on Margaret Fuller (and perhaps Hawthorne's sister-in-law Elizabeth Peabody), seems in search of the limelight and a man, and throughout seems hostile to the one woman (Priscilla) who yearns for sympathy from her feminist sister; Westervelt, while talking of universal reform, seems little more than a patriarchal enslaving master. Though the Blithedale community embraces gender reforms, women continue to do the cooking and men the physical labor, and Coverdale (and

---

7. Similar conflicts inform Hawthorne's presentation of reform in "The Hall of Fantasy" (1843), a sketch written shortly after his experience at Brook Farm. Though the sketch satirizes reformism as a narcissistic fantasy that, like the edifice of the Hall of Fantasy, "give[s] the impression of a dream, which might be dissipated and shattered to fragments, by merely stamping the foot upon the pavement," central to the complexity and power of the sketch is the narrator's admiration for the idealism, energy, and commitment of actual social reformers: "I love and honor such men" (*Hawthorne: Tales and Sketches*, ed. Roy Harvey Pearce [New York: Library of America, 1982], pp. 734, 740).

Westervelt) strongly suggest that Zenobia commits suicide out of her frustrated love for Hollingsworth (whereas Fuller in *Woman in the Nineteenth Century* [1845] had mocked the idea that women live only for the love of a man).

Hawthorne's representation of spiritualism and mesmerism further contributes to the apparently skeptical portrayal of reform at Blithedale farm. Whereas some Americans of the 1840s and 1850s regarded mesmerism—a species of hypnotism—as a reformatory science potentially bringing individuals and nature into a state of perfect harmony, Hawthorne presents it, particularly through Westervelt's and Hollingsworth's manipulations of Priscilla and Zenobia, as the selfish enactment of hyperintrusive patriarchal power. (Hawthorne's anxieties about the invasive, controlling aspects of mesmerism had important sources in his concerns about Sophia's use of a mesmerist to treat her recurrent headaches, and inform as well his depiction of Matthew Maule's cruel domination of Alice Pyncheon in *The House of the Seven Gables*.[8]) Similarly, while some Americans regarded the 1848 "spirit-rappings" of the adolescent Fox sisters of Rochester, New York, as a sign that spiritualism as a social reform could help to link the visible and invisible worlds, in *Blithedale* Hawthorne analogizes Westervelt's decadent spiritualistic (and mesmerical) practices, which link mediums in "one great, mutually conscious brotherhood" (III: 200), to the communitarian practices at Blithedale, which link reformers in a "general brain" (III: 140)—with the large intention of suggesting both groups' propensities toward anarchic revolutionism. This is especially clear near the end of the novel when the scene shifts from Westervelt's lyceum display to the festive masquerade at Blithedale, where the communitarians, as Coverdale describes them from his hiding place in the hermitage, whirled "round so swiftly, so madly, and so merrily, in time and tune with the Satanic music, that their separate incongruities were blended all together" (III: 210). In his imaging of communitarianism and spiritualism as forms of demonic revolutionism, Hawthorne would seem to be in the same reactionary camp as the Roman Catholic convert Orestes Brownson, whose novel *The Spirit-Rapper* (1854) portrayed spiritualism as Satan's invisible tool for bringing forth the French Revolution, the European Revolution of the 1840s, and the emerging women's rights

8. See Hawthorne to Sophia Peabody, letter of 18 October 1841, *Letters*, xv: 588–91. On Hawthorne and mesmerism, see Maria M. Tatar, *Spellbound: Studies on Mesmerism and Literature* (Princeton, NJ: Princeton University Press, 1978), pp. 189–229; Taylor Stoehr, *Hawthorne's Mad Scientists: Pseudoscience and Social Science in Nineteenth-Century Life and Letters* (Hamdon, CT: Archon Books, 1978); and Samuel Chase Coale, *Mesmerism and Hawthorne: Mediums of American Romance* (Tuscaloosa: University of Alabama Press, 1998).

movement. In addition to satirizing women's rights, spiritualism, mesmerism, and communitarianism, Coverdale (or Hawthorne) over the course of the novel also suggests the limits of other key social reforms of the period, such as temperance and prison reform.[9]

But *Blithedale* is more than a merely satirical (or reactionary) novel, in large part because of Hawthorne's use of the first-person narrator Coverdale to enact both a suspicion of and desire for reform. As presented in the novel, Coverdale is simultaneously an insider and an outsider, a fully energetic participant and a more ironic retrospective narrator, a character who, leading an aimlessly drifting life in the anomic city, deeply desires the structure, the community, and perhaps even the reforms offered by Blithedale.[1] He is a narrator, too, whose sexual anxieties and insecurities, and chronic cynicism, make him an unreliable critic of reform, particularly given that, as he confesses at the end of the novel, "I exaggerate my own defects" (III: 247). (One of his exaggerated "defects," of course, is his chronic cynicism.) The novel, to a large extent, is a study in desire and anxiety, as the voyeuristic Coverdale, simultaneously attracted to and frightened by Zenobia's sexuality, Hollingsworth's patriarchal fixedness of purpose, and, indeed, the carnivalesque energies of the festive Blithedalers, weaves melodramatic tales of flight and entrapment suggestive of his own wavering desires. One way of reading Coverdale's exaggeratedly self-critical confessional narrative, then, is to regard it as his somewhat coy and embarrassed effort at reading himself as a reformer. In this respect, the novel both puts on display and attempts to cover up the emotional life of a sentimental man.[2]

With its emphasis on tropes of interiority, Coverdale's confessional narrative can be taken as an extended representation of the problem of sympathy in sentimental culture. Very specifically, the novel foregrounds in the workings of Coverdale's first-person narrative what Christopher Castiglia has identified as one of the obsessive concerns of antebellum reform culture: "the middle-class subject engaged in

9. On antebellum reform and the novel, see my "Fiction and Reform 1," in Emory Elliott *et al.*, eds., *The Columbia History of the American Novel: New Views* (New York: Columbia University Press, 1991), pp. 130–54. My discussion of *Blithedale* and reform draws on several paragraphs in that chapter. See also Ronald G. Walters, *American Reformers, 1815–1860* (New York: Hill and Wang, 1978).

1. For a reading of Coverdale's insider/outsider narrative strategies in the context of antebellum nativism, see my *Conspiracy and Romance: Studies in Brockden Brown, Cooper, Hawthorne, and Melville* (New York: Cambridge University Press, 1989), ch. 3.

2. On male sentimentalism, see Mary Chapman and Glenn Hendler, eds., *Sentimental Men: Masculinity and the Politics of Affect in American Culture* (Berkeley: University of California Press, 1999).

the act of reform."[3] That focus makes *Blithedale* as profoundly *about* reform as any reformist novel of the period, even as the matter of Blithedale's specific reform mission is often occluded by Coverdale's tendencies toward a voyeuristic self-reflection. In *Blithedale*, Coverdale affirms his identity as a sentimental reformer by repeatedly reflecting on his efforts to sympathize with others. Because of the apparently selfish and narcissistic form that Coverdale's efforts take, the problem of sympathy remains at the thematic center of the novel—or perhaps it would be more precise to say that sympathy remains the central problem of Coverdale's narrative, given how little his sympathetic imaginings would appear to accomplish.

Consider the opening of the novel, which for the most part can be taken as a study of the failure of sympathy. On the day before heading off to Blithedale farm, Coverdale attends the public performance of the Veiled Lady. Watching her from a distance with the other male spectators, he describes himself as "wrought up by the enigma of her identity" (III: 6), but he remains content to regard the display as mere entertainment. As we soon learn, however, the Veiled Lady (Priscilla) could have used the help of a rescuer. Shortly after the performance, Coverdale is beseeched by the downtrodden Moodie, who would like him to be that rescuer, and Coverdale fends him off with a show of sympathy so false ("But it is late! Will you tell me what I can do for you?" [III: 8]) as to prompt Moodie to turn to Hollingsworth for help. Coverdale continues to express sympathy while holding himself apart in his account of his next day's journey to Blithedale farm, in which he both expresses his allegiance to the communitarians while pointing to their (and his) distance from the villagers whose interests they claim to be advancing. Encountering a traveler who refuses to return their friendly greeting, Coverdale laments with megalomaniacal flair: "This lack of faith in our cordial sympathy, on the traveller's part, was one among the innumerable tokens how difficult a task we had in hand, for the reformation of the world" (III: 12). As an insider, Coverdale betrays no sympathy for those who fail to appreciate the Blithedalers' beneficent designs.

Coverdale's feelings about reform and sympathy remain at the center of the narrative with the arrival of Hollingsworth and Priscilla. How should he respond to the sad situation of the newly arrived Priscilla? At first he feels some sympathy for her plight, but upon reflection, he exhibits a proto-Oscar Wildean amusement at such bathetic sufferings, confiding to the reader "that I could not help smiling at this odd scene of unknown and unaccountable calamity"

3. Christopher Castiglia, "Abolition's Racial Interiors and the Making of White Civic Depth," *American Literary History* 14 (2002): 37.

(III: 29). Subsequently, while being nursed by Hollingsworth during his illness, Coverdale reflects on the male tendency, which he had exhibited in relation to Priscilla, *not* to be able to sympathize. "Most men," he claims, "have a natural indifference, if not an absolutely hostile feeling, towards those whom disease, or weakness, or calamity of any kind, causes to faulter and faint amid the rude jostle of our selfish existence," though he suggests that "the sympathy of a like experience, and the example of women, may soften, and possibly subvert, this ugly characteristic of our sex" (III: 41). Despite his initial hard-headed (ostensibly male) inability to sympathize with Priscilla, Coverdale quickly distances himself from such conventional notions of sympathy, regularly insisting on his ability to cross the traditionally gendered lines of affect. And he suggests that the same is potentially true for Hollingsworth, whom he states has "something of the woman moulded into [his] great stalwart frame" (III: 42).

Coverdale's meditation on the prison reformer's sympathies and womanly qualities can thus be regarded as a displaced meditation on his own relation to sympathy and reform. The large question on his mind is whether Hollingsworth's reformist desires will reveal him to be the sort of sentimental man Coverdale imagines himself to be, and for the most part his answer is no. Hollingsworth, Coverdale asserts, joined the Blithedalers "actuated by no real sympathy with our feelings and our hopes" (III: 54–55). (Note the implication here that Coverdale *was* actuated by real sympathy for the Blithedalers' feelings and hopes.) He refers to Hollingsworth's "divine power of sympathy" (III: 55) when tending to Priscilla, and Coverdale himself is privy to that same apparent sympathy when he is convalescing from his illness. But he soon comes to regard Hollingsworth's "more than brotherly attendance" (III: 41) at his sickbed as motivated less by sympathy than by his efforts to gain converts to his prison-reform cause. Regarding himself, Priscilla, and Zenobia as all the potential victims of Hollingsworth's false sympathy, he presents him as typical of certain types of reformers who, rather than using their imaginations to build connections between themselves and others, try to take in others as part of their imperial project. As he bluntly remarks on the philanthropist as a moral and social type: "They have no heart, no sympathy, no reason, no conscience" (III: 70).

And yet Coverdale admires Hollingsworth as a leader with whom he would like to share a common cause. He also experiences an extraordinary attraction to the charismatic philanthropist: "I loved Hollingsworth, as has already been enough expressed" (III: 70). The homoerotic subtext of Coverdale's attraction to Hollingsworth is consistent with the portrayal of unconventional Blithedale as a site of erotic freedom, which "seemed to authorize an individual, of either sex, to fall in love with any other, regardless of what would elsewhere be judged suitable and prudent" (III: 72).[4] But during the key scene at Eliot's Pulpit, Coverdale attempts to differentiate himself from Hollingsworth and reinstate the heteronormative by invoking traditional notions of the gendered quality of sympathy. Coverdale portrays himself to Priscilla and Zenobia as a sentimental man who would gladly allow himself to be guided by women, while Hollingsworth, John Eliot redux in his desire to gain converts, is depicted as so manly, so in the tradition of the New England Pilgrims whom the Blithedalers regard as their holy progenitors, as to be untouched by sympathy (or the womanly). Declaiming from Eliot's Pulpit, Hollingsworth states that woman's principal role is to follow male leaders as sympathizers: "Her place is at man's side. Her office, that of the Sympathizer" (III: 122). And he asserts that he would use force to keep women in their assigned place—thereby making sympathy into little more than the handmaiden to patriarchy. Presenting Zenobia as offering a tortured consent to Hollingsworth's proposition through her surreptitious pressing of his hand to her bosom, Coverdale uses the scene, in part, to deflate Zenobia's feminism by revealing her inability to transcend the personal. He also anticipates the presentation of his own personal crisis with Hollingsworth and the Blithedale community by depicting the drooping Priscilla, woman as unthinking sympathizer, as under thrall not only to Westervelt but also to Hollingsworth.

Given Coverdale's sense of himself as a womanly sympathizer, or male sentimentalist, he realizes that there are disturbing similarities between his and Priscilla's attraction to Hollingsworth. Like Priscilla, he desires to be the sort of sympathizer that Hollingsworth describes: free of ego, a true believer. Hollingsworth appeals to those very desires shortly after his speech at Eliot's Pulpit, approaching Coverdale in private and promising to reinvest the life of the drifter with what he has all along been seeking, "a purpose in life, worthy of the extremest self-devotion—worthy of martyrdom, should God so order it!" (III: 133). His hands outstretched, his eyes welling with tears, Hollingsworth beseeches in Christ-like fashion: "Coverdale . . . there is not the man in this wide world, whom I can love as I could you. Do not forsake me!" (III: 133). Seemingly a Veiled Lady on the verge of entering the trance state, Coverdale makes the monumental effort and wills a response to the mesmerical philanthropist's direct demand for an unquestioning sympathizer: "No!" (III: 135). Subsequently

---

4. On the novel's sexual politics, see Lauren Berlant, "Fantasies of Utopia in *The Blithedale Romance*," *American Literary History* 1 (1989): 30–62; and Benjamin Scott Grossberg, "'The Tender Passion Was Very Rife Among Us': Queer Utopia and *The Blithedale Romance*," *Studies in American Fiction* 28 (2000): 3–25. See also Barbara F. Lefcowitz and Allan B. Lefcowitz's still provocative "Some Rents in the Veil: New Light on Priscilla and Zenobia," *Nineteenth-Century Fiction* 21 (1966): 263–75.

feeling "an absolute torture of the breast" (III: 135), he soon after takes leave of Blithedale, returning to the city as an outsider.

In Adam Smith's model of sympathy, as Castiglia explains, "self-transformation lies with the person who extends sympathy," the person who interiorizes the other. But such self-transformation risks becoming "the basis of differential power: the sympathizer extends agency over the sufferer, while the latter controls only him or herself."[5] In the crucial scenes with Hollingsworth that precipitate his flight to the city, Coverdale presents himself as the sufferer, the possible victim of a sympathetic relation that would rob him of his selfhood. In contrast, he presents his own efforts at sympathy as existing apart from power. Perched aloft in his hermitage while watching Westervelt with the despairing Zenobia, for example, he had compared himself to "the Chorus in a classic play" governed by a deep concern for others in which "sympathy is the only bond" (III: 97). But is sympathy a "bond" or a form of bondage? That is the question begged by Coverdale's relationship with Zenobia, which from beginning to end is defined by acts of viewing, performance, and interiorization that make it difficult to say who controls whom.

In the depiction of the mesmerical power that Westervelt wields over Priscilla and Zenobia, and of Hollingsworth's assumption of analogous forms of power over the two women, Hawthorne shows an acute awareness of how the male gaze can keep women in literal and metaphorical forms of bondage. As the voyeuristic pursuer of secrets, Coverdale participates as well in the novel's depiction of what Lori Merish calls "the gendered disequilibrium in social power that structures relations of vision."[6] But things are not quite so asymmetrical in the specific relationship between Coverdale and Zenobia. Coverdale obsesses on Zenobia's bare shoulder, hot-house flower, and sensual body, but his looking is often elicited by Zenobia's deliberate design. Her artful ability to display her body and theatricalize her sufferings allows her to retain more than a modicum of control over Coverdale, who never has access to her private imagination and history. Regarding Zenobia from his sickbed as "womanliness incarnated" (III: 44), he concludes that she lacks the virginal innocence that he demands of True Womanhood: "There is no folded petal, no latent dew-drop, in this perfectly developed rose" (III: 47). But even as he meditates on her supposed lack of innocence, he feels himself to be a kind of Veiled Lady, a "mesmerical clairvoyant" (III: 47), with the suggestion, then, that

5. Castiglia, "Abolition's Racial Interiors," p. 39.
6. Merish, *Sentimental Materialism*, p. 172. See also Gillian Brown, *Domestic Individualism: Imagining Self in Nineteenth-Century America* (Berkeley: University of California Press, 1990), ch. 4.

Zenobia is to him as, say, Westervelt is to Priscilla—the dominant subject who has cast her spell on the hapless innocent (Coverdale), who knows next to nothing of her sexual past or present circumstances. He nonetheless persists in attempting to make her the object of his sympathy, even as she challenges him to sympathize not by "becoming" her through scopic appropriation but by listening to her story. She tells part of that story in her utterance of "a helpless sort of moan" (III: 104) that Coverdale apprehends while watching her from his hermitage as she interacts with Westervelt, and that moan does have an impact on him, "affect[ing] me more than if she had made the wood dolorously vocal with a thousand shrieks and wails" (III: 104). She tells her story a second time in her legend of "The Silvery Veil," which is usually read as an allegory of Coverdale's failure to help Priscilla but is also Zenobia's own story of her painful temptation to betray her sister to a patriarchal master, whether Westervelt or Hollingsworth. Even here, though, she chooses to theatricalize her confession rather than make herself vulnerable to Coverdale's sympathetic embrace.

Tensions between Coverdale's violating sympathetic imagination and Zenobia's theatricalized resistance culminate in a confrontation in the city that stages a debate on sympathy in terms straight out of Adam Smith. Attempting to peer through the window of Zenobia's drawing-room, where she, Priscilla, and Westervelt are gathered, Coverdale affirms his

> quality of the intellect and the heart, which impelled me (often against my own will, and to the detriment of my own comfort) to live in other lives, and to endeavor—by generous sympathies, by delicate intuitions, by taking note of things too slight for record, and by bringing my human spirit into manifold accordance with the companions whom God assigned me—to learn the secret which was hidden even from themselves.   (III: 160)

In Stowe-like fashion, he conceives of his spying in providential terms; God assigned him to his task of doing good. But when this self-celebrating sentimentalist confronts Zenobia to express his beneficent wish to bring his spirit into accord with her own, the other talks back, denouncing his "indefatigable human sympathy" (III: 163) as little more than a grotesque projection of his ego:

> I know precisely what it signifies. Bigotry; self-conceit; an insolent curiosity; a meddlesome temper; a cold-blooded criticism, founded on a shallow interpretation of half-perceptions; a monstrous skepticism in regard to any conscience or any wisdom, except one's own; a most irreverent propensity to thrust

> Providence aside, and substitute one's self in its awful place—
> out of these, and other motives as miserable as these, comes
> your idea of duty! (III: 170)

This exchange enacts the dialectic of sympathy informing the novel,
though Zenobia's complaints about the egotistical limits of Coverdale's
imperial fantasies of communion seem mostly on the mark. Coverdale's
efforts at sympathy, at least with respect to Zenobia, are very much
grounded in (and undone by) his private confusions about identity, sexuality, gender, and desire.

The one moment in which Coverdale does manage to make a
connection through sentimental identification occurs in a tavern
with another man, Moodie, which may seem odd given that the
book begins with Coverdale fending off Moodie. But it is Moodie
as much as any of the other characters who interests Coverdale,
arguably because Coverdale shares more with Moodie than he
would like to allow. Both men are drinkers and drifters in search of
fraternal community, and in drinking, as Hawthorne's punning
suggests, these topers share in a form of utopian desire. Coverdale
earlier had mentioned his effort to view the world through
Moodie's eyes—"I tried to identify my mind with the old fellow's,
and take his view of the world" (III: 84)—and at the tavern he is
able to achieve this sympathetic identification. Guided, he says, by
"a sort of sympathetic impulse that often controlled me" (III: 179),
Coverdale plies Moodie with wine, and he does so in secret sympathy as he marvels at the alcohol's ability to make toper into
utopian. During the time that they drink together, they both
experience camaraderie and regeneration, "the renewed youth
and vigor, the brisk, cheerful sense of things present and to come"
(III: 178). Whether at tavern or at Blithedale, communitarian
inebriation induces regenerative "associations" (III: 181) possessing "an indescribable, ideal charm" (III: 176).

These particular "associations"—Moodie-Fauntleroy's tale of his
two fragmented families and economic fall—allow the sympatheti-
cally responsive Coverdale both to fill in details of the family plot
and to heighten the sentimental contrast between Priscilla and
Zenobia. The offspring of Moodie's superficial first marriage to a
wealthy beauty, Zenobia is regarded by Moodie as just "another
jewel" (III: 182). After perpetrating a secret economic crime in an
attempt to preserve his dwindling wealth, Moodie retreats to the
cramped Irish quarters of a colonial governor's degenerated mansion, marries a feeble seamstress, and fathers feeble Priscilla,
whose renowned spiritualistic gifts eventually attract the attention
of the spiritualist Westervelt. While Zenobia grows to adulthood
amidst great wealth, Priscilla "was enthralled in an intolerable

bondage, from which she must either free herself or perish" (III: 190). Underscoring the contrast between Zenobia's power and Priscilla's vulnerability, Coverdale appends to Moodie's history a sketch of a meeting between Zenobia and Moodie, drawn, Coverdale confesses, "mainly from fancy, although with some general grounds of surmise in regard to the old man's feelings" (III: 190). As Coverdale imagines the scene with respect to Moodie's "feelings," Moodie beholds the bejeweled Zenobia, asks the puzzled heiress to treat Priscilla kindly as a sister, and upon her departure, shouts in his lonely chamber: "Zenobia take heed! Priscilla shall have no wrong!" (III: 193). Linking this imagined scene to the unfolding narrative of Priscilla's entrapment, Coverdale suggests that Zenobia may well have betrayed her familial trust: "that very evening, so far as I can adjust the dates of these strange incidents—Priscilla—poor, pallid flower—was either snatched from Zenobia's hand, or flung wilfully away!" (III: 193).

As the adoption of Moodie's point of view makes clear, the account of Moodie's precipitous loss of financial and familial stability quite unexpectedly makes an impact on Coverdale, who in his own way had been adrift in the democratic marketplace before finding temporary sanctuary at Blithedale. While with Moodie, Coverdale, almost against his will, experiences his strongest sense of fraternity in the romance. His intuition of his kinship with the broken Moodie staggers him: "Well! I betook myself away, and wandered up and down, like an exorcised spirit that had been driven from its old haunts, after a mighty struggle" (III: 194). In his responsiveness to Moodie, which derives from a rather moving moment of imaginative communion, he seems to realize why he had thrown in his lot with the communitarians in the first place, and he subsequently privately reaffirms his connections to Priscilla, Zenobia, and Hollingsworth. Even so, only a fortuitous meeting at the lyceum hall performance of the Veiled Lady recalls Coverdale to the vortex of community, and he once again prefers to watch.

In choosing to watch, Coverdale joins the crowd—the restless, bored New Englanders whose distance from the other (the Veiled Lady) points to the failure of sympathy in antebellum culture.[7] The crowd's "straining eyes" (III: 201) take in the scene, but there is no human connection to the mesmerized Veiled Lady, just the demand that the spiritualist Westervelt provide his paying customers with

---

7. For a reading of the public entertainment of the Veiled Lady in the context of the increasingly privatized nature of domestic life, see Richard H. Brodhead, *Culture of Letters: Scenes of Reading and Writing in Nineteenth-Century America* (Chicago: University of Chicago Press, 1993), ch. 2.

entertainment. To some extent, then, the scene replays Coverdale's viewing of the Veiled Lady in the opening chapter. As in that earlier chapter, Westervelt attempts to spiritualize the entertainment, presenting the display not just as an occasion for the predominately male eyes to gaze upon a spectacular female body, but as a reformist fulfillment of desires for communion between self and other with millennialist implications. Priscilla, he claims, "is, at this moment, in communion with the spiritual world" (III: 201), and that world, he predicts, shall soon be available to the masses: "He spoke of a new era that was dawning upon the world; an era that would link soul to soul, and the present life to what we call futurity, with a closeness that should finally convert both worlds into one great, mutually conscious brotherhood" (III: 200). That image of a utopian, spiritualistically linked brotherhood echoes Coverdale's more critical view of the Blithedalers as linked through "a species of nervous sympathy," so that "[i]f one of us happened to give his neighbor a box on the ear, the tingle was immediately felt, on the same side of everybody's head" (III: 139). Presenting sympathy and reformism as equivalent to a decadent spiritualism, Coverdale manages to undercut Hollingsworth's "rescue" of Priscilla by suggesting that the philanthropist's desire for a sympathizer does not greatly differ from the depraved Westervelt's desire for a medium. From his position as a watcher who claims to sympathize with Priscilla's plight, Coverdale rather meanspiritedly suggests that whether on stage or at Eliot's Pulpit, Hollingsworth seeks to keep his own medium within her "proper bounds."

For all of his protestations of sympathy, however, Coverdale never seems to connect with anybody for very long, or to find a way of moving from sympathy to some sort of action along the lines of Hollingsworth's bold move at the lyceum. But perhaps that is the whole point of sympathy: to feel good about one's virtuous sympathetic imagination while realizing that nothing much can be done for the other beyond simply proffering sympathy. In *The Theory of Moral Sentiments*, Adam Smith suggests as much, proclaiming that sympathy generally cannot significantly help "those who have suffered," precisely because they *are* other, and sympathy "is always extremely imperfect." And not only does sympathy usually prove not to be terribly efficacious for those in need, but according to Smith, the failure of sympathy only adds to the emotional pain of the sentimentalist, who is already "burdened" by an imaginative conception of the sufferings of the object of his or her gaze: "That our sympathy can afford them no consolation seems to be an addition to their calamity; and to think that all we can do is unavailing, and that, what alleviates all other distress, the regret, the love, and the lamentations of their friends, can yield no comfort to them,

serves only to exasperate our sense of their misery."[8] That exasperation becomes the very mark, indeed the redemptive cross (as it
were), of the virtuous sympathizer.

Coverdale's own virtuous exasperation is precisely what is acti-
vated and displayed in his final exchange with Zenobia, which
occurs soon after he returns to Blithedale farm. Apparently dis-
tressed that her imminent loss of Moodie's wealth has motivated
Hollingsworth to jettison her in favor of Priscilla, she is a character
in need of sympathy. Though Coverdale views Zenobia in very conventional terms as a jilted woman, he rises to the occasion, doing his
best to summon a sympathetic response to her sufferings (no matter
that he lacks full access to what those sufferings might be). Convinced of his heartfelt understanding of her "tearless agony" (III:
222), Coverdale rhetorically asks his readers: "Was it wrong, therefore, if I felt myself consecrated to the priest-hood by sympathy like
this, and called upon to minister to this woman's affliction, so far as
mortal could?" (III: 222). Zenobia implies that the answer is yes,
because she regards Coverdale as narcissistically imprisoned in his
imagination and blind to her sufferings. She ironically states that
"you have really a heart and sympathies, as far as they go" (III: 226),
and then mocks the man who aspires to be her priestly confessor by
mocking his metaphors, declaring her intention of taking on a veil
and "going into a nunnery" (III: 227). In response, Coverdale pro-
fesses himself exhausted by his virtuous emotional interactions,
"worn-out with emotion on my behalf, and sympathy for others"
(III: 228). The implication of the syntax here, as throughout the
novel, is that Coverdale's "sympathy for others" is primarily based on
and advances only "emotion on my behalf"—which is why he is the
model sentimentalist.

But is the model sentimentalist the model reformer? On the basis
of Coverdale's own self-representation in his confessional narrative,
the answer would appear to be no, for it is clear to most readers that
Coverdale is a self-celebrating and for the most part deluded voyeur
whose efforts as reformer and sympathizer remain ineffective. But
here is where things get tricky. Coverdale clearly knows this about
himself, and seems to take a perverse pleasure in exaggerating his
defects. Those exaggerations, which regularly depict Coverdale as
an uncomprehending prig, are central to *Blithedale*'s humor. It
could be argued, then, that if we were to evaluate Coverdale in completely negative terms with respect to sympathy and reform, we
would be missing the joke, falling into the trap of a narrative that

8. Smith, *The Theory of Moral Sentiments*, pp. 13, 11, 13.

seems calculated to elicit from readers a self-congratulatory, self-righteous outrage.[9]

We need to move beyond such outrage. I would suggest that Coverdale's retrospective (anti)sentimental narrative is comically informed by his acute awareness of his limitations as a reformer (even as he clings to desires for reform) and as a sympathizer (even as he desires closer and more efficacious connections to others). Viewed in this way, his confessional narrative can be read as both an implicit critique of the limits of sympathy in the sentimental reform culture of the 1850s and as a provocation to readers who resist the terms of his deliberately limited confessional narrative (that is, the majority of readers) to consider alternative models of sympathy and reform.

Certainly there are characters in the novel who adopt different, less imperial perspectives on sympathy and reform, most notably Zenobia, whose feminist reform vision survives as an embodied perspective that ultimately resists appropriation by either Coverdale or Hollingsworth. Theatrical to the very end, Zenobia masks her inner self and desires, even as she calls attention to how difficult it is for women to challenge the assumptions of patriarchal culture. Any attempt to imagine Zenobia's point of view apart from Coverdale's would lead readers toward a radical critique of the patriarchal authority assumed by the mesmerical Westervelt and Hollingsworth, and by Coverdale's gaze.[1] Such a critique would have the potential of encouraging readers to think more seriously about the kinds of structural changes that would be needed to enhance women's power and possibilities in the culture. Though Priscilla and Moodie are hardly radicals, efforts to imagine their situations apart from Coverdale's appropriations would likewise encourage thinking about the need for economic reforms that would address the problem of urban poverty, which is precisely one of the aims of the Blithedale community (and of Brook Farm).

---

9. See, for example, David Leverenz's lively (but self-righteous) recoil from Coverdale in *Manhood and the American Renaissance* (Ithaca: Cornell University Press, 1989), pp. 247–58. For a useful discussion of Hawthorne's deliberate efforts to alienate his readers from Coverdale, see E. Shaskan Bumas, "Fictions of the Panopticon: Prison, Utopia, and the Out-Penitent in the Works of Nathaniel Hawthorne," *American Literature* 73 (2001): 121–45. See also Jonathan Auerbach, *The Romance of Failure: First-Person Fictions of Poe, Hawthorne, and James* (New York: Oxford University Press, 1989), ch. 2; and Dana Brand, *The Spectator and the City in Nineteenth-Century American Literature* (New York: Cambridge University Press, 1991), ch. 7.

1. See, for example, Mary Suzanne Schriber, "Justice to Zenobia," *New England Quarterly* 55 (1982): 61–78; Beverly Hume, "Restructuring the Case Against Coverdale," *Nineteenth-Century Fiction* 40 (1986): 387–99; Leland S. Person, Jr., *Aesthetic Headaches: Women and a Masculine Poetics in Poe, Melville, and Hawthorne* (Athens: University of Georgia Press, 1988), pp. 146–60; and Joel Pfister, *The Production of Personal Life: Class, Gender, and the Psychological in Hawthorne's Fiction* (Stanford, CA: Stanford University Press, 1991), ch. 3.

Hawthorne does give us at least one character capable of a non-appropriative form of sympathy, and that is the working-class farmer Silas Foster. In a provocative discussion of *Blithedale*, Russ Castronovo presents Foster as a "radical democrat" who "acknowledges contingency" and recognizes the specificity, the *otherness*, of embodiment and materiality.[2] It is Foster who realizes that Priscilla needs food and sustenance, while Coverdale contents himself to fantasize about her origins and desires, and it is Foster who voices what could be taken as the most sincere (and non-interiorizing) moment of sympathy in the novel. This occurs when he helps to retrieve Zenobia's dead body from the pond. Here is Coverdale's account of all that Foster has to say upon laying her body out on shore: "'Poor child!' said Foster—and his dry old heart, I verily believe, vouchsafed a tear—'I'm sorry for her!'" (III: 235). The simplicity of his statement and tear provide an attractive alternative to the other forms of sympathy depicted in the book. While Westervelt scornfully comments on Zenobia's "heart" (III: 240), and Coverdale works at making her into a feminist manqué, Foster as a male sentimentalist recognizes her pain while not claiming to feel her pain. In this respect, despite his sometimes brash masculinity, he can be linked with the tire-women, who quietly take Zenobia's body away from the gaze of Coverdale and Hollingsworth.

Arguably, Foster provides Coverdale himself with a model of sympathy that holds out the promise of making him a better reformer, an aim that he suggests he has in the final chapter. Though Coverdale jokingly reflects on the limits of his social reformist energies, proclaiming that he would join hands with Hungarian revolutionaries if the revolution were brought "within an easy ride of my abode" (III: 247), he asserts just before his melodramatic and pointless confession of his love for Priscilla that the reader must not "believe me altogether changed from the young man, who once hoped strenuously, and struggled, not so much amiss" (III: 247). We should take this statement of his reformism seriously, because in important ways Coverdale has learned how to sympathize in the manner of Silas Foster. He displays that less appropriative form of sympathy in his final encounter with Hollingsworth. Journeying to visit Hollingsworth and Priscilla a number of years after the death of Zenobia and the failure of Blithedale, Coverdale confronts a reformer who is intent on self-reform. In response to Coverdale's cutting question of "how many criminals have you reformed?" (III: 243), Hollingsworth says, "Not one! . . . Ever since we parted, I have been busy with a single murderer!" (III: 243). Coverdale's reaction is

2. Russ Castronovo, *Necro Citizenship: Death, Eroticism, and the Public Sphere in the Nineteenth-Century United States* (Durham, NC: Duke University Press, 2001), p. 142.

both moving and confused: "Then the tears gushed into my eyes, and I forgave him" (III: 243). The spontaneity of the tears suggests a non-violative form of sympathy that is honest and potentially productive. The confusion lies in the question of who should be forgiving whom.

In light of this closing image of tears and retreat, we might ask, then, where is social reform at the end of the novel? For many readers, it is dead in the water, an impossibility in a world of decadent spectacle, materialism, and selfishness. Gordon Hutner states that Coverdale's "beleaguered first-person narrative replicates the very disintegration of self which reformist movements mean to correct but which ultimately, for Hawthorne, exhibits their failure"; Richard Millington remarks on the novel's depiction of the "emptiness at the center of the self and of the culture that enfolds it"; Gillian Brown and Lori Merish see in Coverdale's (and the Blithedalers') reformism little more than a consumerism that reenforces the culture's misogyny, homophobia, and materialism.[3] The same year that Hawthorne published *Blithedale* he also published his campaign biography for his Bowdoin College friend Franklin Pierce. Hawthorne's reactionary attack on abolitionists in that volume, along with his apolitical assertion that God will cause slavery "to vanish like a dream" at the point when "all its uses shall have been fulfilled," have further contributed to a general consensus that *Blithedale* has to be read in conservative terms as an attack on the sentimental culture of reform.[4]

But such a thoroughgoing conservative or apolitical reading, as I have been suggesting, would only replicate the surface cynicism of Coverdale's knowing, ironic, self-protective, and self-parodic narrative. (It would also make too much of a campaign biography that was more a letter of recommendation for a friend than an impassioned statement of Hawthorne's political convictions.[5]) In the figures of Silas Foster and Zenobia there are attractive representatives of reform and sympathy; and in Coverdale's retrospective declarations of his solidarity with the aspirations of the Blithedalers, there remains a commitment to the pos-

---

3. Hutner, *Secrets and Sympathy*, p. 103; Richard H. Millington, *Practicing Romance: Narrative Form and Cultural Engagement in Hawthorne's Fiction* (Princeton, NJ: Princeton University Press, 1992), p. 172; Brown, *Domestic Individualism*, ch. 4; Merish, *Sentimental Materialism*, ch. 3. For a seminal study of the novel as a meditation on the breakdown of the authority and values of New England culture, see James McIntosh, "The Instability of Belief in *The Blithedale Romance*," *Prospects* 9 (1984): 71–114.
4. Nathaniel Hawthorne, *Life of Franklin Pierce* (1852), in Hawthorne, *Miscellanies: Biographical and Other Sketches and Letters* (Boston and New York: Houghton Mifflin Company, 1900), p. 166.
5. When Hawthorne hooked up with Franklin Pierce and other future Democrats at Bowdoin College during the 1820s, Jacksonian Democrats were socially progressive, anti-elitist, and, like most other whites of the time, irrespective of party, racist. Over time, Hawthorne's passions were more for his friends, whom he loved, than for their politics.

sibilities of reform. What Hawthorne is challenging through Coverdale's narrative are the untroubled connections between sympathy and reform that permeated sentimental culture. In *Blithedale*, Hawthorne gives life to radical possibilities of reform, particularly through the magnificent characterization of Zenobia. It is of course characteristic of Hawthorne that he seeks to contain precisely the radical forms of dissent and alterity that engage his fictional imagination. As he famously intones after boldly limning Hester Prynne's feminist revolutionism in chapter 13 of *The Scarlet Letter*: "The scarlet letter had not done its office" (I: 166). In Coverdale's narrative, Hawthorne attempts similar forms of containment and control, particularly with respect to Zenobia, but ultimately his imaginative and political sympathies are too complex and contradictory to be reduced to a simple conservatism or reactionism.

In a pioneering essay published in 1968, "*The Blithedale Romance*: A Radical Reading," Nina Baym made claims for *Blithedale*'s radicalism by underscoring the novel's "attack on repressive social organization," its celebration of "the creative energy both of nature and the self," and its feminism, which "outperforms the feminists in the decisive way in which [Hawthorne] links the liberation and fulfillment of the male to his understanding of and relation to women."[6] In my own effort to re-radicalize *Blithedale* in the wake of much critical writing that insists upon its conservatism and cynicism, I have been making two large arguments: (1) that Coverdale's limitations as a critic of reform are part of a deliberate narrative strategy of self-presentation that is intended to provoke negative responses from his readers and to mask his genuine commitment to reform; and (2) that in working with sentimental notions of sympathy, Hawthorne through his narrator exposes the limits of contemporaneous formations of sympathy, encouraging his readers to imagine a subaltern world of the poor and disenfranchised that eludes the appropriative gazes of reformers. A recognition of otherness, of difference, Hawthorne suggests, is what is missing from antebellum reform as sentimentally conceived. It is only from within that world, which needs to be apprehended in a manner very different from Coverdale's, that meaningful social change can come about. That prospect both engages and frightens Coverdale (and Hawthorne), but it gives life and energy to *Blithedale*.

In many respects *Blithedale* is one of the boldest reform texts of the 1850s, powerfully exposing the hazards of trying to make the other into what Zenobia calls "all self!" (III: 218). In simultaneously

---

6. Nina Baym, "*The Blithedale Romance*: A Radical Reading," *Journal of English and Germanic Philology* 67 (1968): 546, 553.

participating in and critiquing sentimentalism by reminding us of the great distance between self and other, *Blithedale* has the potential to provide its readers with a more compelling understanding of what could be called the socio-emotional dynamics of reform than a work like *Uncle Tom's Cabin*, precisely because of its perverse insistence on regularly frustrating the reader's desires for some sort of communion with the other. Unlike readers of *Uncle Tom's Cabin*, the reader of *Blithedale* has to recognize difference and the existence of alternative histories and perspectives, and to that extent *Blithedale* importantly clears the ground for the possibility of social reforms that are not simply the reflections of imperial selves. To be sure, *Uncle Tom's Cabin* may have helped to inspire a war against slavery while *Blithedale* has had a more rarefied existence as a novel that seems simply to satirize reform. But if *Uncle Tom's Cabin* truly inspired a war against slavery by encouraging white middle-class readers to feel close imaginative connections to black people, then the continuing racial prejudice and violence during and after the war—for instance, the New York City draft riots, the resistance of prominent feminists to the Fifteenth Amendment, the failure of Reconstruction—do not make much sense. Stowe's sentimentalism exacerbated contemporaneous sectional conflicts, but it did not bring blacks and whites together, a fact she recognized by positing at the end of her novel that Liberian colonization may prove to be the best solution for a nation facing intractable racial conflicts. Hawthorne had very different designs on the world than Stowe, and his novel of social reform has provoked current critics to wrestle with the problem of sentimentalism's dependence on sympathetic identification.[7] If *Blithedale* did not accomplish much cultural work in its own time, it has the potential, through its insistence on the reality of a recalcitrant otherness, to do some cultural work in our own, even if it is work that Hawthorne, with his fairly conservative views, would probably find himself unable to sympathize with.

---

7. Hawthorne's *Blithedale* has an important place in recent studies of sentimental culture, such as Brown's *Domestic Individualism* and Merish's *Sentimental Materialism*. Noble's *Masochistic Pleasures* concludes with a discussion of *Blithedale* (pp. 195–98). Recent critical assessments of sentimental culture would appear to have been inspired by Hawthorne's.

Nathaniel Hawthorne:
A Chronology

1804   Born Salem, Massachusetts, July 4, second child of
        Nathaniel Hathorne, a ship's captain, and Elizabeth
        Manning Hathorne, member of an enterprising Salem
        family. Descended on father's side from prominent Puri-
        tan colonists. Sisters: Elizabeth (1802–1883) and
        Louisa (1808–1852). (Hawthorne will add the w to the
        family name in his early twenties.)

1808   Father dies of yellow fever in Surinam (Dutch Guiana);
        family joins Manning household. Begins schooling.

1809   Sophia Amelia Peabody, later Sophia Hawthorne, born
        September 21 in Salem.

1813   Injures his foot playing ball; suffers from lameness for
        the next fourteen months. Is tutored at home.

1818   Moves with his family to Raymond, Maine. Attends
        school briefly but enjoys considerable freedom, hunting,
        fishing, reading, and running "quite wild."

1819–20 Returns to Salem, living with his Manning relatives
        while his mother and sisters remain in Raymond.
        Attends school, then prepares for college under the tute-
        lage of a Salem lawyer.

1821–25 Attends Bowdoin College in Brunswick, Maine, where
        he forms lifelong friendships with Horatio Bridge,
        Jonathan Cilley, and Franklin Pierce (fourteenth presi-
        dent of the United States) and meets Henry Wadsworth
        Longfellow, who becomes a good friend in later years.
        An admittedly "idle" student, he is fined for card-playing
        and begins writing fiction. Graduates eighteenth in a
        class of thirty-five.

1825   Returns to Salem after college graduation. Lives in
        Salem with his mother and sisters for the next ten years,
        working to establish himself as a professional writer.
        While some of his best stories are written during this

period and his reputation grows, he struggles to make money in an immature literary marketplace; he abandons ambitions to publish thematically linked collections of his tales and sketches and burns one such manuscript.

1828   Publishes his first novel, *Fanshawe,* anonymously and at his own expense. Later repudiates this book, destroying his own copy and eliminating it from all accounts of his career. (Unsold copies of the novel burn in a Boston book store fire in 1831).

1830   Publishes first tale, "The Hollow of the Three Hills," in the *Salem Gazette.*

1830–33 Other early publications, all anonymous. The sketch "Sights from a Steeple" appears in *The Token,* an annual gift book, for 1831; the 1832 *Token* includes the extremely popular "The Gentle Boy," "My Kinsman, Major Molineux," and "Roger Malvin's Burial."

1834   Proposes a collection of tales and sketches, "The Story Teller," to Samuel Goodrich, who refuses it. The contents of the projected volume will be scattered among various gift books and magazines.

1835   Contributes stories and sketches, including "The Minister's Black Veil" and "The May-Pole of Merry Mount," to *The Token* for 1836; "Young Goodman Brown" appears in *New-England Magazine.*

1836   Moves to Boston to edit, with the help of his talented sister Elizabeth, the *American Magazine of Useful and Entertaining Knowledge.* Resigns editorship when publisher goes bankrupt, and returns to Salem. With his sister he works on *Peter Parley's Universal History, on the Basis of Geography,* part of a popular series for young readers, which appears the following year.

1837   Succeeds in publishing *Twice-told Tales,* a collection of his earlier work, when Horatio Bridge, without his knowledge, agrees to secure the publisher against losses. A favorable review by Longfellow helps establish Hawthorne's reputation as a promising American writer. Meets Sophia Peabody, his future wife, and her sister Elizabeth (a friend of Emerson and powerful presence in intellectual circles and reform movements), who begins her support of his career.

1838   Nearly challenges John L. O'Sullivan, editor of the *United States and Democratic Review* and later promoter of the idea of "manifest destiny," to a duel over Mary Silsbee, a Salem belle. The two men become friends, and Hawthorne

will publish frequently in this notable magazine, associated
with the Democratic Party, during the next seven years.
College friend Jonathan Cilley killed in a duel with a fellow
congressman; Hawthorne writes memorial essay in the
Democratic Review.

1839   Accepts appointment as measurer in the Boston Custom
House; becomes engaged to Sophia Peabody, to whom he
addresses the first of a remarkable series of love letters.

1841   Leaves Boston Custom House. Joins Brook Farm community (the model for the utopian community depicted in
The Blithedale Romance) in April, becoming a trustee and
director of finance. Hoping to establish a home for
Sophia, purchases two shares in the Brook Farm Association for $1,000, but leaves the community in late Octo-
ber. Publishes three historical books for children,
Grandfather's Chair, Famous Old People, and *Liberty Tree*.

1842   Publishes second, expanded edition of *Twice-told Tales*.
Marries Sophia Peabody, July 9; they settle at the "Old
Manse" in Concord.

1842–45   The "Old Manse" period. Encounters transcendentalist
circle gathered around Ralph Waldo Emerson; friend-
ships with Emerson, Henry David Thoreau, Margaret
Fuller, and Ellery Channing. Writes many tales and
sketches, including "The Birth-mark," "Rappaccini's
Daughter," "The Artist of the Beautiful," and "The
Celestial Rail-road," later collected in *Mosses from an
Old Manse*.

1844   Daughter Una (1844–1877), named after a heroine of
Edmund Spenser's *Faeirie Queene*, born March 3.

1845   Edits Horatio Bridge's *Journal of an African Cruiser*.
Cash-strapped, the family returns to Salem, where they
move in with his mother and sisters. Seeks political
appointment through influential friends, Bridge and
Franklin Pierce; nominated for position of custom
house surveyor by Salem Democrats.

1846   Appointed surveyor in the Salem Custom House; publishes *Mosses from an Old Manse*; son Julian
(1846–1939) born, June 22.

1849   Removed from surveyorship in June by new Whig
administration; considerable public controversy ensues.
Mother dies, July 31. By September is "writing
immensely" on "The Custom-House" and *The Scarlet
Letter*.

1850   *The Scarlet Letter* published by Ticknor and Fields (the latter a key figure in the promotion of American literature),

who remain Hawthorne's publishers for the rest of his career. Having resolved to leave the "abominable" Salem forever, moves family to Lenox in the Berkshire Mountains of western Massachusetts. Meets Herman Melville; the two form a profound friendship. Melville publishes "Hawthorne and His Mosses," a manifesto for a distinctive American literature, in *The Literary World*.

1851   Publishes *The House of the Seven Gables, A Wonder-Book for Girls and Boys*, a new edition of *Twice-told Tales*, and *The Snow-Image, and Other Twice-told Tales*, which contains uncollected tales and sketches, including "Ethan Brand," "The Wives of the Dead," and "My Kinsman, Major Molineux." For the first time, earns enough from his writing to support his family. Daughter Rose (1851–1926) born, May 20. Melville dedicates *Moby Dick* to the "Genius" of Nathaniel Hawthorne.

1852   Publishes *The Blithedale Romance* and *The Life of Franklin Pierce*, the presidential candidate's campaign biography. Returns to Concord, Massachusetts, purchasing Bronson Alcott's former house (renamed "The Wayside"); sister Louisa dies in a steamboat accident on the Hudson River, July 27.

1853   Pierce appoints him American Consul at Liverpool, one of the most lucrative posts in the Consular Service; his fee-based salary will make him a rich man. Publishes *Tanglewood Tales for Girls and Boys*. Family leaves for England in July.

1853–57   Lives in England, performing his consular duties conscientiously and traveling in the British Isles; records his impressions of English life in his notebooks. Publishes second, revised edition of *Mosses from an Old Manse* in 1854. Last visits with Melville in the autumn of 1856 and the spring of 1857.

1858–59   Hawthornes travel to France and on to Italy, living first in Rome, then in Florence, then again in Rome. Records impressions in notebooks; becomes friendly with members of British and American expatriate artistic community, including Robert and Elizabeth Barrett Browning, Harriet Hosmer, Louisa Lander, and William Wetmore Story. Begins writing *The Marble Faun* in July 1858, finishing rough draft in January 1859. Daughter Una contracts malaria in October 1858 and becomes gravely ill; near death in April 1859. Family returns to England in May, where Hawthorne finishes revising *The Marble Faun*.

1860   Publishes *The Marble Faun* (released in England under the title *Transformation*). The Hawthornes sail for America, returning to Concord and the Wayside. In the four years until his death, will begin and abandon three new romances, "The American Claimant," "The Elixir of Life," and "The Dolliver Romance."

1862   Visits Horatio Bridge in Washington, D.C.; meets Lincoln. Publishes an essay on the Civil War, "Chiefly About War Matters," in the *Atlantic Monthly*; the essay attracts criticism for its irreverent portrayal of Lincoln. Several pieces on England appear in the same magazine.

1863   Publishes *Our Old Home*, based on *Atlantic Monthly* sketches on England; dedication to Franklin Pierce, now seen as Southern sympathizer, is harshly criticized.

1864   His health deteriorating, he leaves with Pierce on a carriage tour of northern New England. Dies in his sleep at Plymouth, New Hampshire, on May 19. Buried in Sleepy Hollow Cemetery, Concord, Massachusetts; pallbearers include Longfellow, Emerson, Alcott, and Holmes. Pieces of his last work appear in the July *Atlantic Monthly*, under the title "Scenes from 'The Dolliver Romance.'"

Selected Bibliography

• indicates works included or excerpted in this Norton Critical Edition.

Nathaniel Hawthorne's Writings

Hawthorne, Nathaniel. *The Centenary Edition of the Works of Nathaniel Hawthorne*. 23 vols. Ed. William Charvat et al. Columbus: Ohio State University Press, 1962–97.

Bibliographies and Collections

American Literary Scholarship: An Annual. Durham, N.C.: Duke University Press, 1963–present. [Annual bibliographic essay on Hawthorne.]

Bell, Millicent, ed. *Hawthorne and the Real: Bicentennial Essays*. Columbus: Ohio State University Press, 2005.

Cohen, B. Bernard, ed. *The Recognition of Nathaniel Hawthorne*. Ann Arbor: University of Michigan Press, 1969.

Crowley, J. Donald, ed. *Hawthorne: The Critical Heritage*. New York: Barnes and Noble, 1970.

Faust, Bertha. *Hawthorne's Contemporaneous Reputation: A Study of Literary Opinion in America and England, 1828–1864*. New York: Octagon, 1968.

Idol, John L., Jr., and Buford Jones, eds. *Nathaniel Hawthorne: The Contemporary Reviews*. New York: Cambridge University Press, 1994.

——— and Melinda Ponder, eds. *Hawthorne and Women: Engendering and Expanding the Hawthorne Tradition*. Amherst: University of Massachusetts Press, 1999.

Millington, Richard H., ed. *The Cambridge Companion to Nathaniel Hawthorne*. New York and Cambridge: Cambridge University Press, 2004.

Nathaniel Hawthorne Review. 1986–present. [Annual annotated bibliography on Hawthorne.]

Person, Leland S. "Bibliographic Essay: Hawthorne and History." In *A Historical Guide to Nathaniel Hawthorne*. Ed. Larry J. Reynolds. New York: Oxford University Press, 2001, pp. 183–209.

Reynolds, Larry J., ed. *A Historical Guide to Nathaniel Hawthorne*. New York: Oxford University Press, 2001.

Ricks, Beatrice, Joseph D. Adams, and Jack O. Hazlerig, eds. *Nathaniel Hawthorne: A Reference Bibliography, 1900–1971*. Boston: G. K. Hall, 1972.

Scharnhorst, Gary, ed. *Nathaniel Hawthorne: An Annotated Bibliography of Commentary and Criticism before 1900*. Metuchen, N.J.: Scarecrow, 1988.

Biographies

Hawthorne, Julian. *Nathaniel Hawthorne and his Wife: A Biography*, 2nd ed. 2 vols. Boston: James Osgood, 1885.

Herbert, T. Walter. *Dearest Beloved: The Hawthornes and the Making of the Middle-Class Family*. Berkeley: University of California Press, 1993.

Miller, Edwin Haviland. *Salem Is My Dwelling Place: A Life of Nathaniel Hawthorne*. Iowa City: University of Iowa Press, 1991.

Moore, Margaret B. *The Salem World of Nathaniel Hawthorne*. Columbia: University of Missouri Press, 1994.

Stewart, Randall. *Nathaniel Hawthorne: A Biography*. New Haven: Yale University Press, 1948.

Turner, Arlin. *Nathaniel Hawthorne: A Biography*. New York: Oxford University Press, 1980.

Wineapple, Brenda. *Hawthorne: A Life*. New York: Alfred A. Knopf, 2003.

Woodson, Thomas. "Introduction: Hawthorne's Letters, 1813–1853." In *The Letters, 1813–1843*. Vol. 15, *The Centenary Edition of the Works of Nathaniel Hawthorne*. Columbus: Ohio State University Press, 1984, 3–89.

Historical Studies

A brief selection of historical studies and collections of materials useful to the study of the novel.

Delano, Sterling G. *Brook Farm: The Dark Side of Utopia*. Cambridge: Harvard University Press, 2004.

Fourier, Charles. *The Theory of the Four Movements*. Ed. Gareth Stedman Jones and Ian Patterson. Cambridge: Cambridge University Press, 1996.

Fuller, Robert C. *Mesmerism and the American Cure of Souls*. Philadelphia: University of Pennsylvania Press, 1982.

Guarneri, Carl J. *The Utopian Alternative: Fourierism in Nineteenth-Century America*. Ithaca: Cornell University Press, 1991.

Halttunen, Karen. *Confidence Men and Painted Women: A Study of Middle-Class Culture in America, 1830–1870*. New Haven: Yale University Press, 1982.

Myerson, Joel. *The Brook Farm Book: A Collection of First-Hand Accounts of the Community*. New York: Garland, 1987.

Sams, Henry W., ed. *Autobiography of Brook Farm*. Englewood Cliffs, N.J.: Prentice-Hall, 1958.

Critical Studies

Anderson, Douglas. "*The Blithedale Romance* and Post-Heroic Life." *Nineteenth-Century Literature* 60 (2005): 32–56.

Arvin, Newton. *Hawthorne*. Boston: Little, Brown, 1929.

Auerbach, Jonathan. *The Romance of Failure: First-Person Fictions of Poe, Hawthorne, and James*. New York: Oxford University Press, 1989.

Bauer, Dale M. *Feminist Dialogics: A Theory of Failed Community*. Albany: State University of New York Press, 1988.

• Baym, Nina. *The Shape of Hawthorne's Career*. Ithaca: Cornell University Press, 1976.

Bell, Michael Davitt. *The Development of American Romance: The Sacrifice of Relation*. Chicago: University of Chicago Press, 1980.

Bell, Millicent. *Hawthorne's View of the Artist*. New York: State University of New York Press, 1962.

Bellis, Peter. *Writing Revolution: Aesthetics and Politics in Hawthorne, Whitman, and Thoreau*. Athens: University of Georgia Press, 2003.

• Berlant, Lauren. "Fantasies of Utopia in *The Blithedale Romance*." *American Literary History* 1 (1989): 30–62.

Brand, Dana. *The Spectator and the City in Nineteenth-Century American Literature*. New York: Cambridge University Press, 1991.

Brodhead, Richard H. *Hawthorne, Melville, and the Novel*. Chicago: University of Chicago Press, 1976.

———. *The School of Hawthorne*. New York: Oxford University Press, 1986.

• ———. "Veiled Ladies: Toward a History of Antebellum Entertainment." *American Literary History* 1 (1989): 273–94.

Brown, Gillian. *Domestic Individualism: Imagining Self in Nineteenth-Century America*. Berkeley: University of California Press, 1990.

Bumas, E. Shaskan. "Fictions of the Panopticon: Prison, Utopia, and the Out-Penitent in the Works of Nathaniel Hawthorne." *American Literature* 73 (2001): 121–45.

————. "'The Forgotten Art of Gayety': Masquerade, Utopia, and the Complexion of Empire." *Arizona Quarterly* 59 (2003): 1–30.

Carton, Evan. *The Rhetoric of American Romance: Dialectic and Identity in Emerson, Dickinson, Poe, and Hawthorne.* Baltimore: Johns Hopkins University Press, 1985.

• Castronovo, Russ. *Necro Citizenship: Death, Eroticism, and the Public Sphere in Nineteenth-Century United States.* Durham: Duke University Press, 2001.

Chai, Leon. *The Romantic Foundations of the American Renaissance.* Ithaca: Cornell University Press, 1987.

Chase, Richard. *The American Novel and Its Tradition.* Garden City, N.Y.: Gordian Press, 1957.

Christianson, Frank. *Philanthropy in British and American Fiction: Dickens, Hawthorne, Eliot, and Howells.* Edinburgh: Edinburgh University Press, 2007.

Coale, Samuel Chase. *Mesmerism and Hawthorne: Mediums of American Romance.* Tuscaloosa: University of Alabama Press, 1997.

————. "Mysteries of Mesmerism: Hawthorne's Haunted House." In *A Historical Guide to Nathaniel Hawthorne.* Ed. Larry J. Reynolds. New York: Oxford University Press, 2001, 49–78.

Colacurcio, Michael J. "Nobody's Protest Novel: Art and Politics in *The Blithedale Romance.*" *Nathaniel Hawthorne Review* 34 (2008): 1–39.

Crews, Frederick. *The Sins of the Fathers: Hawthorne's Psychological Themes.* New York: Oxford University Press, 1966.

Dauber, Kenneth. *Rediscovering Hawthorne.* Princeton: Princeton University Press, 1977.

Davis, Clark. *Hawthorne's Shyness: Ethics, Politics, and the Question of Engagement.* Baltimore: Johns Hopkins University Press, 2005.

DeSalvo, Louise. *Nathaniel Hawthorne.* Atlantic Highlands, N.J.: Humanities Press, 1987.

Dolis, John. *The Style of Hawthorne's Gaze: Regarding Subjectivity.* Tuscaloosa; University of Alabama Press, 1993.

Dryden, Edgar A. *Nathaniel Hawthorne: The Poetics of Enchantment.* Ithaca: Cornell University Press, 1977.

Dunne, Michael. *Hawthorne's Narrative Strategies.* Jackson: University Press of Mississippi, 1995.

Fisher, Lydia. "The Savage in the House." *Arizona Quarterly* 64 (2008): 49–75.

Flynn, Kelley M. "Nathaniel Hawthorne Had a Farm: Artists, Laborers, and Landscapes in *The Blithedale Romance.*" In *Reading the Earth: New Directions in the Study of Literature and the Environment.* Ed. Michael P. Branch et al. Moscow, Idaho: University of Idaho Press, 1998.

Fogle, Richard H. *Hawthorne's Fiction: The Light and the Dark.* Norman: University of Oklahoma Press, 1964.

Fryer, Judith. *The Faces of Eve: Women in the Nineteenth Century American Novel.* New York: Oxford University Press 1976.

Gable, Harvey L., Jr. "Inappeasable Longings: Hawthorne, Romance, and the Disintegration of Coverdale's Self in *The Blithedale Romance.*" *New England Quarterly* 67 (1994): 257–78.

Goddu, Teresa A. *Gothic America: Narrative, History, and Nation.* New York: Columbia University Press, 1997.

Gollin, Rita K. *Nathaniel Hawthorne and the Truth of Dreams.* Baton Rouge: Louisiana State University Press, 1979.

Greenwald, Elissa. *Realism and the Romance: Nathaniel Hawthorne, Henry James, and American Fiction.* Ann Arbor: University of Michigan Press, 1989.

Greven, David. "In a Pig's Eye: Masculinity, Mastery, and the Returned Gaze of *The Blithedale Romance.*" *Studies in American Fiction* 34 (2006): 131–59.

————. *Men Beyond Desire: Manhood, Sex, and Violation in American Literature.* New York: Palgrave Macmillan, 2005.

Grossberg, Benjamin Scott. "'The Tender Passion Was Very Rife Among Us'": Coverdale's Queer Utopia and *The Blithedale Romance.*" *Studies in American Fiction* 28 (2000): 3–25.

Harris, Kenneth Marc. *Hypocrisy and Self-Deception in Hawthorne's Fiction.* Charlottesville: University Press of Virginia, 1988.

• Howe, Irving. *Politics and the Novel.* New York: Horizon Press, 1957.

• Howells, William Dean. *Heroines of Fiction.* 2 vols. New York: Harper & Brothers, 1901.

Hume, Beverly. "Restructuring the Case Against Coverdale." *Nineteenth-Century Fiction* 40 (1986): 387–99.

Hutner, Gordon. *Secrets and Sympathy: Forms of Disclosure in Hawthorne's Novels.* Athens: University of Georgia Press, 1988.

• James, Henry. *Hawthorne.* English Men of Letters Series. London: Macmillan, 1879.

Johnson, Claudia Durst. *The Productive Tension of Hawthorne's Art.* Tuscaloosa: University of Alabama Press, 1981.

Kaul, A. N. *The American Visiton: Actual and Ideal Society in Nineteenth-Century Fiction* (New Haven: Yale University Press, 1963).

• Lawrence, D. H. *Studies in Classic American Literature.* 1923. New York: Penguin Books, 1977.

Lefcowitz, Barbara F. and Allen B. Lefcowitz. "Some Rents in the Veil: New Light on Priscilla and Zenobia." *Nineteenth-Century Fiction* 21 (1966): 263–75.

Leverenz, David. *Manhood and the American Renaissance.* Ithaca: Cornell University Press, 1989.

Levine, Robert S. *Conspiracy and Romance: Studies in Brockden Brown, Cooper, Hawthorne, and Melville.* Cambridge: Cambridge University Press, 1989.

• ———. "Sympathy and Reform in *The Blithedale Romance.*" In *The Cambridge Companion to Nathaniel Hawthorne.* Ed. Richard H. Millington. New York and Cambridge: Cambridge University Press, 2004, 207–29.

• Levy, Leo B. "*The Blithedale Romance*: Hawthorne's 'Voyage Through Chaos.'" *Studies in Romanticism* 8 (1968): 1–15.

Long, Robert Emmet. *The Great Succession: Henry James and the Legacy of Hawthorne.* Pittsburgh: University of Pittsburgh Press, 1979.

Mackenzie, Manfred. "Colonization and Decolonization in *The Blithedale Romance.*" *University of Toronto Quarterly* 62 (1993): 504–21.

Maibor, Carolyn R. *Labor Pains: Emerson, Hawthorne, and Alcott on Work and the Woman Question.* New York and London: Routledge, 2004.

Male, Roy R. *Hawthorne's Tragic Vision.* Austin: University of Texas Press, 1957.

Margolis, Stacey. *The Public Life of Privacy in Nineteenth-Century American Literature.* Durham: Duke University Press, 2005.

Martin, Terence. *Nathaniel Hawthorne,* rev. ed. Boston: Twayne, 1983.

McCall, Dan. *Citizens of Somewhere Else: Nathaniel Hawthorne and Henry James.* Ithaca: Cornell University Press, 1999.

• McIntosh, James. "The Instability of Belief in *The Blithedale Romance.*" *Prospects* 9 (1984): 71–114.

Merish, Lori. *Sentimental Materialism: Gender, Commodity Culture, and Nineteenth-Century American Literature.* Durham: Duke University Press, 2000.

Miller, John N. "Eros and Ideology: At the Heart of Hawthorne's *Blithedale.*" *Nineteenth-Century Literature* 55 (2000): 1–21.

• Millington, Richard H. *Practicing Romance: Narrative Form and Cultural Engagement in Hawthorne's Fiction.* Princeton, N.J.: Princeton University Press, 1992.

Mills, Angela. "'The Sweet Word,' Sister: The Transformative Threat of Sisterhood and *The Blithedale Romance.*" *American Transcendental Quarterly* 17 (2003): 97–121.

Mitchell, Thomas R. *Hawthorne's Fuller Mystery.* Amherst: University of Massachusetts Press, 1998.

———. "In the Whale's Wake: Melville and *The Blithedale Romance.*" In *Hawthorne and Melville: Writing a Relationship.* Ed. Jana L. Argersinger and Leland S. Person. Athens: University of Georgia Press, 2008, 249–67.

Mueller, Monika. *This Infinite Fraternity of Feeling: Gender, Genre, and Homo-erotic Crisis in Hawthorne's "The Blithedale Romance" and Melville's "Pierre."* Rutherford: Fairleigh Dickinson University Press, 1996.

Newfield, Christopher and Melissa Solomon. "Few of Our Seeds Ever Came Up at All: A Dialogue on Hawthorne, Delany, and the Work of Affect in Visionary Utopias." In *No More Separate Spheres: A Next Wave American Studies Reader*. Ed. Cathy Davidson and Jessamyn Hatcher. Durham: Duke University Press, 2002.

Noble, Marianne. *The Masochistic Pleasures of Sentimental Literature*. Princeton: Princeton University Press, 2000.

Pearce, Roy Harvey. *Gesta Humanorum: Studies in the Historicist Mode*. Columbia: University of Missouri Press, 1987.

Person, Leland S. *Aesthetic Headaches: Women and a Masculine Poetics in Poe, Melville, and Hawthorne*. Athens: University of Georgia Press, 1988.

———. *The Cambridge Introduction to Nathaniel Hawthorne*. Cambridge and New York: Cambridge University Press, 2007.

• Pfister, Joel. *The Production of Personal Life: Class, Gender, and the Psychological in Hawthorne's Fiction*. Stanford: Stanford University Press, 1991.

Poirier, Richard. *A World Elsewhere: The Place of Style in American Literature*. New York: Oxford University Press, 1966.

Porte, Joel. *The Romance in America: Studies in Cooper, Poe, Hawthorne, Melville, and James*. Middletown: Wesleyan University Press, 1969.

• Rahv, Philip. "The Dark Lady of Salem." *Partisan Review* 8 (1941): 362–81.

Reynolds, Larry J. "Hawthorne's Labors in Concord." In *The Cambridge Companion to Nathaniel Hawthorne*. Ed. Richard H. Millington. New York and Cambridge: Cambridge University Press, 2004.

Rowe, John Carlos. *Through the Custom House: Nineteenth-Century American Fiction and Modern Theory*. Baltimore: Johns Hopkins University Press, 1982.

Schriber, Mary Suzanne. "Justice to Zenobia." *New England Quarterly* 55 (1982): 61–78.

Snyder, Katherine V. *Bachelors, Manhood, and the Novel, 1850–1925*. Cambridge: Cambridge University Press, 1999.

Stoehr, Taylor. *Hawthorne's Mad Scientists: Pseudoscience and Social Science in Nineteenth-Century Life and Letters*. Hamden, Conn.: Shoe String, 1978.

Stubbs, John Caldwell. *The Pursuit of Form: A Study of Hawthorne and the Romance*. Urbana: University of Illinois Press, 1970.

Swann, Charles. *Nathaniel Hawthorne: Tradition and Revolution*. New York: Cambridge University Press, 1991.

Tanner, Tony. *The American Mystery*. Cambridge: Cambridge University Press, 2000.

Tatar, Maria. *Spellbound: Studies on Mesmerism and Literature*. Princeton: Princeton University Press, 1978.

Temple, Gale. "His Delirious Solace": Consummation, Consumption, and Reform in Hawthorne's *The Blithedale Romance*. *ESQ: A Journal of the American Renaissance* 49 (2003): 285–321.

Tracy, Laura. *"Catching the Drift": Authority, Gender, and Narrative Strategy in Fiction*. New Brunswick: Rutgers University Press, 1988.

Updike, John. "Hawthorne Down on the Farm." *New York Review of Books*, 9 Aug. 2001; 48 (13): 48–49.

Waggoner, Hyatt H. *Hawthorne: A Critical Study*. Rev. ed. Cambridge: Harvard University Press, 1963.